# CONGRESS
## A to Z

CQ'S ENCYCLOPEDIA OF AMERICAN GOVERNMENT

# CONGRESS
## A to Z

SECOND EDITION

# A READY REFERENCE ENCYCLOPEDIA

CONGRESSIONAL QUARTERLY INC.
WASHINGTON, D.C.

*Book Design by Kachergis Book Design, Pittsboro, North Carolina.*

Printed in the United States of America.

*cover images*

1. Carol Moseley-Braun, R. Michael Jenkins
2. Joseph Cannon, Library of Congress
3. New Deal cartoon, Library of Congress
4. Vietnam protestors, Bettmann
5. John Kennedy and Mike Mansfield, Senate Historical Office
6. Bill Clinton addressing a joint session of Congress, R. Michael Jenkins
7. Andrew Jackson, Daniel Webster, and Henry Clay, New-York Historical Society
8. Farmers protesting at U.S. Capitol, *Washington Post*
9. Senate election cartoon, Library of Congress
*frontispiece* Library of Congress

*Library of Congress Cataloging-in-Publication Data*
Congress A to Z : a ready reference encyclopedia — 2nd ed.
     p.  cm.
    Includes bibliographical references and index.
    ISBN  0-87187-826-7 (hard) — ISBN  0-87187-988-3 (pbk.)
    1. United States.  Congress—Dictionaries.  I. Congressional Quarterly, inc.
JK1067.C67   1993
328.73'003'—dc20                     93–25926
                                           CIP

# Contents

# Preface

*Congress A to Z,* second edition, is one of three comprehensive volumes from Congressional Quarterly offering quick and accurate answers to your questions about the United States government. This volume and its companions, *The Presidency A to Z* and *The Supreme Court A to Z,* make up *CQ's Encyclopedia of American Government,* a set we believe provides the most concise and accessible ready-reference information about the history, powers, and operations of the three branches of government.

This volume is a product of Congressional Quarterly's nearly half-century of reporting on America's national legislature. *Congress A to Z,* like its companions, is intended for anyone who has an interest in national government and politics. High school students researching term papers, political activists working on an issue or a campaign, as well as political buffs following activities on Capitol Hill in Washington, D.C.—whether through newspaper or radio and TV reports or by continuous congressional coverage available on cable systems carrying C-SPAN—all can benefit from this encyclopedia.

The editors and writers have sought to provide, in a readily accessible form, all the basic information most readers will need to understand the structure and operations of the legislative branch of the federal government. *Congress A to Z* offers nontechnical explanations of congressional operations, as well as background on the development of the modern Congress. The entries are arranged alphabetically and are extensively cross-referenced to guide you to related information. A detailed index is available to guide you to the exact information sought.

The core of this volume is a series of essays that provide overviews of broad subject areas, such as the legislative process and the congressional committee system. Those essays are supported by more than 200 additional entries that flesh out details of material covered in the broader essays or provide specific explanations of important technical matters such as recommittal motions and suspension of the rules. Also included are profiles of individual committees and short biographies of important members of Congress, past and present. A separate appendix contains many tables of data and other information about Congress. A general bibliography supplements suggested readings in the individual entries.

For this edition, CQ editors have updated most of the articles that appeared in the first edition in 1988. Although only a few years have elapsed, much has changed. Most notable was a further decline in the already low esteem in which Congress as a whole is held by Americans. The "image" problem belied the serious and responsible work Congress does every year, but even many members could not deny that events—some of their own making—raised more and more legitimate questions about the role of this institution in the governing process. The difficulties arose from varied sources. There were the volatile social issues, such as abortion, gay rights, and racial divisions, on which opposing sides were closely matched in strength and legislative strategy—often reflecting the unresolved nature of the controversies in the public. There were the intractable financial issues in which a huge budget deficit and the constraining impact of uncontrollable entitlement programs left legislators with few options. And there were the self-inflicted wounds of congressional ethical controversies that left a public image of self-serving members-for-life senators and House members who cared more about their own privileges and perquisites than about the problems of the nation. Many parts of the bill of indictment were off the mark, but enough were not to leave Congress at the beginning of 1993 with as serious a problem as it had faced in decades in showing the voters it had a meaningful role to play in government.

Out of this malaise grew important developments. The 1992 elections saw a record number of incumbents retiring or defeated and replaced by a more diverse collection of politicians that included increased numbers of African-Americans, Hispanics, and women. Redistricting for House seats that reflected population movements documented in the 1990 census uprooted comfortable seats of the past decade and led to a larger number of minorities elected from districts drawn expressly for the purpose of increasing their numbers in Congress. Internally, a serious effort was begun to examine the structure and operations of Congress. In early 1993 a few minor House committees were eliminated, but real changes in which power would be redistributed lay in the future and were by no means certain. Outside the halls of Congress and the rarefied political atmosphere of Washington, D.C., there loomed—with a growing momentum—the ultimate threat to members of Congress: terms limits. Experts argued the wisdom of such a dramatic change in the nation's political system, but few doubted the movement was wildly popular with the voters and many agreed it was only a matter of time before that popularity broke through to change political life in Washington fundamentally. CQ editors have attempted throughout the book to bring these trends and developments into focus and to provide coverage current as of mid-1993.

*Congress A to Z* reflects the work of many persons at CQ over many years. Ann O'Connor served as general editor of this edition. Mary Cohn, who was the editor of the first edition and conceived and planned the work in the mid-1980s, wrote much of the text that is retained here. Her contribution to this as well as many other CQ reference books has been unparalleled. They have been ably assisted in both editions by the writing and editing talents of many current and former CQ staff members including Prudence Crewdson, Harrison Donnelly, Pam Fessler, Tom Galvin, Steve Gettinger, Hoyt Gimlin, Marty Gottron, Nancy Kervin, Julia McCue, Barbara Miracle, John Moore, Ann Pelham, Mike Wormser, and Dick Worsnop. Nancy Lammers, assistant director of the Book Editorial Department, devised and executed the plan to turn text into a finished book. Lys Ann Shore served as editor, adding clarity and tightness to the articles. Jamie Holland selected and gathered the hundreds of images that bring this text to visual life. Laura Carter coordinated with great efficiency the many details of this project. Joyce Kachergis and her talented staff are responsible for the book's design and production.

We hope this volume on Congress and the others on the Supreme Court and the presidency that comprise *CQ's Encyclopedia of American Government* will help readers understand, appreciate, and appraise—critically but fairly—the governmental institutions under which we live.

David R. Tarr
Editorial Director

# CONGRESS
## A to Z

# A

## Abscam Scandal

An undercover operation by the Federal Bureau of Investigation (FBI) in 1980 implicated seven members of Congress in criminal wrongdoing. Called Abscam, the operation was a "sting" that used FBI agents posing as wealthy Arabs to offer bribes to an undisclosed number of legislators.

By May 1981 seven who took the bait—six House members and one senator—had been convicted. Within a year all seven were gone from Congress, one of them having been expelled. Some of the members had been asked if they could use their positions to help the "Arabs" obtain U.S. residency. Others were offered money to use their influence in obtaining gambling licenses or federal grants, or in arranging real estate deals.

Four of the House members convicted in the affair were videotaped accepting money. They were Republican Richard Kelly of Florida and Democrats Raymond F. Lederer and Michael J. "Ozzie" Myers, both of Pennsylvania, and Frank Thompson, Jr., of New Jersey. John W. Jenrette, Jr., a South Carolina Democrat, was recorded on tape saying he had been given the cash by an associate. John M. Murphy, a New York Democrat, allegedly told an associate to take the cash. A seventh House member, Pennsylvania Democrat John P. Murtha, was named as an unindicted co-conspirator. He later was cleared by the House Ethics Committee.

The only senator caught in the sting was New Jersey Democrat Harrison A. Williams, Jr. Although Williams turned down a cash bribe, he was convicted for his agreement to participate in a bogus mining venture. He maintained that the government "manufactured" the crimes of which he was accused.

*Harrison A. Williams resigned from the Senate in 1982 as his colleagues debated expelling him. Williams had been convicted on criminal charges in the Abscam scandal.*
*Source: AP/Wide World Photos*

All seven of the convicted members served prison sentences. On October 2, 1980, the House expelled Myers. He was only the fourth representative ever to be expelled and the first since the Civil War. No other member of Congress had been expelled for corruption. Kelly, Murphy, and Thompson were defeated for reelection before their convictions and thus escaped House disciplinary action. Jenrette, Lederer, and Williams resigned. By leaving the Senate voluntarily in 1982, Williams avoided becoming the first senator to be expelled since the Civil War and the first ever ejected on grounds other than treason or disloyalty. (See DISCIPLINING MEMBERS.)

## Adams, John Quincy

John Quincy Adams (1767–1848), the sixth president of the United States, represented Massachusetts in both the Senate and House of Representatives during his long career in public life.

The son of John Adams, the nation's second president, John Quincy Adams was a man of uncompromising rectitude and inflexible purpose. Adams entered the Senate in 1803 as a Federalist, but he soon ran into trouble for supporting Jeffersonian policies. He resigned his Senate seat in 1808. After holding various diplomatic posts, he served with distinction from 1817 to 1825 as President James Monroe's secretary of state. He was chiefly responsible for the Monroe Doctrine, which barred colonization in the Western Hemisphere by European nations.

Adams ran for president in 1824, in an inconclusive four-way race that ultimately had to be decided by the House of Representatives. Although Andrew Jackson was the leading candidate in both the popular and the electoral votes, the House chose Adams. Lacking political or popular support, Adams was not a successful president; Jackson defeated him in 1828.

In 1830 Adams was elected to the House of Representatives, where he served for seventeen years until his death. Known as "Old Man Eloquent," he conducted an almost single-handed attack on so-called gag rules that prevented discussion of antislavery proposals. The House repealed the rules in 1844.

Known as "Old Man Eloquent," John Quincy Adams was one of two presidents to serve in Congress after leaving the White House. (Andrew Johnson was the other.) Adams served in the Senate prior to his presidency and in the House after it.
Source: Library of Congress

On February 21, 1848, the eighty-year-old Adams was stricken ill at his desk in the House chamber. He was carried to the Speaker's room, where he died two days later.

Adams was one of two presidents to serve in Congress after leaving the White House. Andrew Johnson, also a former senator, returned to the Senate for five months before his death in 1875. (See ELECTING THE PRESIDENT.)

## Adjournment

Adjournment is the action of Congress in bringing its meetings to a close. In the congressional context the word has several different meanings.

## End of Session

The terms of Congress run in two-year...
Congress must hold a regula...
called a session, each...
SIONS OF CO...
the Senate and...
meaning "witho...
makers do not in...
session. Adjournn...
ally the final actio...
dent has authority...
special sessions of Co...
thorize their leaders t...
well. Unless called bac...
the constitutionally fixe...
uary 3 of the next year...
president power to adj...
houses can't agree about...
but this has never happene...

## Mid-session

Within a session Congress...
observances, vacations, or ot...
practice is known as adjournn...
Lawmakers set a date for the sess...
constitutional directive neither ch...
for more than three days without...
other.

## Daily

In the House of Representatives d...
most always end in adjournment. Th...
also adjourn, but it is far more likely to...
cessing it continues the same LEGISLATI...
the next calendar day, an arrangement th...
tain procedural benefits under Senate rul...
legislative day may go on for weeks and do...
until the Senate next adjourns.

## Advice and Consent

*See* APPOINTMENT POWER.

### PRINTS & PHOTOGRAPHS DIVISION
### LIBRARY OF CONGRESS
### www.loc.gov/rr/print

**ONLINE RESOURCES:**

**Prints & Photographs Online Catalog**
Online access to P&P holdings; many catalog records are accompanied by digital images.

**Reference and Copying Services**
Services and procedures for researchers working onsite or from a distance.

**Rights and Restrictions Information**
Library of Congress policy on permissions and sources of information on rights and restrictions for materials in the Division's collections.

**Guides, Reference Aids, and Finding Aids**
Overviews of collections and lists of images on popularly requested topics, many accompanied by digital images.

**Exhibits and Exhibit Loans**
Links to exhibits and information on loan procedures.

**Acquisition and Appraisal Information**
Procedures and policies relating to offers and appraisal of works on paper.

**Cataloging Tools and Resources**
Cataloging tools maintained by Prints & Photographs Division staff, including subject and genre/physical characteristics thesauri.

**Caroline and Erwin Swann Foundation**
Supporting activities relating to original caricature and cartoon drawings, including acquisition, preservation, exhibition and scholarship.

**Center for American Architecture, Design and Engineering Project**
Supporting ongoing processing, preservation, and interpretation of the Library's architecture, design and engineering collections.

*Woman assembling B-25 bomber motor, Inglewood, California, by Alfred Palmer, 1942. Entire photograph: LC-USW361-453.*

## Aging Committees, House and Senate

Two congressional committees on aging served as
...ective platforms for advocates of the elderly for
...ny years, but in 1993 the House panel went out of
...ence. Although the committees were barred by
...ressional rules from handling legislation, their
...gs, investigations, and reports gave the prob-
...the elderly increased visibility.

...n the 103rd Congress, which began in 1993,
...to cut costs throughout the federal govern-
...ven by efforts to reduce the federal budget
...mpted legislators to kill a number of special
...in the House, including Aging. However,
...1993 rejected proposals to terminate its
...ittees.

...Special Committee on Aging was set
...1960s. In 1977 a proposal to kill the
...ved the votes of only four senators af-
...mpaign by the senior citizens' lobby
...live.

...t Committee on Aging was estab-
...Claude Pepper, a Florida Demo-
...rom 1977 to 1983 and made the
...oice in Congress for the elderly.
...another committee chairman-
...ssues concerning the elderly
...e in high profile. Many ideas
...curbs on mandatory retire-
...e law. But after Pepper's
...r of his stature pressed for
...the Committee on Aging

### , House

...House Agriculture
...ral government's
...tance to farmers.
...present heavily
...n the House for

The most important element of the committee's jurisdiction is farm price supports. Through a variety of mechanisms, such as government loans and direct cash payments, these federal programs determine the minimum prices farmers will receive for their wheat, corn, cotton, and other crops. The goal of these programs is to provide farmers with some protection against wide swings in market prices for farm products. In addition, the committee is responsible for other agricultural issues, such as the federal law regulating use of pesticides. Also under the committee's authority is the federal food stamp program, which helps poor people buy food.

Although the committee works on legislation in every session of Congress, its principal work comes in years when it must report a comprehensive "farm bill," establishing the overall shape of farm programs for the next four or five years. The year in which the farm bill comes up for renewal is a time of intense activity for committee members.

Most of the members of the Agriculture Committee come from southern and midwestern states, where farm issues are a prime concern. Some of the members are farmers themselves or come from districts where farming remains an important part of the local economy. Few members come from big cities or industrial regions.

Politically, the most important aspect of the Agriculture Committee's work is the "farm coalition." This coalition is essential because no single crop is important everywhere in the United States. In the Midwest wheat and corn are the dominant crops, and farmers there are most concerned with preserving federal assistance to those products. In the South farmers mostly grow cotton and rice, and they care much more about price supports for these crops than about assistance for wheat or corn.

Similarly, each committee member is primarily concerned with protecting the interests of the crops most important to his or her own constituents, while

*The House and Senate Agriculture committees represent farmers' interests in Congress. Their efforts depend on a coalition of members from the Midwest, where wheat and corn are the dominant crops, and the South, where cotton, tobacco, and rice predominate.*

paying less attention to the interests of crops that are grown in other regions. As a result, no one crop commands the allegiance of a majority of the committee or of the House as a whole. If each crop were considered separately, it would be politically weak and would have little chance of obtaining generous price supports.

Long ago committee members learned that it was in their interest to join together in a common front for all farm products. Groups supporting each crop found that they were better off supporting all the other crops and receiving those groups' support in return. For example, members from Georgia, where peanuts are predominant, agreed to support special programs for Michigan potato growers. In turn, Michigan members voted in favor of peanut programs, even though that crop was not important in their state.

By sticking loyally to the farm coalition, Agriculture Committee members were able for many years to win House approval of legislation providing increased federal support for their crops. If opposition developed to price supports for any one crop, committee members usually were able to overcome it by offering to increase federal aid to other crops as well. In this way they won over enough members to obtain a majority.

The growth of the food stamp program has added significantly to the strength of the farm coalition. Food stamps are important to House members from big cities, who otherwise have little interest in supporting farm programs. By including generous funding for food stamps in farm legislation, Agriculture Committee members were able to win the support of many liberal, urban Democrats for farm programs.

In the 1970s and 1980s several factors began to undermine the strength of the farm coalition in the House. The foremost of these was the declining political importance of farmers. The continuing decrease in the number of people living in rural areas meant that fewer House members were primarily concerned with farm interests. Moreover, the spiraling cost of federal farm programs increased opposition to the farm coalition and to Agriculture Committee legislation, as the government continued to run large budget deficits.

In the 1970s federal farm programs typically cost about $3 billion a year. By the 1980s the amount had swollen to more than $20 billion annually. As a result, Agriculture Committee members found themselves under heavy pressure from other House members to hold down the cost of farm programs. At the same time more and more farmers found themselves in deep financial trouble. The 1985 farm bill addressed both problems, pumping in some $80 billion in federal subsidies over five years while altering subsidy formulas so payments would be smaller in the future. Legislators from rural districts found the bill hard to accept, but it served the purpose. By 1990, when the next farm bill was written, the financial health of the farm sector was much improved, and only modest changes were made to federal programs.

## Agriculture, Nutrition, and Forestry Committee, Senate

The Senate agriculture committee shares with its House counterpart the jurisdiction over federal farm programs. The amount of economic help the federal government provides to farmers depends in large part on the decisions made in the committee and on the skill of committee members in guiding their legislation through the full Senate. The committee is formally known as the Agriculture, Nutrition, and Forestry Committee.

As is true of the House Agriculture Committee, the main work of the Senate agriculture committee takes place only every four or five years, when Congress considers renewal of legislation authorizing federal farm price supports, food stamps, and related programs. In between, the committee considers a variety of legislation responding to changes in the agricultural economy, from help for farmers hit by droughts or floods to emergency assistance for the banks that provide operating loans to farmers. (See AGRICULTURE COMMITTEE, HOUSE.)

In many respects, the political situation of the Senate agriculture committee is similar to that of its House counterpart. Both panels are dominated by members from states where agriculture is a key factor in the local economy. Senate committee members also share with their House colleagues the primary goal of protecting the interests of farmers in the competition for federal resources. Furthermore, the Senate committee, like the House committee, traditionally has depended on the farm coalition, in which advocates of various crops band together for mutual political support.

For many years, the Senate panel's work consisted largely of tallying up the requests of various special-interest lobbies, and so fashioning farm programs to cover each group's particular desires. The farm coalition on the committee came under increasing pressure in the 1980s as the rapidly growing costs of farm programs collided with the spiraling federal budget deficit. The strain on the coalition, within the committee and in the full Senate, was shown clearly by action over the 1985 farm bill. The bill sparked bitter debates over the efforts of President Ronald Reagan to hold down the cost of farm programs. But the measure achieved its purpose, nursing the nation's farmers back to health and at the same time reducing federal payments in the future. The 1990 farm bill included only modest revisions over the 1985 act.

The farm coalition on the Senate agriculture committee remained more powerful politically than its House counterpart because of the differences in representation in the two chambers. In the House, sparsely populated farm states, such as North Dakota, had very little voting strength. But the same states each had two votes in the Senate, giving them far more power and making farm issues considerably more important.

# Albert, Carl B.

Carl B. Albert (1908–   ) was a Democratic member of the House for thirty years and its Speaker for six. An Oklahoma lawyer and former Rhodes scholar, Albert entered the House in 1947.

On the day of his arrival, legend has it, the tiny (five feet, four inches) newcomer was mistaken for a congressional page by a veteran representative who called him over and directed, "Son, take these papers over to my office."

During his career in the House, Albert traveled a careful political road along which he made few enemies. He was a protégé of Speaker Sam RAYBURN, who chose him to become majority whip in 1955. Albert moved on up the Democratic leadership ladder to become majority leader in 1962 and Speaker in 1971. He was acceptable to most factions of the party and won election as Speaker with only token opposition.

Because of his low-key style, Albert did little either to help or to impede liberal reform efforts of the early 1970s, and his passive manner soon drew criticism. Some freshman Democrats talked openly of removing him after the House in 1975 upheld Republican president Gerald R. Ford's veto of a Democratic-backed bill to control strip mining. No effort was made to oust Albert, however, and criticism subsided by 1976. He did not run for reelection that year.

# Aldrich, Nelson W.

Nelson W. Aldrich (1841–1915) was arguably the most influential member of the Senate from the 1890s until his retirement in 1911. A staunch conservative, he allied himself with other like-minded Republican senators to control the first powerful party leadership organization in the Senate.

Aldrich was elected to the House of Representatives from Rhode Island in 1879. In 1881 he resigned from the House to fill a vacant Senate seat, and he later won election to the Senate in his own right. A successful financier, Aldrich conformed to the contemporary stereotype of the Senate as a "millionaires' club." Wealth, however, was not his only claim to the job. He was accomplished at parliamentary tactics and had a strong interest in the economic affairs of the country.

Until the 1890s members of the Senate had only experimented with leadership by political party. In the last decade of the nineteenth century, a group of Republican senators led by Aldrich and William B.

*A successful financier in the late nineteenth century, Nelson W. Aldrich conformed to the contemporary stereotype of the Senate as a "millionaires' club."*    Source: Library of Congress

President Theodore Roosevelt's progressive policies and to force concessions from Roosevelt.

A champion of commercial interests, Aldrich opposed any substantive regulation of business and was able to temper restrictions imposed by the Interstate Commerce Act of 1887 and the Sherman Antitrust Act. He supported protective tariffs and clashed with Roosevelt over tariff reform. A protectionist tariff bill sponsored by the Aldrich party machine proved so unpopular with the public that it contributed to Republican defeats in the 1910 elections, and the backlash gave impetus to the formation of the Bull Moose or Progressive party. (See PARTIES, POLITICAL.)

## Allison, William B.

William B. Allison (1829–1908) represented Iowa in both the House of Representatives and the Senate. He was counted among the most influential senators of his day.

Allison entered the House of Representatives in 1863 and continued there until 1871. As a representative he served on the Ways and Means Committee and championed the interests of the nation's railroads. He served in the Senate from 1873 until 1908.

During his thirty-five years in the Senate, Allison was known more as a power broker than as a legislator. With Nelson W. ALDRICH of Rhode Island, Allison was a leader of the conservative Republicans who controlled the Senate around the turn of the twentieth century. Allison's influence and authority originally derived from his position as chair of the Appropriations Committee. In 1897, as the most senior Republican in the Senate, he became chair of the Republican Caucus. He was the first to realize that the position might be a useful tool in building and consolidating power.

He believed that "both in the committees and in the offices, we should use the machinery for our own benefit and not let other men have it." Acting on that belief, he took control of the Republican Steering Committee. Through the steering committee he took over the scheduling of legislation and the proceedings

ALLISON of Iowa pooled influence so that they might control the Senate. Calling themselves the School of Philosophy Club, members of the group cemented their ties during after-hours poker games. With the help of his friends, and through force of personality, Aldrich wielded tremendous power even though he held no leadership position until 1899, when he became chair of the Finance Committee.

With Allison, Aldrich effectively controlled committee assignments, the scheduling of legislation, and the business of standing committees. Loyalty to Aldrich and his group was rewarded by good committee assignments and timely consideration of legislation. Rebellious Republicans were punished with the opposite treatment. The Aldrich "machine" was so effective that it was able to hinder the enactment of

*During his thirty-five years in the Senate, William B. Allison was known more as a power broker than as a legislator.*    Source: Library of Congress

on the floor of the Senate. His authority over the Committee on Committees allowed him to fill committee vacancies to punish or reward fellow Republicans.

Under the leadership of Allison and Aldrich, conservative Republicans were transformed into a cohesive political force that scored many victories over the more progressive Republican president, Theodore Roosevelt. On occasion Roosevelt was able to split the two senators, but for the most part Allison and Aldrich worked successfully with each other and their supporters to challenge Roosevelt's policies.

# Amendments

Amendments are proposals to alter or rewrite legislation being considered by Congress. The amending process provides a way to shape bills into a form acceptable to a majority in both the Senate and House of Representatives.

The process of amending legislation has three aspects. First, it is one of the chief functions of the legislative committees of Congress. Second, it is an important element of floor debate in both chambers. Third, it is vital to working out compromises on bills during House-Senate conference negotiations. (See LEGISLATIVE PROCESS.)

Amendments have many objectives. Members may introduce amendments to dramatize their stands on issues, even if there is little chance that their proposals will be adopted. Some amendments are introduced at the request of the executive branch, a member's constituents, or special interests. Some become tools for gauging sentiment for or against a bill. Some may be used as "sweeteners" to broaden support for the underlying measure. Others are used to stall action on or to defeat legislation. In the House, where debate is strictly limited, amendments are often used to buy time; a member may offer a pro forma amendment, later withdrawn, solely to gain a few additional minutes to speak on an issue.

Amendments themselves are frequently the targets of other amendments offered by members having different points of view. The amending process becomes the arena for a struggle among these diverse viewpoints. Very frequently amendments become the most controversial elements in a bill.

Some amendments take on an identity of their own, regardless of the legislation to which they are attached. In the 1970s the Hyde amendment, a proposal to ban federal funding for abortions, touched off an emotional lobbying crusade. The name of its sponsor, Rep. Henry J. Hyde, an Illinois Republican, became a household word.

## In Committee

Legislation comes under sharp congressional scrutiny at the committee stage. Typically a bill first undergoes section-by-section review and amendment by a specialized subcommittee, a process known as "marking up" the measure. Occasionally the subcommittee may approve the legislation unaltered, but it is more likely to amend the bill or even to substitute an entirely new version. The legislation then goes to the full committee, where the process may be repeated. The committee may accept the subcommittee amendments with little or no change, or it may make additional amendments.

If the changes are substantial and the legislation is complicated, the committee may introduce a "clean bill" incorporating the proposed amendments. The original bill is then put aside and the clean bill, with a new bill number, is reported to the full chamber. If committee amendments are not extensive, the original bill is "reported with amendments." Later, when the bill comes up on the floor, the House or Senate must approve, alter, or reject the committee amendments before the bill itself can be put to a vote.

## On the Floor

During floor action members may seek to change the intent, conditions, or requirements of a bill; modify, delete, or introduce provisions; or replace a section or the entire text of a bill with a different version. In the Senate a member may offer an amendment that is entirely unrelated to the bill under consideration. Such an amendment, called a RIDER, usually is not permitted in the House.

All these attempts to alter legislative proposals involve one of three basic types of amendments: those that seek to add text, those that seek to substitute alternative language for some or all of the existing text, and those that seek to delete some or all of the existing text.

Amendments that seek to revise or modify parts of bills or other amendments are called perfecting amendments. SUBSTITUTE amendments aim to replace previously introduced, or pending, amendments with alternatives. A variation of the substitute, referred to as an "amendment in the nature of a substitute," seeks to replace the pending bill with an entirely new version.

Although the rules are interpreted somewhat differently in the House and Senate, both chambers prohibit the offering of amendments past the "second degree." An amendment offered to the text of a bill is a first-degree amendment. An amendment to that amendment is a second-degree amendment and is also in order. But an amendment to an amendment

to an amendment—a third-degree amendment—is not permissible. The rule, simply laid out in JEFFERSON'S MANUAL in the late 1700s, is more complex than it sounds. In practice, it is possible to have four or more amendments pending at one time, depending on how each chamber interprets the first- and second-degree requirement.

Generally speaking, bills in the House are considered section by section, with floor amendments in order only to the section of the bill then being considered. In the Senate amendments usually are in order to any section at any time, unless such practices are prohibited by unanimous consent. It is a basic concept of the amending process that once an amendment has been rejected, it may not be offered again in precisely the same form (although sometimes another vote can be forced on the same amendment).

Committee amendments—those made by the committee that reported the bill—normally are considered before amendments introduced from the floor. However, committee amendments themselves are subject to floor amendments. Both chambers vote on second-degree amendments before voting on first-degree amendments, although the precise order varies from House to Senate because of differing interpretations of the rules.

## In Conference

Legislation cannot go to the president for signature until both chambers of Congress approve it in identical form. When the two chambers pass different versions of a bill, they usually appoint a conference committee to resolve the differences. (See CONFERENCE COMMITTEES.)

Sometimes House and Senate conferees are unable to reach agreement on every difference in a bill sent to conference; such differences are called "amendments in disagreement." Differences on which compromises are reached are incorporated in a conference report, on which each chamber votes as a whole. But amendments in disagreement must be resolved separately in each chamber once the conference report itself has been adopted. The bill will fail unless the two chambers reach compromises on all amendments in disagreement or agree to drop them altogether.

Conferees generally are able to reach agreement,

*The Hyde amendment, which banned federal funding for abortions, touched off an emotional lobbying crusade in the 1970s and brought fame to its sponsor, Rep. Henry J. Hyde, a Republican of Illinois.    Source:* The Washington Post

and Congress approves the bill. On occasion there are irreconcilable disagreements over content, but more frequently amendments are reported in disagreement because the rules of one chamber prohibit its conferees from accepting certain provisions added by the other chamber. This frequently occurs when the Senate adds unrelated, or nongermane, amendments to legislation passed by the House. House rules permit separate votes by the full House on nongermane portions of a conference report.

A House rules change adopted in 1993 tackled an ongoing turf battle between appropriating and authorizing committees. When a Senate appropriations bill includes legislative language, which is barred by House rules, the House authorizing committee with jurisdiction over the topic may offer a preferential motion to insist on disagreement with the Senate.

Rules in both chambers require conference committees to reach compromises within the bounds of the subject matter on which the House and Senate versions of a bill differ. If conferees go beyond those bounds, they may report an "amendment in technical disagreement." This commonly occurs when conferees exceed the levels of funding passed by the House and Senate for some program in an appropriations bill. In such cases, conferees draft an amendment recommending that the House and Senate concur in the agreed-upon amount.

## Appeal

In both the Senate and House of Representatives, a member may challenge a parliamentary ruling of the PRESIDING OFFICER if he or she believes it violates the chamber's rules. Such a challenge is known as an appeal.

A senator appeals to fellow senators to overturn the presiding officer's decision, which can be done by majority vote. In the House, the ruling of the Speaker traditionally has been final, and members are seldom asked to reverse the Speaker's stand. To appeal a ruling is considered an attack on the Speaker. The Senate is more likely to overturn the rulings of its chair, often on political grounds that have little to do with the parliamentary situation.

## Appointment Power

The Constitution gives the Senate the right to confirm or reject presidential appointments to many government positions. Senators sometimes use this "advice and consent" power to press for their own political beliefs and to assert Congress's independence from the executive branch.

Like the authority to approve or reject treaties, the right to review presidents' choices for jobs within the government is given only to the Senate. The House does not vote on presidential nominations, and members rarely have much influence in decisions about which people the president will appoint.

Senators participate in the selection of Supreme Court justices, cabinet officers, ambassadors, and other high-level government officials. Only the president has the formal right to select someone to fill one of those positions. But the Senate has used its power to reject presidential appointments and pressure the president into selecting people more to its liking. In some cases, such as certain federal judgeships, senators traditionally have dictated the selection of nominees.

It has been said that the Senate's decisions on presidential appointments amount to "a cumulative act of choice" as important as "the electorate's single act of choice" in selecting a president every four years. In the vast majority of cases, however, the Senate's power over appointments is little more than a bureaucratic chore. In 1989, the first year of President George Bush's administration, the Senate received more than 48,000 nominations, but fewer than 600 involved high-level positions that might invite Senate scrutiny. Almost 45,000 of the nominations consisted of routine military commissions and promotions. Lists of routine civilian nominations—to the Foreign Service and Public Health Service, for example—accounted for nearly 3,000.

The president's nominations even for high-level positions normally are approved by the Senate with little debate or objection. Most senators believe that the president has a right to pick his own cabinet officers, unless one of his choices has committed some illegal or unethical action or holds beliefs that are repugnant to most Americans. Since Congress first convened, the Senate has rejected only nine nominees for cabinet positions.

A similar argument often is made about Supreme Court nominations: that the president, who was endorsed by the people in the last election, has the right to name a justice who agrees with the president's legal philosophy. That argument has less force, however, because Supreme Court justices serve for life rather than just for the term of the incumbent president. Twenty-eight Supreme Court nominations have been rejected or dropped as a result of Senate opposition. (See COURTS AND CONGRESS.)

The effect of the Senate's power is seen most clearly in the small number of cases in which a nominee encounters real opposition. Such opposition may crystallize during committee hearings on a nomination. In many instances presidents or the nominees themselves withdraw an appointment when it becomes clear that many senators are prepared to vote against it. Less often, presidents continue to press an appointment in the face of possible defeat on the Senate floor. An outright rejection of an important nomination usually represents a major political setback for a president.

The Senate rejects presidential appointments for several reasons. Partisan political considerations play a role, as do concerns about the personal conduct and ethics of a nominee. Interest groups and the press also influence the confirmation process.

Presidents have one way to get around the Senate confirmation process, although it works only temporarily. The Constitution allows the president to fill vacant positions between sessions of Congress, when the Senate is not meeting. These "recess appointments" are allowed to stand until the completion of the Senate's next session.

## History

Senatorial confirmation of executive appointments is a distinctly American practice. It was included in the Constitution as the result of a compromise. Some delegates to the Constitutional Convention favored giving the Senate the exclusive right to select people to fill important nonelected offices. Others argued that the president should have complete control of appointments. The compromise gave the president the power to choose nominees, subject to the approval of the Senate. The president "shall nominate, and by and with the Advice and Consent of the Senate, shall appoint" officials, the Constitution states.

The framers disagreed on the consequences of the compromise. Alexander Hamilton thought it was not especially important, because the Senate would have no power to select officeholders independent of the president. But John Adams thought that the Senate's power would inevitably be used for partisan political purposes. Adams was quickly proved correct, during his own term as president. By 1800 it was clear that Senate approval of nominations would depend on political considerations.

Virtually every president since then has faced difficult confirmation battles with the Senate. Presidents with solid political support in the Senate generally fared better than those who had to contend with a hostile Senate. But even strong chief executives sometimes were subjected to embarrassing defeats of their nominees.

In many cases the confirmation battles of the past seem trivial, even if their political consequences were significant. In the 1870s, for example, Senate Republican leader Roscoe CONKLING resigned from the Senate as a result of a dispute with President James A.

Garfield over appointments for the port of New York. Other confirmation battles have been events of lasting importance to the nation. The long and bitter fight that led to the confirmation of Louis D. Brandeis as a Supreme Court justice in 1916 marked a crucial turning point in the direction of legal philosophy in the twentieth century.

The details of most confirmation disputes have faded with time, but two long-term trends stand out. One is the rise and decline of the president's control over relatively minor but well-paying government positions. The other is the development of senators' power to control nominations that concern their own states.

By 1820 the so-called spoils system was solidly established in the awarding of government jobs. The term comes from the expression "to the victor belong the spoils." This tradition held that the party that had won the last presidential election had a right to put its own people in government offices, regardless of whether or not the previous officeholders were doing a good job. That rule still holds for top-level government offices, such as members of the cabinet and their ranking subordinates. But in the nation's early days the principle of party control of government jobs extended to lesser positions. Jobs such as postmaster and collector of import duties at a port were eagerly sought after, and victorious political candidates rewarded their supporters with them.

The Senate soon moved to take over its own share of the PATRONAGE bonanza. In 1820 it enacted a law limiting the terms of federal officials to four years. That ensured constant turnover, allowing senators to give many more jobs to friends and relatives. The period from 1837 to 1877 marked the high point of Senate efforts to control executive appointments. During this period the spoils system reached its peak, and all presidents were subject to intense pressure for patronage appointments.

The excesses of the spoils system eventually became so serious that Congress reacted against political patronage. President Rutherford B. Hayes began to fight against the system in 1877, and in 1883 Congress established a civil service system to award most government jobs on the basis of merit.

A key element of the Senate's confirmation power

was the notion of SENATORIAL COURTESY. This custom, initiated in the 1780s, provided that the Senate would refuse to confirm a nomination within a particular state unless the nominee had been approved by the senators of the president's party from that state. In practice, this meant that senators usually could select many officeholders directly—a power that enhanced their political strength at home. When neither of the senators from a state was of the president's party, the right of senatorial courtesy often was given to House party members or to local party officials. The tradition of senatorial courtesy declined in importance as patronage declined and more government jobs moved into the civil service system. But senators still exert a strong influence over certain federal judgeships and other offices within their states.

## Politics and Ethics

In recent decades confirmation debates have shifted from the issue of patronage to questions about the political beliefs and ethics of nominees. Far more than in earlier years, nominees are subjected to searching inquiries—by the press and interest groups as well as the Senate.

The inquiries may focus on political views. Sometimes questions are raised about financial dealings that may be illegal or may pose a conflict of interest for the potential officeholder. In recent confirmations, questions have been raised about aspects of personal conduct never before discussed so openly. Recent nominees to high posts have faced allegations of marijuana use, alcohol abuse, and sexual harassment.

### Political Views

Confirmation debates that center on political opinions often involve appointments to independent boards, commissions, and agencies, such as the Legal Services Corporation or the Federal Election Commission. Most of these agencies were created by act of Congress and are not subordinate to any executive department. Thus, members of Congress tend to see these agencies as arms of Congress and expect to play a larger role in appointments to them.

Arguments over political views also crop up in relation to appointments to major cabinet offices or to the Supreme Court. Between 1933 and 1945 several of President Franklin D. Roosevelt's cabinet nominees faced vocal opposition because of their allegedly radical views, although all were confirmed. Roosevelt also won confirmation of Hugo L. Black as a Supreme Court justice in 1937, despite charges linking Black, an Alabama senator, to the Ku Klux Klan.

Robert H. Bork, who was nominated to the Supreme Court in 1987 by President Ronald Reagan, lost his confirmation battle at least in part because a majority of senators believed that his judicial views on subjects such as civil rights and privacy were so conservative as to be outside the mainstream of American legal philosophy.

### Personal Ethics

The issue of conflict of interest is a frequent topic of concern. Present-day nominees are expected to avoid all situations in which their official decisions could benefit their own personal interests, or in which they receive money from people who stand to benefit from their actions. Financial dealings that appear shady can cause serious trouble for a nominee. One well-known example is the case of Abe Fortas, the Supreme Court justice nominated to the post of chief justice by President Lyndon B. Johnson in 1968. Critics blocked the nomination, partly on the grounds that Fortas had accepted money from past business associates, creating a conflict of interest or at least the appearance of conflict.

President Richard M. Nixon's appointment of Clement F. Haynsworth, Jr., to the Supreme Court was defeated because of charges that Haynsworth had failed to show sensitivity to ethical questions and the appearance of a conflict of interest—even though critics conceded that he was not personally dishonest. And President Ronald Reagan's nominee for attorney general, Edwin Meese III, endured a thirteen-month delay in his confirmation because of concern over the legality and propriety of his financial dealings.

A nominee's personal behavior also comes under scrutiny. In 1987 Douglas Ginsburg, President Reagan's second Supreme Court nominee that year, withdrew his name after the press reported that he had smoked marijuana some years before.

Personal ethics and conduct were at issue again in 1989 when the Senate rejected President George

Bush's nomination of former Texas senator John Tower as secretary of defense—the first rejection of a cabinet nominee since 1959. Democratic opponents of the nomination questioned Tower's fitness for office, citing allegations of alcohol abuse and sexual harassment. Tower's work as a consultant for defense contractors also was questioned as a possible conflict of interest. Republicans countered that the allegations against Tower were unfounded and that the Democrats simply wanted to eliminate a strong advocate for policies they opposed.

Tower was only the ninth cabinet-level nominee that the Senate had ever turned down. His rejection marked the first time the Senate had rejected a president's cabinet nominee at the beginning of his first term. Bush watched another intense confirmation battle with the Senate unfold two years later, when he nominated Judge Clarence Thomas to the Supreme Court. Thomas won confirmation, but only after an unprecedented public airing of allegations about his work life.

Thomas was Bush's choice to succeed Thurgood Marshall as the only black on the Court. In October 1991 the Senate confirmed Thomas's appointment by a 53–48 vote, after charges of sexual harassment against him had been aired during an extraordinary

*Senators participate in the selection of Supreme Court justices, cabinet officers, ambassadors, and other high-level government officials. The Senate sometimes turns down presidential appointments. In 1989, for example, the chamber rejected, by a vote of 47–53, the nomination of former senator John Tower to be secretary of defense.*    Source: AP/Wide World Photos

## SENATE REJECTIONS OF CABINET NOMINATIONS

| Nominee | Position | President | Date | Vote |
|---------|----------|-----------|------|------|
| Roger B. Taney | Secretary of Treasury | Jackson | 6/23/1834 | 18–28 |
| Caleb Cushing | Secretary of Treasury | Tyler | 3/3/1843 | 19–27 |
| Caleb Cushing | Secretary of Treasury | Tyler | 3/3/1843 | 10–27 |
| Caleb Cushing | Secretary of Treasury | Tyler | 3/3/1843 | 2–29 |
| David Henshaw | Secretary of navy | Tyler | 1/15/1844 | 6–34 |
| James M. Porter | Secretary of war | Tyler | 1/30/1844 | 3–38 |
| James S. Green | Secretary of Treasury | Tyler | 6/15/1844 | not recorded |
| Henry Stanbery | Attorney general | Johnson | 6/2/1868 | 11–29 |
| Charles B. Warren | Attorney general | Coolidge | 3/10/1925 | 39–41 |
| Charles B. Warren | Attorney general | Coolidge | 3/16/1925 | 39–46 |
| Lewis L. Strauss | Secretary of commerce | Eisenhower | 6/19/1959 | 46–49 |
| John Tower | Secretary of defense | Bush | 3/9/1989 | 47–53 |

SOURCE:   Adapted from George H. Haynes, *The Senate of the United States: Its History and Practice*, 2 vols. (Boston: Houghton Mifflin, 1938).

three days of televised hearings before the Senate Judiciary Committee.

Thomas's accuser was Anita F. Hill, a law professor who said verbal sexual harassment by Thomas had hindered her ability to work while she held jobs in two federal agencies where he was her boss during the 1980s. Thomas flatly denied the charges. Although Hill also was black, he likened the hearings to a "high-tech lynching" and suggested that Hill was acting for unnamed people who wanted to ruin him.

Although Thomas was confirmed, the battle was bitter and divisive. Many people, especially women, believed that Hill had been treated unfairly. Thomas's confirmation was complicated by the belief of many members of the Democratic-controlled Congress that Thomas was too conservative in his judicial philosophy.

In 1993 personal conduct took a different twist when President Bill Clinton had to drop two female candidates for attorney general. The first nominee, corporate attorney Zoë Baird, was withdrawn by Clinton amid a public uproar about the decision she and her husband had made in 1990 to hire two undocumented aliens as domestic workers. The couple also did not pay federal taxes on the workers' wages even though Baird's salary alone was in the range of $500,000 annually. A second leading candidate, federal judge Kimba M. Wood, dropped out because of her own, albeit less severe, "nanny problem." Wood had hired an illegal alien for child care at a time when it was legal to do so. Wood did pay taxes but withdrew anyway, saying: "In the current political atmosphere proceeding further . . . would be inappropriate."

Senators are likely to face criticism regardless of what stance they take on a particular nomination. If too aggressive, they will be charged with interfering with the president; if too deferential, with neglecting their responsibilities in the appointment process.

### Additional Readings

Bronner, Ethan. *Battle for Justice: How the Bork Nomination Shook America.* New York: W. W. Norton, 1989.

Harris, Joseph P. *The Advice and Consent of the Senate: A Study of the Confirmation of Appointments by the United States Senate.* Westport, Conn.: Greenwood, 1968.

Mackenzie, G. Calvin. *The Politics of Presidential Appointments.* New York: The Free Press, 1981.

Simon, Paul. *Advice & Consent: Clarence Thomas, Robert Bork, and the Intriguing History of the Supreme Court's Nomination Battles.* Washington, D.C.: National Press Books, 1992.

Thurber, James A. *Divided Democracy: Cooperation and Conflict between the President and Congress.* Washington, D.C.: CQ Press, 1991.

## Appropriations Bills

One of Congress's most important duties each year is to pass bills appropriating money to operate government agencies and programs. The Constitution says money cannot be drawn from the U.S. Treasury except "in consequence of appropriations made by law." If Congress did not provide money in appropriations bills, the government would have to shut down. Indeed, brief shutdowns do occur from time to time when Congress fails to appropriate funds in time.

Appropriations bills provide legal authority to spend money previously approved in AUTHORIZATION BILLS, but they need not provide all of the money authorized. By custom, the House acts first on appropriations bills; the Senate revises the House version, although on occasion it has written its own separate measure.

Each year Congress must pass thirteen regular appropriations bills by October 1 to fund the various parts of the federal government. About one-half of federal spending each year is funded through this process. The other half is funded automatically, by the authority granted by laws governing ENTITLEMENTS and other mandatory programs. Each of the thirteen regular appropriations bills covers one governmental function, such as defense, or more than one function, such as the appropriation for labor, health and human services, and education.

In addition to regular appropriations bills, Congress usually passes one or more supplemental appropriations bills annually to provide funds for unbudgeted programs or events. In 1991 a supplemental appropriation was used to supply money for the Persian Gulf War. A supplemental appropriation for emergency urban aid was passed after the Los Angeles riots in 1992. If one or more of the regular appropriations bills have not been enacted by October 1, Congress must pass a CONTINUING RESOLUTION to keep agencies operating temporarily. The continuing resolution may last only a few days or up to an entire fiscal year. It can cover one function or the whole government in an omnibus bill. (See BUDGET PROCESS; OMNIBUS BILLS.)

## Appropriations Committee, House

The House Appropriations Committee is the largest standing committee in Congress, and one of the most powerful as well. Its members play a crucial role in the annual process by which Congress determines funding levels for government agencies and programs. In early 1993 the committee numbered sixty members, thirty-seven of whom were Democrats and twenty-three, Republicans.

By custom, all spending bills begin in the House of Representatives. The job of the Appropriations Committee is to write the first versions of the regular AP-PROPRIATIONS BILLS each year, as well as any emergency funding measures that may be required. In the 1980s long budget battles caused the Senate to take the lead on some spending bills.

The full Appropriations Committee looks to its subcommittees to make most of the important decisions. The recommendations of the subcommittees—one for each of the customary thirteen annual spending bills—are generally accepted by the full committee without substantial change.

The real work of the Appropriations Committee is done in the subcommittees. Subcommittee members each year listen to many hours of testimony from government officials, who come to explain the dollar amounts requested for their agencies in the federal government's budget as prepared by the president. Subcommittee members and staff then meet—more than half the time in private session—to go over programs line by line and decide the exact dollar amounts to be given to each.

Subcommittee members follow closely the activities of the agencies under their jurisdiction, year after year. As a result they often acquire a great deal of knowledge about and power over government programs. Rep. Jamie L. Whitten, a Mississippi Democrat, became chair of the full Appropriations Committee in 1979. Whitten remained chair of the panel's agriculture subcommittee, which he had headed since 1949. He was often referred to as "the permanent secretary of agriculture," because his influence went on and on while the real secretaries of agriculture came and went.

The Appropriations Committee has lost some of its influence since the 1970s. The congressional BUDGET PROCESS now limits the freedom of the Appropriations Committee to set spending levels. In 1990 a further, if temporary, restriction was put on the Appropriations Committee by a budget agreement negotiated by Congress and President George Bush. The deal provided for annual spending limits in three categories—defense, domestic, and international spending—during 1991–1993. New rules limited the committee's flexibility by barring the transfer of funds from one category, such as defense, to another, such as domestic spending.

A more significant and lasting limitation on the Appropriations Committee is the existence of entitlement programs, such as Social Security. An increasing share of the federal budget is consumed by such programs, which the government is legally required to pay for completely. The Appropriations Committee has little or no ability to alter the amounts required for ENTITLEMENTS.

One development in the 1980s was used to shore up the committee's power to make decisions. This was the practice of bundling appropriations for most or all federal agencies into a single omnibus bill, known as a CONTINUING RESOLUTION. These comprehensive spending bills usually were passed toward the end of a congressional session in an atmosphere of haste and pressure, hiding many of the committee's funding decisions. In the 1990s, after criticism from presidents Ronald Reagan and George Bush, Congress backed away from using the continuing resolution as a permanent appropriations measure.

Service on the Appropriations Committee continues to be one of the most sought-after positions for House members. Representatives lobby vigorously to be appointed to the committee, and only those who

*The bulk of the spending decisions made by Congress are made in the House Appropriations Committee. Members meet in this room to consider funding requests of government agencies.*    Source: Ken Heinen

have either the backing of important House leaders or strong regional support are likely to gain a seat there. Members who win a spot on the panel give up their chance to participate in the shaping of new government activities, since the Appropriations Committee does not have the power to prepare legislation establishing government programs. Instead, members have the opportunity to steer funds to activities that are important to them or their constituents.

Turnover on the Appropriations Committee is very low. In 1993, however, nineteen members left the committee due to retirements and defeats. The turnover set the stage for a new era in the committee's history.

### History

Until the Civil War, spending matters were considered along with tax legislation in the House Ways and Means Committee. Overseeing both revenues and spending became too large a task for one committee, however, so in 1865 the Appropriations Committee was established.

The spending panel quickly became a powerful committee. Under the leadership of Democrat Samuel J. Randall of Pennsylvania, the Appropriations Committee became the object of hostility from other members, who thought it was too tightfisted. That resentment gave rise to a move to curb the committee's power. House members voted to take away the panel's jurisdiction over several government programs, including defense, river and harbor projects, agriculture, and the Post Office. By 1885 the committee had lost control over half the federal budget.

But dispersal of spending power to several different committees frustrated efforts to establish control over government budget policy. To centralize spending power, the House in 1920 restored to the Appropriations Committee the exclusive right to approve appropriations bills.

Appropriations Committee members gained more power and independence in the following decades. Committee members often won reelection easily year after year. Because of their long years of service the SENIORITY SYSTEM placed them in positions of power as chairs of the committee and key subcommittees, where they became politically entrenched. They were thus able to pursue their own goals with little interference from the House leadership.

Committee meetings were almost always held in secret, and even the records of hearings were usually withheld from outsiders until shortly before the appropriations bill came to the floor. Consequently, few members who were not on the subcommittee were in a position to challenge the bill. Two of the most powerful committee chairs were Clarence CANNON of Missouri, chair for most of the period between 1949 and 1964, and George H. Mahon of Texas, who held the post from 1964 to 1979.

In the 1970s House leaders began to curb the autonomy of the Appropriations Committee. The Legislative Reorganization Act of 1970 caused most Appropriations subcommittee hearings to be opened to the public, although many bill-drafting sessions remain closed. In 1971 the seniority system was attacked and changed by many younger and more recently elected House members, who wanted to share in the power then concentrated in the hands of their more senior colleagues. One major change allowed committee and subcommittee chairs to be selected without regard to seniority. (See REFORM, CONGRESSIONAL.)

In 1975 the Democrats, who were in the majority, emphasized the importance of the Appropriations subcommittees by requiring that the chairs of those panels, like the chairs of full committees, be elected by a secret vote of all House Democrats. This raised the threat that senior chairs might be voted out by colleagues. It tended to make chairs more responsive to the needs and interests of other House members, including the elected party leadership. Another Democratic party action that year also was aimed at Appropriations: a rule barring members from serving on

more than two subcommittees. The rule was intended to prevent senior Appropriations Committee members from monopolizing key positions.

## Appropriations Committee, Senate

The Senate Appropriations Committee is the largest committee in the Senate and one of the most important. But traditionally its role in the Senate has been considered less significant than that played by its counterpart in the House. (See APPROPRIATIONS COMMITTEE, HOUSE.) In early 1993 the committee had twenty-nine members, of whom sixteen were Democrats and thirteen, Republicans.

Like the House panel, the Senate committee is responsible for preparing the annual bills that provide money for federal government agencies. The committee reviews the spending proposals of the executive branch and can recommend to the full Senate changes in the amounts requested for various programs. For decades the Senate Appropriations Committee existed in the shadow of its more powerful House counterpart, because an unwritten rule in Congress requires that the House be the first chamber to act on these annual spending bills (called APPROPRIATIONS BILLS).

In the 1980s Senate committee members sought to strengthen their role. Members worked to unite their committee and to establish a more unified stance in negotiations with the House in CONFERENCE COMMITTEES. The committee gained a new focus when former Senate majority leader Robert C. BYRD, a West Virginia Democrat, became chair in 1989.

The Senate Appropriations Committee normally takes up a spending bill only after it has passed the House, although preliminary subcommittee work on the bills begins earlier. In the 1980s the Senate Appropriations Committee took action before its House counterpart in several instances because of House delays caused by long budget battles. For the most part, however, Senate committee members find themselves in the position of reacting to a completed bill that has already been approved by the House. As a result, Senate members are likely to allow much of the

House bill to go through unchanged, while focusing their attention on increasing or reducing funding for a few highly visible programs.

For many years the Senate committee operated largely as a "court of appeals." Supporters of programs whose funding had been cut by the House would try to lobby Senate committee members to restore some or all of the money. Senators frequently sought to increase funding levels approved by the House, and they rarely proposed funding reductions. After the 1990 budget agreement between Congress and President George Bush, the Senate Appropriations Committee several times scaled back House proposals, bringing them closer to the president's position.

The heavy and diverse workloads of senators put the Senate Appropriations Committee at a disadvantage in dealing with the House spending panel. Senate committee members serve on one or two other major committees in addition to Appropriations, while House Appropriations Committee members generally serve only on that committee. In consequence senators often have less time than House committee members to master the details of spending bills.

---

# Armed Services Committee, House

The House Armed Services Committee has jurisdiction over most aspects of U.S. national defense. Along with its Senate counterpart, the House committee each year prepares the legislation that sets the upper limits on how much the Defense Department can spend for weapons, troops, and military facilities.

Some $270 billion was spent on national defense in 1991. The enormous size of the defense budget makes Armed Services one of the most important and powerful committees in the House. Its importance is sure to continue as the United States develops its strategy for the post–Cold War era amid expectations for reduced defense budgets.

Committee members spend much of their time reviewing requests for funding of new and existing weapons programs submitted by military and civilian officials in the Pentagon. The committee largely determines the size, strength, and fighting ability of the

nation's armed forces. The committee does not, however, have complete control over spending for defense. The Budget Committee sets an overall limit on the amount of money available for defense each year, and the Appropriations Committee determines the exact dollar amounts for individual defense programs. But the Armed Services Committee plays the most important role in determining how the money will be spent. (See APPROPRIATIONS COMMITTEE, HOUSE; BUDGET COMMITTEE, HOUSE.)

The committee is also a significant arena for debate over issues of strategic defense. In the 1980s and early 1990s committee members were deeply involved in controversies over nuclear arms control, as well as proposals for new nuclear missiles and an antimissile defense program. The committee took the lead in the House in shaping the U.S. defense program following the disintegration of the Soviet Union.

The members of Armed Services traditionally have been conservative and strongly prodefense. Both Democratic and Republican members worked closely over the years with Pentagon officials and supported their budget requests, sometimes at levels considerably higher than those favored by a majority of the House. For many years there was a strongly bipartisan atmosphere on the committee. But in the early 1990s Democrats solidified their control of the committee and began forcing through bills that were more partisan.

### History

The origin of the Armed Services Committee goes back to the creation of the Military and Naval Affairs committees in 1822. The modern history of the committee began in the years after World War II, about the time the unified Department of Defense was created. The actual committee was created by the Legislative Reorganization Act of 1946 out of the combination of the Military and Naval Affairs committees.

For more than three decades the committee was dominated by a solid core of conservative southern Democrats and Republicans, who ensured that the annual defense bills closely followed Pentagon recommendations. The committee was chaired by a succession of powerful southern Democrats, who ran it with an iron hand.

*The House and Senate Armed Services committees are the central arena for debate on arms control and the defense budget. Committee members spend much of their time reviewing Defense Department requests for funding of military programs. The House committee holds hearings in this room.    Source: Teresa Zabala*

The first of the autocratic chairs was Carl Vinson, a Georgia Democrat who controlled the committee from 1949 to 1965, except for the years from 1953 to 1955, when Republican Dewey Short of Missouri was chair. Next came South Carolina Democrat L. Mendel Rivers (1965–1971), who was frequently accused of running the committee as his personal domain, dictating its agenda and rarely allowing junior members to have much of a voice. Rivers worked hard to steer Pentagon spending projects, such as military bases and defense contracts, to South Carolina. Cynics said he was so successful that the entire state would sink into the ocean if another military base were estab-

lished there. Rivers's strenuous efforts to bring job-creating military bases and contracts to his home state were typical of the concerns of many committee members during this period.

Major changes in the committee began to occur in the 1970s. One new factor was the arrival on the committee of a small number of liberal Democrats. These Democrats, who were strongly opposed to U.S. military involvement in Vietnam, soon became vocal critics of the committee's prodefense majority. Members such as Les Aspin of Wisconsin and Patricia Schroeder of Colorado used their committee positions to highlight their attacks on what they saw as wasteful and excessive military spending. But they were overwhelmingly outnumbered on the committee and rarely had the strength to influence committee decisions.

Another factor that began to affect the committee in the 1970s was the House attack on the SENIORITY SYSTEM. Reform-minded Democrats sought to replace the existing method of selecting committee chairs according to length of service with a method based on elections within the House Democratic Caucus. The Armed Services chair at the time, F. Edward Hébert of Louisiana, was one of the prime targets of reformers. The House Democratic Caucus, the organization of party members, deposed Hébert in 1975, replacing him with seventy-year-old Melvin Price of Illinois.

Price chaired the committee for the next ten years. During that time the committee prepared legislation authorizing the massive buildup in military spending sought by President Ronald Reagan in the early 1980s. But Price was not a strong chair. Many of his colleagues saw him as too aged and infirm to run the committee effectively. At the same time, the small group of liberals on the committee was slowly gaining influence.

The turning point in the history of the Armed Services Committee came in 1985. Arguing that the committee needed more effective leadership, Aspin challenged Price. Price was supported strongly by the House Democratic leadership but was defeated by widespread doubts among members about his continued ability to manage the committee as its chair. In a highly unusual move the Democratic Caucus chose as his replacement Aspin, who jumped over five more senior Democrats to become chair.

But Aspin soon ran into problems himself, when he angered many of the liberal Democrats who had voted for him by supporting some of Reagan's key defense proposals. Early in 1987 Aspin was initially ousted as chair by the caucus. He fought back, however, and later won reelection over three opponents.

Although he was sometimes at odds with the liberal-dominated House Democratic Caucus, Aspin emerged as the House Democrats' most savvy and politically influential spokesperson on defense. In 1991, for example, Aspin was instrumental in lining up the majorities that voted to go to war with Iraq. With the disintegration of the Soviet Union, House Democrats looked to the Armed Services Committee chair to articulate a Democratic defense program for the new post–Cold War era.

Aspin's mastery of defense issues won him the post of secretary of defense in President Bill Clinton's cabinet in 1993. The new chair of the Armed Services Committee was California Democrat Ronald V. Dellums, a self-described socialist who regularly denounced Pentagon spending plans. But along with gritty integrity and 1960s rhetoric, Dellums also displayed an acute sense of how to play the legislative game. During a decade of chairing Armed Services subcommittees, Dellums demonstrated a consistent pattern: He would craft consensus bills that enjoyed wide support among his colleagues and then vote against them, on grounds that they earmarked too much money for defense. His political finesse fostered the high regard in which he was held by even some of the most conservative members of the House.

---

# Armed Services Committee, Senate

Like its House counterpart, the Senate Armed Services Committee has responsibility for most aspects of U.S. national defense. Because it has authority over the vast array of Defense Department programs, the committee usually is considered to be among the most influential committees in the Senate. (See ARMED SERVICES COMMITTEE, HOUSE.)

The work of the Armed Services Committee revolves around the annual Defense Department authorization bill. This measure must be reported and passed each year to give the Defense Department authority to spend money. Once it has been passed, Congress may approve appropriations bills for purchase of weapons, military operations, and construction of military facilities.

The Senate committee resembles House Armed Services in many ways. Their jurisdictions are basically the same, with the exception of the Senate panel's jurisdiction over defense-related executive nominations. The two committees also have a similar political approach to defense issues. The Senate committee historically has had a prodefense majority, which has tended to give strong support to Pentagon requests for funding of proposed new weapons systems.

Senate Armed Services has faced challenges to its authority over defense spending similar to those that have confronted the House committee in recent decades. The development of the congressional BUDGET PROCESS and a newly assertive attitude on the part of the Appropriations Committee both posed threats to the Armed Services panel's control over the amount of money available for defense spending. (See APPROPRIATIONS COMMITTEE, SENATE.)

The Senate Armed Services Committee for the most part did not face the kind of political problems that often plagued its House counterpart during the 1970s and 1980s. Senate committee members generally proposed defense policies and spending levels that enjoyed broad support in the Senate. This was in marked contrast to the House, where Armed Services Committee proposals often were opposed by a majority of Democrats in the whole House. But with the demise of the Soviet Union in the early 1990s, even the Senate committee felt increased pressure from Democrats to make deep cuts in the defense budget.

### History

Since its creation by the Legislative Reorganization Act of 1946, the Senate Armed Services Committee has frequently been controlled by a strong chair who has put a personal imprint on Senate defense policy. The first and most powerful of these was Richard B.

RUSSELL, a Georgia Democrat who ran the committee for a total of sixteen years, from 1951 to 1953 and then again from 1955 to 1969.

Russell, whose Senate career had begun in 1933, was one of the most powerful senators of his day. He was a dominant force on defense policy for nearly two decades. He towered over Senate debates on defense bills, because of both his mastery of defense issues and the immense respect his colleagues had for him. He was rarely challenged, either in the committee or on the Senate floor. His control of defense topics became even more entrenched in the 1960s, when he also became chair of the Defense Subcommittee of the Appropriations Committee.

Russell's successor, Mississippi Democrat John C. STENNIS, chaired the committee from 1969 to 1981. He also wielded considerable influence, because he chaired both Armed Services and the defense spending subcommittee. Despite the personal admiration many senators felt for him, however, Stennis did not dominate defense debates the way Russell had. Another committee member, Washington Democrat Henry M. Jackson, was widely viewed as the Democrats' defense expert. His knowledge of defense issues and advocacy of a strong defense posture made him a major force in the Senate and a leader among the section of the Democratic party that favored a tough stance toward the Soviet Union.

The Republican takeover of the Senate in 1981 put Texan John Tower in the Armed Services chair. Tower, a strong-willed negotiator who favored a hard line toward the Soviet Union, guided President Ronald Reagan's massive defense buildup through the Senate in the early 1980s. Later, when enthusiasm for defense increases cooled, Tower was a key force in protecting Pentagon spending requests from budget cuts. He was followed for two years (1985–1987) by Arizona Republican Barry M. Goldwater, a blunt-spoken conservative who had been his party's nominee for president in 1964.

Democrat Sam Nunn, who took over Armed Services in 1987, was a chair in the Russell tradition. Nunn, also from Georgia, was universally recognized as the most knowledgeable senator on defense issues even before he became chair. His expertise on both broad strategic questions and technical defense mat-

ters made him the Senate's dominant force on defense issues beginning in the late 1980s. For example, in 1987 Nunn stopped Reagan's effort to reinterpret a 1972 U.S.-Soviet treaty so it would not conflict with the president's proposed antimissile defense system. In 1989 he spearheaded the Democratic defeat of the nomination of former senator Tower to be President George Bush's secretary of defense. The chair successfully resisted Democratic pressure to slash the post–Cold War defense budget in the early 1990s.

Some observers believed that Nunn lost clout in 1991 when he voted against the Persian Gulf War. But others disagreed and felt, as one of his Senate colleagues put it, that Nunn was "still the man to beat" on defense issues.

---

## Army-McCarthy Hearings

*See* MCCARTHY, JOSEPH R.

---

## At-Large Representative

*See* HOUSE OF REPRESENTATIVES.

---

## Authorization Bills

Congress passes authorization bills to determine which programs and agencies the federal government is allowed to operate. Authorization bills may create legal authority for new programs or continue the operation of existing ones, either indefinitely or for one or several years. They set policy and procedures for government programs. Some authorizations set a ceiling on the amount of money that may be appropriated for the programs; others are open-ended, simply permitting the appropriation of "such sums as may be necessary."

Authorization bills do not themselves provide money; that requires separate action through the appropriations process. Congressional rules state that programs must be authorized before money can be appropriated for them, but the requirement is often waived. (See APPROPRIATIONS BILLS.)

# B

## Baker, Howard H., Jr.

Howard H. Baker, Jr. (1925– ), of Tennessee was first elected to the Senate in 1966 and served until his retirement in 1985. From 1981 to 1985 he was majority leader.

Defeated in his first campaign for the Senate in 1964, Baker ran again and won in 1966, becoming the first popularly elected Republican senator from Tennessee. Baker had strong roots in Congress: Both of his parents served in the House of Representatives, and his father-in-law, Everett McKinley DIRKSEN, was minority leader of the Senate.

Baker gained national prominence in 1973 for his participation in Senate hearings on the WATERGATE SCANDAL. Disclosure of administration efforts to cover up political sabotage in the Watergate affair ulti-

mately drove President Richard Nixon out of office. As vice chair of the Select Committee on Presidential Campaign Activities, Baker impressed his colleagues and the country at large with his calm and measured approach. The question he posed to witnesses, "What did the president know, and when did he know it?" entered the language.

In 1977, after a last-minute campaign and by a slim margin, Baker was elected Senate minority leader. He became majority leader in 1981, after Ronald Reagan was elected president and Republicans won control of the Senate. Despite some philosophical differences with the president, Baker decided that he would become, in his own words, Reagan's "spear-carrier in the Senate." It was a role he filled faithfully during his four years as majority leader.

Baker's style was relaxed and effective. Under his

*Back home in Tennessee, Sen. Howard H. Baker, Jr., shares a laugh with constituents on the courthouse steps in 1973.*
*Source: AP/Wide World Photos*

leadership the Republicans in the Senate became a voting bloc that handed Reagan significant victories on taxation and budget issues. As majority leader, he also played a large part in the Senate's decision to allow television coverage of Senate floor proceedings.

In 1984, saying that "eighteen years is enough," Baker announced that he would retire from the Senate to practice law. He had run unsuccessfully for the Republican presidential nomination in 1980 and was widely expected to try again in 1988. But in February 1987, under pressure in the IRAN-CONTRA AFFAIR, Reagan asked Baker to become White House chief of staff. By accepting the appointment, Baker removed himself from the 1988 presidential contest.

## Banking, Finance, and Urban Affairs Committee, House

The House banking committee is responsible for regulation of the complex U.S. financial system and focuses primarily on the rapidly changing financial world. Today it spends comparatively little time on the urban problems that dominated its agenda in the 1960s. In recent years the House Committee on Banking, Finance, and Urban Affairs has had to adjust the rules of the financial system in response to the now global world of finance.

The committee deals with a wide range of authorizing legislation, from the Export-Import Bank to rehabilitation of rental housing, and it shares responsibility for overseeing international trade. Financial troubles in the savings and loan industry dominated the panel's attention in the late 1980s and early 1990s, as hundreds of savings and loan institutions went bankrupt under the weight of bad loans, recession, and a collapsed commercial real estate market. The committee had to craft several bills to pay for the multibillion-dollar bailout.

The savings and loan crisis came after the committee had deliberated for years on how to respond to revolutionary changes in the financial industry. When money-market funds began offering high interest rates in the 1970s, banks had to wait for permission to compete. New computer technologies made interstate banking attractive, but federal rules kept banks from competing across state lines. Then corporations such as Sears, Roebuck, and Co. began to take deposits and offer bank services—eroding territory banks had once

*The Banking, Finance, and Urban Affairs Committee deals with a wide range of authorizing legislation, from the Export-Import Bank to rehabilitation of rental housing. It shares responsibility for overseeing international trade. Here representatives talk at the start of markup of banking legislation.*
Source: R. Michael Jenkins

had to themselves. Banks argued that they were hindered by Depression-era laws designed to insulate the banking system from the more volatile world of stock trading and land transactions. They wanted the rules changed so that they could compete in insurance, real estate, and securities—arenas closed to them since the 1930s. Congress considered such legislation in the early 1990s, but opposition from the securities and insurance industries defeated the proposals.

The banking committee's other role, as monitor of urban affairs, has received little attention in recent years. Membership on the committee was once sought after by liberal legislators from urban districts and is still popular among representatives from New York City. In the 1980s the committee drew moderates whose districts serve as regional banking centers. But despite the higher visibility of banking questions, the committee continued to advocate public housing.

The banking committee was established in 1865 along with the Appropriations Committee, when the overloaded Ways and Means Committee was split into three parts. However, the banking committee has never matched the standing of the other two panels.

The committee was called Banking and Currency until 1975, when the word *Housing* was added. In 1977 it was renamed Banking, Finance, and Urban Affairs. Wright Patman, the Texas Democrat who chaired the panel from 1963 to 1975, was a consummate populist who used the committee as a pulpit to attack Federal Reserve Board restraints on credit. Patman ran the committee with a firm hand until age made it difficult for him to keep the fractious panel in line. In 1975, when he was eighty-two years old, Patman was one of three chairs ousted by the Democratic Caucus after a loosening of seniority rules.

The next chair, Wisconsin Democrat Henry Reuss, had an almost academic interest in both banking and urban affairs; he focused attention on the latter with a special Subcommittee on the City. Reuss lacked political skills, however. He had trouble with the back-room bargaining needed to pass legislation, and he suffered some embarrassing floor defeats.

After Reuss stepped down for health reasons in 1980, the top post went to Fernand St Germain, a Rhode Island Democrat. St Germain had chaired the preeminent banking subcommittee, the subcommittee on financial institutions, since 1971. St Germain, considered to be politically shrewd, held on to the post of subcommittee chair. As committee chair, he relished being able to orchestrate the committee's every move and seldom shared his plans. Though always careful to speak for the consumer, St Germain was criticized for his close financial ties with the banking and housing industries. The House ethics panel in 1987 absolved him of allegations that he had grown rich through abuse of his office. In 1989, after fresh allegations were made, St Germain lost a reelection bid and was replaced by Texas Democrat Henry B. Gonzalez, a populist who sought to focus more attention on housing issues.

---

## Banking, Housing, and Urban Affairs Committee, Senate

Watching over the nation's banking industry is the chief responsibility of the Senate Committee on Banking, Housing, and Urban Affairs. The committee is responsible for legislation dealing with regulation of the U.S. financial system. The Federal Reserve System, the comptroller of the currency, the Federal Deposit Insurance Corporation, and the Resolution Trust Corporation fall within its purview. The banking committee also shares oversight of international economic policy, including foreign trade.

Although the panel also has jurisdiction over housing and urban issues, the savings and loan bailout and banking regulation dominated lawmakers' attention in the 1980s and early 1990s. Under the direction of committee chair Donald W. Riegle, Jr., a Michigan Democrat, the panel crafted legislation that overhauled the savings and loan industry and provided $50 billion in cleanup costs. Additional money was approved in following years as bailout demands grew. In the late 1980s hundreds of savings and loan institutions went bankrupt under the weight of failed loans, a national recession, and the collapse of the commercial real estate market. The federal government was left to pay off depositors.

At the same time Riegle and Alan Cranston of California, the number-two committee Democrat, were charged with using their positions to influence federal regulators' oversight of a savings and loan owned by Charles H. Keating, Jr., a political contributor. Riegle was rebuked for showing poor judgment, while Cranston received a more serious reprimand. (See KEATING FIVE SCANDAL.)

Since the banking committee is required to take on some of the most unpopular issues in Congress, membership on the committee is less sought after than posts on the Finance or Appropriations committees, for example. Most of its legislative business is handled in the full committee, instead of in subcommittees.

The senator who was probably the best known for drafting banking legislation was Virginia Democrat Carter Glass. Glass was coauthor of one of the major banking laws of 1933, the Glass-Steagall Act, which prohibited banks in the Federal Reserve System from selling stocks and bonds. Glass, who chaired a key Senate banking subcommittee, also played a major role in the creation of the Securities and Exchange Commission in 1934. A senator from 1920 until his death in 1946, Glass had previously served in the House; as chair of the House banking committee, he had helped establish the Federal Reserve System in 1913. In that same year the Senate set up its Banking and Currency Committee.

Like the House, the Senate changed its banking committee's name in the 1970s to reflect its role in housing and urban affairs. William Proxmire, an independent-minded Wisconsin Democrat, chaired the committee from 1975 to 1981 and from 1987 to 1989. Utah Republican Jake Garn held the post during the intervening years, when Republicans controlled the Senate. After Proxmire retired, Riegle took over the committee in 1989, just as the savings and loan bailout, bank troubles, and the Keating Five scandal became public knowledge.

## Barkley, Alben W.

As majority leader of the Senate from 1937 to 1947, Alben W. Barkley (1877–1956) played an important role in the passage of President Franklin D. Roosevelt's NEW DEAL legislation. Barkley was a sup-

porter of Roosevelt but not blindly loyal to him, and on occasion he differed strongly and publicly from the president.

Barkley began his career in Congress in 1912, when he was elected as a Democrat to represent Kentucky's First District. After seven terms in the House of Representatives, he was elected to the Senate in 1926, where he spent the remainder of his congressional career.

In 1937, upon the death of Majority Leader Joseph T. Robinson of Arkansas, Barkley waged a hard-fought campaign to succeed him. He defeated his rival for the post, Pat Harrison of Mississippi, by a narrow margin—just one vote. His success was attributed to a perception that Roosevelt favored his candidacy. The contest brought to the surface deep rifts in the party between conservative southerners and New Deal Democrats. Once revealed, the division among the Senate Democrats contributed to the defeat of some of Roosevelt's domestic initiatives—most notably, his attempt to increase the number of justices on the Supreme Court.

As majority leader, Barkley loyally supported Roosevelt's policies and served as a spokesperson for the president in his relations with Congress. In the fall of 1938, at Roosevelt's request, Barkley agreed to punish senators who worked to defeat the president's Court-packing scheme. But he was angered by Roosevelt's unprecedented veto of a tax bill in 1944.

Barkley spoke forcefully against the president on the floor of the Senate, calling the veto "a calculated and deliberate assault upon the legislative integrity of every member of Congress." He said, "Other members of Congress may do as they please, but as for me, I do not propose to take this unjustifiable assault lying down. . . . I dare say that during the last seven years of tenure as majority leader, I have carried the flag over rougher territory than ever traversed by any previous majority leader. Sometimes I have carried it with little help from the other end of Pennsylvania Avenue." Barkley promptly resigned as majority leader and was just as promptly reelected by a unanimous vote of the Senate Democrats.

In 1948 President Harry S. Truman persuaded Barkley to leave the Senate and run for election as his vice president. The ticket won, and Barkley became a popular public figure, known affectionately as "the Veep." After serving one term as vice president, Barkley was reelected to the Senate in 1954. A campaigner to the end, he died while making a political speech in 1956.

## Bells, Legislative

Business on Capitol Hill is often interrupted by the jarring noise of bells that signal a floor vote in the House or Senate. Committee hearings and bill-drafting sessions stop while representatives and senators listen to the signal; even the congressional handball court is equipped with a buzzer.

New members quickly learn that one ring has a different meaning from three or five. The sound of five bells means that only a few minutes remain on a recorded vote. Fast walkers may ignore the first warning and wait until the last minute to leave their office building for a vote, but others respond immediately to the first warning. Usually a fifteen-minute period is set aside for votes, and slow-moving legislators need every minute to reach the Capitol, even with subways to speed their trip. When five bells ring, members race for the floor. Every police officer, door attendant, and elevator operator helps clear the way for senators and representatives on their way to vote.

The system of legislative bells has been operating in Congress for decades; wiring for buzzers was installed as early as 1912. Many legislators have now supplemented the buzzers with beepers and portable telephones. Neighborhood restaurants, which once rang dinner bells or buzzers to signal a vote, have mostly abandoned the practice.

## Benton, Thomas Hart

Thomas Hart Benton (1782–1858) served as one of Missouri's first senators upon its admission to the Union. A man of strongly held opinions and a colorful past, Benton represented western agrarian interests and championed equality of opportunity at a time

Engraved by J C Buttre

*Source: Library of Congress*

when western expansion and the issue of slavery preoccupied the Senate.

Benton was editor of the St. Louis *Enquirer* when he was elected to the Senate as a Democrat in 1821. An advocate of popular democracy, he supported western expansion and the availability of cheap land. He led the fight in the Senate against rechartering the Bank of the United States; the bank, a private corporation, engaged in commercial banking activities as well as issuing currency and serving as the official depository for federal funds. He opposed the use of paper currency and thereby acquired the nickname "Old Bullion."

Benton supported Andrew Jackson's unsuccessful bid for the presidency in 1824 even though he and

Jackson had fallen out some years earlier. Benton had served on Jackson's staff during the War of 1812, but their friendship ended in a brawl in which Jackson attacked Benton with a horsewhip and was himself shot in the shoulder. When Jackson won the presidency in 1828, however, Benton became one of his most valuable supporters in the Senate. Jackson's withdrawal of government funds from the Bank of the United States led the Senate to censure him in 1834; Benton led a successful fight to expunge the censure resolution from the Senate *Journal*.

Although Benton himself owned slaves, he believed that economic influences, aided by the country's geographic expansion, would ultimately destroy the system. To this end he supported new western states' constitutions barring slavery. During the heated debate on the floor of the Senate over the Compromise of 1850, which brought California into the Union as a free state, Benton so enraged Sen. Henry S. Foote of Mississippi that Foote threatened him with a cocked pistol.

Benton's belief that slavery had reached its geographic limits, coupled with the expansion of business interests in Missouri that were unsympathetic to his populist ideals, caused him to lose his Senate seat in 1851. He later served one term in the House (1853–1855) but was defeated for reelection over his opposition to the Kansas-Nebraska bill, which allowed settlers in those territories to decide whether or not they wanted slavery there.

## Beveridge, Albert J.

Albert J. Beveridge (1862–1927), an Indiana Republican, was elected to the Senate in 1899. As a freshman senator, he pledged his support to the ruling Republican clique led by Nelson W. ALDRICH of Rhode Island and William B. ALLISON of Iowa. Soon, however, Beveridge became one of a small group of Republicans who supported the policies of President Theodore Roosevelt and opposed the more conservative views espoused by powerful Senate Republicans.

Upon joining the Senate Beveridge sent Allison, who had absolute control over committee assignments, a list of preferred committees with a statement of loyalty: "I feel that the greatest single point is gained in the possession of your friendship. I will labor very hard, strive very earnestly to deserve your consideration." That loyalty was short-lived.

When Roosevelt became president in 1901, Beveridge found a Republican leader more to his liking. Against the pressure of the majority of his Republican colleagues, Beveridge became an enthusiastic and vocal advocate of a strong federal government and progressive domestic policies.

Beveridge failed to win reelection in 1910. In 1912 he served as chair and keynote speaker at the national convention of the Progressive party, which nominated Roosevelt as its presidential candidate. Beveridge ran unsuccessfully for governor of Indiana and twice again for his Senate seat. He received the Pulitzer Prize in 1920 for his *Life of John Marshall.*

## Bill

*See* LEGISLATION.

## Blacks in Congress

Black Americans were excluded from Congress for most of its history. Since the civil rights movement of the 1960s they have been elected in slowly but steadily growing numbers. In 1992 thirty-nine were elected, an increase of fourteen members and the largest number of African Americans ever elected to Congress. The dramatic gain was in large measure a result of redistricting aimed at increasing minority strength in Congress—a legacy of the civil rights era.

The 103rd Congress elected in 1992 counted several firsts for black Americans. Carol Moseley-Braun of Illinois became the first black woman ever elected to the Senate. The first African American to serve in the Senate since Edward W. Brooke, a Massachusetts Republican, was defeated in 1978, she also became the first black Democrat elected to the Senate. For the first time since the Reconstruction era, the House delegations from Alabama, Florida, North Carolina, South Carolina, and Virginia included black members. Georgia elected its first black woman representative, Cynthia McKinney.

All of the black members elected in 1992 were Democrats except one, Republican Gary Franks of Connecticut. In addition to the thirty-eight voting House members, Democrat Eleanor Holmes Norton was elected to a second term as delegate from the District of Columbia. (See DISTRICT OF COLUMBIA AND CONGRESS.)

Despite the dramatic gains of the 1992 election and the growing power of senior black members, African Americans remained numerically underrepresented in Congress. They made up about 12 percent of the population, but only 9 percent of the House and 1 percent of the Senate.

## Background

The first black member of Congress, Mississippi Republican Hiram R. Revels, entered the Senate in 1870. From 1870 through 1991, three black senators and sixty-five black representatives served in Congress. Twenty-two of these served in the nineteenth century, all of them belonging to the party of Abraham Lincoln, the Republican party. In the twentieth century almost all black legislators have been Democrats.

The key to election of blacks after the Civil War was that southern states were not allowed to reenter the Union until they had enfranchised black voters. The Fifteenth Amendment to the Constitution, adopted in 1870, barred states from denying voting rights on the basis of race. Sixteen of the twenty-two blacks who served in Congress during the nineteenth century were elected in the 1870s, primarily from the South, where most black Americans lived.

As federal troops were withdrawn, southern states began to erode the voting rights of black citizens. By the end of the century, literacy tests, poll taxes, and other devices designed primarily to prevent blacks from voting had been established. Between 1901 and 1929 no blacks sat in Congress.

The long period without a black American in Congress ended when Chicago's south side sent Republi-

can Oscar De Priest to the House in 1929. That same Chicago area continued to provide Congress with its sole black legislator—De Priest and two successors—until 1945, when the black representative from Chicago was joined by Democrat Adam Clayton POWELL, Jr., of Harlem in New York City. Powell, a flamboyant personality, chaired the Education and Labor Committee from 1961 until 1967, when the House stripped him of the post after finding that he had misused committee funds.

Another watershed came in 1965, when Congress approved the Voting Rights Act, an aggressive move to end literacy tests and other requirements that kept African Americans off voter registration lists in the South. The year before, the Supreme Court had boosted black influence by endorsing the principle of "one person, one vote." That decision eventually put an end to the practice in southern states of diluting black voting power by drawing district lines to break up black communities. Another step toward increased black voting was ratification in 1964 of the Twenty-fourth Amendment, which outlawed payment of any poll tax or other tax as a voter qualification in federal elections.

The laws passed in the civil rights era did not change Congress immediately. Southern voters, who had last elected a black American in 1899, broke the long dry spell in 1972. In that year Democrats Barbara Jordan of Texas and Andrew Young of Georgia won seats in the House. In 1986 Mississippi elected its first black representative since Reconstruction.

The election of a record number of African Americans to the House in 1992 was largely a result of judicial interpretations of the Voting Rights Act requiring that minorities be given maximum opportunity to send members of their own racial or ethnic group to Congress. After the 1990 census, maps in thirteen states were redrawn to increase the number of so-called majority-minority districts, where minorities made up the majority of voters. (See REAPPORTIONMENT AND REDISTRICTING.)

Among the African Americans reelected in 1992 were some who had been in the House for more than twenty years: William L. Clay of Missouri, chair of the Post Office and Civil Service Committee; John Conyers, Jr., of Michigan, chair of the Government Oper-

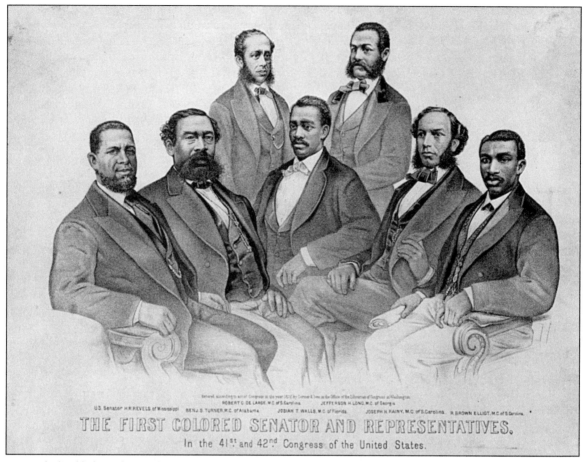

ROBERT C. DE LARGE, M.C. of S.Carolina        JEFFERSON H. LONG, M.C. of Georgia

U.S. Senator H.R.REVELS of Mississippi    BENJ.S. TURNER, M.C. of Alabama    JOSIAH T. WALLS, M.C. of Florida    JOSEPH H. RAINY, M.C. of S.Carolina    R. BROWN ELLIOT, M.C. of S.Carolina

## THE FIRST COLORED SENATOR AND REPRESENTATIVES.
### In the 41ˢᵗ and 42ⁿᵈ Congress of the United States.

*Congress had no black members until 1870. The key to election of blacks after the Civil War was that southern states were not allowed to reenter the Union until they had enfranchised black voters. This Currier and Ives lithograph shows the first black senator and six representatives holding seats in the 41st and 42nd Congress.    Source: National Portrait Gallery, Smithsonian Institution*

ations Committee; and Ronald V. Dellums of California, chair of the Armed Services and District of Columbia committees. Two other black senior members of Congress who had chaired committees in the past were Charles B. Rangel of New York and Louis Stokes of Ohio.

The election of Bill Clinton as president in 1992 brought new prominence to two black House members. Dellums took over as chair of the high-profile Armed Services Committee in 1993 when the previous chair, Les Aspin of Wisconsin, became secretary of defense. Mike Espy, who in 1986 became the first black since Reconstruction elected to represent Mis-

sissippi in the House, left Congress in 1993 to become the first black secretary of agriculture.

Another veteran black representative, William H. Gray III of Pennsylvania, held the third most powerful position among House Democrats—the post of majority whip—when he retired in 1991 to become president of the United Negro College Fund. From 1985 to 1989 Gray had chaired the Budget Committee, one of the most visible and challenging posts in the House.

In 1968 Shirley Chisholm, a New York Democrat, became the first black woman to be elected to the House. The 1992 election made Carol Moseley-Braun of Illinois the first black woman senator and brought five new black women to the House for a total of eight. Cardiss Collins of Illinois, the most senior member of the group, was elected in 1973 to replace her late husband, George W. Collins.

The new generation of African Americans elected to Congress in 1992 reflected the changes begun during the civil rights era. Many came to Congress with considerable experience in state legislatures and other local government positions. Bobby L. Rush of Illinois, a leader of the militant Black Panther movement during the 1960s, had served for a decade on the Chicago city council. Earl F. Hilliard, Alabama's first black representative since Reconstruction, was an eighteen-year veteran of his state's legislature. Walter R. Tucker had been mayor of Compton, a mostly black and Hispanic working-class town in southern California. Cynthia McKinney had been a member of the Geor-

gia state legislature, and Corrine Brown had served in the Florida legislature.

## Black Caucus

The formal organization of black members of Congress is the Congressional Black Caucus, founded in the early 1970s when only a handful of African Americans had been elected. The caucus worked for passage of legislation endorsed by its members and took positions that sometimes were at odds with those of the majority of Democrats, as when it opposed the Persian Gulf War in 1991. Although it was sometimes confrontational, the caucus also sought a role in the House power structure, lobbying to win seats for blacks on key committees.

The dramatic increase in black representatives as a result of the 1992 election swelled the ranks of the caucus and gave it the potential to wield more influence than ever before. Observers of Congress pointed out that the increased size and diversity of the caucus might also make for some internal disagreements among members of the caucus. "I think this is a watershed point in the history of African Americans in American politics," predicted Rep. Conyers, a cofounder of the caucus and its senior member. "The caucus now will be a more powerful influence in a Congress with fewer senior members and more new members. The programs of the caucus will receive a much improved hearing."

*Shirley Chisholm was the first black woman to be elected, in 1968, to the House. A New York Democrat, Chisholm also made a bid for her party's presidential nomination in 1972.*
Source: Congressional Quarterly

# Blaine, James G.

James G. Blaine (1830–1893), a Maine Republican, had a long and varied career in public life. As an influential newspaper editor he helped establish the Republican party in Maine. His congressional service, from 1863 to 1881, included three terms as Speaker of the House. Blaine was the unsuccessful Republican candidate for president in 1884; he twice served as secretary of state.

As Speaker (1869–1875), Blaine reorganized committees to advance his party's legislative priorities. A powerful and effective leader, he urged committee chairs who were grateful to him for their positions to

*James G. Blaine's congressional service included three terms as Speaker of the House. He also ran, though unsuccessfully, for the presidency in 1884 and served twice as secretary of state.*
Source: Library of Congress

pass Republican legislation favorable to the railroads and business in general.

During Blaine's tenure as Speaker, a corruption scandal came to light in the House of Representatives that cast a shadow over his later career. Blaine was accused of having received bribes from Crédit Mobilier of America and the company for which it was building railroad lines, the Union Pacific Railroad. Blaine was implicated in the scandal by letters indicating that he had done legislative favors for railroads in return for gifts of stock. On the floor of the House, Blaine forestalled a move to censure him by reading (but refusing to show) excerpts from the letters.

In July 1876 Blaine left the House to fill an unexpired Senate term. He was later elected to a full term but relinquished his seat in 1881 to become secretary of state for the newly elected president, James A. Garfield. He left the cabinet post after Garfield's assassination the same year.

In 1884 the Republicans chose Blaine as their presidential candidate. The campaign against Democrat Grover Cleveland was characterized by ill feeling and bitter rhetoric. Blaine's involvement in the railroad bribery scandal hurt his candidacy. Cleveland supporters chanted, "Blaine, Blaine, James G. Blaine! Continental liar from the state of Maine." Blaine lost the election but later reentered public life to serve as an able and effective secretary of state under Benjamin Harrison (1889–1892).

## Bolling, Richard

Richard Bolling (1916–1991), a Democrat from Missouri, became one of the most powerful members of the House of Representatives. Although he never became Speaker, as he had hoped to do, Bolling may have influenced the House more than any other member of his generation. He assembled coalitions to pass major domestic programs and was the guiding spirit behind the reform movement that changed the institution in the 1970s. (See REFORM, CONGRESSIONAL.)

Bolling was a master parliamentarian and had a practical grasp of intricate House rules. He wrote several books on the workings of the House and led a bold but unsuccessful move in the early 1970s to restructure the jurisdictions of the House standing committees. He was a principal architect of the congressional BUDGET PROCESS.

Bolling was first elected to the House in 1948. A protégé of Speaker Sam RAYBURN, he joined the Rules Committee in 1955. There, as a loyal lieutenant to Rayburn, he plotted strategy against the Republicans and conservative Democrats who had effective control of the committee. In 1961 Bolling and fellow liberals talked Rayburn into enlarging the Rules Committee and adding more Democratic members to help outvote the old conservatives. Bolling became chair in 1979, by which time the committee stood firmly with the Democratic leadership.

Bolling failed to win leadership elections in 1962, when Carl ALBERT defeated him for majority leader, and in 1976, when he fell three votes short in a contest eventually won by Jim WRIGHT. He was excluded from the Democratic center of power while John W. MCCORMACK was Speaker (1962–1971), but returned to the inner circle when Albert became Speaker in 1971. Bolling was a close adviser to Speaker Thomas P. O'NEILL, Jr., who succeeded Albert in 1977. Bolling retired in 1983.

## Borah, William E.

William E. Borah (1865–1940) was a Republican senator from Idaho for thirty-three years. He is best known for his efforts in 1919 to prevent the United States from signing the Versailles Treaty after World War I and to keep it from joining the League of Nations and the World Court. A man of strong principles, Borah was not so much an isolationist as one opposed to international treaties enforced by anything more concrete than moral sanctions.

Borah, a Boise lawyer, was elected to the Senate by the Idaho legislature in 1907. Later he was a strong supporter of the Seventeenth Amendment to the Constitution, which provided for the DIRECT ELECTION OF SENATORS. During his first term Borah sponsored legislation to establish the Department of Labor. He also strongly supported ratification of the Sixteenth Amendment, which cleared the way for the imposition of an income tax.

Although Borah supported President Woodrow Wilson during World War I, he vigorously opposed Wilson's peace proposals. He was one of the group of "irreconcilables" or "bitterenders" who objected to the treaty. The irreconcilables feared that Article Ten of the League Covenant, which stated that League members would support each other against external aggression, would involve the United States in armed conflicts not central to its interests. Borah also viewed the League Covenant as a "scheme which either di-

rectly or indirectly, greatly modifies our governmental powers."

Borah was the author of a resolution calling for the Washington Conference on the Limitation of Armament, convened in 1921–1922 to discuss naval disarmament. He served as chair of the Senate Foreign Relations Committee from 1924 until 1933. He endorsed the Kellogg-Briand Pact of 1928, which sought to outlaw war, and supported U.S. recognition of the Soviet Union. He died in office on the eve of World War II.

## Budget Committee, House

Of all House committees, the Budget Committee is the one most concerned with broad questions about the overall shape of federal spending and taxation. Established by the Congressional Budget and Impoundment Control Act of 1974, the committee has responsibility for ensuring that the House complies with the budget-planning process created by the same law. In early 1993 the committee had forty-three members, twenty-six of whom were Democrats and seventeen, Republicans.

Like its Senate counterpart, the House Budget Committee does not have authority to directly approve substantive legislation or spending bills. Instead its task is to set out guidelines and goals for bills approved by other committees. To do that, the Budget Committee has two main duties. One is to propose an annual budget resolution, which establishes targets for total federal spending and revenue, and the amounts that can be spent on broad categories of federal programs, such as defense or welfare. The other duty is to try to make other committees and the whole House comply with those spending targets.

The committee is also the first House committee to examine the president's proposed budget each year. It thus influences the tenor of the budget debate for the whole year. In addition the committee may prepare instructions, included in the annual budget resolution, that require other committees to cut programs to meet budget targets. The committee cannot tell other committees how to comply with savings instructions, but sometimes there are few options for meeting the targets. This procedure is known as reconciliation. (See BUDGET PROCESS.)

By the 102nd Congress of 1991–1993, however, the House Budget Committee had lost much of its power to shape budget policy, at least temporarily. The deficit reduction agreement—$500 billion over five years—negotiated by Congress and President George Bush in 1990 set spending limits, defined pay-as-you-go rules for mandatory spending, and allowed the deficit to keep growing. In effect it stripped the Budget Committee of its power to make decisions about the budget. During this period, however, the House Budget Committee continued to draft budget resolutions that stated the committee's priorities.

Even before the 1990 deficit reduction agreement, the House Budget Committee had become a relatively weak player in the budget process. One problem was that most members of the House panel were allowed to serve for only six consecutive years. As a result House committee members usually did not have a chance to build up experience and knowledge of budget issues to match that of Senate Budget Committee members, who had no such limit. Another major problem of the House Budget Committee was its deep partisan divisions between Democratic and Republican members. Unlike the Senate committee, where bipartisanship usually prevailed, House committee members of the two parties rarely were able to agree on anything. The budget resolutions produced by the House committee were largely written by the committee's Democratic majority, with little Republican participation. On the floor they usually were protected from specific amendments; the minority could offer only complete substitutes.

### History

The short-term nature of the post of Budget Committee chair, along with other factors, reduced the power of the panel's chair from the beginning. The first four Budget Committee chairs struggled to assert their influence in the budget process.

The first chair was a Washington Democrat, Brock Adams, who served for only two years before resigning in 1977 to become President Jimmy Carter's sec-

retary of transportation. Adams steered a policy of accommodating other committees and avoiding confrontation over spending limits.

The next chair, Robert N. Giaimo, a Connecticut Democrat, more frequently found himself at odds with other House members. Particularly in the Ninety-sixth Congress (1979–1981), Giaimo had the difficult task of developing controls on the rapid growth of federal spending, while at the same time putting together a coalition that could command a majority of the House.

The tenure of Oklahoma Democrat James R. Jones was even stormier. Jones had the misfortune of becoming the Budget Committee chair in the wake of Ronald Reagan's 1980 presidential victory and heavy losses by House Democrats in that election. The new president demanded drastic spending cuts in domestic social programs. In response Jones tried to put together a coalition of moderates from both parties. However, he was overwhelmed by an alliance of conservative Republicans and "Boll Weevil" southern Democrats, backed by Reagan's great popularity.

By his second term (1983–1985) Jones was able to establish an effective relationship with House Democratic leaders to regain control of the budget process. The pattern was continued by William H. Gray III, a Pennsylvania Democrat. The first black chair of the committee, Gray was successful in guiding budget resolutions through the House, although less so in fashioning workable budget agreements with the Senate.

In 1989 one of Congress's most respected budget experts, California Democrat Leon Panetta, became chair. Panetta's training for the job included a six-year term as a member of the Budget Committee from 1979 to 1985. Panetta in 1993 became President Clinton's director of the Office of Management and Budget. He was succeeded as committee chairman by Martin O. Sabo, a Minnesota Democrat.

## Budget Committee, Senate

The Senate Budget Committee was established by the Congressional Budget and Impoundment Control Act of 1974. Ever since its creation it has been an im-

*Each year, like its House counterpart, the Senate Budget Committee must prepare a budget resolution setting out goals for spending and revenues in the coming fiscal year. The committee's task is particularly difficult in times of budgetary stress, when the federal government consistently takes in less money than it spends.    Source: Sue Klemens*

portant player in the Senate spending debate. Although their efforts have had limited success, Senate Budget Committee members have been among the leaders of Congress's attempt to control federal spending and reduce the growing budget deficit. In early 1993 the committee had twenty-one members, including twelve Democrats and nine Republicans. (See BUDGET PROCESS.)

Like its House counterpart, the Senate Budget Committee faces an exceptionally difficult task each year. The committee must prepare a budget resolution setting out goals for spending and revenues in the next fiscal year and must struggle to resist the many changes proposed as amendments on the Senate floor.

The committee's task is even harder in times of budgetary stress, when the federal government takes in less money than it spends. These conditions defined budget debates in the 1980s and early 1990s and put the committee under conflicting pressures. The committee had to try both to limit the growth of federal spending and to protect funding for popular programs.

The committee has only limited power to make and enforce its spending decisions, especially since the 1990 deficit reduction bill put many restrictions on the budget in following years. Despite all their efforts, Budget Committee members were not able to bring annual deficits under control by the early 1990s. Still, the Senate committee has been far more successful in its history than has the House Budget Committee. The Senate Budget Committee has played a greater role in shaping spending decisions and has more power to make other committees accept its views.

There are several reasons for the Senate committee's greater influence. One is that committee members serve continuously and so build up considerable experience and knowledge about budget issues. This is not true in the House, where most committee members can serve for no more than six years in any ten-year period.

Unlike the House Budget Committee, the Senate committee has a strong tradition of bipartisan cooperation. The Senate committee chair and ranking minority member usually cooperate to form a consensus on issues, which usually wins the backing of the full Senate. The committee also has a tradition of strong leaders who are deeply committed to the budget process.

The Senate committee has sought to establish its influence by focusing on broad budget issues, while avoiding specific policies that are under the jurisdiction of the authorizing committees. Instead of going over the budget line by line, as the House committee typically does, the Senate committee concentrates on the overall shape of the budget and the long-term implications of budget policy.

Although it cannot propose substantive legislation to the Senate on its own, the Budget Committee has several ways to try to enforce the fiscal policies embodied in the budget resolution each year. One is a process known as reconciliation, under which spending programs are altered through legislation to reduce their costs. The Budget Committee can direct other committees to approve legislation reducing spending under their jurisdiction by a certain amount, although it cannot tell the committees exactly how to achieve those savings. For several years after the 1990 deficit reduction agreement, reconciliation was not needed or used.

Senate Budget Committee members have successfully challenged spending proposals on the Senate floor. Under the 1974 Budget Act, legislation that calls for spending more than the amounts set by the budget resolution is subject to a point of order, or parliamentary challenge. Senate Budget Committee leaders have used this tactic frequently and have usually had the floor votes to make the spending limits stick.

## History

In its early years the Budget Committee was shaped by its first chair, Maine Democrat Edmund S. Muskie. A veteran senator and one-time Democratic vice-presidential candidate, Muskie was a major figure in the Senate. His decision to devote much of his energy and influence to the committee was an important factor in establishing its importance. Muskie was greatly aided in his efforts by his alliance with ranking minority member Henry S. Bellmon, a conservative Republican from Oklahoma who was deeply committed to the budget process.

The committee's role was easier in the early years because there was less pressure to cut spending. Instead of having to make painful choices about which programs to cut, the committee tried to accommodate the spending needs of most federal programs. But Muskie and Bellmon tried to ensure that Congress stuck with its budget, by challenging proposals that exceeded its limits. The committee had less success, however, in making sure that tax bills written by the Finance Committee complied with the budget.

The Budget Committee became more prominent in the late 1970s and early 1980s, as Congress confronted the growing deficit and runaway inflation. First in 1980 and again in 1981 the committee used the reconciliation process to direct other committees to recommend savings in politically popular programs. The 1981 bill, written by the committee's new Republican majority, embodied the Reagan administration's plan for major cutbacks in federal social programs for the poor.

In the years that followed, Chair Pete V. Domenici, a New Mexico Republican, and colleagues struggled to keep the budget process alive. Each year they had to overcome seemingly insurmountable political obstacles to have a budget approved at last, even if months after the official deadline. One of Domenici's most dramatic victories came in 1985, when he and the new majority leader, Kansas Republican Robert DOLE, produced a budget that passed only after an ailing Republican senator was brought from the hospital by ambulance in the middle of the night to cast the deciding vote.

Florida Democrat Lawton Chiles became Budget chair in 1987 when the Democrats regained the Senate. He and Domenici were able to force closer adherence to spending targets in appropriations bills by staging parliamentary attacks on them on the Senate floor on the grounds that they exceeded the spending targets of the budget resolution.

In 1989 Jim Sasser, a Tennessee Democrat, became chair of the Budget Committee after Chiles left the Senate, partly out of frustration over the budget. After the 1990 deficit reduction agreement stole much of the power from the budget committees in both the House and Senate, Sasser and Domenici crafted budget resolutions that had a limited impact on policy but served to keep the budget process on the minds of members.

## Budget Process

Since the mid-1970s Congress has used a budget process to determine government spending requirements, decide how to pay for them, and examine the relationship between spending and revenues. The process requires legislators to set overall goals for government spending and revenues—and then to tailor their actions to meet those goals. Congress makes many of its most difficult policy decisions during this exercise.

The budget process is a cyclical activity that starts early each year when the president sends budget proposals to Capitol Hill. The president's budget lays out priorities for the fiscal year that will begin October 1. Before Congress adjourns for the year, the Senate and House of Representatives will have created their own budget and provided the money needed to carry it out. Negotiations with the White House may narrow the differences between the two plans, but the congressional budget is likely to differ in important respects from that proposed by the president.

Lawmakers set their own priorities, deciding how much the government should spend and on what, whom to tax and by how much, and what gap should be allowed between spending and revenues. These decisions often bring Congress into sharp conflict with the president.

In 1990 a budget agreement between Congress and the president limited Congress's ability to change spending priorities for a five-year period. The bill set spending limits for discretionary spending in three categories—domestic, defense, and international spending—for 1991–1993. For 1994 and 1995, the legislation set overall limits for discretionary spending. The agreement also specified that any change in law that would result in decreased revenues or increased spending for entitlement programs, such as Social Security and Medicare, must be accompanied by revenue increases that would make up the shortfall or pay for the expanded entitlements.

### Beginnings

Through most of its history Congress acted piecemeal on tax bills and spending bills; it had no way of assessing their impact on the federal budget as a whole. Although the Constitution entrusted Congress with the power of the purse, primary control over budget policy passed to the executive branch. (See PURSE, POWER OF.)

Congress first conferred budget-making authority on the president in passing the Budget and Accounting Act of 1921. That law required the president to submit to Congress each year a budget detailing actual spending and revenues in the previous fiscal year, estimates for the year in progress, and the administration's proposals for the year ahead. The law also created a Bureau of the Budget (renamed the Office of Management and Budget in 1970) to assist the president.

Congress was not bound by the president's recommendations. It could provide more or less money for particular programs than the president requested, and it could change tax laws to draw in more or less revenue. But half a century went by before lawmakers began drawing up their own comprehensive budget plans.

*Richard Darman, director of the Office of Management and Budget during the Bush administration, testifies in 1991 before the Senate Budget Committee on the mid-session review of the budget.*    Source: R. Michael Jenkins

## Budget Act of 1974

The congressional budget process grew out of fights over spending control in the 1970s. Angered by President Richard M. Nixon's refusal to spend money it had appropriated—a practice known as IMPOUND-MENT OF FUNDS—Congress decided to set up its own budget system. The Congressional Budget and Impoundment Control Act of 1974 established a budget committee in each chamber to analyze the president's budget proposals and to recommend a congressional budget policy. (See BUDGET COMMITTEE, HOUSE; BUDGET COMMITTEE, SENATE.) The CONGRESSIONAL BUDGET OFFICE was created to provide data and analyses to help Congress make its budget decisions.

The law required Congress each year to adopt a budget resolution setting overall targets for spending and revenues and establishing congressional spending priorities. (Originally, two budget resolutions were required, but the second was eventually dropped.) Budget resolutions did not require the president's approval—but the president retained veto power over legislation to carry out the congressional plans.

Once a budget resolution was in place, Congress was required to pass legislation making any changes in law needed to ensure that spending and taxing guidelines were met. These changes were made through the appropriations process and through reconciliation, a procedure under which individual committees were required to cut programs within their jurisdictions to meet assigned quotas. APPROPRIATIONS BILLS were required to conform to limits established in the budget resolution. The 1974 act set a timetable for action to be completed before the start of the fiscal year on October 1.

## Changes in Law

The process seldom worked as intended. Deadlines were rarely met, Congress's budgetary restraint was weak, and federal deficits ballooned to more than $200 billion annually. In 1985 reformers pushed through a drastic change in the procedure. The Balanced Budget and Emergency Deficit Control Act of 1985—known as the Gramm-Rudman-Hollings Act for its congressional sponsors—established annual deficit reduction requirements that were designed to lead to a balanced budget by fiscal 1991. The law invented a new weapon, called sequestration, to make automatic the tough decisions on spending reduction that members were unwilling to face. It accelerated the budget timetable and strengthened procedures to make Congress meet its schedule.

Like the 1974 act, the Gramm-Rudman-Hollings Act did not work exactly as intended, and Congress voted a further revision in 1987. The new measure promised a balanced budget by fiscal 1993, two years later than required in Gramm-Rudman-Hollings. It also revised the procedures for automatic spending cuts to meet objections the Supreme Court had raised the previous year.

Congress overhauled its budget procedures once again in 1990. The revised law allowed Congress to pay less attention to the deficit. Any increases in the budget deficit that were the result of either economic conditions or spending required for new people eligible for entitlement programs would not be subject to the automatic spending cuts. Congress had only to abide by new discretionary spending limits and pay-as-you-go rules for mandatory spending on new or expanded entitlement programs or tax cuts. The mea-sure abandoned the idea of a balanced budget dead-line.

In 1992 there was a significant movement in Congress toward enactment of a constitutional amendment for a balanced budget. In the end, the amendment fell nine votes short of the two-thirds necessary for adoption in the House. The Senate did not vote on the measure. President George Bush, along with Republicans and conservative Democrats, supported the legislation, which would have required the president to submit a balanced budget and would have prohibited deficit spending unless a three-fifths majority of both chambers approved a specific deficit amount. The amendment would have taken effect in fiscal year 1998 at the earliest.

### Competition for Dollars

In the early years of the process, congressional budget making was largely a process of accommodation. House and Senate leaders, anxious to keep the process going, proposed budget resolutions that left

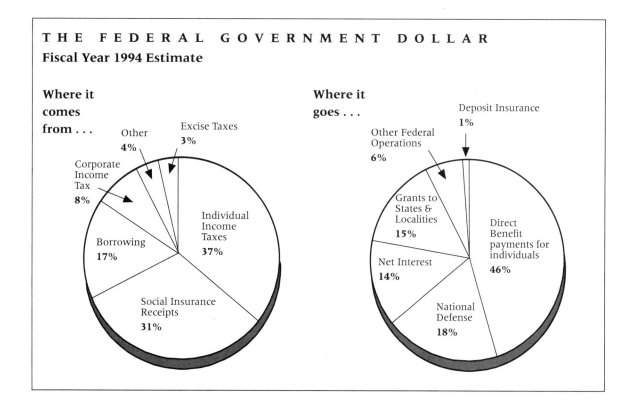

**THE FEDERAL GOVERNMENT DOLLAR**
**Fiscal Year 1994 Estimate**

**Where it comes from . . .**

Other 4%
Excise Taxes 3%
Corporate Income Tax 8%
Borrowing 17%
Individual Income Taxes 37%
Social Insurance Receipts 31%

**Where it goes . . .**

Deposit Insurance 1%
Other Federal Operations 6%
Grants to States & Localities 15%
Net Interest 14%
Direct Benefit payments for individuals 46%
National Defense 18%

room for new programs and additional spending. As long as Congress remained in an expansive mood, the House and Senate were able to construct budgets that satisfied the particular interests of various committees and groups.

When Congress tried to shift to more austere budgets in the 1980s, it encountered much rougher going. While acknowledging the need to hold down spending, members sought to avoid cuts in programs important to their constituents. That became increasingly difficult as the competition for federal dollars increased.

Budget battles with the White House consumed Congress during the administration of President Ronald Reagan. Upon taking office in 1981 Reagan used the congressional budget machinery to carry out sweeping cuts in spending and taxes, as he had promised in his election campaign. In later years Congress routinely dismissed Reagan's budgets, but it had trouble developing plans of its own that also were acceptable to the president. Each year witnessed the two branches battling over the federal deficit, which more than doubled during Reagan's first term.

"The budget process has . . . made it plain that there is no such thing as a free lunch," wrote Sen. William L. Armstrong, a Colorado Republican, in 1984. "A lawmaker who wishes to spend more for some program—whether welfare or defense—must explain where he intends to get the money to pay for it: by reducing spending on other programs, by raising taxes, or by incurring a larger deficit."

The stalemate between Congress and the president led to a new form of budget negotiations in the late 1980s, called summits. An October 1987 crash in the stock market propelled a reluctant President Reagan into a budget summit with congressional leaders of both parties. Congress approved their work—a deficit reduction package of $76 billion over two years—but the experience did not make the summits popular. Many senators and representatives felt they had been excluded from the most important decisions of the session. "You work all year in your committees and then end up with three-quarters of the government run by a half-dozen people locked up in a room for three or four weeks," said Rep. Marvin Leath, a Texas Democrat. "I resent that."

Despite the anger over the 1987 budget summit, in 1990 Bush and the Congress attempted to use a budget summit to negotiate a massive deficit reduction package. Again, the summit alienated many members of Congress who were excluded from the negotiations. For ten days the negotiators met in seclusion at Andrews Air Force Base in suburban Maryland, but they failed to reach agreement. As a last resort, a "hyper-summit" of only eight White House and congressional leaders drafted a deficit reduction plan. The alienated members had their say, soundly defeating the plan and embarrassing the president. Congress finally passed a compromise $500 billion plan that was drafted by the Senate Finance Committee and House Ways and Means Committee.

## Budget Terms

### Appropriations

Acts of Congress that provide actual funding for programs within limits established by authorizations. Appropriations usually cover one fiscal year, but they may run for a definite or indefinite number of years. More than half of all federal spending—for programs such as Social Security and interest on the federal debt—has permanent appropriations, which do not have to go through the annual appropriations process. (See APPROPRIATIONS BILLS.)

### Authorizations

Acts of Congress that establish discretionary government programs or entitlements, or that continue or change such programs. Authorizations specify program goals and, for a discretionary program, set the maximum amount that may be spent. For entitlement programs, an authorization sets or changes eligibility standards and benefits that must be provided by the program. (See AUTHORIZATION BILLS.)

### Budget

A financial plan for the U.S. government prepared annually by the executive branch. The budget sets out in fine print how government funds have been raised and spent and what the president plans for the country in the fiscal year ahead. It is sent to Congress each year in early February. The budget provides for both discretionary and mandatory expenditures. Discretionary funds are appropriated by Congress each year. Congressional appropriations bills are not required to follow the guidelines specified in the president's budget. Mandatory spending is for entitlement programs such as Medicare and veterans' pensions. An entitlement can be changed only by a separate authorizing bill.

## Budget Authority

Legal authority to enter into obligations that will result in immediate or future government spending, called outlays. Budget authority is provided by Congress through appropriations bills.

## Budget Resolution

A congressional spending plan that does not require the president's signature. A budget resolution sets binding totals for broad categories of spending—expressed in budget authority and outlays—and for revenues. Authorization and appropriations bills must then observe these totals. The resolution assumes that certain changes will be made in existing law, primarily to achieve savings assumed in the spending totals. These savings are legislated in appropriations bills and sometimes in reconciliation bills. Each year Congress is supposed to complete action by April 15 on a budget resolution for the fiscal year that will begin October 1. (See BUDGET PROCESS.)

## Congressional Budget and Impoundment Control Act

The 1974 law that established the congressional budget process and created the CONGRESSIONAL BUDGET OFFICE.

## Deficit

The excess of spending over revenues. A surplus exists if revenues are greater than spending. Between 1961 and 1992, the government ran a budget surplus only once, in fiscal 1969. Throughout the 1980s and into the 1990s, the federal budget deficit, which was hundreds of billions of dollars each year, became one of the most intractable issues in government.

## Entitlement

A program that must provide specified benefits to all eligible persons who seek them. Social Security, Medicare, and Medicaid are examples of entitlements. Generally, these programs are permanently authorized and are not subject to annual appropriations. (See ENTITLEMENTS.)

## Fiscal Year

The federal government's accounting period. The fiscal year begins on October 1 and ends on September 30 of the following year. A fiscal year (FY) is designated by the calendar year in which it ends, so that FY 1993 began on October 1, 1992. (See FISCAL YEAR.)

## Gramm-Rudman-Hollings Act

A 1985 act of Congress that set a timetable for achieving a balanced budget and specified a procedure designed to accomplish that goal through mandatory automatic spending cuts. Originally, the act called for achieving a balanced budget by 1991. The timetable was amended in 1987 and again in 1990, at which time the size of the deficit was downplayed and a balanced budget target date was deleted. The act is properly called the Balanced Budget and Emergency Deficit Control Act of 1985. It quickly became known by the names of its three Senate sponsors: Phil Gramm of Texas and Warren B. Rudman of New Hampshire, both Republicans, and Ernest F. Hollings, a South Carolina Democrat.

## Impoundment

A president's refusal to spend money appropriated by Congress. The Congressional Budget and Impoundment Control Act of 1974 established procedures for congressional approval or disapproval of presidential impoundments. (See IMPOUNDMENT OF FUNDS.)

## Outlays

Actual cash expenditures made by the government. In passing appropriations bills, Congress does not directly vote on the level of outlays. Each year's outlays derive in part from budget authority provided in previous years. Outlays also include net lending—the difference between what the government lends and what borrowers repay—such as payments on student loans.

### Receipts (Revenues)

Government income from taxes and other sources, such as user fees and sales of federal assets.

### Reconciliation

Legislation that revises program authorizations to achieve savings required by the budget resolution. Reconciliation bills usually also include revenue increases. The bills are based on instructions in the budget resolution that require authorizing committees to draft legislation specifying cost-cutting changes in programs under their jurisdiction.

### Sequestration

An automatic procedure for making spending cuts required by the Gramm-Rudman-Hollings law if Congress and the president fail to make them legislatively. Under the Gramm-Rudman-Hollings law, as revised, the president's Office of Management and Budget (OMB) determines whether the estimated budget deficit and discretionary spending will fall within the range set by law and whether new mandatory spending or revenue legislation will add to the deficit. If the legal limit is exceeded, OMB determines how much needs to be cut, or sequestered, from the budget. The Congressional Budget Office plays an advisory role. About two-thirds of federal spending is exempt in some way from the automatic cuts. If cuts are needed, they are imposed fifteen days after Congress adjourns.

*Senate Democratic leader for twelve years, Robert C. Byrd later became president pro tempore and handed the gavel over to his colleague, Sen. George Mitchell.    Source: Marty LaVor*

## Byrd, Robert C.

Robert C. Byrd (1918–  ), Democratic floor leader of the Senate from 1977 to 1989, performed his duties with old-fashioned courtesy and consummate parliamentary skills. But his silver hair and the stiff, formal cadence of his speech were poorly suited, some colleagues felt, to his role in the image-conscious Senate.

In 1988, after a productive 100th Congress, Byrd did not seek reelection to the LEADERSHIP post. Instead the West Virginia senator in 1989 became PRESIDENT PRO TEMPORE as the most senior member of the majority party. He retained much power in the chamber by taking over as chair of the Appropriations Committee. Byrd vowed to bring his state $1 billion in federal spending, and he did so in less than two years.

Byrd began his legislative career in 1946, when he won election to the West Virginia state legislature. He was elected to the House of Representatives in 1952. His campaign had been threatened by disclosure that he had joined the Ku Klux Klan when he was twenty-four. Byrd explained the membership as a youthful indiscretion committed because of his alarm over communism. Elected to the Senate in 1958, Byrd combined his Senate duties with law school, finally earning a degree in 1963. In 1967 he won his first leadership post, secretary of the Democratic Conference.

In 1971 Byrd became majority whip, replacing Massachusetts Democrat Edward M. Kennedy. Byrd had assiduously courted his colleagues by arranging schedules to suit their convenience, sharing campaign funds, even sending birthday cards. "My role will be that of a legislative tactician," he said. "I don't want to thrust an ideological position on anyone."

By the time then-majority leader Mike MANS-FIELD retired in 1977, Byrd had made himself indispensable to colleagues, and he had the votes to succeed the Montana Democrat.

With President Jimmy Carter in the White House, Byrd found himself cast as the experienced insider. His legislative skills several times saved Carter's programs, particularly his energy bills and, in 1978, the Panama Canal treaties.

When Ronald Reagan assumed the presidency in 1981, Republicans won control of the Senate and Byrd became minority leader. He tried to unite Democrats by holding weekly meetings and weekend retreats, and he became more aggressive in responding to Reagan.

When Democrats regained control of the Senate in 1987, Byrd became majority leader for the 100th Congress. After giving up the leadership post, he enlarged the office of president pro tempore and became the most assertive Appropriations chair in many years. His prime role was as guardian of Senate traditions and powers. Beginning in 1981 he gave a series of addresses tracing the history of the Senate that were published in 1989–1990 and became an authoritative reference work.

# C

## Calendar

A list of business awaiting floor action by Congress is called a calendar. The House of Representatives has an elaborate system of calendars to help schedule its work. In the smaller Senate, the scheduling system is more flexible.

A House bill goes on one of five different calendars: the Union Calendar, House Calendar, Private Calendar, Consent Calendar, and Discharge Calendar. They are collected in one document entitled *Calendars of the House of Representatives and History of Legislation.* The document, a valuable tool for congressional researchers, is published daily when the House is in session. The first issue of the week lists all House and most Senate measures that have been reported by committees, with a capsule history of congressional action on each. It also includes a general index. Midweek issues deal only with that week's action.

The five House calendars split up bills by broad category. The CLERK OF THE HOUSE assigns bills to one of the calendars when they are reported from committee. They are listed in the order in which they are reported, although they are not necessarily called up for floor action in that order.

Bills that have any effect on the Treasury—revenue bills, general APPROPRIATIONS BILLS, and AUTHORIZATION BILLS—go on the Union Calendar. Most other major bills, which generally deal with administrative or procedural matters, go on the House Calendar. If all these bills had to be taken up in the order in which they are listed on the calendars, as was the practice in the early nineteenth century, many would not reach the House floor before Congress adjourned. Instead, most major legislation reaches the floor by being granted a special rule that allows it to be considered out of order. (See LEGISLATIVE PROCESS.)

Bills involving private matters are referred to the Private Calendar. They cover a range of purposes, from claims against the government to waivers of immigration requirements. Under House procedures, the Speaker is supposed to call up private bills on the first Tuesday of each month and may call them up on the third Tuesday as well.

The CONSENT CALENDAR is reserved for noncontroversial measures. The first and third Mondays of the month are Consent Calendar days. Bills brought up under this procedure almost invariably pass without debate or amendment. A single objection is enough to block consideration the first time a bill is called up. If called up again, it may be blocked only if at least three members object.

The final House calendar, the Discharge Calendar, is rarely used. It comes into play only when 218 representatives (a majority of the total House membership) have signed a petition to take a bill away from the committee that is holding it. This practice, known as discharging a committee, makes it possible for the full House to act on measures that otherwise would remain buried in a hostile committee. Discharge measures may be considered on the second and fourth Mondays of each month. (See DISCHARGE, COMMITTEE.)

In the Senate, all bills are placed on a single legislative calendar, called the Calendar of General Orders. In addition, the chamber has an Executive Calendar listing treaties and nominations, which require the Senate's advice and consent. Schedules for floor action in the Senate are worked out informally, and bills need not be taken up in calendar order.

## Calendar Wednesday

House rules provide a way for committee chairs to force House debate on bills that have been reported by their committees but not scheduled for floor action by the Rules Committee. (See RULES COMMITTEE,

HOUSE.) Under the procedure, known as Calendar Wednesday, bills may be brought directly to the floor on Wednesdays as the Speaker calls each committee in alphabetical order. General debate is limited to two hours, and action must be completed in the same legislative day. The procedure is vulnerable to delaying action and is seldom used. It is not observed during the last two weeks of a session and may be omitted at other times by a two-thirds vote. In practice the House almost always dispenses with Calendar Wednesday by unanimous consent.

The procedure was adopted in 1909 in protest against the autocratic rule of Speaker Joseph G. CANNON, an Illinois Republican who maintained tight control over the House agenda.

## Calhoun, John C.

A brilliant philosopher and an eloquent champion of states' rights, John C. Calhoun (1782–1850) was the foremost spokesperson for the South in the troubled period leading to the Civil War. As lawyer, state legislator, U.S. representative, senator, secretary of war, secretary of state, and vice president, he played a critical role in the course of U.S. foreign and domestic policy in the first half of the nineteenth century.

Calhoun entered the House of Representatives in 1811. During his six years in the House he was a nationalist, supporting efforts to strengthen the central government. With Speaker Henry CLAY, he was one of a group known as the War Hawks who helped push the nation into the War of 1812.

Calhoun left Congress in 1817 to become President James Monroe's secretary of war. In 1824 he was elected vice president under John Quincy ADAMS, a position that made him presiding officer of the Senate. More loyal to Andrew Jackson than to Adams, Calhoun assigned supporters of Jackson to key committee posts. The Senate, which had only recently extended the assignment power to the presiding officer, quickly took back that power.

Calhoun was reelected to the vice presidency in 1828, this time under Jackson, but he and Jackson soon were at odds. Jackson believed in a strong cen-

*With Speaker Henry Clay, John C. Calhoun was one of a group known as the "War Hawks" who helped push the nation into the War of 1812.    Source: Library of Congress*

tral government, while Calhoun had become an advocate of states' rights. Angered by high protective tariffs, Calhoun became an eloquent advocate of the doctrine of nullification, which held that individual states had the right to annul federal laws they considered illegal.

Calhoun resigned as vice president in 1832 and returned to the Senate, where he defended states' rights in a succession of dramatic debates with Daniel WEBSTER. He became an apologist for slavery and fought efforts to prohibit slavery in new states and territories. Except for a brief period (1844–1845) as secretary of state under John Tyler, Calhoun remained a senator for the rest of his life.

Shortly before his death in 1850, Calhoun dragged himself into the Senate chamber to hear a colleague read his final speech in what has been called the greatest debate in the Senate's history. It marked the final appearance in the Senate chamber of the "great triumvirate": Calhoun, Webster, and Clay.

Calhoun in that speech attacked northern opponents of slavery and opposed Clay's final attempt to forestall the South's secession from the Union. Clay's proposals included, among others, a measure clearing the way for California's admission as a free state. They were subsequently adopted and became known as the Compromise of 1850.

## Call of the Calendar

Senate bills that are not brought up for debate by a motion, unanimous consent, or a unanimous consent agreement may be brought before the Senate for action when the CALENDAR listing them is "called." Under the procedure, which is used infrequently, bills must be called in the order in which they are listed on the calendar. Measures considered by this method are usually noncontroversial, and debate is limited to five minutes for each senator. (See LEGISLATIVE PROCESS.)

## Campaign Committees

*See* LEADERSHIP.

## Campaign Financing

Being elected to Congress requires money. Most candidates for House and Senate seats raise a great deal of money to pay for campaign staff salaries, travel costs, mailings, print advertising, radio and television commercials, political consultants, and many other expenses of campaigning.

Perhaps no other aspect of the American political system has aroused so much concern in recent years as the financing of political campaigns. Debate on this subject involves basic issues of representative democracy and the integrity of Congress. As one reform advocate put it, "There are no fights like campaign finance fights because they are battles about the essence of politics and power."

Over the years, congressional candidates have raised money from businesses, labor unions, individuals, and political organizations. The candidates themselves have been important sources of funds at different times during the history of Congress. Today businesses and unions are barred from contributing directly to campaigns. But they contribute indirectly through separate funds called POLITICAL ACTION COMMITTEES (PACs). Other organizations, such as ideological and issue groups, also have PACs. By the end of the 1970s PACs and individuals had become the major sources of campaign funds. Spending by political parties has also risen sharply but is still small compared to PAC and individual spending.

The enormous expense of modern campaigns has made the ability to raise funds crucial to political strength. The amount spent on congressional campaigns more than doubled during the 1980s, and the upward trend continued in the early 1990s. The two major-party candidates in a House race often spend a total of $1 million or more. An incumbent senator in a contested race may spend more than $4 million, while his or her challenger spends at least $1 million.

The ability to raise money often is a key factor in determining a candidate's chances of being elected. This is particularly true for challengers, who must work hard to raise enough money to pay for the political advertising needed to make their names familiar to the voters. Incumbents almost always have an easier time raising money. Particularly if they hold positions of influence in Congress, most incumbents can count on ample contributions from organized interest groups. Often incumbents are able to raise so much money in advance of an election that potential challengers decide not to run against them.

The campaign finance system depends on the willingness of individuals and organizations to make donations. People give to candidates for many reasons. Ideally, contributions are made because the giver agrees with the candidate on important issues and thinks the candidate would do a good job of governing. Viewed this way, political contributions offer a constructive way for citizens to participate in political life.

But another view shows political contributions and the current system of campaign finance in a negative light. From this perspective, contributions are given with the expectation that a successful congressional candidate will reciprocate by supporting issues of importance to the giver—in effect, an exchange of money for votes. Even if no such deal is made, members who become dependent on certain interests for campaign financing are likely to favor those interests in drafting legislation and voting. Although members of Congress may vote against the interests of their major contributors, they place themselves at risk of losing that financial support in the next election.

Critics of the current system of financing campaigns worry that many members of Congress have become captives of special interests that pour money into campaign treasuries in return for favorable treatment on Capitol Hill. There is also concern that the huge contributions made by special interests undermine loyalty to constituents and party while encouraging unnecessary expenditures. Many of these contributions are made to incumbents. Politicians themselves are frustrated by the current system, which can force them into a constant and demeaning quest for contributions, often at the expense of their congressional responsibilities.

Legislation passed in the 1970s set limits on the amounts that can be given to congressional candidates in one election. (A primary is considered as a separate election.) Individual donors may give $1,000 per candidate per election, with a limit of $25,000 a year to all candidates. Most PACs may donate $5,000 per candidate, with no overall limit on donations. Candidates must disclose the sources of their funds.

One gap in the law allows unlimited contributions to state and local party organizations for activities, such as voter registration drives, that indirectly benefit candidates. Such "soft money" contributions have become increasingly helpful to presidential candidates and candidates in hotly contested congressional races.

Dissatisfaction with the campaign finance system grew during the 1980s and early 1990s. Democrats and Republicans, however, could not agree on additional reforms. Democrats favored public financing of congressional campaigns, while Republicans wanted stricter limits on PACs.

## History

Campaign financing was rarely controversial during Congress's first century. Fund raising at that time was completely unregulated. Most candidates paid their own campaign expenses or relied on a few wealthy backers.

By the 1860s federal workers had become the chief source of campaign money. The party that held the White House and controlled federal PATRONAGE was able to persuade or require government workers to contribute to its campaign coffers. In the 1868 election, for example, about three-quarters of the Republican Congressional Committee's campaign money came from federal employees.

The pressure on federal workers to contribute became one of the most unpopular aspects of the "spoils system," under which the party in power was entitled to distribute jobs and contracts to its supporters. As early as 1867 Congress passed a law to protect workers in federal shipyards from having to make political contributions to keep their jobs. Agitation against the spoils system continued until 1883, when Congress passed the Civil Service Reform Act, which barred mandatory political contributions for federal workers and made it a crime for a federal employee to solicit campaign funds from another federal employee.

Political campaign managers next turned for funds to wealthy individuals and to corporations. Large companies had begun to exert increasing control over the economy in the last decades of the nineteenth century. The high point of corporate involvement in political campaigns came in 1896, when financier Marcus A. Hanna raised $3.5 million in corporate donations, a staggering amount for the time, to finance the successful campaign of Republican presidential candidate William McKinley.

The unrestrained spending by big business on behalf of favored candidates became a chief target of the reformist Progressive movement, which sought to end corruption and increase public involvement in

*Links between money and politics were a target for editorial cartoonists even before Thomas Nast drew this in 1871.*

political life. With the backing of President Theodore Roosevelt, Congress in 1907 passed the Tillman Act, which prohibited any corporation or national bank from making contributions to candidates for federal office.

In 1910 came the Federal Corrupt Practices Act, which established the first requirement that political committees backing candidates for the House disclose the names of their contributors. The following year reporting requirements were extended to the Senate, which in 1913 became for the first time subject to direct election by the voters. (See DIRECT ELECTION OF SENATORS.) The 1911 law also set limits on the amounts that candidates could spend on their campaigns: $10,000 for Senate candidates, and $5,000 for House candidates.

The federal law governing campaign finance was further overhauled in 1925, with passage of a new Federal Corrupt Practices Act. That law, which formed the basis of federal campaign law for nearly half a century, limited the amounts that general-election candidates could spend. The new limits were $25,000 for the Senate and $5,000 for the House. The act continued the existing prohibitions on corporate contribu-

tions and solicitation of federal employees, and extended the reporting requirements for campaign funds.

Laws enacted in the following decades expanded the scope of the 1925 act but left its basic structure intact. One change was the extension of reporting requirements and spending limits to primary campaigns. Another made labor unions subject to the ban on political contributions that already applied to businesses.

The 1925 law had little impact on the practices of congressional candidates. Spending limits and reporting requirements were widely violated over the years, but no one was ever prosecuted under the act. Candidates soon learned that they could ignore the law, raising and spending money freely with only token efforts to comply. Indeed, there were so many ways for candidates to get around the statute that it was often said to be more loophole than law.

Contributors and candidates developed a variety of ways to evade the law. The reporting requirement for contributions of $100 or more, for example, encouraged givers to make multiple contributions to candidates of $99.99. The law limited the amount an individual could give to a candidate to $5,000, so wealthy people channeled much larger sums to candidates through family members and friends, each of whom was allowed to contribute up to $5,000. Similarly, corporations were able to make contributions by awarding special bonuses to executives, who in turn gave the money to candidates.

For candidates, the chief loophole was the provision of the law that applied the spending and reporting requirements only to financial activity made with the "knowledge and consent" of the candidate. As a result, candidates could receive and spend as much as they wanted simply by maintaining the legal fiction that they did not know the transactions were taking place. Frequently, candidates who conducted expensive campaigns reported that they had received and spent little or nothing.

## Reform Efforts

By the beginning of the 1970s television advertising was having a growing impact on political campaigns. This, together with the weakness of the existing law, convinced Congress that new campaign finance legislation was needed. Within the next few years Congress passed major laws changing the way both presidential and congressional campaigns were financed and conducted.

The first major change in campaign law since 1925 was the Federal Election Campaign Act of 1971. That legislation combined two different approaches to reform. One part of the law set strict limits on the amounts that federal candidates could spend on communications media. The law essentially limited spending on media advertising by House and Senate candidates to ten cents for each voter in the congressional district or state. In addition, no more than 60 percent of the total media amount was allowed to go for television and radio advertising.

The other part of the law tightened the reporting requirements for contributions to candidates. Backers of the law hoped that full FINANCIAL DISCLOSURE would prevent abuses by reducing candidates' excessive dependence on a single giver. If the voters saw that a candidate received too much money from a single special interest, the theory went, they would vote against the candidate.

The 1971 law was praised by many reformers for improving disclosure of campaign finances and limiting media spending. The law did little, however, to prevent widespread illegal campaign finance activities. A pattern of such activities was revealed by investigation of the WATERGATE SCANDAL. Although most of those abuses involved the 1972 reelection campaign of President Richard M. Nixon, public outrage over the revelations led to pressure for further reforms in congressional as well as presidential campaigns.

The result was the federal election law of 1974, the most comprehensive such legislation ever enacted. It overhauled the existing system for financing federal elections and established the Federal Election Commission, a six-member body responsible for overseeing campaign finance activities. The law also imposed limits on the amounts that could be given to candidates in an election. Individuals were limited to a gift of $1,000 to one candidate and $25,000 to all candidates in a single year; political committees could give no more than $5,000 to one candidate but were not limited in the total amount they could give to all candidates. In addition, the law tightened reporting requirements and established a system of public financing of presidential elections.

The 1974 law repealed the media spending limits adopted in 1971 and replaced them with overall spending limits for Senate and House candidates. A candidate for the House could spend no more than $70,000 in a general election; a Senate candidate could spend no more than $150,000 or twelve cents per eligible voter, whichever was greater.

The Supreme Court overturned the candidates' spending limits in the landmark case of *Buckley v. Valeo* (1976). Both liberal and conservative plaintiffs in the case had argued that the law represented an unconstitutional restraint on the free expression of citizens and political candidates. Although the Court struck down the limits on the amounts that candidates could spend on campaigns, it upheld provisions of the law limiting the amounts that individuals and PACs could contribute to specific candidates, as well as the reporting and disclosure requirements.

Congress amended the campaign finance law in 1976 to bring it into line with *Buckley.* The amendments included a restructuring of the Federal Election Commission, and new limits on the amounts that individuals could contribute to PACs and national political parties, and that PACs could contribute to national political parties. Further amendments to the campaign finance law enacted in 1979 reduced the paperwork involved in complying with the law, but compliance remained complex and time-consuming.

The Supreme Court decision in *Buckley* had upheld the provisions of the campaign finance law regarding presidential elections. The law provided public financing for candidates while limiting the amounts that could be spent by presidential candidates who accepted the federal funds. As a result, attempts to reform congressional campaigns after 1976 focused on proposals for public financing of political campaigns. Under such proposals congressional candidates in primary and general elections would receive federal funding, but they would have to limit the total amount they spent.

Backers of public financing argued that it would reduce the influence of special interests in congressional campaigns. They contended that public financing had cleaned up the previously corrupt campaign finance system for presidential candidates. Opponents of public financing responded that it would give too great an advantage to incumbents. If challengers were blocked by law from outspending the incumbent, opponents argued, they would have little chance against the advantages of incumbency, such as free mailings under the congressional franking privilege and greater recognition among voters. Although President Jimmy Carter supported the idea, public financing bills were defeated in Congress several times in the late 1970s.

Throughout the 1980s efforts to rewrite the campaign finance rules ended in stalemate. Democrats contended that the campaign finance system operated like an arms race, with candidates engaged in a never-ending quest for the financial edge. They insisted that any new law had to limit campaign spending. Most Democrats endorsed the idea of public funding to replace the loss of funds from private sources, but this idea was controversial even among Democrats, and proponents differed on exactly where the money was to come from. Republicans asserted that the problem with the existing system of campaign finance lay with tainted sources of money, not with the amounts contributed. Instead of spending limits, they proposed curbs on specific sources of funds, such as PACs. Republicans feared that spending limits would help lock in a Democratic majority in Congress.

In 1992 congressional Democrats pushed through the most extensive legislation on campaign finance since the 1974 law, but they could not muster the votes to override the veto of Republican president George Bush. Pressure for reform had built up in the wake of scandals that had tarnished Congress, most notably the KEATING FIVE SCANDAL. Televised hearings in 1990–1991 revealed how a wealthy businessman, Charles H. Keating, Jr., used campaign donations to further his own interests on Capitol Hill. Revelations about mismanagement of the House's internal post office and bank added fuel to the fire of voter outrage. (See HOUSE BANK SCANDAL.)

The campaign finance bill vetoed by Bush in 1992 set an optional spending limit for House candidates of $600,000. The optional limit for Senate general-election campaigns was between $950,000 and $5.5 million, depending on state size. In exchange for compliance with these spending limits and additional limits on how money could be raised, House candidates could get up to $200,000 in federal matching funds. Senate candidates could obtain public funds of up to 20 percent of the spending limit in the form of federal vouchers for television advertising time.

Bush said the bill would help Democrats and would put challengers at a disadvantage. The bill placed new limits on the amounts PACs could contribute, but Bush wanted to abolish PACs altogether. He opposed the public funding of campaigns as "a raid on the Treasury" that would hurt taxpayers. Proponents of campaign finance reform were encouraged by the election in 1992 of a Democratic president, Bill Clinton, who during his campaign had endorsed reforms even more stringent than those included in the measure vetoed by Bush.

### The System in Operation

As the Democrats and Republicans fought over ways to reform campaign financing, spending on congressional campaigns continued to grow at a steady pace throughout the 1970s and 1980s. House and Senate candidates spent a total of $66 million in the 1976 election cycle, which includes primaries. By 1988 the total had risen to $459 million. The 1990 total of $445 million marked the first drop in spending since the Federal Election Commission began keeping records in the 1970s. But the dip did not mean that senators were spending less; instead, it reflected the fact that many senators ran uncontested. The 1992 congressional races continued the upward trend, especially on the House side, where competition was intensified by high turnover and redistricting.

A breakdown of the 1990 congressional spending totals gives some idea of the advantage of incumbency. House and Senate incumbents together spent a total of $276.5 million, while challengers spent $101 million. Candidates for open seats (where no incumbent was running) spent $67 million. Incumbents ended the campaign with a $95 million cash surplus—proof that they had plenty of funds in reserve.

How much money is spent varies from one campaign to another. The needs of a challenger differ from those of an incumbent. A Senate candidate in a large state runs a different campaign than does a candidate in a small state. Campaigns for Congress depend on the character of the district—whether it is urban, suburban, or rural—and on the candidates' personal styles.

House and Senate campaign spending differs in some important respects. Senate campaigns, because they cover an entire state, usually rely heavily on media advertising. House races more often feature personal campaigning. In general, Senate candidates receive more of their funds from individuals than from PACs, while House candidates rely more heavily on PACs than on individual donors.

Even when inflation is taken into account, the cost of congressional campaigns has increased dramatically since the 1960s. Population growth has contributed to this trend; as the electorate expands, so does the cost of reaching voters. But more important, campaigning has become a sophisticated enterprise. Campaigns that once featured volunteers stuffing envelopes and canvassing voters now rely on computerized mass mailings, slick radio and television ads, and well-paid political consultants.

A study of how candidates actually spent their campaign funds in the 1990 elections concluded that the cost of running for Congress had skyrocketed because more money was available, and not because of the factors most often blamed by politicians, such as the high cost of television advertising and airline tickets. Incumbents in 1990 used less than half their campaign funds to communicate with voters in traditional ways, such as media advertising and rallies. Instead, they used the funds to build and maintain their political organizations. Even when incumbents ran unopposed, they spent considerable sums to maintain their organizations: an average of $250,000 for unopposed House candidates, and $668,000 for their Senate counterparts.

#### Additional Readings

Alexander, Herbert E. *Financing Politics: Money, Elections and Political Reform.* 4th ed. Washington, D.C.: CQ Press, 1992.

Drew, Elizabeth. *Politics and Money: The New Road to Corruption.* New York: Macmillan, 1983.

Fritz, Sara, and Dwight Morris. *Handbook of Campaign Spending: Money in the 1990 Congressional Races.* Washington, D.C.: Congressional Quarterly, 1992.

Makinson, Larry. *Open Secrets: The Encyclopedia of Congressional Money and Politics.* Washington, D.C.: Congressional Quarterly, 1992.

Sabato, Larry J. *Paying for Elections: The Campaign Finance Thicket.* New York: Priority Press/Twentieth Century Fund, 1989.

## Cannon, Clarence

During his four decades in the House of Representatives, Missouri Democrat Clarence Cannon (1879–1964) earned a reputation as a tough Appropriations Committee chair and as the House's foremost authority on parliamentary procedure. He was the author of *Cannon's Procedure* and *Cannon's Precedents,* both still used by Congress.

Cannon arrived in Washington in 1911, three years after receiving his law degree, to work as confidential secretary to House Speaker James B. "Champ" CLARK, also a Missouri Democrat. After Clark died in 1921, Cannon ran for his seat and won election to the House in 1922. He remained in the House until his death in 1964.

Cannon was chair of the Appropriations Committee from 1941 to 1964, except for two brief periods (1947–1949, 1953–1955) when Republicans controlled the chamber. In 1950 he was one of the chief proponents of a move to lump all regular appropriations for government agencies into a single bill. The experiment was unsuccessful, and in 1951 Congress returned to the practice of passing separate appropriations measures.

Cannon was a stickler for what he viewed as the prerogatives of the House. He reacted angrily in 1962 when the chair of the Senate Appropriations Committee, Arizona Democrat Carl HAYDEN, demanded equal status in the appropriations process—an area in which the House traditionally had claimed primacy. The feud between the two, both of whom were in their eighties, held up action on spending bills for much of the 1962 session.

## Cannon, Joseph G.

Joseph G. Cannon (1836–1926), a conservative Republican from Illinois, was the last in a succession of autocratic Speakers who dominated the House of Representatives during the late nineteenth century and the first decade of the twentieth.

Cannon was the most powerful Speaker in history from 1903 until 1910, when Republicans and Democrats revolted against his arbitrary rule. He was stripped of most of his power by new rules that prohibited the Speaker from naming or serving on the Rules Committee, through which Cannon had controlled the shape and fate of many bills; removed the authority to make committee assignments; and reduced the power to deny recognition to members during House floor debate. (See RULES COMMITTEE, HOUSE; SPEAKER OF THE HOUSE.)

"Uncle Joe" Cannon served in the House for half a century, from 1873 until 1923, with two short breaks (1891–1893, 1913–1915). He was never associated with any particular piece of legislation or cause, although he opposed the progressive policies of President Theodore Roosevelt. His seniority made him chair of the Appropriations Committee in 1897, and he became Speaker six years later.

Cannon fully exploited the authority established by his predecessors. As Speaker, he was chair of the Rules Committee, and he used this position to prevent legislation from coming to the House floor. He also took full advantage of his power over committee assignments: Members loyal to Cannon could be confident of good committees, while dissidents were banished to unpopular ones. Using his power of recognition, Cannon arbitrarily determined which members could speak on the floor. His counting of voice votes was suspect. "The Ayes make the most noise, but the Nays have it," he once ruled.

In 1909 the House rejected a resolution to curtail the Speaker's powers. The resolution was introduced by James B. "Champ" CLARK, who succeeded Cannon in the post two years later. Nebraska Republican George W. NORRIS introduced another such resolution in 1910. Although Cannon tried to prohibit de-

*Joseph G. Cannon was the most powerful Speaker in history from 1903 until 1910, when Republicans and Democrats stripped him of most of his power.    Source: Library of Congress*

bate on the measure, the House overruled him and adopted it after twenty-nine hours of debate. Cannon then offered to resign as Speaker. Because he was well liked by many, the House refused to consider his resignation, and he remained Speaker until the Sixty-first Congress ended the following year.

## Cannonism

*See* CANNON, JOSEPH G.; SPEAKER OF THE HOUSE.

## Capitol Building

It was a "pity to burn anything so beautiful," a British officer reportedly said before setting fire to the U.S. Capitol during the War of 1812. Even at so early a date, the seat of Congress was the most striking public building in Washington, D.C. It remains so to this day.

Although it may appear to the first-time visitor as a unified whole, the Capitol is not one structure but several. There have been many additions to the original building over its nearly two centuries of existence,

and the process has by no means ended. A three-year-long restoration of the Capitol's West Front—the side that faces the Washington Monument midway down the Mall—was completed in November 1987.

The Capitol is constructed of sandstone and marble in the classic style. It rests on an elevated site chosen by George Washington in consultation with Major Pierre L'Enfant, a French engineer and city planner. In 1792 a competition was held to choose an architect; William Thornton gained the president's approval with a plan submitted after the deadline. Washington praised Thornton's design for its "grandeur, simplicity, and beauty of the exterior." In

*This is the earliest known photograph of the East Front of the U.S. Capitol, taken in about 1846. It shows the original, low dome designed by Charles Bulfinch.    Source: Library of Congress*

*Under Abraham Lincoln's orders, construction of the larger Capitol dome continued during the Civil War "as a sign we intend the Union shall go on."*
*Source: Library of Congress*

1793 the president set the cornerstone, with Masonic rites, and the building was begun.

The north, or Senate, wing of the Capitol was finished in 1800. In October of that year records, archives, and furniture arrived by ship from Philadelphia, the former seat of the federal government. Congress convened in the Capitol for the first time on November 21, 1800. President John Adams addressed the members the next day, congratulating them "on the prospect of a residence not to be changed." The Senate then consisted of 32 members from 16 states, while the House of Representatives numbered 105.

All three branches of the national government have had close association with the Capitol. For 134 years the building was the home of the Supreme Court. Starting with Thomas Jefferson in 1801, most presidents have taken the inaugural oath of office in the Capitol or on its grounds. Also, the Capitol long housed the LIBRARY OF CONGRESS, which now occupies three nearby buildings.

**Fire and Reconstruction**

A British expeditionary force set fire to the Capitol on the night of August 24, 1814. Only the exterior walls were left standing. The damage might have been still greater if a violent thunderstorm, typical weather for that time of year in Washington, had not extinguished the flames.

Restoration work began in 1815 under the direction of Benjamin H. Latrobe, who had been appointed twelve years earlier as surveyor of public buildings. The central portion of the Capitol, with a low dome designed by Latrobe's successor, Charles Bulfinch, was completed in 1827.

After Bulfinch's appointment ended in 1829, his position remained vacant until 1851, when President Millard Fillmore appointed Thomas U. Walter to oversee an urgently needed enlargement of the building. By that time 62 senators and 232 House members were jammed into space designed to accommodate a much smaller number. Besides new Senate and House wings, Walter suggested the addition of a larger dome to replace the original one of copper-sheathed wood.

The new House chamber was occupied December 16, 1857. A little over a year later, on January 4, 1859, the Senate moved into its new quarters. The Supreme Court took over the former Senate chamber the following year, and in 1864 the old House chamber became Statuary Hall by act of Congress.

Even after the outbreak of the Civil War, work continued on the Capitol dome. "If the people see the Capitol going on," President Abraham Lincoln said, "it is a sign that we intend the Union shall go on." On December 2, 1863, a great crowd gathered to watch Thomas Crawford's sculpture of Freedom placed atop the dome, fulfilling Lincoln's vision.

## The Capitol Today

The Capitol has undergone only one major structural change since the 1860s. Under provisions of the Legislative Appropriations Act of 1956, a new marble East Front was erected, faithfully reproducing the design of the old sandstone facade. The new front was placed 32 feet east of the original walls, which were retained to serve as interior walls. Work on the extension began in 1958 and was completed four years later, adding 100 rooms at a total cost of $11.4 million.

For the next two decades controversy raged over a proposed extension of the Capitol's West Front. In 1983 Congress voted instead to restore the West Front, which includes the last remaining portions of

*On January 20, 1993, Bill Clinton took the oath of office, becoming the forty-second president. Beginning with Andrew Jackson in 1829, thirty-five inaugural ceremonies have been held outdoors near the East Front portico of the Capitol and three on the West Front, including Clinton's.*  Source: The White House

the Capitol's original exterior. Unlike most other federally funded construction projects in the nation's capital, the West Front restoration was completed well ahead of time and under budget. The refurbished building, said the architect of the Capitol, George M. White, "will look exactly [as] it did when it was new, but it will be structurally sound for the foreseeable future."

Several important rooms in the Capitol may be vis-

*The Speaker's Lobby reflects the opulence of the Capitol's interior.*
*Source: Architect of the Capitol*

*The Capitol's decoration includes elaborate brasswork, marble staircases, carved wood and etched glass, intricate masonry, bronze railings, and crystal chandeliers. Shown here is the main stairway on the House side of the Capitol.* *Source: Ken Heinen*

ited by the public without advance notice. These include the Rotunda, situated under the dome and decorated with statues and large-scale historical paintings, and Statuary Hall, which contains a collection of bronze and marble statues presented by the various states to commemorate distinguished citizens.

The bodies of many celebrated Americans have lain in state in the Rotunda. The list includes nine presidents: Lincoln, Garfield, McKinley, Harding, Taft, Kennedy, Hoover, Eisenhower, and Lyndon B. Johnson.

The Capitol is 751 feet, 4 inches long and 350 feet wide. It contains 16 acres of floor space, an area

slightly smaller than the White House grounds. The building's height at its tallest point, the top of the Freedom statue, is 287 feet, 5 inches. The Senate and House occupy opposite ends of the building; the Senate chamber is in the north wing, the House in the south. The Capitol also includes committee chambers, offices, restaurants, repair shops, and other rooms. Tunnels and subways link the Capitol to Senate and House office buildings nearby.

### Raising the Flags

Since 1937 employees of the flag office of the architect of the Capitol have raised and lowered thousands of American flags each year over the roof of the Capitol. Having flown over the Capitol, the flags are then shipped to citizens or organizations that request one in writing from their member of Congress. In 1991 a total of 154,224 flags—423 a day, on average—were run up a flagpole set aside for the purpose and lowered almost instantly. When mailed, each flag is accompanied by a certificate of authenticity. The recipient is charged a fee according to the type of fabric used, cotton or nylon. Senators and House members may forward to the flag office as many constituent requests as they wish.

### Additional Readings

Aikman, Lonnelle M. *We the People: The Story of the United States Capitol.* 13th ed. Washington, D.C.: United States Capitol Historical Society, 1985.

## VISITORS' INFORMATION

Public tours of the Capitol are offered at no charge between 9 a.m. and 3:45 p.m., seven days a week, except for Thanksgiving, Christmas, and New Year's Day. Tours start from the central Rotunda at least every fifteen minutes. During the peak season from April to August the tours take place as often as every two minutes. Free concerts also are performed on the Capitol grounds during the summer.

Groups and individuals may gain admission to the of time to the member of Congress representing their state or locality. Senate and House gallery passes are not interchangeable, nor do they admit the bearer to special events or to joint sessions of Congress.

The U.S. Capitol Historical Society, a nongovernmental body, maintains information centers in the building.

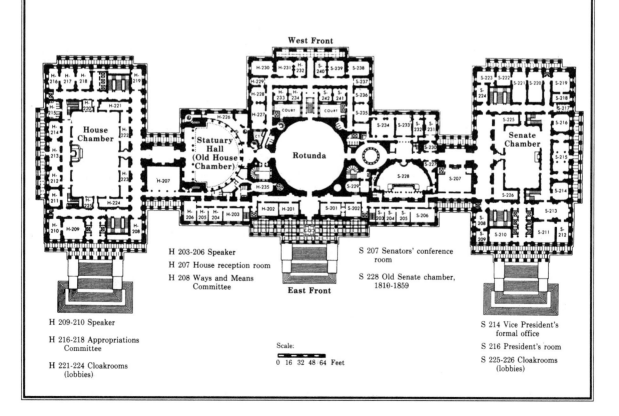

West Front

House Chamber

Statuary Hall (Old House Chamber)

Rotunda

Senate Chamber

East Front

H 203-206 Speaker
H 207 House reception room
H 208 Ways and Means Committee

S 207 Senators' conference room
S 228 Old Senate chamber, 1810-1859

H 209-210 Speaker
H 216-218 Appropriations Committee
H 221-224 Cloakrooms (lobbies)

Scale:
0  16  32  48  64  Feet

S 214 Vice President's formal office
S 216 President's room
S 225-226 Cloakrooms (lobbies)

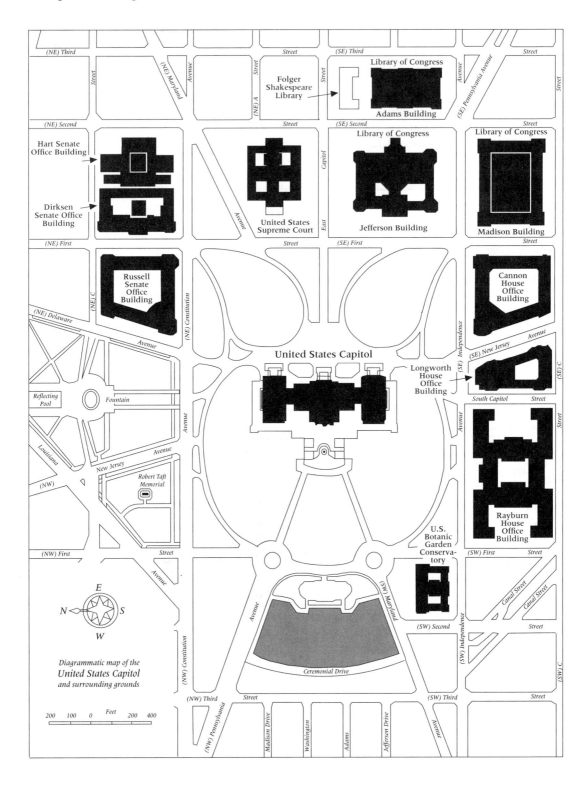

Diagrammatic map of the
*United States Capitol*
and surrounding grounds

Brown, Glenn. *History of the U.S. Capitol.* 2 vols. Washington, D.C.: Government Printing Office, 1903. Rpt., New York: Da Capo Press, 1970.

## Capitol Hill

When Pierre L'Enfant laid out the streets of Washington in the 1790s, he called the hill on the eastern end of town a "pedestal waiting for a monument." L'Enfant placed the CAPITOL BUILDING there, housing the legislative and judicial branches. It stood a mile from the White House, which he located at the other end of Pennsylvania Avenue.

Known then as Jenkins Hill, the site had a sweeping view to the west of swampy land and the Tiber Creek, a finger of the Potomac first straightened into a canal and then captured in pipes and buried. Now Capitol Hill overlooks a formal panorama: the tree-lined lawn of the Mall, surrounded by museums and punctuated by the Washington Monument in the distance. Congress guaranteed its view in 1901, when it banned buildings higher than the Capitol dome—the equivalent of about thirteen stories.

The Capitol itself stands alone on a city block, its grounds a combination of gardens and parking lots. The grounds still reflect the design created in the 1870s by noted landscape architect Frederick Law Olmsted. Flanked on the north by Senate office buildings and on the south by House office buildings, the Capitol has on its eastern side the Supreme Court and the Library of Congress. Collectively, these buildings make up the area referred to as Capitol Hill.

Capitol Hill is also the name for the neighborhood of homes and commercial establishments radiating eastward of the congressional enclave. Developed to serve legislators and their families early in the nineteenth century, the villagelike community serves the same function today. Restaurants and shops are filled at lunchtime with congressional employees. Many senators and representatives live in the restored townhouses common in the area. Two lines of the Washington subway system serve the community.

As a neighbor, Congress has not always been popular. In the mid-1970s, plans to build a fourth House office building where homes already existed prompted an outcry from residents. The plans were modified. Since then schemes for expanding Congress have been replaced by concerns about controlling staff size and the legislative budget.

## Caucuses, Party

Party caucuses are the formal organizations of Democratic and Republican members within the House and Senate. Every two years as members organize for a new Congress, representatives and senators vote in their party caucuses on party leadership, committee chairmanships, and committee assignments. Contests for House Speaker, Senate majority leader, and other top posts can be controversial, but many other caucus votes simply endorse the leaders' recommendations. (See LEADERSHIP.)

Only one of the four party caucuses in Congress actually calls itself a caucus; the others call themselves conferences. The Senate Democratic Conference and Senate Republican Conference meet about once a week to discuss legislation, though attendance varies and the sessions are informal. The House Republican Conference gathers each week, and the House Democratic Caucus usually meets once or twice a month. Meetings of House caucuses are more formal than those in the Senate and are usually well attended. Caucus sessions are closed to the public.

Within each caucus are committees that recommend party positions on bills, help schedule legislation, and make committee assignments. These groups handle most caucus business. Each caucus also has a campaign committee that raises and distributes money and provides other assistance to candidates for congressional office.

The full caucus is rarely asked to settle questions about legislative policy. Instead the leadership and party committees try to help different factions reach a consensus. Budget questions, for example, often involve party task forces and hours of negotiations. If the leadership does bring a policy question to the caucus, the decision is often made by voice vote, which tends to suggest unity and mask any opposition.

Caucus votes have been used as a tool when a large bloc of the caucus was unhappy with the leadership and wished to express its discontent. That happened in the 1970s, when the House Democratic Caucus voted on the Vietnam War, Social Security, and other controversial issues. Such votes are divisive, however, and party leaders try to avoid them.

### Changing Caucus Role

From 1800 to 1824 party caucuses in the House doubled as the national organizations for the major parties, choosing the nominees for president and vice president. By the 1830s national party conventions had begun to select presidential nominees, and the importance of both major parties' caucuses had diminished. Late in the nineteenth century the caucuses became forums for discussion of legislative strategy.

The party caucus was overshadowed by strong Speakers at the turn of the century. (See SPEAKER OF THE HOUSE.) The caucus gained new life after the revolt in 1910–1911 against the autocratic rule of Speaker Joseph G. CANNON, an Illinois Republican. The House took away from the Speaker authority to name the floor leader, select committee chairs, and make committee assignments. Those duties were shifted to the political parties. Democrats, when they gained the majority in 1911, used their caucus to solidify control of the House.

The House caucuses were also used as a way to secure votes on political issues. At that time a two-thirds vote of the caucus could bind members to vote a certain way on legislation. House Republicans quickly abandoned this type of caucus; they even renamed their group a conference to clarify its role. Democrats used the binding rule during the first terms of presidents Woodrow Wilson and Franklin Roosevelt but later invoked it only on procedural or party issues.

The Democratic caucus was particularly strong during Wilson's first term (1913–1917). Wilson, a student of Congress, saw the caucus as an "antidote to the committees," providing unity and cohesion to counter committee independence.

The committees grew even more independent as the unwritten SENIORITY SYSTEM became entrenched, beginning in the 1920s. The post of committee chair went almost automatically to the majority member with the longest record of service on a committee. The party leadership and the caucus were rarely involved and, as a result, were less able to hold the chairs accountable.

The Democratic caucus was also one step removed from another set of decisions: committee assignments. As part of the revolt against Cannon, that responsibility had been given to Democrats on the House Ways and Means Committee. (See WAYS AND MEANS COMMITTEE, HOUSE.) Republicans used a Committee on Committees, which included party leaders, to make assignments.

As the committees gained in power, the authority of the party caucus diminished. Party unity among Democrats also suffered because of political differences within party ranks that had conservative southern Democrats often voting with Republicans. (See CONSERVATIVE COALITION.)

The development of party caucuses in the Senate paralleled their course in the House. In 1846 the caucuses won the power to make committee assignments. During the Civil War and Reconstruction, Republicans used their caucus frequently to discuss and adopt party positions on legislation. Republican leaders used the caucus extensively in the 1890s to maintain party discipline.

Senate Democratic leaders adopted a binding caucus rule in 1903 and used it effectively in 1913–1914 in support of Wilson's legislative objectives. Twenty years later, charged with enacting Franklin Roosevelt's New Deal, Senate Democrats readopted the rule. It was not employed, but frequent nonbinding caucuses were held to mobilize support. Since that time neither party has seriously considered using caucus votes to enforce party loyalty on legislative issues.

More recently Senate caucuses have been used to collect and distribute information to members, to perform legislative research, and to discuss political and policy questions.

*During the 1970s, junior members of Congress demanded a greater role in party caucus decisions. In this 1975 photograph, two members of the Senate Democratic Conference, Mississippi's John C. Stennis, left, and Idaho's Frank Church, debate a proposal to elect committee chairmen by secret ballot.    Source: George Tames,* The New York Times

## House Caucus Reborn

Liberal Democrats led a campaign in the late 1960s and early 1970s to revive the House Democratic Caucus. They then used the reborn caucus to make dramatic reforms in House procedures, including a sweeping assault on the seniority system. (See RE-FORM.)

Their first step was to get Speaker John W. MC-CORMACK, a Massachusetts Democrat, to agree in 1969 to hold regular monthly meetings of the caucus. Then in the early 1970s a wave of liberal Democrats was elected to the House, adding to the ranks of those sitting members who were frustrated with the rigid seniority system, which kept members of longest standing, who often were out of step with party politics, in top positions. The larger bloc of reformers made changes possible.

The caucus voted to give responsibility for nominating committee chairs to a new panel, the Steering and Policy Committee, a group of about thirty members headed by the Speaker. The panel, an arm of the leadership, also proposed committee assignments, a job previously handled by Democrats on the Ways and Means Committee. (Republicans since 1917 had given that role to a Committee on Committees; in the Senate, similar policy groups within each party recommended committee posts.)

The caucus also decided to vote, by secret ballot, on nominations for committee chairs and for chairs of subcommittees of the Appropriations Committee. (Beginning in 1991, subcommittee chairs of the Ways and Means Committee also were elected by the party caucus.) The caucus agreed to have Democrats on each committee, instead of the chair, choose subcommittee chairs. Worried that the rule on binding votes might be resurrected after years of disuse, the caucus repealed it.

The reforms—and the new authority of the caucus—were dramatically illustrated in 1975, when the House Democratic Caucus unseated three incumbent chairs. Two years later the caucus for the first time voted to oust a sitting subcommittee chair from the Appropriations Committee. The caucus replaced another full committee chair in 1985, two more in 1991, and one in 1993.

As they organized for the 103rd Congress, Democrats revised the way they vote on committee chairs to allow for a more open, competitive vote if a chair had significant opposition in the Steering and Policy Committee. The caucus also adopted a new rule allowing the policy committee at any time to declare the chairmanship of a committee or a subcommittee vacant, and send the matter to the full caucus for a vote. Any committee member could be removed by the same process.

---

## Caucuses, Special

The many regional, cultural, economic, and ethnic differences that mark American society are also reflected in special caucuses in Congress. These caucuses are unofficial organizations that allow members of Congress to pursue common interests important to them and their constituents. More than a hundred special caucuses have been organized in the House of Representatives and Senate, and most legislators choose to join at least one of these groups. Representatives and senators also are automatically members of their own party caucus or conference. (See CAUCUSES, PARTY.)

A common denominator of some kind draws members to each informal caucus. The link may be race (the Congressional Black Caucus) or geographic location (the Hudson River Caucus). It may be a shared interest, whether narrowly focused (the House Footwear Caucus, the Senate Wine Caucus) or broad in scope (Congressional Clearinghouse on the Future). It may be concern over an issue, from abortion (the Pro-Life Caucus) to tourism (the Congressional Travel and Tourism Caucus).

Some caucuses have only a handful of members, others more than a hundred. Membership is rarely selective, though the House Wednesday Group, a roundtable of Republicans that meets weekly, invites its thirty-five or so members to join. Other caucuses have criteria for membership, such as the caucus set

up at the beginning of each Congress by new House members, or the caucuses with party affiliations. Even a few state delegations have evolved into formal caucuses with staff.

Caucuses have thrived in the House, where many members feel isolated and anonymous, even within their own parties. Many caucuses function almost as internal interest groups, lobbying committees and individuals for a particular cause. Caucuses sometimes send representatives to testify at hearings, and some draft specific legislative proposals. Critics complain that caucuses disperse power in an already fragmented Congress and do little more than add to the swollen legislative bureaucracy.

Unlike legislative committees and the official party groups, which often have to mute conflict to build compromises, caucuses can endorse even the most controversial points of view. In 1987 the staff director of the House Republican Study Committee, a conservatively oriented caucus, praised the cohesiveness of that group: "I've got a core group of people it would be hard to offend no matter how conservative I got." In contrast, the Republican Conference, the party's official caucus, is constrained by the need to satisfy the wide range of political views represented in its membership.

### Party Groups

Legislators have always formed alliances, but the modern special caucus dates from 1959, when liberal members of the House, frustrated by the successes of conservatives, revamped their own loosely knit group into a formal organization, the Democratic Study Group. With about a hundred members, a formal title, and annual dues (at that time, $25), the Democratic Study Group was the prototype for dozens of partisan and bipartisan caucuses organized since then.

The Democratic Study Group provides background reports and daily bulletins on almost every legislative issue to more than two hundred members. On the Republican side, the House Republican Study Committee provides similar support to conservative House Republicans, while the Wednesday Group gives Republican moderates in the House a forum to consider legislative options.

Dissatisfied, narrowly focused groups within a party have used caucuses to draw attention to their demands. Conservative Republicans created the Conservative Opportunity Society in the 1980s; their relationship with House Democrats was more confrontational than the approach favored by Republican party leaders. A group of conservative Democrats organized the Conservative Democratic Forum, known informally as the Boll Weevils.

Some political caucuses are little more than a label for a loose coalition. The Gypsy Moths, also known as the Northeast-Midwest Republican Coalition, mobilized to fight budget cuts by the Reagan administration in the early 1980s. Another Republican-based caucus, the 92 Group, focused on having a Republican majority in 1992.

## Minority Caucuses

Ethnic and minority groups have often banded together when Congress considered issues particularly important to them. Italian Americans, Polish Americans, Irish Americans, and others have periodically spoken in unison. African Americans, Hispanics, and women are also represented by organized caucuses.

Among the most effective of all caucuses has been the relatively small Congressional Black Caucus, which includes every black legislator. When it was formed in 1969 the caucus had only nine members, and they had little role in the congressional power structure. By 1992 the Black Caucus had grown to twenty-six members. Thanks to seniority gains, during the 1980s African Americans became chairs of several committees and subcommittees. (See BLACKS IN CONGRESS.)

The caucus successfully pressured the Democratic leadership to have black members appointed to powerful House committees. For example, William H. Gray III, a black Democrat from Pennsylvania, served as chair of the Budget Committee and then as Democratic party whip before retiring from Congress in 1991 to head the United Negro College Fund. Legislatively, the Black Caucus lobbied for an economic agenda to help the poor, who are disproportionately black, and to strengthen and enforce civil rights laws. A major victory for the caucus was passage in 1986 of

*Among the most effective of all special caucuses has been the Congressional Black Caucus, which includes every black legislator. It began with nine members in 1969 and, although the photo shows only half, the caucus had about forty members by 1993.*
Source: Congressional Black Caucus

legislation imposing economic sanctions against South Africa.

The cohesiveness of the Black Caucus contrasted with the caucus of Hispanic members, which rarely took a unanimous position. The twelve legislators in the Congressional Hispanic Caucus in 1992 ranged from conservative to liberal.

Women in the House formed a caucus in 1977. In 1981 they reorganized the group as the Congressional Caucus on Women's Issues and opened it to male members. In 1992 twenty-six of the thirty-one women members of Congress (including the two women senators) belonged to the caucus, which had more than a hundred members in all. The women

*Women in the House formed a caucus in 1977 and opened it to male members in 1981. Here, several female members of the House talk to reporters before marching to the Senate side of the Capitol to urge a delay in the vote on the confirmation of Judge Clarence Thomas to the U.S. Supreme Court.*
*Source: R. Michael Jenkins*

who did not join the caucus tended to be politically conservative. Among other activities, the caucus supported legislation to improve the economic status of women. (See WOMEN IN CONGRESS.)

## Other Alliances

Energy shortages in the 1970s intensified economic conflicts between southern and western states in the Sun Belt and the older industrialized areas of the Northeast and Midwest. Forming a caucus was a simple, direct way to recognize these complex problems, and accordingly the Congressional Sun Belt Caucus and the Northeast-Midwest Congressional Coalition were established.

Industries such as steel, textiles, and automobiles have firm allies in their lobbying efforts: caucuses specifically to promote each industry. Primarily composed of legislators whose districts depend on a particular industry, the caucuses have focused on limiting imports and removing trade barriers to U.S. products abroad.

## Funding

Unlike the official party caucuses, to which Congress directly appropriates funds, the unofficial caucuses depend on dues from members to cover their expenses. Caucuses that do without separate offices or staff do not usually require dues.

Dues are transferred to a caucus from a legislator's official allotment for office expenses and salaries. Some people have complained about using government money for this purpose. "These caucuses are financed by the federal Treasury and are by their nature lobbies," said Rep. Charles E. Bennett, a Florida Democrat, in 1985. "And I don't think the federal Treasury ought to be financing lobbying groups."

The House adopted new rules in 1981 putting caucuses under close supervision. The new rules were prompted by concerns about groups that depended on both congressional and private funds. In addition to dues from members, several groups also received outside funds through donations, subscriptions to newsletters, and other activities. Under the 1981 rules change, a special caucus seeking House office space and a share of congressional funds has to be certified as a legislative service organization by the House Administration Committee. Financial disclosure reports must be filed, and no private funds can be accepted.

Several groups that once depended on private funds have set up separate institutes or foundations that still accept donations and grants and have offices outside of congressional buildings. For example, the Congressional Black Caucus has a parallel Congressional Black Caucus Foundation. The Environmental and Energy Study Conference has a separate institute that conducts research and publishes a newsletter, and the Northeast-Midwest Coalition operates a research group.

*Additional Reading*

Cigler, Allan J., and Burdett A. Loomis. *Interest Group Politics.* 3rd ed. Washington, D.C.: CQ Press, 1991.

## Censure

*See* DISCIPLINING MEMBERS.

## *Chadha* Decision

*See* LEGISLATIVE VETO.

## Chaplain

Both the Senate and the House of Representatives have a chaplain, who is responsible for opening each daily session with a prayer. The chaplain also serves generally as spiritual counselor to members, their families, and their staffs. The chaplains are officers of the House and Senate and had annual salaries of $119,000 at the beginning of 1993.

The official chaplain does not offer the opening prayer every day. That honor occasionally goes to guest chaplains, who are often from members' home districts. In 1983 the Supreme Court ruled that the practice of opening sessions with a prayer did not violate the ban on establishment of religion contained in the First Amendment to the Constitution. The Court noted that the practice dated back to the First Congress, the Congress that adopted the First Amendment. "The practice of opening legislative sessions with prayer has become part of the fabric of our society," the Court said.

The Senate elected its first chaplain on April 25, 1789, and the House followed suit five days later. Each was paid $500 a year, comparable to the $6 received by members of Congress for each day of attendance.

## Children, Youth, and Families Committee, House Select

Family issues were just emerging as a primary concern of voters when the House in 1982 agreed to set up a select committee to focus on children, youth, and families. From then on, those issues became even more important to the public, and the committee's studies and hearings have gained increased attention.

California Democrat George Miller pushed the House to approve the committee and then became its first chair. He used the panel to focus on numerous problems and to suggest solutions; for example, one committee report showed improvements in infant mortality after a relatively modest investment in prenatal care. Miller resigned as committee chair when he took over the Interior Committee; he was replaced by Patricia Schroeder, a Colorado Democrat.

Like other special and select committees, the Children, Youth, and Families Committee had no authority to write legislation.

In 1993, the House decided to eliminate this and several other select committees as part of an effort to cut congressional costs and simplify the committee structure.

## Christmas Tree Bill

Few sessions of Congress have gone by without passage of a "Christmas tree bill," so called because it was adorned with amendments like baubles on a holiday tree.

The traditional Christmas tree bill was a minor measure passed by the House, on which the Senate hung a variety of unrelated amendments providing benefits for special interests. The amendments most often involved tax or trade treatment. Enactment of these bills often came as Congress was preparing to adjourn for the winter holidays.

Russell B. LONG, chair of the Senate Finance Committee from 1965 to 1981, claimed to be the originator of the Christmas tree bill. The prototype was a measure passed in 1966, in the Louisiana Democrat's second year as Finance chair. The original purpose of the bill was to help the United States solve its balance-of-payments difficulties. But Long's committee transformed it into a gem of legislative vote trading and congressional accommodation that aided, among others, presidential candidates, the mineral ore industry, large investors, hearse owners, and Scotch whisky importers.

The Christmas tree bill in its traditional form became less common in the 1980s. Members of Congress preferred to tuck special-interest amendments into huge OMNIBUS BILLS where their presence was unlikely to be noticed. Emergency funding measures, called continuing resolutions, became magnets for unrelated amendments because they had to be passed quickly to keep government agencies from shutting down. (See CONTINUING RESOLUTION.)

## Clark, James B. "Champ"

James B. "Champ" Clark (1850–1921), a Democrat from Missouri, was a member of the House of Representatives from 1893 until 1921 except for one two-year period (1895–1897). From 1911 to 1919 he was Speaker of the House, succeeding Joseph G. CANNON, whose removal he had helped engineer. In 1912 Clark was a candidate for the Democratic presidential nomination but lost to Woodrow Wilson after forty-six ballots.

Clark was elected Democratic minority leader in the Republican-controlled House in 1907. Opposed to Cannon's iron rule as Speaker, Clark proposed a resolution in 1909 to curtail the Speaker's powers. Although Clark's resolution was defeated, a measure based on his proposal won approval the following year.

In 1911, when the Democrats gained a majority in the House, Clark became Speaker, but without the sweeping powers Cannon had enjoyed. Oscar W. UNDERWOOD of Alabama was elected majority leader and chair of the Ways and Means Committee. The Democratic Caucus decided that the party's members on Ways and Means would make up the Committee

on Committees with responsibility for making committee assignments—a power previously exercised by the Speaker. As a result Underwood, not Clark, functioned as the leader of House Democrats, and the power of the Speaker went into a fifteen-year decline.

## Clay, Henry

Henry Clay (1777–1852) of Kentucky was one of the giants of Congress during the first half of the nineteenth century. Gifted with charm and eloquence, Clay was called "the Great Compromiser" for his efforts to resolve sectional disputes over slavery. His initiatives included two plans to curb the expansion of slave territory: the Missouri Compromise of 1820 and the Compromise of 1850.

A spokesperson for western expansion, Clay proposed an "American System" for economic development that featured a federally financed transportation network and high tariffs to protect American industry. Clay ran unsuccessfully for president as a Democratic-Republican in 1824, as a National Republican in 1832, and as a Whig in 1844. (See PARTIES, POLITICAL.)

Clay began his congressional career with two brief stints in the Senate, where he filled unexpired terms in 1806–1807 and 1809–1810. In 1810 he was elected to the House of Representatives, where he served for most of the next fifteen years. In the House he quickly joined other young "War Hawks" in pushing the nation into the War of 1812 against England.

Clay was chosen as Speaker on the day he took office in 1811, and he remained Speaker as long as he was in the House. Although he resigned his seat twice—in 1814, to help negotiate an end to the War of 1812, and again in 1820—he was reelected Speaker as soon as he returned to the House in 1815 and 1823. A formidable presiding officer and an accomplished debater, Clay kept firm control over the House until he left the chamber for good in 1825.

Running for president in 1824, Clay wound up last in a four-way race that had to be decided by the House of Representatives. There Clay threw his support to John Quincy ADAMS, ensuring Adams's elec-

*Henry Clay was known as the "Great Compromiser" for his efforts to resolve sectional disputes over slavery.    Source: Library of Congress*

tion. When the new president made Clay his secretary of state, critics charged that Clay was being paid off for his election support. (See ELECTING THE PRESIDENT.)

In 1830 Clay was elected to the Senate, where he played a leading role in the debates over slavery that preceded the Civil War. He left the Senate in 1842 but returned in 1849 and served until his death in 1852.

Clay's final effort to prevent the breakup of the Union, known as the Compromise of 1850, attempted to calm rising passions between slaveholding and free states. Among other measures the Compromise of 1850 permitted California to be admitted to the Union as a free state and strengthened the federal law governing capture and return of runaway slaves.

Clay's proposals prompted a debate that has often been called the greatest in the Senate's history. It marked the last appearance in the Senate chamber of the "great triumvirate": Daniel WEBSTER of Massa-

chusetts, an apostle of national unity; John C. CAL-HOUN of South Carolina, the South's foremost defender of slavery and states' rights; and Clay himself. Calhoun, who was fatally ill, sat in the chamber while his final speech was read by a colleague.

## Clerk of the House

The Clerk of the House is the chief administrative officer of the House of Representatives. The Senate counterpart is known as the SECRETARY OF THE SENATE. The clerk's wide-ranging responsibilities include providing stationery supplies, electrical and mechanical equipment, and office furniture; paying salaries of House employees; attesting and fixing the seal of the House to subpoenas; recording and printing bills and reports; reporting debates and keeping the official House *Journal;* certifying passage of bills; compiling lobby registration information; and preparing a variety of periodic reports. The job pays well: $119,000 annually as of early 1993.

Clerk of the House Donnald K. Anderson, who took over the post in 1987, began as a House page in 1960 and worked his way up through PATRONAGE appointments by Democratic members. The clerk is elected by the majority party in the House and generally remains in the job until that party loses control of the chamber. In 1967, however, the House replaced Clerk Ralph R. Roberts, who had served in the post since 1949. Roberts had been criticized for using the chauffeur and limousine that went with his job for trips to his home in Indiana and to racetracks.

## Cloakrooms

The locker rooms of the House and Senate are the cloakrooms, narrow L-shaped rooms along the sides and rear of the two chambers. Originally designed to hold coats, the hideaways now feature well-worn leather chairs, refrigerators stocked with soda and candy, and televisions. When a series of votes is taking place on the floor, legislators congregate in the cloakrooms, where they are able to relax while remaining only steps from the chamber.

Cloakrooms are Democratic or Republican; each party oversees the cloakroom on its side of the chamber. Employees assigned to the cloakrooms prepare messages several times a day describing floor action and floor schedules. These recorded updates are available by telephone. Women members for many years chose not to use the cloakrooms, preferring the separate women's cloakroom set up in 1927. A special room for women members was still provided in the 1980s, though women were also frequent visitors in the majority and minority cloakrooms.

---

## Cloture

*See* FILIBUSTER.

---

## Commerce Power

The Constitution gives Congress the power to regulate commerce with foreign nations and among the states. At first this power was disputed as far as interstate commerce was concerned. But now the "commerce clause" of the Constitution is the basis for a vast array of federal laws that govern how Americans behave and do business.

For many years the Supreme Court resisted a broad use of the commerce power, considering it an intrusion on states' rights and private property rights. But in the late 1930s, under pressure from President Franklin D. Roosevelt, the Court relented. The interstate commerce power eventually became almost limitless, matching the federal government's authority to oversee foreign commerce, which had never been questioned.

Since the Roosevelt era, Congress has continued to expand the federal government's regulation of interstate commerce. The long list of areas covered includes farm prices, banking, labor practices, food and drugs, consumer products, and pollution. Few legal restraints remain on the federal government's use of the commerce clause.

Using its constitutional power to control foreign commerce, Congress authorizes the federal government to regulate international trade, shipping, aviation, and communications. This power is an important aspect of U.S. foreign policy. Congress promotes exchange with some countries while imposing tariffs and embargoes to inhibit trade with others.

Although the courts no longer question the federal role in the regulation of commerce, political debates about the need for specific regulations continue. In the 1970s and 1980s, Democratic president Jimmy Carter convinced Congress to "deregulate" the transportation industry to increase economic competition. The strict federal rules on rates and fares that had controlled the airlines since 1938 were lifted in 1978. Trucking and railroad deregulation followed in 1980, ending most of the economic controls that had governed those industries for decades.

The Republican president who succeeded Carter, Ronald Reagan, promised to get the federal government "off the people's backs." One aspect of Reagan's antigovernment agenda was his campaign to curtail the growing number of federal regulations covering areas such as worker safety and the environment—regulations that often drew complaints from businesses.

During Reagan's two terms there was less federal regulatory activity. Reagan's successor, Republican president George Bush, also criticized federal regulations for hampering businesses. Bush outraged environmental and consumer activists by setting up a Council on Competitiveness, headed by Vice President Dan Quayle, to review proposed regulations that might put an unfair burden on businesses.

In spite of the continued complaints and disputes about federal regulations, by the end of the 1980s deregulation seemed less desirable. In the airline industry, for example, some airlines had gone out of business and others had combined, leaving the industry less competitive than it had been before deregulation. Aging fleets and an overtaxed traffic control system caused safety concerns as well. The need to protect the public interest—the impetus for the original broad application of the commerce clause—once again brought pressure for reregulation of the airlines.

Increasing public concern about the environment

and outrage over the collapse of the multibillion-dollar savings and loan industry helped create a more favorable climate for stricter federal regulation in those areas. As new technologies brought a revolution in communications, Congress struggled with the problem of whether and how to regulate the broadcast, cable television, telephone, and newspaper industries.

## COMMERCE: AN "ALPHABET SOUP" OF AGENCIES

Most modern federal regulatory agencies owe their existence to the Constitution's interstate commerce clause. A look at a few specific agencies shows how broadly the clause has been applied to create an array of agencies, from the ICC to the NRC. Most of these agencies are commonly known by the acronyms formed from their names, creating an "alphabet soup" of agencies.

Among the oldest regulatory groups are the Interstate Commerce Commission (ICC, 1887), Federal Trade Commission (FTC, 1914), and Food and Drug Administration (FDA, 1927). The New Deal era saw a rapid expansion of the federal government and the establishment of many new agencies. Among them were the Securities and Exchange Commission (SEC, 1933), the Federal Deposit Insurance Corporation (FDIC, 1933), the Federal Communications Commission (FCC, 1934), and the National Labor Relations Board (NLRB, 1938).

Still operating under its commerce power and the duty to protect the general welfare, Congress has since added other agencies. These include the Occupational Safety and Health Administration (OSHA, 1970), the Environmental Protection Agency (EPA, 1970), and the Consumer Product Safety Commission (CPSC, 1972). Sometimes Congress abolishes an agency, but it almost always creates a new one to replace it. For example, in 1974 Congress abolished the Atomic Energy Commission (AEC) and authorized the Nuclear Regulatory Commission (NRC) in its place.

## Origins

The Articles of Confederation, adopted in 1777, set up a weak Congress that had little power over the states. The result was conflict and disorder, as the states printed their own money, taxed the goods of other states, and bickered over how the economy should function. To rectify that situation, the framers of the new Constitution wrote a broad "commerce clause" giving Congress the power to "regulate Commerce with foreign Nations, and among the several States, and with the Indian Tribes."

The framers of the Constitution left it to the courts to decide just how broad the commerce clause should be. The Supreme Court first defined congressional power to regulate interstate commerce in the landmark case of *Gibbons v. Ogden* (1824). The case involved a dispute over steamboat navigation rights. On behalf of the Court, Chief Justice John Marshall emphatically asserted the supremacy of federal control over commerce with foreign countries and between the states. More than a century passed, however, before the Court gave full approval to Marshall's expansive interpretation.

Congress too moved only gradually toward a broad application of the commerce clause. In the first part of the nineteenth century, as new frontiers opened up, Henry CLAY envisioned a strong federal role in the development of roads and canals, which he called an "American System." Although Clay won support for this plan in Congress, President James MADISON vetoed the legislation in 1817. Madison's successor, James Monroe, similarly argued that authority over interstate commerce was limited and did not give Congress the power to establish roads and canals.

Within Congress the federal role was hotly debated. Southerners anxious to maintain slavery argued against broad federal power and in favor of states' rights. The opposition was led by John RANDOLPH, an acerbic Virginia representative who opposed Clay's American System. "If the Congress can do that," he argued, "it can emancipate the slaves."

Congress tried to get around the controversy by purchasing stock in private companies that were building roads and canals and by giving land grants to states. But even that approach was unacceptable to

President Andrew Jackson, who in 1830 vetoed the purchase of stock in the Maysville Road, a Kentucky turnpike. He argued that the road was local, not national. Congress was forced to draw back from road building, and the coalition behind the American System fell apart.

Jackson's 1830 veto came just as the nation's railroads were being built. That same year the Baltimore & Ohio Railroad opened. The nation's transportation, and the focus of interstate commerce, shifted from canals and turnpikes to rails. Congress did not become actively involved in highway building again until 1916.

## Regulation Begins

Railroad expansion led Congress to assume new power under the commerce clause. At first the legislators simply promoted the transportation system, giving generous land grants and government credit to the railroad companies.

A network of tracks eventually crisscrossed the nation, but not without controversy. Railroad rate structures favored certain companies and regions over others, and rebates and price fixing were common. Farmers protested loudly, arguing that these practices put them at an economic disadvantage. The states tried to regulate the railroads, with only limited success.

In 1886 the Supreme Court severely limited the states' regulatory authority. The Court said states could not regulate an enterprise engaged in interstate commerce, even if it passed through the states, because interstate matters were a federal concern. Since most railroad companies by then operated in more than one state, this decision ended most state regulation of the railroads.

Congress responded to the need for federal oversight of the railroads by passing the Interstate Commerce Act of 1887. With the new law, Congress began a decades-long expansion of federal regulation of interstate commerce. The Interstate Commerce Commission (ICC), established to carry out the regulation, was the prototype for later regulatory commissions. The ICC was weak, however, and the Supreme Court within a decade weakened it further.

Congress found the Court equally reluctant to allow congressional regulation of huge corporations. The anger against the railroads among farmers, consumers, and small-business owners in the late 1800s was matched by their outrage at the growing power of the trusts that controlled industries such as steel, oil, sugar, and meat packing. The trusts thwarted competition by combining smaller companies into huge corporations and by controlling manufacturing and distribution as well as production of raw materials.

In an attempt to break up the trusts and to "protect commerce against unlawful restraints and monopolies," Congress passed the Sherman Antitrust Act of 1890. But within five years the Supreme Court narrowly limited application of the antitrust law, again reflecting the justices' conservative outlook. Congress did not fully address antitrust law again until 1914, when it passed both the Clayton Act and the Federal Trade Commission Act. That same year the Supreme Court upheld the ICC's authority to set railroad rates. The commerce power had finally become a useful, if controversial, tool for Congress.

As it endorsed an expansion of federal authority over railroads and corporations, Congress also began to experiment with broader federal "police power," to protect public health, safety, and even morals. This responsibility traditionally had been left to the states. Here again, the commerce power was the means for expanding congressional authority.

At first Congress focused on the railroads. It required that safety devices be installed on all railroad cars used in interstate commerce to protect workers from smashing their hands while coupling the cars. Another safety measure limited the number of hours that railroad employees could work at a stretch.

Congress did not stop with railroads. In 1895, concerned about the spread of gambling, Congress used its police power to outlaw the transport of lottery tickets across state lines. That expansion of federal police power ended up before the Supreme Court, as had so many other acts based on the commerce clause. In 1903 the Court agreed with Congress that lottery tickets were commerce, thus upholding the federal government's power to regulate transport of the tickets.

*Here, in 1916, President Woodrow Wilson signs legislation intended to discourage child labor. The Supreme Court struck down the law in 1918, ruling that Congress had exceeded its authority under the commerce clause. The Court overturned the decision in 1941.*   Source: *Library of Congress*

## The "Stream of Commerce"

Gradually, the Supreme Court was accepting a broader view of the commerce clause. The landmark decision in *Swift & Co. v. United States* (1905) introduced the term *stream of commerce.* Justice Oliver Wendell Holmes, Jr., wrote that Congress had authority over the production, marketing, or purchase of a product even if this took place entirely within one state, because it was part of the overall stream of commerce.

After that decision, Congress moved into new areas, enacting laws that prohibited the interstate transportation of explosives, diseased livestock, insect pests, falsely stamped gold and silver articles, narcotics, and prostitutes.

An important new realm, protection of the consumer's health and safety, was opened to federal control in 1906. In that year Congress passed the Pure Food and Drug Act, which banned all harmful substances from food and provided penalties for false labeling. Congress went on to require inspection of red meat being shipped across state lines and, in 1910, to authorize federal action against misbranded or dangerous poisons, such as insecticides. In 1914 deceptive advertising came under the federal regulatory umbrella. In each case, Congress depended on the commerce clause.

The new and broader interpretation of the commerce power took Congress back into highway building, an area it had largely avoided since the Maysville Road veto of 1830. The 1916 Federal Road Aid Act provided federal money to states to help build highways. After passing that law, Congress steadily expanded its financial commitment, eventually paying for 90 percent of the nationwide interstate highway system.

## New Deal Expansion

The commerce power had never been extended so broadly or rapidly as it was by President Franklin D. Roosevelt. The nation's economy was in a shambles when he took office in 1933. Roosevelt promptly launched a bold attack on the Great Depression. Spurred by the president, Congress invoked its commerce power and other authority to undergird his NEW DEAL programs.

Roosevelt's efforts were hampered by the Supreme Court. By mid-1936 the Court had found unconstitutional eight of ten New Deal laws. "We have been relegated to the horse-and-buggy definition of interstate commerce," Roosevelt complained. His running battle with the Court eventually ended with victory for the president. From 1937 on, the Court consented to an unprecedented expansion of federal authority. The first step was its ruling in favor of the 1935 National Labor Relations Act, which gave workers the right under federal law to organize and bargain collectively. The Court had made a major shift since its earlier ruling that unions violated antitrust laws.

## Civil Rights

The commerce clause played a special role in congressional battles over civil rights legislation in the 1960s. The Fourteenth Amendment had been added to the Constitution after the Civil War to clarify individual rights, but its scope was limited. Supreme Court decisions had restricted its application to actions carried out by states, and not to those by individuals and private organizations.

To close that gap Congress turned to the commerce clause. The Supreme Court had already used the clause to restrict segregation. In 1946, for example, the Court upheld a black woman's refusal to give up her bus seat to a white. Such rules burdened interstate commerce, the Court ruled.

President John F. KENNEDY used the commerce clause as the basis for his 1963 legislation to end discrimination in restaurants, hotels, and other public accommodations. It seemed the best legal route for requiring those outside of government to end racial discrimination. Use of the commerce clause was also a way to outwit southern opponents of the proposed civil rights law in Congress. Because of its wording, Kennedy's bill was sent to the Senate Commerce Committee; it thus bypassed the chair of the Judiciary Committee, a southerner who had buried many civil rights bills. The Commerce Committee acted quickly on the measure, and its members served as key supporters on the floor. (See COMMERCE, SCIENCE, AND TRANSPORTATION COMMITTEE, SENATE.) After various compromises, Congress passed the sweeping Civil Rights Act of 1964.

Challenges to the law were quickly filed, but Supreme Court decisions upheld its application even

*The commerce power played an important role in congressional battles over civil rights legislation in the 1960s. A landmark 1964 civil rights law was rooted in the interstate commerce clause.    Source: U.S. Information Agency*

to local enterprises. The classic case involved a Birmingham, Alabama, restaurant that claimed not to be covered by the law because its clientele was strictly local. The federal government successfully argued that 46 percent of the food served had been supplied through interstate commerce, and the restaurant's refusal to serve blacks was declared illegal.

These civil rights decisions left little doubt that the Supreme Court had rejected its nineteenth-century view that the federal government's authority to regulate commerce should be limited in favor of states' rights and a free market. Almost no restriction remained on federal authority under the commerce clause.

### Additional Readings

Gavit, Bernard C. *Commerce Clause of the United States Constitution.* New York: AMS Press, 1970.

Lofgren, Charles A. "'To Regulate Commerce': Federal Power under the Constitution," in *This Constitution: Our Enduring Legacy.* Washington, D.C.: Congressional Quarterly, 1986.

Maxey, Margaret N., and Robert L. Kuhn. *Regulatory Reform: New Vision and Old Curse.* New York: Praeger, 1985.

Tolchin, Susan, and Martin Tolchin. *Dismantling America: The Rush to Deregulate.* Boston: Houghton Mifflin, 1983.

# Commerce, Science, and Transportation Committee, Senate

The Senate Commerce, Science, and Transportation Committee has jurisdiction over all forms of transportation, from boats to jets. It also handles legislation dealing with communications, consumer protection, interstate commerce, ocean policy, science, technology, and space.

During the 1980s the committee played a central role in the deregulation of the transportation industry. In the early 1990s the committee shifted its focus to the complex and controversial task of revising regulation of the telephone, broadcast, and print industries to keep up with technological advances. Still it was not among the most sought-after committee assignments in the Senate. Unlike committees such as Appropriations or Finance, the Commerce, Science, and Transportation Committee did not command the Senate's attention.

The committee spent most of the late 1970s and 1980s deregulating the airlines and the trucking industry—and then reexamining what it had done. Faith in the magic of the free market was shaken by complaints about bad service and by mergers and bankruptcies. The committee never considered undoing its work, but its members did discuss tinkering with the remains of the regulatory structure in order to regain some federal control.

The Commerce Committee, set up in 1816, was among the first committees created in the Senate. Its name was changed in 1961 from the Interstate and Foreign Commerce Committee to Commerce Committee. In 1977 it became the Commerce, Science, and Transportation Committee.

For more than two decades, from 1955 to 1977, the Commerce Committee was chaired by Warren G. Magnuson, a Washington Democrat who was the most senior member of the Senate when he lost his seat to a Republican in 1981. A close friend of Lyndon B. Johnson, Magnuson in the 1960s worked to implement the president's policies on consumer issues. He fought for automobile safety standards and tougher safety requirements for other consumer products. He led an unsuccessful campaign to introduce federal no-fault automobile insurance.

Nevada Democrat Howard W. Cannon served as chair from 1978 to 1981, a period of difficult negotiations between the House and Senate over deregulation of the transportation industry. Cannon quickly became known as a tough negotiator in conference who always carried enough proxies in his pocket to back up his position. Cannon lost the 1980 election to one of the Republicans who tipped control of the Senate to the Republican party.

Republican Bob Packwood of Oregon, who chaired the committee from 1981 to 1985, tried to continue the wave of deregulation, focusing on loosening federal controls on the broadcasting industry. But his efforts failed. For the next two years, John C. Danforth, a Missouri Republican, served as chair. Skeptical of complete deregulation, he favored national licensing standards for truck and bus drivers.

When Democrats regained control of the Senate in 1987, Ernest F. Hollings, an imposing and sometimes caustic South Carolina Democrat, became chair. As chair of the Appropriations subcommittee on commerce, Hollings was able to fight for funding to back up legislation from the Commerce Committee. Under Hollings's leadership, the committee plunged into the controversial area of communications regulation. Legislation to reregulate the cable television industry led the list of communications issues the panel took on in the early 1990s.

## Committee Action

*See* LEGISLATIVE PROCESS.

## Committee of the Whole

The House of Representatives considers almost all important bills within a parliamentary framework known as the Committee of the Whole. This is one of the most important stages in the LEGISLATIVE PROCESS and comes after the House legislative committees have studied and drafted the bills. The Committee of the Whole is not a committee as the word is usually understood; it is the full House meeting under another name for the purpose of speeding action on legislation.

The committee is formally known as the Committee of the Whole House on the State of the Union. It includes all 435 members of the House, plus most of the time—under a controversial rules change adopted at the beginning of the 103rd Congress—the five DELEGATES to Congress. Meeting on the floor of the House chamber and using special parliamentary rules, the Committee of the Whole debates and amends legislation. It cannot pass a bill. Instead it reports the measure to the full House with whatever changes it has approved. The full House then may pass or reject the bill—or, on occasion, return it to the legislative committee where it originated. Amendments adopted in the Committee of the Whole may be put to a second vote in the full House of Representatives.

Far fewer members must be on the House floor to conduct business in the Committee of the Whole than in a regular House session. This may be an advantage when busy representatives cannot be rounded up to attend a floor meeting. A quorum for doing business in the Committee of the Whole is only 100 members, in contrast to 218 in the full House. The Speaker does not preside but selects another member of the majority party to take the chair. AMENDMENTS are considered under a rule, often ignored, that limits debate to five minutes for those who favor the amendment and five minutes for those opposed.

Until 1971 many important issues were decided in the Committee of the Whole by voting methods that provided no record of how individual members stood. That was an attraction for representatives who wanted to avoid publicity on politically difficult issues. But under rules in force today, a recorded vote must be ordered in the Committee of the Whole if twenty-five members (one-fourth of a quorum) demand it. An electronic voting system is used, and each member's vote is displayed beside his or her name on panels above the Speaker's desk. The vote is also published in the *CONGRESSIONAL RECORD*. (See VOTING IN CONGRESS.)

The Committee of the Whole has no counterpart in the Senate. The concept originated in the British House of Commons, where it was used during periods of strained relations with the king to evade the normal restrictions of a formal House of Commons session.

## Committee on Committees

*See* LEADERSHIP.

## Committee System

Committees are Congress's workshops. Almost every piece of LEGISLATION introduced in the Sen-

## CONGRESSIONAL COMMITTEES, 103RD CONGRESS

**House**
Agriculture
Appropriations
Armed Services
Banking, Finance, and Urban Affairs
Budget
District of Columbia
Education and Labor
Energy and Commerce
Foreign Affairs
Government Operations
House Administration
Judiciary
Merchant Marine and Fisheries
Natural Resources
Post Office and Civil Service
Public Works and Transportation
Rules
Science, Space, and Technology
Small Business
Standards of Official Conduct

Veterans' Affairs
Ways and Means

**House Select and Special**
Aging [1]
Children, Youth, and Families [1]
Hunger [1]
Intelligence
Narcotics Abuse and Control [1]

**Senate**
Agriculture, Nutrition, and Forestry
Appropriations
Armed Services
Banking, Housing, and Urban Affairs
Budget
Commerce, Science, and
    Transportation
Energy and Natural Resources
Environment and Public Works
Finance

Foreign Relations
Governmental Affairs
Judiciary
Labor and Human Resources
Rules and Administration
Small Business
Veterans' Affairs

**Senate Select and Special**
Aging
Ethics
Indian Affairs
Intelligence

**Joint Committees**
Joint Economic
Joint Library
Joint Organization of Congress
Joint Printing
Joint Taxation

1. Abolished as of April 1, 1993.

ate or House of Representatives initially is sent to a committee for review and recommendations. Committees do not have to wait for bills to be referred to them; they often write their own bills from scratch.

Specialized subcommittees usually consider the legislation first, frequently making substantial changes before sending the bill to the full committee for action. A committee or subcommittee often holds hearings at which those who favor and those who oppose a measure have an opportunity to express their views. The committee may decide to approve the bill, with or without changes, and "report" it to the parent chamber, or it may decide to kill the measure altogether. It is very difficult for a bill to reach the Senate or House floor without first winning committee approval. The committee also manages the debate once the measure has arrived on the floor. Later, after both the Senate and House have passed the bill, committee members from both chambers work out any differ-

ences and put the measure into final form. (See LEG-ISLATIVE PROCESS.)

In addition to their legislative role, committees conduct INVESTIGATIONS that highlight national problems or disclose official wrongdoing. They are also responsible for congressional oversight of government programs and agencies. (See OVERSIGHT POWER.)

Congressional committees have changed dramatically in recent decades. Subcommittees have taken over much of the work once performed by full committees, and junior members now share the power once exercised by authoritarian committee chairs. A rapid expansion of STAFF has eased the congressional workload, although some observers now complain that committee aides have undue influence on legislative policy.

The prestige of individual committees rises and falls as national issues change. Still, some panels remain at the center of power. That inner circle includes House Ways and Means and Senate Finance, which are responsible for tax legislation, and House and Senate Appropriations, which have jurisdiction over federal spending. One of the most influential committees in either chamber is the House Rules Committee, which controls access to the House floor for all major bills and sets the terms of floor debate. (See APPROPRIATIONS COMMITTEE, HOUSE; APPROPRIATIONS COMMITTEE, SENATE; FINANCE COMMITTEE, SENATE; RULES COMMITTEE, HOUSE; WAYS AND MEANS COMMITTEE, HOUSE.)

## Types of Committees

There are several types of congressional committees, each with its own purpose. Below the committee level are a multitude of subcommittees.

### Standing Committees

Standing committees handle most of the legislation considered by Congress. They are permanent bodies with responsibility for broad areas of legislation, such as agriculture or foreign affairs. The Senate has sixteen standing committees, and the House has twenty-two; they are organized on roughly parallel lines in each chamber and generally follow the major organizational divisions of the executive branch.

The number of members varies from committee to committee. In the 102nd Congress (1991–1993), for example, House standing committees ranged in size from eleven (District of Columbia Committee) to fifty-nine (Appropriations); Senate standing committees ranged from twelve (Veterans' Affairs) to twenty-nine (Appropriations).

Committee membership is generally in proportion to the overall party breakdown in the parent chamber. Thus the majority party in the chamber maintains a majority in its committees. On some key committees—such as House Rules or Ways and Means—the majority party often gives itself an extra edge so it can maintain strong control.

### Subcommittees

Most standing committees divide their work among subcommittees. As in the full committees, membership is weighted toward the majority party in the parent body. Subcommittees vary in importance from committee to committee. Some, such as the thirteen subcommittees apiece of the House and Senate Appropriations committees, have great authority; much of their work is routinely endorsed by the full Appropriations committees without further review.

Subcommittees provide the ultimate division of labor within the committee system. They help Congress handle its huge workload, and they permit members to develop specialized knowledge in a particular field. But they are often criticized for fragmenting responsibility and increasing the difficulty of policy review, while adding substantially to the cost of congressional operations.

Subcommittees are often less important in the Senate than in the House. Senate committees frequently take up bills without formal subcommittee action (except on Appropriations); House committees do this far less often.

The number of subcommittees exploded as a result of the reforms of the 1970s, and both chambers took steps to reverse that trend. Although their numbers have dropped since then, standing committees in the 102nd Congress had some 220 subcommittees in all. Some committees had seven or eight subcommittees—still too many for some critics. At the beginning of the 103rd Congress (1993–1995), the House voted to reduce the number of its subcommittees by restricting most committees to either five or six subpanels. House Democrats also set new limits on a member's subcommittee assignments.

### Select Committees

Both chambers from time to time create select or special committees to study special problems or concerns, such as aging, hunger, or narcotics abuse. The Senate and House committees that investigated the IRAN-CONTRA AFFAIR were select committees, as was the panel set up in the Senate to look into POW/MIA Affairs. (See POW/MIA AFFAIRS COMMITTEE, SENATE SELECT.)

These committees may make recommendations, but they usually are not permitted to report legislation. In most cases they remain in existence for only a few years. Exceptions are the Select Intelligence committees in both chambers, which do consider and report legislation. They are standing committees in everything but name. Because their subject matter is

*A House-Senate conference on clean air legislation in 1990 included more than 140 members representing nine House and Senate committees.*
Source: R. Michael Jenkins

narrower than that of most standing committees, the Intelligence panels were designated as select rather than standing committees. (See INTELLIGENCE COMMITTEES, HOUSE AND SENATE SELECT.)

### Joint Committees

Joint committees are usually permanent panels composed of members drawn from both the Senate and House; their composition reflects the party ratios in each chamber. Chairmanships generally rotate from one chamber to the other every two years, at the beginning of each new Congress.

Of the five joint committees in existence in early 1993, two had policy roles. The Joint Economic Committee studied economic problems and made recommendations to Congress but could not report legislation. The Joint Committee on the Organization of Congress was a temporary panel set up in 1992 to recommend reforms in legislative operations. (See ECONOMIC COMMITTEE, JOINT; ORGANIZATION OF CONGRESS COMMITTEE, JOINT.)

The Joint Committee on Taxation performed staff work for the House Ways and Means and Senate Finance committees. (See TAXATION COMMITTEE,

JOINT.) The two remaining joint committees—those on printing and the library—dealt with administrative matters, including the GOVERNMENT PRINTING OFFICE and the LIBRARY OF CONGRESS, respectively. (See LIBRARY COMMITTEE, JOINT; PRINTING COMMITTEE, JOINT.)

### Conference Committees

CONFERENCE COMMITTEES, a special kind of joint committee, are temporary bodies that have important powers. Their job is to settle differences between bills that have passed the House and Senate. They go out of business when the job is done.

## Development

The congressional committee system had its roots in the British Parliament and the colonial legislatures. In the earliest days of Congress, legislative proposals were considered first on the Senate or House floor, after which a temporary committee was appointed to work out the details. The committee then reported its bill to the full chamber for further debate, amendment, and passage. Once the committee had reported, it was dissolved.

Gradually the temporary panels were replaced by permanent committees, and legislation came to be referred directly to the committees without prior consideration by the full Senate or House.

By the end of the nineteenth century these small groups had developed such great power that Congress was said to have abdicated its lawmaking function to its committees. Although committees were created by and responsible to their parent bodies, they functioned with almost total independence. The panels tended to be dominated by their chairs, whose power resulted from the rigid operation of the SENIORITY SYSTEM. Under that system the member of the majority party with the longest continuous service on a committee automatically became its chair. The formal title of a person who heads a committee is "chairman."

The chairs often did not share the prevailing views of Congress as a whole or even of the membership of their own party. Yet their powers were so great that Woodrow Wilson in 1885 described the system as "a government by the chairmen of the standing committees of Congress."

One of the last old-time committee czars was Rep. Howard W. SMITH, a conservative Virginia Democrat who chaired the House Rules Committee from 1955 until 1967. The Rules Committee is the gateway through which major bills must pass to reach the House floor, and Smith made the most of his power to censor the legislative program of the House. He regularly blocked civil rights legislation sought by the Democratic leadership.

Congress did not take major steps to curb committee powers until the 1970s, when junior House members demanded and won fundamental changes in the way Congress, and particularly the committees, operated. The changes diluted the authority of committee chairs and other senior members and redistributed power among their younger and less experienced colleagues. Many of these junior members became chairs of newly created subcommittees. By the 1980s the full committees had lost some of their influence to subcommittees, whose chairs became powers in their own right. (See REFORM, CONGRESSIONAL.)

The most significant of the 1970s reforms was a decision by House and Senate Democrats to allow the caucus of party members in each chamber to elect committee chairs. (See CAUCUSES, PARTY.) Although most chairs continued to be chosen on the basis of seniority, the election requirement made them accountable to their colleagues for their conduct. Its force was illustrated in 1975, when three House chairs were deposed in caucus elections. Several others have lost their posts since then.

Caucus election of committee chairs was only one of the changes that restricted the chairs' authority. Most House committees were required to establish subcommittees; House Democrats adopted a subcommittee "bill of rights" that transferred authority over subcommittee organization from committee chairs to subcommittee Democrats. Committees were required to have written rules, and limits were placed on the number of chairmanships members could hold. Members were given their own professional staff to help them with committee work. Committee and subcommittee staff increased.

The diffusion of committee power ended the era of autocratic committee chairs. From that time on a chair's authority depended on the support of a committee majority and his or her own personal and legislative skills. In the 1960s, during his heyday as chair of the House Ways and Means Committee, Arkansas Democrat Wilbur D. MILLS enjoyed almost unchallenged authority over his panel. But the political climate had changed by the time Oregon Democrat Al Ullman succeeded Mills in 1975.

## Power Centers

Committees vary greatly in how much power they have. A panel may be powerful because of the subjects it handles or because an aggressive chair has expanded its turf. Another may be formally classified as a "minor" committee.

Money committees are enduring centers of power. The House Ways and Means and Senate Finance committees write tax bills that govern the flow of revenues into the federal treasury. They also have jurisdiction over billions of dollars in federal spending for Social Security, Medicare, welfare, unemployment, and other programs. The House and Senate Appropriations committees, which prepare annual funding bills for government agencies, oversee the full range of federal activity. Control over federal spending gives Appropriations members considerable influence with their colleagues, as well as with the executive branch. The House and Senate Budget committees exert power more subtly. They set broad spending limits that other committees are expected to observe. But the limits can be violated whenever the political will to meet them is lacking.

The power a committee wields may change with the times. Under an aggressive chair with expansionist aims, the House Energy and Commerce Committee emerged in the 1980s as a major power center. Chair John D. Dingell, a Michigan Democrat, became known for his skill at capturing jurisdiction over additional areas of legislation. The committee laid claim to measures touching major regulatory agencies, nuclear energy, toxic wastes, health research, Medicaid and Medicare, railroad retirement, telecommunications, tourism, and more. It developed the largest staff and budget of any House committee. (See ENERGY AND COMMERCE COMMITTEE, HOUSE.)

As Energy and Commerce gathered influence, some power centers of an earlier era were in marked, though perhaps temporary, decline. The House Education and Labor Committee had its days in the sun in the 1960s, when Congress was enacting landmark school aid laws; the Senate Energy Committee shone in the 1970s, when energy policy was a major economic issue.

The House Rules Committee suffered a brief decline in the 1970s but remains one of the most influential panels in either chamber. With authority to draft ground rules for floor debate on most major bills, the Rules Committee can limit or bar amendments to a bill, or prevent its consideration altogether. The House seldom rejects the panel's recommendations on such matters.

## Members' Assignments

Members' influence in Congress often is closely related to the committee or committees on which they serve. Assignment to a powerful committee virtually guarantees plentiful campaign contributions. Many members seek a particular committee because they have an interest in the panel's jurisdiction, while others stake out committee assignments according to political need. Members from large agricultural districts gravitate toward the agriculture committees. Those whose districts have major military installations often seek out the Armed Services committees.

The political parties in each chamber assign members to committees. The assignments are then routinely approved by the full House or Senate at the beginning of each two-year Congress. The specific process varies by chamber and party.

Just wanting to be on a committee is not enough to ensure assignment to it. In most cases members have to fight for assignments to the more influential panels. In each chamber membership in a few powerful committees, such as Finance and Ways and Means, is difficult to achieve. By contrast, congressional leaders often have to seek "volunteers" to serve on less popular panels, such as the House District of Columbia Committee. A member's rank on a committee is determined by his or her length of service, or seniority, on the panel, and a new member must start at the bottom.

Representatives typically serve on only two committees. Senators often serve on four. Although some veteran members do switch committees, most keep their assignments throughout their careers, gradually advancing through the seniority system to the coveted position of chair (or ranking minority member, depending on which party is in power).

### Additional Readings

Davidson, Roger J., and Walter J. Oleszek. *Congress and Its Members.* 4th ed. Washington, D.C.: CQ Press, 1993.

Fenno, Richard F., Jr. *Congressmen in Committees.* Boston: Little, Brown, 1973.

Goodwin, George, Jr. *The Little Legislatures: Committees of Congress.* Amherst: University of Massachusetts Press, 1970.

Smith, Steven S., and Christopher J. Deering. *Committees in Congress.* 2nd ed. Washington, D.C.: CQ Press, 1990.

Unekis, Joseph K., and Leroy N. Rieselbach. *Congressional Committee Politics: Continuity and Change.* New York: Praeger, 1984.

## Concurrent Resolution

*See* LEGISLATION.

## Conference Committees

Conference committees play such an important part in the LEGISLATIVE PROCESS that they are sometimes called the third house of Congress. A bill cannot be sent to the president for signature until it has been approved in identical form by both the Senate and House of Representatives. Frequently, however, the two chambers pass different versions of the same bill, and neither is willing to accept the version passed by the other. The bill then goes to a conference committee, a temporary Senate-House panel established solely to work out the differences between the two chambers on a particular bill. Although conferences are convened on a relatively small number of measures, these bills generally include the most important LEGISLATION before Congress.

Conference committee members are formally appointed by the Speaker of the House and the presiding officer of the Senate. In practice they are chosen by the chair or senior minority party member of the committee (or committees) that originally handled the bill. These members usually select themselves to serve on the conference committee, as well as other members of their panel. If a subcommittee has exercised major responsibility for a bill, some of its members may be chosen. Seniority, or length of service, once governed the selection of conferees, but it is quite common today for junior members in each chamber to be chosen, especially if they are particularly knowledgeable about or interested in the bill. (See SENIORITY SYSTEM.) Occasionally a member from another committee with expertise in the subject matter of the bill may be named to the conference. Both political parties are represented on the conference committee.

There need not be an equal number of conferees, known as managers, from each house, because a majority vote determines the position of each chamber's delegation on all decisions made in the conference. Conference committees vary widely in size. The conference committee on a 1990 bill to improve emergency medical services consisted of seven members. That same year the clear air act had a conference of 149 members: 140 from the House, representing seven committees, and 9 from the Senate, representing two committees. More than 250 members were appointed as conferees on a 1981 budget reconciliation bill. Such large conferences usually divide up into smaller groups to consider separate sections of the bill.

Senate and House conferees vote separately on each issue, and a majority of both delegations must agree before a compromise provision is included in the final bill. Conferees are supposed to defend their own chamber's provisions even if they disagree with them. At the beginning of the 103rd Congress the House adopted a rule allowing the Speaker to remove any House member from, or add additional ones to, a conference committee.

Conferees are not supposed to insert new material in a bill or reconsider provisions that are the same in both the House and Senate versions. In practice, however, many bills are largely rewritten in conference. Conferees are not always able to compromise on all their differences; in such case they may leave final decisions on some matters to the full House and Senate. A majority of conferees from each chamber must sign the conference report containing the compromise.

The Senate and House must approve the conference report and resolve any remaining differences before the compromise bill can go to the White House. Conference reports are rarely rejected and cannot be amended on the floor under ordinary procedures. The conference committee dissolves after approval by one chamber; should the conference report be rejected, a new conference could be required.

The conference system, used by Congress since 1789, had developed its modern practice by the middle of the nineteenth century. Until 1975 most conference committees met in secret, but House and Senate rules changes have broken down the secrecy and seniority that once were the norm. However, some conferences, such as those dealing with secret intelligence activities, still are closed, and others are settled by a small number of senior members negotiating behind closed doors. (See REFORM, CONGRESSIONAL.)

### Additional Readings

Longley, Lawrence D., and Walter J. Oleszek. *Bicameral Politics: Conference Committees in Congress.* New Haven, Conn.: Yale University Press, 1989.

Volger, David J. *The Third House: Conference Committees in the United States Congress.* Evanston, Ill.: Northwestern University Press, 1971.

---

## Confirmation

*See* APPOINTMENT POWER.

---

## Conflict of Interest

*See* ETHICS.

---

## Congressional Budget and Impoundment Control Act

*See* BUDGET PROCESS.

---

## Congressional Budget Office

Congress has its own office of budget specialists and economists to provide budgetary analyses and economic forecasts. The Congressional Budget Office (CBO) is intended to give legislators nonpartisan information and set out policy options without making recommendations. CBO acts as a scorekeeper when Congress is voting on the federal budget, tracking bills to make sure they comply with overall budget goals. The agency also estimates what proposed legislation would cost over a five-year period.

CBO works most closely with the House and Senate Budget committees. All three were established in 1974 by a new congressional budget law. The intent of that law was to force Congress to consider the overall federal budget, with projected revenues, spending, and deficits. In the past legislators had made spending decisions haphazardly, rarely considering future costs or how new programs fit into the overall budget. (See BUDGET PROCESS.)

The new budget process was also an attempt to regain fiscal control that had been lost to the executive branch. Congress created CBO to give it the kind of expert budgetary support that the president receives from the Office of Management and Budget.

The CBO director is appointed for a four-year term by the Speaker of the House and the president pro tempore of the Senate. Alice M. Rivlin, a Democrat, was CBO director from 1975 to 1983. She was followed by Rudolph Penner, a Republican, who left in 1987. Two acting directors, Edward M. Gramlich and James L. Blum, led CBO during a two-year period in which House and Senate budget leaders were unable to agree on a replacement for Penner. In March 1989 Robert D. Reischauer, a Democrat, was named CBO director. Reischauer's term expires in January 1995.

---

## Congressional Directory

The *Congressional Directory* is the official "Who's Who" of Congress. The thick volume, published at the beginning of each two-year term of Congress, contains biographies of each senator and representative, as well as a hodgepodge of other information: lists of committees, telephone numbers, maps of congressional districts, diagrams of Capitol offices, staffs of executive agencies, and a roster of ambassadors, among other material.

The *Directory* has been published since 1821. The postmaster printed it until 1857, when the Joint Committee on Printing took over. The format of the book has changed little over the years, although it has grown larger. The 1877 edition had 160 pages; the 1993 edition had ten times that number. Single copies of the *Directory* can be purchased from the GOVERNMENT PRINTING OFFICE.

## Congressional Record

The *Congressional Record* is the primary source of information about what happens on the floors of the Senate and House of Representatives. The *Record*, published daily when Congress is in session, provides an officially sanctioned account of each chamber's debate and shows how individual members voted on many issues.

By law, the *Record* is supposed to provide "substantially a verbatim report of the proceedings." Exchanges among legislators during debate can be quite lively and revealing. But senators and representatives are able to edit their remarks for the *Record*, fixing grammatical errors or even deleting words spoken in the heat of debate. Speeches not given on the floor are often included, although both the Senate and House have tightened rules about "inserting remarks," as the process is known. The full texts of bills and other documents, never read aloud on the floor, are often printed in the *Record*.

Because much of what Congress does takes place off the House and Senate floors, reading the *Record* gives only a limited sense of how Congress works. Despite these drawbacks the *Record* is an essential tool for students of Congress and for anyone following a specific issue. In addition to floor debate and vote tallies, the *Record* notes past and future committee meetings and hearings, as well as the next day's schedule for floor action. (See LEGISLATIVE PROCESS.)

The *Record* is not the official account of congressional proceedings. That is provided in each chamber's *Journal,* which reports actions taken but not the accompanying debate. The *Record* is used to determine what Congress intended when it passed a law. For example, federal agencies drafting regulations sometimes turn to recorded debate to gain a better understanding of legislative intent.

The *Record* contains four sections: House proceedings, Senate proceedings, Extensions of Remarks, and the Daily Digest. An index published twice a month helps readers find their way around the gray pages, which typically have three columns of tightly spaced text. Tables and charts rarely appear. Newspaper arti-

*The* Congressional Record *comes off the presses at the Government Printing Office. The* Record *is published daily when Congress is in session.* Source: Government Printing Office

cles are often inserted by legislators, but editorial cartoons are taboo. Smaller type and other typographical devices identify inserted articles and speeches not actually delivered on the floor.

Since 1979 time cues have marked House floor debate to show roughly what time a particular discussion occurred; Senate proceedings have no indication of time. Speakers during debate are identified by name, but not by party or by state, unless to distinguish between two legislators with the same last name.

The cost of printing the *Record* was about $20 million a year in the early 1990s. About 20,000 copies of each day's issue are printed. Each senator is entitled to fifty free copies (thirty on paper and twenty on microfiche), and each representative to thirty-four (twenty on paper and fourteen on microfiche). Several additional copies are provided for office use. Twice as many free copies were provided until a rules change in 1977.

An annual subscription to the *Record* cost $225 in the early 1990s; an individual copy cost $1.50. Until 1970 a subscription cost only $1.50 a month.

Rules require that any insert of more than two printed pages include an estimate of printing costs by the Government Printing Office, which has printed the *Record* since 1873. One of the most expensive inserts appeared in the issue of June 15, 1987, when Rep. Bill Alexander, an Arkansas Democrat, inserted 403 pages covering three and a half years of congressional debate on an amendment barring military aid to the "contra" guerrillas in Nicaragua. The estimated cost of the insertion was $197,000. Republicans said they would object automatically to any future inserts costing more than $10,000.

## Congressional Research Service

*See* LIBRARY OF CONGRESS.

## Conkling, Roscoe

A skilled political operator, Roscoe Conkling (1829–1888) always managed to have a role in power struggles, whether in the Republican party, Congress, or his home state of New York. Conkling seemed to relish conflict and to invite confrontation with his arrogant manner and back-room machinations. In the end, however, he pushed too far, ending his political career.

Conkling first served in the House from 1859 to 1863 and from 1865 to 1867. He then served in the Senate from 1867 to 1881. In the Senate Conkling led a Republican faction that usually controlled the Committee on Committees, rewarding supporters with valuable committee appointments. He eventually chaired the Senate Foreign Relations Committee.

Control of appointments was also the key to the New York political machine that Conkling headed. Two of his allies ran the customhouse in New York, where U.S. customs revenue was collected and where hundreds of people worked at PATRONAGE jobs. When President Rutherford B. Hayes, a supporter of civil service reform, took office in 1877, he attempted to curb patronage abuses. Conkling's two allies refused to comply with a ban on partisan political activities by federal employees, and Hayes called for their resignations. When they refused to resign, he nominated others to replace them. The Senate declined to approve Hayes's nominees after Conkling invoked SENATORIAL COURTESY (a custom permitting senators of the party in office to control selection of local federal officials). The Senate did, however, confirm two later nominations by Hayes. (See APPOINTMENT POWER.)

When James A. Garfield was elected president in 1880, Conkling expected a return to the patronage system. But Garfield was overwhelmed by competing Republican party factions, all demanding patronage slots. When Garfield did not accept Conkling's choices for the customhouse, Conkling tried to have the Senate reject Garfield's nominations. The effort failed. In a risky power play, Conkling resigned his Senate seat in May 1881, as did his ally and fellow New York senator, Thomas C. Platt. Conkling expected the state legislature to reelect them, thus strengthening his hand. But the legislature refused, and Conkling's political career was over.

## Connally, Tom

Tom Connally (1877–1963), a Texas Democrat, was chair of the Senate Foreign Relations Committee from 1941 to 1953, except for two years when Republicans controlled the Senate. He entered the Sen-

*Sen. Tom Connally shows his relief upon completion of the Lend-Lease Act of 1941, which allowed the president to ship supplies to the Allies during World War II.*
*Source: Library of Congress*

ate in 1929, after serving twelve years in the House of Representatives, and remained until his retirement in 1953. He played an important role in U.S. foreign policy in the post–World War II period.

Connally supported successive Democratic administrations on foreign policy. He helped Franklin D. Roosevelt plan the United Nations and was one of the eight representatives of the United States at the San Francisco Charter Conference in 1945. As a result of membership in the United Nations, the United States became a member of the International Court of Justice. Connally also played an important part in persuading the Senate to accept membership in the court.

In 1946 the Senate considered a resolution allowing the International Court jurisdiction over all matters that it did not deem purely domestic. Although President Harry S. Truman urged that the Senate agree to the resolution, senators were reluctant to let the court decide what was or was not a matter under domestic jurisdiction. Connally offered a compromise that became one of the most notable reservations to

an international treaty. The Connally reservation provided that the Senate would decide what are matters "within the domestic jurisdiction of the United States."

Although he lost his post as chair of Foreign Relations in 1947, when Republicans gained control of the Senate, Connally helped win Senate approval of the Marshall Plan for postwar European recovery. When he regained the post two years later, he championed the North Atlantic Treaty Organization.

## Consent Calendar

Members of the House of Representatives may place on the Consent Calendar any bill on the Union or House CALENDAR that is considered to be noncontroversial. Bills on the Consent Calendar normally are called on the first and third Mondays of each month.

When such a bill is called up for the first time, consideration of it may be blocked by the objection of a single member. If objection is made, the bill is carried over to the next day on which the Consent Calendar is called. If three members object the second time the bill is called up, it is stricken from the Consent Calendar (but still remains on the House or Union calendar). If fewer than three members object, the bill is considered immediately and usually passed without debate.

Official objectors are appointed by each party at the beginning of every Congress to guard against passage of important measures on which there may be substantial opposition. Objectors police bills on the Consent Calendar and act for absent members.

## Conservative Coalition

The most potent congressional alliance of the last sixty years has been the conservative coalition, which has never had a staff or formal organization. From the 1930s through the 1970s and later Republicans and southern Democrats combined to exert powerful conservative influence in both the House and Senate.

Disillusioned with NEW DEAL economic policies, southern Democrats began banding together with Republicans to defeat or weaken President Franklin D. Roosevelt's proposals. The coalition dominated the House in the 1950s, and in the early 1960s it defeated many initiatives of President John F. Kennedy. It was less powerful in the Senate but still had an important influence on legislation.

By the mid-1980s institutional changes in Congress and demographic changes in southern states had weakened the conservative coalition. Many southern Democrats had abandoned coalition politics, saying they did not expect to return to it any time soon.

### The Changing South

For reasons that go back to the Civil War, the "solid South" evolved as a one-party region. Well into the 1960s most congressional districts in the South were overwhelmingly rural, with a one-party political system and, in the Deep South, an all-white electorate. Southern members of Congress controlled most of the

important committees. Together with conservative Republicans they could often block civil rights and other social legislation proposed by the national Democratic party.

The situation in the South began to change as early as 1948, when the Democratic party under President Harry S. Truman added civil rights for blacks to its agenda. Over the next three decades, southern allegiance to the Democratic party steadily eroded, and the Republicans gained a firm foothold in the region.

By the 1980s the South was transformed, and the Democratic party in the South had changed with it. The South had become much less Democratic, less rural, more suburban, less poor, and more educated. As northern natives moved into the South, the region became less "southern." The upshot was that southern voters became less conservative.

The southern electorate changed in other ways as well. The enfranchisement of blacks in the 1960s and 1970s made southern politicians of both parties far more sensitive to civil rights and other liberal social issues. Blacks made up a larger proportion of all southern voters. Republicans, meanwhile, gained a foothold in many parts of the South, although they remained far short of a majority. Many voters came to think of themselves as independents, not aligned with either party.

These changes were felt in Congress. Southern states elected a new breed of Democrats who showed little interest in following traditional conservative leadership. They moved closer to their party's national leadership and no longer cast many votes with Republicans. For their part, Republicans made fewer attempts to promote unified positions with the southern Democrats.

The coalition was expected to all but disappear in the 103rd Congress (1993–1995) because of the presidential victory of Arkansas governor Bill Clinton. Southern Democrats were expected to exert their power within the Democratic caucus rather than by joining Republicans to block programs of the Democratic leadership. (See CAUCUSES, PARTY.)

The decline of the conservative coalition can be seen by charting the percentage of floor votes on which a majority of southern Democrats and a majority of Republicans voted together against a majority of Democrats from outside the South. During the coalition's heyday in the 1960s and 1970s, the coalition appeared on 20 percent to 30 percent of Senate and House floor votes. In 1991 it appeared on only 11 percent of the votes and in 1992 on just 12 percent.

---

## Constitutional Amendments

The framers of the Constitution gave Congress a key role in amending the nation's fundamental body of law. They wanted to be sure that the amendment process embodied the principle of checks and balances, the division of authority among the various branches of government. Thus, they divided the power to amend between Congress, the law-making branch of government, and the states, whose ratification of the Constitution originally gave it force.

The Constitution's framers wanted to incorporate some flexibility into their document without making it too easy to change. The method of amending the Articles of Confederation, the nation's first legal charter, had proved to be impractical. Any change in that document required the consent of the Continental Congress and every one of the states. At the other extreme, the British Parliament could change England's unwritten constitution at will.

Under Article V of the Constitution, Congress plays a leading part in proposing amendments. The final decision on amendments still rests with the states, but unanimity is not required. Amending the Constitution nonetheless remains difficult. The first ten amendments, known as the Bill of Rights, are considered practically a part of the original document. Aside from those, the Constitution has been amended only seventeen times in more than two hundred years.

The most recent amendment, ratified in May 1992, prohibits midterm changes in congressional salaries. Proposed by James Madison and approved by the first Congress in 1789, the amendment was sent to the states as part of a package of twelve, ten of which became the Bill of Rights. Six states had ratified the pay raise amendment by 1792; a seventh state did so in 1873 and an eighth over a hundred years later in 1978. By 1992 thirty-three more states had ratified the amendment.

Widespread discontent with Congress inspired the push to ratify the Madison amendment more than two hundred years after it was proposed. Some legal scholars and members of Congress questioned its legitimacy, arguing that the ratification had taken place over too long a span of time.

Thousands of proposed amendments have not become part of the Constitution. Between 1787 and 1992, Congress had submitted only thirty-three amendments to the states; six of those were not ratified.

One recent notable proposal was the Equal Rights Amendment (ERA), which died on June 30, 1982. Although Congress extended the original 1979 deadline for ratification, the ERA fell three states short of the thirty-eight needed for ratification. The amendment, championed by women's rights advocates, stated: "Equality of rights under the law shall not be denied or abridged by the United States or by any state on account of sex." Congress had approved the proposal in 1972, forty-nine years after it was first introduced.

An amendment that would have given the District of Columbia voting representation in Congress died in 1985. Only sixteen state legislatures ratified that proposal within the seven-year deadline set by Congress.

Several proposed amendments circulated in Congress in recent years, including measures to require a balanced federal budget, permit prayer in public schools, ban abortion, and prohibit the use of busing to desegregate public schools. Congress repeatedly considered several versions of the most popular of these, the balanced budget amendment, during the 1980s and early 1990s, but it always backed away from approval.

### Amendment Procedures

The Constitution provides two procedures for amendment, but only one has been used. The process begins with Congress, which by two-thirds majority votes of the Senate and House of Representatives may send amendments to the states for ratification. Under the second, untried method, amendments may be

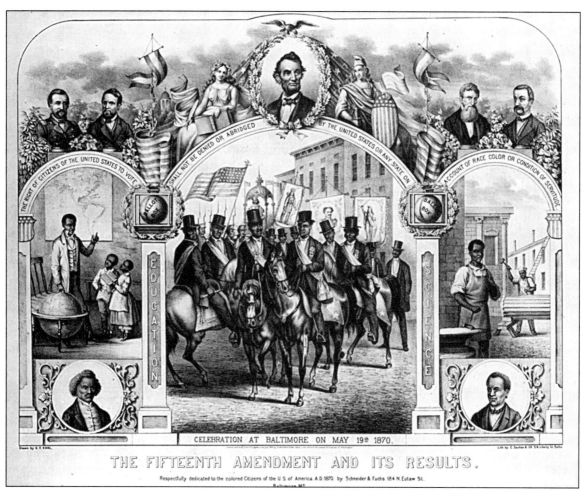

THE FIFTEENTH AMENDMENT AND ITS RESULTS.

Respectfully dedicated to the colored Citizens of the U.S of America A.D.1870. by Schneider & Fuchs 184 N.Eutaw St. Baltimore M.

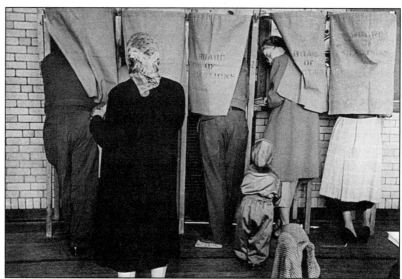

*The Fifteenth Amendment, ratified in 1870, prohibited denial of the right to vote on the basis of race, color, or previous condition of servitude. Ratified in 1920, the Nineteenth Amendment finally cleared the way for women's suffrage.* Source: Library of Congress and U.S. Information Agency proposed by a constitutional convention, which Congress must convene if requested to do so by the legislatures of two-thirds (thirty-four) of the states.

In either case a proposed amendment becomes part of the Constitution if it is ratified, or approved, by three-fourths (thirty-eight) of the states. Congress can set a deadline for state ratification of proposed amendments; in recent cases, the limit has been seven years. Congress also has the power to determine which of two procedures states must use to ratify a proposed amendment: approval by either state legislatures or state conventions. In every case but one Congress has prescribed approval by legislatures. The exception was the Twenty-first Amendment, repealing Prohibition.

The president cannot veto constitutional amendments, and governors cannot veto approval of amendments by their legislatures.

## Convention Controversy

No procedures have been established for determining what is a valid state call for a constitutional convention, or for actually running one. As a result, there are no guidelines on what a convention could debate, how the delegates would be selected, or who would preside. Many people fear a convention might be carried away and open the entire Constitution for amendment. Congressional moves to establish convention procedures never have become law.

Backers of a proposed constitutional amendment that has been bottled up in Congress sometimes campaign for a convention to consider their proposal. While no such campaign has yet succeeded, the effort sometimes spurs Congress to act on the proposed amendment. The Seventeenth Amendment was forced on the Senate in the early 1900s by popular pressure for a constitutional convention to take the selection of senators out of the hands of state legislatures. Fearing that such a convention might go too far, senators decided to submit a specific direct-election proposal to the states. (See DIRECT ELECTION OF SENATORS.)

Some convention campaigns have come close to success. In the 1960s thirty-three states petitioned Congress for a convention on a constitutional amendment permitting one house of a state legislature to be apportioned on some basis other than population. In the 1970s and 1980s thirty-two states petitioned for a convention on an amendment requiring a balanced federal budget.

The balanced-budget campaign illustrates the concern the prospect of a convention can arouse. Responding to a convention drive launched in 1975, Congress began considering a balanced-budget amendment, while intensifying its own efforts to bring the budget under control. The state convention drive lost steam in 1984. In 1982 the Senate had passed a balanced-budget amendment by slightly more than the two-thirds majority needed for passage. Members of the House tried in 1982 and again in 1986, but the measures were defeated both times.

In the spring of 1992, with an election approaching and public concern about the deficit running high, Congress at last appeared on the verge of ratifying a balanced-budget amendment. Supporters predicted victory when an amendment came to a vote in the House in June, but pressure by the Democratic leadership helped defeat it by nine votes. Opponents argued that amending the Constitution was a politically popular but unreliable way to cut the deficit. Even some conservatives opposed the amendment because they feared it would give Congress an excuse to raise taxes. The defeat also reflected the uneasiness many legislators feel about tinkering with the Constitution.

## Successful Amendments

The Constitution has proved remarkably durable. Although the country has changed dramatically in the past two hundred years, only a handful of amendments have changed the document drafted in 1787.

The first ten amendments, known as the Bill of Rights, were passed almost at the beginning. Omission of a bill of rights was the principal source of dissatisfaction with the new Constitution in the state ratifying conventions held in 1788. Congress and the states moved quickly, and the amendments were approved in 1791. The Bill of Rights added explicit guarantees of fundamental civil liberties, such as freedom of speech and trial by jury, that had not been spelled out in the original document.

A Supreme Court decision and a crisis in presidential election procedures prompted the next two amendments. The Eleventh Amendment (1795) stated that the power of the federal judiciary did not extend to private suits against states. The Twelfth Amendment (1804) provided for separate balloting for president and vice president in the electoral college.

**Civil War Era**

The Civil War inspired three amendments. The Thirteenth Amendment (1865) abolished slavery. The Fourteenth Amendment (1868) was designed to protect the basic rights of freed slaves, most significantly by forbidding states to deprive any person of life, liberty, or property without due process of law, or to deny anyone equal protection of the laws. The Fifteenth Amendment (1870) prohibited denial of the right to vote on the basis of race, color, or previous condition of servitude.

The due process and equal protection clauses of the Fourteenth Amendment have served as the basis of controversial shifts in the government's role. Until the mid-1930s the amendment was used more often to protect property rights than to safeguard individual liberties. But in the years following World War II, the Supreme Court began to use the Fourteenth Amendment to restrict state action infringing on civil and political rights. By invoking the due process clause, the Court gradually extended the guarantees of the Bill of Rights to cover actions by state governments. Relying largely on the equal protection clause, the Court brought about fundamental reforms in state policies on racial segregation and legislative malapportionment. The equal protection clause was the basis for the Court's historic 1954 decision outlawing racial segregation in public schools.

**Twentieth Century**

Four amendments were ratified from 1913 to 1920, largely in response to the Progressive movement. (See PROGRESSIVE ERA.) The Sixteenth Amendment (1913) gave the United States the income tax, the Seventeenth (1913) provided for direct election of senators, the Eighteenth (1919) prohibited the manufacture, sale, or transportation of alcoholic beverages, and the Nineteenth (1920) cleared the way for WOMEN'S SUFFRAGE.

Two more amendments were ratified in 1933. The Twentieth Amendment altered the dates for the beginning of a new Congress and of the president's term. The Twenty-first Amendment repealed the Eighteenth, thus ending Prohibition.

Six amendments have been added to the Constitution since World War II. The Twenty-second Amendment (1951) limited presidents to two terms in office. The Twenty-third (1961) gave citizens of the District of Columbia the right to vote in presidential elections. The Twenty-fourth Amendment (1964) outlawed poll taxes in federal elections. The Twenty-fifth (1967) set procedures for handling presidential disability, and the Twenty-sixth (1971) lowered the voting age to eighteen. (See YOUTH FRANCHISE.)

The Twenty-seventh Amendment (1992) reads in full: "No law varying the compensation for the services of the Senators and Representatives shall take effect, until an election of Representatives shall have intervened." The ratification of this amendment more than two hundred years after it was proposed by James Madison was a result of public resentment of congressional pay raises.

Earlier amendments had taken an average of about a year and a half for ratification. A court challenge to the Twenty-seventh Amendment appeared possible on the grounds that it did not reflect "a contemporaneous consensus," a requirement the Supreme Court had set for constitutional amendments.

*Additional Readings*

Burns, James MacGregor, Jack W. Peltason, and Thomas E. Cronin. *Government by the People.* 13th ed. New York: Basic Books, 1987.

Katz, William L. *Constitutional Amendments.* New York: Franklin Watts, 1974.

Mansbridge, Jane J. *Why We Lost the ERA.* Chicago: University of Chicago Press, 1986.

## Contempt of Congress

A person who refuses to testify or to produce documents demanded by a congressional committee risks being cited for contempt of Congress, a criminal offense. This ability to punish for contempt reinforces the congressional INVESTIGATIONS process.

The Constitution does not specifically grant Congress the power to punish for contempt, except in the case of one of its own members. But from the beginning Congress assumed that it could jail persons who were judged in contempt. It even confined some of them in the Capitol. At first Congress imposed punishment itself, but since the 1930s contempt cases have been prosecuted in the courts.

When a committee wishes to begin criminal proceedings against an uncooperative witness, it introduces a resolution in the Senate or House citing the witness for contempt. If the full chamber approves the resolution, as it generally does, the matter is referred to a U.S. attorney for prosecution in a federal court. Contempt of Congress is a misdemeanor punishable by a fine of $100 to $1,000 and one to twelve months' imprisonment.

On rare occasions contempt citations stem from acts, such as bribery or libel, that obstruct the proper functions of Congress. Most contempt citations in recent decades, however, have resulted from refusal to cooperate with congressional committees. The peak period for contempt citations came in the years following World War II. In those years the House Un-American Activities Committee zealously pursued people suspected of association with organizations that were considered subversive, such as the Communist party. In 1950 the House voted fifty-nine contempt citations, fifty-six of them recommended by the Un-American Activities Committee. Many cases involved private persons who invoked Fifth Amendment protection against self-incrimination.

More recently, most contempt disputes have been triggered by the refusal of executive branch officials to supply documents sought by Congress. These disputes have tested the limits of EXECUTIVE PRIVILEGE to withhold confidential information. They have often been settled through compromise. That was the case

in 1982 when a House committee recommended that Interior Secretary James G. Watt be cited for contempt for refusing to turn over documents sought by committee investigators. President Ronald Reagan eventually settled the dispute by giving committee members limited access to some of the documents for one day.

A contempt citation against Anne M. Burford, former head of the Environmental Protection Agency, was canceled in 1983 after the White House agreed to meet subcommittee demands for access to some of that agency's documents. Acting on Reagan's orders, Burford had refused to turn over the documents; she was the first person to be held in contempt of Congress for refusing to produce information on grounds of executive privilege.

## Continuing Resolution

A continuing resolution is a measure to keep government agencies operating when regular APPROPRIATIONS BILLS have not been enacted by the beginning of the government's FISCAL YEAR on October 1. The resolution takes its name from the fact that if it does not become law, the agencies could not continue working because they would run out of money.

Congress has used continuing resolutions (called CRs in Capitol Hill jargon) for more than a century as a temporary expedient to buy time for completing action on regular appropriations bills. Between 1954 and 1991 Congress approved at least one continuing resolution every year, except in 1988 when lawmakers completed the final appropriations bill one minute before the start of the new fiscal year. Most continued funding for a few days, weeks, or months. In the late 1970s, however, Congress began putting into continuing resolutions the entire text of appropriations bills that had not cleared. It also began to make the resolutions cover the full fiscal year. This trend reached its peak in 1986 and 1987, when Congress swept all thirteen regular appropriations measures into huge continuing resolutions that provided funding for entire fiscal years.

By the early 1990s continuing resolutions were once again being used primarily to continue funding for a period of days or weeks. For fiscal year 1992 Congress adopted a total of four continuing resolutions, but the final one contained funding for only one of the thirteen regular appropriations bills.

For decades the executive branch had shifted funds to bridge short gaps between the end of the fiscal year and the enactment of new appropriations. But in 1980 the attorney general prohibited that practice for all but essential costs; instead, agencies had to shut down if their funding lapsed. The impact of the ruling was dramatically illustrated the following year, after President Ronald Reagan vetoed a full-year continuing resolution for virtually the entire government. Federal workers were sent home, the Statue of Liberty and Washington Monument were closed, and the Constitution was lowered into a protective vault at the National Archives. Congress and the president hastily agreed on a substitute measure. Reagan vetoed continuing resolutions twice more during his presidency, shutting down the government for only a few hours each time.

Because of their urgency, continuing resolutions increasingly became magnets for controversial bills and amendments, or riders, that might not pass on their own. (See RIDER.) When President George Bush vetoed a short-term continuing resolution in October 1990, the resolution included funding for the entire federal government, an extension of the federal debt limit, and the suspension of automatic budget cuts that were to take effect in a few days. Three days later Bush signed a revised version of the continuing resolution.

---

# Courts and Congress

The federal judiciary and Congress have the power to check each other's authority. Congress determines the courts' jurisdictions, confirms their members, and pays their bills. The judiciary—most particularly, the Supreme Court—defines the limits of congressional authority.

Both branches have exercised these powers with restraint. Leaving aside the frequent disagreements and heated rhetoric, there have been few instances of direct conflict between the judiciary and Congress.

## Judicial System

The framers of the Constitution left much unwritten regarding the judicial branch. Unlike Articles I and II of the Constitution, which listed the powers and prerogatives of Congress and the executive, Article III simply sketched the outline of a federal judiciary. "The judicial power of the United States shall be vested in one supreme court, and in such inferior courts as the Congress may from time to time ordain and establish," the Constitution stated. The existence and structure of any federal courts lower than the Supreme Court were left entirely to the discretion of Congress.

Congress exercised that discretion early in its history. The Judiciary Act of 1789 established the Supreme Court, three circuit courts of appeal, and thirteen district courts. Thereafter, as the nation grew and the federal judiciary's workload increased, Congress established additional circuit and district courts. By 1992 the system had grown to include thirteen circuit courts and ninety-four district and territorial courts.

## Judicial Review

The Constitution is silent on the question of judicial review. It grants various powers to the judiciary but does not mention the authority to declare unconstitutional a law passed by Congress and to nullify it.

Many constitutional scholars agree that most of the framers intended the Supreme Court to assume the power of judicial review. Writing under the name of Publius in *The Federalist Papers,* Alexander Hamilton argued that "the courts were designed to be an intermediate body between the people and the legislature in order, among other things, to keep the latter within the limits assigned to their authority."

The question whether the Supreme Court could nullify an act of Congress remained unanswered until 1803. In *Marbury v. Madison,* a case that had begun as a relatively unimportant controversy over a presidential appointment, the Court laid down the principle of judicial review. Chief Justice John Marshall declared that "a law repugnant to the Constitution is void." In so doing, he firmly asserted the power of the Supreme Court to make such determinations: "It is, emphatically, the province and duty of the judicial department to say what the law is."

Although *Marbury* is perhaps the most famous decision in the Supreme Court's history, the Court's assertion of its power to nullify a law attracted little attention at the time. More than fifty years elapsed before the power was exercised again.

Of the many thousands of acts passed by Congress in its first two centuries, only a hundred and some have been declared unconstitutional. Most scholars agree that the primary significance of judicial review is to make every member of Congress aware that the laws Congress passes can be nullified by the Supreme Court if they violate the Constitution. (See LEGISLATION DECLARED UNCONSTITUTIONAL.)

## Congressional Influence

Congress has several ways of influencing the judicial branch. It does so mainly through selection, confirmation, and impeachment of justices; institutional and jurisdictional changes; and direct reversal of specific decisions.

### Individual Pressures

The Constitution requires that the Senate give its "advice and consent" to appointments to the federal judiciary. Through the custom of SENATORIAL COURTESY the Senate has wielded considerable influence over appointments to federal district courts. The Senate generally refuses to confirm a nomination within a particular state unless the nominee has been approved by the senators of the president's party from that state. Once a candidate is selected, the nomina-

*The president nominates members of the Supreme Court, but they cannot take their seats until confirmed by the Senate. On occasion the Senate will reject the president's choice. In 1987 the Senate denied confirmation to Robert H. Bork, shown here as he arrived for hearings before the Senate Judiciary Committee.*    *Source: Ken Heinen*

# SUPREME COURT NOMINATIONS NOT CONFIRMED BY THE SENATE

| Nominee | Year | President | Action[1] |
|---|---|---|---|
| William Paterson[2] | 1793 | Washington | Withdrawn (for technical reasons) |
| John Rutledge[3] | 1795 | Washington | Senate rejected |
| Alexander Wolcott | 1811 | Madison | Senate rejected |
| John J. Crittenden | 1828 | J. Q. Adams | Postponed, 1829 |
| Roger B. Taney[4] | 1835 | Jackson | Postponed |
| John C. Spencer | 1844 | Tyler | Senate rejected |
| Reuben H. Walworth | 1844 | Tyler | Withdrawn |
| Edward King | 1844 | Tyler | Postponed |
| Edward King[5] | 1844 | Tyler | Withdrawn, 1845 |
| John M. Read | 1845 | Tyler | No action |
| George W. Woodward | 1845 | Polk | Senate rejected, 1846 |
| Edward A. Bradford | 1852 | Fillmore | No action |
| George E. Badger | 1853 | Fillmore | Postponed |
| William C. Micou | 1853 | Fillmore | No action |
| Jeremiah S. Black | 1861 | Buchanan | Senate rejected |
| Henry Stanbery | 1866 | Johnson | No action |
| Ebenezer R. Hoar | 1869 | Grant | Senate rejected, 1870 |
| George H. Williams[3] | 1873 | Grant | Withdrawn, 1874 |
| Caleb Cushing[3] | 1874 | Grant | Withdrawn |
| Stanley Matthews[2] | 1881 | Hayes | No action |
| William B. Hornblower | 1893 | Cleveland | Senate rejected, 1894 |
| Wheeler H. Peckham | 1894 | Cleveland | Senate rejected |
| John J. Parker | 1930 | Hoover | Senate rejected |
| Abe Fortas[6] | 1968 | Johnson | Withdrawn |
| Homer Thornberry | 1968 | Johnson | No action |
| Clement F. Haynsworth, Jr. | 1969 | Nixon | Senate rejected |
| G. Harrold Carswell | 1970 | Nixon | Senate rejected |
| Robert H. Bork | 1987 | Reagan | Senate rejected[7] |

SOURCE: Library of Congress, Congressional Research Service.

[1] A year is given if different from the year of nomination.

[2] Reappointed and confirmed.

[3] Nominated for chief justice.

[4] Reappointed and confirmed as chief justice.

[5] Second appointment.

[6] Associate justice nominated for chief justice.

[7] President Reagan's nomination of Douglas H. Ginsburg in 1987 was withdrawn before it was officially submitted to the Senate.

tion usually receives a perfunctory hearing and quick approval. (See APPOINTMENT POWER.)

Although the Senate has little to say in the selection of Supreme Court nominees, it does play a significant role once the nomination has been submitted for its approval. Of the 147 Supreme Court nominations submitted to the Senate by the end of 1992, 28 had failed to receive Senate confirmation (29, if the count includes Douglas H. Ginsburg, whose nomination in 1987 was withdrawn before it was officially submitted to the Senate). In contrast, only nine cabinet nominees had been rejected by the end of 1992.

Congress's IMPEACHMENT POWER is rarely used, most often against federal judges. Federal judges made up thirteen of the sixteen officials who had been impeached by the House of Representatives by the end of 1992, and all seven of the officials convicted by the Senate. Three of the judges were convicted under Senate procedures in which a twelve-member panel heard evidence in the cases. The full Senate then voted on the recommendations of the panel.

Only one Supreme Court justice—Samuel Chase—has ever been impeached by the House, but he was acquitted in 1805 following a sensational Senate trial. Two other Supreme Court justices have faced serious threats of impeachment. William O. Douglas weathered impeachment inquiries in 1953 and 1970; Abe Fortas retired from the Court in 1969 after the House threatened an inquiry.

Congress has even used its power of the purse to show displeasure with the Court. (See PURSE, POWER OF.) In 1964, when legislation was passed authorizing federal pay increases, Supreme Court justices were given $3,000 less than the increase for other federal executives. The action was generally seen as retaliation for recent Court decisions on such issues as obscenity, school prayer, and desegregation.

### Institutional Pressures

Congress sometimes tries to influence the judiciary through institutional or procedural changes, but it has considered many more proposals than it has approved.

Congress has the power to create judgeships, and it is in this area that politics historically has played a

*President Franklin D. Roosevelt caused a furor in 1937 with his plan to increase the membership of the Supreme Court. The existing Court had struck down a series of New Deal statutes, and Roosevelt hoped to add six new justices who would support his programs. His Court-packing plan was strongly opposed within and outside of Congress and was never enacted.*

most important role. In 1801, for example, the Federalist-dominated Congress created additional circuit court judgeships to be filled by a Federalist president. But when the Jeffersonians came to power in the midterm elections, the new posts were abolished.

Congress has increased or reduced the number of justices on the Supreme Court seven times. Generally, laws decreasing the number of justices have been motivated by a desire to punish the president; increases have been aimed at influencing the philosophical balance of the Court.

The size of the Supreme Court has remained at nine since passage of the Judiciary Act of 1869, but proposals to change the number of justices have occasionally been put forward. The most serious proposal in the twentieth century came not from Congress but from the president. Franklin D. Roosevelt in 1937 proposed legislation that would have made it possible to appoint six additional justices. The increase was portrayed as an effort to improve the efficiency of the Court. In reality it was designed to allow Roosevelt to appoint new justices who would support the constitutionality of his NEW DEAL programs. A series of New Deal statutes had been struck down by the existing Court. The Court-packing plan was strongly opposed within and outside of Congress and was never enacted. Nonetheless, it coincided with a change of attitude on the part of the Supreme Court. Shortly after the proposal was made public, the Court upheld revised versions of several key statutes in quick succession.

Proposals have occasionally been made to require two-thirds of the Court to concur in order to declare unconstitutional an act of Congress or a state statute. However, Congress has seldom seriously considered such proposals.

In 1802 Congress delayed a decision by abolishing a Supreme Court term altogether. Once, in *Ex parte McCardle* (1868), Congress prevented the Court from deciding a pending case by repealing its appellate jurisdiction over the subject matter of the case. Several other such attempts have been made, but they have been defeated, most of them by large margins.

### Reversals of Rulings

Of all the methods of influencing the Supreme Court, Congress has had most success in reversing individual Supreme Court rulings through adoption of CONSTITUTIONAL AMENDMENTS or passage of legislation.

Four of the twenty-seven amendments to the Constitution were adopted specifically to overrule the Supreme Court's interpretation of the Constitution. The amendments reversed rulings on the ability of citizens of one state to bring suit against another state (Eleventh Amendment), the application of the Bill of Rights to the states (Fourteenth Amendment), the income tax (Sixteenth Amendment), and the extension of voting rights to eighteen-year-olds (Twenty-sixth Amendment).

The most frequently used method of reversing the Supreme Court is for Congress to repass a statute after modifying it to meet the Court's objections. This kind of reversal through legislation is easily accomplished if the Court has interpreted a statute contrary to the construction intended by Congress. The House and Senate may then pass new legislation explicitly setting forth their intention. In many cases of this type, the Court suggests the course the legislation should take to achieve its original purpose.

### Additional Readings

Baum, Lawrence. *The Supreme Court.* 4th ed. Washington, D.C.: CQ Press, 1992.

Berger, Raoul. *Congress vs. the Supreme Court.* Cambridge, Mass.: Harvard University Press, 1969.

O'Brien, David M. *Storm Center: The Supreme Court in American Politics.* 3rd ed. New York: W. W. Norton, 1993.

Witt, Elder. *Congressional Quarterly's Guide to the U.S. Supreme Court.* 2nd ed. Washington, D.C.: Congressional Quarterly Inc., 1990.

# D

## Debt Limit

Since 1917 Congress has set an overall debt ceiling that fixes the limit for federal government borrowing from the public. Over the years the limit has been lifted many times to accommodate increased borrowing as the federal government expanded and deficits became routine.

Today Congress generally passes one or more bills each year to raise the debt limit. In 1990 Congress passed a record seven debt-limit bills, including one bill that raised the debt limit by more than a trillion dollars, from $3.123 trillion to $4.145 trillion. Because of the 1990 increase, Congress did not have to address the debt-limit issue in 1991.

Conservative members often use debt-limit debates to protest high federal spending, and the bills may give rise to political conflict. Yet many members of Congress have a love-hate relationship with bills that raise the debt limit because such bills often serve as a way to get around the regular legislative process in Congress. Congress has little choice but to pass debt-limit bills, since if the increases are not approved, the government will be unable to pay its bills. Congress must act on them quickly, and a president is likely to think twice before vetoing them.

This gives debt-ceiling measures a special urgency that makes them a natural target for unrelated amendments. (See RIDER.) Members whose pet proposals are languishing in committee frequently try to slip them through as amendments to debt-ceiling bills.

Many major proposals have become law as amendments to debt-limit measures. A 1985 debt-limit increase included a radical overhaul of the congressional BUDGET PROCESS. Known as the Gramm-Rudman-Hollings act, the budget measure swept through Congress without committee consideration or extensive floor debate. Two years later another debt bill was used to make major repairs in the original Gramm-Rudman-Hollings law.

Although crises over debt-limit bills frequently bring the government to the brink of default, Congress has brushed aside suggestions that it eliminate the ceiling. The House in 1979 adopted a system that permitted it to approve debt-limit increases through its budget process without voting separately on the issue. The new system was supposed to end House wrangling over debt bills, but instead the House has been forced to pass frequent short-term extensions of the debt limit because of delays in the congressional budget process. In the Senate, which chose not to go along with the House system, debt bills continue to provoke extended debates and streams of unrelated amendments.

## Deferral

*See* BUDGET PROCESS; LEGISLATIVE VETO.

## Deficit

*See* BUDGET PROCESS.

## Delegates

In addition to its 435 voting members, the House of Representatives has 5 members with limited powers. They represent the District of Columbia and four islands closely linked to the United States: Puerto Rico, the Virgin Islands, Guam, and American Samoa. All are known officially as delegates except the Puerto Rican, who is called a resident commissioner. The delegates are elected for two-year terms, while the resident commissioner serves for four years.

Until 1993 these five limited members could make speeches and vote in committees but could not vote on the House floor. At the beginning of the 103rd Congress in 1993, Delegate Eleanor Holmes Norton of the District of Columbia led a successful drive to allow the five to participate in many key floor votes. A new rule permitted delegates and the resident commissioner to participate in votes taken when the House constitutes itself as the COMMITTEE OF THE WHOLE, a parliamentary condition rather than a committee in the usual sense of the word. Since many of the votes on amendments to legislation are taken while the House is in Committee of the Whole, the change increased the political power of Norton and the other four limited members.

The new rule outraged many House Republicans, who charged that their voting power had been diluted in violation of the Constitution. (All five of the limited members were Democrats, the majority party in the House.) In response, House Democrats agreed to soften the rule by stipulating that the House could reverse any vote that was so close that the delegates' votes were decisive. As the 103rd Congress went to work in January 1993, the future of the new rule remained in question while House Republicans challenged it in court.

Nonvoting positions have existed in some form or other since 1794, when the House received James White as the nonvoting delegate from the Territory South of the Ohio River, which later became the state of Tennessee. Most of the current positions date from the 1970s; Puerto Rico's position was granted in 1900.

In addition to its House delegate, the District of Columbia in 1990 gained two "shadow" senators and one "shadow" representative. These three unofficial, unsalaried spokespersons were elected by District voters with a mandate to lobby Congress for District statehood. The "shadow member" tradition dates to the early nineteenth century, when six territories sent shadow senators to Congress before their admission as states. (See DISTRICT OF COLUMBIA AND CONGRESS.)

# Dies Committee

*See* INVESTIGATIONS.

# Direct Election of Senators

Like members of the House, senators are chosen by a vote of the people in each state. But it has not always been that way. Only since 1913 have U.S. voters had the right to vote directly for the men or women they want to represent them in the Senate. Before 1913 senators were selected by the legislatures of each state. The voters had only an indirect voice in the choice of senators, through their right to elect members of the state legislature. It required a decades-long battle, leading to the Seventeenth Amendment to the Constitution, to establish the direct election of senators.

Under the Constitution states were given seats in the House according to the size of their population. But seats in the Senate were equally divided, with each state having two senators. The framers of the Constitution thought of the House and Senate in basically different ways. House members were to be representatives of the people, elected by the voters. Senators, by contrast, were to be representatives of the sovereign states —"ambassadors," in effect, to the federal government. As a result the framers believed that the people should not elect senators. They believed that the legislatures would be more thoughtful and responsible in selecting people qualified to represent the interests of the states in Congress.

The Constitution gave Congress the right to establish specific rules governing the election of senators by the legislatures. For more than seventy-five years, however, Senate election procedures were left up to the individual states. The election system used by most states proved to have serious flaws. Most states required candidates to win majorities in both houses of the legislature. But since members of the two houses often disagreed on candidates, the system produced many deadlocks. Frequently all other legislative business ground to a halt as members of the legislature struggled vainly to agree on a candidate. Sometimes the legislature was simply unable to elect anyone, leaving the state without full representation in the Senate.

Congress reacted to the problems by passing a Senate election law in 1866. The law required the two

THE MAKING OF A SENATOR.

WHEN WILL THE PEOPLE STAND FROM UNDER?

Until the early twentieth century, senators were selected by the legislatures of each state. Voters had only an indirect voice in the choice of senators, through their right to elect members of the legislature. It required a decades-long battle, leading finally to ratification of the Seventeenth Amendment in 1913, to establish the direct election of senators.     Source: Library of Congress houses of a state legislature first to vote separately on candidates. If no candidate received a majority in both houses, then members of both chambers were to meet together and vote jointly, until one candidate received a majority of all votes.

Unfortunately, the 1866 law did little to correct the problems surrounding Senate elections. Deadlocks and election abuses continued to occur as political factions in each state fought for control of its two Senate seats. The stakes were high because senators customarily controlled much of the federal PATRONAGE—government jobs and contracts—available in the state. In many cases the election of a senator became the dominant issue in the legislature, causing other important state business to be virtually ignored.

A dispute in Delaware at the end of the nineteenth century illustrates how bitter and prolonged the fights over Senate elections could be. Divisions in the Delaware legislature were so fierce that no Senate candidate was elected for four years. For two years, from 1901 to 1903, Delaware was left entirely without representation in the Senate because members of the legislature could not agree on candidates.

The system also encouraged corruption. Because of the importance of Senate seats, and the relatively small numbers of state legislators who controlled them, candidates frequently were tempted to use bribery and intimidation to win. Controversies over alleged election fraud often had to be resolved by the Senate.

The basic criticism of legislative elections of senators, however, was that they did not reflect the will of the people. For more than a century the American political system had gradually tended to give the mass of voters more power. By the early years of the twentieth century the Senate was the most conspicuous case in which the people had no direct say in choosing those who would govern them.

### Reform Efforts

Efforts to establish direct election of senators followed two different strategies. One involved a constitutional amendment, which passed the House on five separate occasions. But the Senate, all of whose members had been chosen by the legislatures, was adamantly opposed to direct election. Even after the legislatures of thirty-one states petitioned for a constitutional amendment for direct election, the Senate did not consider the proposal for many years. (See CONSTITUTIONAL AMENDMENTS.)

The other approach was through changes in state laws. Although the legislatures were required by the Constitution to select senators, reformers sought ways to ensure that the will of the people would control the legislatures' choices.

Oregon, which had a strong tradition of political reform, made the most determined attempts to guarantee the popular choice of senators. In 1901 the state established a system in which voters cast ballots for Senate candidates. Although the results were not legally binding, they were supposed to guide the legislature in selecting candidates.

The system initially was unsuccessful. The first time it was used, the legislature selected a candidate who had not received any votes at all in the popular election. Soon after, however, Oregon reformers devised a system in which candidates for the legislature promised to support the popular choice for Senate regardless of their own preference. Once most members of the legislature were committed to backing the candidate who won a majority of popular votes, the legislative election became a mere formality ratifying the choice of the people.

Other states soon adopted the "Oregon plan," so that by 1910 nearly half the senators chosen by the legislatures had already been selected by popular vote.

The state reform plans put more pressure on the Senate to approve a constitutional amendment. Fearing that the states would demand a new constitutional convention, senators finally agreed in 1910 to vote on a constitutional amendment for direct election. But opposition in the Senate remained strong.

After a long and heated battle in the Senate, Congress approved the amendment on May 13, 1912. The amendment became part of the Constitution on May 31, 1913, after the required three-fourths of the states had given their approval. The direct-election amendment did not have dramatic consequences. Most of the senators who had been elected by the legislatures were reelected by the people. But over the years since 1913 the selection of senators by the people has become a key part of the American political system.

*Senate leader Everett McKinley Dirksen in the Oval Office in the late 1960s with President Lyndon B. Johnson.*
*Source: Senate Historical Office*

## Dirksen, Everett

Everett McKinley Dirksen (1896–1969) was one of the most colorful members of Congress in the twentieth century. He was known as "the Wizard of Ooze" for his florid speaking style. As minority leader of the Senate from 1959 to 1969, Dirksen proved himself to be a master of compromise and persuasion. He used his great skills as an orator and negotiator to unify and strengthen the Republican voting bloc. His remark that "the oil can is mightier than the sword" spoke both to his skill in managing his flock and his ability to bring Republican legislation before a Democratic Senate.

Dirksen began his congressional service in the House of Representatives in 1933, but in 1949 illness forced him to leave the House. Upon his recovery, in 1950 he ran successfully for the Senate, where he served until his death in 1969. Dirksen endorsed all of President Dwight D. Eisenhower's major policies and was elected minority whip in 1957, at the beginning of his second Senate term. Two years later he advanced to minority leader.

Dirksen was unpredictable, often switching positions at critical moments. He publicly opposed the Civil Rights Act of 1964 and the nuclear test ban treaty but then voted for them. He played an important role in the passage of the 1968 Civil Rights Act. "One would be a strange creature indeed in this world of mutation if, in the face of reality, he did not change his mind," the senator once said.

Dirksen was unable to persuade the Senate to approve two of his favorite legislative projects, both of which would have reversed Supreme Court decisions of the early 1960s. In the wake of the Court's "one person, one vote" decision, he worked for a constitutional convention to restructure legislative apportionment. He also repeatedly sponsored resolutions to allow voluntary school prayer.

## Discharge, Committee

Both the House of Representatives and the Senate have procedures by which committees may be relieved, or discharged, of legislation under their jurisdiction. The discharge mechanism was designed as a way to keep committees from blocking action on controversial bills.

The House procedure, first adopted in 1910, works through a rarely used device called the discharge petition. If a bill has been held up by a legislative committee for at least thirty days, or if the Rules Committee refuses to clear it for floor action within seven days, any member may offer a motion to discharge the committee of the bill. (See RULES COMMITTEE, HOUSE.) The CLERK OF THE HOUSE draws up a discharge petition, and if 218 members (a majority of the House) sign on, the discharge motion goes on the Discharge CALENDAR. The names of members signing the petition are published in the *CONGRESSIONAL RECORD*. After a seven-day grace period, if the committee still has not acted on the bill, any member may move to call up the discharge motion on the floor. If that motion is approved, a motion to call up the bill itself follows. Discharge measures may be considered on the second and fourth Mondays of each month.

Discharge efforts are seldom successful, since members are reluctant to disregard a committee's judgment and the committee review process. Still, the threat of such a move may spur a committee to act. That happened in 1983, when the House Ways and Means Committee cleared a controversial tax-withholding bill only after 218 members had signed a discharge petition to force the bill to the floor.

Attempts to discharge a committee occur even less often in the Senate than in the House. Because the Senate allows nongermane AMENDMENTS on most legislation, it has little need for procedures to wrest bills out of reluctant committees. A member may simply offer the legislation blocked by a committee as an amendment to another measure being considered on the floor. Moreover, many members believe the discharge procedure undercuts the committee system.

The Senate discharge procedure is cumbersome and rarely effective. Discharging a committee from a particular bill does not automatically bring the legislation to the Senate floor for immediate consideration—the primary reason for using this motion. Instead, in virtually all cases, the legislation discharged is placed on the Senate calendar. Legislation listed on the calendar can be brought up on the floor only by unanimous consent or by MOTIONS, which are debatable and thus open to a FILIBUSTER.

## Disciplining Members

Congress is legally responsible for monitoring the behavior of its members. The Constitution states that Congress should "determine the rules of its proceedings, punish its members for disorderly behavior and, with the concurrence of two-thirds, expel a member." On that authority the House and Senate have sometimes voted to expel, censure, or reprimand an erring colleague. Other offenders have been stripped of chairmanship or fined.

Until Congress adopted formal, enforceable ethics codes in 1977, it followed informal guidelines. After charges were made against a member, a special investigation was usually carried out; then the full House or Senate acted on the results. The formal codes generally follow that same procedure, although responsibility for investigating charges and recommending penalties now falls to permanent House and Senate committees on ethics. The ethics committees also may express disapproval of a member's behavior without recommending formal sanctions by their parent chambers. (See ETHICS.)

The most serious rebuke, and the rarest, has been expulsion, which under the Constitution requires support from two-thirds of those voting. Only a majority is required for a vote to censure, reprimand, or fine a member. Discipline involving a loss of chairmanship or committee membership is usually handled by the caucus of party members, instead of the full House or Senate, because the caucus is responsible for those assignments. (See CAUCUSES, PARTY.)

### Expulsion

Except for expulsions of southerners loyal to the Confederacy during the Civil War, Congress has rarely used its powerful authority to remove a legislator

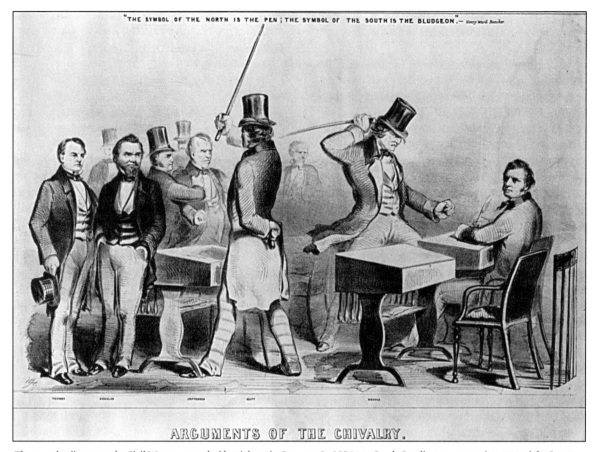

"THE SYMBOL OF THE NORTH IS THE PEN; THE SYMBOL OF THE SOUTH IS THE BLUDGEON." — *Henry Ward Beecher*

ARGUMENTS OF THE CHIVALRY.

*The years leading up to the Civil War were marked by violence in Congress. In 1856 two South Carolina representatives entered the Senate chamber, where Rep. Preston S. Brooks proceeded to bludgeon Massachusetts Sen. Charles Sumner while he sat at his desk. This Winslow Homer political caricature is entitled "Arguments of the Chivalry."*    Source: Library of Congress

from office for misconduct. The first expulsion occurred in 1797, when the Senate ousted William Blount of Tennessee for inciting members of two Indian tribes to attack Spanish Florida and Louisiana. The expulsion followed a House vote to impeach Blount—the only time the House, which originates all impeachment proceedings, has ever voted to impeach a senator or representative. The Senate headed off the impeachment proceedings by voting to expel Blount, something the House had no authority to do. (See IMPEACHMENT POWER.)

During the Civil War fourteen senators and three representatives were expelled. On a single day, July

11, 1861, the Senate expelled ten southerners for failure to appear in their seats and for participation in secession from the Union. One of the ten expulsions was rescinded after the expelled member's death.

From the Civil War to 1993, formal expulsion proceedings were instituted ten times in the Senate and thirteen times in the House. Only once during that time, however, was a member actually expelled. That one member was Rep. Michael J. "Ozzie" Myers, a Democrat from Pennsylvania. The House voted in 1980 to expel Myers after he was caught in the AB-SCAM SCANDAL, a sting operation conducted by the Federal Bureau of Investigation (FBI). Myers, who had accepted money from an FBI agent posing as an Arab sheik, was the first member of Congress ever expelled for corruption.

In most other cases the House shied away from expulsion and instead opted for a lesser form of punishment. Ten of the House expulsion cases resulted in censure.

Several members resigned to avoid expulsion proceedings. Among them was Mario Biaggi, a New York Democrat who had been convicted in 1987 of accepting illegal gratuities from a ship-repair company. Early in 1988 the House ethics committee recommended expulsion of Biaggi. The House delayed action, however, because Biaggi was about to be tried for accepting bribes from another company, Wedtech Corp. After that trial resulted in his second conviction, Biaggi avoided expulsion by resigning from Congress.

The Senate Committee on Ethics in 1982 recommended the expulsion of New Jersey Democrat Harrison A. Williams, Jr., another Abscam target. Senate floor debate had already begun by the time Williams, realizing that a vote to expel him was likely, announced his resignation.

In 1989 House Democratic leaders Jim WRIGHT of Texas and Tony Coelho of California resigned to avoid possible disciplinary action because of their financial activities. Wright, who was accused of using a book deal to evade House limits on outside earned income, became the first Speaker forced out of office at midterm. Coelho, the majority whip, resigned amid controversy over his role in a "junk bond" deal.

## Censure

By 1993, there had been ten times in the Senate and twenty-two times in the House that a majority of legislators had voted to censure a colleague for misconduct. Censure is a formal show of strong disapproval that requires a legislator to listen as the presiding officer reads aloud the condemnation of his or her actions. In the House the member must stand at the front of the chamber while being censured. Censured House Democrats also automatically lose their posts as committee or subcommittee chairs under rules adopted by the House Democratic Caucus in 1980.

A typical censure was the wording read aloud in 1967 to Sen. Thomas J. Dodd, a Democrat from Connecticut. Dodd, who had been charged with pocketing for personal use more than $100,000 in campaign contributions, heard that his conduct was "contrary to accepted morals." The censure said Dodd's behavior "derogates from the public trust expected of a senator and tends to bring the Senate into dishonor and disrepute."

Censure has been prompted by a wide variety of actions, including disloyalty during the Civil War, a fistfight on the Senate floor, insulting remarks made to colleagues, acceptance of stock for legislative favors, and use of campaign contributions for personal expenses. Probably the most publicized was the censure of Sen. Joseph R. MCCARTHY in 1954. Although his tactic of labeling colleagues and others as communists had long been controversial, the Senate for almost three years did nothing to curb the growing power of the Wisconsin Republican. Only after the nationally televised Army-McCarthy hearings, when McCarthy's arrogance and abuses were seen by the public, did the Senate act to "condemn" McCarthy, an action historians consider equal to a censure. (See INVESTIGATIONS.)

Among those censured have been the following:

*Laurence M. Keitt*, censured by the House in 1856 for not acting to stop an assault on a senator, even though he knew of the plan in advance and actually witnessed the attack. Keitt, a South Carolina Democrat, allowed a fellow South Carolinian, Rep. Preston S. Brooks, to strike Sen. Charles SUMNER, a Massachusetts Republican. Brooks attacked Sumner with a heavy walking stick while Sumner sat at his desk in the Senate chamber. Brooks was also censured.

*Oakes Ames*, a Massachusetts Republican, and James Brooks, a New York Democrat, censured by the House in 1873 for accepting stock in Crédit Mobilier, a railroad construction company, in return for legislative favors.

South Carolina Democrats *Benjamin R. Tillman* and *John L. McLaurin*, censured by the Senate in 1902 for engaging in a fistfight in the Senate chamber.

*Hiram Bingham*, a Connecticut Republican, censured by the Senate in 1929 for placing on his staff a

*(Above) The Senate in 1990 voted 96–0 to denounce Dave Durenberger, R-Minn., for his financial dealings, which they deemed "clearly and unequivocally unethical." Shown here are Durenberger (center) with his attorney and chief of staff at the Ethics Committee hearing.    Source: R. Michael Jenkins*

*(Left) The Keating Five hearings were conducted under the glare of television lights in this Senate hearing room. Eight long tables were reserved for the press.    Source: R. Michael Jenkins*

manufacturing association employee whose assignment was to advise on tariff legislation.

*Charles C. Diggs, Jr.,* a Michigan Democrat, censured by the House in 1979 for taking kickbacks from the salaries of his office employees.

*Charles H. Wilson,* a California Democrat, censured by the House in 1980 for using campaign contributions to cover personal expenses

*Gerry E. Studds* and *Daniel Crane,* censured by the House in 1983 in separate cases of sexual misconduct. Studds, a Democrat from Massachusetts, had admitted having a homosexual relationship with a teenager working as a congressional page. Crane, a Republican from Illinois, had an affair with a female page.

Although the Senate in effect censured six members between 1902 and 1991, it used the word *censure* against only one of them, Dodd, in 1967. As in the McCarthy case, historians have regarded the Senate's substitute terms as synonyms for *censure.* These have included the *condemnations* of Bingham and McCarthy; the *denouncements* of Herman E. Talmadge, a Georgia Democrat, in 1979, and Dave Durenberger, a Minnesota Republican, in 1990 (both for financial misconduct); and the *reprimand* of Alan Cranston, a California Democrat, in 1991 for improper conduct as one of the senators involved in the KEATING FIVE SCANDAL.

## Reprimand

The case of Cranston marked the Senate's first use of reprimand, which the House had employed several times since 1976 as a much milder form of punishment than censure. A reprimanded House member is spared the indignity of standing before his or her colleagues to be chastised. But in the Senate there was little or no difference between the reprimand of Cranston and the censure of other senators. The language was equally severe, but the sanction was new because the Ethics Committee offered it on behalf of the Senate, with Cranston listening and speaking in rebuttal. The full body did not vote.

The House ethics committee—established in 1968 and formally known as the Committee on Standards of Official Conduct—first suggested a reprimand instead of censure in 1976. The committee made that recommendation after investigating charges that Florida Democrat Robert L. F. Sikes maintained a business interest in companies dealing with the defense subcommittee he chaired.

The House again opted for the lesser penalty in 1978, when John J. McFall, Edward R. Roybal, and Charles H. Wilson, all California Democrats, were reprimanded for mishandling cash contributions from South Korean rice dealer Tongsun Park. In 1983 the ethics committee recommended a reprimand for Studds and Crane, but the House instead chose to censure them. George Hansen, an Idaho Republican, was reprimanded in 1984 after being convicted of violating federal financial disclosure laws. The next member to be reprimanded was Pennsylvania Democrat Austin J. Murphy; the House said Murphy had diverted government resources to his former law firm, allowed another member to vote for him on the House floor, and kept a "no show" employee on his payroll.

Rejecting calls for expulsion or censure, the House in 1990 went along with the ethics panel in reprimanding Massachusetts Democrat Barney Frank for using his office to help a male prostitute. Frank, who acknowledged in 1987 that he was homosexual, had befriended the man two years earlier.

## Rebuke

The Senate Ethics Committee introduced yet another form of chastisement, the formal rebuke, in August 1992 as a disciplinary action against Oregon Republican Mark O. Hatfield. The committee resolution rebuked Hatfield for violating the 1978 ethics act by neglecting to report the receipt of several expensive gifts. Most of the gifts were from a former president of the University of South Carolina, which had received a federal grant while Hatfield headed the Appropriations Committee.

As in the Cranston reprimand, the committee said it was acting against Hatfield "on behalf of and in the name of" the full Senate, with no further action recommended. But the unusual floor presentation of the Cranston case was not repeated. In other cases, both the House and Senate ethics committees issued "letters of reproval" to members where more stringent action was not deemed necessary.

### Loss of Chairmanship

Loss of chairmanship did not become a common method for disciplining unethical behavior until the 1970s. Earlier the loss of seniority or chairmanship had been primarily a tool that party caucuses used to punish disloyalty. By 1980 the House Democratic Caucus had made loss of a chairmanship automatic for members censured by the House, or those indicted or convicted of a felony carrying a sentence of at least two years.

In the mid-1970s two powerful House Democrats resigned their positions as committee chairs to avoid having them taken away by the party caucus. Wilbur MILLS, an Arkansas Democrat who chaired the House Ways and Means Committee, came under fire after publicity about his affair with an Argentine strip dancer, Fanne Foxe. Mills, who was eventually treated for alcoholism, gave up his influential position in late 1974 but served out the term to which he was reelected that year.

Two years later the spotlight was on Wayne L. Hays of Ohio, who chaired both the House Administration Committee and the Democratic Congressional Campaign Committee. Hays was accused of keeping a mistress, Elizabeth Ray, on his payroll. He was about to be stripped of both positions by the Democratic Caucus when he gave them up. Hays resigned from the House before any further disciplinary action was recommended.

An earlier link between loss of chairmanship and unethical behavior involved Adam Clayton POWELL, Jr., a Democratic representative from New York's Harlem district, who in the 1960s was the most prominent African American in Congress. Powell came under investigation for misuse of committee funds and other alleged abuses. He was deposed as chair of the Education and Labor Committee in a 1967 vote by the Democratic Caucus. The full House then voted to exclude Powell from membership, an action that the Supreme Court overturned two years later.

In 1979 Michigan Democrat Charles C. Diggs, Jr., who had been reelected despite being convicted of taking kickbacks, voluntarily stepped down as chair of the House District of Columbia Committee. He also gave up a post as a subcommittee chair.

In the first twelve years (1980–1992) that the House's automatic rule was in effect, seven representatives were stripped of posts as committee or subcommittee chairs after being censured, indicted, or convicted. In the Senate the three committee leaders who had been censured or convicted soon lost their posts as chairs because of a change in party control of the Senate (McCarthy and Williams) or election defeat (Talmadge).

## Loss of Vote

When a member of Congress is convicted of a crime, the question arises of whether that senator or representative should continue to vote on the floor or in committee. To deny that right also denies representation to the people of the legislator's state or district. Many years ago indicted senators voluntarily remained off the floor and did not vote. But in 1924 Montana Democrat Burton K. Wheeler continued to vote before he was acquitted of bribery, a charge he said was trumped up by the Harding administration. Since then senators have kept on voting. Williams did so until he resigned following his Abscam conviction in 1981.

For representatives suspension was voluntary until 1975, when the House adopted a rule barring floor or committee votes by convicted members until they were cleared or reelected. On the latter basis, Diggs continued to vote in 1979 until the House censured him.

## Exclusion

Exclusion is a disciplinary procedure that applies to those not yet formally seated in the House or Senate. One purpose of the procedure is to resolve debate over whether just-elected legislators meet the basic constitutional qualifications for office; Congress has found some who did not. Legislators have also tried, sometimes successfully, to exclude Mormons who practiced polygamy, colleagues considered disloyal because of the Civil War, and individuals charged with misconduct.

The broad use of exclusion as a disciplinary tool was apparently ended by the Supreme Court decision in *Powell v. McCormack* (1969), which limited exclusion to cases in which constitutionally set qualifications for office were not met. Powell, who had challenged his exclusion from the House, had a flamboyant lifestyle that fueled colleagues' anger over his frequent absences, his extensive use of public funds for travel, and his use of his payroll to hire relatives and friends. Powell's response to the criticism was to insist that he was a victim of racism. In his appeal to the Supreme Court Powell argued that Congress could refuse to seat an elected legislator only if the individual did not meet the qualifications spelled out in the Constitution: age, citizenship, and residence in the appropriate state or district. (See STRUCTURE AND POWERS.)

The Supreme Court agreed with this argument and sharply limited the application of exclusion. However, the Court left up to Congress the discipline of members already seated. Powell, who had been reelected in 1968, took his seat in 1969 after the Court decision. The House then fined him $25,000 for his earlier misuse of government funds. After returning to Congress Powell rarely attended sessions, lost his seat in 1970, and died two years later.

# District of Columbia and Congress

The framers of the Constitution gave Congress the exclusive right to legislate for the nation's capital. Striking a balance between federal and local interests has been difficult, however. The District's residents have continued to press a reluctant Congress for more autonomy ranging from additional voting rights in Congress to complete statehood. Some opponents of increased District self-rule argue that the drafters of the Constitution never intended the area to have the same authority as states in the union, a decision that only a constitutional amendment can change. Political and racial issues also have been important. The District is heavily Democratic and politically liberal, which has prompted many Republicans and conservatives to resist giving it more voting power in Congress. In addition, the District's population is heavily black, which has been depicted as creating racial overtones with a predominately white Congress that includes many members from areas of the nation where race remains a volatile issue.

Congress granted limited self-government to the District of Columbia in 1800, a situation that lasted for nearly seventy years. Then in 1874, after a brief experiment with a territorial system, Congress took back virtually all government authority over the District. For the next century Congress acted as the city's governing council while the president chose its administrators.

The Senate passed home-rule measures six times between 1949 and 1965. These were blocked in the House by the chair of the DISTRICT OF COLUMBIA COMMITTEE, Democrat John L. McMillan of South Carolina, with the support of other southerners on the panel.

Pressure for home rule grew in the civil rights era. In the late 1960s President Lyndon B. Johnson persuaded Congress to loosen its grip on the District government, but the changes fell short of full home rule. Finally, in 1973, with McMillan and many of his supporters no longer in the House, Congress once more gave local residents limited control over their own affairs.

Under the 1973 home-rule law, Congress retained veto power over legislation approved by the District's elected government, as well as control over the District budget. In the years that followed, the House and Senate continued to intervene from time to time in District affairs.

On a separate track from the home-rule debate was a drive by the District to give its residents a voice in national politics. The Twenty-third Amendment to the Constitution, ratified in 1961, permitted District residents to vote in presidential elections. The 1964 presidential election marked the first time since 1800 that citizens in the nation's capital had voted in a national election.

District residents have had a nonvoting delegate in the House since 1971. In 1990 Eleanor Holmes Norton, a civil rights lawyer and constitutional scholar, was elected to succeed Walter E. Fauntroy, who had served as the District delegate since the office was created. Norton took Fauntroy's seat on the District Committee and assumed his leadership role in the fight for more autonomy for the District. She led a successful effort in 1993 to expand the power of the House's five nonvoting DELEGATES by allowing them for the first time to participate in some key floor votes.

In 1978 Congress approved a proposed constitutional amendment that would have given the District of Columbia full voting representation in Congress— two senators and at least one House member. The proposal died, however, when it failed to win ratification by three-fourths of the states as required by the Constitution.

A movement to make the District a separate state gained momentum during the 1970s. It lost steam in the 1980s, however, as relations between Congress and the D.C. government deteriorated. In 1990 District voters elected a nonvoting, unpaid delegation of two "shadow" senators and one "shadow" representative with a mandate to lobby Congress for statehood. One of the senators was Jesse Jackson, Jr., a nationally prominent black leader.

The House District Committee in 1992 approved legislation that would transform the District into the fifty-first state, called New Columbia, and would establish a separate enclave made up of the White House, the Supreme Court, the Capitol, and other federal buildings. Proponents of statehood argued that to deny District residents a voice in Congress amounted to taxation without representation. Opponents countered that statehood for the District would lead to similar claims from territories, such as Guam and the Virgin Islands. Sen. Edward M. Kennedy of Massachusetts, a statehood proponent, revealed the strong feelings underlying the D.C. statehood issue when he blamed the measure's failure to win congressional approval on a "harsh plantation mentality."

## District of Columbia Committee, House

Representatives do not scramble for seats on the House District of Columbia Committee. The District Committee oversees the municipal affairs of Washington, D.C.—a matter of little concern to voters elsewhere in the country. The committee's work has been sharply curtailed since 1973, when Congress granted the District of Columbia limited self-government. (See DISTRICT OF COLUMBIA AND CONGRESS.)

For many years before 1973 southern conservatives had dominated the committee, maintaining strict control over the District and its predominantly black population. South Carolina Democrat John L. McMillan served as the committee's chair from 1949 until 1973. Under his leadership, the committee blocked a succession of bills to grant self-government to D.C. residents.

The committee's makeup changed dramatically in the wake of the 1972 congressional elections. McMillan was defeated in a primary runoff, and five other southern Democrats on the committee either lost their bids for reelection or retired. When the committee convened in 1973, its chair was Charles C. Diggs, Jr., a Michigan Democrat and an African American. That year the committee approved a home-rule bill, and a compromise version of the bill became law.

Ronald V. Dellums, a California Democrat and also an African American, became chair of the committee in 1979. In 1987 the committee overcame sharp internal divisions to approve a bill to grant statehood to the District, but that measure succumbed to tough opposition in Congress as a whole. In 1992, the committee approved another statehood bill.

The committee has no counterpart in the Senate, which dropped its District of Columbia committee after the District gained home rule. District matters now fall within the broad jurisdiction of the Senate Governmental Affairs Committee. In addition, each chamber's Appropriations Committee has a separate District of Columbia subcommittee.

## Dole, Robert

Through a combination of legislative skill and a forceful personality, Robert Dole (1923–    ) became a formidable figure in the Senate in the 1980s, first as a committee chair and then as majority leader from 1985 to 1987. The Kansas Republican scored major legislative victories, proving that the Senate could indeed be led. After his party lost control of the chamber in the 1986 elections, Dole's pragmatism kept him ahead of impatient younger conservative activists.

When his former rival George Bush lost the presidency in 1992, Dole was quick to claim the authority to speak for the Republican party, and also for the 19 percent of voters who had supported a third-party bid by a business executive named Ross Perot. Dole portrayed himself as the personification of the American dream, battling back from a World War II combat injury that had crippled his right arm and damaged his left.

He was first elected to the House in 1961 and remained there until he moved to the Senate in 1969. When the Republicans came to power in the Senate in 1981, Dole became chair of the Finance Committee. In that position he guided difficult legislation through an often chaotic and stubborn Senate. Dole oversaw passage of three major tax bills—including President Ronald Reagan's sweeping 1981 tax-cut program—and an overhaul of the Social Security program. He also remained a key player on agriculture bills, protecting Kansas farm interests.

Dole was often able—through a mixture of negoti-

*Sen. Robert Dole speaks to reporters at the White House after a budget meeting in 1990.*    Source: R. Michael Jenkins

Nicaragua. As minority leader in 1991 he helped win approval for the Persian Gulf War.

Not all of Dole's political endeavors have met with success. After chairing the Republican National Committee from 1971 to 1973, Dole in 1976 was Gerald R. Ford's vice-presidential running mate on the losing Republican ticket. He failed in his 1980 and 1988 bids for the Republican presidential nomination. He overcame bitterness over his 1988 loss to Bush in the primaries to serve the president's cause in the Senate with unflagging loyalty and energy.

## Doorkeeper, House

The House doorkeeper introduces, at the door of the chamber, official guests, visitors attending joint sessions, and the bearers of messages from the Senate and the president. The doorkeeper is responsible for House documents, publications distribution, CLOAK-ROOMS, and telephone service. The doorkeeper also supervises door attendants, pages, and barbers; issues passes for seats in the House galleries; and performs a variety of custodial services. In the Senate, these functions are performed by the SERGEANT-AT-ARMS. The annual salary of the House doorkeeper was $119,000 as of December 1992.

ation, compromise, arm twisting, and verbal lashing—to bring competing interests into line behind a controversial bill. He seasoned his legislative skill with a quick wit and a sharp tongue.

His leadership style was in marked contrast to that of the amiable Howard H. BAKER, Jr., the Tennessee Republican whom he succeeded as majority leader in 1985. Dole's strong will and aggressive use of power gained significant legislative victories and undermined the ability of small groups of senators to bring the chamber regularly to a standstill. Legislation passed with Dole's help included a major revision of the tax code, a new farm bill, and aid to the "contra" rebels in

## Douglas, Stephen A.

Called "the Little Giant" for his small stature and formidable talents, Stephen A. Douglas (1813–1861) was a skilled and energetic orator. He is best remembered as Abraham Lincoln's opponent in the Lincoln-Douglas debates of 1858. At the time of the debates Douglas was campaigning for his third term in the Senate, where he had served as a Democrat since 1847. He also served in the House of Representatives for two terms (1843–1847).

As chair of the Senate Committee on Territories, Douglas opposed anything that would hinder the organization of new territories or the entrance of new

*Stephen Douglas, best remembered as Abraham Lincoln's opponent in the Lincoln-Douglas debates of 1858, was called the "Little Giant" for his small stature and formidable talents.*
*Source: Library of Congress*

states into the Union. Because slavery proved to be just such a hindrance, Douglas searched for a com-promise on the issue. He became an advocate of popular sovereignty, under which new states and territories could decide whether or not to allow slavery. In 1854 he sponsored the Kansas-Nebraska bill, allowing those territories to determine for themselves whether to allow slavery within their borders. The measure angered both North and South and led to violence in the territories.

In 1857 the Supreme Court handed down the Dred Scott decision *(Scott v. Sandford)*, which held that Congress did not have the power to curtail the expansion of slavery. In 1858 Douglas and Lincoln, his opponent for the Senate, debated the Dred Scott decision. Douglas took the position that although the national legislature could not limit slavery, state legislatures could do so. Douglas won the election, but his position angered many southerners. In 1859, to punish him for his perceived opposition to slavery, the Senate Democratic Caucus voted to remove him as chair of the Committee on Territories.

Douglas opposed Lincoln in the presidential election of 1860 and lost in part because the Democratic ticket was split. He loyally supported the new president, and in 1861 he undertook a trip at Lincoln's request to encourage support for the government's policies. During the trip he contracted typhoid and died.

# E

## Economic Committee, Joint

Since 1946 the House and Senate have had a joint committee to monitor the nation's economy. The Joint Economic Committee has a much broader focus than most congressional committees. It tries to provide an overview of the economy and a look at long-range economic trends. Although it cannot write legislation, the Joint Economic Committee issues reports and holds hearings on a variety of topics, ranging from Russian economic reforms to U.S. unemployment figures.

Most widely known are the committee's annual March report and its midyear report, usually issued in August. The March report responds formally to the economic report issued early each year by the president's Council of Economic Advisers; both reports are mandated by the Employment Act of 1946, which set up the committee and the council. The goals of that act were "maximum employment, production, and purchasing power."

Because Democrats and Republicans have traditionally had such different expectations for the economy, the two parties have often written separate reports. During the Reagan administration, for example, Republicans usually predicted a healthy economy and Democrats forecast calamity.

Since 1967 the committee has had ten members from the Senate and ten from the House, with six majority and four minority members from each chamber. The post of committee chair rotates between the House and Senate every two years. The chair often initiates studies, directing the staff to work on a particular topic.

Two individuals put their personal stamp on the committee in the 1950s and 1960s. Rep. Wright Patman, a Texas Democrat, served as chair five times between 1957 and 1975. An outspoken critic of powerful commercial banks and the politics of the Federal Reserve Board, Patman used the Joint Economic Committee as yet another platform for his attacks.

On the Senate side, the chair was held three times in the 1950s and 1960s by Democrat Paul Douglas of Illinois, a prominent liberal who had been a well-regarded professor of economics at the University of Chicago.

Another longtime member of the panel was Senate Democrat William Proxmire of Wisconsin, who did not run for reelection in 1988. He served twenty-seven years on the joint committee, including two terms as chair and two as vice chair. Sen. Paul S. Sarbanes, a Michigan Democrat, has served as chair of the panel since 1989.

## Education and Labor Committee, House

The House Education and Labor Committee has responsibility for many of the programs established by the federal government to attack poverty and other social problems. Its jurisdiction includes federal spending for education and job training, as well as a wide range of efforts to aid children, the poor, and the disabled.

During the 1960s the committee was the originator in the House of much of the legislation sought by President Lyndon B. Johnson for his GREAT SOCIETY. Most important, it helped write the 1965 legislation that for the first time provided federal financial support for locally controlled elementary and secondary education. In later years the committee approved legislation that greatly expanded financial aid to college students, set up programs for health and safety in the workplace, and banned discrimination against the disabled.

The committee continues to have jurisdiction over

many of those programs. However, the political climate in the House has changed greatly since the 1960s, and the committee's degree of influence has been sharply curtailed as a result. Budget restrictions have limited the committee's ability to offer new social programs, and it is now considered a second-tier panel that is often left out of serious policy debate.

One of the reasons for this state of affairs was President Ronald Reagan's opposition to an expanded federal role in education. Many House members also became skeptical of the value of federal involvement in social problems. Few members favored creation of new social programs, and many advocated substantial reductions in spending on existing programs. As a result, the members of the Education and Labor Committee found themselves increasingly isolated in the House.

A majority of committee members, particularly on the Democratic side, continued to favor strong federal involvement in social issues. In 1990 the panel shepherded through Congress the Americans with Disabilities Act, which prohibits job discrimination against the disabled. But for the most part the Education and Labor Committee has concentrated on defending existing programs. Bills to reauthorize higher and secondary education programs and the Older Americans Act occupy most of the panel's time.

---

## Electing the President

Many Americans are dimly aware that something called the electoral college plays a role in presidential elections, but few are able to say just what it is or how it works. The framers of the Constitution conceived the electoral college system as a compromise between direct popular election of presidents and the less democratic option of election by Congress. The system they established has been a source of confusion and controversy almost from the beginning.

Voters cast their ballots for president in November of every fourth year. Their choice is not final, however, until the following January when Congress meets to count the votes of the "electors" chosen in each state. Each state has as many electors as it has senators and representatives, and the District of Columbia has three electors, for a total of 538.

Counting the electoral votes is almost always a ceremonial function. But if no candidate for president or vice president wins a majority of electoral votes, the House of Representatives must choose the president and the Senate must choose the vice president. The House has chosen a president only twice. But several campaigns have been designed deliberately to throw elections into the House, where each state has one vote and a majority of states is needed for election.

Few decisions of the framers have received more criticism than the constitutional provisions governing the selection of the president. Thomas Jefferson called them "the most dangerous blot on our Constitution." A proposed constitutional amendment to reform the system was introduced in Congress as early as 1797. Since then hardly a session of Congress has passed without the introduction of one or more such measures.

In 1969 the House voted 338–70 for a constitutional amendment to replace the electoral college with direct popular election of the president, but the amendment was derailed in the Senate. In 1979 the Senate voted 51–48 in favor of a similar amendment—a margin far short of the two-thirds majority needed for approval of constitutional amendments. In both cases, senators from small states were among the most vocal opponents. This was not surprising, since small states have disproportionate influence in the electoral college and would pull extra weight if the House elected a president.

### Electoral Vote System

The Constitution provided that each state should appoint presidential electors, known collectively as the electoral college, equal to the total number of its senators and representatives. The electors, chosen as each state legislature directs, would meet in their separate states and vote for two persons. The votes would be counted in Congress, and the candidate who received a majority of the total would become president. The candidate who received the second highest number of votes would become vice president.

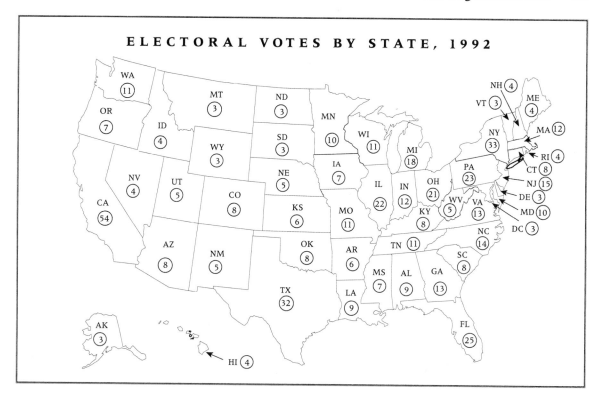

**ELECTORAL VOTES BY STATE, 1992**

If no candidate won a majority of electoral votes, the House of Representatives was to select the president; each state would have one vote, and a majority of states would be required for election. Selection of the vice president would fall to the Senate, with a majority required.

At first no distinction was made between ballots for president and vice president. This caused confusion when national political parties emerged and began to nominate party tickets for the two offices. All the electors of one party tended to vote for the two nominees of their party. But with no distinction between the presidential and vice-presidential nominees, there was the danger of a tie vote. This actually happened in 1800, leading to adoption of the Twelfth Amendment to the Constitution, which required separate votes for the two offices.

The framers of the Constitution intended that each state should choose its most distinguished citizens as electors and that they should vote as individuals. But with the development of political parties, the electors

came to be chosen merely as representatives of the parties. At first some state legislatures chose electors, but by the 1830s most states chose electors by statewide, winner-take-all popular vote. Independent voting by electors disappeared almost entirely. Occasionally electors have voted for someone other than their party's candidate. These "faithless electors" never have affected the outcome of an election.

## Counting the Electoral Vote

In modern practice, the electors meet in their states to cast their ballots in December following a presidential election. In most states the candidate who carried the popular vote wins all the state's electoral votes. Maine and Nebraska are exceptions, awarding electoral votes based on popular vote winners in particular districts. The ballots of all the states are opened and counted before a joint session of Congress in early January, clearing the way for inauguration of the president on January 20.

The Constitution did not say what to do if there

*Counting electoral votes in Congress is not always just a formality. This picture shows a special electoral commission taking testimony on disputed electoral votes in the 1876 presidential election. Congress gave the election to Rutherford B. Hayes even though Democrat Samuel J. Tilden had a majority of the popular vote.    Source: Library of Congress*

were disputes about electors' ballots. This became a critical concern following the 1876 election. That year, for the first time, the outcome of the election had to be determined by decisions on disputed electoral votes. The 1876 campaign pitted Republican Rutherford B. Hayes against Democrat Samuel J. Tilden. Tilden led in the popular-vote count by more than a quarter of a million votes but trailed by one vote in the electoral college; the votes of three southern states were in dispute. A special electoral commission, set up to settle the dispute, awarded the votes to Hayes.

Democrats in the House objected but, after Republicans agreed to withdraw federal troops from the South, southern conservatives allowed the electoral count to continue and Hayes became president.

In 1887 Congress passed permanent legislation on the handling of disputed electoral votes. The 1887 law, still in force, gives each state final authority to determine the legality of its choice of electors. Majorities of both the Senate and House are needed to reject any disputed electoral votes.

## Election by Congress

The election of 1800 was the first in which the House of Representatives elected the president. Candidates of the Democratic-Republican faction had more electoral votes than the Federalists, but their electors unintentionally cast equal numbers of votes for Thomas Jefferson, their choice for president, and Aaron Burr, their choice for vice president. The tie vote threw the election into the House, where the losing Federalists insisted on backing Burr over Jefferson, whom they considered a dangerous radical. It took thirty-six ballots to arrive at a decision; on the final tally ten states voted for Jefferson, four for Burr. Thus Jefferson became president, and Burr automatically became vice president.

The Jefferson-Burr contest dramatized the dangers of the constitutional double-balloting system. The Twelfth Amendment, requiring separate votes for president and vice president, was proposed by Congress and quickly adopted by the states in time for the 1804 election.

The only other time the House elected a president was in 1825. There were four chief contenders in the 1824 presidential campaign: John Quincy ADAMS, Henry CLAY, William H. Crawford, and Andrew Jackson. When the electoral votes were counted, Jackson had 99; Adams, 84; Crawford, 41; and Clay, 37. Jackson led in the popular vote, but he failed to win a majority of the electoral vote. As required by the Twelfth Amendment, the names of the top three contenders—Jackson, Adams, and Crawford—were placed before the House. Clay threw his support to Adams, who narrowly won election. Adams in turn made Clay his secretary of state, lending credence to charges that Clay had agreed to support Adams in return for the appointment. Adams took office under a cloud from which his administration never recovered; he lost the presidency to Jackson four years later.

On one occasion, in 1837, the Senate was forced to decide a vice-presidential contest. That year Democrat Martin Van Buren was elected president with 170 electoral votes, while his vice-presidential running mate, Richard M. Johnson, received only 147—one short of a majority. The Senate elected him, 33–16.

No presidential election has gone to the House in modern times, but several three-way races with potential for electoral deadlock have aroused concern. The threat of House election hung over the presidential campaign of 1968, when George C. Wallace of Alabama was a serious third-party candidate. Wallace predicted that he would win a majority of the electoral votes. His backup plan was to hold the balance of power in the electoral college voting, forcing political concessions from one of the major-party candidates in exchange for the support of his electors. The election was close, and Wallace won forty-six electoral votes, but Republican Richard M. Nixon defeated Democrat Hubert H. Humphrey without help from Wallace's electors.

The possibility of House election became real to Americans again during the 1980 presidential race, when the independent candidacy of Illinois representative John B. Anderson briefly threatened to disrupt the contest between incumbent president Jimmy Carter and Republican challenger Ronald Reagan. But Reagan won in a landslide, while Anderson received less than 7 percent of the popular vote and no electoral votes.

Discussion of the electoral college and House election of the president revived once again in 1992 when the independent campaign of Texas business executive H. Ross Perot showed surprising early strength. Perot's campaign faltered, and he won no electoral votes, yet he ended up with 19 percent of the popular vote. The winner, Democrat Bill Clinton, outpolled incumbent Republican president George Bush in the popular vote. Clinton won even more decisively in the electoral college, 370–168.

As in 1980, the specter of deadlock in 1992 brought renewed calls for abolition of the electoral college and warnings that the House was ill-prepared to elect a president. "We must have clear and concise rules in place, just in case," argued Rep. Dan Glickman of Kansas. A 1980 study had pinpointed several vague areas, but Congress had done nothing to clarify them. For example, no rules existed to specify whether the old or newly elected Congress would elect the new president, whether the House vote could be televised, or what would happen if the

House itself became deadlocked. Clinton's decisive electoral victory took the edge off those concerns—at least for another four years.

## Vice-Presidential Vacancies

The Twenty-fifth Amendment to the Constitution, adopted in 1967, gave Congress additional authority over vice-presidential selection. The amendment, which established procedures to be followed if the president became disabled or died, also gave directions for filling a vacancy in the office of vice president. Whenever a vice president died, resigned, or succeeded to the presidency, the president was to nominate a successor. A majority vote of both houses of Congress was required to confirm the nominee. (See APPOINTMENT POWER; PRESIDENTIAL DISABILITY AND SUCCESSION.)

The vice-presidential selection system was used for the first time in 1973 after the resignation of Vice President Spiro T. Agnew, who was under investigation on criminal charges. President Richard M. Nixon nominated Rep. Gerald R. Ford of Michigan, the House Republican leader, to succeed him. Ford was confirmed by the House and Senate in less than two months.

In 1974 the Twenty-fifth Amendment was used again, after Nixon resigned as president to avoid impeachment because of the WATERGATE SCANDAL. Ford succeeded to the presidency, thus becoming the first president in U.S. history who had not been elected either president or vice president. Ford nominated Nelson A. Rockefeller, the governor of New York, to succeed him as vice president. Rockefeller's great wealth provoked controversy, but he, too, was confirmed.

### Additional Readings

Glennon, Michael J. *When No Majority Rules: The Electoral College and Presidential Succession.* Washington, D.C.: CQ Press, 1993.

Heard, Alexander, and Michael Nelson, eds. *Presidential Selection.* Durham, N.C.: Duke University Press, 1987.

Nelson, Michael, ed. *Congressional Quarterly's Guide to the Presidency.* Washington, D.C.: CQ Press, 1989.

Peirce, Neal R., and Lawrence D. Longley. *The People's President: The Electoral College in American History and the Direct Vote Alternative.* Rev. ed. New Haven, Conn.: Yale University Press, 1981.

## Enacting Clause

"Be it enacted by the Senate and House of Representatives of the United States of America in Congress assembled. . . ." This imposing language is the standard opening for bills introduced in either chamber. Known as the enacting clause, it gives legal force to measures once they have been approved by Congress and signed by the president. During House floor action, opponents of a bill sometimes offer a motion to "strike the enacting clause." Such a motion, if approved, kills the measure.

## Energy and Commerce Committee, House

With its sweeping jurisdiction and colorful personalities, the House Energy and Commerce Committee is a congressional hot spot. Topics such as auto emission controls, oil industry pricing, and regulation of cable television trigger showdowns at both the subcommittee and the committee levels. The panel attracts more than its share of lobbyists representing the many industries and environmental, medical, and consumer groups whose interests are affected by its actions. The high level of controversy means votes are often close, with the outcome in suspense until the last moment—in sharp contrast to many other committees where consensus is the norm.

An octopus of a committee, Energy and Commerce oversees energy, health, communications, consumer safety, the stock market, part of the transportation industry, and numerous regulatory agencies. The panel's authority extends to "everything that moves, is sold, or is burned," according to Michigan Democrat John D. Dingell, who became the panel's chair in 1981. A tough-talking former prosecutor and powerful member of Congress, Dingell defended his committee's turf aggressively and expanded it whenever he could. As chair of the Energy Committee's Oversight and Investigations Subcommittee, Dingell presided over well-publicized investigations into government practices, increasing his own power and the committee's public profile at the same time.

Although the primary Senate counterpart of the House Energy and Commerce Committee is the ENERGY AND NATURAL RESOURCES COMMITTEE, the jurisdictions of the two do not entirely coincide. The Senate Energy Committee and the House Natural Resources Committee share responsibility for federal lands, most nuclear power matters, and most regulation of the coal industry. The environmental concerns of the House Energy and Commerce Committee, such as air pollution, are the responsibility in the Senate of its Environment and Public Works Committee, not of the Energy Committee. When the House Energy and Commerce Committee tackles communications policy or transportation deregulation, it deals in conference with the Senate Committee on Commerce, Science, and Transportation.

### History

The Interstate and Foreign Commerce Committee, the forerunner of the House Energy and Commerce Committee, was set up in 1795. The panel's authority over interstate commerce expanded dramatically in 1887 when Congress created the Interstate Commerce Commission to regulate the railroads. Since then, federal oversight of the marketplace has become extensive, and the Commerce Committee has helped create a wide variety of regulatory agencies. The committee was renamed Energy and Commerce in 1980. (See COMMERCE POWER.)

The committee's visibility increased in the 1950s as it investigated several scandals. A subcommittee probe revealed that a Boston industrialist had paid hotel bills and given an expensive coat and Oriental rug to Sherman Adams, a top Eisenhower administration aide who later resigned. The panel also looked into rigged television quiz shows and "payola," or payoffs, given by the record industry to radio disk jockeys in exchange for air time.

Among the longest running debates in the com-

mittee was one over energy pricing. In the 1970s top Democrats on the committee, including Dingell and then-chair Harley O. Staggers of West Virginia, were still resisting deregulation of natural gas and oil.

The committee's jurisdiction shifted in the mid-1970s, when the Public Works Committee was assigned responsibility for all forms of transportation except railroads, a special interest of Staggers. The reforms also gave the Commerce panel jurisdiction over health issues not related to taxes, previously a responsibility of the Ways and Means Committee.

The 1970s brought change within the committee as well. Frustrated by Staggers's low-key style, other Democrats on the panel shifted more and more authority to the subcommittees. In 1979 they voted to strip Staggers of his post as chair of the investigations subcommittee of the House Interstate and Foreign Commerce Committee. Dingell, who was chair of the Energy and Power Subcommittee, ran the full committee in all but name until he became chair.

Energy issues dominated the late 1970s, but the Commerce Committee temporarily lost its dominance in that area when the House leadership set up an ad hoc energy panel to push through President Jimmy Carter's energy program. A second challenge to Commerce's primacy in the energy field came in 1979, when a special House committee on reorganization recommended that a permanent energy committee be established. With Dingell leading the opposition, that proposal was defeated. The House instead renamed the committee Energy and Commerce and designated it the House's lead panel on energy issues.

Throughout the 1980s Dingell battled with another forceful member of the committee, Henry A. Waxman, over auto emission controls. Dingell, a liberal on most issues, sided with the auto industry, the economic mainstay of his Detroit district. Waxman, representing a mostly liberal and affluent constituency in smog-choked Los Angeles, fought Dingell for tougher air pollution controls from his own power base as chair of the Subcommittee on Health and the Environment. In 1989 they reached a compromise that contributed to enactment of a new, stricter clean air law the following year.

Its vast legislative jurisdiction was only part of the reason for dominance of the House Energy and Commerce Committee in recent years. Another was the work of Dingell's Oversight and Investigations Subcommittee. Staffed by a team of eager investigators, the panel focused on allegations of government wrongdoing, particularly misuse of government funds. Its investigation of practices at the Environmental Protection Agency (EPA) during the early 1980s led to the resignation of one top EPA administrator and the perjury conviction of another.

Other investigations targeted waste and corruption in defense contracting, fraud in government-financed scientific research, and misuse of federal grants by private universities. Dingell's supporters applauded his use of "whistle blowers" to gather information, his tough questioning of witnesses at hearings, and his flair for publicity. Critics charged that Dingell and his investigators frequently exceeded the bounds of propriety and fairness in their zeal to expose wrongdoing.

---

## Energy and Natural Resources Committee, Senate

Managing federal lands and setting energy policy are the main tasks of the Senate Committee on Energy and Natural Resources. The committee traditionally has been controlled by westerners whose states have vast amounts of federal parks and forests, but it also attracts senators whose states depend on oil and gas. In addition, the committee includes advocates of wilderness and proponents of energy conservation. As a result, the Senate Energy and Natural Resources Committee is sometimes unpredictable, though less so than its counterpart, the House ENERGY AND COMMERCE COMMITTEE.

In the 1970s, when there was widespread concern over U.S. oil imports, the committee focused on energy. The panel struggled to adapt price controls and other federal rules to an energy market dominated by a cartel of oil-rich Middle Eastern countries, which limited supplies and kept prices high. By the 1980s the energy situation had changed drastically; prices, imports, and overall consumption had all declined.

The 1991 Persian Gulf War renewed concern over access to the world's oil, prompting the committee to craft a wide-ranging energy bill that encouraged energy efficiency and the development of alternative fuels.

The committee was first organized in 1816 as the Committee on Public Lands. A 1977 Senate reorganization shifted jurisdiction of some environmental laws to the Environment and Public Works Committee; what was then the Interior and Insular Affairs Committee became Energy and Natural Resources.

Henry M. Jackson, a Washington Democrat, chaired the committee for eighteen years (1963–1981). His leadership had a profound effect on the panel. Jackson, who was both forceful and well liked, managed to keep the committee's concerns in the Senate limelight. Although conservative in matters of foreign policy, Jackson was a liberal on domestic issues. For years he advocated price controls on oil and gas, a position that caused no conflict in his state, which does not produce oil.

When Republicans controlled the Senate from 1981 to 1987, James A. McClure of Idaho was chair. He favored a completely free market for energy and in 1983 pushed a Reagan administration plan to remove all remaining federal controls from natural gas. Despite his opposition to controls, McClure supported federal subsidies for synthetic fuels, such as liquids made from coal. That program, announced with great fanfare in the late 1970s, died in 1985 because of budget constraints.

McClure's successor, Louisiana Democrat J. Bennett Johnston, shared his outlook, preferring a market-oriented approach to energy policy. Johnston was known for his solid grasp of the technical aspects of energy and for his ability to craft compromises. He disliked the label "oil-state senator," arguing that his decisions were not governed by the industry position on an issue. Johnston showed his willingness to compromise during work on a wide-ranging energy bill in 1992. He wanted to include provisions in the measure to allow oil drilling in Alaska's Arctic National Wildlife Refuge and to require automobile fleets to have better miles-per-gallon averages, but dropped the provisions when they stood in the way of passing a bill.

## Engrossed Bill

An engrossed bill is the final copy of a measure as passed by either the Senate or House of Representatives, including changes made during floor action. It must be certified in its final form by the secretary of the Senate or the clerk of the House. (See ENROLLED BILL; LEGISLATIVE PROCESS.)

## Enrolled Bill

The final copy of a bill that has been passed in identical form by both the Senate and House of Representatives is known as an enrolled bill. It is certified by the secretary of the Senate or the clerk of the House, depending on where the bill originated, and is then sent on for the signatures of the House Speaker, the Senate president pro tempore, and the president of the United States. An enrolled bill is printed on parchment-type paper. (See ENGROSSED BILL; LEGISLATIVE PROCESS.)

## Entitlements

An entitlement is a federal program that guarantees a certain level of benefits to persons or other entities that meet requirements set by law. Some examples of entitlements are Social Security and Medicare, farm price supports, and unemployment benefits. Congress cannot refuse to provide funding for these programs.

Since the 1970s the largest component of federal spending has gone for programs that provide payments to individuals. Many of these programs have been established as entitlements. Congress has found it almost impossible to gather the political will to reduce spending for entitlement programs. Legislators would have to make significant policy changes, such as raising the age requirements for Social Security benefits, in order to reduce the cost of these programs.

In 1990 Congress did take a step toward curbing new entitlements when it enacted a pay-as-you-go requirement for mandatory spending on entitlements. The law requires that any new entitlements or policy changes that would increase the cost of existing entitlements must be matched by revenue increases to pay for the new programs.

Some entitlements carry permanent appropriations, while others must go through the annual appropriations process. Programs without permanent appropriations also may require a supplemental appropriation to provide the required funds to program beneficiaries.

## Environment and Public Works Committee, Senate

Two markedly different responsibilities fall to the Senate Committee on Environment and Public Works: watching over the nation's environment, and building its highways, dams, and sewers. By 1993 neither task was as easy or popular as it had been twenty years before.

The decade of the 1970s probably was the heyday of the committee, a time when landmark environmental laws were passed and federal money still flowed freely. In the 1980s efforts to clean up the environment were stymied by complex problems, such as toxic waste disposal and acid rain. Glamorous public works projects lost out in the federal budget squeeze and gave way to concerns about the deterioration of existing dams and bridges. The early 1990s brought action on a Clean Air Act and a major reauthorization of federal highway programs.

When Republicans controlled the Senate, from 1981 to 1987, Robert T. Stafford of Vermont chaired the committee. He was forced to take defensive action, deflecting attacks on environmental laws by industry; Stafford was often on the opposite side from the Reagan administration. Stafford also helped win extensions of water pollution controls and the "superfund" program to clean up toxic waste. He concentrated on the environment rather than highways, reflecting his years spent on the Environmental Protection Subcommittee.

Quentin N. Burdick, a North Dakota Democrat, became the committee's chair in 1987. It was his first top post in almost three decades as a senator. Never one to seek power or publicity, Burdick brought his low-key style to the Environment and Public Works Committee. He gave great latitude to active, aggressive subcommittee chairs, such as Democrats George J. Mitchell of Maine and Frank R. Lautenberg of New Jersey.

Burdick died in 1992, and Daniel Patrick Moynihan, a well-known New York Democrat, became chair. Moynihan used his slot on the panel to address constant water shortages for his state. In early 1993 Moynihan became chair of the Senate Finance Committee. He resigned as chair of the environment committee to take the second-ranked position. The new chair of the environment committee was Max Baucus, a Montana Democrat.

## Ervin, Sam J., Jr.

Sam J. Ervin, Jr. (1896–1985), served twenty years as a Democratic senator from North Carolina. He is best remembered as chair of the Senate Watergate committee, which investigated charges that led to the resignation of President Richard Nixon in 1974. (See WATERGATE SCANDAL.) During the committee's televised hearings, Ervin's knowledge of and respect for the Constitution, his courtly manner, and his pithy quotations made him an admired national figure.

Before his Senate service, Ervin practiced law in North Carolina, served in the state legislature, and sat on the bench of the criminal and supreme courts within the state. In 1946 Ervin served one year in the U.S. House of Representatives to finish the term of his brother Joseph, who died while in office.

Ervin was appointed to fill a vacant Senate seat in 1954 and was elected to full terms starting in 1956. As a freshman senator, he was a member of the select committee that recommended Senate censure of Sen. Joseph R. MCCARTHY, a Wisconsin Republican

whose investigations of communism had drawn great criticism.

Ervin construed the provisions of the Constitution strictly. On the grounds of protecting states' rights, he rejected civil rights legislation and other Democratic domestic programs, such as health care for the elderly and school busing. But as a member of the Judiciary Committee he worked to strengthen the civil rights of government workers, Native Americans, and mental patients. He often criticized the government practice of gathering information on private citizens. "It is my belief that the Recording Angel drops a tear occasionally to wash out the record of our human iniquities," he said. "There is no compassion to be found in computers."

As chair of the Separation of Powers Subcommittee of the Judiciary Committee, Ervin recommended procedures to be followed in a convention held to consider CONSTITUTIONAL AMENDMENTS; although such a convention had never been held, the prospect troubled many leaders. Ervin's bill passed the Senate in 1971 and 1973, but the House did not vote on the measure.

In 1973 Ervin was chosen to head the Senate Watergate committee, formally called the Senate Select Committee on Presidential Campaign Activities. He was chosen because of his knowledge of the Constitution and also because, earlier that year, he had declined to run for reelection in 1974. He was therefore unable to benefit from the publicity generated by the committee's investigations. Quoting the Bible and Shakespeare, Ervin immediately caught the attention of the public. A self-described "old country lawyer," Ervin seemed the antithesis of the Watergate conspirators. He became a folk hero and retired in 1974 on a wave of public admiration.

## Ethics

Daniel WEBSTER, a respected Massachusetts statesman in the nineteenth century, openly demanded money from the railroads in return for his support of a bill before the Senate. James A. Garfield, an Ohio representative who became president in

1881, accepted a gift of stock from Crédit Mobilier of America, a company seeking legislative favors. Emanuel Celler, a New York Democrat who chaired the House Judiciary Committee for almost twenty-five years, continued even in the 1970s to practice law alongside partners who handled cases before the federal government.

These actions, which went unpunished, likely would be seen in the 1990s as blatant conflicts of interest. They would come under scrutiny by one or more of the three groups that monitor a legislator's behavior: the courts, House or Senate colleagues, and the voters.

The courts handle indictments of legislators charged with bribery and other financial corruption prohibited by federal criminal statutes. They also review violations of the 1989 Ethics Reform Act. Federal laws for CAMPAIGN FINANCING, which require public disclosure of donations and monitor use of funds, are also designed to expose, or at least discourage, corruption. Regulation is handled by the Federal Election Commission, which can fine violators or take them to court.

The House and Senate ethics codes are the internal guidelines for how legislators behave. Personal finances must be disclosed, income earned outside Congress is restricted, and use of public funds is carefully monitored. The House Committee on Standards of Official Conduct and the Senate Select Committee on Ethics investigate allegations and make recommendations to the House and Senate, which then decide whether to discipline a legislator. (See STANDARDS OF OFFICIAL CONDUCT COMMITTEE, HOUSE; ETHICS COMMITTEE, SENATE SELECT.)

The remaining judge of representatives and senators is the electorate. Voter approval or disapproval means the extension or the end of an official's political life. Voters can be the toughest critics of all: They apply an unwritten set of rules and standards to an official's performance and then hand down their verdict at the polls. This was demonstrated most forcefully in 1992 when the voters showed their displeasure with members involved in the HOUSE BANK SCANDAL. Of the 269 sitting members who had overdrafts at the bank, more than one in four were defeated or chose to retire.

For a man like Webster, who openly complained when payments to him for favors were late, the modern guidelines would leave little room to operate. Yet, despite the proper behavior of the majority, members of Congress continue to be accused of bribery, influence peddling, misuse of funds, sexual misconduct, violations of campaign disclosure laws, and breach of security. The standards for a politician's conduct are high; so are the temptations.

## Punishing Misconduct

For most of its history, Congress operated under an unwritten ethics code, backed by a constitutional directive that legislators should oversee their own behavior. The Constitution states that Congress should "determine the rules of its proceedings, punish its members for disorderly behavior, and, with the concurrence of two-thirds, expel a member." However, the framers left it to the legislators to determine the rules and decide who was breaking them.

Thomas Jefferson set the tone in 1801, while he was vice president and presiding officer of the Senate. In *JEFFERSON'S MANUAL* he wrote, "Where the private interests of a member are concerned in a bill or question he is to withdraw." Jefferson was suggesting that a legislator avoid what is known today as a conflict of interest, when the chance for personal gain influences a decision ostensibly made for the public good. The rules of both chambers permit members not to vote on matters affecting their personal interests.

The policing of Congress has been done on an ad hoc basis. When someone complains about a colleague's behavior, the House or Senate usually investigates. The most drastic step Congress can take is to expel a member, but that constitutional right has been used only nineteen times. Most of those cases occurred during the Civil War, when southerners were expelled for disloyalty.

Between 1861 and 1993 only one member was removed: Rep. Michael J. "Ozzie" Myers, a Pennsylvania Democrat who was expelled in 1980 after he took bribe money from an agent of the Federal Bureau of

# Congress—Who's In It and Who Owns It

## MARGUERITE YOUNG

*Congress here is depicted as the creature of J.P. Morgan, the most powerful figure in U.S. finance and industry at the turn of the twentieth century.     Source: Library of Congress*

Investigation (FBI) who was posing as a wealthy Arab.

Congress has turned more often to another formal punishment: censure, in which a member's conduct is condemned in a formal hearing before the entire House or Senate. More recently Congress devised a new version of censure, called a reprimand, which allows a member to avoid being present in the House or Senate chamber while his or her behavior is condemned. Loss of chairmanships, suspensions, and

fines have also been used as punishment. (See DISCIPLINING MEMBERS.)

House Democratic Caucus rules require that indicted members step down from their posts as committee or subcommittee chairs for the duration of the session or until the charges are dismissed.

Politics, a member's personal popularity, and even the customs of the times play a part in the judgment. When one member of the House shot another to death in a duel in 1838, the House declined to expel the murderer or to censure two colleagues who had served as seconds in the duel. As another legislator noted, dueling by members had been frequent and generally had gone unnoticed by the House. Just six years earlier, when the House for the first time had formally censured a member, the reason for the censure was simply a remark. The representative had told the Speaker his eyes were "too frequently turned from the chair you occupy toward the White House."

Congress has traditionally been reluctant to discipline its members. Many agree with the opinion voiced by Sam RAYBURN, House Speaker for most of the period between 1940 and 1961, who believed the voters, and not fellow politicians, should be the ultimate judge of behavior. The House and Senate have often delayed their investigations and decisions until after an election; the voters often defeat the colleague under fire.

Legislators have another way to avoid disciplining a colleague: resignation. Two House members and one senator used resignation in 1980–1982 to duck their almost certain expulsion following indictments for conspiracy and bribery in the ABSCAM SCANDAL. In 1988 the House ethics committee recommended dismissal of New York Democrat Mario Biaggi, who resigned after his second conviction for bribery. Two House Democratic leaders, Speaker Jim WRIGHT of Texas and Majority Whip Tony Coelho of California, left Congress in 1989 to head off punishment in separate investigations of their financial activities.

Representatives and senators have also retired in the midst of investigations or following disciplinary action. After the House ethics committee in 1986 found that Democrat James Weaver of Oregon had filed incomplete financial reports, Weaver amended the reports; the changes helped him avoid any disciplinary action, but so did his plans not to seek reelection. In 1976 the Senate Republican leader, Hugh Scott of Pennsylvania, was accused of receiving up to $100,000 in illegal campaign contributions from a lobbyist for Gulf Oil Corp. After Scott denied any impropriety, the ethics committee voted not to pursue its investigation; Scott retired from Congress three months later.

Congress's reluctance to discipline members varies depending on the nature of their misconduct. Both Congress and the voters have tended to forgive those with personal problems and those who admit their wrongdoing and repent. Criminal misconduct and a refusal to promise better behavior tend to result in disciplinary action and/or election defeat.

## Ethical Questions

The smell of money pervades most ethical questions, but legislators have also been disciplined for insults, questions of loyalty, sexual misconduct, and other offenses. For example, Joseph R. MCCARTHY, a Wisconsin Republican who gained notoriety for his anticommunist investigations in the early 1950s, was censured by the Senate in 1954 for insulting his colleagues and obstructing the constitutional process. Two House members were censured in 1983 for sexual misconduct. Disloyalty was the charge in the many cases of censure during the Civil War; southerners had supported the Confederacy rather than the Union.

Much more common are allegations of bribery, kickbacks, misuse of public funds, or improper campaign contributions. Scrutiny of a legislator's financial accountability has centered on income, including outside sources, such as legal fees and honoraria for speeches; on campaign contributions; and on the member's access to and use of public funds and privileges.

The criminal code has long prohibited a member of Congress from acts such as soliciting or receiving a bribe in return for a vote or other favor, benefiting from a contract with a federal agency, or promising to influence an appointment in return for something of value, including a political contribution. These laws are enforced by the Justice Department, which investigates the accusation and then can indict a legislator for illegal activity. But such blatant influence peddling is just part of the picture. Critics have argued that a legislator can also be improperly influenced by receiving a generous fee for giving a speech or writing an article, a large retainer for legal services, or a handsome salary for serving on a corporate board. The question of whether to limit such income has been the most controversial aspect of ethics reform, which culminated in 1978 in a formal federal code of ethics.

*Robert G. "Bobby" Baker, right, resigned his post as secretary for the Senate majority in 1963 after influence-peddling charges were raised against him.*
Source: Library of Congress

Amended and tightened in 1989 and 1991, the ethics law banned honoraria, the last remaining source of sizable outside earnings for members of Congress.

A murkier area concerned large campaign contributions and their effect on a legislator's decisions. Concern over undue influence and the escalating costs of elections prompted several reforms of campaign finance laws, beginning in 1971. But there was wide agreement in the early 1990s that too many loopholes still existed.

## Scandals Prompt Reforms

The movement toward a formal code of conduct took twenty years. Congress first endorsed a list of ten guidelines in 1958; the formal codes finally took effect in 1978. The initial set of rules was simply advice about how to behave properly, with no enforcement mechanism. Only after a series of scandals did Congress slowly begin to move toward a formal ethics code and a way to enforce it.

The Senate set up a permanent ethics committee in 1964; the House followed suit in 1967. Politicians found that votes in favor of ethics were a good way to quiet negative news coverage. Bad publicity plagued Congress from the 1960s to the 1990s. In 1963 Bobby Baker, the powerful secretary for the Senate majority, resigned under fire after allegations that he had used his office to promote his business interests. The Senate then went through a painful examination of how Sen. Thomas J. Dodd, a Connecticut Democrat, had misused campaign contributions; Dodd was censured in 1967.

The House was rocked in 1967 by its decision not to seat New York Democrat Adam Clayton POWELL, Jr. In July 1969 a car driven by Sen. Edward M. Kennedy, a Massachusetts Democrat, plunged off a bridge on Chappaquiddick Island near Martha's Vineyard, drowning twenty-eight-year-old Mary Jo Kopechne. The incident raised many questions, and Kennedy said his failure to report it until the next morning was "indefensible."

The WATERGATE SCANDAL provided a flood of examples of improper behavior by top officials during President Richard Nixon's reelection campaign. In

*After the Keating Five investigation, members of the Senate Ethics Committee announce their findings at a press conference. Committee Chairman Howell Heflin stands at the podium.    Source: R. Michael Jenkins*

1973, as the Watergate scandal unfolded, Vice President Spiro T. Agnew resigned; he had been charged with taking money in return for government contracts. In 1974 the influential chair of the House Ways and Means Committee, Democrat Wilbur D. MILLS of Arkansas, resigned his committee post after a well-publicized escapade with an Argentine strip dancer, Fanne Foxe.

One of the worst years was 1976. In that year Rep. Robert L. F. Sikes, a Florida Democrat, was reprimanded for investing in companies that had business before the defense subcommittee he chaired. Ohio Democrat Wayne L. Hays, another highly placed veteran representative, resigned his posts and then left the House in the midst of an investigation into charges that he had kept a mistress, Elizabeth Ray, on his payroll. That same year Congress was also stung by a report that Gulf Oil had illegally contributed more than $5 million to the campaigns of dozens of legislators during the previous decade.

In response, the House in mid-1976 appointed a special ethics study commission chaired by David R.

Obey, a Wisconsin Democrat; the Senate then set up its own special group. Early in 1977 the House approved the Obey commission's recommendations almost intact, despite controversy over income limits and other key issues. The Senate somewhat reluctantly approved a similar code.

More reforms in the late 1980s followed another spate of investigations. These investigations led to the Senate disciplining Minnesota Republican Dave Durenberger and California Democrat Alan Cranston for financial misconduct. Durenberger's case involved book and real estate deals, while Cranston was one of the senators who had accepted campaign contributions from savings and loan operator Charles H. Keating, Jr. (See KEATING FIVE SCANDAL.) In the House, besides the Wright and Coelho resignations, there were probes that resulted in reprimands of Democrat Austin J. Murphy of Pennsylvania for misuse of his office and of Barney Frank, a Massachusetts Democrat, for disgracing the House by improperly using his office to help a male prostitute.

## Formal Ethics Code

Senators and representatives must now obey two separate ethics codes, one internal and another external.

The internal House and Senate codes, adopted in 1977 and periodically updated, provide the framework for the enforcing committees: the House Committee on Standards of Official Conduct and the Senate Committee on Ethics. Both committees have equal representation from Democrats and Republicans.

The external code is the Ethics Reform Act of 1989, which supplanted the landmark Ethics in Government Act passed in 1978. The 1989 revision closed several loopholes that enabled members and other federal officials to skirt the older law's FINANCIAL DISCLOSURE provisions. It brought all three branches of government under the same disclosure law, with each branch responsible for its own administration of the requirements. The restrictions and cutbacks in perquisites, or "perks," were intended to offset public hostility to the 25 percent pay raise also provided in the measure for the House, along with provisions for cost-of-living adjustments. (See PAY AND PERQUISITES.)

At first under the act senators received $23,200 less than the $125,100 salary of House members although senators could continue to receive honoraria for their speeches and articles. But after chafing under the lower pay, the Senate voted in July 1991 to scrap the honoraria and take the same salary as the House. Although senators, representatives, and other federal officials could no longer keep honoraria, they could request that such fees be paid in their name to charities, with a limit of $2,000 per contribution and with mandatory disclosure of the sources and amounts. The receiving charities would be identified only in confidential reports to the ethics offices.

The 1991 legislation raising Senate pay to the House level also eased some of the 1989 gift laws. Members and employees of Congress could accept gifts worth up to $250 a year from any one person; gifts below $100 do not count toward the ceiling. Almost all requirements to disclose such gifts were eliminated.

Enactment of the 1989 and 1991 laws required some revision of the internal House and Senate rules affecting conflict of interest, acceptance of gifts, financial disclosure, and limits on outside earned income (unearned income, such as that from real estate holdings, bonds, or stocks, generally was unrestricted). For the 103rd Congress (1993–1995) the rules were being rewritten to conform to the broader legislation. The existing House and Senate ethics codes also prohibited unofficial office accounts, which had been financed with private contributions; banned personal use of campaign funds; restricted use of the FRANKING PRIVILEGE; limited government-paid FOREIGN TRAVEL by retiring members; and prohibited travel reimbursement if costs had been met by other sources.

The new law eliminated, beginning in 1993, a loophole that had allowed legislators elected before 1981 to convert to personal use any remaining campaign funds when they left office. Congress had already prohibited nepotism by senators and representatives under a 1967 law. Nepotism—the hiring of spouses, children, and close relatives—had given rise to criticism from the press. Over the years certain members had been accused of padding their official staffs with relatives who did little or no work for their government paychecks.

## Outside Income Controversy

The limit on outside earned income, by far the most controversial aspect of the ethics law, took several years to evolve. Congress had first set income limits in the 1974 campaign finance law, but it applied the ceiling only to honoraria from speeches and articles. The objective was to reduce the number of instances in which a legislator was paid thousands of dollars for a half-hour speech to an association or industry lobbying Congress. The ethics code proposed to Congress in 1977 tightened those limits, both by lowering the allowed amount and by broadening the definition of honoraria to include all earned income.

A respected advocate of reform, Morris K. Udall, was among those who objected. "You're saying that if I have all kinds of inherited wealth in stocks and bonds, it's okay," the Arizona Democrat told the House. "But if I get out on weekends and hustle and get some money from speaking engagements, it's not okay." But then-Speaker of the House, Massachusetts Democrat Thomas P. O'NEILL, Jr., argued that the limit was needed to restore the "collective integrity of the House." The House Democratic leadership, which had often protected members by preventing votes on controversial questions, in this case forced a public accounting. Another factor was a pay raise for Congress that took effect at the same time. In the end, reluctant to appear opposed to ethical reform and anxious to appease voters upset about higher pay, a majority voted for income limits and eventually endorsed the full ethics code.

The first House limit on outside income was 15 percent of a member's salary; by 1981 the proportion had been raised to 30 percent. Senators, who generally made more than representatives from speaking fees, balked at a limit even though they were subject to a $25,000 ceiling contained in the 1976 campaign finance law. In 1981 the Senate removed itself from that cap. Not until mid-1983 did the Senate accept an income limit, and then only after the House tacked the 30 percent level onto a pay increase for senators. The Senate found even a 30 percent limit too confining and in 1985 increased it to 40 percent.

No longer allowed to keep honoraria, members of Congress are also limited under the Ethics Reform Act in how much they can make from other types of outside work. House members, senior staff, and top federal officials could earn up to 15 percent of the Executive Level II salary (then $96,600) beginning in 1991. Senators could earn 15 percent of their $125,100 base pay, or $18,765. Legislators no longer could be paid for serving on boards of directors. And House members were barred from outside law practice, as senators had been since 1983.

## Sexual Behavior

Next to money, sex is perhaps the leading cause of ethical lapses by legislators. Behavior that might have been winked at in the past is no longer tolerated by the public or Congress itself. The women's movement, scandals in the navy and in the clergy, and allegations of sexual misconduct made in 1991 by Anita Hill against Clarence Thomas, whom President George Bush had nominated to be a Supreme Court justice, have sensitized the nation to sexual harassment as never before.

In late 1992 ten women complained of unwanted sexual advances from Sen. Bob Packwood, an Oregon Republican known for his strong support of women's rights. Pending the outcome of an Ethics Committee investigation, Packwood apologized and began treatment for alcohol abuse.

Two years earlier a young woman acquaintance had accused another senator, Washington Democrat Brock Adams, of sexual assault. Adams denied her accusations, and similar ones from other women, but he did not seek reelection. The House ethics committee has investigated complaints from women about several representatives, issuing rebukes in some cases. One member, Ohio Republican Donald E. "Buz" Lukens, resigned in 1990 after a Capitol elevator operator complained that he had fondled her. Lukens had been convicted in 1989 of having sex with a minor. As in the Mills and Hays cases in the 1970s, sexual indiscretion has ruined many promising or established congressional careers.

### Additional Readings

Drew, Elizabeth. *Politics & Money: The New Road to Corruption.* New York: Macmillan, 1983.

Garment, Suzanne. *Scandal: The Culture of Mistrust in American Politics.* New York: Doubleday, 1992.

Simon, Paul. *The Glass House.* New York: Continuum, 1984.

Stern, Phillip M. *STILL the Best Congress Money Can Buy.* Washington, D.C.: Regnery Gateway, 1992.

## Ethics Committee, House

*See* STANDARDS OF OFFICIAL CONDUCT COMMITTEE, HOUSE.

## Ethics Committee, Senate Select

The six members of the bipartisan Senate Select Committee on Ethics have the awkward responsibility of making sure their colleagues behave properly.

They are charged with enforcing the Senate code of ETHICS, a formal set of rules adopted in 1977. The three Democrats and three Republicans are expected to act collectively as investigator, prosecutor, and jury. In practice, committee members rarely conduct an official probe, preferring to handle potential problems in private before they escalate into scandals.

Most ethics questions focus on finances. Senators are required to keep separate their personal, office, and campaign funds, and they must file FINANCIAL DISCLOSURE statements with the Ethics Committee. Senators must also avoid situations where they benefit personally from their official acts. Bribery is the most blatant example of this, but less obvious corruption also occurs, such as an inside financial deal with an industry seeking a legislative favor.

In recent years the committee has also had to deal with sensitive issues of harassment and other types of sexual indiscretion. In late 1992 the committee began investigating complaints lodged against Oregon Republican Bob Packwood by female staff members and lobbyists who accused the senator of having made unwanted sexual advances to them.

## Committee Actions

The Senate voted in 1964 to establish an ethics committee. By 1993 four disciplinary cases had been brought to the Senate floor for a vote. The Senate endorsed the committee's recommendation in three of the four cases. The exception was the 1982 case of New Jersey Democrat Harrison A. Williams, Jr., the only senator convicted in the ABSCAM SCANDAL. Debate over Williams's expulsion was cut short by his resignation. The Senate had already indicated its reluctance to handle the controversy by delaying its debate for seven months after receiving the unanimous recommendation of the Ethics Committee. In the other cases, three senators were censured or denounced for financial misconduct: Connecticut Democrat Thomas J. Dodd in 1967, Georgia Democrat Herman E. Talmadge in 1979, and Minnesota Republican Dave Durenberger in 1990. (See DISCIPLINING MEMBERS.)

A fifth disciplinary case went to the floor in 1991, but not for a vote. Instead, the Senate heard the committee's reprimand of California Democrat Alan Cranston for improper conduct in the KEATING FIVE SCANDAL. The committee used reprimand because it lacked authority to issue a censure on its own. But in other respects the reprimand was no less harsh than in the three previous cases.

Critics complain that the Ethics Committee has not aggressively policed the Senate. But committee members have said they want to prevent scandals as much as uncover them. To this end the committee published a manual that contains more than four hundred questions senators have asked of the Ethics Committee, along with answers compiled by the committee and its staff.

If a complaint is filed against a senator, rules allow the Ethics Committee to investigate and, if no action is recommended, to keep the matter from public knowledge. In three of its cases—those of Williams, Durenberger, and the Keating Five—the committee brought in a special counsel, Robert S. Bennett, to act as prosecutor. With his aggressive manner and insistence that senators should avoid even the appearance of impropriety, Bennett went a long way toward toughening the committee's image.

## History

The Ethics Committee was established in 1964 and organized in 1965. Its first chair was John C. STENNIS, veteran Mississippi Democrat. A former judge with a reputation for fairness and integrity, Stennis chaired the panel until 1975, when Nevada Democrat Howard W. Cannon took over for two years. Adlai E. Stevenson III, an Illinois Democrat, chaired the committee from 1977 through most of 1979, the year the Senate voted to denounce Georgia Democrat Herman Talmadge. Stevenson resigned in the fall, and Democrat Howell Heflin, a freshman from Alabama, was named chair. This was the first time since 1910 that so new a member had been given a post as committee chair. A former judge, Heflin demonstrated a judicious restraint that his colleagues appreciated. Heflin was chair from 1979 to 1981 and again from 1987, when Democrats regained the Senate, to 1991.

While Republicans controlled the Senate (1981–1987), the committee had two chairs. Malcolm Wallop of Wyoming, who often criticized the Senate ethics code, held the post from 1981 to 1985; Warren B. Rudman of New Hampshire took over from 1985 to 1987. Rudman then served as vice chair under Heflin, continuing the practice of having a minority member in that post. Another freshman, North Carolina Democrat Terry Sanford, succeeded Heflin as chair in 1991. Sanford, a former governor of his state, was defeated for reelection in 1992, and Rudman left the Senate voluntarily. At the start of the 103rd Congress in 1993, Richard Bryan (D-Nev.) and Mitch McConnell (R-Ky.) were respectively named chair and vice chair of the committee.

# Executive Branch and Congress

The legislative and the executive are separate but interdependent branches of government. Although the Constitution vested the president with "the executive power," the president is often referred to as the "chief legislator." Congress was granted "all legislative powers," which gives it significant leverage over the executive branch through its legislative and oversight powers. (See SEPARATION OF POWERS.)

## Constitutional Deliberations

No questions troubled the framers of the Constitution more than the powers to be given the executive branch and how it should be structured. How much authority and independence to give the national executive remained in dispute until the end of the Constitutional Convention.

The convention at first favored a single executive, chosen by Congress for a term of seven years, whose powers would be limited. Congress would appoint judges and ambassadors and would make treaties. This plan for legislative supremacy finally gave way to a more balanced plan, which called for a president to be chosen by electors for a four-year term without limit as to reelection. (The Twenty-second Amendment, adopted in 1951, set a two-term limit for the presidency.) The president was to make appointments and treaties, subject to Senate approval; act as commander-in-chief; and ensure that the laws were faithfully executed. The framers did not attempt to elabo-

rate on how the system would actually work. The provisions on presidential power were brief and ambiguous.

## President as Lawmaker

The president's role as lawmaker begins with the constitutional duty to "from time to time give to the Congress Information of the State of the Union, and recommend to their Consideration such Measures as he shall judge necessary and expedient." To these bare bones, Congress has added further requirements. For example, the president is required to submit an annual budget message and an economic report. (See BUDGET PROCESS.)

Other legislative powers granted by the Constitution to the president include the power to veto bills; the power to make treaties, subject to Senate consent; and the rarely used power to convene one or both houses of Congress. The president's role as lawmaker has been further increased through the authority to issue rules and regulations, proclamations, and executive orders—or administrative legislation.

The president traditionally sets forth a legislative agenda in the annual STATE OF THE UNION address before a joint session of Congress. The president then sends legislative proposals to Congress in the form of draft bills.

What happens to these administration bills after they are introduced depends on a variety of factors, including who is in the White House, which party controls Congress, the times and mood of the country, and the issue itself.

The Constitution said little about how a president would go about persuading Congress to pass presidential proposals. Several tools are available to the chief executive.

### Lobbying

One tool of persuasion is for the president to lobby Congress directly. Early presidents kept their LOBBYING discreet, either doing it themselves or entrusting it to a few helpers. In modern times, executive lobbying has become more open and more elaborate.

President Harry S. Truman set up a small legislative liaison office in 1949, but the staff was inexperienced; Truman and a few top advisers still did the real lobby-

*President Dwight D. Eisenhower poses with congressional leaders in the 1950s.    Source: Dwight D. Eisenhower Library*

ing. Truman's successor, Dwight D. Eisenhower, in 1953 appointed full-time, senior staff to the task. Liaison operations continued to expand and grow more sophisticated in succeeding administrations.

In addition to the White House operation, all federal departments also have their own congressional liaison forces. The practice began in 1945, when the War Department created the office of assistant secretary for congressional liaison, centralizing congressional relations that had been handled separately by the military services. The services and some civilian agencies have liaison offices on Capitol Hill today.

Some legal limits have been placed on executive lobbying. A 1919 criminal statute prohibits the executive branch from spending money to influence votes in Congress. Direct pressure by the executive on Congress is generally understood to be acceptable, but spending money to solicit outside pressure on Congress is not.

### Public Pressure

When direct appeals to Congress fail, presidents often turn to their vast constituency for help. Presidents can mobilize enormous public pressure to persuade Congress to act on legislative programs. Radio and television have been especially effective tools for shaping public opinion.

One of the most skillful users of the media was President Franklin D. Roosevelt. In 1933, at the end of his first week in office, Roosevelt went on the radio to urge support for his banking reforms. He addressed a joint session of Congress, too. His reforms were passed that very day. Similar radio messages, which became known as "fireside chats," followed.

Television gave presidents further power to influence the public. President Lyndon B. Johnson in 1965 made masterful use of television to win support for the most sweeping voting rights bill in ninety years.

*President George Bush signs legislation bailing out the thrift industry in 1989 as congressional leaders look on.*    *Source: R. Michael Jenkins*

Instead of appearing before Congress at the customary hour of noon, he waited until evening, when the television audience would be greater. He then delivered what has been called his best speech as president.

President Ronald Reagan enjoyed great success with his use of television. His 1981 televised appeal to Congress for passage of his budget package, accompanied by vigorous lobbying for public support of the program, was labeled by House Speaker Thomas P. O'Neill, Jr., a Massachusetts Democrat, "the greatest selling job I've ever seen."

### Patronage

Another means for exerting pressure on Congress is PATRONAGE. Over the years presidential patronage has included everything from distributing government jobs to issuing coveted invitations to the White House.

Although the civil service and postal reforms of the twentieth century dramatically reduced the president's patronage, the award of government contracts, selection of sites for federal installations, and other political favors remain powerful inducements in the hands of a president.

### Veto

When all else fails, there is always the veto, the president's most powerful defensive weapon. A president uses the veto to try to kill unacceptable bills and also to dramatize administration policies.

Short of an actual veto, a presidential threat to veto legislation is a powerful persuader. In 1975 both the House and Senate passed a consumer protection bill, but they dropped the measure because President Gerald R. Ford threatened to veto it. George Bush used VETOES and veto threats to force Congress to compromise on key legislation, such as gun control, civil rights, and unemployment compensation.

*Two weeks after their sweeping victory on Election Day 1992, Bill Clinton, left, and Al Gore, second from left, spent the day meeting with congressional leaders. Here House Speaker Tom Foley speaks during a press conference held in the Capitol building's National Statuary Hall after that day's events.    Source: R. Michael Jenkins*

Although the Constitution permits the House and Senate to override a presidential veto by a two-thirds vote in each chamber, in reality vetoes are rarely overridden.

## Congressional Role

Congress plays an important role in the functioning of the executive branch. Its responsibilities range from counting electoral votes, to providing funds for the executive branch, to monitoring the implementation of laws.

The Constitution provides that Congress will count electoral votes for president and VICE PRESIDENT. If no candidate wins a majority, the House chooses the president and the Senate, the vice president. Congress also bears responsibility in the related areas of PRESI-

DENTIAL DISABILITY AND SUCCESSION. (See ELECTING THE PRESIDENT.)

The Senate has the power to confirm executive appointments. (See APPOINTMENT POWER.) Both the House and Senate can launch INVESTIGATIONS into executive activities, and both chambers work together to seek the impeachment and conviction of top officials accused of wrongdoing. (See IMPEACHMENT POWER.)

Congress also shares with the executive important WAR POWERS and responsibility for ratifying treaties. (See TREATY-MAKING POWER.) But the power that gives Congress the most influence is its power of the purse. Through its AUTHORIZATION BILLS and APPROPRIATIONS BILLS, Congress helps formulate and carry out executive policies. It may use its taxing power to raise money to run the country and to regulate government activities. (See PURSE, POWER OF; STRUCTURE AND POWERS.)

Many of these powers help Congress in performing one of its primary responsibilities: oversight. In the laws it passes, Congress often leaves much to the discretion of the president and the federal bureaucracy. Congress must, therefore, ensure that its legislative intent is being carried out and remedy the situation if it is not. (See LEGISLATIVE VETO; OVERSIGHT POWER.)

### Additional Readings

Davidson, Roger H., and Walter J. Oleszek. *Congress and Its Members.* 4th ed. Washington, D.C.: CQ Press, 1993.

Fisher, Louis. *The Politics of Shared Power: Congress and the Executive.* 3rd ed. Washington, D.C.: CQ Press, 1992.

---

## Executive Privilege

Presidents occasionally refuse congressional demands for information or for officials' testimony before committees by claiming executive privilege. The term is modern, but the practice is as old as the nation.

The Constitution does not specifically grant executive privilege, but presidents since George Washington have asserted a right to withhold information from Congress based on the constitutional SEPARATION OF POWERS. Congress has been reluctant to seek a decisive court ruling on the validity of executive privilege. Instead it has tried to rally public opinion in support of congressional demands for information, and occasionally it has cited executive branch officials for CONTEMPT OF CONGRESS.

Presidents have offered a variety of reasons to justify denying information to Congress. Perhaps the most common is the need for secrecy in military and diplomatic activities. Other reasons for withholding information include protecting individuals from unfavorable publicity and safeguarding the confidential exchange of ideas within an administration. Critics frequently charge that an administration's real motive for refusing to supply information is to escape criticism or to cover up wrongdoing.

The most dramatic clash over executive privilege came during an inquiry into the WATERGATE SCANDAL, which brought about the resignation of President Richard M. Nixon in 1974. The Watergate affair began with a 1972 break-in at Democratic National Committee headquarters in the Watergate office building in Washington, D.C. As the scandal unfolded, it revealed administration political sabotage that went far beyond the original incident.

Claiming executive privilege, Nixon tried to withhold tapes and documents demanded by congressional investigators. The Supreme Court ruled unanimously in July 1974 that Nixon must give up tapes showing his own involvement in the scandal. Days later the House Judiciary Committee recommended that Nixon be removed from office for, among other things, failing to comply with a committee subpoena, or demand, for the tapes. The president quickly resigned, ending the NIXON IMPEACHMENT EFFORT.

The Court's ruling on the Nixon tapes was a defeat for one president but a victory for the presidency. In its unanimous opinion in *United States v. Nixon,* the Court said that the public interest outweighed Nixon's need for confidentiality in the case of the tapes, which might contain evidence relevant to a criminal prosecution. But at the same time the Court recognized executive privilege as a legitimate, if limited, aspect of the president's authority.

---

## Executive Session

An executive session is a meeting of a congressional committee—or occasionally the full Senate or House of Representatives—that only its members may attend. Witnesses regularly appear at committee meetings in executive session. Defense Department officials, for example, testify in executive session during presentations of classified defense information. Other members of Congress may be invited, but the public and press are excluded.

## Expulsion

*See* DISCIPLINING MEMBERS.

## Extensions of Remarks

Each issue of the *CONGRESSIONAL RECORD* has a special section that serves almost as a scrapbook of the day. Legislators who want to publicize articles, newspaper stories, or other information can submit the text for a section called "Extensions of Remarks," which is located in the back pages of the *Record.* Any statement expected to take up more than two printed pages must be accompanied by an estimate of printing costs.

Senators usually prefer to have their articles or undelivered speeches printed as part of the day's floor debate, instead of in "Extensions of Remarks." The extra section is popular with House members, who often fill several pages. A special symbol identifies speeches not actually delivered on the floor.

# F

## Federal Register

The *Federal Register* is a daily government publication that provides a wide variety of information on government operations. It contains presidential proclamations, executive orders, and other executive branch documents, including rules, regulations, and notices issued by federal agencies. The *Federal Register* spells out government requirements in many fields of public concern: environmental protection, food and drug standards, and occupational health and safety, to name just a few. It also includes proposed changes in agency regulations, on which the public is invited to comment. The *Federal Register* is published by the National Archives and Records Administration.

## Filibuster

The Senate has long been famous for the filibuster: the use of prolonged debate and delaying tactics to block action supported by a majority of members. Filibusters have been mounted on issues ranging from peace treaties to internal Senate seating disputes. Editorial writers have condemned them, cartoonists have ridiculed them, and satirists have caricatured them. But filibusters also have admirers, who view them as a defense against hasty or ill-advised legislation.

Filibusters are permitted by the Senate's tradition of unlimited debate, a characteristic that distinguishes it from the House of Representatives. The term *filibuster* is derived from a word for pirates or soldiers of fortune; the term originated in the House, although the modern House seldom experiences delay arising from a prolonged debate.

The Senate proudly claims to be a more deliberative body than the House. George Washington described it as the saucer where passions cool. But many people believe the modern filibuster impedes rather than encourages deliberation. Once reserved for the bitterest and most important battles—over slavery, war, civil rights—filibusters today have been trivialized, critics say.

Historically the rare filibuster provided the Senate's best theater; participants had to be ready for days or weeks of free-wheeling debate, and all other business was blocked until one side conceded. In the modern era drama is rare. Disappointment awaits visitors to the Senate gallery who expect a real-life version of actor Jimmy Stewart's climactic oration in the 1939 classic film *Mr. Smith Goes to Washington.* They are likely to look down on an empty floor and hear only the drone of a clerk reading absent senators' names in a mind-numbing succession of QUORUM calls. Often the filibusterers do not even have to be on the floor, nor do the bills they are opposing.

In large part the change dates from 1975, when the Senate made it easier to choke off debate under a cumbersome procedure known as cloture. Despite the new rule, filibusters and threats of filibusters remain a common weapon of senators hoping to spotlight, change, delay, or kill legislation. Frequent resort to the filibuster, real or threatened, often impedes Senate action on major bills. Success is most likely near the end of a session, when a filibuster on one bill may imperil action on other, more urgent legislation.

Dramatic filibusters do still occur on occasion, as demonstrated by a 1988 Republican filibuster against a campaign finance bill. To counter Republican obstruction, the majority leader, Democrat Robert C. Byrd of West Virginia, forced round-the-clock Senate sessions that disrupted the chamber for three days. When Republicans boycotted the sessions, Byrd resurrected a little-known power that had last been wielded in 1942: he directed the Senate SERGEANT-AT-ARMS to arrest absent members and bring them to the floor. In the resulting turmoil, Oregon Republican Bob Packwood was arrested, reinjured a broken finger, and was physically carried onto the Senate

**137**

floor at 1:19 a.m. Democrats were still unable to break the filibuster, and the campaign finance bill was pulled from the floor after a record-setting eighth cloture vote failed to limit debate.

## As Old as the Senate

Delaying tactics were first used in the Senate in 1789, by opponents of a bill to locate the nation's capital on the Susquehanna River. The first full-fledged filibusters occurred in 1841, when Democrats and Whigs squared off, first over the appointment of official Senate printers and then over the establishment of a national bank.

Slavery, the Civil War, Reconstruction, and blacks' voting rights in turn were the sparks for the increasingly frequent and contentious filibusters of the nineteenth century. Opponents had no weapon against them, and proposed rules to restrict debate were repeatedly rejected.

Minor curbs were adopted early in the twentieth century. But they did not hinder Republican filibusterers from killing two of President Woodrow Wilson's proposals to prepare the nation for World War I: a 1915 ship-purchase bill and a 1917 bill to arm merchant ships. As a political scientist in 1881, Wilson had celebrated "the Senate's opportunities for open and unrestricted discussion." After the 1917 defeat he railed, "The Senate of the United States is the only legislative body in the world which cannot act when the majority is ready for action. A little group of willful men . . . have rendered the great government of the United States helpless and contemptible."

Public outrage finally forced the Senate to accept debate limitations. On March 8, 1917, it adopted a rule under which a filibuster could be halted if two-thirds of the senators present voted to do so. The framers of this first cloture rule predicted it would be little used, and for years that was the case. The first successful use of the rule, in 1919, ended debate on the Treaty of Versailles following World War I.

Nine more cloture votes were taken through 1927, and three were successful. The next successful cloture vote did not occur until 1962, when the Senate invoked cloture on a communications satellite bill.

Only sixteen cloture votes were taken between 1927 and the successful 1962 vote, most of which in-

*The longest speech in the history of the Senate was made by Strom Thurmond of South Carolina. Thurmond, a Democrat who later became a Republican, spoke for twenty-four hours and eighteen minutes during a filibuster against passage of the Civil Rights Act of 1957.    Source: The Strom Thurmond Institute*

volved civil rights. Southern Democrats were joined by westerners and some Republicans in an anticloture coalition that successfully filibustered legislation to stop poll taxes, literacy tests, lynching, and employment discrimination.

Many filibusters turned into grueling endurance contests. Strom Thurmond of South Carolina set a record for the longest speech in the history of the Senate. Thurmond, a Democrat who later switched to the Republican party, spoke for twenty-four hours and eighteen minutes during a 1957 filibuster of a civil rights bill. Speakers did not always confine themselves to the subject under consideration. Democrat Huey P. LONG of Louisiana entertained his colleagues during a fifteen-and-a-half-hour filibuster in 1935 with commentaries on the Constitution and recipes for southern "pot likker," turnip greens, and corn bread.

During a 1960 filibuster of a civil rights bill, eighteen southerners formed into teams of two and talked nonstop in relays. Supporters of the bill had to stay nearby for quorum calls and other procedural moves or risk losing control of the floor. Then-majority leader Lyndon B. JOHNSON, a Texas Democrat, kept the Senate going around the clock for nine days in an effort to break the filibuster. That was the longest session ever, but Johnson ultimately had to abandon the bill. Later in the year a weaker version passed.

"We slept on cots in the Old Supreme Court chamber [near the Senate floor] and came out to answer quorum calls," recalled William Proxmire, a Wisconsin Democrat who supported the bill. "It was an absolutely exhausting experience. The southerners who were doing the talking were in great shape, because they would talk for two hours and leave the floor for a couple of days."

## Changing the Rule

Civil rights filibusters in the 1950s stimulated efforts to make it easier to invoke cloture.

As modified in 1949, the cloture rule banned any limitation of debate on proposals to change the Senate rules, including the cloture rule itself. Since any attempt to change the cloture rule while operating under this stricture appeared hopeless, Senate liberals devised a new approach. Senate rules had always continued from one Congress to the next on the assumption that the Senate was a continuing body because only one-third of its members were elected every two years. Liberals now challenged this concept, arguing that the Senate had a right to adopt new rules by a simple majority vote at the beginning of a new Congress.

The dispute came to a head in 1959, when a bipartisan leadership group seized the initiative from the liberals and pushed through a change in the cloture rule. The new version permitted cloture to be invoked by two-thirds of those present and voting (rather than two-thirds of the full Senate membership, as the 1949 rule had required), and it also applied to proposals for changes in the rules.

Once cloture was invoked, further debate was limited to one hour for each senator on the bill itself and on all amendments affecting it. No new amendments could be offered except by unanimous consent. Nongermane amendments and dilatory motions (those intended to delay action) were not permitted. (See AMENDMENTS; RIDER.)

Although they did not address the continuing-body question directly, members added new language to the rules, stating that "the rules of the Senate shall continue from one Congress to the next unless they are changed as provided in these rules."

## The Modern Filibuster

In 1964 the Senate for the first time invoked cloture on a civil rights bill, thus ending the longest filibuster in history after seventy-four days of debate. Other civil rights filibusters were broken in 1965 and 1968. Liberal supporters of civil rights legislation, who had tried repeatedly to tighten controls on debate, became less eager for cloture reform in the wake of these victories. By the 1970s they themselves were doing much of the filibustering—against Nixon administration policies for the Vietnam War, defense weapons systems, and antibusing proposals.

In 1975, however, the liberals tried again to tighten restrictions on debate. They succeeded in easing the cloture requirement from a high of sixty-seven votes (two-thirds of those present and voting) to a flat sixty votes (three-fifths of the Senate membership). The old requirement still applied for votes on changes in Senate rules. The number of cloture votes continued to increase after the rule was eased, and the success rate nearly doubled.

Minorities still found ways to obstruct action on measures they opposed. The most effective tactic was the postcloture filibuster, pioneered by Alabama Democrat James B. Allen, a frequent obstructionist. In 1976, when the Senate invoked cloture on a bill he opposed, Allen demanded action on the many amendments he had filed previously. He required that each be read aloud, sought roll-call votes and quorum calls, objected to routine motions, and appealed parliamentary rulings. Other senators soon adopted Allen's tactics.

As filibusters changed in character, the Senate's enthusiasm for unlimited debate eroded. At the mere threat of a filibuster it became a routine practice to start rounding up votes for cloture—or to seek a compromise—as soon as debate began. Most of that action occurred behind the scenes. If the first cloture vote failed, more were taken. Meanwhile, leaders often shelved the disputed bill temporarily, with members' unanimous consent, so that the Senate could turn to other matters. That tactic, known as double-tracking, "kept the filibuster from becoming a real filibuster," as one senator said.

In 1979 the Senate agreed to set an absolute limit of one hundred hours on postcloture delaying tactics. The television era prompted additional restraints on debate. When live televised coverage of Senate proceedings began in 1986, members gave new thought to their public image. Senators shied away from several proposals designed to quicken the pace and sharpen the focus of their proceedings for television viewers. But they did agree to one significant change in Senate rules. They reduced to thirty hours, from one hundred, the time allowed for debate, procedural moves, and roll-call votes after the Senate had invoked cloture to end a filibuster.

Despite these restrictions, filibusters continue to be an effective tool to obstruct Senate action. In 1992, for example, anticrime legislation and a bill to ban replacement of striking workers were shelved when the Senate failed to halt Republican filibusters. As it came to an end, the 102nd Congress even featured an old-style filibuster, when New York Republican Alfonse M. D'Amato held the Senate floor for more than fifteen hours in a futile attempt to block a tax bill he wanted to amend. While some Senate leaders called for additional restrictions on filibusters, many members were reluctant to curb the hallowed Senate tradition—a tradition cherished by Democrats as well as Republicans.

### Additional Readings

Burdette, Franklin L. *Filibustering in the Senate.* Princeton, N.J.: Princeton University Press, 1940.

Whalen, Charles, and Barbara Whalen. *The Longest Debate: A Legislative History of the 1964 Civil Rights Act.* Washington, D.C.: Seven Locks Press, 1985.

# Finance Committee, Senate

The most heavily lobbied committee in the Senate is the Finance Committee, which handles all federal taxation and more than 45 percent of all federal spending. Because the tax code has so many special provisions, ranging from deductions for home mortgages to credits for child care, the committee has almost unlimited jurisdiction. Its responsibility for Social Security, health care for the poor and elderly, and welfare programs gives it a much larger share of the federal pie than most committees have. The Finance Committee also handles tariffs and other restraints on international trade. In early 1993 the committee had twenty members: eleven Democrats and nine Republicans.

Although efforts to control the federal deficit have put limits on the Finance Committee's authority, it still operates with great latitude. Revenue goals are set through the congressional BUDGET PROCESS, but the Finance Committee decides how the money should be raised. Assignment to the committee is keenly sought by senators.

Because the Constitution says revenue bills must originate in the House, the House Ways and Means Committee has taken the lead on most tax bills. It usually operates under strict rules to shepherd its proposals safely through the House without major amendments. The Senate Finance Committee operates very differently: committee members' special wishes are accommodated, and other senators are allowed to add a string of amendments on the floor. In conference the bills are rewritten again; this may take place in small, closed caucuses or in one-on-one meetings between the House and Senate committee chairs.

Although subcommittees have in many cases diluted the power of full committees, the Finance Committee has resisted such a shift. Its subcommittees do not have separate staff and have almost no role in writing legislation. That leaves the Finance chair better able than most to steer the committee toward his or her own ends. Senators often gather in an "exec room" behind the large hearing room, where they discuss privately what will happen in the public

*The chairman of the Senate Finance Committee is one of the most influential figures in the Senate. Here, Sen. Lloyd Bentsen, chairman from 1987 until 1993, and House Ways and Means Chairman Dan Rostenkowski talk before a House-Senate conference committee begins work on tax legislation. Bentsen became President Clinton's secretary of Treasury in 1993, placing him in charge of financial issues that are the domain of this Senate committee.    Source: R. Michael Jenkins*

markup, or drafting, of the legislation. When the chair is ready, and not before, they take up a matter in formal session.

The federal tax code is extremely complex, riddled with tax incentives treasured by various industries. Any effort to pass new tax legislation attracts a corridor full of lobbyists. Members of the Finance Committee have often been able to accommodate favored lobbyists or even fellow senators by adding a sentence worded in a general way but carefully crafted to benefit a particular case. Russell B. LONG, the Democratic senator from Louisiana who chaired the committee from 1966 to 1981, once asked, "What is a loophole? That is something that benefits the other guy. If it benefits you, it is tax reform."

Reform of the welfare system and changes in health care benefits for the poor and elderly are other subjects that occupied the Finance Committee in re-

cent years. The breadth of its jurisdiction and the importance of its decisions, both financially and socially, have made the Finance Committee a most formidable group of senators. Its members are consistently among those receiving the largest donations from PO-LITICAL ACTION COMMITTEES.

### History

Set up in 1816, the Finance Committee was among the first committees established in the Senate. At first the committee handled all aspects of the federal budget, but it lost responsibility for spending during the Civil War, when a separate Appropriations Committee was established. With the high costs of war, the job had simply become too large for one group to handle. (See APPROPRIATIONS COMMIT-TEE, SENATE.)

In the late nineteenth century the Finance Committee upheld protectionism, advocating tariffs on imports at rates often exceeding 50 percent. Among its leaders at that time were Republicans John SHERMAN of Ohio (1861–1877, 1881–1897), who chaired the committee, and William B. ALLISON (1873–1908), a senior member of Finance who also chaired the Appropriations Committee.

At the turn of the century, millionaire Rhode Islander Nelson W. ALDRICH (1881–1911), also a Republican, took the helm. Aldrich was one of the nation's leading conservatives and consistently supported high tariffs. Politically astute, he won crucial votes from western senators by endorsing new tariffs to protect western-based industries. Often commodities in which Aldrich had personally invested, such as sugar, benefited from the tariff structure he helped create.

After the federal income tax was enacted in 1913, the importance of tariffs and excise taxes as a source of government funds diminished. The Finance Committee's focus shifted as Congress began to write exceptions into the tax code, eventually creating a maze of rules. The pressure for special tax treatment is continual, and the Finance Committee has always been in the center of the clamor.

Two southern Democrats had long tenures as Finance chairs after World War II. Harry Flood Byrd of Virginia chaired the committee from 1955 to 1965. One of the most conservative Democrats in the Senate, Byrd used his position as Finance chair to block much of the social welfare legislation sought by presidents John F. Kennedy and Lyndon B. Johnson. After Byrd's death Russell Long took over as chair. He proved more amenable to social programs—and also to requests for special tax treatment from business and industry, particularly the oil industry. At first, in fights with the House, Long was overshadowed by the more experienced Wilbur D. MILLS, chair of the House Ways and Means Committee. But by 1987, when Long retired after almost forty years of service, he had become a legend in the Senate, confident in his command of complex subjects and skilled at breaking up tense negotiations with a funny story.

Robert DOLE of Kansas became Finance Committee chair when Republicans gained control of the Senate in 1981. That year he helped engineer the passage of sweeping tax cuts sought by President Ronald Reagan. The following year, in a break from the usual procedure, the Finance Committee initiated a major tax bill, and the House did not vote on the measure until it emerged from a Senate-House conference.

When Dole was elected majority leader in 1985 Republican Bob Packwood of Oregon took over as chair of the Finance Committee. He served in that post for just two years, until Democrats won back the Senate majority. Although at first he did not support tax reform, Packwood presided over a major overhaul of the tax code. In 1987 Democrat Lloyd Bentsen of Texas became Finance chair. Bentsen gave up that post in 1993 to become secretary of the Treasury under President Bill Clinton. He was succeeded by Democrat Daniel Patrick Moynihan of New York.

## Financial Disclosure

Financial disclosure, the public exposure of sources of money, is a key principle behind two different reforms: federal ETHICS codes and laws concerning CAMPAIGN FINANCING.

Top federal officials are required to report annually the sources of their income, and candidates for federal office must file detailed reports of campaign contributions and expenditures. The hope is that public scrutiny of financial records will discourage corrupt practices, which range from conflicts of interest to outright bribery.

The Supreme Court, upholding a 1925 law requiring reports on campaign spending, commented in 1934: "Congress reached the conclusion that public disclosure of political contributions, together with the names of contributors and other details, would tend to prevent the corrupt use of money to affect elections. The verity of this conclusion reasonably cannot be denied."

In actual practice, the soundness of the underlying concept made little difference. Until the reforms of the 1970s, the laws on disclosure simply did not work. President Lyndon B. Johnson, in proposing election reforms in 1967, described the campaign laws: "Inadequate in their scope when enacted, they are now obsolete. More loophole than law, they invite evasion and circumvention."

The requirements for financial disclosure, both in the ethics codes and in campaign finance laws, were greatly improved in later years, though critics still complained that they were flawed and inconsistently enforced. The disclosure rules probably helped to keep government officials honest, but no one was sure to what extent. The following paragraphs describe the requirements in force in 1993.

## Income Disclosure

Following passage of the Ethics in Government Act in 1978, top federal officials, in Congress and in the executive and judiciary branches, had to file annual financial reports that covered salaries, honoraria, gifts, reimbursements, income from investments, and the value of assets and liabilities.

In the Ethics Reform Act of 1989 Congress changed some of the figures and added some new requirements, but it retained the structure and spirit of the 1978 law. The 1989 act barred House members from a controversial practice, the acceptance of honoraria (fees received for giving speeches and writing articles). In 1991 the Senate joined in the ban on honoraria in exchange for a hefty raise that made Senate salaries equal to those in the House. The ethics laws did not require specific amounts to be disclosed but instead allowed officials to report within a range of figures set in the law. This gave a rather vague picture of an individual's financial situation, but it did give a sense of his or her wealth and how it was acquired, or of debt and how it was accumulated. However, under the rules details of certain transactions, such as real estate deals, could be omitted. Mortgages, car loans, and other consumer loans did not have to be reported.

Members of Congress filed their reports with the CLERK OF THE HOUSE and the SECRETARY OF THE SENATE, and the House and Senate ethics committees reviewed them and investigated complaints. If the committees found omissions or false reports, they could recommend House or Senate disciplinary action against that member. Expulsion, censure, and reprimand were among the disciplinary actions the legislators could take. Sometimes the ethics commit-

tees recommended against any punishment, even when they concluded that the legislator had broken rules. (See DISCIPLINING MEMBERS.)

Executive branch employees filed their reports with the Office of Government Ethics, and judicial branch employees filed with the Judicial Ethics Committee. The 1989 amendments doubled to $10,000 the maximum civil penalty against anyone who knowingly and willfully filed a false report or failed to file a report. Violators were also subject to criminal penalties under a general statute prohibiting false reporting to the federal government. Breaking that law was a felony, for which the maximum fine was $10,000, and the maximum prison sentence, five years.

Although several members were investigated for not complying with the financial disclosure rules, only one member of Congress was convicted between 1978 and 1993. George Hansen, a Republican representative from Idaho, was convicted in 1984 for failing to report nearly $334,000 in loans and profits be-

*Rep. George V. Hansen, R-Idaho, was the first member of Congress to be convicted for failure to comply with financial disclosure rules. Here he leaves U.S. District Court in Washington with his wife after sentencing. Hansen was subsequently reprimanded by the House.*
*Source: AP*

*House Speaker Jim Wright, D-Texas, addresses charges against him at a press conference. The highly publicized investigation attracted national attention and disrupted House leadership. In 1989 Wright resigned from the House.    Source: R. Michael Jenkins*

tween 1978 and 1981. Hansen was fined and imprisoned for nearly a year. The ethics committees typically did not investigate or make recommendations while a Justice Department probe was taking place, but they did review convictions to see if congressional disciplinary action was warranted. Following Hansen's conviction in April 1984, the House Committee on Standards of Official Conduct, as the ethics panel is formally known, recommended that he be reprimanded for the false reports. The House agreed. Hansen, who declined to change his reports when given a chance by the ethics committee and who maintained his innocence, was narrowly defeated in his reelection bid in November 1984.

The House panel found inaccurate reporting by other members but decided not to recommend disciplinary action against several Democrats. The members included Geraldine Ferraro of New York, in 1984;

James Weaver of Oregon and Dan Daniel of Virginia, both in 1986; Fernand J. St Germain of Rhode Island, in 1987; and Charlie Rose of North Carolina, in 1988.

In Rose's case court action followed. The Justice Department sued Rose in 1989, charging him with "knowingly and willfully" failing to report fully about loans from his campaign funds for personal use. The civil suit requested fines of $30,000. In April 1992 a federal district court refused to dismiss the suit, raising the prospect of an important precedent on how far executive branch officials can go in trying to punish legislators who have already been judged by the ethics committees. Rose contended that the constitutional doctrine of SEPARATION OF POWERS protected him from prosecution because his peers already had acted.

Inaccurate reports were part of the more serious charges of financial misconduct that resulted in the

House censure of Democrats Charles C. Diggs, Jr., of Michigan in 1979 and Charles H. Wilson of California in 1980, and the Senate reprimand of Georgia Democrat Herman E. Talmadge in 1979. In August 1992 the Senate Ethics Committee formally rebuked Oregon Republican Mark O. Hatfield for failing to disclose his acceptance of several expensive gifts in the period 1983–1986. Several of the gifts were from the former president of a university that had received a large federal grant while Hatfield headed the Appropriations Committee.

## Campaign Financing

Under campaign finance laws in effect for the 1992 elections, candidates for federal office were required to keep detailed records of who contributed to their campaigns and how the money was spent. A regulatory agency, the Federal Election Commission, made sure candidates complied with the law. Disclosure rules had a major impact on campaigning. The best evidence of this was the presence of accountants and lawyers on campaign staffs of major candidates.

Financial disclosure was only part of the campaign finance law, which also limited the size of contributions that could be made by individuals and political committees. In presidential campaigns, candidates who accepted public financing also had to comply with spending restrictions.

The Supreme Court in 1976 ruled, in the case of *Buckley v. Valeo,* that spending limits were valid only when accepted voluntarily. Presidential campaigns since 1976 have been publicly funded, but only if the candidates agreed to spending limits. Texas billionaire Ross Perot, who in 1992 waged the most successful independent campaign in modern times, spent his own money and did not have to abide by the limits.

Congressional candidates did not receive public funds and thus were not limited in spending. But they were subject to other aspects of the financing law, including disclosure requirements and contribution limits. The shortcomings of those laws were dramatized in 1990 by the investigation of the so-called KEATING FIVE SCANDAL. The affair involved five senators suspected of having done favors for Charles H. Keating, Jr., a wealthy contributor who headed a failing Cali-

fornia savings and loan. Keating made or solicited $1.5 million for the campaigns or political causes of the senators. In the end all five were rebuked by the Senate Ethics Committee. In addition, one of the five, California Democrat Alan Cranston, was strongly reprimanded. The episode fueled demands for a new and tighter campaign finance law, but the House and Senate failed in 1992 to resolve their differences over the legislation.

## History

The use of disclosure to keep tabs on campaign financing began in 1910 and 1911, when Congress passed and then amended the Federal Corrupt Practices Act. The law required congressional candidates and political organizations operating in two or more states to file financial reports, and it limited spending to $10,000 for Senate candidates and $5,000 for House candidates.

Loopholes and lack of enforcement meant that the law had little effect on campaigns; neither did an overhaul of the statute approved in 1925. A major flaw allowed congressional candidates to report that they had received and spent nothing on their campaigns. They did this by maintaining that campaign committees established to elect them had been working without their "knowledge and consent." No candidate for the House or Senate was ever prosecuted under the 1925 act.

Not until 1971 did Congress again address the financing of campaigns. The Federal Election Campaign Act of 1971 required, for the first time, relatively complete and timely public reports by candidates on who was financing their campaigns and how much they were spending. Less than three years later investigation of the WATERGATE SCANDAL revealed misuse of campaign funds. As a result Congress in 1974 extensively rewrote the existing campaign-financing law. Although the Supreme Court overturned several features of that law, prompting yet another version in 1976, the financial disclosure requirements remained intact. A further revision in 1979 was directed in part toward reducing the red tape associated with financial disclosure. The changes decreased the frequency of required reports, raised the minimum contribution and expenditure that had to be itemized, and exempted candidates who raised or spent less than $5,000.

## Requirements

A complex set of rules defined the various political committees that had to register and file financial reports with either the clerk of the House, the secretary of the Senate, or the Federal Election Commission (FEC). Copies of all reports were kept on file at the FEC and in the relevant state.

Each candidate designated a principal campaign committee that usually solicited and spent the bulk of his or her campaign funds. This committee had to report to the FEC if the candidate spent or received more than $5,000.

Also covered by the financial disclosure rules were political parties and their campaign committees, which had to report when $1,000 or more was spent or received in a year. POLITICAL ACTION COMMITTEES, or PACs (organizations that distribute campaign contributions to candidates for Congress and other offices), also fell into that category. Tighter restrictions applied to the PACs most closely tied to corporations, labor unions, trade associations, or certain other groups. Administration of these PACs, including bank accounts, was often handled by the corporation, union, or association, with the PAC funds kept in what the FEC called "separate segregated accounts." These PACs were required to report any expenditures, even if only $100 was spent in a year.

A separate rule applied to expenditures made without consulting the candidate. Such independent expenditures, either by individuals or political committees, had to be reported once they exceeded $250 in a year. The top independent spenders in the 1980s included Cecil R. Haden, a Texas industrialist and Reagan supporter, and Stewart Mott, heir to a General Motors fortune and a liberal Democrat. Among the groups making large independent expenditures were the Congressional Club, led by conservative Republican senator Jesse Helms of North Carolina, and the National Conservative Political Action Committee, noted for its negative campaigns against several Democratic senators.

## Reports

In addition to details of financial transactions, including total receipts and expenditures, the reports had to identify the source of all contributions in excess of $200. This requirement included a contributor whose smaller donations added up to $200 in a year.

Those who were paid more than $200 by a committee (for advertisements, transportation, management, or other campaign operating expenses) had to be listed by name and address. Rules about when reports must be filed varied according to the type of campaign, whether an election was scheduled, and the amount of money involved. The rules focused on elections, with reports specifically required just before and just after elections.

# Fiscal Year

The financial operations of the federal government are carried out in a twelve-month fiscal year that begins on October 1 and ends on September 30. The president's budget and congressional spending bills are calculated on a fiscal-year basis. (See BUDGET PROCESS.)

The fiscal year carries the date of the calendar year in which it ends. The current fiscal calendar has been in use since fiscal 1977. From fiscal 1844 through fiscal 1976 the fiscal year began July 1 and ended the following June 30.

# Floor Debate

See LEGISLATIVE PROCESS.

# Floor Manager

The floor manager of a bill is responsible for guiding a bill through floor debate and the amendment process to final vote in the House or the Senate. The chair of the committee or subcommittee that handled a bill usually acts as floor manager for its supporters. The committee's ranking member of the minority party often leads the opposition.

In both the House and Senate the floor managers operate from designated aisle seats. Staff members, who rarely come onto the floor, are allowed to sit alongside the floor manager. Regardless of their personal views on a bill, floor managers are under obligation to present the work of their committees in the most favorable light and to fend off undesirable amendments. The mark of successful floor managers is their ability to get a bill passed without substantial change.

## Foley, Thomas S.

The office of SPEAKER OF THE HOUSE returned to a traditional stance above the fray of partisanship when Washington Democrat Thomas S. Foley (1929– ) took the position in mid-1989. Foley's judicious presence was a marked contrast to that of his hard-charging predecessor, Texas Democrat Jim WRIGHT, who quit mid-term after questions arose about his personal finances.

Foley had a somewhat shaky start in the angry atmosphere created by Wright's departure, along with other scandals. He also had to deal with Democrats demanding more confrontation against a Republican administration. But when the Democratic administration of President Bill Clinton began in 1993, the Speaker was expected to be a legislative go-between rather than a national party spokesperson and to capitalize on his skills as an institutionalist and a consensus builder.

Foley's approach resembled those of Speakers such as Sam RAYBURN and Nicholas LONGWORTH more than those of Wright or "Czar" Thomas REED. An intellectual with a sense of detachment rare among politicians, he rose to the post without ever having displayed the vaunting ambition that characterizes many other leaders. He defined his politics more in terms of the institution than in terms of his party.

*House Speaker Tom Foley succeeded Rep. Jim Wright, who was the first Speaker in history to be forced from office. Here Foley is surrounded by reporters and cameras after a 1990 Democratic caucus on the budget.    Source: R. Michael Jenkins*

The first Speaker from west of the Rocky Mountains, Foley came to the House in 1964 from a largely rural district in western Washington. He served on the Agriculture Committee and became its chair in 1975. The previous year he had become chair of the Democratic Study Group, the strategy and research arm of liberal and moderate Democrats. A veteran of numerous reform battles against secrecy and seniority in the committee system, Foley became chair of the Democratic Caucus in 1977. Although he was not particularly active in that post, he caught the eye of Thomas P. O'NEILL, Jr., who was then Speaker.

When Republicans took control of the White House in the 1980 elections and defeated the Democratic whip, O'Neill knew he would need a skilled parliamentary strategist for upcoming battles. Foley, who had been the Democratic National Convention's parliamentarian in 1980, was chosen.

After O'Neill retired in 1987, Foley moved up to majority leader without opposition. Although he sometimes seemed uncomfortable in his role as chief Republican-basher, he took his cues from Wright and solidified his position in the party. His apprenticeship was cut short in the next Congress after Wright abdicated rather than face an extended inquiry into his finances. Foley's reputation for integrity and evenhandedness was an antidote to Wright's style, and he was given the Speaker's gavel.

In his early years as Speaker, Foley was able to lead Democrats on economic issues and to oppose the authorization of the Persian Gulf War in 1991 without opening his party to charges of disloyalty. Some liberal colleagues grumbled about his distaste for fiery torch-bearing and harsh discipline, and there was open dissatisfaction with his handling in 1992 of a scandal involving bad checks written by members at the House's internal bank. (See HOUSE BANK SCANDAL.) But he eventually brought the House back to the business of legislating, and after the 1992 elections brought no anti-incumbency backlash at the polls, he was well positioned to serve as a strong Hill leader for the Democrats, who controlled both branches of government.

*Gerald R. Ford takes the presidential oath.    Source: Gerald R. Ford Library*

## Ford, Gerald R.

Gerald R. Ford (1913–  ) is best known as the thirty-eighth president of the United States. He came to that position after twenty-four years as a Republican representative from Michigan, including nine years as House Republican leader. He also served a brief stint as President Richard Nixon's vice president.

Ford was the first person to assume executive office under provisions of the Twenty-fifth Amendment to the Constitution governing presidential and vice-presidential succession. In 1973 Nixon chose Ford to replace Vice President Spiro T. Agnew, who had resigned in the face of criminal charges. Ford became

president in 1974 when Nixon himself resigned under threat of impeachment. (See NIXON IMPEACHMENT EFFORT; PRESIDENTIAL DISABILITY AND SUCCESSION; WATERGATE SCANDAL.)

Ford was first elected to the House of Representatives in 1948. From the beginning he compiled a strongly conservative voting record. He consistently voted against amendments to limit defense spending and was critical of the policies of the Johnson administration during the Vietnam War. He voted against the 1973 War Powers Resolution, which sought to limit the president's war-making powers, and supported increased bombing of North Vietnam.

On domestic issues, Ford backed attempts to limit federal spending and the expansion of the federal government. He opposed the Medicare program of health care for the elderly and federal aid to education. Although he voted for the civil rights acts of the 1960s, he preferred milder substitutes.

Angry over the Senate's rejection of two of Nixon's appointees to the Supreme Court, Ford in 1970 launched an unsuccessful attack on Justice William O. Douglas. Calling for his impeachment, Ford cited Douglas's financial connections with a private foundation and his defense of civil disobedience as set forth in his book *Points of Rebellion*.

Ford's unwavering loyalty to his party led to his

election as chair of the House Republican Conference in 1962. He was elected House minority leader in 1965. Ford was admired by his peers for his honesty and frankness. His popularity in Congress and loyalty to the administration made him a logical choice for vice president upon Agnew's resignation on October 10, 1973. He was confirmed by the Senate on November 27, 1973, by a vote of 92 to 3.

On August 9, 1974, Nixon resigned, and Ford assumed the office of president. His popularity with Congress and the country at large suffered after he pardoned Nixon on September 8, 1974. Ford ran for president in 1976 but was defeated by Democrat Jimmy Carter. He then retired from public life.

## Foreign Affairs Committee, House

The House Foreign Affairs Committee has broad responsibility for legislation dealing with the relations of the United States with other countries. The most important legislative topics that fall under its jurisdiction are foreign aid programs, which provide economic assistance to poor and developing countries, and military equipment and training for U.S. allies around the world. Despite its seemingly significant responsibilities, the panel has had little impact on the direction of U.S. foreign policy.

The Foreign Affairs Committee was created in 1822. Traditionally, it was overshadowed by its Senate counterpart, the Foreign Relations Committee. To a great extent, this reflects the foreign policy roles of the House and Senate as established by the Constitution. Since the Constitution gives the Senate exclusive control over international treaties and nominations, the Senate Foreign Relations Committee is frequently at the center of debate over major international issues. The House has much less authority over foreign affairs under the Constitution, so the House Foreign Affairs Committee has less authority as well. (See FOREIGN RELATIONS COMMITTEE, SENATE).

The Foreign Affairs Committee receives less public notice than the Senate committee. While Foreign Relations for many decades drew some of the best-known and most respected members of the Senate, the House committee included many obscure junior members, who quickly left for a committee of greater legislative and political importance.

The Foreign Affairs Committee was affected by the same forces that reduced the once-great power of Senate Foreign Relations. The executive branch assumed greater control over foreign issues, thus reducing the foreign policy role of Congress as a whole. In addition, other committees with overseas interests, such as the Armed Services panels, eclipsed the role of the two foreign affairs panels.

Another problem for the Foreign Affairs Committee was the political weakness of foreign aid programs. Although advocates of foreign aid say it can be an effective means of advancing U.S. interests in the world, these programs have long been unpopular among the public and much of Congress. The climate for foreign aid grew even more hostile as the domestic economy declined in the 1980s and early 1990s. Foreign aid programs became so controversial that between 1980 and 1992 Congress only twice completed action on legislation authorizing foreign aid, in 1981 and 1985. So the Foreign Affairs Committee rarely was able to have any legislative impact on how the programs were run.

The inability of Congress to pass foreign aid authorization bills effectively transferred control over the shape and direction of foreign aid to the House Appropriations Committee and its Foreign Operations Subcommittee, which made many of the decisions about the programs during this period. (See APPROPRIATIONS COMMITTEE, HOUSE.) Venting his frustration, Foreign Affairs Committee chair Dante B. Fascell, a Florida Democrat, complained in 1990 that the need for action by the authorizing panels "has been less and less and less. It has made our work almost irrelevant."

Nevertheless, the influence of the Foreign Affairs Committee grew in some ways during Fascell's tenure, from 1983 to 1993. Fascell brought strong leadership to the post. In 1990, for example, when most Democrats opposed authorizing President George Bush to use military force to reverse Iraq's invasion of Kuwait, Fascell helped organize a group of key House committee chairs to back the president.

The committee gained a higher profile as various committee members became more visible participants in foreign policy debates.

Significant changes in the committee's membership came in 1993. Both Fascell and the panel's ranking Republican, William S. Broomfield of Michigan, retired, as did several other members of the committee. Lee H. Hamilton, a Democrat from Indiana, succeeded Fascell as chair.

# Foreign Relations Committee, Senate

The Senate Foreign Relations Committee oversees most aspects of the relations of the United States with other countries. Historically, it has been one of the most important forums for congressional influence in the field of international affairs.

Like its House counterpart, the Foreign Affairs Committee, the Senate Foreign Relations Committee has jurisdiction over foreign aid and legislation concerning the operations of the State Department, which carries out most U.S. foreign policies. Unlike the House committee, Foreign Relations also has the right to recommend Senate approval or rejection of foreign policy nominations and treaties submitted by the president. (See TREATY-MAKING POWER.)

Since the early nineteenth century the Foreign Relations Committee has been one of the most prestigious and powerful committees on Capitol Hill. Its members played important roles in crucial foreign policy debates. In the decades following World War II, for example, the committee helped guide U.S. policy through the Cold War of the late 1940s and 1950s, the Vietnam War in the 1960s, and the Panama Canal treaties in the 1970s. The committee was widely admired as the source of a bipartisan foreign policy consensus that for many years guided U.S. actions.

By the 1980s, however, the committee had lost much of its power and influence. For a variety of reasons, the committee no longer occupied the vital role in decision making for foreign policy that it had in previous decades.

## Loss of Influence

One factor weakening the Foreign Relations Committee was the general decline in the foreign policy authority of Congress. As power shifted from Congress to the executive branch, the Foreign Relations Committee lost its role in many key international issues.

The unpopularity of foreign aid programs also handicapped the committee. One of the committee's most important duties is to write a bill authorizing economic and military aid to other countries. The bill, which sets overall policy guidelines and spending limits for foreign aid programs, was once an important means for Congress to influence U.S. foreign policy. But in recent years the bills approved by the committee have rarely won approval from the Senate or Congress as a whole. From 1980 to 1992 only two authorization bills for foreign aid cleared Congress.

The Foreign Relations Committee's loss was the Appropriations Committee's gain, as the traditional annual or biennial authorization bills for foreign aid were supplanted by appropriations bills. The committee also lost power to other congressional committees, such as the Armed Services Committee, which gained influence over arms control matters.

The political makeup of the Foreign Relations Committee also changed significantly. In its glory days, the committee was dominated by a coalition of moderate Democrats and Republicans, who usually were able to work out a common position on critical issues. But by the late 1980s the committee had become deeply divided between mostly liberal Democrats and a group of very conservative Republicans. Debates on important issues, such as war in Central America and nuclear arms control, were marked by bitter arguments between the two factions.

In an attempt to resolve some of its problems and restore the effectiveness of the panel, Democrats on the committee agreed in the early 1990s to restructure the panel to shift more power to its subcommittees.

*The Senate Foreign Relations Committee has jurisdiction over most international issues, the State Department, treaties, and diplomatic nominations. Here, Senate and House conferees meet on South Africa sanctions.*     Source: The New York Times/*George Tames*

## History

The Foreign Relations Committee was created in 1816 and quickly became one of the most important committees in Congress, primarily because of its jurisdiction over treaties. All treaties, regardless of their subject matter, are referred to the committee.

The committee attracted some of the most illustrious members of the Senate, including Daniel WEBSTER, John C. CALHOUN, Roscoe CONKLING, and Robert A. TAFT. Among its chairs have been Charles SUMNER, Henry Cabot LODGE, William E. BORAH, Arthur H. VANDENBERG, and J. William FULBRIGHT.

The growing importance of the United States in world politics during the twentieth century added to the importance of the Foreign Relations Committee. After World War I, for example, Lodge and other committee members helped determine whether the

United States would ratify the Versailles Treaty and thus join the League of Nations. The committee helped draft limitations on the treaty that were unacceptable to President Woodrow Wilson. As a result the treaty was rejected, and the United States did not join the League of Nations.

After World War II the committee helped commit the United States to a policy of heavy involvement in world affairs and the containment of communism. Before the war Vandenberg and many other committee members had been isolationists who opposed U.S. entanglements with other countries. But Vandenberg, who chaired the committee from 1947 to 1949, became an internationalist after the war. Along with other committee members, he helped create a bipartisan consensus in favor of a strong foreign policy.

Fulbright served as chair from 1959 to 1975. The combination of television and the Vietnam War made him the committee's most famous chair. Fulbright was an outspoken critic of President Lyndon B. Johnson's policy of expanding the U.S. role in the Vietnam War. To dramatize his opposition Fulbright held nationally televised hearings on the war in the mid- and late 1960s. The hearings commanded public interest and attention and helped organize widespread opposition to Johnson's policies.

Fulbright was defeated for reelection in 1974. Most committee chairs after him lacked his ability to lead the committee. Idaho Democrat Frank Church (1979–1981) and Indiana Republican Richard G. Lugar (1985–1987) were widely seen as strong chairs able to restore the committee's influence. For example, Lugar used his position to exercise influence over the policies of the Reagan administration on two important foreign issues: the Philippines, where a popular movement ousted President Ferdinand E. Marcos, and South Africa, where the white minority government continued to deny basic human rights to the nation's black majority. Both Church and Lugar chaired the panel only briefly.

Claiborne Pell, a Democrat from Rhode Island, took over as chair in 1987. Under his leadership the panel continued to lose influence. The problems came partly from Pell's disengaged leadership style, as well as from the tactics of the ranking Republican on the committee, Jesse Helms of North Carolina, a master of parliamentary obstruction. Helms, one of the Senate's most conservative members, often differed not only with the committee's Democratic majority but also with the administration and with more moderate Republicans on the committee. The panel became recognized more for its failure to gain quorums at meetings than as a force in setting foreign policy.

The panel's loss of influence was illustrated by the 1990–1991 debate over the U.S. decision to go to war to end Iraq's occupation of Kuwait. The committee held hearings on the crisis but was even less involved than the House Foreign Affairs Committee in the congressional decision to authorize war against Iraq. The course of that debate was set largely by the Democratic leaders as well as by the chairs of the House and Senate Armed Services committees.

Frustrated by the committee's marginal role in foreign policy debates, committee Democrats, with the quiet backing of a few Republicans, in 1991 developed a plan to strengthen the panel's subcommittees and expedite legislation through the committee. Pell was persuaded to turn over much of his authority to the panel's subcommittee chairs, allowing legislation to be marked up in subcommittee for the first time. As part of the move, the majority staff was enlarged and reorganized along subcommittee lines.

---

## Foreign Travel

Foreign trips by senators and representatives have been one of the most visible and controversial perquisites of serving in Congress. Defenders of foreign travel see it as a valuable way to educate legislators about world problems, particularly when many congressional votes deal with foreign affairs. But critics call the trips junkets—adventures or vacation trips at taxpayers' expense. (See PAY AND PERQUISITES.)

Some legislators are legendary for their traveling, among them Allen J. Ellender, a Democratic senator from Louisiana (1937–1972), and Adam Clayton POWELL, Jr. (1945–1967, 1969–1971), a Democratic representative from New York. Legislators have since learned to be more discreet, but controversy still erupts upon occasion. In 1985 Rep. Bill Alexander, an Arkansas Democrat who served as chief deputy whip, used a military plane at a cost of $50,000 for a solo trip to Brazil; the resulting bad publicity helped end his leadership ambitions.

Most trips are sponsored by congressional committees, but House and Senate leaders receive special travel allowances. In 1988 Jim Wright, a Texas Democrat and House Speaker at the time, caused comment by taking thirteen members and seven staff aides to Australia for a week to celebrate the centennial of that country's parliament. The excursion cost $188,266.

Large delegations also go each year to meetings of the Interparliamentary Union and the North Atlantic Assembly, which bring together U.S. and foreign legislators. Another popular trip is to the Paris Interna-

*Not all foreign trips are the luxurious junkets critics decry. Rep. Mickey Leland, D-Texas, seen here speaking to children, was killed in a 1989 plane crash while on a hunger relief mission in Ethiopia.    Source: Marty LaVor*

tional Air Show, where manufacturers display military hardware and other equipment.

Often congressional delegations travel on military planes, accompanied by Marines or other military escorts who help with baggage and act as flight attendants. Embassy personnel in each city they visit are expected to set up meetings with local officials, arrange tours, and sometimes take the visitors to see night spots. But not all trips are luxury excursions. In 1989, Rep. Mickey Leland, a Texas Democrat, was killed in a plane crash while helping deliver food and supplies to famine-ridden Ethiopia.

Senators and representatives have been required since the 1950s to file accounts of travel spending, but the rules have been rewritten several times since

then. In 1973 Congress voted to stop requiring that travel reports be printed in the CONGRESSIONAL RECORD, but the rule was restored in 1976 after public protest. Under the rules, committees, but not individual members, had to file quarterly travel reports with the CLERK OF THE HOUSE and SECRETARY OF THE SENATE. Although these reports were published in the *Record*, it was virtually impossible to tell the true cost of travel because the reports did not count the true cost of military transportation, for instance.

Reports do not have to be filed on trips funded by the executive branch or by private agencies, but members are required to list private trips on their annual FINANCIAL DISCLOSURE forms. In 1989 Congress declared that members could not accept trips that lasted longer than seven days (excluding travel time) from private interests.

---

## Former Members of Congress

When senators and representatives leave Congress, typically after eight or ten years, their activities are as varied as those they pursued before election. Many return to the practice of law or to business. A few take prestigious posts outside of government. Still others simply retire, living on a congressional pension that can be quite generous. A member with ten years in Congress who retired in 1993 and was part of the Civil Service Retirement System would be eligible for a pension of about $32,000 annually. A member with twenty years' service would get double that. In addition, congressional pensions are automatically adjusted for inflation. Indeed, substantial increases in congressional pensions contributed to the large number of House retirements in 1992. (See PAY AND PERQUISITES.)

Former House members who have found prestigious jobs in the private sector include John Brademas, an Indiana Democrat who was named president of New York University in 1981, and Barber B. Conable, Jr., a New York Republican who became head of the World Bank in 1986. Pennsylvania Democrat William H. Gray III retired from the House in 1991 to become president of the United Negro College Fund, leaving the leadership post of majority whip.

Many members left Congress but stayed in politics. Twenty-seven of the first forty-three presidents served in Congress or its predecessor, the Continental Congress. As of 1993, thirty-five vice presidents had served in the legislative branch.

Some former members of Congress have been appointed to the cabinet or other top posts. After serving in the House and Senate, Albert Gallatin of Pennsylvania became Treasury secretary in 1801, serving for a record thirteen years. Another veteran legislator, John C. CALHOUN of South Carolina, served as secretary of war and secretary of state, as well as vice president, in the pre–Civil War period. Tennessee

Democrat Cordell Hull had spent almost twenty-five years in Congress when he was named secretary of state by Franklin D. Roosevelt in 1933. In the 1980s President Ronald Reagan turned more than once to ex-legislators to staff his cabinet; in the White House itself, Tennessee Republican Howard H. BAKER, Jr., a former Senate majority leader, served as chief of staff.

Some members of Congress have given up congressional seats to accept posts in the executive branch. In the 1840s and 1850s Daniel WEBSTER, a Massachusetts Whig, twice left the Senate to become secretary of state. More recently, Sen. Edmund S. Muskie, a Democrat from Maine, became secretary of state. Stewart Udall, an Arizona Democrat, and Rogers C. B. Morton, a Maryland Republican, each left the House to become interior secretary—Udall in 1961, Morton ten years later. Richard B. Cheney, a Wyoming Republican, left the House in 1989 to become President George Bush's secretary of defense.

Democrat Bill Clinton, elected president in 1992, picked three of his cabinet secretaries from the ranks of Congress. Senate Finance Committee chair Lloyd Bentsen of Texas became Clinton's Treasury secretary; House Armed Services Committee chair Les Aspin of Wisconsin became defense secretary; and Mike Espy of Mississippi, a member of the House Agriculture Committee, became agriculture secretary. Clinton named Leon E. Panetta, chair of the House Budget Committee, as his budget director.

Governors have often been elected to Congress, particularly to the Senate, and the reverse is also true. In the 1980s Louisiana, South Carolina, Maine, and West Virginia were among the states whose governors had previously served in Congress. Republican Henry Bellmon of Oklahoma had an unusual résumé: he served first as governor, then as a senator, and in 1986 he was elected governor again.

Still another career choice for former members has been the judiciary. Although the pattern has been rare since the 1940s, about one-third of all Supreme Court justices had previously served in Congress or the Continental Congress. Other judicial appointments have been more common in recent decades. For example, in 1979 Abner J. Mikva, a Democratic representative from Illinois, accepted a federal judgeship.

Among the most visible former members of Congress are those who stay in Washington as lobbyists, with law firms or organizations whose views they share. They stalk familiar corridors and hearing rooms to win votes from former colleagues—or, in many cases, favorable wording from staff who draft the bills. Although ex-members have lifetime privileges on the House and Senate floors, the House has a rule against LOBBYING on the floor and the practice is frowned on in the Senate. Lobbying is not out of bounds, however, in the Capitol Hill dining rooms and gymnasiums still frequented by ex-members.

Often ex-member lobbyists handle the same issues they concentrated on as legislators. James Abourezk, a South Dakota Democrat, championed the Arab cause in the House and Senate in the 1970s; he later lobbied as chair of the American-Arab Anti-Discrimination Committee. Florida Democrat Paul Rogers became an expert on federal health policy as chair of a key House subcommittee; later, as a Washington lawyer, he was a director of Merck and Co., Inc., a major pharmaceutical manufacturer. Arkansas Democrat J. William FULBRIGHT chaired the Senate Foreign Relations Committee for fifteen years until his 1974 reelection defeat; as a lobbyist he later had clients from Saudi Arabia and Japan, among other countries. Republican Richard S. Schweiker of Pennsylvania served in Reagan's cabinet after he left the Senate in 1981; he then became president of the American Council of Life Insurance.

Several hundred ex-members belong to the U.S. Association of Former Members of Congress. The group, which has a variety of educational programs, hosts a reunion every spring on Capitol Hill. Returning members meet in the House chamber, just before an official session, and have a chance once again to make a speech in the Capitol.

*The franking privilege permits members of Congress to communicate directly with their constituents at government expense. Each member's facsimile signature, or frank, is used in place of a postage stamp.*

## Franking Privilege

Most people receive mail occasionally from their legislators. Instead of a stamp, the envelope may bear the legislator's signature in the upper righthand corner. For senators and representatives this facsimile of their handwriting, called the frank, is an important privilege. It allows them to send newsletters and other mailings to their constituents at government expense. Using the franking privilege, legislators can communicate directly with their constituents to inform them of congressional decisions and pass on useful news about the federal government. In 1988 Congress spent $113 million on its special postage, but new regulations since then have pushed the cost below $100 million.

A franked envelope might contain a legislator's response to a question or request, a copy of a newsletter, a survey, a press release, a packet of voting information, government publications, or other printed matter that in some way relates to the legislator's "official duties." The frank cannot be used to solicit money or votes. Letters related to political campaigns, political parties, or personal business or friendships are not permitted. For example, a legislator cannot use the frank on a holiday greeting, a message of sympathy, an invitation to a party fund-raising event, or a request for political support.

Congress has limited use of the frank in the weeks preceding elections, but the amount of franked mail usually jumps by more than half in election years.

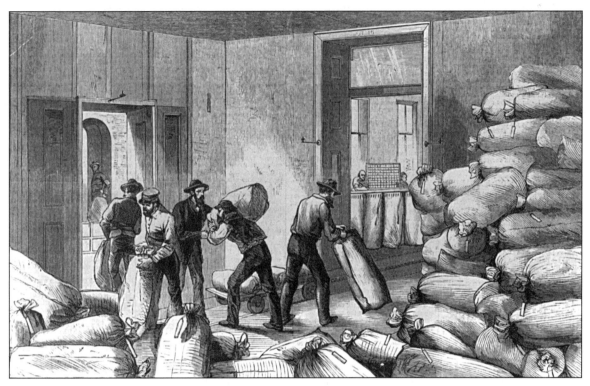

*The concept of the frank goes back to 1775, when the first Continental Congress enacted a law giving its members mailing privileges. In 1990, Congress spent about $15 million a year on its special postage. This 1869 wood engraving shows free bags of mail leaving the Washington, D.C., post office.    Source: Library of Congress*

This has prompted charges from challengers that the privilege is yet another advantage for incumbents.

Those authorized to use the frank include the vice president, members and members-elect of Congress, and certain officers of the House and Senate. Committees and subcommittees send mail under the frank of a committee member.

The concept of the frank is older than Congress itself. The first Continental Congress in 1775 adopted the seventeenth-century British practice of giving its members mailing privileges as a way of keeping constituents fully informed. It was also a way of reminding voters back home between elections that their legislator was thinking of them. A common practice in the nineteenth century was to send home packets of seeds, courtesy of the Agriculture Department. Congress enjoyed the use of the frank almost without re-

striction until 1973, when the first effort at self-policing began.

Although no stamp is needed on a franked letter, such letters are not actually mailed free of charge. The U.S. Postal Service keeps track of how many franked pieces of mail it handles and how much they weigh. At the end of the year the Postal Service sends Congress what amounts to a bill; Congress then transfers the funds to the Postal Service.

The cost of the mailing privilege jumped dramatically in the 1970s and 1980s because of increases in mailing rates and the amount of mail. In 1970 Congress sent 190 million pieces of franked mail at a cost of $11.2 million; by 1988 more than 800 million letters and packages were sent under the frank at a cost of $113 million.

Congress frequently spent more than it appropriated for mailing costs; only after an election would it vote more money to pay the final tab. But concerns about federal budget deficits and political fairness prompted Congress to reduce the flood of mail.

The Senate used improved cost accounting to control its mailings. Beginning in 1986 each senator received a budget showing his or her share of the appropriation for postage, based on population. Each senator also received reports, twice a year, on his or her mass mailings and their cost. Senators were required to disclose how much they had spent.

The power of publicity was demonstrated in 1989, when the Senate temporarily lifted its disclosure requirements. During the first five months of the year, the Senate spent $6 million on official mail; during the rest of the year, with disclosure suspended, mailing costs soared to $29 million. In 1990, once disclosure was again in force, the cost sank to $15 million.

## Advantage to Incumbents

The advantage the frank gives to someone in office running for reelection has been the most controversial aspect of the traditional privilege. The debate intensified after the 1972 election campaign. Several mailings during the campaign were considered improper, since they seemed too much like advertising for members' political campaigns. Twelve cases reached the courts. One case of abuse took place in Georgia. Fletcher Thompson, a Republican representative running for the Senate, used the frank to send mail throughout the state, not just to his congressional district. The mailing, which cost taxpayers more than $200,000, became a campaign issue and a key factor in the representative's loss to Democrat Sam Nunn.

## Restrictions

In response to the abuses and the threat of court intervention, Congress in 1973 passed a new law setting guidelines for use of the frank. These included tighter definitions of the types of mail eligible and a limit on mass mailings (defined as more than 500 pieces of identical mail) during the four weeks before an election, either a primary or a general election. To oversee use of the franking privilege, the House set up a Commission on Congressional Mailing Standards. Later the Senate gave its Ethics Committee a similar responsibility, although its Rules and Administration Committee handles routine administration of the frank.

Additional changes in later years tightened the rules. For example, in 1977 the pre-election cutoff was extended from twenty-eight to sixty days, making it harder to use the frank for political purposes. The growth in franking began to slow down after 1986, when the Senate made members individually and publicly responsible for their own accounts. The House resisted such disclosure until 1990. Disclosure had an effect: In 1992 the House was able to send back to the treasury $20 million of the $80 million it had appropriated for the fiscal year.

Embarrassed by a federal court ruling that the practice was unconstitutional, the House in 1992 changed its rules to stop a particularly blatant form of electioneering: sending newsletters to voters outside a member's district in years when postcensus reapportionment would change the district's boundaries and require the member to face new voters.

---

# Fulbright, J. William

Dean of foreign affairs in the Senate, J. William Fulbright (1905–  ) was a critic of U.S. foreign policy in the decades following World War II. From the beginning of his Senate career, Fulbright advocated the conduct of international relations based on understanding and the exchange of ideas rather than show of force. As chair of the Senate Foreign Relations Committee from 1959 to 1975, Fulbright was at the forefront of Senate opposition to U.S. involvement in Vietnam.

An Arkansas lawyer and educator, Fulbright spent several years as president of the University of Arkansas before entering the House of Representatives as a Democrat in 1943. After one term in the House, he moved to the Senate in 1945 and remained there for thirty years.

In his first year in the House, Fulbright introduced

a resolution advocating the establishment of a postwar organization to maintain world peace. In 1946 he sponsored legislation to establish the educational exchange program that bears his name. In later years Fulbright saw the exchange program as his greatest contribution to international understanding.

In the Senate Fulbright was best known for his opposition to the Vietnam War. He voted for the Gulf of Tonkin resolution in 1964, although he later regretted having done so. The resolution became the primary legal justification for prosecution of the war during the presidency of Lyndon B. Johnson. Fulbright criticized Johnson for his invasion of the Dominican Republic in 1965, and after this incident Fulbright had little influence over Johnson's conduct of the Vietnam War. Fulbright also was an outspoken critic of President Richard Nixon's handling of the war.

In 1973 Congress passed the WAR POWERS resolution, designed to limit the president's power to commit U.S. forces abroad without congressional approval. Fulbright had introduced the forerunner of the measure in 1967 and 1969.

Although liberal on international issues, Fulbright followed the more conservative domestic policies supported by his constituents. He opposed the Supreme Court's 1954 school desegregation decision and voted against the Civil Rights Act of 1964. In the end Fulbright's concentration on international affairs distanced him from his constituents, and he was defeated for reelection in 1974.

# G

## General Accounting Office

Congress has its own agency, the General Accounting Office (GAO), to monitor spending by the executive branch. The largest congressional support agency, GAO has more than 5,000 employees who conduct investigations, perform audits, and offer legal opinions about financial disputes. The office's basic role is to review how the executive branch spends the money Congress appropriates. Individual members of Congress, as well as committees, can ask GAO to investigate specific programs or broad policy questions.

When Congress revamped federal budget making in 1921, two new agencies were set up. The Bureau of the Budget (now the Office of Management and Budget) was to work with the president on proposals for how and where federal funds should be spent. The General Accounting Office, an agency of the legislative branch, was to give Congress an independent review and audit of executive branch expenditures.

During World War II almost 15,000 people worked for the GAO, handling masses of vouchers and routine claims related to the war. In 1950 the GAO was freed from performing regular audits of agencies; the agencies themselves handled the audits, as well as the routine processing of vouchers and claims. As a result, instead of concentrating on details of spending, the GAO was able to review how agencies were managed, with a focus on uncovering waste and fraud. Some people maintain that the office's reports are overly critical; others complain that it waters down its reports to avoid controversy.

### Comptroller General

The comptroller general, who heads the GAO, is appointed by the president and confirmed by the Senate. The comptroller serves a fifteen-year term. Seeking a larger role in filling the position, Congress in 1980 set up a special committee to suggest nominees to the president, though the list would be nonbinding. The sixth head of the office, Charles A. Bowsher, was chosen from the list. Bowsher, who took office in 1981, previously was a partner with the Arthur Andersen accounting firm. The position paid $129,500 annually in 1992.

## Gephardt, Richard A.

Missouri Democrat Richard A. Gephardt (1941– ) was elected House majority leader in 1989, taking over from Thomas S. FOLEY of Washington, who became Speaker of the House. A veteran legislator and party leader with two decades of service in the House, Gephardt took the number-two post in the House Democratic leadership after an unsuccessful bid for his party's 1988 presidential nomination. Like Foley, he was known for his negotiating skills. But Gephardt's aggressive partisanship contrasted with Foley's more detached approach.

Gephardt's consensus-building ability served him well as the House leader responsible for the detail work of moving legislation through the House. Another part of the majority leader's job is to help the Speaker and other party leaders develop and sell their legislative goals within Congress and to the public. Gephardt took on that role with gusto, instituting special morning meetings with other House leaders to plan strategy for getting their message across.

Born in St. Louis, Missouri, Gephardt graduated from Northwestern University in 1962 and received a law degree from the University of Michigan in 1965. He was first elected to Congress in 1974. Gephardt won a seat on the Ways and Means Committee with the help of his mentor Richard BOLLING, who was then dean of the Missouri delegation and chair of the powerful Rules Committee.

Gephardt gave up that seat when he became majority leader, but he kept an ex officio seat on the

*Majority Leader Richard Gephardt speaks to the press during a break in the House Democratic caucus meeting where Persian Gulf legislation was debated.*
Source: R. Michael Jenkins

House Budget Committee. During a long debate over the budget in 1990, Gephardt played a key role in hammering out an agreement between Democrats and Republicans, including Republican president George Bush. When that agreement failed on the House floor, Gephardt led House Democrats in drafting their own proposal.

Gephardt's career has been characterized by political pragmatism. In 1984 he helped found the Democratic Leadership Council, whose goal was to move the party away from its identification with traditional liberal interest groups and toward the center. Yet in 1988 Gephardt ran for president as an angry populist outsider, an approach that helped him win the Iowa Democratic caucuses. The centerpiece of his campaign was a proposal to retaliate against countries that set high barriers to U.S. exports—a "fair trade" amendment that Congress had not been willing to accept. By the time Gephardt sought the presidency he was chair of the House Democratic Caucus, and he gathered scores of endorsements from House colleagues. He kept the pledge he made in 1989 to stay out of the 1992 presidential race.

## Germaneness

*See* AMENDMENTS.

## Gerrymandering

Gerrymandering is the practice of manipulating the shape of legislative districts to benefit a particular politician, political party, or group of voters. The practice is almost as old as the nation. The word was coined in 1812, when the Massachusetts legislature redrew the boundaries of state legislative districts to favor the party of Governor Elbridge Gerry. One of the redrawn districts, it was pointed out, looked like a salamander, a kind of lizard. An artist added a head, wings, and claws to the district map, and a Boston newspaper published the resulting drawing, which it called a "GerryMander."

The oddly shaped district was drawn to encompass most of the state's Federalists. Governor Gerry's strat-

*Gerrymandering is the practice of shaping voting districts to benefit a particular politician, party, or group of voters. It takes its name from a salamander-shaped legislative district created by the Massachusetts legislature under Gov. Elbridge Gerry in 1812.*
*Source: Library of Congress*

egy was to let the Federalists win there and to leave his party, the Anti-Federalists, with the balance of power in all the other districts of the state. The term *gerrymandering* quickly became part of the American political vocabulary, and the practice it describes is still in use. In 1986 the Supreme Court ruled that gerrymanders are subject to federal court review. However, the Court did not rule on the constitutionality of the practice. (See REAPPORTIONMENT AND REDISTRICTING.)

# Governmental Affairs Committee, Senate

The Senate Governmental Affairs Committee is charged with overseeing how the federal government operates. It is able to probe almost every cranny of the bureaucracy. Although it is rarely responsible for ma-

jor legislation, the committee's oversight role is so broad that aggressive senators can use a seat on the Governmental Affairs Committee to pursue almost any matter that interests them, from telling the Defense Department it is a poor shopper to investigating nuclear safety. (See OVERSIGHT POWER.)

The Governmental Affairs Committee looks at the federal government from a different perspective than most. Concerns about personnel management or maintenance of federal buildings cause much of the agenda to appear mundane. But the committee at times focuses on broader trends, such as the government's future role in health care or the effect of increased foreign economic competition.

The committee was established in 1842. It was known as the Committee on Expenditures in Executive Departments until 1952, when it was renamed Government Operations. In 1979 the title was changed to Governmental Affairs. The committee usually operates without much publicity—except for its Permanent Investigations Subcommittee.

Formally created in 1948, the subcommittee grew out of a special committee that then-senator Harry S. TRUMAN convinced the Senate to set up in 1941. The Special Committee to Investigate the National Defense Program, known as the Truman committee, concentrated on uncovering fraud and inefficiency as defense programs multiplied during World War II. The publicity the Missouri Democrat gained on the committee helped him win his party's vice-presidential nomination in 1944. When the Senate in 1948 abolished all special committees, Vermont Republican George Aiken made the Truman committee part of his Committee on Expenditures in Executive Departments, giving it a broader mandate to investigate the management of all government agencies.

Often headed by the chair of the full committee, who has first choice of assignments, Permanent Investigations is considered the most desirable Governmental Affairs subcommittee. In the 1950s it was the setting for the anticommunist INVESTIGATIONS of Joseph R. MCCARTHY. The Wisconsin Republican was chair of both the subcommittee and full committee from 1953 to 1955.

From 1949 until 1972, except during McCarthy's tenure, the full committee was chaired by Democrat

John L. McClellan of Arkansas. McClellan, who was also chair of the investigations subcommittee, initiated highly publicized investigations of organized crime that focused on, among others, the Teamsters Union and its head, Jimmy Hoffa. The panel also probed white-collar crime, including the case of Texan Billy Sol Estes and his paper empire of fertilizer and federal cotton allotments. The subcommittee's chief counsel at that time was Robert F. Kennedy, brother of future president John F. Kennedy. McClellan left the committee in 1972 to become chair of Appropriations.

Other chairs of the Governmental Affairs Committee have included Connecticut Democrat Abraham A. Ribicoff (1975–1981); Delaware Republican William V. Roth, Jr. (1981–1987); and Ohio Democrat John Glenn, who took over the post in 1987. Georgia Democrat Sam Nunn, who had chaired the investigations subcommittee from 1979 to 1981, resumed that post in 1987.

## Government Operations Committee, House

Like its Senate counterpart, the House Government Operations Committee focuses primarily on how the federal government functions. Its sweeping jurisdiction over the entire federal government permits an aggressive chair to pursue almost any issue of interest. But Government Operations is mostly detail-minded, tackling such subjects as computer security and the retirement system for civil servants.

Established in 1816, the committee was originally called the Committee on Expenditures in Executive Departments. Government Operations originates little legislation; most of its bills are written in the Subcommittee on Legislation and National Security. The legislation handled by the committee includes proposals for government reorganization, including new agencies or departments, and intergovernmental relations. Other subcommittees concentrate on investigations, and exposure of waste and fraud is a theme that runs through many reports. The committee has often

focused on procurement—what and how the government buys from private industry.

Long considered a congressional backwater, the Government Operations Committee gained a new image when Texas Democrat Jack Brooks became chair in 1975. Brooks quickly turned it into an aggressive investigatory arm that touched many federal agencies. John Conyers, Jr., a Michigan Democrat, took over the panel in 1989 when Brooks moved to Judiciary. Conyers showed that he intended to keep up the watchdog role. The committee investigated corporate defense-contracting improprieties and allegations of wrongdoing by the Internal Revenue Service.

## Government Printing Office

More than 5,000 people work for the Government Printing Office (GPO), which is one of the largest printing operations in the world. For Congress, the GPO prints, or contracts with commercial companies to print, thousands of publications each year. These publications include bills, public laws, committee re-

*The presses at the Government Printing Office turn out thousands of publications every year.    Source: Government Printing Office*

## Ordering from the Government Printing Office

A wide range of information is provided in government publications. Although many are geared to a small audience and cover extremely technical matters, hundreds of publications are designed for general readers. Government publications are usually reasonably priced, and some are available free of charge. Questions about publications and orders are handled by the Superintendent of Documents, Government Printing Office, Washington, DC 20402 (telephone: 202-783-3238).

The GPO publishes catalogs, including two free publications: U.S. Government Books, which lists about 1,000 best-selling titles, and New Books, a bimonthly list of all GPO publications placed on sale in the previous two months. These catalogs may be ordered from the Superintendent of Documents. Many libraries have in their reference section two other publications: GPO Sales Publications Reference File (PRF), which is on microfiche, and the Monthly Catalog of U.S. Government Publications.

Payment must be received before orders are shipped. Checks or money orders should be made payable to the Superintendent of Documents. MasterCard and Visa are also accepted.

ports, the *CONGRESSIONAL RECORD* and *CONGRESSIONAL DIRECTORY,* legislative calendars, hearing records, and franked envelopes. (*See* FRANKING PRIVILEGE.)

Many books, pamphlets, and reports printed by the GPO may be purchased by the public at the two dozen bookstores it operates throughout the country; they can also be ordered by mail. The GPO also administers the depository library program. Selected libraries throughout the country receive from the GPO copies of important government publications, including those that by law must be made public.

Congress agreed in 1860 to establish the GPO, which has retained the old-fashioned title of public printer for its top official. To set up the printing office, buildings, equipment, and machinery were purchased from Cornelius Wendell, a private printer, for $135,000. A GPO building still stands on the site of the original plant. Oversight of the GPO is handled by the congressional Joint Committee on Printing.

## Gramm-Rudman-Hollings Act

*See* BUDGET PROCESS.

## Great Society

The Great Society is the name given to the sweeping array of social programs proposed by President Lyndon B. JOHNSON and enacted by the Democratic-controlled Congress in the mid-1960s. In his 1964 speech launching the Great Society, Johnson said it rested "on abundance and liberty for all." The Great Society demanded "an end to poverty and racial injustice," but that was "only the beginning."

The Great Society was the most ambitious social agenda advanced by any president since the New Deal era in the 1930s. Great Society programs included medical care for the aged, a historic voting rights law, the first comprehensive plan of federal aid to elementary and secondary education, the War on Poverty, a Model Cities program, and housing, job training, and conservation measures.

Johnson, who became president after John F. Kennedy was assassinated in 1963, opened his War on Poverty in 1964. But most Great Society programs were enacted in 1965, following Johnson's landslide election to a four-year term. By 1966, Johnson's Vietnam War policy had damaged the president's popularity, and Congress became increasingly reluctant to support controversial new domestic programs.

The War on Poverty was the most innovative of

*The Great Society was the most ambitious social agenda advanced by any president since the New Deal era. Here President Johnson signs legislation establishing the Medicare program as former president Harry S. Truman looks on.    Source: AP/Wide World Photos*

Johnson's Great Society initiatives. It was launched under the Economic Opportunity Act of 1964, which established an Office of Economic Opportunity to direct and coordinate a wide variety of new and expanded activities in education, employment, and training. The ten separate programs authorized by the law were designed to make a coordinated attack on the multiple causes of poverty. Together, the programs were to alleviate the combined problems of illiteracy, unemployment, and lack of public services that left one-fifth of the nation's population impoverished, according to the administration's statistics.

Key sections of the law authorized a Job Corps to provide work experience and training for school dropouts, a Neighborhood Youth Corps to employ youths locally, a community action program under which the government would assist a variety of local efforts to combat poverty, an adult education pro-

gram, and Volunteers in Service to America (VISTA), which was billed as a domestic Peace Corps.

The 1964 law was one of the most controversial laws of Johnson's presidency. The poverty program was plagued from the beginning by charges of "boss rule" and rule by the militant poor at the local level, of rioting and excessive costs in the Job Corps, and of excessive salaries in the Office of Economic Opportunity and at local levels.

Such reports, which distressed both conservatives and liberals, eventually led Congress to take a strong stance in molding the program. Republicans made unremitting efforts to abolish the Office of Economic Opportunity, and the agency was finally dismantled during the presidency of Johnson's successor, Republican Richard Nixon. VISTA and the Job Corps continued in the early 1990s.

# H

## Hart, Philip A.

Philip A. Hart of Michigan (1912–1976) entered the Senate in 1959 as one of a class of freshman Democrats destined for prominence. Some, like Eugene McCarthy of Minnesota and Edmund S. Muskie of Maine, ran for president. Another, Robert C. Byrd of West Virginia, became Senate majority leader. Hart distinguished himself in a different way, earning the unofficial title of "conscience of the Senate."

Hart's political views were to the left of the majority, but he was revered for his honesty, fairness, and intellectual depth. A soft-spoken man who did not seek the limelight, Hart worked diligently on the details of legislation and had a talent for making his points without offending those who disagreed. Before he died of cancer in December 1976, at the end of his third term, the Senate voted to name a new office building after him. It was an honor accorded to only two other senators before him, Everett M. DIRKSEN and Richard B. RUSSELL.

Hart played an important role in the framing and passage of major legislation on voting rights, open housing, drug safety, and consumer credit. As chair of the Judiciary Subcommittee on Antitrust and Monopoly, he held extensive hearings on economic concentration, but had difficulty moving legislation because of the opposition of conservatives on the panel. Hart prevailed in 1976 when the subcommittee released, and Congress approved, an antitrust law that authorized the states to bring class-action suits on behalf of citizens.

On the major issues of his time, Hart stood with the liberals. He advocated strict gun control, opposed capital punishment, and refused to join opponents of school busing. He took part in the Democrats' successful efforts to block two of President Richard Nixon's nominees to the Supreme Court: Clement F. Haynsworth, Jr., and G. Harrold Carswell. He fought the controversial antiballistic missile (ABM) system and opposed the war in Vietnam. His wife Jane Hart, an earlier and more militant antiwar activist, was arrested in a demonstration at the Pentagon.

Hart frequently was at odds with Mississippi Democrat James O. Eastland, chair of the Judiciary Committee and a foe of civil rights legislation. Still, Eastland later spoke warmly of Hart and described him as "a man of principle, courage and intellectual honesty." Similar praise came from virtually the entire Senate at the end of Hart's eighteen years there. The Hart Building, opened in 1982 after many delays and revised cost estimates, was the most expensive of the six congressional office buildings, costing close to $140 million.

## Hayden, Carl

Carl Hayden (1877–1972) gave up his job as a county sheriff to become Arizona's first representative in 1912; he was sworn in five days after Arizona became a state. The Arizona Democrat remained in Congress for the next fifty-six years—a record unmatched by any other member of Congress through 1988. (See MEMBERS: SERVICE RECORDS.)

Hayden served fifteen years in the House before moving in 1927 to the Senate, where he served seven six-year terms. When Hayden retired in 1969, at the age of ninety-one, he was president pro tempore of the Senate and chair of the Senate Appropriations Committee, a post he had assumed when he was seventy-eight.

## Hayne, Robert Y.

Almost by accident, Robert Y. Hayne (1791–1839) ended up participating in one of the Senate's most famous debates, the Webster-Hayne debate of 1830. Hayne, then a thirty-nine-year-old senator from South Carolina, spoke boldly for states' rights, arguing that a state could reject a federal law it considered unconstitutional, a concept known as nullification. His chief opponent, Daniel WEBSTER of Massachusetts, said the Union was not a compact of states but a creation of the people. The states, Webster maintained, had no authority to reject a tariff or any other federal law. The debate, which took place over a two-week period, packed the Senate galleries with spectators. Hayne gave a stirring defense of state sovereignty, a key proslavery position, but Webster, with a deep voice and a flair for drama, was more forceful in his defense of federal power over the states. (See STATES AND CONGRESS.)

Hayne had been elected to the Senate in 1823 as a Tariff Democrat, with help from fellow South Carolinian John C. CALHOUN, a leading proponent of nullification. While Hayne was advocating his mentor's position on the Senate floor, Calhoun, then vice president, was presiding. As South Carolina's resistance to high tariffs intensified in 1832, the state legislature named Hayne governor, opening up the Senate seat for Calhoun, whom many considered the more effective statesman. Hayne, though ready to fight any federal troops enforcing the tariff laws, responded favorably to a congressional compromise, which Calhoun had crafted with Henry CLAY.

Before entering the Senate, Hayne served in the South Carolina state legislature and as the state's attorney general. He had only two years as governor; state rules prevented his serving an additional term. In 1834 Hayne became mayor of Charleston. He then devoted his energies to the establishment of a railroad that would link Charleston with the West.

---

## Hispanics in Congress

Like some other underrepresented groups, such as blacks and women, Hispanic Americans won increased representation in Congress in 1992. Among the large freshman class of the 103rd Congress elected in November 1992 were eight new House members of Hispanic descent. That raised the Hispanic membership in the House from eleven to seventeen—a substantial increase but not enough to give Hispanics representation equal to their proportion of the population.

People of Hispanic ancestry with roots in Mexico, Puerto Rico, Cuba, and other Latin American nations numbered 14 million according to the 1980 census: the 1990 census showed a dramatic increase to 22 million. Hispanics accounted for 9 percent of the population but only about 4 percent of the Congress. A variety of explanations were given for this, from the group's ethnic and economic diversity to low voter turnout caused by poverty and the language barrier.

The growth of Hispanic representation in the House was in large part the result of judicial interpretations of the Voting Rights Act requiring that minorities be given maximum opportunity to elect members of their own group to Congress. After the 1990 census, congressional district maps in states with significant Hispanic populations were redrawn with the aim of sending more Hispanics to Congress, a goal accomplished by the 1992 elections. (See REAPPORTIONMENT AND REDISTRICTING.)

Before the new group was elected in 1992, twenty-three Hispanics had served in Congress, one in the Senate only, one in both chambers, and twenty-one in the House only. No Hispanic candidate had been elected to the Senate since 1970, when Joseph Montoya won his second and last term. Dennis Chavez, his fellow Democrat from New Mexico, served in the Senate from 1935 to 1962. (See Appendix.)

Of the seventeen Hispanics elected to the House in 1992, five were from Texas, four from California, two from Florida, two from New York, and one each from Arizona, Illinois, New Jersey, and New Mexico. For Illinois and New Jersey, election of a Hispanic to Congress was a first. Eleven of the newly elected Hispanics were Mexican Americans, three were Cuban Americans, and three were of Puerto Rican descent.

Although Hispanic members had formed a Congressional Hispanic Caucus, they did not always agree on issues. Fourteen of the Hispanics elected in 1992 were Democrats, and three were Republicans. Among the group were eight freshmen and two veteran Texas

Democrats who had attained leadership positions in the House: Henry Gonzalez, chair of the Banking, Housing and Urban Affairs Committee since 1989, and E. "Kika" de la Garza, chair of the House Agriculture Committee since 1981.

In addition to the seventeen voting members elected to the House in 1992, there were two Hispanics in nonvoting seats: Carlos Romero-Barcelo, the resident commissioner from Puerto Rico, and Ron de Lugo, delegate from the Virgin Islands. Both were Democrats. (See DELEGATES.)

The first Hispanic to serve in Congress was Romualdo Pacheco, a California Republican, who entered the House in 1877. After he retired in 1883, there was no Hispanic representation in Congress until Ladislas Lazaro, a Louisiana Democrat, entered the House in 1913.

## Historic Milestones

The history of Congress is studded with events that have helped to shape the legislative branch and define its relations with the nation as a whole. Some of these milestones in congressional history are listed here.

**1787** Delegates to the Constitutional Convention agree to establish a national legislature consisting of two chambers: a HOUSE OF REPRESENTATIVES to be chosen by direct popular vote, and a SENATE to be chosen by the state legislatures. Under the terms of the "Great Compromise" between the large and small states, representation in the House is to be proportional to a state's population; in the Senate each state will have two votes.

**1789** The First Congress is scheduled to convene on March 4 in New York City's Federal Hall. The House does not muster a quorum to do business until April 1, and the Senate, until April 6. Congress continues to meet in New York until August 1790. President George Washington appears twice in the Senate to consult about an Indian treaty. His presence during Senate proceedings creates such tension that later presidents never participate directly in congressional floor proceedings.

**1790** Congress moves to Philadelphia, where it meets in Congress Hall from December 1790 to May 1800.

**1800** Congress formally convenes in Washington, D.C., on November 17. Both houses meet in the north wing of the Capitol, the only part of the building that has been completed.

**1801** In its first use of contingent election procedures established by the Constitution, the House of

*The signing of the Constitution on September 17, 1787.*
Source: Library of Congress

Representatives chooses Thomas Jefferson as president. The election is thrown into the House when Democratic-Republican electors inadvertently cast equal numbers of votes for Jefferson and Aaron Burr, their candidates for president and vice president, respectively. The Twelfth Amendment to the Constitution, requiring separate votes for president and vice president, will be ratified in time for the next presidential election in 1804. (See ELECTING THE PRESIDENT; CONSTITUTIONAL AMENDMENTS.)

**1803** The Supreme Court, in the case of *Marbury v. Madison,* establishes its right of judicial review over legislation passed by Congress.

**1812** Using its WAR POWERS for the first time, Congress declares war against Great Britain, which has seized U.S. ships and impressed American sailors.

**1814** British troops raid Washington on August 24, setting fire to the CAPITOL BUILDING, the WHITE HOUSE, and other buildings. Congress meets in makeshift quarters until it can return to the Capitol in December 1819.

**1820** House Speaker Henry CLAY negotiates settlement of a bitter sectional dispute over the extension of slavery. Known as the Missouri Compromise, Clay's plan preserves the balance between slave and free states and bars slavery in any future state north of 36°30' north latitude.

**1825** The House settles the 1824 presidential election when none of the four major contenders for the office receives a majority of the electoral vote. Although Andrew Jackson leads in both the popular and the electoral vote, the House elects John Quincy ADAMS on the first ballot.

**1830** The doctrine of nullification sparks one of the most famous debates in Senate history. As articulated by Vice President John C. CALHOUN of South Carolina, the doctrine asserts the right of states to nullify federal laws they consider unconstitutional. In a stirring Senate speech, a fellow South Carolinian, Sen. Robert Y. HAYNE, defends the doctrine and urges the West to ally with the South against the North. Massachusetts Whig Daniel WEBSTER responds with a passionate plea for preservation of the Union.

**1834** The Senate adopts a resolution censuring President Andrew Jackson for his removal of deposits from the Bank of the United States and his refusal to hand over communications to his cabinet on that issue. (The censure resolution is expunged from the Senate *Journal* in 1837 after Jacksonian Democrats gain control of the Senate.)

**1846** The House passes the Wilmot Proviso, which would bar slavery in territories to be acquired from Mexico in settlement of the Mexican War. Southerners, led by Calhoun, defeat the measure in the Senate. The proviso—named for its sponsor, Rep. David Wilmot of Pennsylvania—deepens the sectional split in Congress over extension of slavery.

**1850** The Compromise of 1850, Clay's final attempt to keep the South from seceding from the Union, brings together Webster, Clay, and Calhoun for their last joint appearance in the Senate. Ill and near death, Calhoun drags himself into the chamber to hear his speech read by a colleague. Clay, in a speech that extends over two days, urges acceptance of his proposals, which exact concessions from both the North and South. The compromise package clears the way for California to be admitted to the Union as a free state, permits residents of the New Mexico and Utah territories to decide in the future on slavery there, abolishes the slave trade in the District of Columbia, and establishes a strong fugitive slave law.

**1854** Congress passes the Kansas-Nebraska Act, repealing the Missouri Compromise of 1820 and permitting settlers in the Kansas and Nebraska territories to decide whether or not they want slavery. Opponents of the new law establish the Republican party. Conflict over slavery in Kansas leads to violence in the territories—and in Congress.

**1856** During debate on the Kansas statehood bill, two South Carolina representatives attack Sen. Charles SUMNER at his desk in the Senate chamber. They beat him so severely that the Massachusetts senator is unable to resume his seat until 1859.

**1858** Abraham Lincoln, Republican candidate for the Senate from Illinois, challenges Sen. Stephen A. DOUGLAS, his Democratic opponent, to a series of debates on the slavery issue. Lincoln loses the election, but his moderate views recommend him for the presidential nomination two years later.

**1859** The Thirty-sixth Congress convenes on December 5, its members inflamed by the execution of abolitionist John Brown only days before. The House

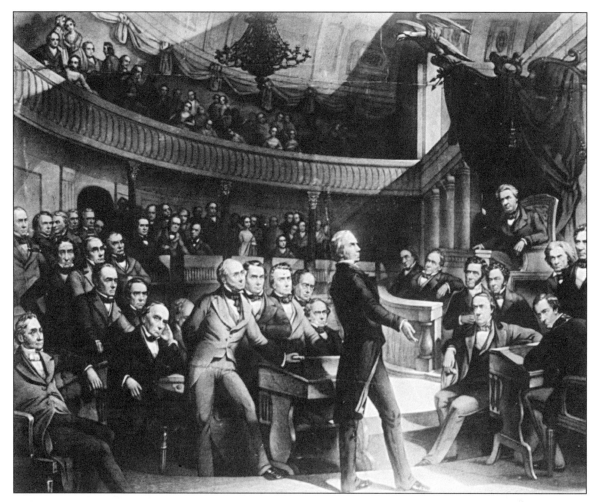

*Henry Clay's last great effort to hold the Union together was known as the Compromise of 1850. Visitors packed the galleries during this debate, which marked the last joint appearance in the Senate of Clay, Daniel Webster, and John C. Calhoun.* Source: Library of Congress

takes two months and forty-four ballots to elect a Speaker; its choice is William Pennington of New Jersey, a new member of the House and a political unknown. The session is marked by verbal duels and threats of secession. Pistols are carried openly in the House and Senate chambers.

**1860** South Carolina secedes from the Union in the wake of Lincoln's election to the presidency. Ten other southern states follow. The Civil War all but eliminates the South from representation in Congress until 1869.

**1861** Congress establishes a Joint Committee on the Conduct of the War. The committee, a vehicle for Radical Republicans opposed to President Lincoln, uses its far-ranging inquiries to criticize Lincoln's conduct of the war.

**1863–1865** The Radicals, opposed to Lincoln's mild policies for postwar Reconstruction of the South, pass a bill placing all Reconstruction authority under the direct control of Congress. Lincoln pocket-vetoes the bill after Congress adjourns in 1864. Radicals issue the Wade-Davis Manifesto, asserting that "the authority of Congress is paramount and must be respected." They put their harsh Reconstruction policies into effect when Andrew Johnson becomes president after Lincoln's assassination in 1865. (See RECONSTRUCTION ERA.)

**1868** The House votes to impeach Johnson for dismissing Secretary of War Edwin M. Stanton in violation of the Tenure of Office Act. In the ensuing Senate trial, Johnson wins acquittal by a one-vote margin. (See JOHNSON IMPEACHMENT TRIAL.)

**1870** The first black members take their seats in Congress, representing newly readmitted southern states. The Mississippi legislature chooses Hiram R. Revels to fill the Senate seat once occupied by Confederate president Jefferson Davis. Joseph H. Rainey of South Carolina and Jefferson F. Long of Georgia enter the House. All are Republicans. (See BLACKS IN CONGRESS.)

**1873** Several prominent members of Congress are implicated in the Crédit Mobilier scandal. A congressional investigating committee clears House Speaker James G. BLAINE, but two other representatives are censured for accepting bribes from Crédit Mobilier of America, a company involved in construction of the transcontinental railroad. (See INVESTIGATIONS.)

**1877** Disputed electoral votes from several states force Congress for the first time to rule on the outcome of a presidential election. Congress determines that Republican Rutherford B. Hayes has been elected president by a one-vote margin over Democrat Samuel J. Tilden. Tilden leads in the popular vote count by more than a quarter of a million votes, but Hayes wins the electoral vote, 185–184. He is sworn into office on March 4.

**1881** The Supreme Court, in the case of *Kilbourn v. Thompson,* for the first time asserts its authority to review the propriety of congressional investigations.

**1890** Republican Speaker Thomas Brackett REED puts an end to Democrats' obstructionist tactics, which have paralyzed the House. The "Reed Rules" are adopted by the House after bitter debate. (See SPEAKER OF THE HOUSE.)

**1910** The House revolts against the autocratic rule of another Speaker, Joseph G. CANNON, and strips him of much of his authority. The power of the Speaker goes into a decline that lasts nearly fifteen years.

**1913** Ratification of the Seventeenth Amendment to the Constitution ends the practice of letting state legislatures elect senators. From now on senators, like representatives, will be chosen by direct popular election. The change is part of the Progressive movement toward more democratic control of government. (See DIRECT ELECTION OF SENATORS.) Also in 1913, President Woodrow Wilson revives the practice of addressing Congress in joint session. The last president to do so was John Adams in 1800.

**1916** Although it will be four more years before women win the franchise, the first woman is elected to Congress: Jeannette RANKIN, a Montana Republican. (See WOMEN IN CONGRESS; WOMEN'S SUFFRAGE.)

**1917** A Senate FILIBUSTER kills the Wilson administration's bill to arm merchant ships in the closing days of the Sixty-fourth Congress. "The Senate of the United States is the only legislative body in the world which cannot act when its majority is ready for action," Wilson rails. "A little group of willful men, representing no opinion but their own, have rendered the great government of the United States helpless and contemptible." The Senate quickly responds by adopting restrictions on debate through a process known as cloture.

**1919** The Senate refuses to ratify the Versailles Treaty ending World War I. Senate opposition is aimed mainly at the Covenant of the League of Nations, which forms an integral part of the treaty. During consideration of the treaty, the Senate uses its cloture rule for the first time to cut off debate.

**1922–1923** A Senate investigation of the TEAPOT DOME oil-leasing scandal exposes bribery and corruption in the administration of President Warren G. Harding. His interior secretary, Albert B. Fall, ultimately is convicted of bribery and sent to prison.

**1933** Franklin D. Roosevelt assumes the presidency in the depths of the Great Depression and promptly calls Congress into special session. In this session, known as the "Hundred Days," lawmakers are asked to pass, almost sight unseen, several emergency economic measures. Roosevelt's NEW DEAL establishes Democrats as the majority party in Congress for most of the next half-century.

**1934** For the first time Congress meets on January 3, as required by the Twentieth Amendment to the Constitution. The amendment, ratified in 1933, also fixes January 20 as the date on which presidential terms will begin every four years; that change will take effect in 1937 at the beginning of Roosevelt's second term.

**1937** Roosevelt calls on Congress to increase the membership of the Supreme Court, setting off a great public uproar. The Court has ruled unconstitutional many New Deal programs, and critics claim the president wants to "pack" the Court with justices who will support his views. The plan eventually dies in the Senate. In the 1938 elections, Roosevelt tries unsuccessfully to "purge" Democratic members of Congress who opposed the plan. (See COURTS AND CONGRESS.)

**1938** The House establishes the Dies Committee, one in a succession of special committees on "un-American activities." The committee is given a broad mandate to investigate subversion. The committee chair, Texas Democrat Martin Dies, is avowedly anti-communist and anti-New Deal.

**1941** The Senate sets up a Special Committee to Investigate the National Defense Program, chaired by Missouri Democrat Harry S. TRUMAN. The committee earns President Roosevelt's gratitude for serving as a "friendly watchdog" over defense spending without embarrassing the president. Truman will become Roosevelt's vice-presidential running mate in 1944 and succeed to the presidency upon Roosevelt's death the following year.

**1946** Congress approves a sweeping legislative reform measure. The most important provisions of the Legislative Reorganization Act of 1946 aim to streamline committee structure, redistribute the congressional workload, and improve staff assistance. Provisions to strengthen congressional review of the federal budget soon prove unworkable and are dropped. A section on regulation of lobbying has little effect. (See REFORM, CONGRESSIONAL.)

**1948** The House Un-American Activities Committee launches an investigation of State Department official Alger Hiss. Its hearings, and Hiss's later conviction for perjury, establish communism as a leading political issue and the committee as an important political force. The case against Hiss is developed by a young member of the committee, California Republican Richard NIXON.

**1953** Sen. Joseph R. MCCARTHY, a Wisconsin Republican, conducts widely publicized national investigations of communism during his two-year reign as chair of the Permanent Investigations Subcommittee of the Senate Government Operations Committee. His investigation of the armed services culminates in the 1954 Army-McCarthy hearings and McCarthy's censure by the Senate that year.

**1957** South Carolina senator Strom Thurmond sets a record for the longest speech in the history of the Senate. During a filibuster on a civil rights bill Thurmond, a Democrat who later switches to the Republican party, speaks for twenty-four hours and eighteen minutes.

**1963** President John F. KENNEDY is assassinated, and Vice President Lyndon B. JOHNSON succeeds him. Johnson is elected president in his own right in 1964. Using political skills he honed as Senate majority leader (1955–1961), Johnson wins congressional approval of a broad array of social programs, which he labels the GREAT SOCIETY. Mounting opposition to his Vietnam War policy leads to his retirement in 1968.

**1964** Congress adopts the Tonkin Gulf Resolution, giving the president broad authority for use of U.S. forces in Southeast Asia. The resolution becomes the primary legal justification for the Johnson administration's prosecution of the Vietnam War. (Congress repeals the resolution in 1970.)

The Supreme Court, in the case of *Wesberry v. Sanders,* rules that congressional districts must be substantially equal in population. Court action is necessary because Congress has failed to act legislatively on behalf of heavily populated but underrepresented areas. (See REAPPORTIONMENT AND REDISTRICTING.)

**1967** The House votes to exclude veteran representative Adam Clayton POWELL, Jr., from sitting in the Ninetieth Congress. Powell, a black Democrat

*These four members, along with others of the House Judiciary Committee, recommended President Richard Nixon's impeachment and removal from office for his role in the Watergate scandal.*
*Source: WETA*

from New York's Harlem district, has been charged with misuse of public funds; he ascribes his downfall to racism. Later, in 1969, the Supreme Court rules that the House improperly excluded Powell, a duly elected representative who met the constitutional requirements for citizenship. Powell is reelected to the House in 1968, but rarely occupies his seat. (See DIS-CIPLINING MEMBERS.)

**1968** New York Democrat Shirley Chisholm is the first black woman to be elected to the House of Representatives. Born in Brooklyn in 1924, she began her career as a nursery school teacher and director, and then headed a child-care center. She was elected to the state Assembly in 1964.

**1970** Congress passes the first substantial reform of congressional procedures since 1946. The Legislative Reorganization Act of 1970 opens Congress to closer public scrutiny and curbs the power of committee chairs. Among other things, the act changes House voting procedures to allow for recorded floor votes on amendments, requires that all recorded committee votes be publicly disclosed, authorizes radio and television coverage of committee hearings, encourages more open committee sessions, and requires commit-

tees to have written rules. (See VOTING IN CONGRESS.)

**1971** Congress passes the Federal Election Campaign Act of 1971, which limits spending for media advertising by candidates for federal office and requires full disclosure of campaign contributions and expenditures. It is the first of three major campaign laws to be enacted during the 1970s; major amendments are enacted in 1974 and 1976. (See CAMPAIGN FINANCING.)

**1973** The Senate establishes a select committee to investigate White House involvement in a break-in the previous year at Democratic National Committee headquarters in the Watergate office building in Washington, D.C. The committee hearings draw a picture of political sabotage that goes far beyond the original break-in. (See WATERGATE SCANDAL.)

In its first use of powers granted by the Twenty-fifth Amendment to the Constitution, Congress confirms President Nixon's nomination of House minority leader Gerald R. FORD to be vice president. Ford succeeds Spiro T. Agnew, who has resigned facing criminal charges.

Congress passes the War Powers Resolution over

Nixon's veto. The resolution restricts the president's powers to commit U.S. forces abroad without congressional approval.

**1974** The House Judiciary Committee recommends Nixon's impeachment and removal from office for his role in the Watergate scandal. Nixon resigns to avoid almost certain removal. Ford succeeds to the presidency; Congress confirms Nelson A. Rockefeller, his choice as vice president. (See JUDICIARY COMMITTEE, HOUSE; NIXON IMPEACHMENT EFFORT.)

Seeking better control over government purse strings, Congress passes the Congressional Budget and Impoundment Control Act. The new law requires legislators to set overall budget levels and then make their individual taxing and spending decisions fit within those levels. (See BUDGET PROCESS.)

**1975** The House Democratic Caucus elects committee chairs for the first time and unseats three incumbent chairs. It thus serves notice that seniority, or length of service, will no longer be the sole factor in selecting chairs. The chairs' defeat is one of the most dramatic manifestations of the reform wave that sweeps Congress in the 1970s. (See SENIORITY SYSTEM.)

**1977** The House and Senate adopt their first formal codes of ETHICS, setting guidelines for members' behavior. Personal finances must be disclosed, income earned outside Congress is restricted, and use of public funds is monitored.

**1979** The House begins live radio and television coverage of its floor proceedings. The Senate will not begin gavel-to-gavel broadcasts until 1986.

**1983** The Supreme Court invalidates the LEGISLATIVE VETO, a device Congress has used for half a century to review and overturn executive branch decisions carrying out laws. In the case of *Immigration and Naturalization Service v. Chadha,* the Court rules that the legislative veto violates the constitutional SEPARATION OF POWERS.

**1987** Senate and House committees hold joint hearings on the IRAN-CONTRA AFFAIR, investigating undercover U.S. arms sales to Iran and the diversion of profits from those sales to "contra" guerrillas in Nicaragua. The committees conclude that President

*House Speaker Jim Wright, standing with other Democratic leaders, talks to reporters about ethics charges made against him. The first Speaker in history to be forced from office at midterm, he resigned and left the House in 1989. Majority Leader Tom Foley, left, succeeded him.    Source: R. Michael Jenkins*

Ronald Reagan allowed a "cabal of zealots" to take over key aspects of U.S. foreign policy.

**1989** House Speaker Jim WRIGHT resigns as speaker, amid questions about the ethics of the Texas Democrat's financial dealings. It is the first time in history that a House Speaker has been forced by scandal to leave the office in the middle of his term.

**1991** A sharply divided Congress votes to authorize the president to go to war against Iraq if that country does not end its occupation of Kuwait. Although this is not a formal declaration of war, it marks

*Carol Moseley-Braun was the first black woman to win a Senate seat. At the 1992 Democratic convention she waves to the audience as other women candidates applaud her.*
Source: R. Michael Jenkins

the first time since World War II that Congress has confronted the issue of sending large numbers of American troops into combat.

**1992** Beset by scandals, legislative gridlock, and public scorn, Congress establishes a Joint Committee on the Organization of Congress to recommend institutional reforms. The committee is patterned after the reform committees of 1946 and 1970. (See HOUSE BANK SCANDAL; ORGANIZATION OF CONGRESS COMMITTEE, JOINT.)

Ratification of a constitutional amendment prohibiting midterm pay raises for members of Congress is completed more than two centuries after the amendment was first proposed. The amendment, proposed by James MADISON, was approved by the First Congress in 1789.

In an election year that ushers in the most diverse freshman class in Senate history, Carol Moseley-Braun is the first black woman elected to the Senate. Moseley-Braun had formerly been a state legislator and the recorder of deeds in Cook County, Illinois. She is one of four women elected to the Senate in 1992, which brought the number of women serving in the Senate to a record total of six. A seventh woman was elected in a special election in June 1993.

### Additional Readings

Byrd, Robert C. T*he Senate 1789–1989: Addresses on the History of the United States Senate*. Washington, D.C.: Government Printing Office, 1988.

Galloway, George. *History of the House of Representatives*. Rev. ed. by Sidney Wise. New York: Thomas Y. Crowell, 1976.

Haynes, George H. *The Senate of the United States: Its History and Practice*. 2 vols. Boston: Houghton Mifflin, 1938.

Josephy, Alvin M., Jr. *On the Hill: A History of the American Congress from 1789 to the Present*. New York: Simon and Schuster, 1980. (Originally published in 1975 under the title *The American Heritage History of the Congress of the United States*.)

## House Administration Committee

Internal operations of the House are handled by the House Administration Committee. Details of committee budgets and decisions about allocating space—housekeeping matters, not the politics of leadership—are the committee's business.

Although committee chairs are usually supreme in their own territory, the House Administration Committee holds a different view. To Administration Com-

mittee members, chairs are an annual parade of sup-
plicants, asking for money to run their committees.
Individual members, too, must deal with the committee, depending on it for office space and allowances,
and approval for various expenditures.

Most spending requests are handled routinely. But
the House Administration Committee has the potential to be both controversial and powerful. Of little
consequence outside the House, the committee looms
large in the world of Capitol Hill. Ohio Democrat
Wayne L. Hays, who chaired the committee from
1971 to 1976, used his authority over money and office space to reward friends and punish enemies. Even
petty matters, such as orders for new telephones,
were reviewed to see whether the request had come
from an ally, or someone who had irritated the prickly
chairman. Hays's empire collapsed after revelations
that he had kept a mistress, Elizabeth Ray, on the
committee payroll; he resigned from the House in
1976.

Although never so manipulative as Hays, New Jersey Democrat Frank Thompson, Jr., also used his authority as chair against those who crossed him.
Thompson was indicted as part of the ABSCAM
SCANDAL, and the scandal was a major factor in his
1980 election defeat.

Frank Annunzio, an Illinois Democrat, chaired the
committee from 1985 to 1991. He also gained a reputation for playing favorites among members. Annunzio was ousted in 1991 partly due to complaints about
his handling of members' requests. Charlie Rose, a
Democrat from North Carolina, became chair in the
102nd Congress, just as the House was rocked with
allegations of wrongdoing at the House bank and post
office. Drug dealing and embezzlement at the House
post office led to a committee investigation, which
was critical of how the bank was run and members'
use of post office employees. (See HOUSE BANK
SCANDAL.)

The Senate counterpart to the House Administration Committee is its Committee on Rules and Administration. The Senate committee also handles legislative matters, such as questions of committee
jurisdiction or floor procedure; in the House, those
matters are in the purview of the Rules Committee.

## House Administrator

The House of Representatives, home to more than
400 legislators and thousands of staff members, has a
variety of support services and amenities available. In
1992 revelations in the press about mismanagement
and abuses of some of these amenities—notably the
House bank and post office—prompted House leaders
to create a new position: a professional administrator
to run their institution in an up-to-date, nonpartisan
style. (See HOUSE BANK SCANDAL.)

The new "director of non-legislative and financial
services" was given responsibility for member and
staff payrolls, the computer system, internal mail, office furnishings and supplies, restaurants, telecommunications, barber and beauty shops, child-care center,
photography office, tour guides, and nonlegislative
functions of the House printing services, recording
studio, and records office.

The position of House postmaster was abolished
along with the scandal-plagued House post office.
(The House bank had been closed earlier.) The re-
sponsibilities of the three other officers in charge of
internal House business—the clerk, the SERGEANT-
AT-ARMS, and the doorkeeper—were scaled back. A
new, bipartisan subcommittee of the HOUSE ADMIN-
ISTRATION COMMITTEE was set up to oversee the
House administrator. (See CLERK OF THE HOUSE;
DOORKEEPER, HOUSE.)

The first person selected to fill the new position
was Leonard P. Wishart III, a retired army lieutenant
general who had run two large bases in Kansas. It was
hoped that Wishart's administrative experience, combined with his status as a nonpartisan outsider, would
bring a new professionalism to the House's internal
operations and help improve its tarnished image.

Traditionally, the party in control of the House has
handed out most of the institution's internal jobs as
rewards for political loyalty, a practice known as PA-
TRONAGE. The House specified that its new administrator was to "hire and fire his or her staff on the basis
of competency and qualifications, not patronage."
When Wishart assumed the position in the fall of
1992, however, less than half of the 600 or so patron-

age jobs in the House had been transferred to his control. The law that created the new position left it up to the House Administration Committee to decide if the new administrator should take on additional responsibilities—an expansion that would further reduce the number of patronage slots left in the House.

## House Bank Scandal

Few if any other congressional abuses of privilege have exploded with the fury of the House of Representatives bank scandal in 1990.

Disclosures that members had written thousands of bad checks without penalty fueled the anti-incumbent mood of the public. Congress's General Accounting Office (GAO) reported that in one year scores of members had kited 8,331 checks, all of them honored by the House bank. Many of the checks were for $1,000 or more.

House Speaker Thomas S. FOLEY, a Democrat of Washington, promptly closed down the bank and launched an investigation. His action, however, did little to calm outraged voters worried about their own bank balances amid a persistent recession. Many vowed revenge at the polls against the check kiters, whose identities were not fully known for more than a year.

### Check-Cashing Service

The so-called House bank was not a true bank but a convenience provided by the SERGEANT-AT-ARMS. Representatives pooled their money by depositing their paychecks. If they were overdrawn, the shortage could be covered by the remaining deposits. The worthless checks thus floated from when they were cashed until they were covered by the writer's next paycheck. Regulated banks would have bounced the checks or provided overdraft protection at extra cost. By honoring the checks, the House bank in effect gave members interest-free loans.

Auditors frowned on the long-standing practice, and in recent years the GAO had urged tighter restrictions. Some warnings were issued, and a few checks were bounced. But most of the reforms affected non-member users, such as journalists, who could cash small checks. Among House members, the problem of floating checks became worse.

After the situation was exposed, Sergeant-at-Arms Jack Russ resigned in March 1992. Full disclosure of the overdrafters' names was made in April 1992, when the House Committee on Standards of Official Conduct, the ethics committee, published the list of 303 current or former members and the number of bad checks each had written. The committee cited twenty-two of those on the list as abusers of the system.

In the 1992 election, overdrafts proved troublesome to incumbents. Of 269 sitting members with overdrafts, 77—one in four—retired or were defeated for reelection. Incumbents with clean bank records did much better, losing only one in six of their number. One of the first casualties in the primaries was Illinois Democrat Charles A. Hayes, who had 716 overdrafts totaling $296,691. The legislator who had written the most overdrafts was Tommy F. Robinson, a Republican who had resigned to run for governor of Arkansas. Publicity over his 996 checks derailed his campaign. The largest single overdraft, $60,625, was made by former majority whip Tony Coelho, a Democrat of California, who resigned in 1989 amid questions about his ethics. (See DISCIPLINING MEMBERS; ETHICS.)

### House Post Office

The bank affair had barely dropped out of the headlines when the House was rocked by another scandal, this one from the members' post office. The affair began as an investigation of embezzling and drug dealing by employees but escalated to possible criminal activity by representatives, including some House leaders.

Operated under contract to the U.S. Postal Service, the House post office had allegedly cashed personal checks in violation of regulations. There were also reports of stamps being bought with campaign money and converted to cash. As the probe was getting under way in March 1992, House Postmaster Robert V. Rota resigned—in the same week as Sergeant-at-

Arms Russ. Rota was replaced by Michael J. Shinay, a career postal manager, and plans were made to shift the five-branch House post office to direct Postal Service control.

Auditors found evidence of sloppiness and shortages under Rota, including an apparent loss of $33,000 to embezzlers. One unlocked vault with keys in it contained $75,000 in money orders. Six employees pleaded guilty to assorted criminal charges. Federal agents tried to determine whether some stamp purchases were in fact sham transactions to get cash from the post office. Members' stamp-buying practices varied widely, from none to tens of thousands of dollars' worth a year. This was a puzzling circumstance because most official mail could be delivered unstamped under the FRANKING PRIVILEGE.

A federal grand jury subpoenaed the postage records of three Democratic members: Dan Rostenkowski of Illinois, and Joe Kolter and Austin J. Murphy of Pennsylvania. A Congressional Quarterly survey of House records from 1986 to 1992 showed that all three were heavy buyers of stamps. Rostenkowski, chair of the Ways and Means Committee, had bought $29,672 worth, more than any other member. Kolter was fourth with $17,374, and Murphy was twenty-fifth with $9,244. The House had reprimanded Murphy in 1987 for misuse of his office. Seeking to avert future scandals and improve the chamber's day-to-day financial management, Speaker Foley obtained approval to create the position of a professional HOUSE ADMINISTRATOR.

## House Manual

The rulebook of the House of Representatives bears a formidable title: *Constitution, Jefferson's Manual, and Rules of the House of Representatives*. It is known informally simply as the House Manual. The House Manual is prepared for each two-year term of Congress by the PARLIAMENTARIAN of the House. In addition to the written rules of the chamber, the document contains the text of the Constitution, portions of *JEFFERSON'S MANUAL*, and the principal rulings and precedents of the House.

## House of Representatives

The 435 members of the House of Representatives share responsibility with the SENATE for writing the nation's laws and overseeing operation of the federal government.

Representatives are elected every two years to represent districts of more than half a million people. Today, they work full time at a job that once took only a few weeks a year. Representatives must attend committee hearings, draft legislation, keep up with floor debate, consider or offer amendments, vote on bills, and respond to constituents' problems. At the same time they must campaign, because a new election is always less than two years away.

The rapid rhythm of House procedures and the hubbub caused by the sheer number of representatives contrast sharply with the slower pace and quieter atmosphere of the Senate. The Senate, with 100 members, is less than one-fourth the size of the House and prefers to operate informally. Senators' six-year terms allow them time between campaigns, a luxury House members do not enjoy.

Maintaining high visibility in their districts and raising campaign funds are part of the routine for most representatives. Most representatives travel home at least every other weekend; travel expenses are usually covered by official allowances. Meanwhile, newsletters are mailed out, letters answered, and individual problems with the federal bureaucracy handled, usually by the representatives' staffs in Washington and in the home district. POLITICAL ACTION COMMITTEES and individuals are asked to contribute campaign funds; the solicitation is often accompanied by an invitation to a cocktail party or a speech by the representative. In 1990 the average House member seeking reelection spent $390,000 on his or her campaign. (See CAMPAIGN FINANCING.)

The House is a complex institution, having 22 standing committees, which have within them 140 subcommittees; decision making is spread broad-

*The House chamber is the setting for the president's annual State of the Union address to a joint session of Congress. Administration officials, justices of the Supreme Court, and other dignitaries also sit in the chamber.*    *Source: Jim Wells Photographers*

ly. The LEADERSHIP controls the key gateways to floor action, but participation is open and usually democratic in the first stages of the LEGISLATIVE PROCESS, when members question witnesses at hearings or debate amendments during bill-drafting sessions. The House has been most effective under strong leaders, who face the difficult task of satisfying a large and diverse body. (See Appendix.)

Two centuries of evolution have given the House thick volumes of rules and procedures, but the insti-

tution is far from rigid. Its decisions can turn in a matter of minutes on what Speaker Sam RAYBURN, a Texas Democrat, called "rolling waves of sentiment." The basic principle in the House is that all points of view should be heard, but that minorities should not be able to block action. Filibusters, which are common in the Senate, are not allowed in the House. The idea of delaying a vote to accommodate a single member, as the Senate sometimes does, is almost unheard of. "Senate rules are tilted toward not doing things,"

# A TYPICAL DAY IN THE HOUSE

A typical day in the House of Representatives might go like this:

• The chaplain delivers the opening prayer.

• The Speaker approves the Journal, the record of the previous day's proceedings. Often a member will demand a roll-call vote on the approval of the Journal.

• At the request of the Speaker, a member comes forward and leads the chamber in reciting the Pledge of Allegiance.

• After some procedural activities—receiving messages from the Senate or the president and granting committees permission to file reports—members are recognized for one-minute speeches on any topic.

• The House then turns to its legislative business. Virtually every major bill is considered under a rule setting guidelines for floor action. The rule is usually approved with little opposition, but the vote may be the first test of a bill's popularity. Those who want a less restrictive rule, so they can offer amendments, often work with opponents of a bill to defeat the rule.

• After the rule is adopted, the House resolves into the Committee of the Whole to consider the bill. The Speaker relinquishes the gavel to a chair, who presides over the committee. The debate time is controlled by the managers of the bill, usually the chair and ranking minority member of the standing committee that has jurisdiction over the measure.

• After time for general debate has expired, amendments that are permitted under the rule can be offered. Debate on the amendments is conducted under a rule that limits each side to five minutes, unless the rule for the bill allows more time, as it usually does for major amendments. Members may obtain additional time by offering pro forma amendments to "strike the last word."

• Voting is usually by voice. Some votes are recorded electronically: members insert a plastic card into one of many voting stations on the House floor and press a button to record a vote of yea, nay, or a present. Their vote is immediately recorded on a big screen on the wall above the Speaker's desk and tabulated, giving a running vote total. Most electronic votes are scheduled for fifteen minutes, though they usually are kept open as long as members are on their way to the chamber.

• After the amending process is complete, the committee "rises," and the chair reports to the Speaker on the actions taken. Acting once again as the House, the members vote on final passage of the bill, sometimes after voting on a motion by opponents to recommit the bill to its committee of origin.

• On many noncontroversial bills, the House leadership wants to speed up action, bypassing the Rules Committee and the Committee of the Whole. It can do that by waiving, or suspending, the rules. Bills under suspension, sometimes as many as a dozen at a time, are usually brought up early in the week. Suspensions cannot be amended. Debate is limited to forty minutes, and then members are asked to vote on whether they want to suspend the rules and pass the bill. A single vote accomplishes both steps. A two-thirds vote is needed to suspend the House rules, making it a gamble sometimes to bring up legislation under suspension. Measures that are even less controversial are placed on the consent calendar or are passed by unanimous consent.

• After the House completes its legislative business, members may speak for up to sixty minutes under special orders. They must reserve the time in advance but may speak on any topic—often to an almost deserted chamber.

said Speaker Jim WRIGHT, also a Texas Democrat, in 1987. "House rules, if you know how to use them, are tilted toward allowing the majority to get its will done." Senators who have been representatives are often frustrated with the slow pace of the Senate and long for the relative orderliness of the House. "Simply to come here and work in a museum is not my idea of a modern legislative process," said South Dakota Democrat Thomas A. Daschle, a senator who had served four terms in the House.

Despite its tight procedures, though, the House often leaves major questions unresolved for years as opposing sides scramble for votes and compromises are drafted. The lack of national consensus on an issue is sure to be reflected in the House. The most difficult choices often are put off, and the last month of a session is a blinding whirl of legislative activity and night meetings. The habit is an old one. Davy Crockett, a legendary frontiersman who served three House terms (1827–1831, 1833–1835), said, "We generally lounge or squabble the greater part of the session, and crowd into a few days of the last term three or four times the business done during as many preceding months." Barber B. Conable, Jr., a New York Republican who served in the House from 1965 to 1985, was untroubled by disorderliness. He enjoyed saying that "Congress is working the way it is supposed to work, which is not very well."

When the pace of voting is particularly frenetic at the end of a session, the House is filled with legislators who mill about, gathering in groups on the floor to talk, or streaming in and out of the chamber into the cloakrooms or nearby hallways. When a vote is close, representatives gather in the well of the chamber, near the rostrum, and watch the electronic voting chart, which displays how each member voted. Like spectators at a horse race, they wait expectantly for any vote switches and react with a collective gasp to any surprises. The Senate, which lacks a tally board, has no such sport.

Although many senators arrive on Capitol Hill as public figures, having served previously as representatives or governors, members of the House face the prospect of anonymity among more than 400 colleagues. New representatives, called freshmen, jockey for spots on favored committees and try to develop expertise on a subject to avoid obscurity and gain credibility in debate. Their ability to act independently is facilitated by their STAFF. Staff help was once reserved for senior members who ran committees, but reforms in the 1970s gave additional staff even to the most junior members. (See REFORM, CONGRESSIONAL.)

Despite its reputation as an open, democratic institution, the House began the 1990s with a new set of concerns. Budget constraints dominated the agenda, and members not on the fiscal committees—Appropriations and Ways and Means—complained that they were left out of major decisions. There was almost no opportunity to initiate new programs. Floor amendments had once offered a way for individuals to influence the committee-driven system of the House. Even this opportunity was limited in the 1980s, as the Democratic leadership convinced the Rules Committee to restrict floor action. "In the retrenchment of the state, power is being concentrated," said California Democrat Vic Fazio in 1986. "There's a certain amount of resentment among members who thought they had achieved power and find it's a blind alley. They are presiding over the dissolution of the empire."

## Origins and Development

The structure of the House was a victory for the more democratic-minded framers of the Constitution. The House "was to be the grand depository of the democratic principles of the government," said George Mason of Virginia. He and his colleagues prevailed over others who wanted state legislatures to elect the House, as they did the Senate until 1913. "The people immediately should have as little to do" with electing the government as possible, argued Roger Sherman of Connecticut, because they lack information "and are constantly liable to be misled."

Although the House and Senate have equal standing on most matters, the Constitution gave each chamber certain duties and responsibilities. The House has three special powers: to originate all revenue bills, to recommend removal of federal officials through the impeachment process, and to elect a

*This drawing captures a nineteenth-century House session packed with visitors.*    Source: *Library of Congress*

president when the electors have failed to do so. (See ELECTING THE PRESIDENT; IMPEACHMENT POWER; PURSE, POWER OF)

Originally the House was a body of just sixty-five legislators, compared with twenty-six in the Senate. In the early years of the nation, the House was seen as more desirable than the Senate. Gradually, however, legislators such as Henry CLAY, John C. CALHOUN, and Daniel WEBSTER shifted to the Senate, cutting what became a well-worn path. The larger, more diverse House could not be easily swayed by an impassioned, eloquent speech. Rules, not orators, had already assumed control.

As early as 1841 the House limited debate, giving each representative an hour to speak on a bill. The rule prevails today, in contrast to the Senate, where a senator's right to speak for as long as he or she wants is curbed only rarely.

The House almost from the start delegated the drafting of bills to committees. At first legislative debate took place on the House floor, and then a select committee was set up to write a specific bill based on floor discussions. The committee would return to the full House with its proposed language for a final vote. Often more than a hundred different select committees would be created in a session. (See COMMITTEE SYSTEM.)

Over time the House established standing committees that had jurisdiction over particular subjects. Among the earliest were the Ways and Means Committee and the Commerce and Manufactures Committee, today called Energy and Commerce. What is now standard House practice began in this period: committee members developed expertise in particular areas and thus gained credibility to back their positions on the House floor. The Rules Committee, set up in 1789 and made a standing committee in 1880, provided further structure to the legislative process. It was responsible for deciding which legislation should reach the floor and what rules should cover floor debate. The Rules Committee usually works with the leadership of the majority party, although it operated independently in the 1940s and 1950s and held up action on an array of liberal programs. (See RULES COMMITTEE, HOUSE.)

### Shifting Power Centers

The center of power in the House has shifted several times during the past two centuries. Strong individuals, such as Henry Clay, Thomas Brackett REED, Joseph G. CANNON, and Sam Rayburn, have used their terms as SPEAKER OF THE HOUSE to consolidate power. At other times the House has been dominated by committee chairs, party caucuses, its Rules Committee, or voting blocs of members. For most of the twentieth century the Democratic party has been in the majority, though it has not always been able to control House action.

The Speaker was the only House officer mentioned in the Constitution, which left undefined the rest of the organizational structure of the House. Only the Speaker is chosen by a formal House vote, though the Speaker is nominated and effectively chosen by the

*Shown here is the rostrum of the House chamber in the U.S. Capitol. On the left the mace, symbol of legislative authority, rests on its pedestal.*    *Source: Architect of the Capitol*

majority party. Each party votes in caucus to elect the majority and minority floor leaders. (See CAUCUSES, PARTY.) The whips, who rank next and are responsible for maintaining party loyalty, are also elected. These officials rank just below the Speaker in the House hierarchy.

The Speaker is usually chosen from among the most senior and loyal party members; since 1925 every Speaker has first served as majority or minority leader. The post of majority leader was formally created in 1899. Before that time the chair of the Ways and Means Committee had been the floor manager and had been considered the deputy leader.

Forging a unified position is a difficult task with 435 members and the array of committees and subcommittees that are the first level of decision making in the House. Each panel competes to have its opin-

ion heard—and its solution selected by the House. Most members serve on as many as six or seven different subcommittees; however, each can chair only one subcommittee.

Legislators also must ultimately answer to the voters in their districts. Although Democrats and Republicans have tried to strengthen party ties by providing campaign funds and other support, ideological differences within each party—and the need to "keep the voters back home happy"—make it difficult to keep the party voting together, particularly on controversial questions.

The House membership, though accustomed to rules, has occasionally revolted when the power structure became too rigid and failed to respond to changing demands. Cannon's autocracy, for example, gave rise to a coalition of Republicans and Democrats who in 1910 reduced the Speaker's powers. Rules changes in the 1970s were prompted by a SENIORITY SYSTEM that had grown more rigid because of the safe seats of conservative southern Democrats. Control of the House rested in the hands of a few elderly men whose ideas about civil rights, conduct of the war in Vietnam, and other major questions were at odds with the views of a growing number of House Democrats.

By the mid-1970s a new generation of legislators, both Democrats and Republicans, had rewritten the rules to make the leadership more accountable to the Democratic Caucus and Republican Conference, the party organizations. The new members of the House, once kept meekly disciplined, suddenly had a voice in picking the leaders.

### Membership

To serve in the House, a representative must have been a U.S. citizen for at least seven years and must be at least twenty-five years old. Members of the House must be residents in the state they represent, but they do not have to live in their particular district. In practice, few legislators need worry about the minimum age, since the average House member is about fifty years old. Most have been citizens since birth. And the overwhelming pattern is for representatives to live in the district they serve.

### Characteristics

In the 103rd Congress (1993–1995) the House was dominated, as it always had been, by middle-aged white men who had a background in law or business and a Christian upbringing. But its membership broadened considerably to include forty-seven women, thirty-eight blacks, and seventeen Hispanics. One hundred ten legislators were new to the House, the largest number of freshmen since 1949. (See BLACKS IN CONGRESS; HISPANICS IN CONGRESS; MEMBERS OF CONGRESS: CHARACTERISTICS; WOMEN IN CONGRESS.)

### Representation

State legislatures redraw the lines of congressional districts every ten years, after the national census, to reflect population increases and shifts. Some states lose seats while others gain, depending on shifts in the national population. Politics plays a major role in the way the new district lines are drawn within each state. (See REAPPORTIONMENT AND REDISTRICTING.)

Under the 1990 census, seven states with small populations were entitled to only one representative each: Alaska, Delaware, Montana, North Dakota, South Dakota, Vermont, and Wyoming. The largest House delegations were those from California (fifty-two representatives), New York (thirty-one), and Texas (thirty).

Until the 1920s the House simply added seats to reflect population increases and to keep states from having the size of their delegations reduced. After a decade of dispute Congress in 1929 agreed to 435 permanent seats, the number reached after the 1910 census. The legislators also voted in 1929 to reapportion the districts after the 1930 census, thus avoiding another lengthy protest from the states losing seats. The 1930 census eventually cost twenty-one states a total of twenty-seven seats in the House. In addition to its full members, the House has five DELEGATES representing the District of Columbia and four islands closely linked to the United States: Puerto Rico, Guam, the Virgin Islands, and American Samoa.

### Incumbency

Although technically it becomes a new body every two years, the House in the mid-twentieth century changed only gradually, with familiar faces retaining the positions they had held for years. The situation contrasted sharply with the mid-nineteenth century. In 1869, 145 of 243 members were new to the House. Most elections after 1949 brought fewer than 80 new members to the House. Turnover of seats averaged around 75 between 1973 and 1983; just 33 new members were seated in 1991. Retirements and defeats caught up with the House in 1993, however, as 110 new members arrived.

Incumbents have a powerful edge in contests for House seats. Roughly three-quarters of all House members routinely win reelection with 60 percent of the vote or more. Since 1946 more than 90 percent of House members seeking reelection have retained their seats. In the 1986 contests, only 8 of the 393 House members who sought reelection were defeated, giving incumbents a success rate of 98 percent. The House leadership makes campaigning easier for members by giving them frequent four-day weekends and scheduling most House business on Tuesdays, Wednesdays, and Thursdays.

#### Additional Readings

Davidson, Roger H., and Oleszek, Walter J. *Congress and Its Members.* 4th ed. Washington, D.C.: CQ Press, 1993.

Fenno, Richard F., Jr. *Home Style: House Members in Their Districts.* Boston: Little, Brown, 1978.

MacNeil, Neil. *Forge of Democracy: The House of Representatives.* New York: David McKay, 1963.

O'Neill, Thomas P., Jr., and William Novak. *Man of the House: The Life and Political Memoirs of Speaker Tip O'Neill.* New York: Random House, 1987.

---

# Humphrey, Hubert H.

The Senate career of Hubert H. Humphrey (1911–1978) spanned four decades, from 1949 until his death. The Minnesota Democrat left the Senate in

*Hubert Humphrey's Senate career spanned four decades. Here he campaigns in the 1968 Democratic presidential race against Richard Nixon.*

the 1960s to serve as vice president and ran unsuccessfully as the 1968 Democratic presidential nominee. But Humphrey ended up back on Capitol Hill in 1971, still the "happy warrior," as enthusiastic and irrepressible as ever.

Perceived as too liberal and garrulous when he first arrived in the Senate, Humphrey eventually became one of the most loved and revered senators in modern history. Many of his original goals, from civil rights to medical care for the elderly, became part of mainstream politics. But Humphrey never achieved his personal dream, to become president. He was never able to overcome his identification with the unpopular war in Vietnam.

Humphrey learned his liberal politics in Minneapolis. He lost his first political race, for mayor of Minneapolis, in 1943, but then won in 1945 and 1947. The mayoral race was nonpartisan, but Humphrey was deeply involved in building the Democrat-Farmer-Labor party. In 1947 and 1948 he and his supporters wrested control of the party from a group of leftists who had ties to the Communist party. Humphrey became his party's nominee for a Senate seat then held by a Republican.

Humphrey made an impression at the Democratic national convention in 1948 with his impassioned plea for a strong civil rights plank in the party platform. "The time has arrived for the Democratic party to get out of the shadow of states' rights and walk forthrightly into the bright sunshine of human rights," he said. When the convention adopted Humphrey's tough stand on civil rights, outraged southern Democrats walked out of the hall.

In the Senate, where southerners held the balance of power, Humphrey began his career at a disadvantage. Nonetheless, by 1961 he was majority whip, the second-ranking party leader. The culmination of his fight for equality came in 1964, when he managed floor action on landmark civil rights legislation. He was in large part responsible for Senate ratification of the 1963 treaty banning some nuclear tests. The 1965 Medicare law built on a concept Humphrey had proposed in one of the first bills he introduced in the Senate.

In 1964 Lyndon B. JOHNSON chose Humphrey as his running mate. For Humphrey the alliance, though successful, proved unhappy. When he made his own bid for the presidency four years later, he was dragged down by his loyalty to Johnson over conduct of the Vietnam War. Still, Humphrey came very close to defeating Richard Nixon, with less than a percentage point of difference in the popular vote. After that defeat, he was out of public office for the first time in more than two decades. He reentered the Senate in 1971.

Humphrey made another run for the presidency in 1972. Still haunted by Vietnam, he lost the Democratic nomination. Back in the Senate, in 1975 he became chair of the Joint Economic Committee, a platform ideally suited to his advocacy of full employment programs. In 1976 he was reelected to the Senate for the last time. Early in 1977 the Senate created a new post, deputy PRESIDENT PRO TEMPORE, to honor Humphrey, now gravely ill with cancer. He died January 13, 1978.

---

## Hunger Committee, House Select

Increased concern about hunger and malnutrition in the United States and in foreign countries prompted the House in 1984 to set up a special hunger committee. Mickey Leland, a Texas Democrat, won bipartisan House support for his proposal and was later named committee chair. When he died in a plane crash in Ethiopia in 1989, Ohio Democrat Tony Hall became chair.

Although quieter than Leland, Hall worked to bring hunger issues to the forefront of congressional debate. In particular, he pushed for greater funding for the Women, Infants and Children (WIC) feeding program.

The Hunger Committee was one of several congressional panels that had to be reauthorized at the beginning of each two-year Congress. However, in 1993 the panel—along with several other select committees—was not reauthorized as Congress attempted to cut legislative costs and simplify the committee structure. It went out of existence on April 1.

The Senate had a special hunger committee from 1968 until 1977, when a reorganization shifted its duties to the Senate Agriculture Committee. George S. McGovern, a South Dakota Democrat, chaired the Senate's hunger committee and used its hearings and studies to build support for the major expansion of federal food programs in the 1970s.

# I

## Immunity, Congressional

The Constitution shields members of Congress from lawsuits or criminal charges that relate to their legislative duties. This congressional immunity, provided by the "speech and debate" clause, was borrowed from British law. Still, questions persist about where to draw the line between official and private acts, and courts have given different interpretations of the extent to which legislators' actions are protected. By shielding lawmakers from retribution for official acts, the framers of the Constitution hoped to guarantee the independence of the legislative branch. They wanted to keep Congress free from executive or judicial scrutiny inappropriate under the SEPARATION OF POWERS. The speech and debate clause states that senators and representatives "shall in all Cases, except Treason, Felony and Breach of the Peace, be privileged from Arrest during their Attendance at the Session of their respective Houses, and in going to and returning from the same; and for any Speech or Debate in either House, they shall not be questioned in any other Place."

### Limits to Immunity

The Constitution appears to give legislators immunity from being arrested while in the Capitol or handling congressional work. But the courts have decided that immunity applies only to arrests for civil, not criminal, matters. This leaves the privilege with limited practical application. Members of Congress are still subject to criminal and civil charges for actions outside of Congress. Their behavior within Congress is monitored by their peers, who have authority to discipline colleagues for any unethical behavior. (See DISCIPLINING MEMBERS; ETHICS.)

In 1992 the possibility arose of an important test case of whether the executive branch can punish a member for an infraction already judged by the ethics committees. A federal judge refused to dismiss a civil suit brought by the Justice Department in 1989 against North Carolina Democrat Charlie Rose for "knowingly and willfully" filing false and incomplete FINANCIAL DISCLOSURE forms. Because the House ethics committee had disciplined him for the violation in 1988, Rose and House leaders contended that the Constitution shielded him from court action. Justice Department lawyers disagreed, saying, "Taking the [House's] argument to its logical conclusion, a congressional investigation of a member of Congress could even be used to immunize a congressman from criminal prosecution. Such a result would be patently unconstitutional."

### Drawing the Line

The speech and debate clause has been controversial because of disputes about how to distinguish between legislative and nonlegislative actions.

As one judge noted, a lawmaker can be immune from legal problems concerning a floor speech but not immune from charges related to circulating a copy of the same speech. The rulings have not always appeared to be consistent. One legislator's bribery conviction was reversed because evidence against him was based on what he had done, as subcommittee chair, to prepare for an investigative hearing. The Supreme Court agreed with him that such activity was shielded by congressional immunity. In another bribery case prosecution continued because the Court found that the actions in question were not part of the legislative process.

Senators and representatives have also used congressional immunity as a shield against civil actions by private citizens. Sen. William Proxmire, a Wisconsin Democrat, was sued for libel in 1975 by a researcher who said his work had been ridiculed by one of Proxmire's Golden Fleece Awards, which claimed to spotlight wasteful government spending. The Supreme Court ruled in 1979 that congressional immunity covered Proxmire's statements on the floor of the Senate, but not his press release or newsletter. The case was eventually settled out of court.

## Impeachment Power

On August 9, 1974, President Richard Nixon relinquished the office to which he had been overwhelmingly reelected less than two years earlier. Nixon's resignation came as the House of Representatives prepared to begin debate on impeaching him. By choosing to become the first president in history to resign, Nixon avoided almost certain impeachment and removal from office on charges arising out of the Watergate scandal. "Our long national nightmare is over," said Nixon's successor, Gerald R. Ford. "Our Constitution works."

The power of impeachment under the Constitution permits Congress to remove officials who are found guilty of grave misconduct. Congress has used that power sparingly. Only seven federal officials, all judges, have been removed from office through the impeachment process in more than two centuries. Others, like President Nixon, resigned voluntarily rather than risk impeachment. Thus the purpose of the impeachment process has been fulfilled, if not in the precise manner the framers of the Constitution envisioned.

The process is similar to an indictment and trial in the criminal court system. First, the House of Representatives approves formal charges, called articles of impeachment, against an official accused of wrongdoing. House members then prosecute the case in a trial held in the Senate chamber. The Senate is judge and jury. The penalty upon conviction is removal from office. There is no appeal.

The two most powerful officials actually impeached by the House were Supreme Court justice Samuel Chase in 1805 and President Andrew Johnson in 1868. Both were acquitted by the Senate after sensational trials. The overwhelming majority of impeachment proceedings have been directed against federal judges. Because they hold lifetime appointments "during good behavior," federal judges cannot be removed by any other means.

### Constitutional Background

The impeachment process outlined in the Constitution had its origins in fourteenth-century England, where Parliament used the procedure to gain authority over the king's advisers. Impeachment was used against ministers and judges whom Parliament believed guilty of breaking the law or carrying out unpopular orders of the king. The king himself was considered incapable of wrongdoing and therefore could not be impeached.

The framers of the U.S. Constitution embraced impeachment "as a method of national inquest into the conduct of public men," in the words of Alexander Hamilton. Details of the process were not settled until the closing days of the Constitutional Convention in 1787, when the delegates determined that "the president, vice president, and all civil officers of the United States" should be subject to impeachment. Conviction was to be followed by "removal from office" and possibly by "disqualification to hold" office in future.

The delegates had difficulty deciding who should try impeachments. They finally agreed to follow the pattern used by Parliament, where charges were brought by the House of Commons and tried before the House of Lords. Thus the House of Representatives was granted sole power to impeach, or charge, a federal official. The Senate was granted sole power to try impeachments.

Another difficult issue involved the definition of impeachable offenses. The language ultimately adopted was "treason, bribery, or other high crimes and misdemeanors," which left many questions unanswered. While treason and bribery have established legal definitions, the meaning of "high crimes and misdemeanors" remains in dispute to this day. As a Republican representative from Michigan, Gerald Ford took a sweeping view. In 1970, during an unsuccessful attempt to impeach Supreme Court justice William O. Douglas, Ford declared, "An impeachable offense is whatever a majority of the House of Representatives considers it to be at a given moment in history."

On one side of the dispute over what constitutes an impeachable offense are the "broad constructionists," who view impeachment as a political weapon.

On the other side are "narrow constructionists," who argue that impeachment is limited to offenses for which a person may be indicted under the criminal code. During President Nixon's impeachment inquiry in 1974, staff members of the House Judiciary Committee argued for a broad interpretation of high crimes and misdemeanors, while the president's attorneys argued for a narrow view. As adopted by the committee, the first article of impeachment charged Nixon with obstruction of justice, a charge falling within the narrow definition of impeachable offenses. The second and third articles reflected the broader definition, charging Nixon with abuse of his presidential powers and contempt of Congress.

## Procedures

In modern practice, impeachment proceedings begin in the House Judiciary Committee, which holds hearings and investigates charges against an accused official. If its investigation supports the charges, the committee draws up articles of impeachment stating the reasons why the official should be removed from office. (See JUDICIARY COMMITTEE, HOUSE.)

A resolution containing the articles of impeachment then goes to the full House of Representatives. The House may approve the committee's recommendations without change, or it may alter or reject them. The accused official is impeached if the House adopts the resolution of impeachment by a simple majority vote. Upon adoption of the impeachment resolution, the House selects several of its members to present the case to the Senate.

The Senate trial resembles a criminal proceeding, with the House managers acting as prosecutors. Senators take a special oath promising to act impartially in the matter. If the president or the vice president is on trial, the Constitution requires the chief justice of the United States to preside. Both sides may present witnesses and evidence; the defendant is allowed counsel, the right to testify in his or her own behalf, and the right of cross-examination.

The Senate votes separately on each article of impeachment; the Constitution requires a two-thirds vote for conviction. If any article receives two-thirds approval, the defendant is convicted. The Senate may also vote to disqualify the convicted person from holding federal office in the future. Only two of the seven convictions have been accompanied by disqualification, which is decided by majority vote.

In addition, the removed officer remains subject to trial in the ordinary courts. As president, Ford granted a pardon to Nixon in 1974, protecting him from possible prosecution in the wake of the impeachment inquiry.

## Notable Cases

Although impeachment proceedings have been launched more than sixty times since 1789, the House has impeached only sixteen officers: one president, one cabinet officer, one senator, and thirteen federal judges. Fifteen cases reached the Senate. Six resulted in acquittal, seven ended in conviction, and two were dismissed before trial because the person impeached left office. One case did not go to the Senate because the accused official had resigned.

### Presidents

The only president before Nixon to face a serious impeachment challenge was Andrew Johnson. In 1868 the House impeached Johnson, and the Senate came within one vote of removing him from office. The JOHNSON IMPEACHMENT TRIAL grew out of a power struggle between Johnson and Radical Republicans in Congress, who opposed his moderate policies toward the South after the Civil War. The president was formally charged with violating the Tenure of Office Act, which required Senate assent for removal of any official appointed through its power of advice and consent. Johnson had fired the secretary of war, a holdover from the Lincoln administration. (See APPOINTMENT POWER.)

In 1974 the House Judiciary Committee recommended that Richard Nixon be impeached for obstruction of justice, abuse of power, and contempt of Congress. The NIXON IMPEACHMENT EFFORT stemmed from a 1972 break-in at Democratic National Committee headquarters in the Watergate complex in Washington, D.C. The break-in was followed by efforts to cover up White House involvement in the burglary. Nixon resigned in the face of almost certain impeachment and conviction.

*Andrew Johnson was the only U.S. president to stand trial in the Senate on impeachment charges. Here Rep. Thaddeus Stevens and, right, Rep. John A. Bingham appear before the Senate to read the charges. Johnson escaped removal from office in 1868 by a single Senate vote.   Source: Library of Congress*

### Judiciary

In 1804 the House impeached Supreme Court Justice Samuel Chase, charging him with partisan behavior on the bench. The Senate trial in 1805 ended in acquittal. Chase, a Federalist, was a victim of attacks on the Supreme Court by Jeffersonian Democrats, who had planned to impeach Chief Justice John Marshall if Chase were convicted.

By the end of 1992 seven judges of lower courts had been impeached by the House and convicted and removed from office by the Senate. The charges ranged from drunkenness to tax fraud and sometimes

were politically motivated. The Senate acquitted three other judges and dismissed charges against a fourth. Federal judges also have been the subject of most of the resolutions and investigations in the House that have failed to result in impeachment.

The three impeachment trials of the 1980s followed a fifty-year period with no judicial impeachments. Judge Harry E. Claiborne of Nevada, convicted by the Senate in 1986, had refused to resign his judgeship even though he was serving a prison sentence for tax fraud. In 1989 the Senate convicted a Florida judge, Alcee L. Hastings, on charges of perjury and bribery. Later the same year Judge Walter L. Nixon, Jr., of Mississippi was convicted by the Senate. He was accused of having lied to a grand jury about his role in trying to win leniency for the indicted son of a business associate.

In those three trials the Senate for the first time used a shortcut procedure authorized in 1935. The shortcut allowed a special twelve-member committee to hear witnesses and gather evidence before the full Senate convened to try the judges. This saved the Senate months of deliberation but resulted in court challenges from the judges, who claimed that their convictions were unconstitutional because the full Senate had not heard the evidence. In 1993 the Supreme Court refused to consider that argument, ruling unanimously in the case of *United States v. Nixon* that the courts could not interfere with the Senate's conduct of impeachment trials because the Constitution gave the Senate "the sole power to try all impeachments."

The Court's ruling was an important affirmation of the Senate's impeachment power, but the unique case of Hastings remained unresolved. Unlike Claiborne and Nixon, Hastings had been impeached and convicted after having been tried and acquitted of criminal charges. In 1992 he made history by winning election to the House as a Democrat from Florida. Hastings's election raised a new constitutional question: whether conviction by the Senate was sufficient to disqualify a person from holding public office, or whether disqualification required a separate Senate vote.

The Constitution states that "judgment in cases of impeachment shall not extend further than to re-

---

### SENATE IMPEACHMENT TRIALS, 1789–1992

Between 1789 and the end of 1992 the Senate sat as a court of impeachment fifteen times, as follows:

| Year | Official | Position | Outcome |
|------|----------|----------|---------|
| 1798–1799 | William Blount | U.S. senator | charges dismissed |
| 1804 | John Pickering | district court judge | removed from office |
| 1805 | Samuel Chase | Supreme Court justice | acquitted |
| 1830–1831 | James H. Peck | district court judge | acquitted |
| 1862 | West H. Humphreys | district court judge | removed from office |
| 1868 | Andrew Johnson | president | acquitted |
| 1876 | William Belknap | secretary of war | acquitted |
| 1905 | Charles Swayne | district court judge | acquitted |
| 1912–1913 | Robert W. Archbald | commerce court judge | removed from office |
| 1926 | George W. English | district court judge | charges dismissed |
| 1933 | Harold Louderback | district court judge | acquitted |
| 1936 | Halsted L. Ritter | district court judge | removed from office |
| 1986 | Harry E. Claiborne | district court judge | removed from office |
| 1989 | Alcee L. Hastings | district court judge | removed from office |
| 1989 | Walter L. Nixon, Jr. | district court judge | removed from office |

NOTE: The House in 1873 adopted a resolution of impeachment against District Judge Mark H. Delahay, but Delahay resigned before articles of impeachment were prepared so there was no Senate action.

---

moval from office, and disqualification to hold and enjoy any office of honor, trust or profit under the United States." In practice the Senate had treated the punishments as distinct and held separate votes on whether to block an impeached official from holding office again. In three of its seven convictions, the Senate had taken separate votes on disqualification from future office and had twice voted to do so. A disqualification vote was not taken for Hastings, and in January 1993 a federal judge rejected a lawsuit claiming that Hastings's Senate conviction disqualified him from holding office. Hastings took his seat with the rest of the 103rd Congress.

### Cabinet

William W. Belknap, President Ulysses S. Grant's fourth secretary of war, is the only cabinet member ever to have been tried by the Senate. He was acquitted in 1876 of bribery charges, largely because senators questioned their authority to try Belknap, who had resigned several months before the trial.

### Congress

The House has impeached only one member of Congress, Sen. William Blount of Tennessee. Blount was impeached in 1797 for having conspired with the British to launch a military expedition intended to conquer Spanish territory for Great Britain. The Senate expelled Blount and later dismissed impeachment charges for lack of jurisdiction.

### Additional Readings

Berger, Raoul. *Impeachment: The Constitutional Problems.* Cambridge, Mass.: Harvard University Press, 1973.

Black, Charles L. *Impeachment: A Handbook.* New Haven, Conn.: Yale University Press, 1974.

Brant, Irving. *Impeachment: Trials and Errors.* New York: Alfred A. Knopf, 1972.

Labovitz, John R. *Presidential Impeachment.* New Haven, Conn.: Yale University Press, 1978.

Smith, Gene. *High Crimes and Misdemeanors: The Impeachment and Trial of Andrew Johnson.* New York: William Morrow, 1976.

# Impoundment of Funds

Presidential refusal to spend money voted by Congress is known as impoundment. The practice has been a thorny issue throughout the nation's history. Although the Constitution gave Congress authority to appropriate federal funds, it left vague whether a president was required to spend the appropriated money or whether he could make independent judgments on the timing and need for spending. (See PURSE, POWER OF.)

Impoundments go back to the administration of Thomas Jefferson, but they became a major dispute only in the late 1960s and 1970s, when Republican president Richard NIXON refused to spend billions of dollars of appropriated funds. Nixon argued that he was withholding the money to combat inflation, but Democrats contended that the president was using impoundment primarily to enforce his own spending priorities in defiance of the will of Congress.

This conflict prompted Congress in 1974 to reassert its control over the federal budget by enacting the Congressional Budget and Impoundment Control Act. In addition to creating the BUDGET PROCESS used thereafter by Congress, the 1974 law established procedures for congressional approval or disapproval of presidential impoundments.

Under this system the president must notify Congress if he intends to cancel spending altogether, a step called a rescission. Rescissions require positive action by Congress. Unless Congress enacts a law approving the rescission within forty-five days, the president must spend the money. In March and April 1992 President George Bush sent four rescission packages—a total of 126 rescissions worth $7.9 billion—to Capitol Hill. Congress responded by passing its own $8.2 billion package of rescissions that ignored many of the cuts recommended by Bush and instead substituted cuts in programs targeted by legislators.

Both presidents Ronald Reagan and Bush called for increased rescission authority through "enhanced rescission" and "expedited rescission" powers. Enhanced rescission authority would allow a request by the president to remain in effect unless Congress rejected it. Expedited rescission authority would ensure timely congressional action on rescission requests.

The original 1974 budget act also permitted the president to delay spending temporarily—called a deferral—unless Congress acted to forbid the delay. Two court decisions in the 1980s restricted the use of deferrals for policy reasons. The Gramm-Rudman amendment to the 1987 debt-limit bill further clarified the matter when it limited the use of deferrals to management issues.

# Indian Affairs Committee, Senate Select

The Indian Affairs Committee was created in 1977 in the midst of a Senate reorganization that was intended to consolidate and eliminate committees, not add new ones. That beginning, against all odds, and the several reauthorizations since then, reflect a recognition within Congress of Native Americans' problems. Legislation related to Indian affairs is referred to the select committee for review, although the panel has no legislative authority. It also conducts studies and holds hearings.

Native Americans have a unique relationship with Congress and the rest of the federal government. Although subject to federal laws and tribal regulations, those living on reservations are covered by state and local laws only when Congress gives its consent, as it has for criminal laws and in many other instances. Indian reservations have a special status under which the federal government acts as trustee.

The primary advocate of establishing the Senate committee in 1977 was Democrat James Abourezk of South Dakota, whose mother was a Native American. After Abourezk left the Senate in 1979, Montana Democrat John Melcher persuaded the Senate to continue the select committee, and Melcher became its chair.

# Intelligence Committees, House and Senate Select

Most of the work of the House and Senate Select Intelligence committees is done in closed session, and even the legislation they report is usually kept secret. These habits reflect their role: oversight of the nation's espionage agencies.

The relationship between Congress and the agencies is uneasy. The intelligence agencies criticize Congress for leaking sensitive information and are wary of any congressional interference. The committees complain that they are not kept informed and insist upon exercising their oversight responsibilities.

Until the special committees were set up, jurisdiction over intelligence operations had been scattered among several committees. Although shared jurisdiction is common on Capitol Hill, it hindered oversight of intelligence activities. When so many people had to be given access to classified information, executive agencies were reluctant to share data with Congress.

Centralizing the reporting in the two intelligence committees did not fully resolve the problem. Critics still claimed that Congress was not careful enough about keeping classified information secret, and the intelligence agencies continued to withhold information from Congress.

The IRAN-CONTRA AFFAIR, which shook the Reagan administration in the 1980s, illustrated the problem. Congress was not fully briefed about the extent of Central Intelligence Agency (CIA) involvement in the "contra" resistance to Nicaragua's Sandinista government, and was not told about secret arms sales to Iran. After Congress banned U.S. aid to the Contras, White House officials orchestrated private donations to them. When questioned by Congress, the officials denied any involvement in illegal aid to the Contras. The administration also kept Congress in the dark for months about the Iranian arms sales and formally notified Congress only after the sales had become public.

Administration officials later argued that they had withheld information from Congress in order to guard against leaks on Capitol Hill. They also complained about Capitol Hill interference in foreign policy. In 1992 former defense secretary Caspar W. Weinberger was indicted on charges of perjury for allegedly having lied to Congress about his knowledge of the affair. Weinberger, however, was pardoned by President George Bush before the case went to trial.

Conflicts over intelligence matters continued in the wake of the Iran-Contra affair, as the intelligence committees pressed for legislation aimed at preventing a similar scandal in the future. Attempts to set a forty-eight-hour limit on how long the president could wait before telling Congress about covert operations ended in a compromise in 1991 that did not include a specific timetable for reporting.

In 1989 a House intelligence subcommittee was refused access to detailed information on the activities of the CIA's inspector general, the agency's internal watchdog who was assigned to root out mismanagement. Congress then established an independent inspector general, subject to Senate confirmation, and mandated that the House and Senate intelligence committees should have access to that official's reports.

Leaders of the intelligence committees in 1992—Sen. David L. Boren and Rep. Dave McCurdy, both Democrats from Oklahoma—launched a high-profile attempt to restructure the nation's multiagency intelligence apparatus for the post–Cold War era. But the Bush administration, on guard against congressional attempts to restructure executive agencies, was cool to the proposals and announced its own overhaul of the CIA and other intelligence operations.

Creation of the two special committees was prompted by revelations in the mid-1970s that intelligence agencies had run illegal covert operations, including plots to assassinate foreign leaders and surveillance of U.S. mail. The disclosures were detailed in news reports and later in investigations by two study committees set up temporarily by the House and Senate. Most notable was the fifteen-month probe headed by Sen. Frank Church, an Idaho Democrat, that chronicled a long list of intelligence abuses. Both the House and Senate decided they needed permanent intelligence committees to monitor how the United States conducted its espionage. The Senate established its permanent panel in 1976.

The House committee, set up on a temporary basis in 1975, had a shaky beginning. Its first chair was replaced after members found out he had not shared inside information about illegal CIA activities. Then in 1976 the House blocked release of the committee's final report in deference to objections from the Ford administration. But the report was leaked and published in the *Village Voice*, a New York City weekly newspaper, prompting an investigation by the House Committee on Standards of Official Conduct. Not until 1977 did the House set up a permanent intelligence committee, and even that was controversial. Republicans argued, without success, that the ratio of nine majority members and four minority members would make the panel too partisan. (By 1992 the House panel had twelve Democrats and seven Republicans.) The first chair was Edward P. Boland, a Massachusetts Democrat, who became a key opponent of undercover U.S. aid to the Contras in Nicaragua.

Membership of the House committee must include a representative from each of several committees: appropriations, armed services, foreign affairs, and judiciary. A member is allowed no more than six years of continuous service on the intelligence committee.

The Senate set up a special committee in 1975 and then voted in 1976 to create a permanent, fifteen-member panel. Like the House, the Senate limits service on the committee, allowing a senator to serve a maximum of eight years. In an effort to create a bipartisan spirit, the post of vice chair is given to a member of the minority party. Membership on the committee must include two members from each of several committees: appropriations, armed services, foreign relations, and judiciary. In 1992 eight Democrats and seven Republicans were serving on the committee.

Although most special or select committees do not handle legislation, the intelligence committees do consider and report legislation. Each year they approve the spending authorization for the intelligence agencies, including the CIA, Defense Intelligence Agency, National Security Agency, intelligence branches of the armed services, and intelligence activities of the Federal Bureau of Investigation. The select committees share with other committees jurisdiction over the intelligence agencies, except for the CIA, but the select committees act first and have primary responsibility.

The Senate committee also handles the confirmation of top intelligence officials, such as the director of central intelligence. (See APPOINTMENT POWER.)

Both intelligence committees had new chairs at the beginning of the 103rd Congress (1993–1995). Boren, whose eight-year term on the Senate committee expired, was succeeded by Dennis DeConcini, a Democrat from Arizona. On the House side, Speaker Thomas S. Foley named Dan Glickman, a Kansas Democrat, to replace McCurdy. The official reason for McCurdy's replacement was that he had been on the committee for nine years, which, although not continuous service, was far longer than the usual six-year term. However, it was well known that McCurdy had been at odds with Foley in the past and, in the wake of the 1992 HOUSE BANK SCANDAL, had considered challenging Foley for the Speakership. Some observers believed Foley had taken the action less out of spite than to better consolidate his powers as Speaker. The move gave the House leadership more control over a committee that was among the few plum assignments handed out by the Speaker.

## Internal Security Subcommittee

*See* INVESTIGATIONS.

## Investigations

Investigations are the eyes and ears of the legislative branch. They test the effectiveness of existing laws and document the need for new legislation. They inquire into the performance of government officials,

*The Senate Caucus Room has been the setting for many of Congress's most spectacular investigative hearings. Here, Sen. Joseph McCarthy in 1954 takes the oath before testifying in the Army-McCarthy hearings.    Source: Wide World Photos*

including members of Congress themselves. They expose waste and corruption in government. They educate the public on great issues of the day.

Investigations have given Congress some of its finest hours, and some of its most deplorable. They have transformed minor politicians into household names and have broken the careers of important officials. Since 1948, television has permitted millions of Americans to witness some of the high drama congressional investigations can generate.

Harry S. TRUMAN and Richard NIXON both gained national fame for their leadership of congressional investigations before they attained the presidency. Truman, a Democratic senator from Missouri, won distinction during World War II for his committee's investigation of the nation's defense program. As a Republican representative from California, Nixon

drew wide attention in 1948 for his zealous investigations of suspected communists in the government.

Soon afterward, Sen. Joseph R. MCCARTHY , a Republican from Wisconsin, captured the spotlight. He skillfully used speeches, press releases, and hearings to accuse—often falsely—many prominent Americans of being communists or communist sympathizers. McCarthy was widely feared, but gradually public sentiment shifted as television cameras displayed his antics during hearings in 1953 and 1954. A Senate inquiry into McCarthy's conduct led to a vote of censure by his colleagues in 1954, ending his political power. (See DISCIPLINING MEMBERS.)

Twenty years later President Nixon was forced from office by the threat of impeachment arising from investigations into the WATERGATE SCANDAL. The House Judiciary Committee recommended his impeachment in the summer of 1974, after a dramatic television debate that helped prepare the nation to accept the resignation of a president it had overwhelmingly reelected less than two years earlier. (See NIXON IMPEACHMENT EFFORT.)

The Senate Select Committee on Presidential Campaign Activities, known as the Watergate Committee, contributed to the impeachment inquiry by exposing the efforts of the Nixon administration to cover up political sabotage and other illegal activities. Sen. Sam J. Ervin, Jr., the North Carolina Democrat who chaired the panel, observed that the power to investigate is a double-edged sword in the hands of Congress. He said, "The congressional investigation can be an instrument of freedom. Or it can be freedom's scourge. A legislative inquiry can serve as the tool to pry open the barriers that hide governmental corruption. It can be the catalyst that spurs Congress and the public to support vital reforms in our nation's laws. Or it can debase our principles, invade the privacy of our citizens, and afford a platform for demagogues and the rankest partisans."

### The Investigative Process

Investigations are not mentioned anywhere in the Constitution, but the Supreme Court has upheld Congress's power to investigate as part of the LEGISLATIVE PROCESS. The Court first asserted its authority to review congressional investigations in the case of *Kilbourn v. Thompson* in 1881.

From the beginning Congress has delegated investigative functions to its committees. A major investigation typically begins when the Senate or House authorizes it, often establishing a temporary committee (known as a select or special committee) to undertake the job. At other times investigations are conducted by the standing committees with jurisdiction over the subject in question.

Following a preliminary inquiry by its staff, the committee holds hearings at which people with knowledge of the matter under investigation are called to testify. At the conclusion of the investigation the committee issues a report summarizing its findings and offering recommendations for future action. Much of the information disclosed in investigations is uncovered during the staff inquiry. The formal hearings, at which witnesses appear, often become dramatic spectacles intended to educate and influence the public through the media, particularly television.

The Senate committee that investigated the Watergate scandal spent several months interviewing people, including scores of Nixon administration officials, before the televised hearings began in May 1973. Similarly, months of spadework preceded the May 1987 opening of joint Senate-House hearings on the IRAN-CONTRA AFFAIR, an investigation of undercover U.S. arms sales to Iran and the diversion of profits from those sales to the "contra" rebels in Nicaragua. Although the House and Senate each established a committee to investigate the affair, leaders of the two committees agreed to merge their investigations and hearings to avoid duplication. That was an unusual procedure for the two houses of Congress, which do not often cooperate on investigations.

Major investigations call for big staffs. At the height of the Watergate investigation, sixty-four professional staff members were working for the committee looking into the scandal. The House Judiciary Committee employed a staff of nearly a hundred, including forty-three attorneys, in its 1974 Nixon impeachment inquiry.

Sometimes people refuse to cooperate with congressional committees that request testimony or demand records and documents. In such cases, legislators can draw upon their SUBPOENA POWER to force compliance. A subpoena is a legal order that requires a person to testify or to produce documents. Those who ignore subpoenas risk being punished for CONTEMPT OF CONGRESS.

Witnesses who appear before a committee may be prosecuted as criminals if they do not tell the truth. Witnesses sometimes avoid testifying by citing the Fifth Amendment to the Constitution, which says a person does not have to be a witness against himself or herself in any criminal case. Witnesses who invoke the Fifth Amendment may be required to testify if they are granted limited immunity from prosecution.

On occasion, government officials either refuse to testify or withhold information by order of the president, citing the president's EXECUTIVE PRIVILEGE to protect sensitive information. Presidents have had considerable success in using executive privilege to refuse demands for information.

Since many congressional investigations target mismanagement or wrongdoing by the administration in power, they tend to have partisan overtones, especially if the House or Senate and the presidency are controlled by different political parties. Partisanship may be the motive for an investigation and can influence how it is conducted. Votes on areas to be investigated, witnesses to be called, and final committee recommendations may divide along party lines.

A House investigation of federal regulatory agencies in 1957–1958 is a case in point. The Democratic chair of the investigating subcommittee insisted that the inquiry was not politically motivated. But its main result was the resignation of White House assistant Sherman Adams, right-hand assistant to Republican president Dwight D. Eisenhower. Adams was accused of having interceded with federal agencies on behalf of a Boston industrialist from whom he had received gifts. Democrats used the Adams affair to embarrass the Republicans on the eve of the 1958 congressional elections.

## Investigative Milestones

Over two centuries Congress has investigated scandals, wars, national security threats, and a host of other topics. Many of the earliest investigations involved charges brought against a senator or representative, but most concerned the civil and military activities of the executive branch.

Between 1880 and World War I (1914–1918) economic and social problems and government operations were the principal fields of investigation. Subversive activities—those aimed at overthrowing the government—emerged as a major investigative concern in the period between the two world wars (1918–1939). They became the dominant concern for the first decade or so after World War II. In later decades headline-making investigations focused on organized crime and abuses of power by government officials and agencies.

### Wartime

The first congressional investigation focused on an Indian massacre of troops sent into the Ohio territory in 1791. A select committee established by the House in 1792 to inquire into the affair absolved Maj. Gen. Arthur St. Clair, the troops' commander, of blame for the disaster. It said the War Department was at fault.

Seventy years later Congress set up its first joint investigating committee in response to another military action, the Civil War. The Joint Committee on the Conduct of the War routinely second-guessed President Abraham Lincoln's military moves and attempted to impose its own military strategy on him.

The committee was controlled by Radical Republicans who were convinced that Lincoln was not acting aggressively enough to secure a Union victory against the southern confederacy. Confederate general Robert E. Lee welcomed the committee's disruption of the northern war effort, observing that the panel was worth about two divisions of Confederate troops.

Aware of the excesses of the Civil War committee, the World War II–era Truman committee, formally titled the Senate Special Committee to Investigate the National Defense Program, scrupulously avoided any attempt to judge military policy or operations. Created early in 1941, the committee worked closely with the executive branch to uncover and reduce wasteful practices in the war mobilization effort. The Truman panel came to be widely regarded as one of the most effective investigating committees in the history of Congress.

### Corruption

Other investigations have dealt with money and favors. Widespread corruption during Ulysses S. Grant's two terms in the White House (1869–1877) sparked numerous congressional investigations. One famous scandal of the time, the Crédit Mobilier affair, tarnished both the legislative and executive branches. The scandal involved wholesale corruption in the construction of the last portion of the transcontinental railroad, which had been completed in 1869 by Crédit Mobilier of America, a company related to the Union Pacific Railroad.

Attempting to head off a legislative inquiry into the affair, Rep. Oakes Ames, a Massachusetts Republican who was a principal shareholder in Crédit Mobilier, arranged to sell $33 million of stock in the company at bargain prices to members of Congress and executive branch officials.

Ames and another House member eventually were censured by the House. Others, including Vice President Schuyler Colfax and Rep. James A. Garfield, were implicated, but no action was taken against them. Garfield, an Ohio Republican, was elected to the presidency in 1880.

Another series of congressional investigations in 1922–1924 uncovered the TEAPOT DOME scandal, which ravaged the administration of President Warren G. Harding. That scandal involved the Interior Department's leasing of naval oil reserves on public lands to private oil companies. The reserves, at Elk Hills, California, and Teapot Dome, Wyoming, were natural deposits of oil that had been set aside for use by the navy. As a result of the investigations Harding's secretary of the interior, Albert B. Fall, served almost a year in prison for accepting a bribe. Two other cabinet members resigned, and other high officials resigned or were fired.

### Finance and Industry

Investigations of American business practices paved the way for several major regulatory laws in the early decades of the twentieth century.

A 1912–1913 House investigation of the "money trust"—the concentration of money and credit in the United States—led to passage of the Federal Reserve Act of 1913, the Clayton Antitrust Act of 1914, and the Federal Trade Commission Act of 1914. A 1932–1934 Senate investigation of the stock exchange and Wall Street financial manipulation paved the way for the banking acts of 1933 and 1935, the Securities Act of 1933, and the Securities Exchange Act of 1934.

The munitions industry was the focus of an investigation by a special Senate committee in 1934–1936. The committee was chaired by Gerald P. Nye, a Progressive Republican from North Dakota. It set out to prove that arms makers were merchants of death who promoted conflicts throughout the world in order to reap enormous profits. The evidence was thin, and the inquiry produced no legislation. Still it established Nye as leader of the movement to curb the arms traffic and as the nation's most eloquent isolationist.

### Subversives

After World War I members of Congress frequently pushed for inquiries into threats to national security posed by groups within the United States that were loyal to other nations. After World War II rising tensions with the Soviet Union raised fears of communist subversion, and investigations of communist activities set the stage for enactment of various antisubversive laws.

In 1938 the House established the Special Committee to Investigate Un-American Activities and Propaganda in the United States. The committee was known popularly as the Dies Committee after its first chair, Rep. Martin Dies, Jr., a Texas Democrat. The committee and its successors weathered nearly four decades of controversy.

In 1945 the Dies Committee was replaced by the House Un-American Activities Committee. Like its predecessor, the new committee carried on a crusade against persons and groups it considered to be subversive. Witnesses who agreed with the committee's activities accused hundreds of citizens of being communists or communist sympathizers. The committee's aggressive style raised concerns about abuse of Congress's investigative powers and the need to safeguard the constitutional rights of those who appeared before or were investigated by the committee.

A remark made to a witness by Rep. J. Parnell Thomas, a New Jersey Republican who was chair of the House Un-American Activities Committee in 1947–1949, was a good indication of the committee's view of its power: "The rights you have are the rights given you by this committee. We will determine what rights you have and what rights you have not got before the committee."

In 1947 the panel trained its sights on the movie industry. Hollywood personalities, including an actor named Ronald Reagan, testified about communist efforts to infiltrate the Screen Actors Guild. It was the year of the Hollywood Ten, mostly screenwriters such as Dalton Trumbo, who defiantly challenged the panel's conduct and later went to jail for contempt of Congress. Nervous studio executives responded with a blacklist of suspected communists, who were barred from Hollywood jobs. The blacklisting practice lingered into the 1950s and beyond.

The Un-American Activities Committee, with Nixon playing a key role, gained the most attention in 1948 with a dramatic confrontation between Alger Hiss, a State Department official, and a man named Whittaker Chambers, who accused Hiss of having been a communist years earlier. While Hiss professed his innocence, Nixon doggedly pursued the matter. He eventually managed to refute Hiss's claim that he did not know Chambers, paving the way for Hiss to be convicted and jailed for perjury.

In the early 1950s the Un-American Activities Committee was overshadowed by Sen. Joseph Mc-Carthy's more flamboyant hunt for communists. But McCarthy's investigation into alleged subversion in the U.S. Army, televised nationwide in 1954, ultimately convinced his Senate colleagues that he had gone too far. The Senate's 1954 vote to censure Mc-Carthy for his tactics ended his crusade, but the Un-American Activities Committee continued its work until the House abolished it in 1975.

### Age of Television

Televised hearings, first used spectacularly by the Un-American Activities Committee in 1948, soon were adopted by other committees as well. Although television exposed witnesses to vast, often damaging, publicity, it enabled ambitious members of Congress to make a name for themselves in national politics.

In 1950–1951 Sen. Estes KEFAUVER, a Tennessee Democrat, used televised hearings by his special investigating committee to spotlight racketeering, drug trafficking, and other organized crime. One of the highlights of the hearings was the appearance before the committee of reputed underworld king Frank Costello. Costello refused to have his face televised, so television audiences viewed only his hands.

The Kefauver hearings were followed by scores of citations for contempt of Congress and many local indictments for criminal activities. In a series of reports the committee claimed that crime syndicates were operating with the connivance and protection of law enforcement officials. Kefauver became a leading presidential candidate after the widely viewed hearings; he was the unsuccessful Democratic nominee for vice president in 1956.

In 1957 another special committee, chaired by Sen. John L. McClellan, an Arkansas Democrat, began investigating shady activities of labor unions. The panel's chief counsel was Robert F. Kennedy, brother of future president John F. Kennedy and himself a future senator and presidential candidate. The committee focused much attention on the Teamsters union and its president, James R. Hoffa, whom it characterized as a national menace running a "hoodlum empire." During the committee's 270 days of hearings, 343 witnesses invoked their Fifth Amendment right against self-incrimination. The inquiry led to the 1959 passage of the Landrum-Griffin Act, a measure designed to fight corruption in union affairs.

### Abuses of Power

The Watergate scandal prompted a 1973–1974 investigation by a Senate select committee that looked into widespread abuses of power by President Nixon and his top aides. The Senate committee was established early in 1973 to investigate White House involvement in a break-in the previous year at Democratic National Committee offices in the Watergate complex in Washington, D.C.

The committee hearings revealed a pattern of political sabotage that went far beyond the original break-in. They also brought to light administration efforts to cover up the affair. The Watergate hearings led to the disclosure of tape recordings of Nixon's White House conversations and revelations of his role in the cover-up. In the summer of 1974 the House Judiciary Committee capped its own investigation by voting articles of impeachment against Nixon. He resigned on August 9, 1974, rather than face a House impeachment vote and probable conviction by the Senate.

Six months later a Senate select committee was established to look into charges of another form of government abuse: activities by the Central Intelligence Agency (CIA) that exceeded its legal authority. The Senate committee conducted a fifteen-month inquiry that confirmed accounts of CIA spying on U.S. citizens, assassination plots against foreign leaders, and other abuses. In the wake of the Senate's CIA investigation, and a parallel one conducted by a House special committee, both chambers created ongoing intelligence committees with oversight jurisdiction over the CIA.

The CIA also figured in 1987 hearings on the Iran-Contra affair. Several witnesses testified that CIA officials had actively participated in a network of aid to the "Contra" guerrillas in Nicaragua at a time when official U.S. assistance was barred by law. The Reagan administration's backing of the Nicaraguan rebels led Democrats to charge that the administration had flouted the will of Congress, endangering the constitutional system of government. In its November 1987 report, a bipartisan majority of the committee faulted the White House for "secrecy, deception, and disdain for the rule of law."

Practices at the Department of Housing and Urban Development (HUD) were the subject of congressional investigations in 1989. Three committees, with a House subcommittee on employment and housing in the lead, uncovered evidence of influence peddling and political favoritism within the agency during the Reagan administration.

Perhaps the most difficult investigations for Congress are those that involve abuses of power by its own members. In the early 1990s, the Senate took on the painful task of investigating five of its own members for actions that at least appeared unethical. After more than a year of investigation and two months of televised hearings, one senator was harshly rebuked and four others reprimanded for their actions on behalf of Charles H. Keating, Jr., the powerful owner of a thrift and real estate empire. (See KEATING FIVE SCANDAL.)

### Additional Readings

Hamilton, James. *The Power to Probe: A Study of Congressional Investigations.* New York: Random House, 1976.

McGeary, M. Nelson. *The Development of Congressional Investigative Power.* New York: Octagon Books, 1966.

Schlesinger, Arthur M., Jr., and Roger Burns, eds. *Congress Investigates: A Documentary History, 1792–1974.* 5 vols. New York: Bowker, 1975.

---

## Iran-Contra Affair

The ongoing debate over Congress's proper role in foreign policy was rekindled in 1986 with the startling revelation of secret U.S. arms sales to Iran. Iran was considered an enemy nation after it held Americans hostage for more than a year beginning in 1979. Moreover, some of the profits from those sales had been diverted to U.S.-backed "Contra" rebels fighting the Sandinista government in Nicaragua. Congress had been kept in the dark about the arms sales and had banned U.S. aid to the Contras.

The disclosures triggered several investigations and curtailed the political effectiveness of a very popular president, Ronald Reagan.

A lengthy probe by an independent counsel resulted in the indictment and conviction of several key participants in the Iran-Contra affair, including former White House aides. Although some of these convictions were overturned, the independent counsel pursued his investigation. In 1992 the scandal jumped back into the headlines with the indictment of Caspar W. Weinberger, Reagan's former secretary of defense for, in part, allegedly lying to Congress. But late in the year President George Bush pardoned Weinberger and five others who had been accused of withholding information or of lying to Congress about the Iran-Contra affair.

### What Happened

Following the trails that brought two countries on opposite sides of the globe—Nicaragua and Iran—together in a U.S. foreign policy scandal was not an easy task for investigators or the American public. A bewildering array of charges, allegations, and facts emerged.

## Contra Aid

U.S. involvement with the Nicaraguan Contras began in the early 1980s when the Reagan administration authorized the Central Intelligence Agency (CIA) to form a paramilitary force to harass the leftist Sandinista government of Nicaragua. The amount of aid provided to the Contra force grew, but in late 1982 a skeptical Congress restricted and ultimately cut off U.S. aid through a series of "Boland amendments," named after Rep. Edward P. Boland, a Massachusetts Democrat who was then chair of the House Intelligence Committee.

As it became clear in 1984 that Congress would block further assistance for the Contras, an alternative network of aid was developed, under the direction of an aide to the president's National Security Council (NSC), Lt. Col. Oliver L. North. North raised funds for the Contras from wealthy Americans, while other members of the administration solicited money from foreign allies. North, apparently working closely with CIA director William J. Casey, provided the Contras with intelligence information and advice on military tactics. He also arranged for the Contras to buy covert shipments of arms. Although providing regular CIA aid was illegal, CIA agents cooperated unofficially with North's private aid network.

When questions about North's activities were raised on Capitol Hill, North's bosses—national security adviser Robert C. McFarlane and his successor, Vice Admiral John M. Poindexter— insisted that the administration was complying with the Boland amendment. North and Poindexter later contended to investigators that the Boland amendment barred involvement with the Contras only by the U.S. intelligence agencies, not by the NSC staff.

In early 1986 the Contra operation crossed paths with another covert operation, arms sales to Iran. Some of the profits from the Iranian sales were used to help finance the Contra-aid network.

## Iran Initiative

Despite a U.S. policy against arms sales to Iran and deep enmity between the United States and the militant Iranian government, the Reagan administration in 1985 approved Israeli sales of U.S. arms to Iran. In 1986 the United States began selling arms directly to Iran. The sales were intended to help win, through Iranian intercession, the release of American hostages kidnapped in war-torn Lebanon by pro-Iranian groups.

In December 1985 Reagan signed a "finding" retroactively authorizing CIA participation in a November 1985 arms sale. In January 1986 he signed another finding, which authorized direct arms sales and contained an important and unusual provision directing that Congress not be told about it. Reagan allowed ten months to pass before he formally notified Congress, and he did so only after his secret was published in a Beirut magazine.

Congressional investigators were later told that about $3.5 million was diverted to the Contras out of the profits from the Iranian arms sales.

## Investigations

When the Iran-Contra story broke in November 1986, investigators scrambled to find out what had happened. Conflicting recollections, contradictory statements from the White House, sloppy record keeping, a misleading chronology prepared by key participants, destruction and alteration of documents, and the illness and death of former CIA director Casey complicated their job.

An inquiry into the Iranian arms sales was made by Attorney General Edwin Meese III. Although much criticized for its investigative techniques, Meese's inquiry uncovered a memo from North that mentioned the diversion of funds to the Contras. In the aftermath of that revelation, North was fired and Poindexter resigned.

Reagan then appointed a prestigious review board, headed by former senator John Tower, a Texas Republican. Other board members were former senator and secretary of state Edmund S. Muskie, a Maine Democrat, and former national security adviser and retired lieutenant general Brent Scowcroft, who later served as President Bush's national security adviser. The Tower commission served up a damning indictment of failures by Reagan and his aides throughout the events of the Iran-Contra affair. The board criticized the president's inattention to detail, euphemistically described as his "management style," and the

White House staff's failure to take compensating steps. It said the administration should adhere to existing structures and procedures instead of creating ad hoc means of carrying out foreign policy and should be more responsive to congressional concerns.

Congress launched its own investigations. The House and Senate Intelligence committees and the House Foreign Affairs Committee held hearings. Each chamber also appointed a select investigating committee. Those committees were headed by Sen. Daniel K. Inouye of Hawaii and Rep. Lee H. Hamilton of Indiana, both Democrats.

In a strongly worded report released in late 1987, the bipartisan majority of the select committees found that the failures of the affair stemmed from White House "secrecy, deception, and disdain for the rule of law." The committees found a pervasive willingness by administration officials to use any means, legal or illegal, to accomplish the president's policy objectives. The majority charged that the administration had "violated," "disregarded," or "abused" a series of laws and executive orders.

The majority devoted a chapter of its report to a defense of the proposition that Congress and the executive branch share power over foreign policy. North and Poindexter had bluntly told the committees that Congress should stay out of foreign policy, and even Secretary of State George P. Shultz, who was considered to be one of the Reagan officials most sensitive to congressional sentiment, had complained about congressional interference in the conduct of diplomacy. (See EXECUTIVE BRANCH AND CONGRESS.)

A Republican minority of the two committees issued a heated rebuttal to the report, acknowledging that Reagan had made mistakes but claiming that most of the fault rested with Congress for interfering with the president's policies.

## Independent Counsel

Shortly after the scandal broke, the Reagan administration, under political pressure, requested appointment of an independent counsel, or special prosecutor. Retired federal judge Lawrence E. Walsh, an Oklahoma Republican, was selected.

Walsh's lengthy probe resulted in indictments of Iran-Contra participants both within and outside of

*Former White House aide Lt. Col. Oliver North is sworn in by Sen. Daniel Inouye, a Democrat from Hawaii, during the 1987 Iran-Contra hearings. Inouye and other members of the House and Senate committees questioned North and others about their role in the scandal.    Source: AP/Wide World Photos*

government, but his efforts in the major cases ultimately proved unsuccessful. North and Poindexter were tried and convicted of felony charges, but their convictions were overturned on the grounds that their trials might have been tainted by their earlier immunized testimony before Congress.

Among other participants convicted in the Iran-Contra scandal were McFarlane, former assistant secretary of state Elliott Abrams, and former CIA official Alan D. Fiers, Jr., all of whom pleaded guilty to charges of withholding information from Congress. A federal jury found former high-ranking CIA official

Clair E. George guilty of perjury and of having made a false statement to Congress about the Iran-Contra scandal.

Former secretary of defense Weinberger was indicted in June 1992 on charges of having lied to Congress and having concealed the existence of his personal notes that detailed the Reagan administration's decision to approve arms sales to Iran. A second indictment against Weinberger, which replaced one that had been dismissed earlier, was obtained in late October. The new indictment was for having made false statements regarding his documents on the Iran-Contra affair.

The indictment contained a previously unreleased note by Weinberger, which indicated that then-vice president Bush was aware of Reagan's arms-for-hostages policy and of opposition to that policy within the administration. This cast new doubt on Bush's assertions that as vice president he had been "out of the loop" during the dealings with Iran. Some Republicans charged that the timing of the indictment—on October 30, just days before the presidential election—was politically motivated and called for an investigation by an independent counsel. The Justice Department rejected that request. The second indictment was eventually thrown out because the five-year statute of limitations had run out. Weinberger's trial on the other charges was scheduled for early 1993.

On Christmas Eve, just a few weeks before leaving office, Bush pardoned Weinberger, along with McFarlane, Abrams, George, Fiers, and Duane R. Clarridge, another former senior CIA official who was awaiting trial. Bush explained the pardons by saying the men were all "patriots" who had given the nation years of public service and had not profited from their involvement in the scandal. He said the prosecutions of the six represented not law enforcement but "the criminalization of policy differences."

The surprise reprieve brought swift condemnations from several key Democrats in Congress, as well as from the independent counsel. Walsh said Bush's action improperly set some former administration officials above the law and constituted a "cover-up" of misdeeds.

# J

## Jefferson's Manual

The Senate's first compilation of procedures was prepared by Thomas Jefferson for his own guidance when he was president of the Senate in the years of his vice presidency (1797–1801). Known as *Jefferson's Manual of Parliamentary Practice,* the work reflected English parliamentary practice of his day. *Jefferson's Manual* was adopted in part by the House of Representatives in 1837 and remains the foundation for many practices in the modern Senate and House. (See HOUSE MANUAL; SENATE MANUAL.)

## Johnson, Hiram

Hiram Johnson (1866–1945), a California Republican, was an isolationist leader in the Senate in the period of World Wars I and II. Before entering the Senate in 1917, Johnson served six years as a reform governor of California. He was Theodore Roosevelt's running mate on the unsuccessful Progressive (Bull Moose) ticket in 1912. In the Senate, Johnson worked to block U.S. participation in the League of Nations and the World Court following World War I. He opposed U.S. participation in World War II and the United Nations Charter in 1945.

## Johnson, Lyndon B.

Schooled in politics on Capitol Hill, Texas Democrat Lyndon B. Johnson (1908–1973) used that expertise when he became president in 1963. He built a working relationship with Congress considered the best of any president in modern times.

As Senate Democratic leader in the 1950s, John-son transformed the job into a powerful, prestigious post. When he became president, he was able to win congressional support for civil rights and for GREAT SOCIETY programs on health, education, and welfare that were more sweeping than any since the New Deal. Eventually, however, Johnson's conduct of the war in Vietnam strained his ties with Congress and split the Democratic party. Although he was expected to seek a second full term as president, Johnson announced in March 1968 that he would not be a candidate.

Johnson first came to Washington in December 1931 to work for a House member from his home state. When a Texas representative died in 1937, Johnson won a special election to fill the vacancy. But he was impatient with the slow pace of the House, where power accrued gradually through the SENIORITY SYSTEM. When a Texas senator died in 1941 Johnson, then thirty-two, ran in a special election to fill the seat. He lost narrowly, despite support from President Franklin D. Roosevelt.

He succeeded on his second try in 1948, winning the primary by a margin of eighty-seven votes—and earning the nickname "Landslide Lyndon." Johnson's experience on the House Naval Affairs Committee helped win him a seat on the Senate Armed Services Committee, then chaired by Georgia Democrat Richard B. RUSSELL. One of the most powerful members of the Senate, Russell led a coalition of Republicans and southern Democrats known as the CONSERVATIVE COALITION. Johnson was friendly with Russell, but he avoided a close alignment with the southern bloc. This decision later made it possible for him to work with both southern and northern Democrats.

An ambitious man who worked hard, Johnson also benefited from a void in the top Democratic leadership ranks caused by election losses. In 1950 both the Democratic floor leader and whip were defeated.

*President Lyndon B. Johnson shakes hands with enthusiastic supporters in 1964.*    Source: *Lyndon B. Johnson Library*

Johnson was still a freshman senator, but with Russell's support he was elected whip. He was elected minority floor leader in 1952, when the top post again fell vacant after an election that also cost the Democrats their majority in Congress. In 1954 the Democrats regained control of the Senate, and Johnson was elected majority leader, a job that had not tempted more senior colleagues away from their committee chairmanships.

Johnson had long been adept at building a network of loyal supporters. With committee assignments, campaign contributions, and a variety of other favors at his disposal, the new majority leader wove a tapestry of alliances with his colleagues. Johnson also had an extraordinary ability to persuade others, in one-on-one encounters, through sheer force of will. The "Johnson treatment" became famous. To make a convert he might urge, threaten, beg, or cajole. "The

only power available to the leader is the power of persuasion," he once said. "There is no patronage; no power to discipline; no authority to fire senators like a president can fire members of his cabinet."

Johnson was often described as crude and sometimes as cruel, but even his detractors had to acknowledge his talent for Senate leadership. As minority leader he worked to maintain amicable relations between President Dwight D. Eisenhower and Senate Democrats. He convinced the Democratic caucus in 1953 to give each senator, regardless of seniority, a seat on a major committee. This move, known as the "Johnson rule," presaged the congressional reform of the 1970s. In 1957 Johnson engineered passage of the first civil rights bill since Reconstruction. A testimony to Johnson's skill as majority leader, it passed without a filibuster and without causing a rift in the Democratic party.

Building on his eight years of success as majority leader, Johnson ran for the presidency in 1960. After an intense battle for the Democratic nomination, he surprised many by agreeing to run for vice president on a ticket headed by John F. KENNEDY. Like other vice presidents, Johnson was never comfortable in the role. He also differed markedly in style and background from Kennedy and his top aides.

Kennedy's assassination on November 22, 1963, elevated Johnson to the presidency. In 1964 he won election to a full term in a landslide victory over Barry Goldwater. Johnson took advantage of an overwhelmingly Democratic Congress to complete action on Kennedy's legislative program and then to win passage of his own Great Society bills. Of the supportive Congress he remarked that it "could be better, but not this side of heaven." Johnson still suffered, however, from the feeling that he remained in Kennedy's shadow. "They say Jack Kennedy had style, but I'm the one who's got the bills passed," Johnson told a group of senators in 1966.

Johnson's good relationship with Congress did not last. The 1966 midterm elections brought forty-seven additional Republicans to the House and three to the Senate. Concerned about the escalating war in Vietnam, the country's economic problems, and urban rioting, Congress and the public expressed growing dissatisfaction with the administration. On March 31, 1968, Johnson announced that he would not seek reelection. At the end of his term he retired to his Texas ranch, where he died of a heart attack on January 22, 1973.

## Johnson Impeachment Trial

Only one president of the United States has ever stood trial on impeachment charges: President Andrew Johnson, who in 1868 escaped removal from office by a single Senate vote.

The IMPEACHMENT POWER granted by the Constitution permits Congress to remove federal officials it finds guilty of grave misconduct. The process requires two steps. An accused official must first be for-

mally charged, or impeached, by the House of Representatives. The official is then tried in the Senate, where a two-thirds majority is required for conviction.

Johnson was charged with having dismissed the secretary of war in violation of the Tenure of Office Act. But his impeachment was part of a larger political struggle with a hostile Congress. A Tennessee Democrat who had remained loyal to the Union at the outbreak of the Civil War, Johnson was chosen as Abraham Lincoln's vice-presidential running mate in 1864. He became president upon Lincoln's assassination the following year. Johnson tried to pursue Lincoln's moderate approach to the South, but this brought him into conflict with the Republican-controlled Congress—particularly the Radical Republicans, who favored harsh treatment of the defeated Confederacy.

On their first attempt to impeach Johnson, in 1867, the Radical Republicans suffered a crushing defeat. The House Judiciary Committee recommended impeachment on general charges, but the full House of Representatives rejected an impeachment resolution by a vote of 57 to 108.

A second impeachment effort was triggered early in 1868 when Johnson dismissed Secretary of War Edwin M. Stanton, a holdover from the Lincoln administration who had close ties to the Radical Republicans. In dismissing Stanton, Johnson defied the Tenure of Office Act, which required Senate approval for removal of government officials who had been appointed with Senate consent. The tenure law had been enacted over Johnson's veto in 1867. Its purpose was to protect Republican officeholders from executive retaliation if they did not support the president. (See REMOVAL POWER.)

Johnson's action infuriated Congress, which moved swiftly to impeach him. The House Committee on Reconstruction, headed by Rep. Thaddeus STEVENS of Pennsylvania, one of the Radical Republican leaders, reported an impeachment resolution on February 22, 1868. The full House approved the measure two days later by a 126–47 vote that divided along party lines.

In early March the House approved specific

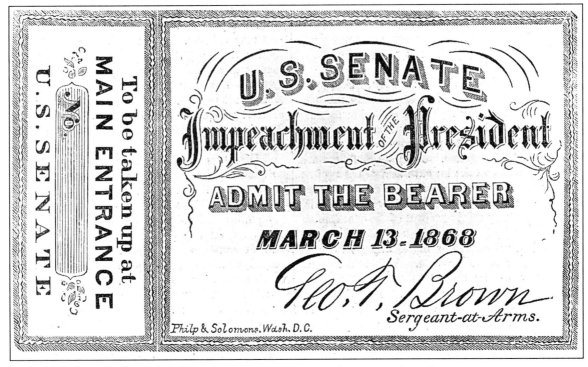

*This ticket allowed admittance to the Senate galleries for the impeachment trial of President Andrew Johnson.*    Source: Library of Congress

charges, called articles of impeachment, against Johnson and chose seven of its members to prosecute the charges before the Senate. There were eleven articles in all, the main one concerning Johnson's removal of Stanton.

The Senate trial ran from March 30 to May 26. Chief Justice Salmon P. Chase presided, as required in a presidential impeachment trial. The president himself did not appear. He was represented by a team of lawyers headed by Henry Stanbery, who had resigned as attorney general to lead the defense.

After weeks of argument and testimony, the Senate on May 16 voted on a catchall charge considered most likely to result in a vote for conviction. The drama of the vote has become legendary. With 36 votes needed for conviction, the final count was guilty, 35, and not guilty, 19. Seven Republicans joined twelve Democrats in supporting Johnson. Votes on two further charges were taken May 26, and again the tally was 35–19. The trial was abruptly

ended to save Johnson's opponents from further defeats.

The Tenure of Office Act was weakened early in the administration of Ulysses S. Grant, once the Republicans had control of the appointing power. It was repealed in 1887. In 1926 the Supreme Court declared that the tenure act had been unconstitutional.

## Joint Resolution

*See* LEGISLATION.

## Joint Session

A combined meeting of the Senate and House of Representatives is called a joint session or a joint meeting of Congress, depending on what arrangements are made.

Joint sessions require adoption of a concurrent resolution by each chamber. Joint meetings are held when one chamber adopts a unanimous consent agreement to recess to meet with the other body.

A combined meeting to hear the U.S. president is called a joint session of Congress. Such sessions are always held in the House chamber, which has a larger seating capacity than the Senate chamber. A joint session usually is held early each year to hear the president's STATE OF THE UNION address. The president may address joint sessions at other times as well.

From time to time foreign leaders are invited to address joint meetings of Congress. Strictly speaking, such occasions are not joint sessions. The first foreign leader to address Congress was the Marquis de Lafayette, the French hero of the American Revolution, who spoke to the legislature in 1824. Eighty foreign dignitaries had addressed joint meetings by the end of 1992. Congress turned down a proposed address by Soviet leader Mikhail S. Gorbachev in 1987; it was said that such appearances should be reserved for world leaders who were friends of democracy.

The Constitution requires that Congress meet jointly every four years to count electoral votes for president and vice president. These meetings are called joint sessions. If no candidate receives a majority of the electoral vote, the House and Senate must vote separately to decide the outcome: The House chooses the president, the Senate the vice president. (See ELECTING THE PRESIDENT.)

# Judiciary Committee, House

Many controversial issues, such as abortion, gun control, and civil rights, must begin their path through the House in its Judiciary Committee.

While most committees concentrate on programs or dollars and cents, the Judiciary Committee often deals with raw emotion. For more than three decades, the panel has had liberal leadership. In the 1960s that gave civil rights legislation a boost; in the 1970s and 1980s the liberal advantage foiled conservatives seeking constitutional amendments to outlaw abortion and busing and to permit school prayer. Critics have called the Judiciary Committee a legislative mortuary.

Texas Democrat Jack Brooks became chair of the committee in 1989. An irascible partisan, though no liberal, Brooks made his mark immediately by approving a vertical price-fixing bill and a civil rights measure.

The Judiciary Committee helped draft a variety of laws in the 1980s and early 1990s. Voting rights laws were extended, anticrime and antidrug programs were passed, and the nation's immigration laws were overhauled.

The Judiciary Committee became widely known in 1974 when it voted three articles of impeachment against President Richard Nixon. Nixon resigned before the House could act on the articles. At that time Peter W. Rodino, Jr., a New Jersey Democrat, was committee chair. At first criticized for moving slowly, Rodino was later praised for his evenhandedness. By avoiding a partisan approach, he was able to pick up impeachment votes from Republicans. (See NIXON IMPEACHMENT EFFORT.)

One of the first standing committees created by the House, the judiciary panel was made permanent in 1813. Because of its responsibility for handling CONSTITUTIONAL AMENDMENTS, the committee has participated in a large share of Congress's most difficult and important decisions over the years.

The Judiciary Committee had only two chairs between the mid-1950s and the late 1980s: Rodino, who announced his retirement in 1988, and New York Democrat Emanuel Celler. No other House committee could make that claim.

Celler first chaired the panel from 1949 until 1953, when Republicans gained the House majority. Then Celler again served as chair from 1955 to 1972. Then, at age eighty-four, he lost a bid for renomination. Rodino took over in 1973; he had been chair for barely a year when the WATERGATE SCANDAL put the committee in the national spotlight.

Under Celler's leadership the committee in the 1950s focused on antitrust violations and monopolies, then shifted to civil rights legislation in the 1960s.

Celler's support of civil rights was crucial because the Senate Judiciary Committee was led by an ardent opponent of the legislation. Celler also was a key advocate of immigration reform, passed in 1965, and gun control. Considered an autocratic chair, he shared little authority with subcommittees.

Rodino continued the tradition of liberal politics and, like Celler, kept action under his control in the full committee. Cautious and deliberate, he usually focused on just a few issues in each Congress. Although a more philosophical, aggressive chair might have served as a visible counterpoint to the Reagan administration's conservative social agenda, Rodino preferred to be a relatively quiet obstructionist. But he still knew how to save faltering legislation; he did so in 1986 on immigration reform, when he successfully pressured key negotiators to keep talking.

The Judiciary Committee in the late 1980s handled the impeachment of several federal judges. Judge Harry E. Claiborne was the first official in fifty years to be removed from office by impeachment and the fifth in the history of the country. The panel then recommended the impeachment of federal judges Walter L. Nixon, Jr., and Alcee L. Hastings. (See IMPEACHMENT POWER.)

---

# Judiciary Committee, Senate

Ideological issues dominate the Senate Judiciary Committee, making it a volatile panel that attracts activists from both ends of the political spectrum. Although committee members manage to compromise on some issues, they also have bitter fights, and the nation's disputes about sensitive issues are often played out in the committee.

Dating from 1816, the Judiciary Committee is one of the oldest Senate committees but has never ranked among the most powerful. Its jurisdiction encompasses CONSTITUTIONAL AMENDMENTS, the federal judiciary, immigration, antitrust laws, and civil liberties. An important duty is recommending to the Senate whether to confirm presidential nominations to the Supreme Court. About one out of five nominees is rejected by the full Senate. (See APPOINTMENT POWER.)

In recent decades the Senate Judiciary Committee has had many shifts in its top post, from a conservative southern Democrat to a liberal northern Democrat, and then to a conservative southern Republican. In 1988 Democrat Joseph R. Biden, Jr., of Delaware became committee chair. The committee's focus tends to shift drastically depending on who is in charge. While the Senate was in Republican hands (1981–1987), the committee pushed through the Senate two bills high on the conservative agenda. But the measures, one to reestablish the federal death penalty and one to add a balanced budget amendment to the Constitution, died in the House and had little chance of resurrection in a Democratic-controlled Senate.

Democrats on the Judiciary Committee brought their ideological differences with the Reagan administration to the fore in 1987 when they rejected one Supreme Court nominee, Robert H. Bork, and forced the withdrawal of a second, Douglas H. Ginsburg. But the panel was widely criticized in 1991, during the confirmation hearings of a Supreme Court appointment made by President George Bush.

Bush had nominated Clarence Thomas, a conservative African American judge, to a vacancy on the Court created by the retirement of black justice Thurgood Marshall. Although his nomination was controversial among groups that opposed his judicial philosophy, Thomas was expected to be confirmed by the Senate. But as the committee hearings concluded, allegations were reported in newspapers that a former employee of Thomas had accused him of sexual harassment. Hearings were reconvened, during which University of Oklahoma law professor Anita Hill, who had worked for Thomas at the Department of Education and Equal Employment Opportunity Commission, testified that Thomas had repeatedly sexually harassed her.

The Thomas-Hill hearings, nationally televised, were sensational and, in many respects, bizarre. The panel heard lengthy descriptions of explicit sexual conduct and body organs. Thomas denied the allegations, and a split Senate later confirmed him by the closest margin in more than a century.

*Among other duties, the Senate Judiciary Committee recommends whether to confirm presidential nominations to the Supreme Court. Clarence Thomas was questioned intensely during his confirmation hearings in 1991, especially after Anita Hill, an attorney and law professor who had worked with him at the Department of Education and the Equal Employment Opportunity Commission, accused him of sexual harassment.   Source: R. Michael Jenkins*

The episode was a huge embarrassment for the committee, which was harshly and widely criticized for not acting on the allegations as soon as it had heard them, which had been early in the committee's deliberation on the appointment. The committee was also criticized for the leak of information about the charges to the press. The episode embarrassed the full Senate as well, which was lambasted for lack of sensitivity to the issue of sexual harassment.

Despite partisan disagreements, the Senate Judiciary Committee has managed to compromise on many issues. In the last decade both a major revision of the criminal code and an overhaul of the nation's immigration laws reflected cooperation between Republicans and Democrats.

Dozens of federal judicial nominees have generated little controversy, although there have been exceptions. The committee has not always reflected the political makeup of the full Senate. Two of President Richard Nixon's nominees to the Supreme Court, Clement F. Haynsworth, Jr., and G. Harrold Carswell, were endorsed by the Judiciary Committee and then rejected by the Senate. In 1987 the committee was more in step with the full Senate, which agreed with the committee and rejected Bork, Reagan's choice for the Court. (Although recommending against confirmation, the committee sent the nomination to the full Senate for a vote.)

For more than two decades, from 1956 to 1979, the Judiciary Committee was chaired by James O.

Eastland, a conservative Democrat from Mississippi known for his fervent obstruction of civil rights legislation. When the Senate leadership began setting deadlines for committee action on voting rights and other bills in the mid-1960s, Eastland called the rules "legislative lynching." He never wavered in his support of conservative causes, endorsing school prayer, opposing the ban on poll taxes, arguing against immigration reform, and voting against gun control. He once claimed in a Senate address that the Supreme Court was biased in favor of communism. As committee chair, however, Eastland mellowed over the years. Autocratic and protective of his power at first, Eastland was pressured into letting subcommittees have more authority. He eventually developed a reputation for evenhandedness.

After Eastland's retirement, Massachusetts Democrat Edward M. Kennedy had two years as chair, from 1979 to 1981. Distracted by his campaign for president, he never took advantage of the post to promote the liberal causes he supported. Kennedy won credit for working well with Republican Strom Thurmond of South Carolina when the latter became chair in 1981. Thurmond was in a position to become chair because he had opted in 1977 for the top minority spot on the Judiciary Committee instead of the Armed Services Committee. That prevented the Judiciary Committee post from going to Charles McC. Mathias, Jr., of Maryland, whose liberal leanings made Republican leaders nervous. When Republicans took over the Senate and Thurmond became chair, he went so far as to abolish an antitrust subcommittee that Mathias was in line to head.

Thurmond served as chair from 1981 to 1987, while his party controlled the Senate. When the Democrats won back control in 1987, the post went to Biden. Biden's chairmanship came under strong criticism because of the committee's handling of the Thomas nomination hearings.

## Junkets

*See* FOREIGN TRAVEL.

## Jurisdiction

*Jurisdiction* is the word used to denote a congressional committee's area of legislative responsibility. Committee jurisdictions are spelled out in each chamber's rules or other documents. They guide the assignment of bills to committees for preliminary consideration in the House and Senate. Most referrals are routine matters handled by the PARLIAMENTARIAN of each chamber. But sometimes matters are not quite so clear.

Many bills do not fall within the subject area of a single committee; in that case, they may be referred to two or more committees before going to the floor—a practice known as multiple referral.

Because jurisdictional boundaries are not always precise, committees sometimes compete for referral of an important bill. Or one committee may try to usurp legislative territory that another committee considers its own. An aggressive chair who became known for his skill at seizing new jurisdictional territory was Rep. John D. Dingell, a Michigan Democrat who became chair of the House Energy and Commerce Committee in 1981.

## Keating Five Scandal

With the reprimand of one senator, the Senate Ethics Committee in 1991 completed a sweeping investigation of possible wrongdoing by five senators in behalf of a failed California savings and loan (S&L) institution. The S&L was headed by Charles H. Keating, Jr., and the investigated senators thus came to be known as the Keating Five. (See ETHICS COMMITTEE, SENATE SELECT.)

The five senators were Democrats Alan Cranston of California, Dennis DeConcini of Arizona, John Glenn of Ohio, and Donald W. Riegle, Jr., of Michigan, and Republican John McCain of Arizona. All had received help from Keating, who had contributed or raised some $1.5 million for their campaigns or favorite political causes. The committee investigated to determine whether the senators, in exchange, had intervened against federal regulators in a vain effort to save Keating's ailing thrift, Lincoln Savings and Loan Association. Lincoln Savings had collapsed in 1989 at a cost to taxpayers of $2 billion.

### Reprimand for Cranston

After months of televised hearings and thirty-three hours of closed deliberations, the Ethics Committee concluded that all five senators had shown poor judgment in dealing with Keating, but that only Cranston's official actions were "substantially linked" to his fund raising. In February 1991 the committee chided the other four senators in writing, but it left Cranston's fate undecided.

Months passed as the members of the bipartisan committee debated the issue. Republicans favored a full Senate censure—next to expulsion, the harshest available penalty—and Democrats attempted to avoid a floor vote. With one Republican abstaining, the committee on November 19, 1991, voted 5–0 for a

*Charles H. Keating, Jr., surrounded by press and police, arrives on Capitol Hill to testify before the House Banking Committee.*
*Source: R. Michael Jenkins*

compromise, halfway between a committee rebuke and a Senate censure. The following day on the Senate floor the committee, without asking for a vote, announced its reprimand of Cranston "in the name of the Senate" for "an impermissible pattern of conduct in which fundraising and official activities were substantially linked."

Cranston, who was seventy-seven years old and suffering from prostate cancer, accepted the rebuke but then derided the committee and said other members had done what he had done or worse. He in turn was criticized by the committee vice chair, New Hampshire Republican Warren B. Rudman. Rudman said Cranston's statement was "arrogant, unrepentant, and a smear on this institution. Everybody does *not* do it." The committee listed as "extenuating circumstances" Cranston's poor health and his decision, announced at the start of the investigation, not to seek reelection. In using the term *reprimand* the committee followed the example of the House of Representatives, which in recent years had used the sanction in place of the more formal *censure*. (See DISCIPLINING MEMBERS; ETHICS.)

### Pressure for Reform

Keating and his associates had begun seeking help from legislators in 1984–1986. They hoped to stop federal regulators from limiting direct ownership of real estate and other assets by savings and loans, which made possible the thrifts' expansion into deals much more profitable than their traditional role as mortgage lenders. The collapse of real estate values in some parts of the country later triggered the failure of many federally insured S&Ls. Twice the Keating Five senators (except Riegle in one case) met privately with officials of the Federal Home Loan Bank Board in April 1987. Much of the Ethics Committee hearings dealt with those meetings and the efforts of special counsel Robert S. Bennett to determine whether the senators had acted improperly on behalf of Keating. All denied any wrongdoing.

Keating, who did not testify at the hearings, was convicted of securities fraud under California law in December 1991. He and his associates faced further action under federal charges. The Keating Five inves-

tigation fueled demands for reform of existing CAMPAIGN FINANCING laws. Keating had used a technique called bundling to circumvent limits on individual contributions. Although direct corporate payments to candidates were prohibited, Keating had channeled some $850,000 in such money to nonprofit voter registration organizations affiliated with Cranston.

## Kefauver, Estes

Estes Kefauver (1903–1963) was an independent-minded Tennessee Democrat who served in the House of Representatives from 1939 to 1949 and in the Senate from 1949 until his death. Kefauver was known for his populist rhetoric and liberal voting behavior; his political trademark was a coonskin cap. He rose to national prominence as chair of a Senate com-

*Sen. Estes Kefauver, second from right, used televised hearings by his special investigating committee to spotlight organized crime in 1950 and 1951.    Source: Library of Congress*

mittee investigating organized crime. (See INVESTI-GATIONS.) The resulting publicity fueled Kefauver's presidential ambitions. He was an unsuccessful aspirant to the presidency in 1952 and 1956.

Kefauver won his House seat in a special election in 1939. As a representative, his particular interest was legislative reorganization; he presented his case for reform in his popular book, *A Twentieth-Century Congress,* published in 1947. The Legislative Reorganization Act of 1946 contained several reforms espoused by Kefauver, including regulation of LOBBYING and expansion of congressional STAFF. (See REFORM, CONGRESSIONAL.)

Kefauver won his Senate seat in 1948 by defeating the powerful Crump machine of Memphis. As a senator, he championed civil liberties—he was one of only seven senators to vote against the Internal Security Act of 1950—and concerned himself with antitrust issues. He urged the Senate to investigate organized crime and in 1950 became chair of the Special Committee to Investigate Organized Crime in Interstate Commerce. The committee heard testimony from Mafia figures and well-known criminals. Hearings were held all around the country, many of them televised. Although the investigation highlighted crime problems, little legislation resulted.

Kefauver did well in the 1952 presidential primaries and was considered the most popular Democratic contender. Still, he lost the nomination to Adlai E. Stevenson at the national convention; his independence appealed to voters, but not to his party. Republican Dwight D. Eisenhower won the presidency that year. Kefauver again entered the primaries for the 1956 election, but he withdrew to support Stevenson's nomination. He was chosen to be Stevenson's running mate after a hard-fought contest with Sen. John F. Kennedy of Massachusetts.

Kefauver returned to the Senate after Eisenhower's landslide win in 1956. There he played a critical role in the adoption of the Twenty-fourth Amendment to the Constitution, which banned poll taxes. He continued to head congressional investigations, most notably into antitrust violations.

*Sen. John F. Kennedy, running in the 1960 presidential race, campaigns in West Virginia.*    Source: *Charleston Gazette; John F. Kennedy Library*

# Kennedy, John F.

John F. Kennedy's (1917–1963) congressional career has been overshadowed by his term as president. Kennedy, a Massachusetts Democrat, served in the House of Representatives from 1947 to 1953 and in the Senate from 1953 to 1960. Much of his career in Congress was spent building a legislative record that would serve him well when he sought higher office. He was elected to the presidency in 1960 and served from 1961 until his assassination on November 22, 1963.

Kennedy was a World War II hero and a member of a powerful political family. After a brief career as a journalist, he ran for the House in 1946. An indefatigable campaigner, he won handily and was returned twice to that office. During his tenure in the House he was preoccupied with serving the needs of his Massachusetts constituents. Liberal in his defense of labor and support of low-cost housing and other domestic issues, he was more conservative when voting on foreign policy measures. He sharply criticized the Truman administration for allowing communist rule in China and gave only grudging support to foreign aid proposals.

In 1952 Kennedy made a successful bid for the Senate seat held by Henry Cabot Lodge, Jr. Although Dwight D. Eisenhower carried the state in that year's presidential election, Kennedy captured the Senate seat from the Republican incumbent with little difficulty. Once in the Senate, Kennedy began to emphasize national issues over northeastern concerns. In 1954 he voted for the St. Lawrence Seaway, a project that his general constituency opposed. He gained a seat on the Foreign Relations Committee in 1957, and this gave him a base from which to criticize the foreign policy of the Eisenhower administration. During his Senate tenure, while convalescing from a grave operation, Kennedy wrote *Profiles in Courage,* sketches of senators who had followed their consciences over the wishes of their constituents.

Kennedy was denied the Democratic nomination for vice president in 1956 in a floor fight at the party's national convention. In 1960 his party nominated him for president, and he won over Richard Nixon by a very slim margin. As president, his most notable achievements were in the area of foreign affairs; his domestic program was planned but not fully implemented during his lifetime. He was assassinated while visiting Dallas, Texas.

Two of John Kennedy's brothers served in Congress after his death. Robert F. Kennedy, who had been attorney general in his brother's administration, was a senator from 1965 until his own death on June 6, 1968; he was assassinated while campaigning for the Democratic presidential nomination. Edward M. Kennedy entered the Senate in 1962; despite repeated efforts to win the Democratic presidential nomination, he was unable to capture the prize.

# L

## Labor and Human Resources Committee, Senate

Among the most liberal committees in the Senate, the Labor and Human Resources Committee has been a key advocate of the federal health, welfare, and education programs it helped create in the 1960s and 1970s.

During the administrations of presidents Ronald Reagan and George Bush from 1981 to 1993, the committee doggedly defended key social programs, not always successfully. Congress cut some programs and consolidated others during the 1980s. A bigger challenge to the committee's standing and power, however, was the bleak outlook for expensive new social programs in the 1990s.

Democratic control of the Senate, regained in 1987, did not mean a return to the days when the committee could champion expansive and costly social programs. Major new initiatives were not possible because of the growing federal budget deficit. Even popular ideas, such as funding for day care and protection against catastrophic medical costs, were blocked by lack of tax revenue to pay for them.

It was ironic and frustrating that a broader political consensus for at least some social programs had been reached at the same time federal funds were drying up. Just three decades before, Congress had vigorously debated a limited federal commitment to education and health care. By the late 1980s the situation was much different. Even Orrin G. Hatch, the Utah Republican who chaired the panel from 1981 to 1987, and other conservatives had endorsed a federal role in providing child care. The price tag was the problem.

The election of a Democratic president in 1992, Arkansas governor Bill Clinton, meant the committee might have a more active legislative agenda beginning in 1993. Observers noted that Clinton's wife, Hillary Rodham Clinton, was active in child welfare and education issues and was expected to influence the new administration's agenda on these issues.

Even though some agreement on education and related human resources issues had developed over a twenty-year period, no similar consensus was reached on labor issues. Traditional labor legislation, such as an increase in the minimum wage, remained on hold during Hatch's chairmanship. Labor issues had been in decline since the late 1970s. In 1978 Hatch had been a major figure in a filibuster that killed a reform bill designed to make it easier for unions to organize.

*Members of the Labor and Human Resources Committee in the 100th Congress meet to mark up a bill.   Source: The Washington Post*

The labor committee is the key Senate panel on education and labor issues. On many health and welfare issues, however, it has been overshadowed by the Senate Finance Committee. The finance panel has jurisdiction over Medicare, Medicaid, and Social Security, as well as Aid to Families with Dependent Children (AFDC), the primary federal income program for the poor. These programs make up the largest chunk of federal spending for health and welfare; only a portion remains for the labor committee, despite its overall responsibility for health and welfare policy. The National Institutes of Health, subsidized school lunches, and Head Start are among the programs the committee handles.

### History

The committee was set up in 1869 as the Education and Labor Committee. The 1946 Senate reorganization gave it a new title, Labor and Public Welfare. Another reform, in 1977, renamed the committee Human Resources. The new title was in effect for only two years before labor advocates convinced the Senate to call the committee Labor and Human Resources.

The legacy of the New Deal guided the committee as it pursued a gradual expansion of the federal social role. A key advocate of that view was Lister Hill, an Alabama Democrat who chaired the committee from 1955 to 1969. Although typical of southerners in his opposition to civil rights laws, Hill had a liberal view of social programs and often backed health proposals opposed by the medical establishment. He favored federal aid for medical research, hospital construction, and training of doctors and nurses. Hill's authority was enhanced because he also chaired the appropriations subcommittee that handled labor, health, and welfare spending.

In the 1970s New Jersey Democrat Harrison A. Williams, Jr., chaired the committee, continuing the liberal tradition. An early proponent of safety in the workplace, Williams worked with labor leaders on various issues, not always with success. Williams's career in Congress was undermined by his conviction on charges that included bribery and influence peddling. When a Senate vote to expel him seemed certain, Williams resigned his seat in 1982.

Hatch, who became chair when Republicans gained control of the Senate in 1981, headed a committee that often deadlocked on votes, as Republicans Lowell P. Weicker, Jr., of Connecticut and Robert T. Stafford of Vermont frequently voted with Democrats. Despite Hatch's reputation as a strident conservative, however, he worked with his colleagues to find acceptable compromises. He quickly learned that his more controversial proposals, such as establishment of a separate, lower minimum wage for young people, had no chance of approval. Massachusetts Democrat Edward M. Kennedy, passing up the chairmanship of the Judiciary Committee, became chair of the Labor and Human Resources Committee in 1987, a position he continued to hold when the 103rd Congress began in 1993.

## La Follette, Robert M., Sr.

Robert M. La Follette, Sr. (1855–1925), was one of the founders of the progressive wing of the Republican party. Progressivism's basic themes of regulation of business, conservation, and dislike of machine politics surfaced in the late nineteenth century.

La Follette was elected to the House of Representatives as a Republican from Wisconsin in 1884. During his years in the House he was not distinguished for the independence and enthusiasm for reform that he later showed. In 1890 La Follette lost his bid for reelection in a wave of Republican defeats, and he resumed practicing law in Wisconsin.

In the decade after his defeat, La Follette formulated a series of reform proposals. Elected governor of Wisconsin in 1901, he worked to implement his proposals. He believed that businesses should bear a heavier burden of taxation consistent with that borne by other sectors. To challenge machine-ruled political conventions, he supported political primaries. La Follette also supported increased regulation and oversight of the railroads. These proposals were eventually accepted by the state legislature; known as the "Wisconsin Idea," they were eventually copied by other states.

La Follette left the statehouse to become a U.S.

*In one of the longest individual filibusters in the history of the Senate, Sen. Robert La Follette in 1908 held the floor for eighteen hours and twenty-three minutes. He was opposing a currency bill supported by conservative senator Nelson Aldrich.    Source: Library of Congress*

senator in 1906. His brand of Republicanism was very different from that of the conservative ruling clique led by Nelson W. ALDRICH of Rhode Island. He opposed Aldrich on several occasions, including a FILIBUSTER on an Aldrich currency bill in 1908. La Follette held the floor for eighteen hours and twenty-three minutes, one of the longest individual filibusters in the history of the Senate.

As a senator, La Follette championed public ownership of the railroads. He once inserted a 365-page speech on railroad rates in the *Congressional Record*. Known as an "insurgent," La Follette so angered the "stalwart" faction of Senate Republicans that on one occasion they voted to elect a Democratic representa-

tive as chair of the Interstate Commerce Committee rather than have La Follette assume that position. However, the Senate refused to expel him for sedition in 1917 when petitioned to do so by the Minneapolis Public Safety Commission. La Follette had given a speech in St. Paul criticizing U.S. involvement in World War I.

Twice an unsuccessful candidate for the Republican nomination for president, in 1908 and 1912, La Follette ran on the Progressive ticket in 1924. He lost the election but garnered 16 percent of the popular vote.

La Follette died in office in June 1925. Two months later he was succeeded by his son, Robert M. La Follette, Jr. ("Young Bob"), who served in the Senate until 1947.

## Lame-Duck Amendment

The Twentieth Amendment to the Constitution, ratified in 1933, is known as the Lame-Duck Amendment. It established the beginning date and frequency of sessions of Congress. The amendment requires the House and Senate to meet at least once a year, and it specifies January 3 as the opening date for each congressional session unless members select another date. Members' terms begin and end on January 3. (See TERMS AND SESSIONS OF CONGRESS.)

The amendment also sets the date for the inauguration every four years of the president and vice president: January 20 of the year following the election. Previously, both presidential and congressional terms had begun and ended on March 4. Other sections of the amendment outline Congress's authority in certain cases involving the death of a president-elect.

The Lame-Duck Amendment was added to the Constitution after a decade-long struggle by its chief sponsor, Sen. George W. NORRIS, a Nebraska Republican. It received its nickname because it was an attack on the long-standing practice of "lame duck" sessions of Congress. In congressional jargon, a lame duck is a member who serves out the balance of his or her term after being defeated or not seeking reelection.

From its earliest days, Congress followed a lopsided schedule that gave ample opportunity for lame ducks to wield considerable influence long after they had been rejected by their constituents. Under the traditional practice, which lasted more than 140 years, the first session of each two-year-long Congress began in December of odd-numbered years. That session, which opened more than a year following the election, customarily lasted for six months or so. The second, "short" session of a Congress typically began in December of the even-numbered years. That session, which ran until March 4 of the following year, was known as the lame-duck session because it was conducted after the election for the succeeding Congress had already been held. As a result, many of the members who served in these sessions were lame ducks.

The traditional schedule had many drawbacks and was widely criticized for a century before it was finally changed. The long delay in beginning each Congress slowed the government's response to public opinion as expressed through the elections. It also allowed presidents to make recess appointments and other moves without any interference from Congress. (See APPOINTMENT POWER.)

In addition to allowing defeated members to retain power for a few more months, the short sessions were rarely productive. The fixed adjournment date was an invitation to a FILIBUSTER, and members frequently took advantage of it as the session drew to a close. Merely by talking long enough, members could kill a bill by blocking action until the old Congress expired.

The short session survived for so long because it was advantageous to congressional leaders, particularly in the House. House leaders liked the short session because its automatic termination strengthened their ability to control the legislative output of the House. The House Republican leadership was the strongest opponent of the proposed Twentieth Amendment during more than ten years of congressional debate.

## History

The practice of long and short sessions began early in Congress's history. The 1st Congress met for the first time on March 4, 1789, and soon decided that

*The Lame-Duck Amendment was added to the Constitution in 1933, after a decade-long struggle by its chief sponsor, Sen. George Norris.    Source: Library of Congress*

congressional terms would begin and end on that date each year. But the Constitution directed that Congress should meet each year early in December. The congressional schedule soon accommodated both requirements by use of long and short sessions.

Later Congresses sometimes were called into special session by the president, and often they fixed earlier dates for meeting. But the basic pattern of long and short sessions did not change much.

Dissatisfaction with lame-duck sessions grew more intense in the early twentieth century. The use of the filibuster was seen by reformers as a major obstacle to legislative progress. During the Wilson administration (1913–1921), each of four second sessions of Congress ended with a Senate filibuster and the loss of important legislation.

Norris advocated revision of the congressional schedule to abolish lame-duck sessions as a way of undermining use of the filibuster. His plan was in the form of a constitutional amendment because the Constitution specifically mentioned the first week in December as the opening date for a congressional session. Norris's amendment ended the gap between the start of congressional terms and the opening day of annual sessions by putting both in early January.

The Norris amendment was popular in the Senate, which was searching at this time for ways to control the legislative havoc created by filibusters. The amendment was first passed by the Senate in 1923, on a 63–7 vote that far exceeded the two-thirds majority needed for approval. However, the plan soon ran into trouble in the House. The Senate joint resolution was approved by the House Election Committee, and won the support of a majority of members of the Rules Committee, whose approval was necessary for floor consideration of the measure. But the Rules Committee chair, Philip P. Campbell, a Kansas Republican who was himself a lame duck, refused to act on the resolution, and the proposal died for that session.

Consideration of the Norris amendment followed the same pattern for many years. The Senate approved the amendment six times before it finally won House approval. In the Sixty-eighth Congress (1923–1925), the Senate-passed measure was again blocked in the Rules Committee, causing Norris to charge that his amendment was "being held up because machine politicians can get more out of this [legislative] jam than the people's representatives can get." When the Norris amendment did reach the House floor, in 1929, a majority of members supported it. But the 209–157 vote for the proposal was short of the two-thirds majority required under the Constitution.

In 1931 the House passed an amended version of the Norris plan, but the House and Senate could not agree on a final version, and it died once again. The Democratic takeover of the House in the 1930 elections cleared the way for final approval of the amendment. The Senate adopted the joint resolution on January 6, 1932, and the House followed a month later with a 335–56 vote. The amendment became part of the Constitution less than a year later, when it had been ratified by three-quarters of the states. (See CONSTITUTIONAL AMENDMENTS.)

The amendment helped reduce the dangers of delay in postponing a new president's assumption of office for four months after the November elections. It did so by moving the inauguration date to January 20, from March 4. The dangers of that long delay were shown by the inauguration that took place while the amendment was still in the process of being ratified. After the 1932 election, president-elect Franklin D. Roosevelt was not able to take over from defeated incumbent Herbert Hoover for four months. During that period the nearly leaderless nation, in the throes of the Great Depression, veered to the edge of economic catastrophe. (See NEW DEAL.)

## Lame-Duck Session

A lame-duck session of Congress is one held after a successor Congress has been elected in November of an even-numbered year but before it is sworn in the following January. Senators and representatives who have been rejected at the polls can vote in a postelection session, as can those who are about to retire from Congress by choice. Such members are known as lame ducks.

Lame-duck sessions are not noted for legislative accomplishments. They frequently bog down in partisan bickering, especially if party control of one or both chambers is about to shift in the new Congress.

Before adoption of the Twentieth Amendment to the Constitution in 1933, the so-called LAME-DUCK AMENDMENT, postelection sessions were a regular feature of the congressional calendar. The amendment advanced the starting date of a new Congress to January from March. No further postelection sessions were held until after World War II. Six were held between 1945 and 1992, the last in 1982.

Among the notable lame-duck sessions since World War II was one in 1950, when Congress met in a marathon session to act on a "must" agenda presented by President Harry S. Truman; the session ended only a few hours before the new Congress took over. In 1954 the Senate alone reconvened and voted to censure Sen. Joseph R. MCCARTHY, a Wisconsin Republican whose anticommunist investigations had rocked the nation. In a 1974 lame-duck session Congress approved the nomination of Nelson A. Rockefeller as vice president under President Gerald R. Ford and passed several major bills.

## Laws

Each bill that is passed and signed by the president, or passed over the presidential veto, becomes a law. Eventually the law is incorporated into the *U.S. Code,* which is organized according to subject matter and divided into titles, chapters, and sections. The *Code* is updated annually by the House Office of the Law Revision Counsel, and a new set of bound volumes is published every six years. (See LEGISLATION.)

Laws are also given numbers separate from their designation in the *U.S. Code.* A new series of numbers is assigned at the beginning of each two-year term of Congress; thus, the first public law passed in the 102nd Congress (1991–1993) was labeled Public Law 102-1, or PL 102-1. Private laws, which deal with individuals and not the general public, have a separate numbering system (Private Law 102-1, etc.). Laws are also referred to by their formal titles, such as the Legislative Reorganization Act of 1946 or the Ethics in Government Act of 1978.

Although a bill technically becomes an act as soon as it has been passed by one chamber of Congress, the term *act* is generally reserved for measures that have become law. *Statute* is used interchangeably with *law.*

At the end of each session of Congress, all the public and private laws, as well as concurrent resolutions, are compiled and published as *U.S. Statutes at Large* by the Office of the Federal Register, which is part of the National Archives and Records Administration. Throughout the year, the same office publishes "slip laws," which are single sheets or pamphlets containing the text of a bill as enacted and a summary of its legislative history. In the margin, alongside the legal language, are notes that identify a section as dealing with a particular subject.

## Leadership

*Leadership* is the term used to describe, collectively, the Democratic and Republican leaders in Congress and their lieutenants. These leaders play a dual role: they attempt to win support in Congress for their party's goals, and they are responsible for operating Congress as an institution. The party that commands a majority in a chamber has primary direction of its operations.

In both the House and Senate, the organizations of party members, known as conferences or caucuses, vote on top leaders at the start of each two-year term of Congress. The elected leaders then make several key appointments to complete the leadership structure of each party. Committee chairs, always from the majority party, are also part of the leadership. Nominated by party leadership groups, usually on the basis of seniority, they must win approval from the party caucuses. (See CAUCUSES, PARTY; COMMITTEE SYSTEM; SENIORITY SYSTEM.)

Control over legislative activity is a powerful tool for leaders of the majority party. If they oppose a bill, they can usually keep it from coming to the floor, while a measure they favor receives top priority. Depending on the minority party's numbers and its degree of unity, minority leaders also can help, or hurt, the progress of legislation.

The majority leadership is particularly powerful in the House, where strict rules govern floor debate. Strong leaders are able to orchestrate how the rules are applied and enforced in order to benefit party-backed legislation. In the Senate the rights of minority members are protected by tradition; they can bottle up legislative work with prolonged debate (known as a FILIBUSTER) and other delaying tactics. As a result, Senate majority leaders, in the hope of avoiding such obstructions, are usually more sensitive to the minority's viewpoint than are House majority leaders.

The structure and practices of congressional lead-

*House Speaker Tom Foley, left, and Senate Majority Leader George Mitchell— with representatives Robert H. Michel and Richard Gephardt and Sen. Bob Dole looking on—speak to the press outside the White House in 1991, after meeting with President George Bush to discuss the Persian Gulf War.*
*Source: R. Michael Jenkins*

ership have evolved. The Constitution established a PRESIDING OFFICER for each chamber, but other leaders have little written authority for their roles. Their positions and duties are based on tradition within the parties rather than on formal rules that apply to Congress as a whole.

In acknowledgment of their special duties, top party leaders receive additional pay, enjoy spacious offices in the Capitol, and are allotted extra funds to hire staff. A car and driver are usually assigned to each.

## House

### Speaker

The most visible and prestigious officer within Congress is the SPEAKER OF THE HOUSE. The Constitution made the Speaker the presiding officer of the House; custom has made the Speaker also the leader of the majority party in the House.

The Speaker is formally elected by the House at the start of each two-year term of Congress. The House chooses between candidates selected by the party caucuses, and the vote follows party lines. The majority's candidate becomes Speaker, and the minority's candidate becomes minority leader.

The modern Speaker is often the chief spokesperson for the party nationally, as well as the leader of its members in the House. Most of the time the Speaker does not actually preside over floor debates but delegates that role to another member of the same party. In practice, the Speaker takes the chair primarily when important matters are before the House. Then the Speaker's authority to recognize members, resolve disputes over rules, and oversee roll-call votes may be used to partisan advantage.

The Speaker traditionally gives up seats on legislative committees and rarely votes except to break a tie.

In the 1800s the Speaker was often a forceful orator, elected because of the ability to command attention and articulate ideas. Seniority, or length of service, which later became an important factor, was hardly considered. For example, Henry CLAY was elected Speaker the day he entered the House in 1811. In contrast, since 1925 every Speaker has first served as majority or minority leader.

Before the two political parties became dominant, the candidates' stands on certain issues often turned the contest. The issue of slavery, in particular, often had a role. The 1855 race was so bitterly divided by the slavery question that resolving it took two months—and 133 ballots. By the twentieth century, with the Democratic and Republican parties well established, topical issues were rarely a factor in the contests. Instead, the Speaker was chosen from the most senior and most loyal party members.

Twice in the twentieth century the Speaker's role has undergone significant changes. In 1910 the House revolted against the autocratic rule of Speaker Joseph G. CANNON and sharply curtailed the Speaker's powers. Power shifted to committee chairs and the Rules Committee, which had been freed from the Speaker's domination. In the 1970s the Speaker regained some of the authority that had been lost sixty years earlier. (See REFORM, CONGRESSIONAL; RULES COMMITTEE, HOUSE.)

The office of the Speaker came under a cloud in the late 1980s, when its occupant, Texas Democrat Jim WRIGHT, became embroiled in an ethics scandal. Wright became the first House Speaker in history to be forced by scandal to leave the office in the middle of his term.

### Floor Leaders

The floor leaders for each party are responsible for handling legislation once it reaches the full House; they oversee debate, amendments, and voting. (See Appendix.)

The majority leader is the number two official in the House. The post was formally created in 1899. Until then, the chair of the Ways and Means Committee had served so often as floor manager that he was considered the deputy leader. The Speaker chose the majority leader until Democrats gained control of the House in 1911, when that authority was shifted to the Democratic Caucus. In most cases the majority leader has continued to be the Speaker's chief lieutenant, rather than a rival.

The minority leader is the minority party's top official. Ever since the post was first recognized in 1883 the minority leader has been that party's nominee for Speaker. The minority leader monitors floor activity but can only try to influence scheduling, lacking direct control over it. The minority leader also serves as top party spokesperson and performs other duties that the Speaker handles for the majority party.

### Whips

Ranking after the majority and minority leaders are the whips, who try to convince party members to follow the leadership's program. The title *whip* was borrowed from the British Parliament and first used in the U.S. Congress in 1897. The term comes from the fox-hunting term *whipper-in,* the person assigned to keep hunting dogs in a pack.

The whips handle the mechanics of polling members on their views on issues and their stands on specific floor votes. They inform members about upcoming floor action and make sure members are present for tight votes. Whips and their assistants sometimes stand at the door of the House chamber, signaling the leadership's position on a vote by holding their thumbs up or down.

Whips are elected by each party. The Democratic whip was chosen by the Speaker and majority leader until 1987, when the Democratic Caucus began electing the whip. One reason for the change was that the whip often moved up to the positions of majority leader and Speaker; junior members in the caucus wanted a say in who got the inside track. The Republican whip has traditionally been elected by the party conference.

Each party designates numerous members as assistants to the whips. In the 102nd Congress (1991–1993), the Democratic whip had an organization of more than 100 members, among them 3 chief deputy whips, 1 floor whip, 13 deputy whips, 6 representatives of special caucuses, and 18 zone whips, each of whom represented and focused on a specific area of the country. The Republican whip had 2 chief deputy whips, 5 deputy whips, 3 assistant deputy whips, and 4 regional whips.

### Party Committees

House Democrats have a Steering and Policy Committee, whose thirty-one members make Democratic committee assignments and help develop party strategy and programs. The top elected leaders, chairs of key committees, and several legislators appointed by the Speaker serve with twelve regional representatives on the policy committee.

While organizing for the 103rd Congress (1993–1995), House Democrats created a new policy council to help the party set a legislative agenda for the House and see that it was followed. The twenty-member panel, officially called the Speaker's Working Group on Policy Development, was to be appointed by the Speaker. Half of its members would come from the Steering and Policy Committee and half from the rank and file.

Republicans have three committees handling these various duties. The minority leader chairs the Republican Committee on Committees, and two other legislators chair the Republican Policy Committee and Republican Research Committee.

Both parties also have congressional campaign committees that provide campaign money and advice to party candidates. In the House, these are the Democratic Congressional Campaign Committee and the National Republican Congressional Committee. The campaign committees, appointed in part by party leaders, help identify potential candidates, brief them on issues, and assist them with all phases of campaigning. The committees also raise and disburse campaign funds to candidates for Congress. The first congressional campaign committee was formed in protest against the national party committee in the mid-nineteenth century. Radical Republicans opposed to President Andrew Johnson, who ran the national committee, set up their own group. Democrats soon adopted the practice. (See CAMPAIGN FINANCING.)

### Senate

### Presiding Officers

No post comparable to that of Speaker exists in the Senate. The Constitution named the vice president "president of the Senate" and authorized him to vote in case of a tie. But the vice president, who is elected as a member of the executive branch, is the president's choice; the vice president's party affiliation may differ from that of the Senate majority. In modern practice, the vice president seldom visits the Capitol and presides over the Senate only occasionally, for example, when it appears that the vice president's vote might be needed to break a tie.

The Constitution also directed the Senate to elect a PRESIDENT PRO TEMPORE to handle the vice president's duties in his absence. *Pro tempore* is a Latin phrase meaning "for the time being"; the title is commonly shortened to president pro tem. The Senate has not given much parliamentary authority to the post, but the president pro tem does preside or select a substitute to oversee floor debate. Until 1890 the post was filled, on a temporary basis, only when the vice president was absent. During some sessions no president pro tem was appointed. Since 1945 custom has given the job to the member of the majority party with the longest record of Senate service. (The one exception was Arthur H. Vandenberg of Michigan, who was the second-ranking Republican when elected president pro tem in 1947.)

### Floor Leaders, Whips

Both Democrats and Republicans developed a centralized leadership structure in the late 1890s. The position of floor leader probably emerged around 1911, though the official titles of leader or floor leader apparently were not used until the 1920s. The position of whip was established by Democrats in 1913 and by Republicans in 1915.

Duties and roles are less institutionalized than they are in the House. The leadership's authority has been hampered by the Senate tradition of giving strong rights to individual senators, instead of to any group. The majority leader schedules floor action in consul-

*The "Senate Four" dominated the Senate at the turn of the century. They were senators Orville H. Platt, John C. Spooner, William B. Allison, and Nelson W. Aldrich. Here they meet informally at Aldrich's Newport, Rhode Island, estate in 1903.    Source: Senate Historical Office*

tation with the minority leader, and much of the Senate's business is conducted by UNANIMOUS CONSENT of the members.

### Party Committees

The Senate parties each have a Policy Committee and a panel that makes committee assignments (the Democratic Steering Committee and the Republican Committee on Committees). Traditionally, the Democratic leader has chaired these committees as well as the party conference, positions that gave the leader significant potential power to control the party apparatus. But George MITCHELL of Maine, who became majority leader in 1989, broke with that custom when he chose someone else to chair the Steering Committee and selected a cochair of the Policy Committee. Republicans elect other senators, not the top leader, to chair their party committees and conference.

As in the House, both parties also have campaign committees, known as the Democratic Senatorial Campaign Committee and the National Republican Senatorial Committee, to aid their candidates.

## Leadership Tactics

Modern senators and representatives rarely follow their leaders blindly and often take pride in their independence. To encourage a strong party alliance, party leaders can use several kinds of rewards—and a few punishments. A legislator who votes with his or her party might be rewarded with a better committee assignment or a visit by party leaders to his or her district at campaign time. A pet program could be handled sympathetically by a committee or attached to an important bill heading for the floor.

Leaders are also aware of the local slant on everyday congressional business; they can steer to loyal members what their district or state needs, whether a tax break for a key industry, a new flood control project, or an exemption from clean air rules. Campaign funds are also spread judiciously to encourage loyalty.

Punishment for disloyal behavior can be subtle. A member's bid for a local dam or scheme to revamp national education grants could languish in an unresponsive committee. A request to switch committees or add another staff member could be denied. In rare cases, legislators have been stripped of committee seniority or a committee post for repeatedly betraying the party position. Democratic leaders removed then-representative Phil Gramm of Texas from his seat on the House Budget Committee in 1983, after Gramm masterminded enactment of budgets proposed by Republican president Ronald Reagan. Gramm resigned his House seat, won reelection as a Republican, and soon rejoined the committee as a Republican member.

The need to satisfy diverse groups within their party has kept congressional leaders from taking bold political stands. An emphasis on ideology would split the party. Instead, the neutral role of sharing information has become a vital way of building party unity. Background reports and whip advisories prepared by the leadership are a key link in the network of party members.

Congressional leaders often serve as national party spokespersons, publicizing their party's programs and achievements. Their role becomes especially visible when the president is of the opposing party. Critics at times have pointed to this role in complaining about the practice, particularly among Democrats, of promoting the next in line when the party's top leadership post is open. Party leaders have not always been noted for their charisma or ability to articulate party policy, shortcomings less important within Congress than outside it.

## Styles

Personal style can contribute to or detract from a leader's effectiveness. In his ten years as House Speaker (1977–1987), Massachusetts Democrat Thomas P. O'NEILL, Jr., depended on close personal relationships and a warm, friendly manner to win support. A game of golf with colleagues was O'Neill's way of building close ties.

Jim Wright, who became Speaker in 1987, was a backslapper with a broad grin and confident manner. But Wright, the one modern Speaker to push his leadership close to the limits of its power, caused resentment by acting without first consulting other party leaders or the rank and file. That exclusion, coupled with his aggressive and sometimes abrasive style, left him politically vulnerable when the challenge to his personal ethics arose.

Wright's successor, Thomas S. Foley, was known as a consensus builder. He was thought to be well equipped to help the Democrats and the House put the divisions of the Wright era behind them. But Foley's hands-off leadership style sparked criticism from some rank-and-file Democrats in 1992, when the chamber was rocked by scandals involving the House bank and post office. Some critics wanted the leadership to move more aggressively and decisively to contain the volatile situation. Foley, however, survived the criticism and was secure in his position following the Democratic victories at the polls in 1992. (See HOUSE BANK SCANDAL.)

As Senate majority leader from 1955 to 1961, Lyndon B. JOHNSON was known for his extraordinary ability to persuade colleagues to support him. In one-on-one encounters Johnson applied "the treatment," cajoling, touching an arm or shoulder for emphasis, leaning closer to make a point. The treatment was extremely effective.

Johnson was a protégé of another forceful personality, fellow Texan and Democrat Sam RAYBURN,

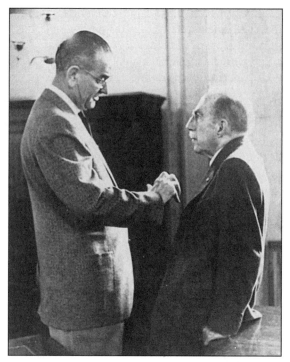

*As Senate majority leader from 1955 to 1961, Lyndon B. Johnson was known for his extraordinary ability to persuade colleagues to support him. In one-on-one encounters, Johnson applied "the treatment"—cajoling, touching an arm or shoulder for emphasis, leaning closer to make a point.* Source: George Tames, The New York Times

who served a record seventeen years as Speaker (plus four years as minority leader) between 1940 and 1961. Like Johnson, Rayburn demanded loyalty and responded ruthlessly to disobedience. He skillfully mixed political and personal relations, gathering favorite colleagues in a hideaway Capitol office to share a drink and stories. This "board of education" carried on a tradition begun by another House Speaker, Republican Nicholas LONGWORTH of Ohio, who ran the House from 1925 to 1931.

Among Senate Republicans, Howard H. BAKER, Jr., of Tennessee brought an open personal style to the floor leader's job, which he held from 1979 to 1985. His steady, low-key performance stood in sharp contrast to that of his father-in-law, Everett DIRKSEN of

Illinois, who was Republican leader from 1961 to 1970. Dirksen's florid style and distinctive bass voice caused him to be called the "Wizard of Ooze."

After four years of Baker's easygoing stewardship, Republican senators opted for a leader who could restore some discipline and sense of purpose to a chamber increasingly bogged down in procedural chaos: Robert DOLE of Kansas. In addition to his image as a decisive leader, Dole was known as a superb negotiator able to find compromises where others had failed. During his two years as majority leader, Dole produced some significant victories.

West Virginian Robert C. BYRD served as Democratic majority leader from 1977 to 1981 and again from 1987 to 1989, and as the minority leader in the intervening years. He built a solid political base with diligence, loyalty to allies, and unsurpassed knowledge of the Senate's arcane rules and procedures. Most senators were indebted to him for practical reasons: for years, Byrd meticulously accommodated his colleagues' personal and political needs. Although some criticized him for being more interested in procedure than substance, Byrd could use his knowledge as a powerful weapon to disadvantage or circumvent legislative opponents.

In contrast to the strong-willed Byrd, his successor George Mitchell brought a more accommodating, consensus-oriented style to the leadership. His collegial approach was evident at the outset when, unlike his Democrat predecessors, he chose to share the responsibilities of the party committees.

## Challenges

Today the job of leading Congress is perhaps more challenging than ever before. Reforms of the 1970s swept away old autocratic ways of doing business and empowered individual members of Congress. A new generation of members was elected, one that was less bound by tradition and much less dependent on the political party apparatus for electoral survival. Opening Congress to greater public scrutiny made members more accountable, but it also made debate more partisan, unruly, and beholden to special interests.

Party leaders' hold on their rank and file was weakened. Today they must spend more time consulting with and responding to the demands of their party members. Failure to do this could mean stalemate or humiliating defeat. A widely publicized example of this was the budget debacle in 1990, when House Democratic and Republican leaders agreed to a budget deal with the White House, but neither party was able to deliver its share of the votes. The agreement was defeated.

In the early 1990s a variety of proposals were being made to change the way Congress operates. Among these were ideas to give congressional leaders more power.

The 1993 decision by House Democrats to create a new policy council named by the Speaker was seen as a move toward strengthening the leadership's hand in setting the party's legislative agenda, rather than letting it be dominated piecemeal by Congress's many committees.

### Additional Readings

Baker, Richard A., and Roger H. Davidson, eds. *First among Equals: Senate Leaders of the 20th Century.* Washington, D.C.: CQ Press, 1991.

Davidson, Roger H., and Walter J. Oleszek. *Congress and Its Members.* 4th ed. Washington, D.C.: CQ Press, 1993.

Kornacki, John J., ed. *Leading Congress: New Styles, New Strategies.* Washington, D.C.: CQ Press, 1990.

Mackaman, Frank H., ed. *Understanding Congressional Leadership.* Washington, D.C.: CQ Press, 1981.

Peabody, Robert L. *Leadership in Congress: Stability, Succession, and Change.* Boston: Little, Brown, 1976.

Sinclair, Barbara. *Majority Leadership in the U.S. House.* Baltimore: Johns Hopkins University Press, 1983.

## Legislation

Congress uses various types of legislation to differentiate how the thousands of bills and resolutions introduced each term are handled by the committees and scheduled for floor action. Different types of legislation receive different treatment. (See LEGISLATIVE PROCESS.)

Both chambers use four types of legislation. Two of these, bills and joint resolutions, become law if passed in identical form by both houses and signed by the president. In the House of Representatives, these measures are labeled "HR" for a bill and "H J Res" for a joint resolution. In the Senate "S" denotes a bill, and "S J Res," a joint resolution.

Every legislative proposal is given a number that reflects the order in which it is introduced during each two-year congressional term (HR 1, 2, 3, etc.; S 1, 2, 3, etc.). If passed and signed by the president, a bill that is public in nature receives another designation, a public law (PL) number. Public law numbers also include the Congress in which they are enacted; thus, "PL 102-1" identifies the first public law enacted in the 102nd Congress. (See LAWS.)

The vast majority of legislative proposals—recommendations dealing with either domestic or foreign issues and programs affecting the U.S. government or the population generally—are drafted in the form of bills. These include AUTHORIZATION BILLS and APPROPRIATIONS BILLS.

Joint resolutions—the other form of legislation that can become law—have a more limited focus, though occasionally they may be used for omnibus legislation. Proposed CONSTITUTIONAL AMENDMENTS also are drafted in the form of joint resolutions, as are some emergency and catchall appropriations measures. In addition, routine measures making technical or minor changes in existing law or correcting errors in newly enacted legislation may be drafted as joint resolutions.

There are no significant differences in consideration of joint resolutions and bills. Both must be passed in identical form by the House and Senate and signed by the president to become law. There is one major exception, however: Joint resolutions embodying proposed constitutional amendments are not sent to the president for signature after they have been approved by Congress (by a two-thirds vote in each house). Instead, they are forwarded directly to the fifty states for ratification, which requires approval by a three-fourths majority (thirty-eight states).

One other form of legislation can be enacted into law: private bills (also labeled either "HR" or "S"). If enacted, these bills have a separately numbered system of laws. Private bills deal primarily with matters for the relief of individuals or private parties and are not of a general nature affecting the nation. Immigration cases and grievances or claims against the United States constitute the largest categories of private bills today.

The other two forms of legislation are concurrent resolutions and, simply, resolutions. These are labeled "H Con Res" and "H Res" in the House, "S Con Res" and "S Res" in the Senate. Unlike bills and joint resolutions, concurrent resolutions and resolutions are not signed by the president, do not become law, and thus do not receive PL numbers. Concurrent resolutions are internal measures of Congress and are considered by both the House and the Senate. Simple resolutions are considered only by the chamber in which they are introduced.

House and Senate concurrent resolutions address matters involving Congress itself as well as some wider issues that do not require the president's signature. Examples of the first category are the resolution that fixes the time of adjournment of a Congress and the so-called sense of Congress resolutions, which are expressions of congressional sentiment that do not have the force of law. Of potentially greater impact is the second category of concurrent resolutions, such as the annual congressional budget resolutions setting Congress's revenue and spending goals for the coming fiscal year. These are drafted as concurrent resolutions because they are not binding on the federal government and thus do not have to become law. Instead, they are statements of congressional intent or expressions of Congress's budgetary priorities.

House and Senate resolutions deal with internal matters of each chamber, often of a housekeeping nature. For example, resolutions are used periodically to set the spending levels for the various legislative committees or to revise the standing rules of each chamber. In the House, resolutions also embody the rules granted by the Rules Committee setting the guidelines for floor debate on each bill. (See RULES COMMITTEE, HOUSE.)

## Introducing Bills

Legislation can be introduced only by senators and

representatives and only when Congress is in session. All bills must be printed and made available to the public as well as to members of Congress. There is no limit on the number of cosponsors a bill or resolution may have or on the number of bills a member may introduce. Once it has been introduced, assigned a number, and printed, a bill is referred to the appropriate legislative committee.

Frequently, identical legislation is introduced in both houses. So-called companion bills are employed primarily to speed the legislation through Congress by encouraging both houses to consider the measure simultaneously. Sponsors of companion bills also may hope to dramatize the importance or urgency of the issue and show broad support for the legislation.

Major legislation undergoes changes in nomenclature as it works its way through the legislative process. When a measure is introduced and first printed, it is officially referred to as a bill and is so labeled. When the bill has been passed by one house and sent to the other body, it is reprinted and officially labeled an act. If cleared by Congress and signed by the president, it becomes a law (and also may still be referred to as an act).

When legislation is heavily amended in committee, all the changes, deletions, and additions, together with whatever is left of the original bill, may be organized into a new bill. Such measures, which are reintroduced and given a new bill number, are referred to as clean bills. For parliamentary reasons, this procedure is a timesaver once the bill reaches the floor of either house. If the original bill, with all the changes, is considered by the House or Senate, every change made in committee must be voted on individually. In a clean bill, all the changes made in committee become part of the new bill, so that only one vote is needed to approve it, unless additional amendments are introduced from the floor.

### Treaties

In the Senate a unique type of resolution, known as a resolution of ratification, is used for consideration of treaties. These resolutions have their own "treaty document" number, which indicates the Congress and the order in which treaties are submitted to the Senate. For example, "Treaty Doc 102-1" indicates the first treaty to be submitted in the 102nd Congress. Before the 97th Congress (1981–1983), resolutions of ratification were listed in alphabetical order along with the Congress and the session in which they were submitted (Exec [for Executive] A, 96th Cong., 1st sess.).

Of all the varieties of legislation used by Congress, resolutions of ratification are the only ones that do not lapse at the end of the Congress in which they are introduced. If not acted upon by the Senate, these resolutions are held by the Senate Foreign Relations Committee and may be brought before the Senate during any future Congress. (The Senate also can show its lack of enthusiasm for a treaty by voting to return it to the president.) Approval of resolutions of ratification requires a two-thirds vote of senators present. The House does not participate in the ratification process. (See TREATY-MAKING POWER.)

## Legislation Declared Unconstitutional

The Supreme Court early in its history asserted the right to review acts of Congress to determine whether they were constitutional, and the right of review has been an accepted fact ever since. It serves as a constant reminder to Congress that the laws it passes will be measured against the provisions of the Constitution and nullified if found in conflict.

The Missouri Compromise, a federal income tax, child labor laws, New Deal statutes, and the LEGISLATIVE VETO (a device used by Congress to block executive branch actions) are some notable examples of laws struck down by the Court. But cases such as these are rare.

Of the thousands of federal laws enacted in more than two centuries, only 127 had been invalidated in whole or in part by 1992. Of these, only a handful were laws of major significance for Congress, the Court, and the country.

The Court invalidated only two statutes from 1789 to 1865. But as Congress began to exercise its powers more fully in the late nineteenth century, the number of federal laws declared unconstitutional increased.

From 1918 to 1936, the Court and Congress were in sharp conflict. In those years the Court overturned twenty-nine laws, many of which were important pieces of legislation. Among these were several statutes of President Franklin D. Roosevelt's NEW DEAL program.

Since 1963 the Court has overturned fifty-four laws, but—in contrast to the earlier period—few of these were major laws, and many were rather old. Some, however, were of more recent vintage. In addition to the 1983 legislative veto decision, the Court struck down provisions of campaign finance legislation in 1976, a new bankruptcy court system in 1982, and in 1986 the method for automatic budget cuts included in an antideficit statute. (See BUDGET PROCESS; CAMPAIGN FINANCING.)

## Judicial Review

Although the Constitution made no mention of judicial review, its framers seem to have intended for the Supreme Court to determine whether acts of Congress conformed to the Constitution. But the question of whether the Court could actually nullify an act of Congress as unconstitutional remained unanswered until 1803. At that time a rather minor political controversy over a presidential appointment turned into what many regard as the most important decision in the Supreme Court's history: *Marbury v. Madison.* (See COURTS AND CONGRESS.)

Democratic-Republican Thomas Jefferson defeated Federalist John Adams in his quest for reelection to the presidency in 1800. Before the Democratic-Republican took office, Adams nominated several Federalists to judicial posts created by legislation passed by the lame-duck Federalist Congress. The nominations were confirmed by the Senate and the commissions signed by Adams, but not all the commissions were delivered before Jefferson entered office. Jefferson promptly ordered that these commissions be withheld. William Marbury, who had been named justice of the peace for the District of Columbia, asked the Supreme Court to order Jefferson's secretary of state, James MADISON, to deliver his commission. Marbury filed suit under the Judiciary Act of 1789, which empowered the Court to issue writs of mandamus compelling federal officials to perform their duties.

The Supreme Court, led by Chief Justice John Marshall, held that Marbury should have received his commission but that the Court lacked the power to order that the commission be delivered. The Court ruled that the provision of the Judiciary Act empowering the Court to issue such an order was unconstitutional because Congress had no power to enlarge the Court's original jurisdiction.

Marshall stated that it was "the province and duty of the judicial department to say what the law is." This claim was not seen as particularly important at the time. Instead, the Court's opinion that mandamus should have been granted if the Court had had jurisdiction attracted most of the attention.

## Major Decisions

The following paragraphs list some significant laws declared unconstitutional by the Supreme Court.

### Missouri Compromise

Not until 1857—fifty-four years after *Marbury*—was a second act of Congress declared unconstitutional by the Supreme Court. In the infamous Dred Scott case *(Scott v. Sandford),* the Court held that the Missouri Compromise of 1820 was unconstitutional because Congress lacked the power to exclude slavery from the territories. The decision intensified the debate over slavery, which eventually exploded into civil war. The Dred Scott ruling was undone by the Thirteenth and Fourteenth amendments.

### Test Oath Law

The Court in 1867 declared invalid an 1865 law that required attorneys, as a condition for practicing in federal courts, to swear that they had never engaged in or supported the southern rebellion against the Union. The Court's opinion in this and other cases indicated that it would not look favorably on other federal legislation of the RECONSTRUCTION ERA. To avoid this possibility, Congress removed from the Court's jurisdiction cases arising under certain of those laws. This was the only time in the Court's history that Congress specified a group of laws the Court could not review.

### Legal Tender Acts

The Court in 1870 struck down the 1862 and 1863 acts of Congress that had made paper money legal tender in payment of debts incurred before the passage of the acts *(Hepburn v. Griswold)*. The outcry from debtors and the potential economic repercussions from this decision were so great that within fifteen months the Court—with two new members—reconsidered and overturned its earlier decision *(Knox v. Lee)*. Critics contended that the administration of President Ulysses S. Grant had packed the Court to win the reversal and thus establish paper money as a legal currency.

### Civil Rights Act

In 1883 the Court struck down the Civil Rights Act of 1875, which barred discrimination in privately owned public accommodations, such as hotels, theaters, and railway cars. The decision was one in a series that weakened Congress's power to enforce the guarantees given to blacks by the Thirteenth and Fourteenth amendments. Almost a century passed before Congress and the Court effectively overturned this series of rulings.

### Federal Income Tax

The Court in 1895 struck down the first general peacetime income tax enacted by Congress. The decision *(Pollock v. Farmers' Loan and Trust Co.)* was bitterly attacked by Democrats in Congress and was reversed in 1913 by the Sixteenth Amendment.

### "Yellow Dog" Contracts

The Supreme Court opposed the organized labor movement in its early years. In 1908 the Court invalidated a section of an 1898 statute that had made it unlawful for any railway employer to require as a condition of employment that employees not join a labor union—so-called yellow-dog contracts. Not until 1930 did the Court sanction a federal law guaranteeing collective bargaining rights for railway employees.

### Child Labor Laws

The Court in 1918 struck down a two-year-old law that sought to end child labor. Congress responded in 1919 by passing a second child labor statute. When this law was struck down in 1922, Congress adopted a constitutional amendment to overturn the decisions. But the amendment failed to win ratification by a sufficient number of states before the Court itself in 1941 overruled its earlier decisions.

### New Deal Laws

President Franklin Roosevelt's New Deal program provoked an unprecedented clash between the Court and the legislative and executive branches. At Roosevelt's instigation, Congress in the 1930s enacted a series of laws aimed at ending the Great Depression and restoring the nation's economic well-being. Of eight major statutes to come before the Court, only two were upheld. Laws that were struck down included the Agricultural Adjustment Act of 1933, the National Industrial Recovery Act of 1933, and the Bituminous Coal Conservation Act of 1935. The Court came under heavy fire for its decisions, and Roosevelt proposed a controversial plan to increase the size of the Court, presumably to ensure a majority sympathetic to the New Deal. Shortly after the plan was proposed, the Court defused the issue by upholding a series of revised New Deal laws.

### Legislative Veto

In a 1983 decision the Court declared the legislative veto to be unconstitutional *(Immigration and Naturalization Service v. Chadha)*. Not since the New Deal era had Congress felt so keenly the power of the Supreme Court to curtail its actions. By denying Congress the use of the legislative veto, a device it had employed in more than 200 laws since 1932, the Court seemed to alter the balance of power between Congress and the executive branch.

### Gramm-Rudman

In 1986 the Court invalidated a key enforcement provision of the Balanced Budget and Emergency Deficit Control Act *(Bowsher v. Synar)*. The Court ruled that the law violated the constitutional SEPARATION OF POWERS by requiring that the comptroller general determine how much federal spending needed to be cut to meet certain deficit goals. Congress responded by passing a revised version of the so-called Gramm-Rudman-Hollings law that essentially put the power in the hands of the White House Office of Management and Budget.

### Additional Readings

Baum, Lawrence. *The Supreme Court.* 4th ed. Washington, D.C.: CQ Press, 1992.

Berger, Raoul. *Congress v. the Supreme Court.* Cambridge, Mass.: Harvard University Press, 1969.

Warren, Charles. *The Supreme Court in United States History.* 2 vols. Boston: Little, Brown, 1922, 1926. Rpt. 1987.

Witt, Elder, ed. *Congressional Quarterly's Guide to the U.S. Supreme Court.* 2nd ed. Washington, D.C.: Congressional Quarterly Inc., 1990.

## Legislative Day

In congressional usage, a legislative day extends from the time either chamber of Congress meets after an ADJOURNMENT until the time it next adjourns. The rules in each chamber call for certain routine business at the beginning of each legislative day. (See MORNING HOUR.)

The House normally adjourns at the end of a daily session, so its legislative days usually correspond to calendar days. The Senate, however, frequently goes days and sometimes weeks or even months without an adjournment; instead, it recesses. By recessing, it continues the same legislative day and avoids interrupting unfinished business.

## Legislative Obstruction

*See* FILIBUSTER.

## Legislative Process

The procedures Congress uses to write the laws of the land are collectively known as the legislative process. Through this process the ideas of presidents, members of Congress, political parties, interest groups, and individual citizens are transformed into national policy. The lawmaking function as set forth by the Constitution is complicated and time-consuming. It is governed by detailed rules and procedures, as well as more than 200 years of customs and traditions.

To become law a proposal must be approved in identical form by both the SENATE and the HOUSE OF REPRESENTATIVES and signed by the president—or else, infrequently, approved by Congress over the president's veto or allowed to become law without his signature during a session of Congress. Legislative proposals usually follow parallel paths through the two chambers of Congress. Bills are referred to committees for preliminary consideration, then debated, amended, and passed (or rejected) by the full House or Senate. The process is repeated in the other chamber. When the House and Senate pass different versions of a major bill, a temporary Senate-House conference committee normally is appointed to work out a compromise. Both chambers must approve the conferees' changes before the bill can be sent to the president for signature.

Not surprisingly, relatively few bills make it through this complex process. In the 101st Congress (1989–1991) nearly 12,000 bills and resolutions were introduced, but only 650 were enacted into law.

Bills that are not passed die at the end of the two-year term of Congress in which they are introduced. They may be reintroduced in a later Congress. (See TERMS AND SESSIONS OF CONGRESS.)

A typical bill that survives the many roadblocks to enactment generally travels the route described in the remainder of this article. (See Appendix.)

### Introducing Legislation

All legislation must be formally introduced by members of Congress, although members themselves

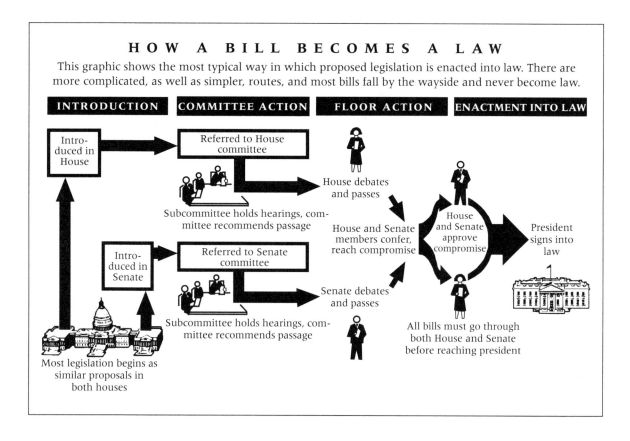

## HOW A BILL BECOMES A LAW

This graphic shows the most typical way in which proposed legislation is enacted into law. There are more complicated, as well as simpler, routes, and most bills fall by the wayside and never become law.

**INTRODUCTION**   **COMMITTEE ACTION**   **FLOOR ACTION**   **ENACTMENT INTO LAW**

Introduced in House

Referred to House committee

Subcommittee holds hearings, committee recommends passage

House debates and passes

Introduced in Senate

Referred to Senate committee

Subcommittee holds hearings, committee recommends passage

Senate debates and passes

House and Senate members confer, reach compromise

House and Senate approve compromise

President signs into law

All bills must go through both House and Senate before reaching president

Most legislation begins as similar proposals in both houses

---

do not originate most bills. The vast majority of legislative initiatives today are proposed by the executive branch—the White House and federal agencies—and by special-interest organizations, such as trade unions or business associations. But there are many other sources as well, including Congress itself, state and local government officials, and ordinary citizens.

LEGISLATION is drafted in various forms. Bills originating in the House are designated "HR," and resolutions are labeled "H J Res," "H Con Res," or "H Res," depending on the type of resolution. Senate measures are designated "S," "S J Res," "S Con Res," or "S Res." Each measure carries a number showing the order in which it was introduced: "HR 1" or "S 1" would be the first bill introduced at the beginning of a new Congress. Many bills fall into one of two categories:

AUTHORIZATION BILLS, which establish or con-

tinue government programs or policies and set limits on how much money may be spent on them, and

APPROPRIATIONS BILLS, which provide the actual funds to carry out authorized programs or policies or provide funds to operate government agencies.

Authorization bills may be valid for several years, but appropriations bills generally are valid for only one year.

### Committee Action

Once a bill has been introduced by a member, it is generally referred to a committee that has specialized knowledge of the subject matter. Bills that involve more than one subject may be referred to two or more committees, a practice known as multiple referral. Senators and representatives are far too busy to follow every bill that comes before Congress, and they cannot be experts in all the different subjects bills cover. They must rely on the committees to screen most of this legislation. (See COMMITTEE SYSTEM.)

A bill usually faces the sharpest scrutiny in committee. It is here that most deliberation and rewriting are done. This is especially true in the House; in the Senate deliberation and revision by the full chamber sometimes are equally important in determining a measure's final form.

Bills may be considered by the full committee initially or, as happens more frequently in the House, by a subcommittee. Sometimes the major review of a bill takes place at the subcommittee level, and the full committee simply endorses the subcommittee's recommendations.

The committee or subcommittee generally holds hearings on legislation before taking further action on it. Comment is requested from administration spokespersons and federal bureaucrats who run the programs that might be affected by the bill. Heads of cabinet-level departments of the government testify on the most important proposals. Scholars and technical experts also may appear at hearings. LOBBYING groups and private citizens may testify for or against the legislation.

Committee hearings are very important in setting the legislative agenda and shaping its political tone. They are one of the most important forums for finding out what the public thinks about national problems and how to solve them. Hearings also may have an educational function. Members of Congress need political support for the actions they take, especially when controversial issues or remedies are involved. Hearings assist Congress in developing a consensus on proposed legislation.

After the hearings, committee members may meet to consider the provisions of the legislation in detail, a process known as marking up the bill. Many bills are heavily amended—that is, revised—or entirely redrafted in committee. Votes may be taken on controversial amendments and, finally, on whether to approve the bill and recommend that the full House or Senate pass the measure.

When committee action has been completed, the panel prepares a written report describing the bill and its amendments, and explaining why the measure should become law. Both the members supporting the bill and those opposed may include their views in the report, which is filed with the parent chamber. At this point a bill is said to be reported to the House or Senate.

The fate of most bills is sealed in committee. Bills that gain committee approval do not always win consideration by the parent chamber, but those that do are likely to pass—although they may be revised on the floor. Most bills simply die in committee. Procedures to remove a bill from an unsympathetic committee seldom succeed. (See DISCHARGE, COMMITTEE.)

## Scheduling Floor Debate

### House

The House Rules Committee functions as a sort of traffic cop for bills reported from the legislative committees. Its power is considerable, and its role in the legislative process is crucial. The power of the Rules Committee comes from its authority to control the flow of legislation from the legislative committees to the full House and to set the terms of debate for almost every major bill that reaches the floor of the House. In today's greatly decentralized House, it is one of the few centralizing forces of the leadership. Generally, it acts on behalf of the Speaker in facilitating and promoting the majority party's program. (See RULES COMMITTEE, HOUSE.)

The chair of the Rules Committee has wide discretion in arranging the panel's agenda. The decision to schedule, or not to schedule, a hearing on a bill will usually determine whether the measure ever comes before the House for debate. Under regular House rules, bills must be brought up and debated in the order in which they are reported from the committees. The large volume of bills vying for action makes it necessary to have some system of priority selection. In the modern Congress there is just not enough time to act on all the legislation working its way through the legislative process.

Once the Rules Committee has given a bill the go-ahead for floor debate, it drafts a special RULE FOR HOUSE DEBATE, which is custom-made for each bill.

*Representatives testify before the House Rules Committee on an energy bill.*    *Source: R. Michael Jenkins*

The committee decides how many hours the House may have to debate the bill and whether all amendments, some amendments, or no amendments may be introduced from the floor. Although it has no authority to amend bills that come before it from other committees, the Rules Committee can strike bargains on proposed amendments desired by various members in return for granting the rule.

Until the 1980s the vast majority of rules were open, allowing any germane amendment to be offered on the floor at the appropriate time. Closed rules, barring all but committee amendments, generally were reserved for tax bills and other measures too complicated or technical to be tampered with on the House floor. But in recent years the Rules Committee has drafted an increasing number of modified rules, specifying which amendments can be offered and often stipulating in what order they will be considered.

The kinds of modified rules vary considerably. They may, for example, allow amendments only to specific sections of a bill, or permit only amendments that have been drafted and printed in the *Congressional Record* in advance of the debate.

The drafting of legislation in the modern Congress is very complicated. In many cases, more than one committee works on a bill before it goes to the full House. Frequently their work involves fragile compromises, which lead to demands to keep these bills intact. Modified rules help to avoid hasty and sometimes ill-advised writing of legislation on the House floor. There also are political benefits for the leadership in controlling the amending process on the most controversial elements of a major bill. In the 1980s the Republican minority in the House skillfully used the amending process to frustrate the Democratic leadership's floor strategy. Modified rules can often be used to head off embarrassing defeats or surprises during debates. The Rules Committee has become increasingly innovative in designing rules to keep floor debate under control and achieve the objectives of the LEADERSHIP.

The rule from the Rules Committee also may waive points of order—that is, objections raised during the debate because something in the bill or a procedure used to bring the bill to the floor violates a House rule. A POINT OF ORDER is often used by a bill's opponents when they do not have enough votes to defeat the bill outright, in order to delay action and perhaps win concessions from the sponsors of the legislation. The Rules Committee can set aside temporarily any rule of House procedure—except those ordered by the Constitution—in order to facilitate action.

Like the bill to which it is attached, the rule for full House action requires the approval of a simple majority of the House. It is possible to amend the rule on the floor, but this happens infrequently. Rules are seldom rejected. Once the rule is adopted, the bill itself can be debated.

There are special procedures for bringing up measures stymied in legislative committees or in the Rules Committee: the discharge petition and CALENDAR WEDNESDAY. In addition, the Rules Committee has a special power to draft rules dislodging bills from balky legislative committees. These procedures are seldom used.

There also are procedural shortcuts for bringing routine legislation to the floor. Most legislation—about 70 percent—is passed this way. The SUSPENSION OF THE RULES procedure is the most frequently used. Bills debated under this shortcut can be passed quickly if they can garner a two-thirds majority vote.

### Senate

Scheduling legislation for debate in the Senate is a more informal process. Senators have nothing comparable to the House Rules Committee. Nevertheless, the Senate faces the same problem of having to set priorities. Instead of trying to legislate by its cumbersome and rather archaic rules, the Senate legislates often through what is called a UNANIMOUS CON-SENT AGREEMENT. This informal agreement geared to a particular bill is the functional equivalent of a rule issued by the House Rules Committee.

Such an agreement may limit debate time on a bill and on proposed amendments and may specify what amendments can be introduced and by whom. It may set a time and date to consider the bill and, leaving nothing to chance, may even set a time for a final vote. However, unlike a House rule, a unanimous consent agreement is drawn up privately, without committee hearings, by the majority and minority leadership and other interested senators. Because a unanimous consent agreement cannot take effect if any senator objects, the drafters must be sensitive to the rights of all 100 members of the Senate.

Once an agreement has been struck, the measure is brought to the floor at the prearranged time. Unless the agreement prohibits them, nongermane amendments, or extraneous policy provisions, may be offered. (See RIDER.)

Bringing up controversial legislation by any other method—for instance, by offering a motion to do so—is risky, since most Senate motions are debatable. Any senator may engage in unlimited debate on the motion, so that a time-consuming attempt to cut off this "debate" may be necessary even before the bill is formally before the Senate. (See FILIBUSTER.)

Like the House, the Senate has several ways of bringing to the floor legislation stalled in committee or never considered in committee: bypassing the committee stage and placing the bill on the legislative CALENDAR; suspending Senate rules; discharging the bill from the committee blocking it; or attaching the bill as a rider to another already on the floor. Of these, only the last is generally effective. Unlike the House, the Senate does not have a germaneness rule; there is nothing to prevent a senator from offering a measure concerning, say, water quality or civil rights as a rider to a health bill.

### Floor Action

There are marked differences in how the two chambers debate and dispose of legislation. This stage in the legislative process is called floor action. The House, because of its size, must adhere strictly to detailed procedures. It is organized to expedite legislative business. The SPEAKER OF THE HOUSE controls the agenda and is easily the most powerful member in either chamber. The smaller Senate operates more informally. Power is less centralized, and no Senate leader wields the power the Speaker of the House possesses. Scheduling in the Senate traditionally has been the joint work of the majority and minority leaders.

The philosophy behind the rules of the two chambers also is different. Senate procedures are intended to give great weight to the minority, even at the expense of legislative efficiency, while House rules emphasize majority rights.

Approval of bills and amendments in either chamber requires a majority of the members voting. Thus a tie vote spells defeat. In the Senate the VICE PRESIDENT of the United States, who under the Constitution is the Senate's PRESIDING OFFICER, may vote to break a tie. But this is the only circumstance in which the vice president may vote. In the House the Speaker traditionally votes only to break a tie, although as an elected member of that chamber the Speaker may vote at any time on any proposal.

### House

Most bills are debated and disposed of in the House in one afternoon, although some bills take two or three days. Rarely is action drawn out over many days or even weeks, as occurs in the Senate. House rules make filibusters and most other stalling tactics impractical. The House uses a parliamentary tool known as the PREVIOUS QUESTION to close debate and guarantee that a bill will come to a final vote.

House parliamentary procedures are the same for most major bills, except those handled under shortcut methods. The rule, presented in a resolution reported by the Rules Committee, is debated and adopted. The House debates most legislation in the Committee of the Whole House on the State of the Union, or more simply, the COMMITTEE OF THE WHOLE. This is nothing more than the House sitting in another form. When functioning as the Committee of the Whole, the House uses special rules designed to speed up floor action. On each bill there is a period for general debate, as regulated by the Rules Committee's rule, and

separate debate and votes on all amendments introduced and allowed under the rule.

General debate is controlled by floor managers for the majority and minority parties, who often are the chair and ranking minority member of the committee or subcommittee with jurisdiction over the bill. (See FLOOR MANAGER.)

After general debate, which usually lasts one or two hours, the bill is read section by section for amendment. The House considers amendments under guidelines that give both the proponents and opponents at least five minutes to discuss each one. But a legislator can gain extra time by employing certain parliamentary MOTIONS.

Since the majority party sets the agenda, the minority party underlines its policy differences by trying to amend the bill. Amendments publicize the minority's positions even if there is little chance they will be adopted. Amendments also may be used as part of a strategy to defeat a bill. Opponents may attempt to weigh down the legislation with so many amendments that the bill will lose support. Some members, particularly on the minority side, develop great parliamentary expertise and act as self-appointed watchdogs of the rules and tactics of the majority.

Some votes in the House are taken by methods that make it impossible to tell how individual members voted. Others are taken by an electronic system that provides a public record of each member's vote on an issue. The Constitution spells out certain instances when votes must be individually recorded. (See VOTING IN CONGRESS.)

When all amendments have been disposed of, the Committee of the Whole dissolves and the bill is reconsidered by the members, now sitting as the House of Representatives. The House then proceeds through a series of parliamentary motions and votes that give opponents a final opportunity to influence the outcome while guaranteeing that the proponents—assuming they are in the majority—will be able to pass the bill. Unlike the situation in the Senate, a determined House majority can always be expected to prevail on a particular bill.

Bills that reach a final passage vote are seldom defeated outright. By that time the support or opposi-

*Senate Banking Committee members gather for the markup of banking legislation. Stacks of papers in front of each senator are amendments to the legislation.    Source: R. Michael Jenkins*

tion has been clearly established, while attempts to revise the legislation have already been made during floor debate.

### Senate

In the Senate much of what goes on has been planned in advance. Senators read speeches on legislation written by their staffs, and action on bills and amendments is by prior arrangement under unanimous consent agreements. Spontaneous debate is the exception. Normally there are few senators on the floor, except when crucial votes occur. Nevertheless, floor debate and procedural strategies are important in the Senate. One reason is that Senate rules make the legislative outcome less certain than in the House. The play of personalities and political influence affects the result to a much greater extent.

Floor action bears little resemblance to the proce-

dures outlined in the formal rules. Scheduling is quite flexible. Debate is unstructured; for example, no period is reserved for general debate. The Senate often conducts its business by setting aside its rules and operating through unanimous consent agreements. All senators can participate in scheduling. If there is broad backing for a bill, the Senate can act quickly. But if a political consensus is lacking, Senate action can be held up almost indefinitely.

On controversial bills for which agreements cannot be reached ahead of time, the majority leader may put the Senate on a track system. Tracking permits the Senate to have two or more bills pending simultaneously, with a specific time of the day designated for each bill. If one bill is being filibustered, the Senate can turn to another and thus not hold up all floor action.

The majority leader's greatest influence comes

from control of the legislative agenda. The majority leader can schedule bills to suit certain senators or the White House, and can hold votes at times that benefit a bill's supporters or minimize the opposition's strength.

The Senate mostly relies on two types of votes, voice votes and roll calls. The roll sometimes is called slowly to give absent senators time to hustle to the floor from their offices in nearby buildings. Senators have a second chance to vote when the roll call is repeated. Much legislation is passed by unanimous consent. Even measures on which the Senate is closely divided may be passed without a roll call because the controversial issues already have been resolved, either by approval or rejection of key amendments or by procedural votes that reflect the Senate's positions before the bill itself is voted on.

The Senate does not use such House parliamentary tools as the previous question to end debate. Debate can be cut off only by informal agreement or by cloture; for most legislation a vote of three-fifths of the entire Senate, or sixty members, is needed to end debate. Even without the filibuster, senators have many devices at their disposal for sidetracking legislation. Certain rules may delay consideration of a bill after it has been reported by a committee, and an informal practice allows senators to place "holds" on bills for varying lengths of time.

## Action in Second Chamber

After a bill has been passed by one chamber it is sent to the other. At this point several parliamentary options are available. The normal practice for all but the most routine legislation is for the measure to go to committee, where there will be more hearings, followed by markup, a vote to approve the bill, and the drafting of a committee report. (In most cases, the other chamber has already begun action on its own version of a bill.) It may then go to the floor. If passed by the second chamber, the bill in all likelihood will have been substantially amended. It may now be totally different from the first chamber's version. Both chambers usually agree to send such bills to a House-Senate conference committee to negotiate a compromise. (See CONFERENCE COMMITTEES.)

In certain situations the second chamber may approve the bill as passed by the first chamber, without further amendment, thus clearing the legislation for the president.

## Conference Action

The House-Senate conference is the last major hurdle for most legislation. Everything the bill's sponsors have worked for may be won or lost during these negotiations, and all the effort exerted by the executive branch and private interests to help pass or defeat it may have been in vain.

Either chamber may request a conference with the other to resolve the differences between the versions passed by the House and Senate. Conferees are appointed from each chamber. They are generally chosen by the chair and highest ranking minority member of the committee or subcommittee in which the bill originated.

Before House and Senate conferees begin their negotiations, each delegation may meet separately to work out its positions on the key differences. They decide what they are willing to sacrifice and what provisions they will not bargain away.

Conferences are more informal than regular committee bill-drafting sessions. The staffs play a more obvious role in the final bargaining. Spokespersons for the administration usually are present, and lobbyists try to influence proposed compromises during breaks in the meetings. In theory, conferees must observe certain rules: They may not amend or delete any section of the bill that is not in dispute, and they may not introduce new provisions not relevant to the differences already in the bills. In practice, however, many bills are largely rewritten in conference.

If there are disagreements among House conferees or among Senate conferees, such disputes must be settled by majority vote. Each chamber's delegation may be of any size, but each side votes as a unit on each provision in disagreement. The political influence and skill of conference leaders play an important part in the outcome.

After conferees have agreed to a compromise bill, they write a conference report, explaining specific changes they have made. The legislative intent of certain provisions may be written into the conference report rather than into the bill itself. The report becomes official once a majority of conferees from each chamber has signed it.

Finally, after the report has been printed, the two houses vote on the compromise. Under legislative rules, bills that have been approved in conference are not supposed to be further amended by the House or Senate. But if conferees have been unable to agree on any of the amendments in disagreement, separate votes are taken in both houses to resolve the disputed provision. The House also can vote separately, in most circumstances, on any provision added by the Senate that is not germane to the bill. Sometimes bills are sent back to conference for further compromise efforts. The final version is rarely defeated, although this happens on occasion when wholesale changes are made in a long, controversial conference. Once the compromise has been approved, the bill is sent to the White House for the president's review.

### President's Role

When a bill reaches the president's desk, he has three choices:

• He may sign it, thus enacting the measure into law.

• He may veto it and return it to Congress with a statement giving his objections. Congress may override the veto by a two-thirds majority vote of both chambers. The bill then becomes a law without the president's approval. (See VETOES.)

• He may take no action, in which case the bill will become law without his signature after ten days excluding Sundays—provided Congress does not adjourn for the year during that period. Should Congress adjourn, however, the legislation does not become law. This is known as a pocket veto.

#### Additional Readings

Birnbaum, Jeffrey H., and Alan S. Murray. *Showdown at Gucci Gulch.* New York: Random House, 1987.

Davidson, Roger H., and Walter J. Oleszek. *Congress and Its Members.* 4th ed. Washington, D.C.: CQ Press, 1993.

Oleszek, Walter J. *Congressional Procedures and the Policy Process.* 3rd ed. Washington, D.C.: CQ Press, 1989.

Redman, Eric. *The Dance of Legislation.* New York: Simon & Schuster, 1973.

Reid, T. R. *Congressional Odyssey: Saga of a Senate Bill.* New York: W. H. Freeman, 1980.

Smith, Steven S. *Call to Order: Floor Politics in the House and Senate.* Washington, D.C.: Brookings Institution, 1989.

## Legislative Veto

Congress lost one of its most useful oversight devices in 1983, when the Supreme Court ruled that most legislative vetoes were unconstitutional. Congress had used the legislative veto with increasing frequency in the 1970s and early 1980s. The device allowed either one house or both houses of Congress, and in some instances even legislative committees, to reject regulations and policies recommended by the president or various federal departments and independent agencies.

In its 1983 decision the Court held that most legislative vetoes were unconstitutional because they barred the president from having any role in Congress's veto process. The Court ruled that the Constitution requires final legislative decisions to be approved by both houses of Congress and presented to the president for signature or veto. Congress's self-styled veto was criticized as a backhanded, even careless way of legislating that was outside the bounds of legitimate legislative procedures. The Court held that the legislative veto violated the constitutional SEPARATION OF POWERS by expanding Congress's powers from lawmaking and oversight to "shared administration" of the laws.

Nevertheless, the legislative veto served many useful purposes from the point of view of both lawmakers and presidents. Although presidents since Herbert Hoover had denounced the procedure as an infringement on executive powers, they had accepted it in order to gain additional authority and flexibility in administering certain laws. As a result Congress and federal agencies developed several informal methods that allow Congress to continue to veto proposed agency actions.

### Background

The legislative veto is a relatively recent congressional tool for controlling the executive branch. It was first written into law in 1932, when Congress passed legislation that gave President Hoover the authority to reorganize U.S. government departments. That legislation allowed either house of Congress, by majority vote, to "veto" the president's recommendations for reorganization. Just a year later the House exercised that veto, blocking Hoover's plan. Hoover later vetoed an emergency appropriations bill that would have allowed a single committee—the Joint Committee on Taxation—to exercise a veto over certain tax legislation.

Hoover's initial acquiescence in and later opposition to the legislative veto set the pattern for future presidential views on the issue. Presidents after Hoover voiced strong objections to it, but most of them chose not to confront the issue directly. An exception was President Gerald R. Ford, who in 1976 dramatized his opposition by vetoing an environmental bill because it contained a veto provision. As a candidate for president in 1980, Ronald Reagan gave some support to Congress's use of the legislative veto, but once in office he reversed his position. In 1982 Reagan's solicitor general urged the Supreme Court to declare the veto unconstitutional.

The legislative veto was seldom used until the early 1940s, when lawmakers saw it as an effective way to check the vast war-making and emergency powers Congress had granted the Roosevelt administration during World War II. Its use then declined in the 1950s and 1960s.

In the 1970s Congress began adding legislative veto provisions to a wide range of legislation, especially in foreign policy and defense, energy, and environment. This trend was fueled by the Democratic Congress's growing distrust of President Richard Nixon's actions and by public criticism of excessive federal regulation.

The Vietnam War and the Watergate scandal weakened the presidency and led to a more assertive Congress. It was no coincidence that this period saw a rapid expansion of the legislative veto. Some of the most important laws of the period contained legislative vetoes, including the 1973 War Powers Act, the 1974 Congressional Budget and Impoundment Control Act, and the 1974 Federal Election Campaign Act. By the time the Reagan administration took office in 1981, there were well over 200 laws containing leg-islative veto provisions. Of these, more than one-third had been enacted since the mid-1970s. A bill enacted in 1980 to deal with future domestic energy shortages contained twenty-one separate veto provisions.

## Types of Legislative Vetoes

Over the years Congress devised several types of legislative vetoes. Most of them had one feature in common: they allowed Congress, by one method or another, to block executive branch actions without the president having the opportunity to reverse the vetoes. Usually Congress gave itself thirty to sixty days in which to consider and approve a veto. In some cases lawmakers were free to apply the veto at any time.

Probably the most common form of the veto procedure was the two-house veto, which required a majority vote in both the House and Senate to block an executive branch policy. Concurrent resolutions were used to approve two-house vetoes because they were not sent to the president for signature or disapproval. (Some two-house vetoes were provided in bills requiring the president's signature.)

Congress also used one-house legislative vetoes. These allowed either chamber to block a regulation of a government department or independent agency by adopting a simple resolution of disapproval. A variation permitted either chamber to veto a federal regulation unless the other chamber overturned the action of the first chamber within a specified period. Still another form of the veto gave certain House and Senate committees the power to block or delay a department's regulation.

All these veto procedures allowed federal departments or agencies to implement certain rules or programs unless Congress intervened to block them. However, another variation of the veto blocked or delayed certain regulations from taking effect unless lawmakers took the initiative and voted to approve them. This in effect constituted a veto in advance, which could be reversed only if one, or both, houses voted to let stand a proposed regulation or policy.

## Supreme Court Ruling

The Supreme Court reached its decision in *Immigration and Naturalization Service v. Chadha* on June 23,

1983. In that ruling and in follow-up decisions soon thereafter, the Court held that all forms of the legislative veto that did not give the president the opportunity to respond to Congress's action were unconstitutional. The Court said the legislative process outlined in the Constitution demanded that all acts of Congress must include the president's participation, through his approval or veto, to be enforceable. Thus, if Congress gives federal departments and agencies the authority to issue certain regulations or make policy decisions, it "must abide by its delegation of authority until that delegation is legislatively altered or revoked." In the majority decision in *Chadha,* Chief Justice Warren E. Burger said it was beyond doubt "that lawmaking was a power to be shared by both houses [of Congress] and the president."

The only type of veto not affected by the Court's rulings was the two-house veto by joint resolution, which must be sent to the president for signature or disapproval. This procedure essentially is the same as passing a new law. (See LEGISLATION.)

Congress has taken steps to conform to the Supreme Court's decisions by repealing some legislative vetoes and amending others. But many legislative vetoes are still incorporated in current law despite their doubtful constitutionality. In many other cases federal agencies find it politically prudent to agree to informal legislative review—and implicit rejection—of their activities.

### Additional Reading

Fisher, Louis. *Constitutional Dialogues.* Princeton, N.J.: Princeton University Press, 1988.

## Library Committee, Joint

The Joint Library Committee oversees the LIBRARY OF CONGRESS, dealing primarily with legal matters and general questions of policy. More detailed oversight of the library's budget and operations is handled by the House and Senate appropriations subcommittees. The Joint Library Committee also rules on proposals to erect statues or other memorials on the Capitol grounds. The committee consists of five members of the House Administration Committee and five members of the Senate Rules and Administration Committee; the post of chair rotates between the House and Senate every two years. The Library Committee usually meets only once or twice in each two-year term of Congress, although members are frequently polled between meetings. Nominations for librarian of Congress are handled solely by the Senate Rules Committee, since that is a Senate duty.

## Library of Congress

The Library of Congress has the dual role of assisting Congress and serving as the nation's library. With more than 80 million items in its collection, the library is one of the largest in the world. The collection grows each year, usually by more than a million new items. The librarian of Congress oversees the library and its staff of more than 5,000 people. The annual budget exceeds $230 million. The librarian is a presidential appointee, confirmed by the Senate, but reports to Congress, which has a ten-member Joint Committee on the Library. (See LIBRARY COMMITTEE, JOINT.)

The thirteenth librarian of Congress, historian James H. Billington, was appointed in 1987. Members of Congress are privileged users of the library. Their requests for books or background information are handled by a separate division, the Congressional Research Service (CRS). It has more than 800 employees whose duties range from answering simple queries to spending several months on a complicated analysis. CRS receives and answers more than 450,000 inquiries from Congress each year.

The library is housed in three sprawling buildings on Capitol Hill. Its holdings include one of three known perfect copies of the Gutenberg Bible (which is on display), a set of stringed instruments made by Antonio Stradivari, Thomas Jefferson's rough draft of the Declaration of Independence, a nearly complete set of Matthew Brady's photographs of the Civil War, and the personal papers of twenty-three presidents, from Washington through Coolidge.

The earliest known motion picture, *Fred Ott's Sneeze,* copyrighted in 1893 by Thomas Edison, is part of the library's collection, as is the world's smallest book, *Ant,* which is 1.4 millimeters square.

Not every book published in the United States enters the library's collection. Although the library buys books and subscribes to periodicals, its collection also benefits from copyright laws. Authors seeking U.S. copyright protection for books, music, photographs, art, movies, or other work must deposit one, and sometimes two, copies at the Library of Congress. The library does not keep every copyrighted work, but it adds to its collection thousands of the more than half a million items that are copyrighted each year.

Works in more than 460 different languages are included in the library's holdings; about two-thirds of its books are not in English.

A major library service is cataloging books published in the United States and abroad. U.S. libraries buy catalog cards, computer tapes, and other materials from the Library of Congress. The Library of Congress gives a catalog number to every book published in the United States (and many published abroad) that reflects the book's subject matter. The library also maintains the Dewey Decimal Classification System, which is used by most public libraries.

The library produces books in Braille and records books on tape for distribution to 160 cooperating libraries that provide services to blind or partially sighted people. About 2,500 book titles and a variety of music scores are selected each year for Braille transcription or for recording.

Scholars from all over the world are attracted to the Library of Congress and its extensive holdings. Their appreciation of its resources was given a rare public display in 1986, when more than 100 researchers protested early closing hours. Some protesters refused to leave the main reading room at the new closing time of 5:30 p.m., and several were eventually arrested. Others marched in front of the building. A public relations success, the protest prompted Congress to provide additional funds and earmark them for operating the library during evening hours. (Not all reading rooms are open during the evening, and many are closed on the weekend.)

## USING THE LIBRARY OF CONGRESS

The main building of the Library of Congress is across from the Capitol on First Street, S.E. Two additional buildings are nearby. Visitors of any age may tour the library, which attracts more than 2 million people each year. The library also hosts concerts, poetry readings, and lectures.

Anyone over high school age is allowed to use the library's materials; high school students may do so if their principal writes that other searches for material have been unsuccessful.

The Library of Congress does not usually loan out its books. Instead, users request materials, and staff then retrieve them from the stacks. As a last resort, books can be checked out through interlibrary loan. This means the Library of Congress will lend a book, through another library, if it cannot be found anywhere else.

Visitors often wait for their books in the main reading room, an ornate, domed chamber decorated with stained glass, enormous pillars, and elaborate statues. The central card catalog is housed there—and spills into other nearby areas. Also available are computer terminals the public can use for searching records that the library has computerized.

The Library of Congress has several other reading rooms for particular subjects or collections; these are scattered throughout the library and are also open to the public. Library hours vary; each reading room has a separate schedule.

### Jefferson's Library

When Congress decided in 1800 to transfer the U.S. government to Washington, D.C., the legislators set aside $5,000 to buy books and set up a congressional library. After a Joint Committee on the Library made a list, London booksellers supplied 152 works in 740 volumes. The new Library of Congress was given a room in the north wing of the Capitol. Most of the library's books were burned or pillaged in 1814 when British troops attacked Washington.

After the war Thomas Jefferson, then in retirement at Monticello, offered to sell Congress his distinguished collection of more than 6,000 volumes. Despite some grumbling from critics of Jefferson, the legislators agreed to pay about $24,000 for the library, pricing each book by size and format.

Congress further boosted the library's status in 1815 by appointing James MADISON as librarian. He was the first person to hold the post on a full-time basis. The library suffered from another major fire in 1851, when 35,000 of its 55,000 books were lost. After the Civil War the library benefited from a new, stronger copyright law, passed in 1865. It required anyone applying for a copyright to deposit a copy of the publication in the library.

A major advocate of that law was Ainsworth R.

Spofford, who in 1864 began thirty-two years of service as the librarian of Congress. A bookseller, publisher, and writer, Spofford had been assistant librarian. Under his tenure, the number of books and pamphlets the library owned grew from about 100,000 to more than 1 million. He was one of three librarians to serve more than three decades; the others were John S. Meehan (1829–1861), a newspaper publisher, and Herbert Putnam (1899–1939), librarian of the Boston Public Library and member of a family of book publishers. The twelfth librarian of Congress, Daniel J. Boorstin, a historian, was appointed in 1975 and served until 1987, when Billington was named to the post.

**Three Library Buildings**

In 1886, while Spofford was librarian, Congress agreed to construct a separate building for the library. The collection was moved in 1897 from crowded

*In 1897, after the demand for space became overwhelming, the Library of Congress moved out of the Capitol and into its own building.    Source: Library of Congress*

*The Great Hall of the Library of Congress.    Source: Library of Congress*

quarters in the Capitol to the new $6.36 million facility, modeled after the Paris Opera in the Italian Renaissance style and located across the street from the Capitol to the east. It has been called the Jefferson Building since 1980. An annex was authorized by Congress in 1930 and occupied in 1939. The white marble building, which cost $9 million, is behind the main library. Originally it was called the Jefferson Building; Congress in 1980 renamed it the John Adams Building. The third building, called the Madison Building, received congressional approval in 1965, but Congress for years postponed appropriating the money to build it. Construction was finally completed in 1982 at a cost of more than $130 million, substantially more than the original estimate of $75 million. About 1.5 million square feet in size, the Madison Building is one of the largest in Washington. About 80 percent of the library's employees work in the building, which stands across Independence Avenue from the main library.

---

# Lobbying

A retiree buttonholes her representative at a Fourth of July picnic to complain about Medicare. A hiker writes his senator urging an end to logging in national forests. A teacher sends her dues to the National Education Association, which then fights cuts in federal education funds. A lawyer phones an old friend newly elected to the House and makes a pitch for a corporate client's military aircraft. An aide to the president drops in on a committee meeting to suggest new wording for an amendment. An angry farmer drives his tractor to the steps of the Capitol to join a protest against low crop prices.

All these people are lobbying Congress, trying to win support for a certain point of view. Thousands of voices compete for congressional attention as laws are written and money provided for everything from health care to weapons. Individuals, organizations, corporations, and even governments can influence the way laws are made and carried out.

The term *lobbying* comes from England, where in the mid-seventeenth century citizens would wait in an anteroom, or lobby, near the House of Commons to see members of Parliament. Lobbying is sanctioned by the Constitution. The First Amendment protects the right of the people to "petition the government for redress of grievances."

Central to a democratic society is the freedom to ask questions, make suggestions, and debate results. Lobbying is an element of such widespread political participation. It allows competing points of view to be heard and provides information to those making decisions. It is how the wronged and needy, as well as the greedy, call attention to their cause. But there is no guarantee that all the voices will be heeded, or even heard.

## How Lobbyists Work

Unlike voters, who each get one ballot, lobbyists are not equal: some are clearly more powerful than others. The most visible lobbyists are those who work full time in Washington. Their employers include trade or professional associations, law firms, public relations firms, large corporations, organizations with particular interests, and other groups. Political insiders populate the field; many lobbyists once held jobs on congressional staffs or in federal agencies. Former members of Congress frequently find jobs as lobbyists or "rainmakers" and are valued by law firms because they attract clients eager for inside contacts.

Some lobbyists focus on esoteric details of specific laws, while others concentrate on broader policy changes. Many handle a range of issues and a variety of clients, while others specialize in a single area. Whatever their approach, lobbyists are important players in the LEGISLATIVE PROCESS. Although representatives and senators still bristle at the notion of being "in someone's pocket," most would count a lobbyist or two in their circle of close advisers.

Often a lobbyist's best technique is simply to provide accurate information, either directly to a legislator or at a committee hearing. The credibility gained then gives the lobbyist more influence when arguing his or her point of view. A record of reliability can win a quick hearing if a lobbyist should find a minor clause that is damaging to a client. Information packets, drafts of bills, and scenarios of how a bill would

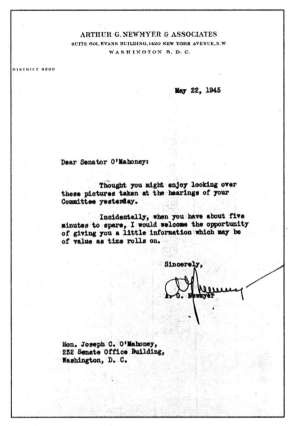

ARTHUR G. NEWMYER & ASSOCIATES
SUITE 601, EVANS BUILDING, 1420 NEW YORK AVENUE, N.W.
WASHINGTON 5, D. C.

DISTRICT 0000

May 22, 1945

Dear Senator O'Mahoney:

Thought you might enjoy looking over these pictures taken at the hearings of your Committee yesterday.

Incidentally, when you have about five minutes to spare, I would welcome the opportunity of giving you a little information which may be of value as time rolls on.

Sincerely,

A. G. Newmyer

Hon. Joseph C. O'Mahoney,
252 Senate Office Building,
Washington, D. C.

*This 1945 letter shows the old-fashioned give-and-take relationship between senator and lobbyist.*    Source: Library of Congress

affect an industry are among the ways lobbyists approach legislators and their staffs.

Lobbying has a rather unsavory reputation. A century ago lobbyists were widely portrayed as less than scrupulous characters, hanging out in the halls and lobbies of the Capitol. That reputation was reinforced whenever bribery and other improper practices were exposed. Industry's apparently excessive influence on the Senate was a major factor in the push for DIRECT ELECTION OF SENATORS; until 1913, senators were chosen by state legislatures, where moneyed interests reigned supreme.

Among the most colorful lobbyists of the past was the self-described "King of the Lobby," Samuel Ward, whose legislative successes in the mid-1800s were so dazzling that Congress decided to investigate him.

When the investigating committee asked Ward about the well-known elegant dinners he hosted for politicians, he replied, "At good dinners people do not talk shop, but they give people a right, perhaps, to ask a gentleman a civil question and get a civil answer."

At dinners and cocktail parties, at plush resorts where legislators combine speech making and vacationing, well-heeled lobbyists continue to use Ward's methods. Less prosperous groups emphasize letter writing and telephone calls. In the White House, the president can use the prestige of his office to impress legislators. Federal agencies have their own professionals assigned to monitor Congress.

Senators and representatives still find lobbyists waiting for them as they step off elevators, heading for votes on the Senate or House floor. Thumbs pointing up or down, to signal a yes or no vote, were once very common and can sometimes still be seen. But most lobbying is done long before a bill reaches the floor.

In addition to direct lobbying contacts, organizations can influence legislators by giving money to their political campaigns. Although CAMPAIGN FINANCING laws restrict donations, powerful lobbies make certain that responsive legislators receive sizable contributions. Lobbyists often direct fund-raising efforts for members they support. Corporations and labor unions are not allowed to make direct campaign contributions, but their employees and members can form POLITICAL ACTION COMMITTEES (PACs), which then channel their donations to particular candidates. Trade associations and membership groups also form PACs. The richest PAC in the 1990 election cycle was the Teamsters' Democratic Republican Independent Voter Education Committee. It gave $2.3 million directly to congressional candidates and spent another $8.3 million to support the election of sympathetic candidates. Overall PACs provided about a third of the $445 million raised for 1990 congressional campaigns.

Too close a relationship with a lobbyist can be dangerous for a politician. In 1989, for example, House Speaker Jim Wright, a Texas Democrat, and Democratic whip Tony Coelho of California both resigned because of questions about whether their personal finances had become intertwined with favor-seeking private interests. Rep. Robert Garcia, a Democrat from New York, was convicted of extortion and conspiracy for taking payments and loans from a defense contractor. In the same year the Senate opened a sweeping investigation into the favors that five of its members had done for a wealthy savings-and-loan operator, Charles H. Keating, Jr., who had contributed heavily to their political causes. (See KEATING FIVE SCANDAL.)

## Regulation of Lobbying

Lobbying is a constitutionally protected activity, but the combination of special interests is not always for the public good. Woodrow Wilson, when campaigning for president in 1912, said, "The government of the United States is a foster child of the special interests. It is not allowed to have a will of its own."

Lobbyists have resisted efforts to regulate their activity. Congress also has found it difficult to restrain lobbying without infringing on the right to free speech. Rules on domestic lobbying were considered in every Congress after 1911 but were not approved until 1946, when Congress passed the Federal Regulation of Lobbying Act.

The principle behind the 1946 law was disclosure, not regulation. The law simply required lobbyists for corporations and organizations to register their names and subjects of interest, along with how much they had spent. But the law left loopholes, so that not all individuals and groups were listed and financial reports did not accurately reflect expenditures.

The Supreme Court in 1954 upheld the constitutionality of the law, but its narrow interpretation made the statute less effective. The Court ruled that the law applied only to funds directly solicited for lobbying, thereby exempting organizations that used general funds for lobbying purposes. Another ruling required registration only for individuals whose primary job was contact with Congress—a definition that allowed many lobbyists to avoid registering. Only contacts with members of Congress counted; lobbying staff aides did not count. Court interpretations made enforcement of the law almost impossible. There were only six prosecutions between 1946 and 1980.

Critics of the 1946 law have fought for new rules.

They came close to success in 1976, when both the House and Senate passed revision bills, but senators and representatives could not resolve their differences. The legislation was unpopular with many lobbyists, who found themselves working together for the first time as they fought the bill.

In May 1993 the Senate—spurred by voters' complaints that special interests exert too much influence over government—passed a far-reaching overhaul of lobby legislation. The Senate bill would require anyone paid to lobby members of Congress, their staffs, or senior executive branch officials to register at a new office within the Justice Department. Similar legislation was pending before a House Judiciary subcommittee.

The Senate-passed bill would also replace a 1938 law regulating lobbyists representing foreign governments and companies, whose ranks swelled in the 1980s. The Foreign Agents Registration Act of 1938, later amended several times, imposed tighter rules than the domestic law, but it was aimed more at controlling "propaganda" than at influencing Congress. In 1991 there were 788 agents registered. A 1990 report by the General Accounting Office said fewer than half of those who should register had done so.

Congress has attempted to weaken the influence of former insiders. In 1978 former executive branch officials were barred from lobbying their ex-associates for a year after leaving government. In 1988 similar limits were placed on former military officers. In 1989 one-year limits were put on former members of Congress and top staff aides.

## Powerful Voices

The first step of the legislative process is committee hearings. The hearings are familiar turf for lobbyists. A trade association often sends its president to testify, instead of its Washington-based legislative representative, on the assumption that someone from outside Washington has more credibility. The witness spells out the organization's view of the legislation, and that position becomes the lobbyist's theme as he or she follows the bill through subcommittee or committee, onto the House or Senate floor, to a conference between the two houses, and then back to each house again for final passage. If necessary, the lobbyist may

*Some groups resort to dramatic demonstrations to get the attention of Congress. In 1979 farmers drove their tractors and other farm machinery to the Capitol to protest government farm policies.*    Source: The Washington Post

then try to convince the executive branch to veto the bill.

In a parallel move, an interest group may ask its members to write directly to their states' legislators. This grass-roots lobbying can be extremely effective. Often an association, in its newsletter or a separate mailing, provides a sample letter or even a stamped postcard for members to sign and mail. The huge membership of some associations can result in formidable amounts of mail to legislators. For example, one of the largest associations is the American Association of Retired Persons, which in 1991 had 33 million members and its own postal ZIP code in Washington.

Just as a huge membership gives an organization credibility, so does a group's economic power. For example, the Business Roundtable, which consists of the chief executive officers of major corporations, always receives a respectful hearing on Capitol Hill. Other groups, lacking such ready access, may resort to dramatic demonstrations to draw attention to their cause. For example, in May 1932 more than 12,000 World War I veterans gathered in Washington to protest delays in payment of their bonuses and their inability to find jobs during the Depression. An estimated 200,000 people, black and white, massed before the Lincoln Memorial in August 1963 in support of civil rights legislation pending in Congress. Marchers gathered in November 1969 to press for an end to the war in Vietnam. Just a few months later, in April 1970, environmentalists held the first Earth Day to galvanize support for laws to clean up the air and water.

Farmers borrowed the tactic in 1979, when they brought tractors and other farm machinery to Washington to protest farm policies. Anti-abortion groups have skirmished on the steps of the Supreme Court each January 22 to mark the anniversary of the court's 1973 *Roe v. Wade* decision that legalized abortion.

### Associations

Certain groups have become legendary for their lobbying influence. One such is the National Rifle Association (NRA), with almost 3 million members. The NRA has such a strong grass-roots organization that going against the NRA position may cost a politician votes. Those with pro-NRA records receive big campaign contributions from the organization's richly endowed political action committee; those who favor any form of gun control find themselves the targets of hard-hitting advertisements.

Another influential organization is the American Medical Association (AMA). Once known for its adamant opposition to federal health programs, such as Medicare, the AMA has since softened its stand, a change that has made it even more influential. The AMA is known for its favorite lobbying technique: having campaign contributions delivered in person by a member's family doctor.

The U.S. Chamber of Commerce follows a long list of business issues before Congress and backs up its position with an extensive network of local chambers. Geographically scattered membership is an important advantage for both the AMA and the Chamber, as it is for organizations of pharmacists, insurance agents, teachers, and home builders, among others. The same large groups, however, may be handicapped by the need to satisfy a diverse membership. Trying to reach a consensus so as to speak with one voice in Washington can hinder an organization's effectiveness.

### Industry Groups

Even within an industry, certain groups become more adept than others at presenting their point of view. The Independent Petroleum Association of America, for example, has often effectively opposed stands taken by the major oil companies.

Because of the billions spent on defense by the federal government, the weapons industry has an array of Washington representatives who make up an extremely powerful group. Simple geography helps make the American Trucking Associations influential: the group's headquarters building near Capitol Hill has rooms readily available for campaign fund-raising events. Knowing how to throw a good party is a special talent of some groups: the International Ice Cream Association throws a lavish ice cream party every June to which many members of Congress bring their children.

### Iron Triangles

Some groups develop a cozy relationship with a congressional committee or subcommittee and an executive agency or department. This set of lobbyists, legislators, and bureaucrats is sometimes called an "iron triangle," providing three-sided protection against budget cuts or program changes advocated by "outsiders." Veterans' groups, for example, have always had a close relationship with key congressional committees, such as the House Veterans' Affairs Committee, and with the Veterans Administration. Few such triangles are so tightly knit, however, and complex issues keep the relationships fluid.

### Labor Unions

Labor unions once had enough clout to influence union members at election time. In recent years, however, the unions have found it harder to deliver voting blocs, and hence to have an impact on Capitol Hill. Union membership declined from 35 percent of the work force in the 1950s to 16 percent in the 1990s. Labor was stung twice in the 1970s by failing to win passage of an important picketing bill. In the 1980s and 1990s it piled up defeats under the Reagan and Bush administrations, but its fortunes seemed to be improving in the early months of Bill Clinton's term.

### Forming Coalitions

Lobbyists have learned to form coalitions among themselves. As Congress prepared in the late 1970s to decide what parks and wilderness areas to create from

*Lobbyists opposing the MX missile compare notes on the Capitol steps in 1985.*
*Source: Teresa Zabala*

federal lands in Alaska, environmental groups formed an alliance. Although the groups did not always agree on every point, they compromised on major areas and together presented their case to Congress. Their united front helped convince Congress in 1980 to accept many of their recommendations.

### Government Organizations

Governments have become lobbyists, too. The National Governors' Association, the League of Cities, and the National Conference of Mayors are among the leading groups. States and cities also have their own representatives in Washington, many housed together in the Hall of the States just a few blocks from the Capitol. Though at first preoccupied with getting a bigger share of the federal budget, the government associations have become sophisticated lobbyists on a variety of issues. In 1988, for example, then-governor Bill Clinton of Arkansas, a Democrat, and Delaware governor Michael N. Castle, a Republican, went door-to-door on Capitol Hill to promote a welfare reform plan

hammered out a year earlier by the National Governors' Association. The group's emphasis on work and training programs bridged a liberal-conservative gulf and provided the impetus for the most significant overhaul of the welfare system in half a century.

Foreign governments usually are most effective when U.S.-based groups argue their position for them. Israel, Greece, and Ireland have loyal friends in Congress in part because Americans of those heritages belong to strong, well-financed associations with political influence, such as the American Israel Public Affairs Committee.

### Former Officials

Military officers and Pentagon officials often retire and then turn up as employees of defense contractors. Former White House officials also are popular lobbyists. Michael K. Deaver, former deputy chief of staff for President Ronald Reagan and confidant of Nancy Reagan, moved so quickly to set up his public relations firm and take on clients that he was convicted in

1987 of perjury for having lied to investigators about his activities. Another former political adviser to Reagan, Lyn Nofziger, was convicted in 1988 of having violated federal ethics laws that require officials to wait a year before lobbying former colleagues; the conviction was overturned the next year.

### Citizens' Groups

Broad-based citizens' groups sprang up in the 1970s that claimed to give the public the same lobbying sophistication as big business and unions. Common Cause, founded in 1970 by John Gardner, a former cabinet secretary, concentrated on "good government" issues, such as campaign finance and ethics. Public Citizen was founded in 1971 by lawyer-activist Ralph Nader to work on consumer and safety issues. These groups combined grass-roots activism with publicity seeking and traditional lobbying, but avoided campaign contributions and election endorsements. By 1990 some 2,500 organizations called themselves "public interest" groups.

### The President as Lobbyist

Standing above all other lobbyists is the president himself. The White House has its own legislative agenda and its own "congressional liaison" staff, a euphemism for lobbyists. Representatives and senators feel the pull when invited to the White House for a chat with the nation's most powerful politician.

The president possesses a powerful tool that other lobbyists can only dream of: the veto. By threatening to veto a bill he does not like, the president can quickly get the attention of the House and Senate and may win changes in the measure. Most presidents use the veto as a last resort, relying instead on their ability—like other lobbyists—to persuade legislators to support their agenda. (See VETOES.)

The most successful presidential lobbyist was Franklin D. Roosevelt, whose legislative victories in the 1930s were the basis of the NEW DEAL. Another sweeping domestic program, the GREAT SOCIETY, was enacted in the 1960s at the behest of President Lyndon B. JOHNSON. Johnson had worked at the Capitol for thirty-two years—as a congressional aide, member of the House, senator, Senate minority leader, majority leader, and vice president. With Presi-

dent Johnson lobbying vigorously for his agenda, Congress endorsed new federal programs on poverty, voting rights, and health care for the aged.

Less successful at lobbying was President George Bush, a former member of the House who retained many personal friends on Capitol Hill. In spite of his experience and contacts, Bush was able to get little legislation enacted during his four years in office, after promising to put out his hand in openness to a Democratic Congress.

## Congressional Reform

A series of congressional reforms in the 1970s opened up the legislative process with the intention of freeing Congress from the hidden influence of powerful groups. Steps such as making committee meetings public and recording individual votes allowed voters to see more, but they hardly squelched lobbying. As power was decentralized throughout the Capitol, there were more people to persuade, and consequently the ranks of lobbyists swelled.

Members of Congress found that they were often uncomfortable publicly taking an action that would antagonize powerful interests. After the changes, the House Appropriations Committee, traditionally known as a bastion of anonymous skinflints, became a magnet for glad-handing lobbyists. In writing the 1986 tax overhaul, the House Ways and Means Committee voted repeatedly to close its doors in order to make tough choices between competing industries. "Members ought to have the courage to look the lobbyists right in the eyes and go against them," said committee member Don J. Pease, an Ohio Democrat who supported open meetings. "But as a practical matter, that's hard to do."

## Group against Group

A lobbying story can be found behind every major bill that goes through Congress. Most intriguing are those that pit powerful groups against one another.

### Steamships and Railroads

In the late 1850s Commodore Vanderbilt, the steamship king, found his lucrative contracts with the post office challenged by the railroads. Directing the lobbying effort himself, Vanderbilt successfully fought off the railroads, who wanted major help from Congress in building the transcontinental railroad. The railroad was put off until after the Civil War; by then Vanderbilt had sold his steamships and gotten into the railroad business, which Congress embraced with generous land grants and special financial treatment.

### Prohibitionists and the Liquor Industry

Convincing Congress to act on a controversial subject can take years, as the Anti-Saloon League found during its campaign for a national ban on alcoholic beverages. Impatient with the milder tactics of the Woman's Christian Temperance Union, the Anti-Saloon League in the 1890s beefed up its own efforts and began to raise money, make campaign contributions, and rally local leaders. Eventually the league dispatched field organizers across the country to develop local groups. Opposing the league was the well-financed liquor industry, for which the fight against prohibition appeared to be a matter of survival. The league's persistence finally paid off in 1919, when its supporters won ratification of a constitutional amendment banning the sale of alcoholic beverages. (The Eighteenth Amendment remained in effect until 1932, when another constitutional amendment repealing Prohibition was ratified.)

### NRA and the Police

The National Rifle Association for years fought a rear-guard action against gun control laws enacted in 1968 as a response to political assassinations. On several occasions the NRA had to contend with opposing police organizations, which brought state and local police officers in full-dress uniform to the Capitol to stand as silent witnesses—thus skirting rules against demonstrations inside the building. The NRA, using its millions of members and hard-ball election tactics, was able to win some key victories: relaxation of the 1968 laws (1986); sidetracking of proposals to ban high-powered "assault weapons" (1990); and death of a crime bill that would have required a waiting period for handgun purchases (1992).

### Environmentalists and the Auto Industry

A fashionable and broad-based movement to protect the environment waged a battle against a main-stay of the U.S. economy, the auto industry, which had close ties to the American way of life. At first environmentalists had the upper hand. The Clean Air Act of 1970 led to auto emission tests in most states, and the Energy Policy Act of 1975 set minimum standards for gas mileage that auto manufacturers had to meet. But concern over the nation's energy crisis came to be overshadowed by the economic problems of the manufacturing sector. As a result the auto industry was able to hold its own in the 1990 rewrite of the Clean Air Act and the 1992 energy strategy law.

### Additional Readings

Birnbaum, Jeffrey H., and Alan S. Murray. *Showdown at Gucci Gulch: Lawmakers, Lobbyists, and the Unlikely Triumph of Tax Reform.* New York: Random House, 1987.

Cigler, Allan J., and Burdett A. Loomis. *Interest Group Politics.* 3rd ed. Washington, D.C.: CQ Press, 1991.

Levitan, Sar, and Martha R. Cooper. *Business Lobbies: The Public Good and the Bottom Line.* Baltimore: Johns Hopkins University Press, 1983.

Wolpe, Bruce C. *Lobbying Congress: How the System Works.* Washington, D.C.: CQ Press, 1990.

# Lodge, Henry Cabot

Henry Cabot Lodge (1850–1924) played an important role in the conduct of U.S. foreign policy from the Spanish-American War through World War I. An influential member of the Senate (1893–1924), Lodge was an intimate of Theodore Roosevelt and an enthusiastic imperialist. He believed that military strength, not law and moral suasion, was the determining factor in the conduct of international affairs. As chair of the Foreign Relations Committee and as Senate majority leader (1919–1924), he mobilized opposition to the post–World War I Treaty of Versailles, which contained the Covenant of the League of Nations.

Lodge received the first Ph.D. in political science granted by Harvard University. He then wrote several historical works and taught. Turning from theory to practice, he entered state politics and was elected to the U.S. House of Representatives in 1887. He served as a Republican representative from Massachusetts until 1893, when he entered the Senate.

As a representative, Lodge played an important role in support of the so-called "Force Bill" in 1890–1891. The bill would have promoted black suffrage by authorizing the presence of federal officers at polling places from which blacks might be excluded during national elections.

Lodge supported Roosevelt's domestic reforms, although without much enthusiasm. His real interest was in the conduct of foreign affairs. His support of the Spanish-American War in 1898 led him to advocate the annexation of all of Spain's colonial holdings.

In 1919 Lodge gained international notoriety as the most powerful congressional opponent of the League of Nations. As chair of the Senate Foreign Relations Committee, Lodge wrote the majority report on the committee's consideration of the Treaty of Versailles. In it he endorsed ratification, but only with the addition of four reservations and forty-five amendments. The changes Lodge proposed strongly rejected any infringement on the sovereignty of the United States. Under his leadership the Senate rejected the treaty and membership in the League of Nations in 1919 and 1920.

Lodge's grandson and namesake, Henry Cabot Lodge, Jr., served in the Senate in the World War II era (1937–1944, 1947–1953). He was an unsuccessful Republican vice-presidential candidate in 1960.

*An influential member of the Senate, Henry Cabot Lodge mobilized opposition to the post–World War I Treaty of Versailles.*    Source: Senate Historical Office

## Logrolling

Members of Congress often trade their votes so that each may attain his or her goal. Senators and representatives eager for passage of a bill win votes from colleagues by promising them support on future legislation. Such mutual aid, known as logrolling, has been practiced in Congress since the early days of the republic. The term originated in the nineteenth century, when neighbors used to help each other roll logs into a pile for burning.

A classic example of logrolling occurred in 1964, when northern Democrats convinced southern Democrats to vote for a permanent food-stamp program.

In return the northern Democrats agreed to vote for a bill providing price support for wheat and cotton, which was sought by the southern Democrats. Republicans, who opposed the food-stamp bill, were not able to break up the Democratic coalition.

In the 1980s, when efforts to reduce the federal budget deficit held a high priority, members bargained with each other to distribute the effects of spending cuts. In this case logrolling was a way to share burdens rather than win rewards.

Logrolling is probably most common on legislation that benefits particular districts. The practice is also more common when party discipline is weak, as legislators cross party lines to cast votes they believe are—or promise to be—of particular benefit to their home districts or states.

## Long, Huey P.

Huey P. Long (1893–1935) was governor of Louisiana when he was elected to the Senate in 1930. Determined to prevent his lieutenant governor, whom he disliked, from taking over, Long delayed entering the Senate until 1932, after his preferred successor had been elected governor. This determination to control politics in Louisiana was typical of "the Kingfish," as Long was called.

Long was a Democrat and a populist. He began his political career in 1918 as a member and later commissioner of Louisiana's railroad (or public service) commission, where he argued the consumers' case against the utilities. Unsuccessful in his first run for the governor's seat, he ran again and was elected in 1928. As governor, Long built roads and bridges, eliminated the poll tax, and provided free textbooks for schoolchildren. He also built a strong state organization through what many said was a combination of coercion and political favors. Even after he entered the U.S. Senate, Long continued to dominate Louisiana politics and government.

Championing the poor against the interests of big business and the wealthy, Long had a strong appeal for a populace battered by the Depression. He sup-

*Serving as Louisiana's Democratic governor and later as senator, Huey Long was one of the most flamboyant figures in American politics in the 1920s and 1930s.    Source: Senate Historical Office*

ported the campaign of Franklin D. Roosevelt but later opposed the president's NEW DEAL, believing that it was not radical enough. Instead, in 1934 he proposed a Share Our Wealth Society that would have put a limit on personal wealth and guaranteed a minimum income and homesteading allowance.

Regarded in Washington as an eccentric (he reportedly wore green pajamas to greet formal callers), Long was famous for his lengthy and colorful Senate filibusters.

Furious with Roosevelt for withholding patronage prizes, Long threatened to leave the Democratic party, and in August 1935 he declared his candidacy for president. Before his campaign got under way, Long was assassinated on September 8, 1935, in the Louisiana state capitol in Baton Rouge. His son, Russell B. LONG, served in the Senate from 1948 to 1987.

## Long, Russell B.

When Russell B. Long (1918–  ) entered politics in 1948, he was following in the steps of other members of the Long family of Louisiana. His father was Huey P. LONG, a flamboyant governor and senator, assassinated in 1935. One uncle and a cousin were members of the House of Representatives, and another uncle was governor of Louisiana. Unlike his father, an ardent champion of the poor, Long spent much of his career aiding home-state businesses—specifically oil and gas producers—through the Internal Revenue Code. In his thirty-five years on the Senate Finance Committee, Long became a master of the tax code and oversaw its many revisions.

A Democrat, Long was elected to fill a vacant Senate seat in 1948 shortly before his thirtieth birthday. He joined the Finance Committee in 1953 and was its chair from 1965 to 1981. The committee has jurisdiction over almost half of the federal government's spending, including Social Security and many social programs, as well as jurisdiction over the federal tax code. (See FINANCE COMMITTEE, SENATE.)

His style of committee leadership was based on rewards. In exchange for members' support of legislation, Long allowed them to add provisions benefiting interests in their states. Critics complained that this led to unwieldy legislation that was not always the best. But Long had few critics within the Senate. Wily, candid, and generous with fund-raising help, Long was well liked by colleagues. But their affection for him did not blind them to his shortcomings. Elected majority whip in 1965, Long was judged unreliable in that post and was removed in 1969. He retired from the Senate in 1987.

## Longworth, Nicholas

Nicholas Longworth (1869–1931) served as a Republican representative from Ohio from 1903 to 1913 and from 1915 to 1931. He was a conservative rather than a progressive Republican. In 1912 he supported the presidential candidacy of William Howard Taft over that of his own father-in-law, Theodore Roosevelt. This contributed to his defeat in the 1912 elections. Longworth had little sympathy for partisan squabbles, believing that order and a spirit of cooperation were essential for the smooth running of the House of Representatives. Elected SPEAKER OF THE HOUSE in 1925, Longworth restored much of the power of that office, which had been greatly reduced when the House in 1910 revolted against the dictatorial rule of Joseph G. CANNON.

A lawyer by training, Longworth became involved in politics first in Cincinnati and then at the state level. In the U.S. House he was one of Speaker Cannon's trusted lieutenants, a member of Cannon's inner circle and poker group. Longworth became majority leader in 1923 and was elected Speaker two years later.

As Speaker, Longworth was determined to centralize authority in his office. One of his first acts was to demote thirteen progressive Republicans to the bottom of committee rosters. The loss of seniority was punishment for their votes in favor of a progressive candidate for Speaker and against a rules change that Longworth favored. Longworth bypassed the party steering committee and, like Cannon, relied on a few trusted colleagues to control the House. Unlike Cannon, however, Longworth did not rule through arbitrary interpretation of House rules but through persuasion and mediation. He prized and achieved the efficient and dignified conduct of the House.

# M

## McCarthy, Joseph R.

Joseph R. McCarthy (1908–1957), a Republican senator from Wisconsin from 1947 to 1957, was Congress's most notorious anticommunist investigator of the post–World War II period. He gave his name to the atmosphere of fear and intimidation that pervaded American politics in the 1950s.

As chair of the Senate Permanent Investigations Subcommittee in 1953–1954, McCarthy conducted a series of wide-ranging and controversial INVESTIGATIONS; the State Department and the armed services were primary targets.

The hearings were the high-water mark of the "McCarthy era." National television exposure of the senator's abrasive and aggressive character, particularly during the Army-McCarthy hearings, began to turn public sentiment against McCarthyism. McCarthy's behavior led to his censure by the Senate in 1954. (See DISCIPLINING MEMBERS.)

### McCarthy's Tactics

In February 1950 McCarthy gave a speech in Wheeling, West Virginia, in which he claimed many government officials were communists. He followed up this charge with six hours of accusations on the Senate floor. McCarthy charged that fifty-seven people, "known to the secretary of state as being communists," were still working and shaping policy at the State Department.

Democrats, forced to respond to attacks on a Democratic administration, set up a special subcommittee of the Foreign Affairs Committee to investigate. During the panel's thirty-one days of hearings, McCarthy charged ten people by name with varying degrees of communist activities. He claimed he was hampered by President Harry S. Truman's refusal to release the confidential personnel files of federal workers. However, the investigating panel, chaired by Maryland

*Joseph McCarthy was Congress's most notorious anticommunist investigator of the post–World War II period.   Source: Wide World Photos*

Democrat Millard E. Tydings, found most of McCarthy's charges to be false and rejected others because the person charged had never worked for the government. In its report the panel said, "We have seen how, through repetition and shifting untruths, it is possible to delude great numbers of people." In response, the Republican Policy Committee said the report was "of a purely political nature and is derogatory and insulting to Senator McCarthy."

The investigation, one of the most bitterly controversial in the history of Congress, became an important issue in the 1950 elections. Charges of "softness" toward communism were a major factor in Tydings's defeat and in several other campaigns. McCarthy, who took an active role in the Tydings race, was criticized in a later Senate investigation that called it a "despicable, back-street type of campaign." In 1951 and 1952 investigations of alleged communism were carried out by both the House Un-American Activities Committee and the newly formed Senate Judiciary Subcommittee on Internal Security. In 1953, when Republicans gained control of Congress, McCarthy launched his own investigations and hearings as chair of a third "anticommunist" panel, Government Operations Permanent Subcommittee on Investigations.

McCarthy, who had just been reelected, focused on a wide range of topics, questioning the Voice of America, the condition of State Department personnel files, trade with China, the loyalty of a Harvard University professor, and army operations in New Jersey. His aides toured Europe, checking out the holdings of State Department libraries, which they complained included thousands of books written by communists or "communist sympathizers." In its year-end report, the subcommittee included among its accomplishments several resignations from the government of what it called "Fifth Amendment communists."

### Army-McCarthy Hearings

The subcommittee was continuing its probe of possible spies in the army in 1954 when McCarthy hit an unexpected roadblock. McCarthy had told a brigadier general he was questioning that the general was "not fit to wear that uniform" and did not have "the brains of a five-year-old." Army Secretary Robert T. Stevens announced he would appear in the officer's place. Stevens said he was "unwilling to have so fine an officer . . . run the risk of further abuse." Eventually the army charged that McCarthy and his staff had used improper means to seek preferential treatment for a private, G. David Schine, who had been a consultant to the subcommittee and a friend of committee counsel Roy M. Cohn. McCarthy, in turn, claimed the charges were an attempt to force the subcommittee to

call off its probe of the army. The result was an investigation by the subcommittee of both sets of charges. McCarthy temporarily resigned his chairmanship. The thirty-five days of televised hearings offered an unprecedented look at the phenomenon, which by then was widely known as McCarthyism.

In charges and countercharges Stevens, army counsel John G. Adams, McCarthy, Cohn, and several other witnesses told their stories, often contradicting one another. McCarthy, who managed to convince his fellow Republicans that he personally was innocent, made a poor impression on the television audience and on the Senate as a whole. The committee's report said that McCarthy should have kept better control of his staff, especially Cohn, who was "unduly aggressive and persistent." Democrats, in a minority report, said McCarthy "fully acquiesced in and condoned" the "improper actions" of Cohn.

### Censure by the Senate

By the time the reports were issued, McCarthy was already the subject of a censure resolution. Sen. Ralph E. Flanders, a Vermont Republican, had introduced the resolution charging McCarthy with, among other things, "personal contempt" of the Senate for refusing to answer questions and "habitual contempt of people." On August 31, the same day the investigations subcommittee filed its report, two weeks of censure hearings began before a special bipartisan committee. The special committee recommended censure on two counts: McCarthy's conduct during the investigation of the Tydings election and his treatment of the brigadier general in early 1954. The Senate, voting after the November elections, accepted the first charge but rewrote the second to focus on McCarthy's conduct during the censure hearings. The vote to censure McCarthy was 67–22.

With the return of the Senate to Democratic control in 1955, McCarthy lost his subcommittee chairmanship. His influence and his ability to command publicity had already been curbed by the Senate censure. McCarthy died of a liver ailment on May 2, 1957.

## McCormack, John W.

Seventy years old when he became SPEAKER OF THE HOUSE in 1962, Massachusetts Democrat John W. McCormack (1891–1980) never managed to get the House running smoothly. Frustrated liberal Democrats tried to oust him in 1969. Their attempt failed, but such an attack on a sitting Speaker was unprecedented. McCormack retired the next year, after forty-three years in the House. He was the first casualty of an increasingly impatient crowd of young Democrats who went on to reform House procedures in the 1970s. (See REFORM, CONGRESSIONAL.)

McCormack, a Boston native, never attended high school, but he read law books at the law firm where he worked as an office boy. At the age of twenty-one, McCormack passed the bar. After a stint in the state legislature, he lost his first bid for Congress in 1926 but then, after the incumbent died, won the seat in 1928.

McCormack was an early ally of Texas Democrat Sam RAYBURN, who was elected majority leader in 1936. McCormack became secretary and then chair of the House Democratic Caucus. When Rayburn became Speaker, he backed McCormack as majority leader, a key factor in McCormack's victory.

McCormack's poor reputation as Speaker overshadowed his more effective performance in the number-two Democratic post. Rayburn decided when to bring legislation to the floor and how to craft it for the best chance of success; McCormack did the legwork, rounding up votes and speaking for the Democratic leadership during the debate.

McCormack was comfortable on the floor. "I believe in fighting hard, but I don't like personal fights," he once said. "I go down on the floor of the House and take on my Republican friends." Although he consistently backed liberal positions on domestic issues, McCormack was never passionate about his beliefs. Not naturally forceful, he had little chance to act independently while Rayburn was in charge.

When Rayburn died in November 1961, McCormack was heir-apparent and succeeded him without challenge. But McCormack was seen as a weak leader by the increasingly active liberal Democrats who were frustrated by the CONSERVATIVE COALITION of southern Democrats and Republicans. When Republican gains in the 1966 elections reduced the Democratic majority, McCormack drew even more criticism for not bringing southern Democrats into line. His enthusiastic support of the war in Vietnam also put him out of step with many younger members.

In 1969 Rep. Morris Udall, an Arizona Democrat in his forties, ran for Speaker against McCormack. Although Udall received only fifty-seven votes, the challenge was a sign of how the Speaker's authority had declined. McCormack did not run for reelection in 1970.

## Mace, House

The most treasured possession of the House of Representatives is the mace, a traditional symbol of legislative authority. The concept, borrowed from the British House of Commons, had its origin in republican Rome, where the fasces—an ax bound in a bundle of rods—symbolized the power of the magistrates.

The mace was adopted by the House in its first session in 1789 as a symbol of office for the SERGEANT-AT-ARMS, who is responsible for preserving order on the House floor. The first mace was destroyed when the British burned the Capitol in 1814, and for the next twenty-seven years a mace of painted wood was used.

The present mace, in use since 1841, is a replica of the original mace of 1789. It consists of a bundle of thirteen ebony rods bound in silver, terminating in a silver globe topped by a silver eagle with outstretched wings. It is forty-six inches high and was made by William Adams, a New York silversmith, for the sum of $400.

On several occasions in the history of the House the sergeant-at-arms, on order of the Speaker, has lifted the mace from its pedestal and " presented" it before an unruly member. On each such occasion, order is said to have been promptly restored. At other times the sergeant-at-arms, bearing the mace, has

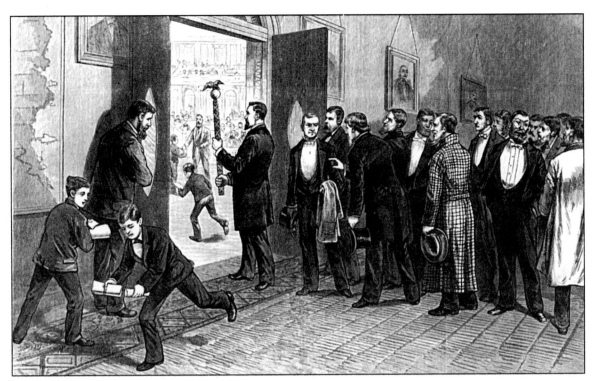

The mace was adopted by the House in its first session in 1789 as a symbol of office for the sergeant-at-arms, who is responsible for preserving order on the House floor.    *Source: Library of Congress*

passed up and down the aisles to quell boisterous behavior in the chamber.

When the House is in regular session, the mace rests on a tall pedestal beside the Speaker's desk. When the House is sitting as the COMMITTEE OF THE WHOLE, the mace is moved to a low pedestal nearby. Thus it is possible to tell at a glance whether the House is meeting in regular session or as the Committee of the Whole.

## Madison, James

When James Madison (1751–1836) was in his mid-twenties he suffered from melancholia, leading him to conclude that he was fated to die young and that, faced with eternity, earthly matters had little im-

portance. When he died at age eighty-five, he could look back on a life distinguished by extraordinary service to his country. Wide reading and observation combined with concern for the needs of the United States led him to formulate many of the precepts later set forth in the Constitution.

As a young man, Madison was caught up in the political affairs of Virginia. In 1776 he was a delegate to Virginia's Revolutionary Convention, serving on the committee responsible for the drafting of Virginia's constitution and bill of rights. In 1780 he was elected to the Continental Congress, where he became a leader of those who favored the interests of national government over state sovereignty. Returning to Virginia, Madison entered the Virginia legislature in 1784.

Convinced that the Articles of Confederation were inadequate, Madison called for a convention to re-

*James Madison, one of the key framers of the Constitution, also wrote the* Federalist Papers *with Alexander Hamilton and John Jay.*    Source: Library of Congress

solve problems plaguing the union of states. He played a leading role in the Constitutional Convention held in Philadelphia in 1787.

Madison was one of the authors of the "Virginia Plan," which proposed a tripartite national government, reflecting his belief that the governing power should be shared among three separate but dependent branches of government. Madison also advocated representation in Congress on the basis of state population, the right of the government to raise revenue, and the popular election of national legislators and executives. He kept a detailed diary of the proceedings of the convention, published in 1840 as the *Journal of the Federal Convention.* With Alexander Hamilton and John Jay, he wrote the *Federalist Papers,* a series of commentaries on the Constitution aimed at building support for its ratification.

In 1789 Madison entered the new U.S. House of Representatives, where he served four terms. He introduced the Bill of Rights, fought for revenue legislation, and took part in shaping the executive branch. Angry over John Jay's 1796 treaty with Great Britain, Madison left Congress in 1797.

Madison served as secretary of state under President Thomas Jefferson and was elected to succeed him in 1808. Madison's presidency was plagued by political dissension and his inability to organize the country and armed forces for the War of 1812. After ratification of the Treaty of Ghent in 1815, Madison turned his attention to domestic problems and retired in 1817 with his popularity restored.

## Majority Party Control

*See* LEADERSHIP.

## Mansfield, Mike

Mike Mansfield (1903–   ), a Montana Democrat who followed Lyndon B. Johnson as majority leader of the Senate, exercised a permissive style of leadership that contrasted sharply with Johnson's methods. A representative for ten years and a senator for nearly twenty-five, Mansfield brought a wealth of congressional experience to the leadership post. His sixteen-year tenure as leader (1961–1977) was the longest in Senate history. After Mansfield retired, President Jimmy Carter named him to be U.S. ambassador to Japan; the Japanese respected Mansfield so highly that President Ronald Reagan kept him in the post throughout his administration.

Mansfield left a career as a professor of Latin American and Asian history to run for a House seat. Unsuccessful in 1940, he won in 1942. He gained a seat on the Foreign Affairs Committee, and in 1944 President Franklin D. Roosevelt sent him to China on a fact-finding mission.

Moving to the Senate in 1953, Mansfield was

given a seat on the Foreign Relations Committee. He was one of the first two freshman senators to benefit from Johnson's decision to place newcomers on key committees. In the Senate as in the House, Mansfield compiled a liberal voting record on domestic and foreign issues.

A taciturn man, Mansfield often answered questions simply with "yep" or "nope." But his spareness with words did not keep him from the leadership track. In 1957 he became majority whip under Johnson. When Johnson moved to the vice presidency in 1961, Mansfield took over the majority leader's post. Johnson had been assertive, powerful, and manipulative; Mansfield was known as "the gentle persuader" because he held that each senator should conduct his affairs with minimal pressure from the leadership. Besides, he said, "Sooner or later they'd just tell you to go to hell and do what they wanted to anyway."

Mansfield held the respect of his colleagues, but he was not an aggressive leader. Under him the Johnson system of rewards and punishment gave way to a col-

legial pattern in which the Democratic Policy Committee and the legislative committees played important roles. He was one of the first Democrats to differ openly with Johnson on the Vietnam War. Later he was a leader of efforts to cut off funds for the war and thus force President Richard Nixon into negotiations to end it.

## *Marbury v. Madison*

*See* COURTS AND CONGRESS.

## Markup

*See* LEGISLATIVE PROCESS.

*Mike Mansfield's sixteen-year tenure as majority leader was the longest in Senate history. He is shown here, left, with colleague Hugh Scott.*
*Source: Senate Historical Society*

## Martin, Joseph W., Jr.

A representative from Massachusetts for forty-two years, Joseph W. Martin, Jr. (1884–1968), was leader of the House Republicans from 1939 to 1959. For most of those twenty years he was minority leader. But in the two Congresses in which the Republicans controlled the House (1947–1949, 1953–1955), Martin served as Speaker. He was the only Republican SPEAKER OF THE HOUSE between 1931 and the end of the Bush administration in 1993. Martin also served as chair of the Republican National Committee from 1940 to 1942.

Martin was a newspaper publisher in North Attle-

boro before he became involved in Republican politics in Massachusetts. After six terms in the state legislature, in 1925 he entered the U.S. House, where he remained until 1967. He served on the Foreign Affairs Committee and later the Rules Committee. Martin's name is not associated with any major legislation, and he was not known as an orator. A consummate politician, he was mainly interested in the day-to-day workings of the House. "We are not reformers, not do-gooders, not theorists. . . . We are just practical Americans trying to do a practical job to reach practical goals," he said of members of Congress.

In 1933 Martin became minority whip. In this position and later as minority leader and Speaker, Martin worked to defeat the domestic initiatives of

*House Speaker Joseph Martin swears in members of the House of Representatives as the 83rd Congress convenes.*
*Source: U.S. Information Agency*

Franklin D. Roosevelt and Harry S. Truman. To this end he helped form an alliance of southern Democrats and Republicans, known as the CONSERVATIVE COALITION, which proved both durable and powerful. His efforts to defeat the NEW DEAL, together with the opposition of New York Republicans Bruce Barton and Hamilton Fish, Jr., so enraged Roosevelt that during his 1940 presidential campaign he referred sarcastically to the three men as "that historic trio . . . Martin, Barton, and Fish."

If Martin's relations with Democratic presidents were bad, his understanding with House Democratic leader Sam RAYBURN of Texas was good—too good for many House Republicans. Martin had an amicable and cooperative relationship with Rayburn, who both preceded and succeeded him as Speaker.

In 1959 Republicans took the unusual step of ousting Martin as party leader, complaining that he was too old for the post and too conciliatory to the Democratic leadership. They replaced him with Charles A. Halleck of Indiana, an outspoken conservative.

## Members of Congress: Characteristics

Congress has been dominated from the first by middle-aged white men with backgrounds in law or business. But the institution's group portrait gradually has acquired more variety, and the new class of freshmen who entered the House and Senate in 1993 altered it further. They were younger than the returning incumbents and included a record number of women and members of minority groups.

African Americans and women, shut out of Congress for decades, were well integrated into Congress by the late 1980s, but their numbers remained small. The 103rd Congress, which convened in 1993, had thirty-nine black members and seventeen Hispanics, dramatic increases over previous congresses.(See BLACKS IN CONGRESS; WOMEN IN CONGRESS.)

Asians and Pacific islanders gained two voting seats over the three they had had in the House in the 102nd Congress. Including senators Daniel K. Inouye and Daniel K. Akaka of Hawaii, there were seven members of Congress of Asian or Pacific island de-

scent. The 103rd Congress included the first Korean American to serve in the House, Republican Jay C. Kim of California, as well as a senator of Native American descent, Democrat Ben Nighthorse Campbell of Colorado.

The average age of members of Congress increased substantially between the post–Civil War period and the 1950s and has fluctuated since then. The relative youth of the 1993 freshmen tempered a decade-long aging trend, a result of the aging of the population in general and of low turnover in Congress. On average, the Senate in 1993 was a year older than previously at fifty-eight; the House was a year younger at an average age of fifty-two, as was the Congress as a whole at fifty-three.

Half the freshmen who entered Congress in 1993 were under forty-five, while only one-fifth of the returning incumbents were that young. The newcomers also tended to lack military experience. In all, 98 of the 121 members of the freshman class reported no service in the armed forces. In contrast, well over half of the returning members had served in the military, most of them during wartime.

Most members of Congress have undergraduate degrees, and many have additional training. By occupation, senators and representatives are primarily from law or business. In the 1980s roughly two-thirds of the Senate and almost half of the House were lawyers, though the number of lawyers in Congress has gradually declined since the 1970s. The 103rd Congress continued the decline, with the number of lawyers dropping from 244 to 239.

A new breed of legislator emerged in the 1970s: the career politician whose primary earnings had always come from political office at the local, state, or federal level. This trend became possible because states and localities had begun to think of political positions as full-time jobs and had raised salaries accordingly. In addition, the rigors of modern political campaigns demanded increased expertise and commitment on the part of candidates and left less time for the pursuit of other careers.

In the 103rd Congress, ninety-seven members—including one-fourth of the freshman class—listed public service as their primary occupation. Freshman House member James A. Barcia of Michigan typified

## LONGEST SERVICE IN CONGRESS

| Member | Years of Service | Total Years[1] |
|---|---|---|
| Carl T. Hayden, D-Ariz. | 1912–1927(H), 1927–1969(S) | 57 |
| Jamie L. Whitten, D-Miss. | 1941–   (H) | 51[2] |
| Carl Vinson, D-Ga. | 1914–1965(H) | 50 |
| Emanuel Celler, D-N.Y. | 1923–1973(H) | 50 |
| Sam Rayburn, D-Texas | 1913–1961(H) | 49 |
| Wright Patman, D-Texas | 1929–1976(H) | 47 |
| Joseph G. Cannon, R-Ill. | 1873–1891(H), 1893–1913(H), 1915–1923(H) | 46 |
| Adolph J. Sabath, D-Ill. | 1907–1952(H) | 46 |
| Lister Hill, D-Ala. | 1923–1938(H), 1938–1969(S) | 45 |
| George H. Mahon, D-Texas | 1935–1979(H) | 44 |
| Warren G. Magnuson, D-Wash. | 1937–1944(H), 1944–1981(S) | 44 |
| Justin S. Morrill, R-Vt. | 1855–1867(H), 1867–1898(S) | 44 |
| Melvin Price, D-Ill. | 1945–1988(H) | 44 |
| William B. Allison, R-Iowa | 1863–1871(H), 1873–1908(S) | 43 |
| Henry M. Jackson, D-Wash. | 1941–1953(H), 1953–1983(S) | 43 |

SOURCE: Congressional Research Service.

NOTES: H = House, S = Senate.

[1] As of the end of 1992. Totals, based on exact dates of service, are rounded to nearest year. Minor differences in days or months of service determine rankings of members with the same total of years.

[2] Service record as of the end of 1992. Whitten was reelected in 1992.

these professional politicians. Barcia was elected to the Michigan house at the age of twenty-four and later moved to the state senate. When he entered Congress at forty-one, he listed his occupation as "public official."

Whether or not a politician has a career outside of public service, his or her route to Congress typically begins with local or state politics. Senators often have served in the House or as governor, while representatives frequently emerge from state legislatures or city councils. For some, however, Congress is the first elective office. Alabama Republican Terry Everett, for example, won a House seat in 1992 after a successful career in business. Some, like Democratic senators Bill Bradley of New Jersey and John Glenn of Ohio, were celebrities before they came to Congress. Bradley was a basketball star and Glenn, an astronaut.

Protestantism has been the most common religious affiliation for legislators, with over two-thirds of the members listing some Protestant denomination as their religion. The number of Catholics and Jews in Congress has been growing since the 1960s. In the 103rd Congress, 141 members listed their religion as Roman Catholic and 42 as Jewish.

Although the House and Senate in many ways do not mirror the electorate, the House does reflect geographic shifts in the nation's population. After each ten-year census, the 435 districts are reapportioned, with a few states gaining or losing representatives. In the 1980s and early 1990s Congress had far more Californians, Texans, and Floridians than in the 1930s. New York, Illinois, Ohio, and Pennsylvania, on the other hand, continued to lose seats. The election of record numbers of minority members in 1992 was largely a result of congressional redistricting aimed at increasing minority representation in Congress. (See REAPPORTIONMENT AND REDISTRICTING.)

Change in the characteristics of members has come slowly on Capitol Hill, in part because turnover rates have been low in the twentieth century. Incumbents usually have sought reelection and have been successful. From 1984 to 1990 more than 95 percent of incumbents who ran for reelection were successful. In 1992, despite widespread dissatisfaction with Congress and reports of anti-incumbent sentiment sweeping the nation, 94 percent of incumbents were reelected. Twenty-four House incumbents and three incumbent senators were defeated.

## Members: Service Records

On average, senators and representatives spend about ten years in Congress. The longest congressional career was that of Carl T. HAYDEN, an Arizona Democrat who served in the House (1912–1927) and Senate (1927–1969) for a total of fifty-seven years.

The runner-up, Democrat Jamie L. Whitten of Mississippi, had been in the House for fifty-one years as of the end of the 102nd Congress in 1992. First elected in 1941 when he was thirty-one years old, Whitten was reelected again in 1992 at the age of eighty-two. As chair of the Appropriations Committee from 1978 to 1992, Whitten was sometimes referred to as "the last of the New Dealers."

By the end of 1992 Whitten had surpassed Democrats Carl Vinson of Georgia and Emanuel Celler of New York to become the longest-serving member of the House. Vinson was a long-time chair of the House Armed Services Committee, and Celler chaired the Judiciary Committee. Sam RAYBURN (1913–1961), a Texas Democrat and House Speaker, served for almost forty-nine years.

## Merchant Marine and Fisheries Committee, House

An odd mix of legislation makes the Merchant Marine and Fisheries Committee a hybrid, where supporters of the shipping industry rub shoulders with environmental activists. A primary activity has been to keep in place the massive subsidies and cargo preference rules that have supported the ailing U.S. shipping industry since 1916. But the committee has not had the clout to expand support of the industry, which has been swamped by international competition and hampered by dissension among unions, shipbuilders, and ship operators.

The committee's standing has not been helped by charges of unethical behavior against committee leaders. New York Democrat John M. Murphy was chair of the Merchant Marine and Fisheries Committee in 1980 when he was caught up in the ABSCAM SCANDAL on charges of influence peddling. He lost his reelection bid that year. Mario Biaggi, also a New York Democrat, was vice chair of the committee in 1988 when he was convicted on bribery charges; the House ethics panel recommended his expulsion. (See DISCIPLINING MEMBERS.)

The Merchant Marine and Fisheries Committee was set up in 1887. Considered a secondary committee, it attracts members from coastal and Great Lakes districts. In addition to shipping, the committee oversees the oceans, including fishing policy, wildlife and fisheries, and the Coast Guard. On many environmental issues it shares jurisdiction with other committees. Its Senate counterpart on most questions is the Commerce, Science, and Transportation Committee.

Because of the Merchant Marine and Fisheries Committee's relatively narrow jurisdiction, advocates of reorganization proposed eliminating it in the 1970s. The chair at the time, Missouri Democrat Leonor K. Sullivan, managed to defeat attempts to abolish her committee. North Carolina Democrat Walter B. Jones was chair of the committee from 1981 until his death in 1992. Gerry E. Studds, a Massachusetts Democrat from a district with fishing and shipping interests, took his place.

The Merchant Marine and Fisheries Committee had a spotty record in the 1980s and early 1990s. It was at first unsuccessful in fighting user fees for recreational boaters, but it was able to pass toxic cleanup legislation. The committee also managed to resist efforts by agricultural interests to win an exemption for their products from existing "cargo preference" rules. Those rules required shippers to use U.S.-operated vessels, instead of less expensive foreign-flag ships, for half of all government-generated exports.

## Michel, Robert H.

Robert H. Michel (1923–   ), an Illinois Republican elected House minority leader in 1981, steered his

*House Minority Leader Robert Michel steered the Republican party in the House to unexpected victories during the Reagan administration, but his influence diminished in the late 1980s.* Source: Lisa Berg

party to unexpected victories in the early years of Ronald Reagan's presidency. His influence waned in the late 1980s as Democratic majorities swelled in the House and younger conservatives pressed for a more confrontational stance. But Michel managed to keep his post into the Clinton administration that began in 1993. His strengths were his amiable, optimistic style and his ability to adapt to changing circumstances.

In his first tests as leader, Michel milked Reagan's popularity in the early 1980s for every vote it could yield, holding Republicans together and wooing conservative Democrats to win startling victories on tax cuts and budget bills. In later years his quiet intervention at key moments helped win anticrime measures and the continuation of aid to the Nicaraguan "contra" rebels for Reagan.

This did not ensure his post as leader, given the changing dynamics of the House. For that Michel had to use what he called "gentle persuasion" to balance the demands of junior conservatives urging confrontation with the Democrats against those of moderates in the party. His balancing act became more difficult in 1989, when his colleagues selected conservative advocate Newt Gingrich of Georgia as whip over Michel's candidate, Edward Madigan of Illinois. Michel confessed to discouragement at the end of 1990, but his enthusiasm was revived in early 1991 as he led a divided House to give President George Bush authority to use military force against Iraq.

Michel was first elected to the House in 1956 and spent much of his congressional career as a member of the House Appropriations Committee. During his quarter-century on that committee, he became a top-flight negotiator, skilled in the trade-offs and compromises that are the hallmark of the appropriations process. Michel became minority whip in 1974, a position he held until his election as minority leader, when House Republicans chose his "workhorse" campaign arguments over the oratorical flourishes of opponent Guy Vander Jagt of Michigan. (See LEADERSHIP.)

## Mills, Wilbur D.

An expert on U.S. tax law, Wilbur D. Mills (1909–1992) skillfully used his knowledge and political savvy during seventeen years as chair of the House Ways and Means Committee (1957–1974). Mills's preeminent position made his fall in 1974 even more dramatic. After well-publicized escapades with a striptease dancer, he resigned as chair and entered a hospital for treatment of alcoholism. Mills served the term he had just won and then retired in 1977.

Mills was a judge in White County, Arkansas, when he first ran for Congress in 1938. Friendship with Democratic leader Sam Rayburn won Mills a seat in 1943 on the Ways and Means Committee, a coveted spot usually reserved for more senior members. Mills studied the tax code and by the time he became chair was well known for his grasp of even minor details. Colleagues were awed by his ability to speak, without notes, in favor of his committee's work.

An authoritarian chair, Mills kept control over all tax measures by bringing them before the whole committee and refusing to establish subcommittees to consider different issues. Mills consolidated his power by accurately sensing what the House would support and drafting legislation accordingly. He took tax bills to the floor under ground rules that barred floor amendments, and the full House regularly passed the measures by wide margins.

Mills's personal prestige was enhanced by his role as chair of the Democratic Committee on Committees. Since 1910 the chair of the Ways and Means Committee, along with the panel's Democratic members, had made Democratic committee assignments. Mills was the last chair to have the double responsibility; the Democratic Caucus in 1974 shifted committee assignments to the Democratic Steering and Policy Committee. The caucus also tried to dilute the authority of the chair of the Ways and Means Committee by expanding the panel from twenty-five to thirty-five members. (See CAUCUSES, PARTY.)

Conservative in his politics, Mills still managed to work with Presidents John F. Kennedy and Lyndon B. Johnson, though not on every issue. Opposition from Mills was enough to kill a bill; his resistance to Medicare stalled the legislation for several years.

By the 1970s Mills was a target of Democratic reformers, who considered his accumulation of power improper and a roadblock to a more democratic House. His personal indiscretions simply bolstered their position. In October 1974 police stopped Mills's car near the Tidal Basin, a shallow part of the Potomac River not far from the Washington Monument. One of the passengers, later identified as stripteaser Fanne Foxe, jumped from the car and ended up in the water. Several weeks later Mills appeared briefly on stage with Foxe in Boston.

Although he had just been reelected, his standing in Congress was never the same after the incident. After his retirement in 1977 Mills stayed in Washington working for a law firm, Shea and Gould, and lobbying his former colleagues.

## Mitchell, George J.

George J. Mitchell's (1933–   ) election as Senate majority leader in 1988 surprised those who thought his thoughtful, low-key manner and liberal views would disqualify him. A Democrat from Maine who gave up a federal judgeship to fill a Senate vacancy in 1980, Mitchell won high marks from Democrats during his first years as majority leader. He was respected for his command of legislative detail, his skill at forging consensus, and his strong articulation of positions in opposition to Republican president George Bush.

Mitchell often played the role of adversary during his first four years as majority leader. He managed to kill a capital gains tax proposal favored by Bush, and he spoke eloquently against Bush's use of military force in the Persian Gulf. Mitchell proved an effective negotiator as well, working out a compromise with Republicans that contributed to enactment of a major clean air bill. The election of Democrat Bill Clinton as president in 1992 for the first time put Mitchell in position to cooperate with an administration on legislative goals.

Mitchell began his career in politics as an assistant to Sen. Edmund S. Muskie. Mitchell was named U.S.

*Sen. Robert Byrd, left, who served as Senate Democratic leader for a decade, hands the gavel, the symbol of authority, to Sen. George Mitchell after Mitchell's election as majority leader in 1988.    Source: AP/Wide World Photos*

attorney for Maine in 1977 and two years later became a federal judge. He left that position after only a few months to fill the Senate seat vacated in 1980 when Muskie became President Jimmy Carter's secretary of state.

In the Senate Mitchell quickly caught the attention of his colleagues with his keen memory for detail and his command of facts, particularly on environmental and health care issues. He further impressed his fellow senators with his political skills when he came from behind to win election to a full term in 1982 with 61 percent of the vote. Chosen to chair the Democratic Senatorial Campaign Committee for the critical 1986 elections, Mitchell was instrumental in helping his party regain control of the Senate. As a reward, he was made deputy president pro tempore, a post created for Hubert H. Humphrey in 1977 and not occupied after that.

Appointed in 1986 to the Senate committee investigating the IRAN-CONTRA AFFAIR, Mitchell proved himself to be an able performer before national television cameras, a factor considered crucial to his election as majority leader.

## Morning Business

*See* MORNING HOUR.

## Morning Hour

The morning hour is a time set aside by the Senate at the beginning of a daily session for transaction of routine business. Under Senate rules the morning "hour" may actually extend for up to two hours. During that period members conduct what is known as morning business—introducing bills, filing committee reports, and receiving messages from the House of Representatives or the president. Senators may make brief speeches by unanimous consent. A senator also may move to consider any bill on the CALENDAR, but such motions must be decided without debate. This tactic is rarely used.

The Senate's rules do not call for a morning hour every day. The Senate holds a morning hour only if its previous session ended in ADJOURNMENT, as distinguished from a recess. Even then the morning hour may be limited or dropped by unanimous consent. Between adjournments the Senate conducts morning business by unanimous consent. (See LEGISLATIVE DAY.)

Although House rules also provide for a morning hour, the arrangement is almost never used there.

## Motions

Motions play as important a role as voting in Congress. In fact, without the use of motions members could never reach the voting stage. Virtually every step in the LEGISLATIVE PROCESS is initiated and completed by motions of one type or another. Put another way, motions enable senators and representatives to consider and dispose of legislation in a deliberate and orderly manner. Certain motions are especially important to the opponents of a bill, giving the minority side on any issue an opportunity to be heard and to present its policy choices. (See VOTING IN CONGRESS.)

Motions have specific functions, and their use is governed by the parliamentary situation. Among others, there are motions to adjourn, recess, postpone debate, end debate, withdraw other motions, proceed to the consideration of a bill or conference report, table a bill, reconsider a bill, strike out and insert substitute provisions in a bill, recommit a bill to a committee, discharge a committee from consideration of a bill, move the PREVIOUS QUESTION to bring a measure to a vote, suspend the rules, and make a POINT OF ORDER. A few are used only in one chamber. (See DISCHARGE, COMMITTEE; RECOMMITTAL MOTION; RECONSIDER, MOTION TO; SUBSTITUTE; SUSPENSION OF THE RULES; TABLE, MOTION TO.)

Under normal circumstances members can offer motions or initiate other legislative business only when they are recognized by the chair (the presiding officer). Once a member who has the floor offers, or "moves," a motion or introduces an amendment, he or she gives up the floor.

The standing rules of each house recognize certain motions as having precedence, or PRIVILEGE, over others. A formal hierarchy is necessary to avoid confusion and disputes when several members desire to offer different, and sometimes conflicting, motions at the same time. A tabling motion supersedes a motion to reconsider a previous vote on a bill. A vote therefore would be held on the tabling motion first; if adopted, the motion to reconsider would be nullified. A motion to adjourn in either house takes precedence over all others.

Some motions are more important than others to the everyday operations of the House and Senate, and some are indispensable. Others are clearly intended as delaying tactics. Some are offered merely to gain extra debate time when the House is sitting as the COMMITTEE OF THE WHOLE and debate on amendments is limited to five minutes for each side. Pro forma motions "to strike the last word" or "to strike the enacting clause" of a bill give proponents and opponents each five additional minutes to debate an amendment. However, delays cannot go on indefinitely. Members who thinks debate is dilatory can always offer their own motion to end debate immediately or at a specified time. This procedure for ending debate does not apply in the Senate.

# N

## Narcotics Abuse and Control Committee, House Select

Back in 1977, before the "Just Say No" campaign and proposals for mandatory drug testing, the House set up a select committee to study drug problems. Initially the Select Committee on Narcotics Abuse and Control focused on marijuana and heroin; in the 1980s and early 1990s its primary concern was cocaine and crack. But in 1993 it went out of existence, a victim of government spending cuts.

Like other select committees, the panel could not write legislation but could make recommendations; it also held hearings and conducted investigations. It had to be reauthorized at the beginning of each two-year term of Congress.

In the 103rd Congress, which began in 1993, pressure to cut costs throughout the federal government, driven by efforts to reduce the federal budget deficit, prompted legislators to kill a number of special committees in the House, including Narcotics.

Several other House committees, including Judiciary, Foreign Affairs, and Energy and Commerce, had legislative jurisdiction over various aspects of drugs. When Congress passed a massive antidrug bill in 1986, eleven House standing committees contributed to the measure, which also included some proposals made by the Narcotics Abuse and Control Committee.

## Natural Resources Committee, House

The House Natural Resources Committee oversees the nation's public lands, carrying out the decades-old philosophy that some land should be set aside and managed by the government for the good of all. Conflicts between preserving the land as wilderness and using it for logging, grazing, and mining often fall to the Natural Resources Committee, and then Congress, to resolve. Legislators from the West, where most federal land is located, dominate the committee. The Natural Resources Committee also oversees the federal water projects that subsidize irrigation of arid western areas and make large-scale agriculture possible there.

Among the oldest House committees, the Natural Resources Committee was established in 1805 as the Public Lands Committee; its title was changed in 1951 to Interior and Insular Affairs. It gained its present name in 1993. Although the Natural Resources Committee is not considered a major committee, it is still crucial to representatives from the West.

Many environmental issues, such as clean air and water, lie outside the committee's jurisdiction. Even federal lands are not entirely within its purview; it shares management of wildlife refuges with the Merchant Marine and Fisheries Committee, and oversight of forestry with the Agriculture Committee. The Natural Resources Committee handles some aspects of energy policy, such as regulation of nuclear power and restrictions on the strip mining of coal, but the Energy and Commerce Committee is the primary House energy panel.

### Public Lands

Under Morris K. Udall, the Arizona Democrat who chaired the committee from 1979 to 1991, the Natural Resources Committee was a strong advocate of protecting public lands. Although many committee members still wanted to accommodate the timber and mineral industries, that attitude did not dominate the committee in the late 1970s and 1980s as it had earlier under the lengthy chairmanship (1959–1973) of Colorado Democrat Wayne N. Aspinall. Although Stewart Udall, interior secretary from 1961 to 1969 and Morris Udall's brother, had won support from the Senate to close certain federal lands to commercial use, the proposals had faced opposition from Aspinall and the House. Congress eventually passed the 1964 Wilderness Act, a landmark bill that also included concessions to mineral leasing and other activities.

More than a decade later the House, not the Senate, was the lead player on preservation issues. When Congress was considering what parks, forests—and energy development—were appropriate on the millions of acres of federally owned land in Alaska, the Senate pushed for less protection and more development. In contrast, the Natural Resources Committee won House passage of a conservation-oriented bill. Eventually enacted in 1980, the measure concerning Alaska lands fell short of House goals, but it did reflect earlier concessions by the Senate to the committee's proposals.

George Miller, a California Democrat, ushered in a more combative style when he became committee chair in 1991. Sparks flew almost immediately, with western members opposed to Miller's environmentalist agenda. He sought to limit big farms' use of federally subsidized water, instead diverting it to restore damaged breeding areas for fish and wildlife.

Never were the ideological differences between the parties more apparent than during the early years of Ronald Reagan's presidency in the 1980s. James Watt, secretary of interior from 1981 to 1983, launched an aggressive campaign to allow private industry to develop wilderness areas before a 1984 deadline would close them to commercial use. That legacy from Aspinall's era had permitted an additional twenty years of development in areas designated as wilderness in 1964. Eventually, even Republicans on the natural resources panel objected to Watt's plans, and Congress blocked him from acting. On many other issues, the committee took positions more favorable to conservation than did the Republican-controlled Senate Energy and Natural Resources Committee, which handles most public land questions.

The Natural Resources Committee has a mixed record in one area: water projects. The committee oversees the Bureau of Reclamation, which since 1902 has provided water in the West at subsidized rates. Although sensitive to environmentalists' complaints in most areas, even Udall was a staunch defender of dams and waterworks, particularly the massive Central Arizona Project, which promised to bring water to the arid cities of Tucson and Phoenix in his district.

# New Deal

The period in U.S. history known as the New Deal took in the first two terms (1933–1941) of President Franklin D. Roosevelt. Made up of hundreds of individual programs, the New Deal was designed to rescue the United States from the greatest economic depression in its history. The recovery programs of the Roosevelt administration in turn brought about major changes in American society, economic relationships, and government.

Roosevelt coined the term *New Deal* in his acceptance speech at the 1932 Democratic national convention in Chicago. Breaking with tradition by attending the convention in person to accept the presidential nomination, Roosevelt pledged "a new deal for the American people." He was the overwhelming winner in 1932 against President Herbert Hoover. The election also gave Roosevelt large Democratic majorities in both houses of Congress—a clear mandate to initiate his recovery programs. Roosevelt vowed in his presidential inaugural speech "to treat the task as we would treat the emergency of a war."

## Philosophy

Roosevelt's governing philosophy called for a dynamic role for the federal government, including the responsibility to relieve the nation's poverty and unemployment. His New Deal called for action in many different areas:

• Massive changes in agriculture to improve the lot of the farmer through a variety of assistance programs

• Conservation and development of the nation's resources for the widest benefit of the population

• New protections for working people and reform of labor-management relations

• Rehabilitation of American industry to establish a more productive as well as a more humane economy

• Wholesale changes in the nation's financial system, including tighter federal regulation of banking and securities exchanges

• Lower tariffs and reciprocal trade agreements with foreign nations to stimulate business activity

Many innovative domestic programs and reforms are associated with the New Deal. Roosevelt, however, did not assume office with an overall plan to remake the U.S. economy or institute a welfare state. Rather the New Deal began with a series of stopgap relief measures aimed at revitalizing free enterprise, which was near collapse after four years of massive economic dislocation.

Pragmatic rather than doctrinaire, Roosevelt drew on the ideas of experts in many fields in and out of government. Many of his proposals originated in the PROGRESSIVE ERA and in the Wilson administration's experience in mobilizing the country in World War I. But the New Deal went far beyond any earlier U.S. government involvement in the affairs of its citizens.

## Strategy

Immediately upon taking office, Roosevelt convened a special session of Congress—the famous "Hundred Days" session—to deal with the economic emergency. Congress, acting with breathless speed and virtually without debate, enacted some fifteen landmark bills proposed by the administration, most of them highly controversial. The president himself delivered ten major speeches. He assumed the role of a bipartisan leader reaching out to all groups and interests in a time of crisis. That strategy could not last indefinitely. In fact, the New Deal in later years concentrated on fundamental long-term reforms and programs directed at groups and economic interests that threatened its success. Conservative southern Democrats as well as northern industrialists, whom the president called "economic royalists," increasingly felt uncomfortable and insecure. By early 1935 the more innovative New Deal laws were being challenged directly by the Supreme Court. In the next year and a half, the Court overturned six of the New Deal's most sweeping laws. (See COURTS AND CONGRESS.)

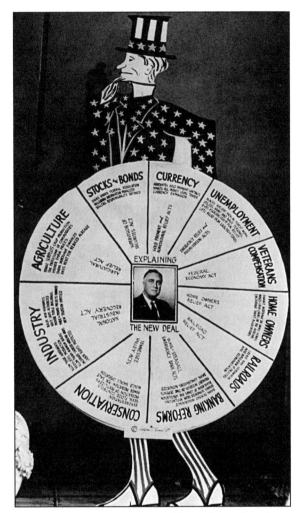

*The New Deal was designed to rescue the United States from the greatest economic depression in its history by implementing massive changes and reforms. Here a figure of Uncle Sam carries a wheel whose spokes contain facts and figures on New Deal legislation.*
*Source: Library of Congress*

In his second term Roosevelt began to focus the New Deal on structural reform and was more outwardly supportive of organized labor, the unemployed and the rural poor, the aged, and small business. At the same time he called for more stringent federal regulation of big business and higher taxation of the more affluent. He tried to meet the Supreme

Court challenge head on by introducing his so-called Court-packing plan. Having just won reelection in the greatest presidential landslide in U.S. history, Roosevelt early in 1937 called for increasing the Court's size as a way to dilute the influence of several old, conservative justices on the nine-member bench. In this the president suffered one of his most humiliating defeats in Congress. He miscalculated public reaction, and the plan divided the ranks of the New Deal coalition.

Although he lost the battle, Roosevelt won the war. Even before Congress debated the controversial proposal, the Court began to show a willingness to accept New Deal policies. Newly passed legislation similar to that declared unconstitutional just a year or two earlier was now upheld. And changes in the membership of the Supreme Court, beginning with the appointment of Hugo Black in August 1937, ensured that a majority of the justices would be sympathetic to the expansive legislation of the New Deal.

Between March 1937 and February 1941 the Court upheld revised versions of virtually all the legislation it had declared unconstitutional in Roosevelt's first term. In doing so, it reversed many of the doctrines it had espoused in curtailing state and federal power over economic matters. The Court's new direction culminated in a 1941 decision upholding the Fair Labor Standards Act of 1935, commonly known as the Wagner Act. That law prohibited child labor, set a maximum forty-hour work week, and established the first national minimum wage (forty cents an hour) for workers engaged in, or producing goods for, interstate commerce. Child labor was prohibited, and severe limits were placed on teenage employment in hazardous occupations. (See COMMERCE POWER.)

Nevertheless, the political costs of Roosevelt's defeat on the Court bill had lasting effects on the New Deal. After 1938 a CONSERVATIVE COALITION of southern Democrats and Republicans repeatedly blocked administration initiatives. At the same time the administration was forced to turn its attention to mobilization for war. Still, as late as 1939 Roosevelt could point to enactment of an impressive list of administrative reforms for controlling the expanded federal bureaucracy.

## Legislation

The National Industrial Recovery Act (NIRA) was the centerpiece of the New Deal recovery plan. Enacted in 1933, the measure established a National Recovery Administration that encouraged cooperation among industry trade groups under exemption from antitrust laws. It also set maximum daily working hours and minimum wage rates, and it guaranteed workers the right to join a labor union and bargain collectively. Other provisions of the law established a Public Works Administration to organize and supervise a network of public works projects. This landmark law was overturned by the Supreme Court in 1935, only to be replaced by the even stronger Wagner Act.

The NIRA was only one of the major New Deal bills. Another was the Agricultural Adjustment Act, which aimed to increase farm income by holding down production. The Wagner-Steagall Act established the Federal Housing Authority and authorized several billion dollars—an unheard-of amount in those days—to supervise and pay for slum clearance and construction of low-income housing. The Home Owners' Loan Act set up the Home Owners' Loan Corporation to help avert foreclosures by refinancing home mortgages at very low interest rates.

The Glass-Steagall Act, part of the Banking Act of 1933, barred commercial banks from operating in the investment banking business. Other provisions of the Banking Act of 1933 established the Federal Deposit Insurance Corporation. The Securities Exchange Act established a commission to fight fraud and misrepresentation in the securities business. Probably the best known and most lasting New Deal accomplishment was federal old age and unemployment insurance: the Social Security Act of 1935.

## Nixon, Richard

The stormy career of Richard M. Nixon (1913–  ) reached heights and fell to lows remarkable in U.S. political history. First elected to the House in 1946 as a Republican representative from California, he served two terms before moving to the Senate. Before he

*Congressman-elect Richard Nixon poses with his mother at his 1946 election victory party.    Source: National Archives*

through his second term he was forced to resign in the wake of the WATERGATE SCANDAL.

Nixon viewed his career in terms of crises and setbacks; he wrote *Six Crises,* a political memoir, in 1972. His rise to high political office was swift, impelled by political leaders who chose him as a candidate before, it seemed, he had declared himself. Nixon was a lieutenant in the navy in 1946 when a California Republican group asked him to run for the House of Representatives. He accepted and was successful; in his campaign he accused his opponent Jerry Voorhis, a New Deal Democrat, of communist sympathies.

As a freshman representative, Nixon served on the Education and Labor Committee, where he helped to draft the Taft-Hartley Act of 1947, a landmark labor law. His career in the House is most notable for his activities on the House Un-American Activities Committee. Over the objections of some committee members, Nixon persuaded the committee chair to allow him to reopen an investigation into charges that Alger Hiss, a former State Department official, had communist affiliations. The investigation led to Hiss's indictment for perjury, the first indictment to result from the committee's investigation into communist activities. The case brought Nixon national recognition and, as he himself acknowledged in *Six Crises,* "it also left a residue of hatred and hostility toward me" that was to wax and wane throughout his public career. (See INVESTIGATIONS.)

Nixon used the country's fear of communism to his advantage in his 1950 Senate bid, linking the voting record of his Democratic opponent, incumbent Helen Gahagan Douglas, with that of an allegedly procommunist representative. Nixon won handily, but many observers called his campaign the dirtiest on record. Nixon's later reputation as a ruthless campaigner stemmed from his conduct in that campaign.

Nixon had been a senator for less than two years when he caught the eye of New York governor Thomas E. Dewey, who was promoting Eisenhower's 1952 bid for the presidency. Soon Dewey also was promoting Nixon for the vice presidency. Nixon came close to being forced off the ticket when charges surfaced that he had used the proceeds of a secret campaign fund to supplement his Senate salary. On Sep-

could complete his first Senate term, he was put on the Republican ticket with Dwight D. Eisenhower in 1952 and became the second-youngest vice president in the nation's history.

In 1960 Nixon lost a close race for the presidency to John F. Kennedy. Two years later he lost a bid for the California governorship and bade a bitter farewell to politics. "You won't have Nixon to kick around anymore," he told members of the press, which he blamed for his two losses. Six years later Nixon was elected president; he was reelected in 1972. Midway

tember 23, 1952, he went on national television to re-
but the charges, referring at one point to his wife's
"respectable Republican cloth coat," and to a dog,
Checkers, that had been given to his children.

Nixon's own presidency was notable for his
achievements in foreign relations, particularly improved relations with the Soviet Union and China and
the ending of the war in Vietnam. His domestic programs, however, suffered gravely from poor relations
with the Democratic Congress. Then came the 1972
break-in at the Democratic National Committee headquarters in the Watergate complex. Revelation of
White House involvement in the burglary and its
cover-up fatally injured Nixon's administration. In the
face of almost certain impeachment and removal
from office for obstruction of justice, Nixon left the
White House on August 9, 1974, the first American
president to resign the office. (See NIXON IMPEACH-
MENT EFFORT.)

*President Richard Nixon's resignation in 1974 cut short the
impeachment effort, thus sparing him almost certain impeachment
and removal from office.*

## Nixon Impeachment Effort

Dusting off a rarely used piece of constitutional
machinery, Congress in 1974 began impeachment
proceedings against President Richard NIXON for his
role in the WATERGATE SCANDAL. Nixon's resignation from the presidency cut short the effort, sparing
him almost certain impeachment and removal from
office.

Under the IMPEACHMENT POWER granted by
the Constitution, Congress may remove the president
and other officials for "treason, bribery, or other high
crimes and misdemeanors." The process requires two
steps. An accused official must first be formally
charged, or impeached, by the House of Representatives. The official must then be convicted on those
charges in a Senate trial. Only one president before
Nixon had faced a serious impeachment threat: Andrew Johnson, who was acquitted by the Senate in
1868. (See JOHNSON IMPEACHMENT TRIAL.)

The House Judiciary Committee adopted three
charges, called articles of impeachment, against Nixon
in late July 1974. The articles charged him with abuse

of his presidential powers, obstruction of justice, and
contempt of Congress. The full House never voted on
these articles because Nixon resigned on August 9.
Republican House and Senate leaders had told him
that the evidence against him virtually ensured that
he would be impeached, convicted, and removed
from office.

The chain of events that ended in Nixon's resignation began with a 1972 break-in at Democratic National Committee headquarters in the Watergate
complex in Washington, D.C. A national scandal un-

folded with discovery of White House involvement in the burglary and other political sabotage, as well as cover-up efforts. The extent of White House activities was spelled out in 1973 hearings before a special Senate committee headed by Sen. Sam J. ERVIN, a North Carolina Democrat noted for his knowledge of the Constitution.

A House impeachment inquiry was triggered in October 1973 when Nixon fired a special prosecutor who had been appointed to investigate the Watergate affair. The prosecutor, Archibald Cox, had tried to force Nixon to release tape recordings of conversations concerning Watergate. In July 1974 the Supreme Court ordered Nixon to release the tapes, which made clear that the president had participated in efforts to cover up White House involvement in the burglary. The Supreme Court action came as the House Judiciary Committee was preparing to vote on impeachment charges against Nixon.

The Judiciary Committee approved three articles of impeachment in a series of votes, July 27–30. The first, adopted 27–11, charged Nixon with obstruction of justice. The second, adopted 28–10, charged him with abuse of power. The third, adopted 21–17, charged him with contempt of Congress.

House debate on impeachment was set to begin August 19. Adoption of the charges was considered a certainty, and the Senate began preparing for a trial. It was at this point that Republican congressional leaders told Nixon the evidence against him almost guaranteed that he would be impeached, convicted, and removed from office. On August 8 Nixon appeared on television to announce that he would resign. The following day his resignation became effective, and Nixon left the White House.

The House Judiciary Committee continued to prepare its report recommending Nixon's impeachment, and the report was later filed in the House. But the impeachment proceedings themselves went no further. Vice President Gerald R. FORD succeeded Nixon as president. A month after taking office, Ford granted his predecessor a "full, free and absolute pardon . . . for all offenses against the United States which he . . . has committed or may have committed" during his years as president.

# Norris, George W.

George W. Norris (1861–1944) entered Congress as a Republican from Nebraska, became a Progressive Republican, and ended his congressional career as an Independent Republican. No matter what his party label, Norris was and remained a reformer. His zeal led him to advocate changes in the House of Representatives, the electoral system, the ownership of utilities, and the resolution of labor disputes.

Norris entered the House in 1903. He joined with Democrats in 1908 to try to curtail the powers of the

*Sen. George Norris, author of the Lame-Duck Amendment, also sponsored legislation that established the Tennessee Valley Authority.    Source: Senate Historical Office*

SPEAKER OF THE HOUSE that had been so abused by Joseph G. CANNON, a Republican. The attempt was unsuccessful, and Norris was reelected by a margin of just twenty-two votes. Norris and his Democratic allies eventually won their goal, however, and in 1910 the post of Speaker was stripped of much of its power.

Norris moved to the Senate in 1913, the year the Seventeenth Amendment, calling for DIRECT ELECTION OF SENATORS, was ratified. Norris had backed the amendment, and he continued to push for presidential primaries and the abolition of the electoral college. He supported President Woodrow Wilson's domestic policies but was one of six senators to vote against entry into World War I. He voted against the Treaty of Versailles, which ended the war and created the League of Nations.

Concerned by filibusters that slowed the proceedings of the Senate, Norris proposed doing away with the LAME-DUCK SESSION at the end of every Congress (held after a new Congress was elected but before it began on March 4). The Senate was most vulnerable to filibuster during the short session. Norris wrote the Twentieth Amendment to the Constitution, ratified in 1933, which abolished the short session by advancing the first day of a Congress to January. (See LAME-DUCK AMENDMENT.)

A supporter of organized labor, Norris sponsored legislation restricting the use of federal injunctions against striking workers. He believed that hydroelectric power should be publicly owned, and he sponsored the legislation establishing the Tennessee Valley Authority.

Never one to take party ties too seriously, Norris endorsed the candidacy of Franklin D. Roosevelt in 1932 and later elections. Norris was defeated for reelection in 1942.

# Oath of Office

Article VI of the Constitution states that senators and representatives, as well as the president and other public officers, "shall be bound by Oath or Affirmation to support this Constitution; but no religious Test shall ever be required as a qualification to any Office or public Trust under the United States." The form of the oath of office was established by law: "I, A B, do solemnly swear (or affirm) that I will support and defend the Constitution of the United States against all enemies, foreign and domestic; that I will bear true faith and allegiance to the same; that I take this obligation freely, without any mental reservation or purpose of evasion, and that I will well and faithfully discharge the duties of the office on which I am about to enter. So help me God."

The oath of office is administered to newly elected members at the start of each new Congress in January of odd-numbered years. Because the entire House is up for election every two years, all representatives take the oath each time. Members first elect their chief presiding officer, the SPEAKER OF THE HOUSE, who is sworn in by the CLERK OF THE HOUSE. The Speaker then administers the oath to all other members as they stand together in the chamber. In the Senate, one-third of whose members are elected every two years, the vice president administers the oath to senators-elect as they come to the front of the chamber in small groups.

*The oath of office is administered to newly elected members at the start of each new Congress in January of odd-numbered years. Here Speaker Thomas S. Foley swears in the 102nd Congress. Source: R. Michael Jenkins*

# Office of Technology Assessment

In 1972 Congress established the Office of Technology Assessment (OTA) to help it evaluate scientific and technical proposals for legislation. The office began operations in January 1974. By law OTA serves congressional committees, not individual members of the House or Senate. Its staff and corps of consultants conduct studies to assess the consequences of technologies and prepare analyses of alternate policies.

OTA is governed by a bipartisan congressional

board, consisting of six Senate and six House members plus a director, who is appointed by the board to a six-year term. It is guided also by a Technology Assessment Advisory Council whose members are the comptroller general (head of the General Accounting Office), the director of the Congressional Research Service (an arm of the Library of Congress), and ten members of the public appointed by the board. OTA also has ties to the National Science Foundation and the Congressional Budget Office.

OTA had a full-time staff of about 140 in 1991. In addition, the office had a list of some 2,000 consultants from industry, universities, private research organizations, and public interest groups who could be called on to do specialized work for periods ranging from a day to several weeks.

## Omnibus Bills

A noteworthy feature of the modern Congress has been its tendency to package many, often unrelated, proposals in a single, very long piece of legislation, called an omnibus bill.

Although omnibus bills have been used throughout the nation's history, they assumed new importance after Congress adopted its BUDGET PROCESS in 1974. Using that process, each year the Senate and House of Representatives adopt a budget resolution setting an overall plan for government spending and revenues. In many years, they have followed up with an omnibus measure revising government programs to conform to the overall plan.

It became common practice in the 1980s for Congress to provide funding for most or all government departments and agencies in a single omnibus bill known as a CONTINUING RESOLUTION. In the 1990s, however, Congress began backing away from using continuing resolutions as omnibus funding bills.

In 1992 Congress used an omnibus bill for a package of rescissions—cuts from funding already enacted but not yet spent—proposed by President George Bush and modified by Congress.

Critics complained that individual provisions of omnibus bills often receive little debate, and members are forced to vote on the mammoth measures without fully understanding what is in them. Others defended the omnibus approach, however, arguing that members benefit from the broad overview of government activities it provides. Some noted that many politically unpopular actions, however necessary, might be impossible unless they were buried in an omnibus bill. Omnibus budget bills often enjoy special protections from floor amendments or filibusters.

## O'Neill, Thomas P., Jr.

As SPEAKER OF THE HOUSE from 1977 until his retirement in 1987, Thomas P. O'Neill, Jr. (1912–   ), found himself playing a new role. Before becoming Speaker, "Tip" O'Neill spent twenty-four years as a Democratic representative from Massachusetts. As a representative, O'Neill practiced insider politics, talking over strategy with close friends during games of poker or golf. The post of Speaker in those years was similarly an inside office. O'Neill's three predecessors all sought to win key showdowns on the House floor by quietly building coalitions within the chamber. O'Neill became Speaker, however, just as House members began to put more stock in independence, rather than party loyalty, and to take their cues from constituencies outside the chamber. O'Neill soon found that he could win more votes by influencing public opinion than by twisting arms. As the one visible Democratic officeholder at the national level during the first six years of the Reagan administration, from 1981 to 1987, O'Neill inevitably became the party symbol to the national press.

O'Neill came to the House in 1953, a cigar-smoking, poker-playing Red Sox fan from Cambridge, proud of his great success in state politics, where he had been his party's first Speaker of the Massachusetts house in the twentieth century. In Congress O'Neill joined the Public Works Committee to make sure that Massachusetts received its share of federal jobs and projects. In his second term he moved to the Rules Committee, which controls access to the floor for major legislation. During his eighteen years on the rules panel, O'Neill nearly always supported the Speaker;

*Thomas P. "Tip" O'Neill, Jr., was a Democratic representative for twenty-four years before becoming Speaker of the House. While serving as Speaker during the first six years of the Reagan administration, O'Neill became his party's symbol to the national press.*
*Source: George Tames/*The New York Times

he was viewed more as a loyal soldier than as a potential House leader. Two events, however, helped change that perception.

In late 1967 O'Neill broke with President Lyndon B. Johnson and publicly opposed the war in Vietnam, thus drawing the attention of younger House liberals. Three years later he worked with many of these same liberals to pass a major reform of House procedure. (See REFORM, CONGRESSIONAL.) In 1971 he won a place on the leadership ladder as majority whip, and in 1973 he became majority leader. When Carl Albert retired as Speaker in 1976, Democrats chose O'Neill by acclamation.

Strongly partisan, more interested in the politics of the House than the content of legislation, O'Neill car-

ried the Democratic banner during the administrations of Democrat Jimmy Carter and Republican Ronald Reagan. Although he had no particular enthusiasm for Carter's programs, O'Neill worked hard to pass them through Congress. He pushed through tough ethics legislation and speedily delivered House approval of Carter's massive energy package. But by the end of Carter's term in 1981 O'Neill was having a difficult time, often unable to break up a united Republican front or to prevent Democratic defections.

With the election in 1980 of a Republican president and a Republican-controlled Senate, O'Neill fell victim to the rising partisan tension on the House floor. He was unable to block House approval of Reagan's economic package. Democrats regained effective control of the House in the 1982 elections. In his final years as Speaker, O'Neill nearly always had the votes to prevail when he wanted.

When he retired, O'Neill published his memoirs (coauthored with William Novak), *Man of the House: The Life and Political Memoirs of Speaker Tip O'Neill.*

## Organization of Congress Committee, Joint

Congress in 1992 created a Joint Committee on the Organization of Congress to recommend changes in its legislative procedures and power structure. The action was taken against a backdrop of headline-grabbing scandals, legislative deadlock, public cynicism, and the retirements of some talented—and frustrated—members of Congress. Some of the most respected members in the House and Senate were calling for major changes.

Creation of the committee reflected members' impatience with the way Congress operated and their desire to rebuild public confidence. But it also represented a concerted strategy to get on top of the issue before the 103rd Congress (1993–1995) arrived with the largest freshman class since 1949. To avoid becoming the object of a freshman revolt, members of the 102nd Congress were trying to draw up an agenda that would harness new members' energies.

Specifically, the new committee was directed to

study the committee system, the relationship between the House and Senate, the relationship between Congress and the executive branch, and the responsibilities and powers of the congressional leadership. The panel was modeled on committees that produced two major reorganizations of Congress in 1946 and 1970. (See REFORM, CONGRESSIONAL.)

The panel numbered twenty-eight members. It included equal numbers of Republicans and Democrats from both the House and Senate, as well as both chambers' majority and minority leaders as ex-officio members. The committee was to make recommendations for change by December 1993. Democrats Lee H. Hamilton, representative from Indiana, and David L. Boren, senator from Oklahoma, were chosen to head the committee.

---

## Oversight Power

Congress has delegated to the executive branch broad authority over agencies and programs it has created. Its oversight power helps ensure that the executive branch performs as Congress intends.

Hearings and INVESTIGATIONS, the most publicized form of oversight, provide some of the most colorful moments on Capitol Hill. The lengthy 1987 hearings on the IRAN-CONTRA AFFAIR exposed a web of covert activities involving members of President Ronald Reagan's National Security Council (NSC). There were moments of high drama as Marine Lt. Col. Oliver L. North, a former NSC staff member, defended his role in U.S. arms sales to Iran and the diversion of profits from those sales to antigovernment guerrillas in Nicaragua.

Oversight takes less spectacular forms as well. The most effective may stem from the power of the purse. Because Congress controls the federal purse strings, it is able to review agencies' performance and demand changes before providing the money needed to operate agency programs. House and Senate Appropriations committees make searching inquiries into agency activities before voting annual appropriations. Other committees review agency performance as they consider renewal of authorizations, without which

programs cannot be funded. (See APPROPRIATIONS BILLS; AUTHORIZATION BILLS; PURSE, POWER OF.)

Lawmakers also exercise their oversight function through informal contacts with executive officials. Staffs of individual members of Congress conduct ongoing oversight through casework—the handling of constituent questions and problems regarding agency actions. The GENERAL ACCOUNTING OFFICE and other support agencies help Congress keep tabs on the executive branch. In addition, many agencies are required to make regular reports to Congress on their activities. In 1990 more than 3,000 reports were submitted to Congress, fueling criticisms that Congress was trying to "micromanage" administrative details.

The Supreme Court in 1983 ruled unconstitutional another widely used oversight device: the LEGISLATIVE VETO. The veto had allowed one or both houses of Congress—or sometimes even a committee—to overrule executive actions. The Supreme Court decision, in the case of *Immigration and Naturalization Service v. Chadha,* was a major defeat for Congress, whose attorneys had argued that the legislative veto was a useful and necessary modern invention that enabled Congress to delegate authority without abdicating responsibility. Congress had included legislative veto provisions in more than 200 laws since 1932.

The *Chadha* decision did not end the use of legislative vetoes, which continued to be included in bills passed by Congress. Legislators and executive branch officials also explored informal alternatives to the legislative veto. The device had been useful to both branches, permitting Congress to give the executive branch broad leeway over administration of programs while retaining ultimate control.

### Developing Role

Congress did not officially acknowledge an oversight role until it enacted the Legislative Reorganization Act of 1946. That law directed the House and Senate standing committees to exercise "continuous watchfulness of the execution by the administrative agencies" of the laws and programs under their jurisdiction. Another reorganization act approved in 1970 called for regular reports on oversight activities. Better oversight of fiscal and budgetary matters was the aim

*Hearings and investigations, the most publicized form of oversight, provide colorful moments on Capitol Hill. The Iran-Contra hearings in 1987 were held under the glare of television lights.    Source: Ken Heinen*

of the Congressional Budget and Impoundment Control Act of 1974. Committee reorganization measures in the mid-1970s required many House committees to set up oversight subcommittees and certain Senate committees to carry out "comprehensive policy oversight."

This new interest in oversight investigations came about in part because of revelations of executive branch abuses, beginning with the WATERGATE SCANDAL that drove President Richard Nixon from office in 1974. Following its investigation of the Nixon White House, Congress investigated the performance of the Central Intelligence Agency (CIA). The fifteen-month inquiry confirmed that the CIA had spied on U.S. citizens, participated in assassination plots against foreign leaders, and engaged in other abuses of its authority. In the wake of the investigation, both the Senate and the House set up permanent intelligence committees with oversight jurisdiction over the agency. Other congressional investigations faulted the performance of the Federal Bureau of Investigation and major regulatory agencies.

Oversight investigations are not always an effective means of monitoring agency performance. The reason may be as simple as inadequate work by committee staff. Sometimes the investigating committee has developed a close working relationship with the agency being investigated; that relationship may color the committee's view of the agency's performance and soften criticism. Effective oversight requires the cooperation of the executive branch, and occasionally the White House may refuse to provide information to Congress during a politically sensitive investigation. Officials may justify their refusal to cooperate by citing EXECUTIVE PRIVILEGE to withhold confidential information. However, Congress may win their cooperation by threatening to cite them for CONTEMPT OF CONGRESS or by granting them immunity from prosecution.

### Additional Reading

Fisher, Louis. *The Politics of Shared Power: Congress and the Executive.* 3rd ed. Washington, D.C.: CQ Press, 1992.

# P

## Pages

Visitors to the Capitol often see young people in dark blue suits hurrying through the corridors with messages or handing out documents on the House or Senate floor. Called pages, the boys and girls are juniors in high school who attend school early in the morning and then run errands for Congress the rest of the day. About sixty-five pages work for the House and about thirty for the Senate. They are housed on two floors of a congressional office building. Pages are PATRONAGE appointees. Those nominated by the more senior representatives and senators have the best chance of being selected. Pages serve for at least one semester; some stay for a full year. There is also a summer program for pages. Pages do not work directly for those who appoint them, but instead report to the House doorkeeper and the Senate SERGEANT-AT-ARMS. (See DOORKEEPER, HOUSE.)

By 1992 Congress was paying pages about $1,000 a month, of which $300 went for room and board (five evening meals a week). Pages are required to follow a dress code. A House description of the page program, noting the extensive walking required on the job, says, "We cannot stress enough that pages bring well broken-in, comfortable shoes."

Congress revamped the page program in the early 1980s after criticism that pages were poorly supervised and schooled. Housing for pages, called the Page Residence Hall, was set up in early 1983. Congress also agreed that only juniors in high school should serve as pages; previously pages had ranged in age

*Records show that boys worked as pages as early as 1827. The first female page was appointed in 1970. Vice President Thomas R. Marshall poses with Senate pages in the early 1900s.*
Source: Library of Congress

*President Ronald Reagan shares a laugh with pages in 1983.*
*Source: The White House*

from fourteen to eighteen, making it difficult to provide an appropriate curriculum. Each chamber has its own school for pages, housed in the Library of Congress and offering an accredited academic program.

Scandals shook the page program in the early 1980s. In news reports in 1982, two unidentified pages told of sexual misconduct on the part of House members. Later they recanted their stories; a House investigation concluded that most of the allegations "were the product of teenage exaggeration, gossip, or even out-and-out fabrication." More painful for the House was its 1983 censure of two representatives who had had sexual relationships with pages. Daniel B. Crane, an Illinois Republican with a wife and six children, admitted that he had had an affair in 1980 with a seventeen-year-old female page. Gerry E. Studds, a Massachusetts Democrat, was found to have had a homosexual relationship in 1973 with a seventeen-year-old male page. (See DISCIPLINING MEMBERS.)

Records as early as 1827 show that boys worked as messengers. The name *pages* came into use a decade later. The first Senate page, Grafton Dulany Hanson, was appointed at the age of nine by Sen. Daniel Webster. Webster's second page served the Senate in various capacities from 1831 to 1895. In the 1800s pages augmented their pay by collecting autographs from members and by arranging for printing and sale of major speeches. Sen. Jacob K. Javits, a New York Republican, broke the color barrier when he appointed the first black page in 1965. Javits also appointed the first female page in 1970, but her employment was delayed until the following May, when the Senate voted to permit girls as pages. Some pages have returned to the halls of Congress as legislators. Rep. John D. Dingell of Michigan and Sen. David Pryor of Arkansas, both Democrats, were once pages.

## Pairs

*See* VOTING IN CONGRESS.

## Parliamentarian

Two of the most powerful employees of Congress are the Senate and House parliamentarians. These officials are the arbiters of legislative practice in each chamber. Their interpretations of the body's rules and precedents can have a profound impact on the shape of legislation and the course of floor action. The parliamentarian or an assistant is always on the floor during House and Senate sessions, whispering advice to the PRESIDING OFFICER.

The parliamentarians do not officially make rulings. But presiding officers rarely ignore their advice, especially in the Senate, where freshman senators traditionally take the chair. The parliamentarians can often anticipate the points of order and parliamentary inquiries likely to be raised. When they cannot do so, they must be able to offer authoritative on-the-spot advice to the presiding officers. (See POINT OF ORDER.)

Parliamentarians also play an important role behind the scenes. As masters of the procedural and technical skills that are the backbone of successful legislating, they are consulted by members of both parties and their staffs. They are acknowledged experts in suggesting ways to route legislation to a sympathetic committee, prepare it for floor debate, and protect it from opposition attacks. The parliamentarians customarily are responsible for referring bills to the committees with appropriate jurisdiction. They also prepare and maintain compilations of the precedents in each chamber.

House parliamentarians build on work prepared earlier in the twentieth century by two House members, Asher Hinds, a Maine Republican, and Clarence A. CANNON, a Missouri Democrat. Senate precedents were compiled by Floyd M. Riddick, Senate parliamentarian from 1965 to 1974.

Parliamentarians are chosen by the leadership of the House and Senate. In the House the parliamentarian is the Speaker's right hand. Lewis Deschler, parliamentarian from 1928 to 1974, was a member of the "Board of Education," a group of House friends of Speaker Sam RAYBURN who met with the Texas Democrat at sundown for drinks and strategy talks. In the Senate, where power is more diffused, parliamentarians have occupied a less central position.

## Parties, Political

A political party is a coalition of people who try to gain governmental power by winning elections. Members of a party in theory share a loosely defined set of beliefs, although there are often extremely wide differences of opinion among members of the same party.

Political parties are not specifically mentioned in the Constitution, yet they are considered essential to the functioning of a democracy. They provide a mechanism for electing leaders, forging compromises, and running governments.

Political parties have been important in Congress almost since it was created. They assist in the election of members. They organize members and elect the formal leaders of Congress. The party that has a majority of seats in each chamber controls all key positions of authority. Parties develop legislative positions and attempt to unify their members behind those policy goals. How strong and effective the parties are in these roles varies from one period in history to another, from the House to the Senate, from party to party, from leader to leader, even from issue to issue.

There have been only two major political parties in Congress, the Democratic and the Republican, since the mid-nineteenth century. Almost all members of Congress have belonged to one of these two coalitions. But it has not always been that way. In the nineteenth century several different parties were significant in Congress. Only after the Civil War did the Democrats and Republicans begin to share complete control of Congress between them. Even since then, however, members of other parties—the Progressive party in the early 1900s, for example—occasionally have been elected. Sometimes a member declines to join either major party and is called an independent.

The Democrats and Republicans have been dominant at different times during the history of Congress. For much of the period between the Civil War and the Great Depression of the 1930s, Republicans held majorities in both the House of Representatives and the Senate. Since the election of 1932, however, Democrats usually have been in control of both chambers.

They have been particularly strong in the House, where for decades they have held a majority solid enough to withstand periodic Republican gains due to that party's landslide presidential victories.

### Congressional Elections

Party affiliation is often a crucial factor in whether a candidate wins or loses a political race. A Democrat running in a traditionally Democratic area will more than likely win, just as a Republican has the advantage in a predominantly Republican region.

Political parties provide a mechanism for choosing and supporting congressional candidates. Without the parties, a congressional election could be a confusing process in which many individual candidates sought votes with the aid of their friends and personal connections alone. Through primary elections held by the parties, the choice is narrowed to two candidates instead of a multicandidate free-for-all.

Primaries were introduced early in the twentieth century to reduce the power of corrupt "party bosses" by giving the choice of the party nominee to party members as a whole. Primaries have had the unintended effect of weakening the parties. Because party leaders no longer control who runs for office on the party ticket, congressional candidates can bypass the established party leadership in their area and appeal directly to voters in primary races. They can generate their own support instead of being recruited and groomed by party leaders. The increasing importance of interest groups and abundance of CAMPAIGN FINANCING sources have made it easier for candidates to campaign independently of the party structure.

During the general election campaigns, parties do provide important campaign assistance and services to their candidates. In addition to traditional campaigning by local party regulars, both parties in the House and Senate have campaign committees. The committees help party candidates in a variety of ways, the most important being financial assistance. The Republicans in particular have successfully developed their campaign committees into sophisticated, high-tech operations.

But here again the party role has been diminished. Party campaign contributions are small when compared to the money that pours in from individuals and the POLITICAL ACTION COMMITTEES of labor, business, and interest groups. Candidates who can tap these sources of money and support no longer have to defer to party leaders or party politics. General election candidates, although chosen in party primaries, frequently campaign on their own, seeking to appeal to voters without reference to party labels.

This independence on the campaign trail often continues on Capitol Hill. Members who make it to Congress largely on their own do not necessarily feel obliged to toe the party line.

### Organizing Congress

Parties play an important role in the internal organization of Congress. Without structures for bringing together like-minded members for common action, Congress might find itself in constant chaos, as 100 senators and 435 representatives each fought solely for his or her individual agenda. Instead, the parties help to create a system in which leaders and followers can work together in pursuit of policy goals.

LEADERSHIP positions are allocated according to party. The party that holds a majority in each chamber has the votes to select leaders, such as the SPEAKER OF THE HOUSE and the PRESIDENT PRO TEMPORE and the majority leader in the Senate. All committee and subcommittee chairs are members of the majority party.

Senators and representatives who are affiliated with a political party, as almost all are, belong to party caucuses or conferences. The caucus as a whole votes on party and committee leaders and committee assignments. Caucuses provide forums for debating substantive legislative issues. They can have a major impact on the procedures of their chambers as well. This was the case in the 1970s when the House Democratic Caucus led the way on reforms that dramatically loosened the hold of the SENIORITY SYSTEM, which had awarded positions of authority on the basis of length of service. Having given itself the power to elect committee chairs, the House Democratic Caucus has used that power several times to oust chairs who were thought to be out of step with the party mainstream. (See CAUCUSES, PARTY; REFORM, CONGRESSIONAL.)

Committees within the party caucuses advise on

policy, make committee assignments, and provide campaign support for their party's candidates. Hopes that the policy committees would evolve into effective policy-making bodies had not been realized as of the early 1990s. Powerful committee chairs were unwilling to give up the control they had over their policy areas, and the diversity within each party made it hard to achieve policy consensus.

Majority party committees set their chamber's legislative schedule. In the House this is done in conjunction with the Rules Committee. In the Senate the majority party committee sets the schedule in consultation with the minority party leaders and any other member who wants a say as to when a bill comes to the floor. (See LEGISLATIVE PROCESS.)

## Party Unity

Once members are united under their party banners, do they stay together? Sometimes—but not consistently and definitely not easily.

In the early part of the twentieth century, parties often exercised significant control over all aspects of Congress, but this is no longer true. The parties of today cannot dictate party policy and expect their members to fall into line. Now party leaders must work hard to persuade members to support party positions and to put together coalitions on specific issues.

This is no easy task. Members who have an electoral base independent of their party do not automatically support party positions or obey party leaders. They know that their constituents, not the party, gave them their seat in Congress and that those same constituents can take it away in the next election. Outside interest groups also compete with the parties for members' attention and support on votes.

The distribution of power within Congress further complicates attempts at party unity. Powerful committees and their chairs are always on the lookout for any encroachment on their turf by rival power centers, including their own parties. The reforms of the 1970s decentralized Congress, and as a result leaders have to build a consensus within a much broader constituency. The party is further fragmented when members join subgroups representing parochial interests or philosophical factions within their parties. (See CAUCUSES, SPECIAL.)

Moreover, party leaders today have a weak hold over their rank and file. The debacle in 1990 over a federal budget agreement dramatically illustrated this. Republican and Democratic leaders agreed on a budget deal with the White House, but neither party in the House was able to deliver its share of the votes. The deal went down to a humiliating defeat.

Yet, with all this working against them, parties still display unity when congressional votes are tabulated. In fact, party affiliation appears to be the most important factor in members' voting decisions. In an annual study of party votes, Congressional Quarterly identifies the votes on which a majority of Republicans opposed a majority of Democrats and calculates the percentage of times members voted with their party. In 1992 the study found partisanship at near record levels, with nearly two-thirds of the roll calls taken in the House and slightly more than half of those in the Senate meeting the definition of a party vote. House Democrats won 82 percent of the party unity votes in 1992, while Senate Democrats prevailed on 57 percent of the votes that split along party lines.

Despite the general lack of party discipline, members vote with their party for several reasons. For one thing, many of them come from more or less similar districts and share certain goals. In addition, it is much easier for them to vote with their party than to oppose it. Leaders may have a weak hold over party members, but they still have some tools to reward or punish party members. Incentives for members to support party positions include desirable committee assignments, campaign assistance, and help with members' bills or amendments. Leaders are also assisted by whip organizations, which gather intelligence, conduct polls, and count and cajole votes. House Democrats have an especially elaborate whip system, in which more than one-third of House Democrats hold positions. Inclusion of so many members in the party hierarchy and the assignment of whips to specific geographic areas (ZONE WHIPS) promote party cohesion.

Party unity has also been enhanced by changes in the parties themselves. Party mavericks are far fewer than they once were. Conservative southern Democrats have been replaced by either moderate Democrats or Republicans, and liberal northern Republicans have been replaced by Democrats. The CONSER-VATIVE COALITION, a voting bloc of Republicans and southern Democrats that held a place in American politics for half a century, has clearly declined in recent years.

Partisanship was heightened during the administrations of Ronald Reagan and George Bush. Republicans rallied behind Republican White House proposals, and Democrats rallied against them. This polarization of parties was particularly noticeable in the House, which is by tradition a more partisan body than the Senate. House rules are designed to let the majority party get things done, and the wishes of the minority party may well be ignored in that large, impersonal chamber. In contrast, the Senate emphasizes individualism and accommodation with the minority party. The bitter partisan battles that are frequently seen in the House are rare in the Senate.

## Development of the Party System

The framers of the Constitution never envisioned the importance that political parties would develop in Congress and the nation. The framers had little understanding of the functions of political parties; they were ambivalent, if not hostile, to the new party system as it developed in the early years of the republic. "If I could not go to heaven but with a party, I would not go there at all," said Thomas Jefferson in 1789.

The Constitution did not mention parties, either to authorize them or prohibit them. It made possible a permanent role for parties, however, by giving citizens civil liberties and the right to organize. At the same time it erected safeguards against partisan excesses by creating a system of checks and balances within the government.

Parties emerged soon after the adoption of the Constitution. Those who favored the strong central government embodied in the Constitution came to be called Federalists. Led by Treasury Secretary Alexander Hamilton, they were drawn mostly from merchants and bankers of the Northeast, who favored strong government action to prevent money from losing its value through inflation. They were opposed by a group that later became known as the Democratic-Republicans. Led by Jefferson and James Madison, the Democratic-Republicans were largely southern and western farmers, who opposed a strong central government and sought government policies to make it easier to borrow money.

Party lines were fluid in the early Congresses, with members drifting between one loose coalition and the other. By the mid-1790s, however, the factions had hardened enough for one senator to observe that "the existence of two parties in Congress is apparent." Federalists generally held the upper hand in these early years, controlling the Senate and contending equally for power with the Democratic-Republicans in the House. By 1800 Jefferson's supporters had become a majority. Their control of Congress continued to tighten in the ensuing years. The 1816 elections signaled the effective end of the Federalist party, whose representation in Congress dropped off to a small minority.

Along with the dominance of the Democratic-Republicans, the first twenty years of the nineteenth century saw growth in the power of the party caucus over Congress's operations. Important decisions were made in private meetings of the Democratic-Republicans, and members were pressed to follow the party's position. The power of the party caucus was increased by its role as presidential nominating committee. Party members in the House and Senate had the authority to name the Democratic-Republican presidential candidate, who at that time was virtually assured of being elected. Caucus nominations continued through 1824.

The size and power of the Democratic-Republican party soon led to the development of internal factions, as different regional groups struggled for influence within the only national political organization. By the mid-1820s two groups had emerged: the National Republicans and the Democrats. The National Republicans favored internal economic development projects and a protective tariff against foreign goods. The Democrats, who represented agrarian interests from the South and West, held that the common people, not the rich, should have the dominant voice in government. The Democrats captured control of Congress in 1826.

The Democrats, who took over the White House in 1828 with the election of Andrew Jackson, remained the dominant party in Congress for the next three decades. The National Republicans, who soon took the name of Whigs, twice won the presidency and always held many seats in Congress. But the Whigs were able to capture a majority of either body on only a few occasions.

The Whigs faded rapidly during the 1850s and ceased to exist in 1856. In their place arose the Republican party of today, which was initially composed of Democrats and Whigs who opposed the extension of slavery. The Republicans won control of the House in 1854, lost it in 1856, and then regained it in 1858. They were not able to muster a majority in the Senate until 1860, on the eve of the Civil War. The young party held a solid majority throughout the war. The Democratic presence in Congress was sharply reduced after its many members from the South quit to join the Confederacy.

## Party Dominance

The Republican party controlled Congress and the presidency for most of the next seventy years. Democrats sometimes were able to win a majority of House seats, and on occasion they won a Senate majority. But the Republicans, who soon gained the nickname of "Grand Old Party" (GOP), dominated the era. They were backed by eastern business interests and favored high tariffs and tight controls of the amount of money in the economy. The Democrats were the party of the South and of disaffected agricultural interests from the West. They generally sought low tariffs and liberal credit.

The role of the parties became much more important during this period. While the Congress of the pre–Civil War period tended to be dominated by brilliant individuals, the postwar Senate and House were the arenas of powerful party leaders. This trend was particularly apparent in the Senate, where many of the members were party bosses who had gained power through political organizations in their own states. These men placed a high value on party loyalty and the need for party discipline. They were often ready to compromise their ideals to maintain harmony within the party.

The first attempt at developing a strong party structure came in the 1870s, when New York Republican Roscoe CONKLING organized a faction that con-

trolled the Senate on procedural matters. Conkling's group had little effect on legislation, however, and the Senate returned to individualistic ways after Conkling left.

The true birth of modern party discipline came in the 1890s. Republican senators William B. ALLISON of Iowa and Nelson W. ALDRICH of Rhode Island organized an informal group of senators, who at first met only for poker and relaxation. After Allison was elected chair of the Republican Caucus in 1897, the group assumed control of the Senate. Allison used his office to consolidate his own control of his party, and his party's control of the Senate. "Both in the committees and in the offices, we should use the machinery for our own benefit and not let other men have it," Allison said.

Allison controlled the Steering Committee, which directed floor proceedings, and the Committee on Committees, which made committee assignments. Although chairmanship of committees was determined solely by seniority, Allison had great leeway to assign committee positions to members who would follow his wishes. Access to positions of influence soon depended on the favor and support of the party leaders.

Republicans used the caucus to work out party positions in private and then to speak with a unified voice on the Senate floor. Although they were not bound to obey the party position, members who ignored it risked losing most of their power in the Senate. The Democrats soon followed the Republicans by organizing their own internal power structure. In the House, majority party control was consolidated under two powerful Republican Speakers: Thomas Brackett REED and Joseph G. CANNON.

By the end of the nineteenth century, the two major political parties had assumed a decisive role in the legislative process. The parties named the committees that initially considered legislation and determined what bills would be brought to the floor. Party members worked out their differences in caucus meetings, then went forth in disciplined ranks to ratify caucus decisions on the floor.

The system of strict party control was not popular among many people outside of Congress, who saw it as violating the principles of representative democracy. Some members of Congress also criticized the system, including the Liberal Republicans of the 1870s and the "Mugwump" antileadership Republicans of the 1880s. Representatives of third parties also attacked the system.

The most important third party was the Populist party, an agrarian reform movement based in the Midwest. The Populists won three Senate seats and eleven House seats in 1892. They reached their peak in the crucial election of 1896, when they and their allies won seven Senate seats and thirty House seats. Much of their program, which stressed loosening of controls on the amount of money circulating in the economy, was adopted by the Democrats, and the Populists soon faded from the scene.

The cause of reform was soon picked up by the progressives. This movement sought both economic changes, such as antitrust legislation and introduction of the income tax, and political measures aimed at opening up the system to public pressure, such as DIRECT ELECTION OF SENATORS and laws against corrupt election practices. The progressives included reformist Republicans and members of the separate Progressive party. The Bull Moose–Progressives, as they were called in honor of their leader, former president Theodore Roosevelt, elected seventeen House members in 1912. The progressives played a key role in the congressional reform movement of the early 1900s, working to reduce the autocratic power of House Speaker Cannon, and pushing through the Senate curbs on the FILIBUSTER and a proposal for direct election. (See PROGRESSIVE ERA.)

The system of party control of Congress that had grown up in the last decades of the nineteenth century developed into a formal institution in the first two decades of the twentieth century. In 1911 Senate Democrats elected a single member to serve both as chair of the party caucus and as floor leader (although the title of floor leader apparently was not used until 1920). Republicans soon followed suit, and by 1915 the majority and minority leaders were the acknowledged spokespersons for their parties in the Senate. In the House the revolt against the power of the Speaker led to a great increase in the power of the party caucuses. The Democrats, who controlled the House from 1911 to 1919, worked out most legislative decisions within the "King Caucus." Members were obliged to vote for the party position if endorsed by a two-thirds majority. The dominant force in the chamber was Democratic majority leader (and Ways and Means Committee chair) Oscar W. UNDERWOOD of Alabama, who had far more power than Speaker James B. "Champ" CLARK of Missouri.

Republicans regained control of both houses of Congress in 1918, and they maintained their power until the early years of the Great Depression. However, the party was torn by deep divisions between regular forces and the progressives, who often cooperated with the Democrats in pushing legislation favorable to the economic interests of western farmers. Progressive Republicans who tried to challenge their party leadership were quickly punished by the loss of seats on important committees.

## Democratic Dominance

The Republicans lost their exclusive control of Congress in 1930, when Democrats gained a narrow majority in the House. That election foreshadowed the results of two years later. The 1932 elections were a watershed in the history of partisan divisions in Congress. Led by presidential candidate Franklin D. Roosevelt, who promised relief from the economic disaster that had befallen the nation, the Democrats gained commanding majorities in both House and Senate. By the 1936 elections the Republicans had been reduced to a small minority.

The Democrats generally remained in control of Congress from then on. Between the 1930s and the early 1990s, they lost their House majority only twice, in the 1946 and 1952 elections. Senate Republicans had brief interludes in power as a result of the same elections, as well as a more significant period of ascendancy in the 1980s. The Republicans controlled the Senate during the first six years of President Reagan's administration (1981–1987). However, Democrats regained a sizable majority in the 1986 elections.

Remarkably, the Democrats' continuing status as the majority party in Congress has survived even when popular sentiment has shifted strongly to the Republicans, as shown by some landslide Republican presidential victories. Several reasons have been cited for the Democrats' long-term dominance of Congress. Among them is the fact that, quite simply, the electorate favored Democratic candidates over Republicans by a small but consistent margin in congressional races. Once in office, members of Congress have the advantage over challengers. Aside from missteps by an incumbent or major scandals that spawn anti-incumbent sentiment, it is very difficult to defeat a sitting member of Congress. Incumbents work hard to stay in office. They campaign constantly, assist and communicate regularly with their constituents, have access to media coverage, and attract campaign money. Democrats have ended up with many "safe" or uncontested seats and, since congressional seats do not often switch from one party to another, the Democrats have remained the majority party.

Still, the significance of this Democratic lock on Congress has been reduced by the decline of the parties as the most important force in Congress. Parties and party leaders have much less power in Congress in the modern era than they did at the beginning of the century. With members of Congress functioning as individuals rather than loyal party members, party leaders work hard to form winning coalitions. Measures to strengthen the hand of congressional party leaders were being proposed in the early 1990s as part of a push for institutional reform.

### Additional Readings

Davidson, Roger H., and Walter J. Oleszek. *Congress and Its Members.* 4th ed. Washington, D.C.: CQ Press, 1993.

Jacobson, Gary C. *The Politics of Congressional Elections.* 2nd ed. Boston: Little, Brown, 1987.

*All formal authority in Congress is decided according to party lines. The party that holds a majority in each chamber has the votes to select leaders. Here Majority Leader George J. Mitchell meets with the Senate Democratic Conference to pick new leaders for the 102nd Congress.*
*Source: R. Michael Jenkins*

Keefe, William J. *Parties, Politics, and Public Policy in America.* 6th ed. Washington, D.C.: CQ Press, 1991.

Truman, David B. *The Congressional Party.* New York: John Wiley & Sons, 1959.

## Party Discipline

*See* LEADERSHIP.

## Patronage

*Patronage* is the term for the use of political power to place favored individuals in jobs. On Capitol Hill doorkeepers, elevator operators, and pages have been among the support jobs filled by senators and representatives who make patronage appointments. In the House, however, the practice dwindled to insignificance after the House in 1992 gave up most of its members' direct control over these positions.

All members of Congress hire their own office STAFF, and committee and subcommittee chairs have even more slots to fill. These legislative jobs are not considered to be patronage. The majority party in the House or Senate fills most patronage slots, although the minority party staffs its own cloakroom and other posts that have a party designation. When control of the House or Senate changes hands, to either a new leader or a new party, the tradition has been to let those in patronage jobs stay on.

The practice of considering political loyalty when filling jobs began with President George Washington. President Andrew Jackson was the first to provoke public criticism by his aggressive use of the "spoils system."

The civil service system was established to insulate most federal employees from political pressures. It was created after the 1881 assassination of President James A. Garfield by a disappointed job seeker. (See APPOINTMENT POWER.)

Patronage was once a source of major political

*The practice of considering political loyalty when filling jobs began with George Washington. The list of patronage jobs controlled by Congress was once very long, extending even to the choice of rural mail carriers.    Source: U.S. Postal Service*

power for senior members, but the list of patronage jobs was gradually shortened to insignificance. In 1969 President Richard Nixon removed from congressional influence 63,000 postmaster and rural carrier jobs, leaving only a few Capitol Hill posts for members to control. Congress itself eliminated patronage from most jobs that required skill and training, such as the Capitol Hill police force.

Patronage employees were hired on the word of senior members. Their supervisors could not fire them without checking with their sponsor, but they could lose their jobs at a moment's notice if their sponsor wanted to give the post to someone else.

The House turned over control of its workforce to a professional HOUSE ADMINISTRATOR in 1992, following a series of embarrassing incidents in the House's own bank and post office involving patronage employees. (See HOUSE BANK SCANDAL.)

A Republican report said the post office was greatly overstaffed, with some functionally illiterate workers who were incapable of sorting mail, and promotions and pay depending on political favoritism. The whole operation was "more akin to a feudal system than a modern business," the report said.

At the time, there were roughly 600 patronage jobs (of which about 50 were allocated to Republicans), mostly for low-level postal clerks, mailroom workers, door attendants, pages, and elevator operators. They were hired by the Democratic Personnel Committee at the recommendation of senior Democrats, and worked for the doorkeeper, clerk, sergeant-at-arms, and postmaster—elected officers whose own jobs were dependent on personal ties and party loyalty. Under the 1992 overhaul, the administrative and financial responsibilities of these officers were given to a director of nonlegislative and financial services, who was required to hire and fire employees on the basis of competency and qualifications.

In the Senate the arrangement for patronage employees has been less formal, with the two party leaders and their staffs allocating the patronage among fellow senators. Although seniority is a factor, party leaders can also make patronage slots available to colleagues in return for favors, such as crucial votes on legislation. Most Senate patronage posts were supervised by the Senate sergeant-at-arms. One remnant of the patronage system was members' ability to make appointments to the Military Academy, the Naval Academy and the Air Force Academy. About three-fourths' of these academies' combined enrollments came through members of Congress. Although candidates were required to meet minimum academic and physical standards, members had great latitude in deciding how to select their nominees.

## Pay and Perquisites

Senators and representatives earn the same amount: $133,600 as the 103rd Congress began in 1993, with automatic cost-of-living increases set for the future to keep pace with inflation. Although members can earn other money from investments, they cannot hold outside jobs or earn significant income in most ways. Federal law and congressional rules have many provisions to prevent members from capitalizing on their office or pocketing money from special interests. (See Appendix.)

The Constitution gave Congress the task of setting its own salaries: a built-in conflict of interest that has caused recurrent political headaches. Members generally have earned less than people who reach the top in other professions, but far more than their constituents. Whenever members of Congress have raised their salaries, they have been accused of lining their own pockets; sometimes a member has lost a seat in the next election because of public outcry.

In 1991 the Senate joined the House, which had acted in 1989, to complete a far-reaching overhaul that blocked members' ability to take money for giving speeches and writing articles. That ended a tradition that had given private interests the opportunity to pay members—a practice long attacked as a legalized form of bribery. The states put the final touch on the overhaul in 1992 by ratifying the Twenty-seventh Amendment to the Constitution, which decreed that no salary increase could take effect until an election had taken place.

In addition to their salaries, members have other benefits and perquisites, such as free travel and an ex-

## CONGRESSIONAL PAY

| Year | Salary |
|------|--------|
| 1789–1795 | $6 per diem |
| 1795–1796 | $6 per diem (House) |
| | $7 per diem (Senate) |
| 1796–1815 | $6 per diem |
| 1815–1817 | $1,500 per year |
| 1817–1855 | $8 per diem |
| 1855–1865 | $3,000 per year |
| 1865–1871 | $5,000 per year |
| 1871–1873 | $7,500 per year |
| 1873–1907 | $5,000 per year |
| 1907–1925 | $7,500 per year |
| 1925–1932 | $10,000 per year |
| 1932–1933 | $9,000 per year |
| 1933–1935 | $8,500 per year |
| 1935–1947 | $10,000 per year |
| 1947–1955 | $12,500 per year |
| 1955–1965 | $22,500 per year |
| 1965–1969 | $30,000 per year |
| 1969–1975 | $42,500 per year |
| 1975–1977 | $44,600 per year |
| 1977–1979 | $57,500 per year |
| 1979–1982 | $60,662.50 per year* |
| December 1982–1983 | $69,800 per year (House) |
| July 1983 | $69,800 per year (Senate) |
| 1984 | $72,600 per year |
| 1985–1986 | $75,100 per year |
| January 1987 | $77,400 per year |
| March 1987–1989 | $89,500 per year |
| 1990 | $96,600 per year (House) |
| 1990 | $98,400 per year (Senate) |
| January 1991–1992 | $125,100 per year (House) |
| | $101,900 per year (Senate) |
| August 1991–1992 | $125,100 per year (Senate) |
| 1992 | $129,500 per year |
| 1993 | $133,600 per year |

SOURCES: Congressional Research Service; House Sergeant-at-Arms; Senate Disbursing Office.

NOTES *Percentage increases in congressional salaries generally are rounded to the nearest $100. The 1979 increase was not rounded because of specific language in the enacting legislation.

cellent pension program. The exact value of those benefits is difficult to calculate.

## A Political Football

Disputes over pay levels have been a feature of congressional politics since the First Congress. The Constitution settled one key question concerning pay by decreeing that members would be paid by the federal government, rather than by the states they represented. But the Constitution left up to members themselves the delicate question of the level of pay. Members have raised their pay many times over the past two centuries but often have suffered politically at the hands of the electorate as a result.

The first pay raise, in 1815, was a 60 percent hike from $6 a day to $1,500 a year in 1815. It had to be repealed the next year after scores of members were defeated for reelection. Congress did not regain an annual salary until 1855.

In the past, economic and political problems have sometimes led Congress to reduce pay levels, or to pay one chamber more than the other, or to leave salaries alone for years as inflation gnawed at purchasing power. Members had no pay raise from 1969 to 1975 while the cost of living rose by nearly 50 percent. Members have tried to avoid political retaliation by devising automatic mechanisms for pay increases, such as independent commissions to recommend pay levels or presidential responsibility for congressional pay raises. But more often than not these mechanisms failed, since there was no way to prevent Congress from voting on the issue. In early 1989 Speaker Jim Wright's maneuvers to prevent the House from voting to block a recommended pay raise provoked severe public criticism. His attempt failed; it also undercut support for Wright's leadership and contributed to his resignation five months later.

Slightly more successful have been annual adjustments for inflation for members, linked to those for all federal employees. Congress in 1989 set these adjustments at slightly less than the rate of inflation. The increases, such as the one that raised pay from $125,100 to $129,500 at the beginning of 1992, could still be challenged by floor votes. The Twenty-seventh Amendment forbade a pay raise from taking effect until a congressional election had taken place. The amendment was first proposed by James Madison in 1789 as part of the group of amendments that became the Bill of Rights. It was originally ratified by six states, was ratified by a seventh in 1873, and then lay dormant until Wyoming picked it up in 1978. Other states followed, and after the large pay raises of 1989 and 1991, enough states ratified it to make it official. Despite lingering questions about whether the early ratifications were still valid, Congress declined to interfere with such a popular proposal.

The terms of debate over congressional pay have not changed much over the years. Supporters of higher pay stress the importance of paying enough to attract talented people to run for Congress. Without adequate pay, only the rich would be able to afford to serve in Congress. Although in comparison with most workers members of Congress seem to be well paid, they argue that they are hard pressed to meet their needs. They must support two residences, one in Washington and one in their home state, on salaries that are often much lower than what they could earn as lawyers or business executives. Often they find themselves being wooed by lobbyists who are paid much more than they are.

Opponents of pay raises traditionally have argued that it is wrong for members to be able to act to raise their own pay. Congressional salaries normally are several times the average wage earner's income and should suffice to attract qualified people. Opponents also contend that members should not be able to protect themselves during times of economic difficulties, while their constituents must struggle with inflation or unemployment.

## Outside Income

Traditionally, service in Congress was a part-time job. Members attended sessions for a few months each year and then returned to their regular jobs, from which they earned most of their income. In recent years, however, Congress has tended to meet for most of the year. The demands of legislation and constituent service make it difficult for members to hold other jobs.

Until 1992, however, many members still received

*One of the many perquisites of members of Congress is a designated parking area at Washington's crowded National Airport.*     *Source: R. Michael Jenkins*

a significant portion of their income from private interests. The principal vehicle for this was the system of honoraria, in which members could keep fees for speeches, writings, or appearances for businesses, labor unions, and trade associations. There were no limits on such payments until 1975, and prominent members sometimes earned more from honoraria than they received as their salaries. The restrictions placed limits on the amount members could keep in total and for any single speech or article. At first the limit per speech or article was $1,000; after 1976 it was raised to $2,000. Members could accept more and give the rest to charity. In 1990 Rep. Dan Rostenkowski, chair of the House Ways and Means Committee, reported that he had received $310,000 in honoraria, of which he had kept the maximum allowed, $26,850.

Common Cause, the self-styled citizens' lobby, and other "good government" groups argued for years that the payments were little more than the purchase of influence by special interests. Gradually members began to refuse honoraria because of the questions they raised. This was especially the case after Speaker Wright was brought down in 1989 by ethics charges stemming from a book deal that seemed designed to evade honoraria limits. Late that year the House banned honoraria as of 1991.

The Senate, which tended to be more supportive of honoraria because its better known members booked more speaking engagements, held on to the system until 1991, when it banned honoraria in return for a 23 percent pay raise that brought it up to the House level. The 1989–1991 changes also cramped members' ability to earn income from outside work. Members could not earn money from law firm affiliations or membership on boards of directors. Book royalties, the cause of Wright's trouble, were limited to conventional arrangements with established publishers. Unearned income, such as that from stocks and bonds, was not limited, but members were required to file annual FINANCIAL DISCLOSURE statements reporting their income from various sources.

### Other Benefits

The list of other financial benefits available to members of Congress is a long one. For example, senators and representatives participate in a federal pension program that provides generous benefits, such as automatic increases for inflation, in contrast with private pensions, which are usually fixed.

Members receive many other benefits. These include health and life insurance, access to health and recreation facilities, and free parking on Capitol Hill and at National Airport. Some benefits are of minor importance or are holdovers from an earlier day. For example, members can receive free plants for their offices and discounts on office supplies, as well as goatskin-bound copies of publications issued by the Government Printing Office.

Another type of congressional benefit is related more closely to members' performance at their jobs. Members receive allowances to pay the salaries of their STAFF and to cover the expenses of offices in Washington and their home districts. They can send postage-free mail to constituents, a practice known as the FRANKING PRIVILEGE. The government pays for their travel home, and they can engage in FOREIGN TRAVEL at government expense.

Although such benefits are intended to help members carry out their duties, they also aid members personally. Most galling to critics is the fact that members can use their staff and travel allowances to build up their political strength at home, thus improving their chances of reelection.

## Petition

The First Amendment to the Constitution guarantees the right of the people "to petition the Government for a redress of grievances."

Organizations and private citizens' groups from time to time exercise this right, petitioning one or both houses of Congress to support particular legislation or to give favorable consideration to a matter not yet receiving congressional attention. Petitions are referred to committees with legislative jurisdiction over the subject matter.

## Point of Order

If a member of the Senate or House of Representatives believes that the chamber is violating rules governing its conduct of business, he or she may enter an objection. This action, known as raising a point of order, usually stops all parliamentary proceedings, except a recorded vote, until the chair sustains or overrules the member's objection. Before ruling, the chair often allows debate on the point of order, giving both sides the opportunity to explain their position. The chair's rulings are subject to APPEAL and may be overturned by the chamber's membership. This occurs more frequently in the Senate than in the House. Some House bills go to the floor under ground rules that prohibit points of order.

When a member in either chamber raises a point of order that a QUORUM—the minimum number of members required—is not present to conduct business, no further legislative activity can take place until enough absent members have been rounded up.

## Policy Committee

*See* LEADERSHIP.

## Political Action Committees (PACs)

Political action committees (PACs) are organizations that raise and distribute campaign contributions to candidates for Congress and other offices. Their rapid growth during the 1970s and 1980s made them one of the most controversial aspects of the CAMPAIGN FINANCING system.

PACs fall into three main categories: business, labor, and ideological or single-issue. Business PACs, such as those sponsored by the National Association of Realtors and the American Bankers Association, distribute their contributions relatively evenly between the two political parties. Labor PACs, such as those of the National Education Association and the Teamsters Union, give primarily to Democrats. Among the single-issue or ideological PACs, the National Rifle Association's PAC gives more to the Republicans, while that of the National Abortion Rights Action League contributes most heavily to Democrats.

During the 1990 elections, business PACs gave a total of $108.5 million, almost evenly split between Republicans and Democrats. Labor PACs gave $36.5 million, of which Democrats received over 90 percent. Ideological PACs gave $14.3 million, with almost two-thirds going to Democrats.

In addition to the three main types of PACs, a small but influential group of PACs called "leadership PACs" exists within Congress. These PACs help members achieve political goals other than reelection, such as election to leadership positions within Congress or even to the presidency.

Under federal law most PACs are permitted to contribute $5,000 per candidate, per election. There is no limit on the total amount they can give to all candidates. They also can spend as much as they want to help candidates—for example, with heavy television advertising—as long as they operate independently of the candidates' campaigns.

Although PACs date back to the 1940s, their significance in political campaigns began with the passage in 1971 and 1974 of laws to reform campaign financing. The laws, along with later court decisions, allowed PACs to become a major factor in the financing of congressional elections. In 1974 only about 600 PACs were registered, and they gave less than $20 million to House and Senate candidates. By 1990 the number of PACs had increased to over 4,000, and the groups gave more than $150 million to all congressional candidates. Most of the contributions come from a small number of large PACs. During the 1990 elections, for example, more than two-thirds of PAC contributions came from less than one-tenth of the PACs.

PACs have provided a growing share of all funds available to congressional candidates. PAC contributions are particularly important in the House, where many candidates regularly receive more than half of their campaign funds from PACs. Senate candidates usually are less reliant on PACs. PACs have little involvement in presidential elections. They provide only a small share of funds needed by candidates seeking their party's presidential nomination, and they are barred from contributing to general election campaigns, which are publicly financed.

### Incumbents' Advantage

Campaign contribution statistics show that PACs have a strong preference for incumbent legislators who are running for reelection. PACs give most often to incumbents because they are in a position to sup-

## TOP PAC CONTRIBUTORS, 1989–1990 ELECTION CYCLE

| | |
|---|---|
| Realtors PAC | $3.1 million |
| American Medical Association PAC | $2.4 million |
| DRIVE (Teamsters Union) | $2.3 million |
| National Education Association PAC | $2.3 million |
| UAW-V-CAP (United Auto Workers) | $1.8 million |
| Committee on Letter Carriers Political Education | $1.7 million |
| American Federation of State, County and Municipal Employees—PEOPLE | $1.5 million |
| National Association of Retired Federal Employees PAC | $1.5 million |
| Association of Trial Lawyers of America PAC | $1.5 million |
| Carpenters Legislative Improvement Committee (Carpenters Union) | $1.5 million |

SOURCE: Federal Election Commission.

port PAC interests when legislation is drafted as well as when it comes to a vote. This is particularly true for committee chairs and party leaders, who have more power than other members to see that legislation is approved.

PACs tend to support current members regardless of party affiliation. Challengers represent a gamble for PACs because only a few defeat incumbents in any election. By contributing to a challenger, PACs risk alienating a successful incumbent. Of the more than $150 million that candidates reported receiving from PACs during the 1990 campaign, about $117 million went to incumbents, $16 million to challengers, and $18 million to candidates for open seats.

### Critics and Supporters

Many people are sharply critical of the role played by PACs, arguing that they allow well-financed interest groups to gain too much political influence. By accepting contributions from PACs, critics say, members of Congress become dependent on them. That may make the members reluctant to vote against the inter-

ests of the PAC, either from fear of losing the PAC's contributions or from fear of having the PAC help finance their political opponents.

Proposals to curb the influence of PACs have been debated by Congress over the years, but none had become law as of mid-1993. One way to weaken PACs would be to provide public funds for congressional campaigns, as the federal government has done for presidential campaigns since 1974. President George Bush vetoed a public-financing bill sent to him by the Democratically controlled Congress in 1992. Bush and other Republicans opposed public financing and wanted to outlaw most PACs instead.

Defenders of PACs argue that the groups provide a legitimate means by which citizens can join together to support candidates. PACs encourage people to participate in politics, they say, and offer the most efficient method for channeling campaign contributions. Spokespersons for PACs say their groups are seeking not to buy votes but to gain access to members of Congress, so that their views will be heard on legislative decisions affecting them.

### *Additional Readings*

Alexander, Herbert E. *Financing Politics: Money, Elections and Political Reform.* 4th ed. Washington, D.C.: CQ Press, 1992.

Makinson, Larry. *Open Secrets: The Encyclopedia of Congressional Money and Politics.* Washington, D.C.: Congressional Quarterly Inc., 1992.

Sabato, Larry J. *PAC Power: Inside the World of Political Action Committees.* New York: W. W. Norton, 1984.

# Pork-Barrel Politics

Since the earliest days of Congress, local concerns have played an important role in decision making on Capitol Hill. Legislators from farm states agitate for price supports, while those from the arid West press for water reclamation projects. The drafting of trade and tax laws is complicated by the efforts of lawmakers to attach provisions that will benefit industries and businesses in their districts or states. When federal funds go to a particular local project or entity, and when the decision is based on political clout rather than an objective assessment of need, pork-barrel politics is at work.

The term *pork-barrel* has been traced to the pre–Civil War practice of distributing salt pork to hungry slaves, who were said to clamber over one another in a mad rush to grab as much as they could from a barrel of pork. Whatever its exact origin, the phrase was applied to congressional practices early in the twentieth century, and it stuck.

Few legislators can resist taking credit for a new park, post office, dam, or sewage treatment plant in their district. Since much of their work in Congress involves broad national issues, senators and representatives are eager to accomplish something concrete for their constituents. In securing the construction of a dam or a defense contract for a local company, a lawmaker contributes directly to the livelihood of his or her constituents—and earns their gratitude. The member with a reputation for "bringing home the bacon" is hard to beat.

In addition to allowing members to boost their image with constituents, pork-barrel politics helps committee chairs and other influential members to en-

hance their power within Congress. For example, Rep. Jim WRIGHT of Texas for many years used his position on the Public Works Committee to help congressional colleagues obtain federal projects for their districts. The favors were returned in 1976, when Wright was elected Democratic majority leader.

Traditionally, "pork" has been identified with public works projects, such as roads, bridges, dams, and harbors. But contemporary lawmakers seek many other benefits for their constituents, including university research grants, corporate tax breaks, and environmental cleanup projects. APPROPRIATIONS BILLS have long been a favorite vehicle for pork-barrel projects. A member who gets a project included in an appropriations bill is bound to support the whole bill. As efforts to trim federal spending intensified in the 1980s, less money was available for traditional pork-barrel spending. The list of projects was shorter, and the fight to get an item included grew more intense. Members who lacked influence within Congress often found their requests ignored. "Those with the clout use the clout to get what they want, and merit selection never enters into the thinking," complained Republican representative Robert S. Walker of Pennsylvania in 1987.

By then, members of the Appropriations committees, once able to accommodate favored colleagues, had little left to share after the needs of top legislators were met. Still, most appropriations bills pass easily. "All of us go begging to the Appropriations Committee for water projects or different things we want in our district," said Rep. Douglas H. Bosco, a California Democrat. "It isn't easy to vote to cut one of these bills because a lot of times you're fearful that the next time you go asking for something, the door will be slammed in your face."

In 1992 George E. Brown, Jr., of California, chair of the House Science, Space, and Technology Committee, won an unusual victory on the House floor when he moved to cut $95 million from an energy and water appropriations bill. The funds, earmarked for university building projects, had been added to the final version of the bill during the House-Senate conference and benefited the home states of some of the conferees. Brown argued that the funds should be authorized only after a competitive selection process. After the House voted to delete the funds, supporters of the projects had them added to a defense appropriations bill despite Brown's objections. "We always try to help as many members as we can," said John P. Murtha of Pennsylvania, chair of the House Appropriations subcommittee that wrote the bill.

Most legislators see their efforts to distribute federal funds back home as a legitimate aspect of their jobs; they apply the term *pork-barrel* to the pet projects of other members, if they use it at all. But critics complain that Congress is overly influenced by parochial concerns and should be more attuned to national needs.

Presidents often share that view, though they also distribute federal largess for political purposes. One of the strongest challenges to the pork-barrel system in recent decades came from President Jimmy Carter, who in 1977 proposed the elimination or modification of five water projects on grounds that they were wasteful or damaging to the environment. Congress rejected most of his suggestions, and the episode soured Carter's relations with Capitol Hill and weakened his presidency.

Carter's successor, Ronald Reagan, also tangled with Congress over pork-barrel spending. Despite Reagan's enormous popularity, even some top Republican leaders in Congress voted to override the president's 1987 veto of an authorization bill for highways and mass transit. A classic pork-barrel bill, the measure set up more than 120 special "demonstration" projects for which members could claim credit back home.

President George Bush continued Reagan's attacks on congressional spending, calling on Congress to vote on specific "items of pork" instead of concealing them within huge multibillion-dollar appropriations bills. "Funds for local parking garages, $100,000 for asparagus-yield declines, meat research, prickly pear research," Bush complained in 1992. "The examples would be funny if the effect weren't so serious."

Several presidents have proposed that they be given a line-item veto over appropriations bills, to enable them to eliminate what they see as wasteful pork-barrel spending projects. (See VETOES.)

## Post Office and Civil Service Committee, House

The policies of the federal bureaucracy—hiring, firing, and retiring—are the concern of the House Post Office and Civil Service Committee. Although agencies and departments usually have little contact with the committee, the panel does handle salary levels and major personnel questions, such as a 1978 civil service reform, a 1986 revamp of the federal retirement system, and a 1990 overhaul of the pay system for federal employees.

The committee is heavily lobbied by the unions that represent federal employees. The Post Office Committee also oversees the U.S. mails, as it has since 1808. It lost much of its control in 1970, when the Postal Service became an independent corporation. But the committee still provides a forum for complaints about deliveries and postal rates, and it continues to influence postal operations. Companies with large postal budgets, such as those that advertise through mass mailings or send material by subscription, keep in close touch with the committee.

The post office committee handles national holidays. In 1983 it won that designation for the birthday of Rev. Dr. Martin Luther King, Jr., the black civil rights leader who was assassinated in 1968. The committee also has jurisdiction over political activity by government workers. In 1990 it approved legislation to overhaul the Hatch Act, which prohibits most political activities by federal workers, but the measure was vetoed by President George Bush.

Within the House the committee has little appeal. Few members who sit on the panel put much effort into its activities. In the Senate the Postal Service and federal personnel are among the subjects handled by the Governmental Affairs Committee.

## Powell, Adam Clayton, Jr.

Rep. Adam Clayton Powell, Jr. (1908–1972), a flamboyant Democrat from New York, provoked a storm of controversy over congressional powers and

*Considered by many to be the most powerful African-American in the United States at the time, Adam Clayton Powell, Jr., was excluded from the 90th Congress for misconduct. Powell was later reelected to Congress, and the Supreme Court declared his exclusion unconstitutional.*     Source: Library of Congress

His downfall began in 1966 as a result of a revolt in his own committee over legislative business. When his long absences delayed passage of antipoverty legislation in 1966, the committee adopted new rules that limited his power as chair.

Following an investigation into Powell's use of committee funds, he was stripped of his committee chairmanship in 1967 and temporarily denied a seat in the House. In March 1967 the House, rejecting the recommendations of a select committee that Powell be punished but seated, excluded Powell from the 90th Congress. (See DISCIPLINING MEMBERS.)

Powell was reelected at a special election and again in 1968. He was seated in January 1969, although he lost his seniority and was fined. Following his swearing in, Powell told a press conference: "I'll behave as I always have."

The Supreme Court in 1969 ruled in *Powell v. McCormack* that the House had acted unconstitutionally in excluding Powell. The Harlem Democrat was defeated in a primary election in 1970 and died in 1972.

ethics in the 1960s. A House vote to exclude Powell from Congress because of misconduct led to a Supreme Court decision prohibiting Congress from adding to the constitutional qualifications for membership. The Powell case was also a key factor in the development of congressional codes of ETHICS.

Powell was pastor of the Abyssinian Baptist Church in Harlem, New York, one of the largest congregations in the country, when he was first elected to Congress in 1944. He rose in seniority to become the chair of the House Education and Labor Committee in 1961 and was considered by many to be the most powerful African American in the United States.

But Powell came under fire on a variety of issues: his involvement in court cases concerning income tax evasion and libel, his numerous well-publicized trips at government expense, and his employment of his wife as a member of his congressional staff while she lived in Puerto Rico.

## POW/MIA Affairs Committee, Senate Select

Because of renewed concern that American soldiers from the Vietnam War might still be alive in Southeast Asia, the Senate in 1991 created a select committee to investigate the fate of American prisoners of war (POWs) and soldiers missing in action (MIAs). Concern about the fate of the long-lost soldiers had been revived by a grainy photo that relatives believed showed several Americans in captivity, although a Defense Department spokesperson questioned its authenticity.

After a fifteen-month investigation, the panel reported in January 1993 that it had found "no compelling evidence" to suggest that any American prisoners were still alive in Southeast Asia, but it held open the possibility that some U.S. soldiers had languished in enemy hands after the end of the Vietnam War almost twenty years earlier. The committee criticized top U.S. government officials for dismissing that possibility but rejected charges that they possessed any "certain knowledge" that prisoners were abandoned.

The final report was signed by all twelve members of the committee—six Democrats and six Republicans. It conveyed a delicately crafted balance of judgments, reflecting the debate that took place within the committee on the emotional question of the warriors who never came home. In a footnote to the report, however, two members dissented from the majority view that there was no evidence for believing that POWs might still be alive today.

The select committee also investigated military personnel unaccounted for from the Korean War, World War II, and the Cold War. But the Vietnam War was the focus of the most attention and debate.

In its investigation of the fate of the 2,264 Americans still unaccounted for from the Vietnam War, the committee sent fact-finding delegations to Southeast Asia, reviewed U.S. government files to determine whether the MIA and POW cases had been handled properly, and held a series of hearings. Two defense secretaries in the Nixon administration, Melvin R. Laird and James R. Schlesinger, testified that the Nixon administration had every reason to believe that Americans were left behind in enemy hands as U.S. troops were withdrawn in 1973. But former secretary of state Henry A. Kissinger called such suggestions "a flat-out lie."

Nearly a dozen congressional investigations had previously been launched into the matter of missing personnel from the war; all ended inconclusively. In late 1992 the Vietnamese government released thousands of photographs of captured and dead U.S. soldiers that helped identify some of the missing men.

The select committee's authorization expired January 3, 1993. But committee chair John Kerry, a Massachusetts Democrat and a decorated veteran of the Vietnam War, said that the panel's final report was not intended to close the issue. Kerry and other members said they would continue to press for more answers to the POW issue in permanent committees of the Senate.

## President and Congress

*See* EXECUTIVE BRANCH AND CONGRESS.

## Presidential Disability and Succession

Congress has broad responsibility for maintaining the continuity of the presidency. The Constitution provides (Article II, Section 1) that Congress should decide who is to succeed to the presidency if both the president and vice president die, resign, or become disabled. Congress enacted a presidential succession law as early as 1792. But for nearly 200 years legislators avoided the question of presidential disability, because they were unable to decide what constituted disability or who would be the judge of it. Those questions were not resolved until adoption of the Twenty-fifth Amendment to the Constitution in 1967.

At least two presidents who served before the amendment was adopted became disabled while in office. James A. Garfield was shot in 1881 and was confined to his bed until his death two and a half months after the shooting. Woodrow Wilson suffered a severe stroke in 1919 but remained in office until his term ended in 1921. In each case the VICE PRESIDENT did not assume any of the duties of the presidency for fear of appearing to usurp the power of that office. The result was uncertainty about who was in charge, especially in Wilson's case.

The Twenty-fifth Amendment permits the vice president to become acting president under either of two circumstances. If the president informs Congress that he is unable to perform his duties, the vice president becomes acting president until the president says he is able to take over again. The vice president also can become acting president if he and a majority of the cabinet (or another body designated by Congress) decide that the president is disabled. The vice president then is to remain acting president until the president informs Congress that he is able to resume his duties; however, Congress can overrule the presi-

*The first vice president to take office under provisions of the Twenty-fifth Amendment was Gerald R. Ford, right, who was nominated by President Richard Nixon and confirmed by Congress in 1973. Ford succeeded Spiro T. Agnew, who resigned under fire.*
Source: Wide World Photos

dent's declaration that he is no longer disabled by a two-thirds vote of both the Senate and the House of Representatives.

Another section of the Twenty-fifth Amendment spells out what will happen if the vice president dies, resigns, or succeeds to the presidency. In such a case the president is to nominate a replacement, who requires confirmation by a majority vote of both the Senate and House.

The presidential disability procedures first came into play in 1985 when President Ronald Reagan underwent cancer surgery. Responding to criticism that he had not invoked the Twenty-fifth Amendment in 1981 when he was seriously wounded in an assassination attempt, Reagan transferred his powers to Vice President George Bush just before receiving anesthesia and signed papers reclaiming them less than eight hours later. The president did not formally invoke the Twenty-fifth Amendment, however. A bipartisan advisory commission, in a 1988 report, criticized Reagan's reluctance to do so; it urged routine use of the disability mechanism in such cases.

The first vice president to be confirmed under the Twenty-fifth Amendment was Gerald R. FORD, who was nominated by President Richard Nixon in 1973; Ford succeeded Spiro T. Agnew, who had resigned as a result of political corruption charges. The second was Nelson A. Rockefeller, whom Ford nominated in 1974 after he replaced Nixon in the White House. (See ELECTING THE PRESIDENT.)

## President Pro Tempore

Officially the highest ranking senator, the president pro tempore (a Latin term meaning the president "for a time," often shortened to "president pro tem") is in practice a largely ceremonial leader. By tradition, the post goes automatically to the senator in the majority party with the longest service record. Because of his seniority, the president pro tempore usually chairs a committee and is counted among the top decision makers in the Senate. However, the position carries far less influence than the party floor leaders. There is no Senate post comparable to the SPEAKER OF THE HOUSE. (See LEADERSHIP.)

The Constitution calls for the president pro tempore to preside when the VICE PRESIDENT, the constitutional president of the Senate, is absent. The post of president pro tempore has never become a politically powerful position, in part because the vice president at any point is able to take the chair, unseating the president pro tempore. One ceremonial task of the president pro tempore is to sign the final version of legislation passed by Congress.

In the nineteenth century the post was filled on a temporary basis, whenever the vice president was not present. But the Senate never let the vice president be an active participant in its affairs; often the vice president was of a political party different from that of most senators. As the vice president spent less time in the Senate chamber, the post of president pro tempore evolved into a long-term position. In 1890 the Senate decided that the president pro tempore should serve until "the Senate otherwise ordered." In effect, it gave tenure to the person elected.

The president pro tem is third in line, behind the vice president and the Speaker, to succeed to the presidency. (See PRESIDENTIAL DISABILITY AND SUCCESSION.)

The practice of electing the most senior member of the majority party in terms of Senate service as president pro tempore has been followed since 1945, with the exception of Arthur H. Vandenberg of Michigan, who was the second-ranking Republican when elected president pro tem in 1947.

Although the president pro tempore occasionally presides over the Senate, the day-to-day routine often is handled by more junior members of the majority party. Senators rotate as PRESIDING OFFICER, usually spending less than an hour at a time in the chair.

Democrat Robert C. BYRD of West Virginia, first elected to the Senate in 1958, became president pro tempore in 1989. Byrd had stepped down from the position of Democratic majority leader in the Senate to become chair of the Appropriations Committee and president pro tem. In this dual role, Byrd remained one of the most powerful members of the Senate. He increased the budget and staff of the president pro tem's office, and he was able to make use of his formidable skill in parliamentary procedure when he exercised his prerogative as president pro tem to oversee debate.

## Presidents Who Served in Congress

President George Bush followed a well-trodden career path when he served in Congress and later became chief executive. Over half of the nation's presidents have entered the White House by way of Congress.

Of the nation's forty-two presidents, twenty-four sat in one or both chambers: nine served in the House of Representatives, six in the Senate, and nine in both. In addition to the nine presidents who sat in the House before assuming the presidency, one served there after leaving it. Another ex-president returned briefly to the Senate, where he had served before becoming president.

The move from Congress to the White House began early. James MADISON, the fourth president, served in the House; his successor, James Monroe, was in the Senate. Both Madison and Monroe also had been members of the Continental Congress, as had their predecessors George Washington, John Adams, and Thomas Jefferson.

Few have moved directly from Congress to the White House. John F. Kennedy made that leap in 1961, as James A. Garfield and Warren G. Harding had before him.

Others advanced through the vice presidency. John Tyler, Millard Fillmore, Andrew Johnson, Harry S. TRUMAN, and Lyndon B. JOHNSON all succeeded presidents who had died in office. Martin Van Buren was vice president when he ran for president, as was Bush. Gerald R. FORD, Richard Nixon's vice president, became president when Nixon resigned.

Others held intervening posts in government: Madison, Monroe, and John Quincy ADAMS were secretaries of state, for example, while James K. Polk,

*Few presidents have moved directly from Congress to the White House. John F. Kennedy made that leap in 1961, as James A. Garfield and Warren G. Harding had done earlier. Here Senator Kennedy, catcher, plays softball in 1954 with Senate colleagues Henry M. Jackson, batter, and Mike Mansfield, umpire.* Source: Senate Historical Office

William McKinley, and Rutherford B. Hayes were governors. Bush took on a variety of jobs, including ambassador to the United Nations, chair of the Republican party, chief envoy to China, and director of the Central Intelligence Agency.

Success in one branch of the government has not always been matched by success in the other. Lyndon Johnson, a Senate majority leader of legendary skill, was a powerful and effective chief executive until his presidency foundered on the Vietnam War. Abraham

Lincoln's single term in the House did not foreshadow his immense stature as president, while Ford's years of House leadership did not translate into White House triumphs. More consistent was the performance of Harding, an ineffectual senator who became an ineffectual president.

Bush served only two terms in the House and then left a safe seat to run an unsuccessful Senate race in 1970; voters thwarted his plans again in 1992, when he was denied a second term as president.

*Lyndon B. Johnson served in the House and Senate for a total of twenty-four years before he became vice president in 1961 and president in 1963. Here he talks with Sen. Thurston Morton, left, in the Senate Reception Room.    Source: Senate Historical Office*

The two presidents who served in Congress after leaving the White House were John Quincy Adams and Andrew Johnson. Adams pursued a seventeen-year career in the House of Representatives; earlier in life he had served in the Senate. Johnson, with a background of service in both chambers, returned to the Senate for five months before his death.

Countless members of Congress have sought the presidency in vain. Aaron Burr, Henry CLAY, Stephen A. DOUGLAS, James G. BLAINE, Robert A. TAFT, Hubert H. HUMPHREY, George McGovern, Robert DOLE, and Tom Harkin are among the many who have tried and failed to win the highest office.

## Presiding Officer

Members of the Senate and House of Representatives take turns presiding over floor debate, a job that is viewed by some as drudgery, by others as an honor requiring finesse and skill. Members may speak on the floor only if the presiding officer permits, or "recognizes," them. The presiding officer also rules on points of order and delivers other pronouncements that regulate floor debate. (See POINT OF ORDER.) The script is usually written by the PARLIAMENTAR-IAN, who cannot directly address the chamber but can prompt the member in the chair. Members may APPEAL, or challenge, the presiding officer's decisions, and the rulings can be overturned by majority vote.

In the Senate it once was common for the VICE PRESIDENT, its constitutionally designated president, to preside over floor debates. In the modern Senate the vice president seldom is called in unless the vote might be needed to break a tie. In 1979, however, Vice President Walter F. Mondale took the chair to help Democratic majority leader Robert C. Byrd of West Virginia quash a filibuster on a natural gas deregulation bill by issuing a series of controversial rulings.

The PRESIDENT PRO TEMPORE, usually the senior member of the majority party in the Senate, may preside in the absence of the vice president, but generally the Senate puts a freshman member in the chair. That relieves senior members of a time-consuming task and gives newcomers experience in Senate rules and procedures. Not surprisingly, new senators are heavily dependent on the parliamentarian for advice.

The House puts no premium on giving new members experience in the chair. Its formal presiding officer is the SPEAKER OF THE HOUSE, the leader of the majority party in the chamber. But the Speaker must appoint other representatives to preside when the House is considering bills for amendment in the COMMITTEE OF THE WHOLE. When sensitive bills are under consideration, the Speaker's choice turns to senior members who are skilled parliamentarians—such as William H. Natcher, a Kentucky Democrat who entered the House in 1953. While senators tend to view presiding as drudgery, some House members actively seek the duty. In an institution as large as the House, it is one way for members to increase their visibility.

In both the House and Senate only members of the majority party preside. Until 1977 members of each party took turns presiding in the Senate. The practice was abandoned following an incident in which the presiding officer, a member of the minority party, broke with Senate custom by denying recognition to the majority leader.

## Press and Congress

Although news coverage of Congress occasionally assumes an adversarial tone, the relationship between the two institutions is one of mutual need. Senators and representatives must cope with constant and sometimes critical press scrutiny, but they also use the news organizations that cover Capitol Hill to keep constituents informed about their legislative accomplishments and to further their own political ambitions. For reporters Congress is an extremely valuable and accessible source of information. Reporters spend long hours cultivating senators and representatives and their staffs to find out what has been taking place backstage and to understand the subtle pressures that shape the legislative process. Most legislators have a staff member whose sole, or primary, responsibility is to deal with the press.

### Covering Congress

Reporters do not cover every event on Capitol Hill or follow every legislative issue. Choices are made, often informally and quickly, to skip floor debate and focus on a hearing or wait outside a room where negotiators might reach agreement. Certain issues receive more attention from the press because they affect more people or cost more money, or because they are interesting or controversial. Reporters talk to certain legislators instead of others because they are more involved in a particular issue, more accessible, more articulate, more powerful within Congress, or more representative of different parts of the country. Reporters say covering Congress is like watching a twenty-ring circus with no clue about where or when the most dazzling act will take place.

Print and broadcast journalists cover Congress from both a national and a local perspective. While major news organizations, such as the *New York Times* or CBS, report on the national or international implications of a congressional decision, dozens of reporters look first at how legislators from their area voted. Instead of seeking comments from the key committee chairs who handled a bill, reporters for regional newspapers interview local representatives and senators. Even congressional leaders who deal often with national reporters maintain a close relationship with reporters from their region. Regional reporters far outnumber those from the major news organizations.

Some legislators prefer local coverage to appearances on a national program. "I can be on Tom Brokaw," said Rep. Dan Glickman, a Kansas Democrat, in 1987, referring to the NBC evening news anchor. "But it is not as important to my reelection as being on the NBC affiliate in Wichita. . . . On national TV, you don't get more than a short bite. On local TV, it's often two or three minutes."

### Attracting the Press

Senators and representatives try in many ways to influence news coverage. Congressional offices issue press releases and newsletters that point out a legislator's accomplishments. Well-equipped Capitol Hill recording studios make it possible for senators and representatives to produce a video version of a press release that can be beamed via satellite to home television stations. Many members are given space on newspaper editorial pages for their own columns.

*House Speaker Tom Foley speaks to a cluster of reporters outside the Capitol.*
*Source: R. Michael Jenkins*

Within Congress traditions have evolved that put the spotlight on individual members, giving them a chance to attract press attention. Both the House and Senate set time aside for floor statements by members on topics that need not relate to the day's legislative debate. Just before committee meetings begin, chairs often give each member a chance to make a statement that is typically directed not at fellow members but at reporters. (See SPECIAL ORDERS.)

About 5,000 journalists, photographers, and other technicians are accredited to the House and Senate press galleries, although only a handful cover Congress full time. Congress has given reporters themselves responsibility for deciding who qualifies for membership in the Senate and House press galleries. For working journalists, accreditation is straightforward, but rules prohibit gallery members from doing paid promotional work or LOBBYING. The restrictions date from the 1880s.

There are four separate press galleries in each chamber, for daily newspapers and news services, periodicals, radio and television correspondents, and photographers. Each looks out over the floor of the House or Senate, and each is staffed by congressional personnel and furnished by Congress with telephones, typewriters, and other equipment. Seats are also reserved for the press at most committee hearings.

Congress is a very open institution, but meetings and even floor debate may be closed to the public. Public access to floor action was greatly enhanced by live TELEVISION coverage, which the House allowed in 1979 and the Senate in 1986. Employees of the House and Senate operate the cameras. C-SPAN, a cable network, provides continuous congressional coverage to its subscribers, and national and local news programs often show brief excerpts from debate. But members have voted to hold secret discussions of sensitive national security matters.

Although committee hearings have been open to the public for decades, the writing of legislation was done primarily in private until the 1970s. Then reform efforts opened up committee sessions unless the members specifically voted to close them. By the mid-1970s even conference committees, which resolve differences in House and Senate versions of bills, were open to reporters. Often those meetings, held in cramped rooms in the Capitol, are able to accommodate only two or three reporters. Some committees, such as the Appropriations committees, meet in such small rooms that public access is always limited. (See REFORM, CONGRESSIONAL.)

By the mid-1980s the push for openness, or "sunshine," on Capitol Hill had begun to fade. Among the committees that frequently closed meetings was the House Ways and Means Committee, which shut the press and public out of its tax-writing sessions. "I hate to say it, but members are more willing to make tough decisions on controversial bills in closed meetings," said committee member Don J. Pease, a Democrat from Ohio, in 1987. Pease usually voted against closing meetings.

Being able to attend hours-long meetings has not made it easier for reporters to write news stories. Legislation must pass through several stages before it becomes law, and the process of crafting compromises and adding detailed amendments is often murky. Only a small part of what Congress does actually is reported.

The difficulty of portraying what 535 different people—100 in the Senate and 435 in the House—are doing on a given day is in sharp contrast to the straightforward nature of most reporting on the presidency. Scholars have argued that television has enhanced the power of the presidency, while Congress has suffered because its activities are decentralized and difficult to present concisely in a brief news story.

For reporters Congress can be an excellent source of information, particularly when the White House has decided not to discuss a subject. Presidents have criticized Congress for news leaks, but legislators are independent-minded and unlikely to end their mutually beneficial relationship with reporters.

### Additional Readings

Graber, Doris A. *Mass Media and American Politics.* 4th ed. Washington, D.C.: CQ Press, 1992.

———. *Media Power in Politics.* 2nd ed. Washington, D.C.: CQ Press, 1989.

Hess, Stephen. *Live from Capitol Hill! Studies of Congress and the Media.* Washington, D.C.: Brookings Institution, 1991.

## Previous Question

The previous question motion is one of the fundamental rules of general parliamentary procedure. Its use is indispensable to the legislative process in the House of Representatives because it is the only way to bring debate to a formal close.

The previous question is adopted, or "ordered," by a majority vote. Adoption of a motion ordering the previous question brings the House to a direct vote on the pending question. The motion itself is not debatable but must be put to a vote immediately. The motion is used not only to bring debate to a close, but also to foreclose the opportunity to revise, or amend, the question or legislation pending before the House. The previous question is used only when members are sitting as the House; it is not permitted in the COMMITTEE OF THE WHOLE, where other debate limitations apply. When the Rules Committee grants a special rule for floor debate on a bill, it routinely adds language "ordering the previous question." (See LEGISLATIVE PROCESS.)

The motion normally is offered by the FLOOR MANAGER of the bill. Adoption of the previous question means essentially that the House thinks the legislation or parliamentary question has been debated adequately and that members are ready to vote. If the House defeats the previous question, debate continues and amendments are in order. In addition, control of the debate passes to those who successfully opposed adoption of the previous question.

Use of the previous question motion in the House distinguishes its debates from those in the Senate. Since it is a debate-limiting device, the previous question is not permitted in the Senate, which cherishes "extended debate." Senate debate can be shut off in only two ways: by unanimous consent or by a three-fifths vote of the Senate membership to invoke cloture. (See FILIBUSTER.)

An example of the importance of ordering the previous question occurred in 1981 on the eve of debate on a $35 billion package of budget cuts that had been proposed by President Ronald Reagan and House Republicans. The rule supported by the House Democratic leadership would have forced the House to vote separately on each proposed cut, making it very difficult for the Republicans to sustain their budget package. But the procedural vote ordering the previous question on the rule, which would have cleared the way for the Democrats' ground rules, failed on a vote of 210–217. That vote opened the rule to amendment, and the Republicans then rewrote the rule to allow a single vote on the entire package of budget cuts; their version was adopted 216–212.

## Printing Committee, Joint

Although the Joint Printing Committee rarely meets, its staff closely monitors the printing operations of the entire federal government. Unlike most congressional committees, which oversee the operations of executive agencies and their implementation of congressional mandates, the Joint Printing Committee actually approves or disapproves specific agency decisions about printing. The purchase of a press by the GOVERNMENT PRINTING OFFICE (GPO) or plans by the Defense Department to buy new data-processing equipment can be vetoed by the Joint Printing Committee. A mandate to reduce inefficiencies and waste in public printing guides the committee, but it also makes sure that agencies comply with laws that require public access to government information.

The Joint Printing Committee has authorized more than 200 government printing plants outside of the GPO, but it also keeps business coming to the GPO that many agencies would rather handle themselves or buy from private companies. Critics say GPO rates and schedules for completing work are not competitive. Congress created the GPO to handle congressional publications. The Joint Printing Committee operates on the premise that the GPO should also be used for other federal printing.

The Joint Printing Committee is responsible for the style and format of the *CONGRESSIONAL RECORD* and for the contents of the *CONGRESSIONAL DIRECTORY*. When the House and Senate each decided to mark in the *Record* those speeches that were not actu-

ally delivered, the Joint Committee chose the mechanism for making that distinction.

The committee acts as a watchdog for Congress, overseeing the way the GPO handles the printing of the *Record* and other congressional publications. The committee consists of the chairs of the House Administration and the Senate Rules committees, and four other members from each panel.

## Private Bill

*See* LEGISLATION.

## Privilege

Privilege relates to the rights of members of Congress and to the relative priority of motions and actions in their respective chambers.

"Privileged questions" deal with legislative business. The order in which bills, motions, and other legislative measures are considered on the floor of the Senate and House is governed by strict priorities. A motion to table, for instance, is more privileged than a motion to recommit, so it would be voted on first. A motion to adjourn is considered "of the highest privilege" and would have to be considered before virtually any other motion. (See MOTIONS.)

"Questions of privilege" concern members of Congress collectively or individually, and they take precedence over almost all other proceedings. Matters affecting the rights, safety, dignity, and integrity of proceedings of the House or Senate as a whole are questions of privilege in both chambers. Questions involving individual members are called "questions of personal privilege."

At the beginning of the 103rd Congress (1993–1995), the House adopted a rules change concerning questions of privilege affecting the House collectively. Under the new rules the Speaker, instead of having to immediately deal with such questions, could delay many of these motions unless they were made by the majority or minority leader.

## Progressive Era

The Progressive Era flourished from about 1900 to 1917, when Americans concluded that the governmental and economic affairs of the country were being run by unscrupulous politicians and powerful corporate interests. Much legislation enacted by Congress was designed to further the influence and financial advantage of these interlocking groups.

The national economy was largely the province of the railroads, manufacturing, and mining corporations, and the large banks and financial institutions. In addition to the collusion between big business and the federal government, almost all state governments and large cities had fallen under the control of these same economic interests.

The Progressive movement was basically a revolt against this conspiracy of politics and economic power. Its roots were in the rural populist protests of the Midwest during the final third of the nineteenth century. Concerned citizens feared that democratic government and the basic well-being of vast numbers of Americans were threatened by this concentration of wealth and political power in a privileged few. Exploitation of the underprivileged, women, and children was widespread. The Progressive Era, therefore, was both a culmination of reform pressures that had been building since the 1880s and the beginning of a new political activism directed at bringing government and economic institutions under genuine popular control. The Progressives sought reform of existing structures rather than revolutionary change.

### Progressive Agenda

The Progressives became an influential force at various levels of American society. Their initial targets were the injustices and political corruption in the cities. Cleaning up the cities required wresting power from bosses of political machines. This led to campaigns to capture control of state governments, since reformers found that in most cases the big-city machines were tied into statewide political networks. Inevitably, the reform pressures affected the two national political parties.

At the local level the Progressive movement sought to relieve problems, such as the substandard living and health conditions in urban areas, unemployment, child labor, exploitation of women and immigrant workers, and the high incidence of industrial accidents. At the state level it tried to break the stranglehold on economic life of the giant trusts and corporations, such as the railroads; to end the exploitation and abuse of natural resources by business interests; and to reform state constitutions.

At the national level the Progressives' concerns centered on the need for a fairer distribution of the country's wealth and an end to social and class divisions along economic lines. Specific proposals included DIRECT ELECTION OF SENATORS; direct primaries; the Australian, or secret, ballot; the initiative, referendum, and recall to give voters more direct control over government; the graduated income tax; postal savings banks; protective labor laws; and regulation of economic power generally.

The quest for social justice, urban rehabilitation, and the health and welfare of working people and the disadvantaged did not always center on economic, political, or administrative solutions. The Eighteenth Amendment to the Constitution, outlawing the sale or manufacture of alcoholic beverages, was in part a Progressive concern.

### Progressivism in Politics

The influence of the Progressives in Congress began with attempts to open up the LEGISLATIVE PROCESS. Politically, the Progressives were an insurgent element within the Republican party. For a few years before U.S. entry into World War I, they held the balance of power. Joining forces with a majority of Democrats in the House, they were able in 1910 to strip the autocratic and conservative Speaker, Illinois Republican Joseph G. CANNON, of most of his power. The revolt against "Cannonism," led by Progressives George W. NORRIS of Nebraska and John M. Nelson of Wisconsin and by Democrats James B. "Champ" CLARK of Missouri and Oscar W. UNDERWOOD of Alabama, was consolidated in 1911. That year House Democrats returned to power and won approval of meaningful reforms in the rules that made it easier to bring to the floor for debate legislation that had been blocked by the conservative leadership. Clark was

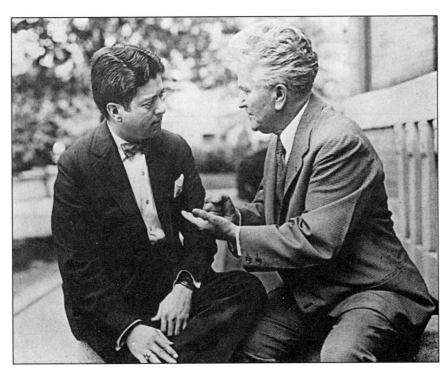

*Sen. Robert La Follette, right, was a leader of Progressive forces in the Senate. His son, Robert, Jr., succeeded him in the Senate in 1925.    Source: Library of Congress*

elected Speaker, but Underwood became the real leader of the House.

Speaker Cannon had opposed much of the Progressive agenda sought by President Theodore Roosevelt (1901–1909). Roosevelt's reputation as a Progressive rested on his policies toward "trust busting," railroad regulation, conservation, his Square Deal for labor, and other efforts. His administration took the first tentative steps nationally to grapple with the complex social and economic problems of a modern industrial nation.

In the Senate the Progressives were led by Robert M. LA FOLLETTE, Sr., of Wisconsin, Albert J. BEVERIDGE of Indiana, and Albert B. Cummins and Jonathan P. Dolliver of Iowa, and by Norris and Underwood, both of whom went from the House to the Senate.

A split in Republican ranks between the Progressives and the conservative backers of President William Howard Taft led Roosevelt in 1912 to form the Progressive (Bull Moose) party. The division among Republicans gave Democrat Woodrow Wilson a landslide victory in that year's presidential election.

Wilson, who initially had championed traditional free enterprise and rejected the activist government role advocated by Roosevelt, eventually supported a dynamic federal role to solve the nation's social and economic problems. By 1916 Wilson had won enactment of most of the demands the rural populists and Progressives had advocated.

## Progressives' Accomplishments

The Progressives achieved an impressive record of social, economic, and political reforms. But many of these programs were disrupted by U.S. entry into World War I, by the disillusionment that followed the failed peace settlement, and later by Supreme Court rulings and the conservative presidential administrations of the 1920s. Many of the changes the Progressives had fought for had to be won anew in the 1930s. To an important degree the philosophical and political foundations of the NEW DEAL had their origin in the Progressive Era.

A few of the landmark initiatives identified with the Progressives and enacted during the Wilson administration were the Federal Reserve Act, Federal

Trade Commission Act, Clayton Antitrust Act, and Rayburn Securities Act. Others included the Adamson Act, which created the first eight-hour workday on interstate railroads, and the first federal law regulating child labor. Although not ratified until 1920, the Nineteenth Amendment, granting suffrage to women, also was a consequence of the Progressive Era. (See WOMEN'S SUFFRAGE.)

## Public Works and Transportation Committee, House

The federal government has spent billions of dollars building roads, airports, dams, and subways—and the House Public Works Committee has had a say in most of those decisions. Even the politics of tight federal budgets have not dimmed the panel's enthusiasm for road building and channel dredging.

Labels like *pork-barrel* are not welcome on the Public Works Committee. Although less sought after than the Ways and Means, Appropriations, or Rules committees, the public works panel has always been popular with legislators eager to show concrete evidence of their work. When the committee is choosing special projects, those located in the districts of committee members usually receive top priority. But the committee also accommodates other members on a bipartisan basis by including dams or roads for those who comply with the unwritten rule: Give full support to bills that contain something for your district. (See PORK-BARREL POLITICS.)

Despite the budget constraints of the 1980s, the public works committee chalked up several successes. In 1991 Congress cleared a six-year, $151 billion authorization measure for federal highway and mass transit programs. After breaking a decade-long stalemate in 1986, the panel has been able to authorize bills for U.S. Army Corps of Engineers water projects every two years.

The public works committee is also responsible for the aviation and trucking industries. It played a key role in ending regulation of airlines in 1978 and of trucking in 1980. (Railroad deregulation was handled by the Energy and Commerce Committee.) In the 1980s the committee raised safety concerns with both industries. Pressure for profits in many cases had led companies to postpone buying new equipment, cut back on maintenance, and ask employees to work extra hours at their jobs.

The committee has been criticized for its commitment to capital improvements. The 1991 surface transportation measure was said to be laden with pork projects. But Robert A. Roe, the New Jersey Democrat who chaired the committee from 1991 to 1993, remained undeterred. "With this bill we are rebuilding America," he said. Roe never objected to pork-barrel charges, contending that the projects were vital for the states' economies and helped create jobs.

## Purse, Power of

The Constitution entrusted to Congress the power to tax and spend. For two centuries this power of the purse has given the legislative branch paramount authority to command national resources and direct them to federal purposes. No other congressional prerogative confers so much control over the goals of government, or so much influence on the nation's well-being.

Since the 1930s Congress has made broad use of its taxing, spending, and borrowing powers to vastly enlarge the government and expand its influence over the U.S. economy. The way the government spends its money—and raises it through taxes or borrowing—carries enormous consequences for the nation's economic performance and its political and social balance. Under congressional direction, the federal government provides income to the poor and health care to the elderly, builds highways and space shuttles, encourages economic development with subsidies and tax advantages, and pays for weapons and soldiers to operate them.

Through the years the House and Senate have jealously guarded most congressional powers to finance the machinery of government. But Congress has had trouble using its taxing and spending powers to shape a coherent federal budget policy. The result has been mounting gaps between spending and revenues and constant battling between Congress and successive presidents for final authority to set budget policy.

Much as it wanted to control the purse strings, Congress rarely bothered until the mid-1970s to tie its separate legislation to tax and spending totals. (Since 1921 the executive branch had drawn up yearly federal budgets setting forth revenue, spending, and deficit or surplus targets.) But in the early 1970s a heavily Democratic Congress fiercely resisted when Republican President Richard NIXON refused to spend billions of dollars already appropriated to federal agencies, a practice known as IMPOUNDMENT OF FUNDS.

Congress responded in 1974 by setting up its own elaborate BUDGET PROCESS, which forced it to weigh spending against expected government revenues and to establish limits for each. Lawmakers continue to make decisions on spending and revenues through separate legislation, written by different House and Senate committees. Budget committees in each chamber draw up overall budget plans, but the actual spending bills are written by the House and Senate Appropriations committees within limits set by AUTHORIZATION BILLS that have been drafted by various other committees. The House Ways and Means and Senate Finance committees control the complicated process of writing tax legislation. (See APPROPRIATIONS BILLS; APPROPRIATIONS COMMITTEE, HOUSE; APPROPRIATIONS COMMITTEE, SENATE; FINANCE COMMITTEE, SENATE; WAYS AND MEANS COMMITTEE, HOUSE.)

## Power to Tax

Without sufficient revenues, no government could function effectively. The Constitution granted Congress the right to enact almost any taxes, except for duties on exports. That power was enlarged in 1913 by adoption of the Sixteenth Amendment to the Constitution, authorizing a federal tax on incomes.

### *Tariffs*

During the nineteenth century the federal government derived the bulk of its revenues from tariffs on imports and other customs duties. Limited funds were also provided by estate or excise taxes.

Disputes over tariff policy were common. At times the nation was divided by region: protective tariffs were popular in the North and East, where manufacturing was important to the economy, and unpopular in the agricultural West and South. Critics were so upset by duties imposed in 1828 that they called the law the "tariff of abominations." In the last part of the nineteenth century tariff policy split the major political parties; Republicans generally favored high tariffs, while Democrats supported low tariffs.

Customs duties provided a smaller share of federal revenue after taxation of incomes began, but the political debate continued. Thinking that higher tariffs would boost the badly ailing domestic economy, Congress in 1930 passed the Smoot-Hawley Tariff Act, which raised duties to the highest levels in U.S. history. The misguided effort was repealed in 1934.

Congress finally delegated virtually all its tariff-making power to the president, beginning with the Reciprocal Trade Agreements Act of 1934. By then individual and corporate income taxes had begun replacing customs receipts as the main source of government revenues. In 1910 customs duties still brought in more than 49 percent of federal revenues; by fiscal 1991 they contributed only 1.5 percent, even though customs receipts were close to the $16 billion level.

### *Income Tax*

Congress first passed taxes on income to finance the Civil War, but the levy expired in 1872. The income tax was renewed in 1894, with the rate set at 2 percent on personal incomes in excess of $3,000. The next year, however, the Supreme Court ruled the tax unconstitutional, stating that it violated a requirement that direct taxes be apportioned among states according to population.

That roadblock was removed by the Sixteenth Amendment, and a new income tax system was established in 1913. Congress exempted families with low incomes from the income tax; over the years a complicated sliding scale evolved that set higher tax rates on higher incomes. Tax deductions, allowed from the start, encouraged specific activities; among the best known is the deduction for interest on home mortgages, a subsidy to encourage home ownership that in the early 1990s "cost" the government more than $42 billion a year in lost revenues.

Congress had no constitutional difficulty with the corporate income tax it first levied in 1909. The Supreme Court let the tax stand as an excise on the privilege of doing business as a corporation. An outright corporate income tax was enacted in 1913.

Federal taxes on individual incomes now make up more than 44 percent of all federal revenues, totaling nearly $468 billion in fiscal 1991. Corporate income taxes amounted to $98 billion.

### Excise, Other Taxes

The power of Congress to tax in other areas is well established. Excise taxes (taxes on the sale of products or services) have always been a part of the federal tax system. The excises levied after ratification of the Constitution included taxes on carriages, liquor, snuff, sugar, and auction sales. Modern excise taxes extend to telephone service and diesel fuel. Another important area of taxation is payroll taxes, which support the Social Security and unemployment compensation systems. Payroll taxes are the second largest source of government revenues, amounting to $396 billion in fiscal 1991.

## Power to Spend

The Constitution gave Congress the basic authority to decide how the government should spend the money it collects. It set few specific limits on the spending power.

By authorizing Congress to collect taxes "to pay the debts and provide for the common defense and general welfare of the United States," the Constitution opened the way for an expansive interpretation of the spending power. The new national government spent $5 million in fiscal 1792, its fourth year in operation. Peacetime spending grew slowly until the 1930s, when President Franklin D. Roosevelt and Congress launched federal programs to pull the economy out of the Great Depression. During World War II federal spending grew tenfold, reaching $92.7 billion in fiscal 1945. Spending dropped off after the war ended, only to rise again during the Korean War. It continued upward in an almost uninterrupted spiral for the next three decades.

Federal spending mounted to more than $1.3 trillion in fiscal 1991, accounting for almost a quarter of the nation's total output of goods and services. As recently as 1980, less than half that amount was spent annually. A combination of factors swelled the federal budget and kept spending at high levels even when revenues, though also increasing, fell behind. Annual deficits, the gap between revenues and spending, first exceeded $200 billion in 1983. After enactment of the Gramm-Rudman-Hollings legislation, deficits dipped below the $200 billion mark for a few years in the late 1980s. By 1992 the deficit had reached more than $290 billion despite the enactment of a major deficit-reduction package in 1990.

Since the 1970s the largest portion of spending has been for payments to individuals: retirement benefits, welfare, disability insurance, and other programs. When inflation in the 1970s made fixed benefits seem unfairly small, Congress provided automatic cost-of-living increases for many programs, a process known as indexing. That increased the government's costs, as did the growing ranks of participants. Many benefit programs were established as ENTITLEMENTS, which required payments to everyone who met legal requirements. Once these programs were in place, Congress found it politically impossible to dismantle them. Payments to individuals—some of which are direct payments while others are made through grants to state and local governments—made up almost 50 percent of federal spending in fiscal 1991, far outstripping defense spending, the second largest category, which accounted for slightly more than 20 percent. Interest on the national debt was an uncontrollable element of the budget, consuming more than 14 percent of spending.

Only about a third of federal spending remained under direct congressional control through the annual appropriations process. Reducing those programs by substantial amounts proved very difficult for the House and Senate. The bureaucracy that operated the programs, and the groups that benefited from them, created a powerful block against budget cuts.

## Power to Borrow

There is no constitutional restriction on the government's power to borrow money on the nation's

*For two centuries the "power of the purse" has given the legislative branch authority to command national resources and direct them to federal purposes. In 1985 senators Ernest F. Hollings, Phil Gramm, and Warren B. Rudman worked together to win passage of the Gramm-Rudman-Hollings antideficit bill.    Source: AP/Wide World Photos*

credit. Congress by statute has set a DEBT LIMIT since 1917, but it has regularly raised the limit, though often with political difficulty. Funds to pay interest on the debt have been permanently appropriated since 1847. Congress protected that obligation from political uncertainty, thus strengthening the nation's credibility as a borrower.

The federal government has incurred debt when it has had to spend more than it collected in tax and other forms of revenue. The deficit must be made up by borrowing.

During most of the nation's history, government has tried to assure that revenues were sufficient to meet spending requirements. This philosophy, which dictated an approximate balance between revenues and spending, was generally accepted until the early 1930s. But then Congress approved major federal projects to stimulate economic recovery. In the process the government began following an economic philosophy, developed by British economist John Maynard Keynes, that justified peacetime deficits to ensure stable economic growth.

As a result, the government abandoned its former insistence on balancing revenues and spending. The practice of using the federal budget to help solve national economic problems was increasingly accepted. Budget deficits and a rapidly increasing national debt were the result. By the end of fiscal 1992 the national debt was almost $4 trillion. Paying interest on those loans cost more than $194 billion in 1991; this was the third largest component of the federal budget, exceeded only by defense and payments to individuals, such as Social Security.

### Additional Readings

Birnbaum, Jeffrey H., and Alan S. Murray. *Showdown at Gucci Gulch: Lawmakers, Lobbyists, and the Unlikely Triumph of Tax Reform.* New York: Random House, 1987.

Fenno, Richard F., Jr. *The Power of the Purse: Appropriation Politics in Congress.* Boston: Little, Brown, 1973.

Schick, Allen. *Congress and Money: Budgeting, Spending and Taxing.* Washington, D.C.: Urban Institute, 1980.

Stockman, David. *The Triumph of Politics: The Inside Story of the Reagan Revolution.* New York: Avon Books, 1987.

# *Q*

## Quorum

A quorum is the minimum number of members who must be present for the transaction of business. In both chambers of Congress it is a majority of the total membership: 51 in the Senate and 218 in the House of Representatives, provided there are no vacant seats. Only 100 members are required when the House is sitting as the COMMITTEE OF THE WHOLE, the parliamentary framework it adopts when it considers bills for amendment.

A quorum is assumed to be present, even when only a few members are on the floor, unless a member suggests otherwise. In that case the roll is called, and absentees quickly stream into the chamber to make up a quorum. Quorum calls are frequently used in the Senate to kill time while groups of senators informally negotiate legislative or procedural disputes or to give a senator time to reach the floor to offer an amendment.

# R

## Randolph, John

John Randolph (1773–1833) represented Virginia in the House of Representatives intermittently from 1799 to 1833. His tenure there was interrupted four times, once to allow service in the Senate from 1825 to 1827. Randolph was a State Rights Democrat who opposed legislation that he believed would strengthen the national government at the cost of state sovereignty. He had a difficult personality, but many in Congress were in awe of his brilliant oratory and his uncompromising beliefs. Henry Adams described Randolph standing to speak to the House "with the halo of youth, courage, and genius around his head—a sort of Virginian Saint Michael, almost terrible in his contempt for whatever seemed to him base or untrue."

Randolph entered Congress as a supporter of Thomas Jefferson and almost immediately became chair of the Ways and Means Committee. He supported Jefferson's purchase of the Louisiana territory but later broke with the president over his attempts to acquire Florida.

A constitutional purist, Randolph refused to bow to necessity if it conflicted with principle. He opposed protective tariffs, roads built by the national government, the chartering of the Bank of the United States, and federal interference in the issue of slavery.

Randolph also was a prominent opponent of the Missouri Compromise of 1820. Ill feeling over this issue between Randolph and Henry CLAY, another great orator, went beyond words in 1826. That year, the two men fought a duel over Randolph's denunciation of Clay's support for John Quincy Adams's selection as president. Neither man was harmed. Clay had been a losing candidate for the presidency in the 1824 election, which had been decided by the House of Representatives. (See ELECTING THE PRESIDENT.)

In 1830 Randolph traveled to St. Petersburg as Andrew Jackson's minister to Russia. He became ill and was forced to leave shortly after his arrival. Having been in ill health for most of his life, Randolph died in 1833 after periods of dementia, alcoholism, and opium use.

## Rankin, Jeannette

Jeannette Rankin (1880–1973) was the first woman to serve in Congress. A suffragist and pacifist, she ran for the House at a time when only a handful of states allowed women to vote and as the nation was about to enter World War I. (See WOMEN IN CONGRESS.)

Born into a family that believed in education for women and political activism, Rankin graduated from the University of Montana and went on to study social work at the New York School of Philanthropy. She then returned west and lobbied for the enfranchisement of women in the states of Washington, California, and Montana.

Rankin ran as a Republican for one of Montana's House seats in 1916 on a platform favoring Prohibition, women's rights, and federal suffrage. (The Nineteenth Amendment giving women the right to vote was not ratified until 1920.) When elected, Rankin said: "I knew the women would stand behind me. I am deeply conscious of the responsibility. I will not only represent the women of Montana, but also the women of the country, and I have plenty of work cut out for me."

In the House Rankin worked to further the cause of women. She introduced legislation to grant women citizenship independent of their husbands and sponsored a bill providing for federally supported maternal and infant health instruction. She helped set up a

House committee on women's suffrage and tried to ensure that employment generated by legislation would include women.

In 1917 the House voted on the entry of the United States into World War I. With forty-nine other representatives Rankin voted no, saying, "I want to stand by my country but I cannot vote for war." Her vote brought national notoriety for her, but not for her forty-nine male colleagues.

After her first term in the House, Rankin ran unsuccessfully for the Senate. Out of office, she continued to work for women's rights, and in 1940 she was reelected to the House. Once again she was faced with a vote on U.S. involvement in a war. Rankin was the only member to vote against entry into World War II. Few people shared the view of Kansas newspaper editor William Allen White, who said of her pacifist stand: "It was a brave thing! And its bravery somehow discounted its folly." After the vote, she was forced to lock herself in a phone booth to escape from the curious and angry crowds.

In 1968, when she was in her late eighties, Jeannette Rankin led a Jeannette Rankin Brigade to the Capitol to protest the war in Vietnam. She died at the age of ninety-two.

*Speaker of the House for seventeen years until his death in 1961, Sam Rayburn held the post longer than any other member in history.*

## Rayburn, Sam

Sam Rayburn (1882–1961) served as SPEAKER OF THE HOUSE longer than any other member in history. He wielded great authority through a combination of personal prestige, persuasiveness, and an almost uncanny sense of the nature of the institution and how it worked.

A Texan and a Democrat "without prefix, without suffix, and without apology," Rayburn entered the House in 1913. In 1931 he became chair of the Interstate and Foreign Commerce Committee, where he managed the regulatory measures of the New Deal. In 1937 he became majority leader, and in 1940, Speaker. Except for stints as minority leader in 1947–1949 and 1953–1955, he retained the post of Speaker until his death.

Rayburn's advice to younger members has often been quoted: "To get along, you've got to go along." The comment reflected a House in which it was no longer possible to exercise the kind of power earlier Speakers had enjoyed. "You cannot lead people in order to drive them," he said. "Persuasion and reason are the only ways to lead them. In that way the Speaker has influence and power in the House."

Rayburn used all the power available to him. He gave out good committee assignments as a reward to members who were sympathetic to the goals of the

Democratic party. In 1961 he gave way to the pressure of party liberals and orchestrated the expansion of the Rules Committee to ease the passage of liberal legislation. Occasionally he could be autocratic. In 1941, for example, he was "suspected of wielding a quick gavel" to prevent reconsideration of a military draft extension that had passed by a 203–202 vote. But mainly Rayburn ruled behind the scenes through conciliation and compromise. Although plagued by a CONSERVATIVE COALITION of southern Democrats and Republicans that stymied much Democratic domestic legislation, Rayburn was generally successful in getting legislation through the House. He oversaw the passage of the civil rights acts of 1957 and 1960 and was able to gain approval for much foreign affairs legislation.

## Readings of Bills

House and Senate rules require that all bills be read three times before passage, in accordance with traditional parliamentary procedure. The original purpose was to make sure legislators knew what they were voting on, but in modern practice usually only the title of the bill is actually read.

When legislators need a delaying tactic, they sometimes object to requests for UNANIMOUS CONSENT to dispense with a reading. Then the drone of the text being read aloud is added to the usual hum of noise on the House and Senate floors. Few members listen to the words.

Senate rules require bills and resolutions to be read twice, on different legislative days, before they are referred to committee. The third and final reading follows floor debate and voting on amendments.

In the House the first reading occurs when the bill is introduced and printed by number and title in the *Congressional Record*. The second reading takes place when floor consideration begins; often the bill is read section by section for amendment. The third reading comes just before the vote on final passage.

## Reapportionment and Redistricting

Reapportionment and redistricting are the two processes that allocate the 435 seats in the House of Representatives. As such, they are central to the American political system. They help to determine whether the House will be dominated by Democrats or Republicans, liberals or conservatives—and whether racial or ethnic minorities will receive fair representation.

Reapportionment is the redistribution of House seats among the states to reflect shifts in population as indicated by the national census, which is conducted every ten years. States whose populations have grown quickly over the previous decade are given additional House seats, while those that have lost population or have grown more slowly than the national average have seats taken away.

Redistricting means that the boundaries of congressional districts within each state are redrawn, based on the number of House seats allotted to the state and population changes within the state. Most House members represent a specific area, or district, within a state, although seven states with sparse populations have only one House member for the entire state. Redistricting usually occurs in the two years following reapportionment; the process is normally controlled by the governor and legislature of the state. Today, maps are often challenged in court. The courts sometimes order a second round of redistricting in the middle of a decade, and on occasion even draw new district maps on their own.

Reapportionment and redistricting have been subjects of debate throughout U.S. history because the Constitution did not specify how they should be done. The framers of the Constitution decreed that House seats would be divided among the states on the basis of population, and that House members would be elected by the people. Beyond that, the Constitution gave little guidance on these subjects, leaving Congress, the courts, and state governments to wrestle with them.

After many decades of debate, the basic goal of reapportionment and redistricting was settled by

Supreme Court rulings in the 1960s. The guiding principle of the two processes is "one person, one vote." Under this principle, fairness requires that each citizen must have approximately the same representation in the House. This means that the 435 congressional districts should be as close to equal in population as possible.

Many other questions about reapportionment and redistricting have yet to be settled. Most important, the courts have not decided definitively whether the Constitution permits GERRYMANDERING, the practice of states drawing the boundaries of House districts so as to favor one party or group.

In contrast to the House, the Senate never undergoes reapportionment or redistricting. The Constitution gave each state two Senate seats, and senators are always chosen on a statewide basis.

## Reapportionment

Reapportionment determines the relative strength of states and regions in the House according to a mathematical formula that distributes House seats to states on the basis of population. It has not been easy to pick the best formula for distributing House seats. Congress has tried different methods over the years, but none, including the one currently in use, has worked perfectly. Many experts believe it is impossible to devise a method of allocating House seats that does not give some states more or less representation than they deserve.

The cause of the difficulty is simple: no state can have a fraction of a representative. Each state must have a whole number of House members, from one to as many as fifty-two in the early 1990s. Even with the complex reapportionment formula now in use, there are variations in the amount of representation states receive based on their populations.

The framers settled the difficult question of distribution of House seats for the first Congresses by specifically listing the number of seats each of the thirteen original states would have. This was necessary because at that time there were no accurate statistics on the populations of the states. After the first census in 1790, the Constitution directed that each congressional district should have at least 30,000 residents.

An exception was made for small states, which were guaranteed at least one representative no matter what their population. In a compromise between the slave-owning South and the rest of the country, the Constitution provided that each slave would be counted as three-fifths of a person.

At first Congress followed the Constitution in basing representation on an ideal population size of a congressional district. As a result, the total number of House members at any time varied widely. In 1832, for example, the standard size of a congressional district was set at 47,700 people, producing a House of 240 members. None of the different allocation methods used in those days could solve the problem of fractional representation, so congressional districts varied widely.

The early reapportionment methods also failed to deal with the rapid growth in the nation's population. No matter what method was used, there seemed to be unanticipated effects that went against common sense. One method was subject to the "population paradox," in which an increase in the total population led to a decrease in the size of the House. Another technique produced the "Alabama paradox," which at times decreased the size of a state's delegation even as the total number of House seats went up.

Finally, around 1850, Congress settled on a method that seemed to solve many reapportionment problems. The size of the House was supposed to be fixed, although Congress regularly voted to add more members as new states entered the Union. The addition of members allowed the House to sidestep the difficult task of cutting back on the representation of existing states to make room for new ones. By the beginning of the twentieth century, however, the process threatened to make the House too large to be a workable legislative body. In 1911 Congress fixed the size of the House at 435, where it has remained except for a brief period (1959–1963) when the admission of Alaska and Hawaii raised the total temporarily to 437.

The decision to freeze the size of the House set the stage for the reapportionment battles of the 1920s. The 1920 census was a landmark event in the nation's history because it showed that for the first time there were more Americans living in cities than in rural areas. States with large cities thus were entitled to many more representatives, while rural states faced sharp cutbacks in their House representation.

Arguing that people who lived on farms and in small towns were the heart and soul of America, rural representatives fought hard to prevent their loss of power. They managed to block reapportionment throughout the 1920s. Redistribution of House seats did not take place until after the 1930 census. That reapportionment led to drastic shifts in power, with California nearly doubling its House delegation, from eleven to twenty, while twenty-one other states lost a total of twenty-seven seats.

The current method of reapportionment, called "the method of equal proportions," was adopted in 1950 and made retroactive to 1941. It allocates House seats according to a complicated mathematical formula designed to minimize population variation among districts. Its adoption put an end to most controversy over reapportionment until the early 1990s, when two states mounted legal challenges. Both succeeded in the lower courts but were rejected by the Supreme Court in 1992.

Massachusetts argued that it deserved one more seat than it received because the census had counted overseas military personnel inaccurately. Montana, which had lost one of its two seats in the 1990 reapportionment, challenged the reapportionment formula on grounds that it was unfair to less populous states. The Supreme Court's refusal to support either claim reflected its traditional reluctance to interfere in the politically explosive issue of reapportionment.

Reapportionment every ten years has continued to exert a major influence on political strength in the House. Because Americans move so often, the populations of many states change substantially in ten years. The political strength of those states in the House can change considerably as well.

The most important change in state populations in recent years has been the shift of people away from the older, industrial states of the Northeast and Midwest to the newly developing states along the nation's southern tier, from Florida to California (the Sun Belt). As a result of the 1980 census, seventeen House seats shifted from the Northeast and Midwest to the

Sun Belt. The state that benefited most was Florida, which picked up four seats, followed by Texas with three and California with two. New York, on the other hand, lost five seats—the sharpest drop in House representation for any state since 1840. Illinois, Ohio, and Pennsylvania lost two seats each.

The 1990 census showed that the trend had continued. California picked up seven seats, reflecting a dramatic westward population shift, while Florida gained another four seats and Texas gained three. New York once again was the big loser, dropping three seats. Illinois, Ohio, and Pennsylvania again lost two seats each, as did Michigan.

Many political analysts predicted that the 1980 reapportionment would alter the political makeup of the House. Most of the states that lost seats tended to favor liberal Democrats, while the states that gained seats were more likely to favor Republicans or conservative Democrats. Because of Democratic successes in the state redistricting battles that followed reapportionment, however, the effects were much less significant than expected. Similarly, Republicans were disappointed in their hopes to substantially reduce the Democrats' majorities in Congress after the 1992 election, the first to reflect reapportionment following the 1990 census.

### Redistricting

Redistricting has become a subject of intense dispute in recent decades as a result of Supreme Court decisions in the 1960s, major population shifts within states, and the development of computer-based technology. The national Republican and Democratic parties devote immense resources to the effort to persuade state legislatures and the courts to approve state district plans favorable to their own candidates.

Some political analysts believe that redistricting is the single most important factor determining political control of the House. They argue that the dominance of the Democratic party, which has controlled the House continuously since 1955, is a result of Democratic control of the redistricting process. Republicans claim that Democratic-dominated state legislatures have devised district plans that give the advantage to Democratic House candidates. They say that this makes it difficult for Republican candidates to win even when they are favored by a majority of the voters. Other political experts disagree. But there is no question that redistricting is crucial to the outcome of many House elections.

The early years of debate over redistricting were dominated by the question of whether there needed to be congressional districts within states at all. The Constitution does not say so, and several states favored at-large elections in which all the voters in the state chose all the state's House members. Use of the system declined because it did not encourage the close ties between representatives and citizens that developed when a member of Congress represented a specific area.

Congress banned at-large House elections in 1842, except in one-member states, although the ban frequently was violated until the 1960s. The 1842 law also established the basic principle that House districts should be contiguous—that is, a single, connected area rather than several separate areas scattered across a state.

For a hundred years redistricting questions received little attention. State legislatures had to draw new district lines when reapportionment cost the state House seats, and occasionally there was a heated dispute over a single congressional district. But state legislatures usually ignored the question of redistricting and rarely acted to change district lines. As a result, cities did not gain additional representatives as their populations grew. Partisan fights over district lines were rare, however, and there was little pressure for major alterations in the shape of most districts.

The situation changed radically when the Supreme Court began to consider redistricting issues in the 1960s, after refusing for decades to become involved in the matter. By the time the Court began to act, there was clear evidence that something was wrong with the way legislative districts were drawn. Particularly in state legislatures, rural areas were vastly overrepresented, while cities did not have nearly as much representation as their populations warranted. In every state the most populous state legislative district had more than twice as many people as the least populous district. Things were not as bad in congressional districts, but wide differences between rural and urban representation remained. For example, in Texas

one urban district had four times as many people as one lightly populated rural district.

The state legislatures, which were dominated by members from rural areas, refused to change the existing districts. Frustrated urban dwellers turned to the courts, arguing that they were being denied fair representation by the legislatures. In its historic decision in *Baker v. Carr* (1962), the Supreme Court ruled that the districts used in the Tennessee state legislature were unconstitutional because they violated the principle of one person, one vote. In 1964 the Court extended that doctrine to the House in the case of *Wesberry v. Sanders,* which concerned congressional districts in Georgia. That decision stated that congressional districts should be as nearly equal in population "as is practicable."

Since then, the Court has continued to tighten the requirement that congressional districts should have equal populations. In *Kirkpatrick v. Preisler* (1969) the Court struck down the district plan of Missouri, where the largest district had a population only 3.1 percent larger than that of the smallest district. Any population difference, "no matter how small," the Court declared, was unacceptable in all but a few cases. The Court set an even more rigorous standard in *Karcher v. Daggett* (1983). In that case the Court overturned New Jersey's congressional map because the difference between the most populated and the least populated districts was 0.69 percent.

Although the principle of "one person, one vote" is now widely accepted in American politics, some political experts are critical of the strict standard of population equality set by the Court in recent years. For one thing, the census figures for district populations are not entirely accurate, and they usually are out of date within a year or two after the census has been taken. The 1990 census was especially controversial because studies showed that certain urban and minority populations were seriously undercounted.

Moreover, districts that are drawn to ensure equal population often cross traditional political boundaries, such as cities, counties, or regions, that help voters develop a sense of identification with and interest in their congressional district. Finally, critics have pointed out that the Court's standard can be satisfied by a district plan that is a grossly unfair case of politi-

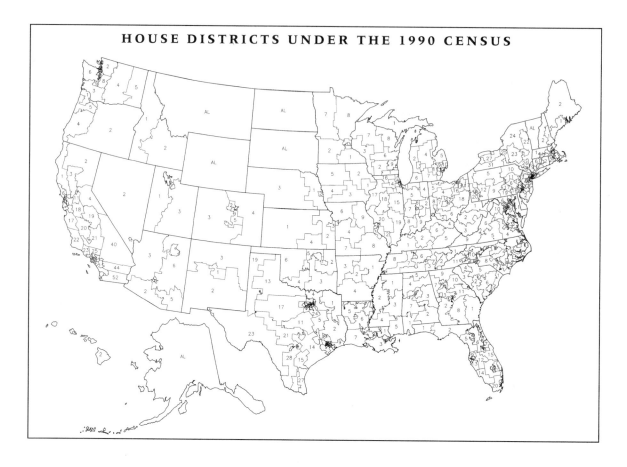

HOUSE DISTRICTS UNDER THE 1990 CENSUS

cal gerrymandering, as long as each district has the same number of people.

The issue of gerrymandering is at the center of current debate over redistricting. The subject is complex, but it boils down to one basic idea: certain areas within each state show a long-term preference for one party over the other. In each election the majority in these areas votes for the candidate of one party, regardless of who is running or what issues are being debated. An area with many working-class people and African Americans, for example, tends to favor Democratic candidates year after year. A wealthy area in the suburbs, on the other hand, may support Republicans in almost every election.

Because these voting habits are well known to political experts in each state, it is possible to create districts that are almost certain to favor candidates of one

party. A district composed solely of blue-collar and inner-city neighborhoods will almost always elect a Democrat, while one made up entirely of well-to-do suburbanites will be a "safe" Republican seat.

State legislators and party strategists have learned over the years to play even more subtle redistricting games. If an incumbent barely survives a tough re-election fight, her friends in the state legislature might agree to redraw that legislator's district to include areas filled with voters who favor her party, while taking out some neighborhoods that usually vote against the party. On a larger scale, "party A" might try to dilute the voting strength of "party B" by spreading B voters among several districts, preventing B candidates from winning a majority in any one. Or else A strategists might concentrate all possible B voters in one district, creating a safe district for party B but making all the other districts in the state favorable to A candidates.

Another potential kind of gerrymandering involves racial or ethnic groups. By dividing up African Americans or other minority voters among several districts, a legislature might be able to ensure that members of a minority group make up no more than half the voters in a district and so prevent election of a minority representative. When blacks in the South began to vote in large numbers in the 1960s, civil rights groups feared that they might be subjected to racial gerrymandering by white-dominated legislatures. To prevent this, Congress added provisions to the 1965 Voting Rights Act barring redistricting plans that dilute the voting strength of blacks.

The law required states with histories of racial discrimination to submit their redistricting plans to the U.S. Justice Department to ensure that African American voters were being treated fairly. Other minorities, including Hispanics, Asian Americans, and Native Americans, were later included in the law's protection. The department and the courts have required changes in redistricting plans in several states to ensure that minority candidates have a chance of being elected. The department required fourteen states to submit their redistricting plans for approval after the 1990 census.

In a ruling on districts in North Carolina *(Thornburg v. Gingles* [1986]), the Supreme Court said that gerrymandering that deliberately diluted minority voting strength was illegal. The burden of proof shifted from minorities, who had been required to show that lines were being drawn to dilute their voting strength, to lawmakers, who had to show that they had done all they could to maximize minority voting strength.

The expansion of minority rights sparked by *Gingles* and later court rulings changed redistricting dramatically. Republicans, many of whom originally had opposed the creation of "majority minority" districts, became promoters of the trend when they saw how it might benefit them. Since minorities usually vote Democratic, concentrating them in one district leaves surrounding districts more favorable to Republican candidates.

In 1992 Republicans in several states expected to profit from legislative or judicial efforts to draw new districts to benefit minority voters—but their hopes were disappointed. Although Republicans failed to make significant gains, the new district maps resulted in record numbers of Hispanics and African Americans being elected to Congress in 1992. (See BLACKS IN CONGRESS; HISPANICS IN CONGRESS.)

## Unresolved Question

The constitutionality of gerrymandering is an important unresolved question in American politics. By one argument it is unconstitutional, since it deprives voters in a gerrymandered district of the right to make an effective choice between candidates of both parties. If a district is set up to make election of a Democrat virtually inevitable, then Republicans in the district have lost the right to cast anything more than a symbolic vote for their candidate. The Supreme Court has been reluctant to address gerrymandering directly. The Court has viewed the issue as a political question outside its jurisdiction. As long as districts are sufficiently similar in population, the Court has not been willing to judge whether they were unfairly gerrymandered—except in cases where racial discrimination is at issue.

In 1986 the Court handed down a significant decision on gerrymandering. In a case involving Indiana's state legislative districts, the Court ruled that political gerrymanders were subject to constitutional challenges for unfairly discriminating against political parties. The case was expected to open the door for many other challenges to allegedly gerrymandered district plans. But in 1989 the Court declined to become involved in the gerrymandering question when it reaffirmed without comment a lower court's decision to uphold California's congressional map, widely recognized as a classic example of a partisan gerrymander.

### Additional Readings

Benenson, Robert, et al. *Jigsaw Politics: Shaping the House after the 1990 Census.* Washington, D.C.: Congressional Quarterly, 1990.

Schwab, Larry M. *The Impact of Congressional Reapportionment and Redistricting.* Lanham, Md.: University Press of America, 1988.

## Recess

*See* ADJOURNMENT.

## Recess Appointment

*See* APPOINTMENT POWER.

## Recommittal Motion

Motions to recommit are used often in the House of Representatives, seldom in the Senate. Although a motion to recommit a bill may be offered for several reasons, usually the purpose is to kill the legislation pending in the full House or Senate. Motions to recommit also may be offered to resolutions, House-Senate conference reports, and, in the House, amendments added to legislation by the Senate. (See LEGISLATIVE PROCESS.)

In the House the motion cannot be used during consideration of a bill for amendment in the COMMITTEE OF THE WHOLE, but it may be offered before a vote on passage of the bill in the full House. If the motion is successful, which it rarely is, the bill is returned to the committee that reported it.

There are two kinds of recommittal motions. A simple motion to recommit, if adopted, kills the bill for all practical purposes. A motion to recommit "with instructions" contains language instructing the committee to report the bill back "forthwith" with certain amendments (or sometimes after a study is completed or by a certain date). If the instructions to report forthwith are adopted, the instructions automatically become part of the legislation; usually the bill is not actually returned to the committee.

The motion to recommit is a standard parliamentary procedure in the House, one of the final steps toward passage of legislation. As such, it is guaranteed by the rules. Opponents must be given preference in offering the motion, and only one such motion is permitted on each bill. If made with instructions to add or amend certain provisions, recommittal motions give opponents of a bill a final opportunity to revise the legislation. They are an important strategic and policy tool of the minority, especially on bills considered under ground rules that bar floor amendments.

The Senate does not routinely use recommittal motions because opponents have many other ways to defeat or amend legislation. Occasionally the Senate will vote to recommit legislation with certain instructions to be reported back to the Senate within a specified period of time.

From time to time the Senate entangles itself in such a parliamentary morass that it uses the recommittal motion to extricate itself. That happened in 1982 when the Senate was considering a bill to raise the national debt limit. Majority Leader Howard H. BAKER, Jr., a Tennessee Republican, had promised senators for months that they could offer their pet proposals as amendments to the debt bill. But when the measure reached the floor, it became bogged down in a debate on controversial amendments dealing with abortion and school prayer. After five weeks, and with more than 1,400 amendments still pending, the Senate recommitted the measure to the Finance Committee, which immediately stripped it of all but the debt limit provisions and returned it to the floor for a final vote.

## Reconciliation

*See* BUDGET PROCESS.

## Reconsider, Motion to

The motion to reconsider is a necessary procedure for the final disposition of legislation in both the Senate and House of Representatives. It is a principle of parliamentary law that floor action on bills and amendments is not conclusive until there has been an opportunity to reconsider the vote by which the question was approved or rejected.

The motion to reconsider usually is followed immediately by a motion to table. Once the motion to reconsider has been tabled, the earlier action on the bill or amendment is final; the act of tabling blocks any future attempt to reverse the result. (See TABLE, MOTION TO.)

In the House, the Speaker usually makes the tabling motion by stating that "without objection a motion to reconsider is laid on the table." Under the rules of both houses, only a member on the prevailing side of the original vote approving or rejecting the bill or amendment (or, in the Senate, someone who did not vote) can make a motion to reconsider.

Besides its importance as a pro forma procedural step in the passage of legislation, the motion to reconsider, followed by a tabling motion, also is used routinely after amendments and other parliamentary questions have been voted on. In the Senate, the results are not always pro forma. Especially on close votes, switches can occur, and reconsideration of bills and amendments gives members another chance to vote on the original question.

The rules in both houses set a time limit for entering motions to reconsider, and the parliamentary situation determines when such motions are in order. For example, a motion to reconsider a vote rejecting an amendment after the bill itself has been passed would come too late.

---

# Reconstruction Era

The period immediately following the Civil War is known as the Reconstruction Era. The name refers to the policies implemented by the victorious Union government in its effort to "reconstruct" the eleven war-torn and economically devastated Confederate states. But Reconstruction, which lasted from 1865 to about 1877, connotes more than merely a sectional administrative matter. It also represents a period of unprecedented radical national leadership dominated by Congress at the expense of the presidency and the judiciary.

## Lincoln's Leniency

Even before the Civil War ended, President Abraham Lincoln had outlined a policy for dealing with the southern states once they capitulated to the Union armies. As early as 1862 he began appointing military governors in areas that had fallen to the Union. He first outlined his Reconstruction policy in December 1863 and eloquently reiterated his views in his last public address, on April 11, 1865. Lincoln's primary goal was to return the seceded states to the Union as quickly and painlessly as possible. Amnesty and restoration of property rights were to be granted to everyone who gave an oath of loyalty to the Union, except for a relatively few Confederate civilian and military leaders. Whenever 10 percent of the electorate of any state made such a pledge, a state government could be established. Once each new state government ratified the Thirteenth Amendment— thereby nullifying its previous secession, repudiating the debts of its Confederate government, and abolishing slavery—the president was prepared to recognize that state as once again a loyal part of the United States. The states of Louisiana and Arkansas promptly accepted Lincoln's terms and adopted new constitutions abolishing slavery even before the president was assassinated.

Such magnanimous treatment of the South was at odds with the will of Congress, which during and after the war was controlled by the Republicans, the most influential of whom were radical abolitionists. They made little attempt to disguise their hatred of southerners and southern institutions, and they refused to accept the validity of Lincoln's terms. In their view Reconstruction was solely the jurisdiction of Congress. When the two readmitted southern states sent their newly elected representatives to Washington, Congress refused to seat them.

## Radical Reconstruction

To the Radical Republicans, the southerners remained traitors and rebels, who could not be restored to citizenship of a country they had rejected without first undergoing rigid tests of loyalty. They devised a punitive plan of their own for implementing Reconstruction. Embodied in the Wade-Davis bill—named for Sen. Benjamin F. Wade of Ohio and Rep. Henry W. Davis of Maryland—the plan required that a majority of the electorate in a state, rather than 10 percent, swear their allegiance to the federal government before the state could be readmitted to the Union.

The Radicals' amnesty excluded even common Confederate soldiers from holding federal office. Such a policy had the effect of excluding the natural leaders and experienced statesmen of the region from participation in its new civilian governments. But that was just the beginning. Underlying all the invective and passion, the Radicals' real goal was to force upon the South the immediate, full equality of all former slaves and to use black votes to ensure Republican domination in southern state governments and in Congress. The collapse of the Confederacy had resulted in the emancipation of some 4 million slaves.

But Lincoln was convinced that leniency was the only way to build loyalty to the Union and establish intersectional peace. Although he pocket-vetoed the Wade-Davis bill, the bill's authors issued the legislation as a manifesto of congressional sentiment and intent. "The president . . . must understand that the authority of Congress is paramount and must be respected . . . and if he wishes our support he must confine himself to his executive duties—to obey and execute, not to make the laws—to suppress by arms any armed rebellion, and leave political reorganization [of the South] to Congress." Confrontation between the legislative and executive branches over Reconstruction now was inevitable.

After Lincoln's assassination his successor, Andrew Johnson, lacking Lincoln's political astuteness, played into the hands of the Radicals. He had the disadvantage of being the nominal leader of a party in which he was not a member. A War Democrat added to the Republican ticket in 1864 to emphasize unity, he had no personal following in either the North or the South. After a brief period of vindictiveness that appeased the Radicals, Johnson reversed positions and adopted Lincoln's mild policies.

The conflict between the two branches was not resolved until Johnson had been impeached, harsh and constitutionally questionable Reconstruction laws enacted, and the Constitution itself amended to suit the Radicals' purposes.

## Committee of Fifteen

The Radicals were led by Rep. Thaddeus STEVENS of Pennsylvania. Stevens's policies were based less on sympathy for blacks than on a desire for political advantage and a cold hatred of the southern gentry.

Although he was not its chair, Stevens dominated a joint committee of the House and Senate, the Joint Committee of Fifteen. This committee was the outgrowth of the Committee on the Conduct of the War that had tried to force its views on Lincoln. The joint committee officially investigated and reported on the credentials of southern members-elect to Congress. In reality, it also wielded the real power in Congress at the time. The Radicals' Reconstruction policies and the tactics used against the president were formulated by this group.

The Radicals' leader in the Senate was Charles SUMNER of Massachusetts. He was not on the Committee of Fifteen, but next to Stevens he was the most powerful figure in the Reconstruction policy. He too believed the Confederate states had committed political suicide and that Congress had exclusive jurisdiction over postwar administration of these outlaw states. As an idealist, lacking any personal knowledge of the slaves' condition, Sumner insisted on giving the freed slaves immediate equality. He lent the Radical cause a tinge of idealism and respectability.

In 1866 Johnson vetoed the first of two Freedmen's Bureau bills, designed to provide services for and protect the rights of the ex-slaves. The Radicals were unable to override that veto, but soon thereafter they did manage to override the veto of a civil rights bill as unconstitutional. Even Radicals had doubts about the bill's constitutionality, however. To allay any doubts they drafted the Fourteenth Amendment, which among other things guaranteed the civil rights of blacks against state interference, reduced the southern states' representation in Congress in proportion to their denial of black suffrage, and disqualified from holding federal or state office ex-Confederates who had formerly held such offices. But the most important provision was the first clause: "No State shall make or enforce any law which shall abridge the privileges or immunities of citizens of the United States; nor shall any State deprive any person of life, liberty, or property, without due process of law; nor deny to any person within its jurisdiction the equal protection of the laws."

The congressional elections of 1866, in which the Radicals were reelected, proved critical to the direction of Reconstruction policy. Using the results as vindication of their policy, the Radicals pushed through Congress a series of punitive laws, including the First Reconstruction Act of 1867. This law declared that there were no legal governments in the southern states (except in Tennessee) and divided the South into five military districts supervised by Union officers. There followed a harsh military occupation of some 20,000 soldiers, including a force of black militia. The military commanders' primary tasks were to create new electorates and establish new state governments. In South Carolina, Alabama, Florida, Mississippi, and Louisiana black voters outnumbered whites. New constitutions were drafted enfranchising blacks, disenfranchising ex-Confederate leaders, and guaranteeing civil and political equality to the freedmen.

The threat of reduced representation in the House, included in the Fourteenth Amendment, failed to prompt southern states to extend the franchise to blacks. As a result, Congress in 1869 submitted to the states the Fifteenth Amendment, which prohibited denial of the right to vote on the basis of race, color, or previous condition of servitude. The amendment was ratified the following year. Congress also passed legislation designed to make the amendment effective, but parts of that law were later held unconstitutional.

### Separation of Powers

The Reconstruction policies threatened more than the South. The Radicals' goal was ultimately to establish a government dominated by Congress and, within Congress, by the Radical Republicans themselves. With pliant executive and judicial branches, the constitutional principle of SEPARATION OF POWERS was in jeopardy. This was the inescapable

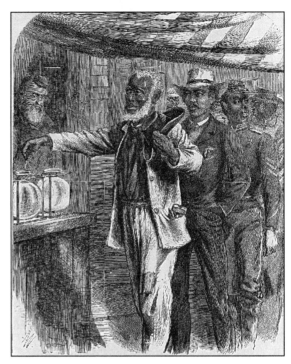

*The collapse of the Confederacy resulted in the emancipation of some 4 million slaves. The Radicals' aim was to use the former slaves' votes to ensure Republican domination in southern state governments and in Congress.    Source: Library of Congress*

implication of passage, over Johnson's veto, of the First Reconstruction Act of 1867, as well as two other laws passed at the same time.

The first, the Command of the Army Act, barred the executive from exercising any control over the army by requiring the president to issue all military orders through the general of the army. The president could not fire or suspend this officer.

The second, the Tenure of Office Act, prevented the president from removing civilians in the executive branch, including members of his own cabinet, without the consent of the Senate. This, of course, made it impossible for a president to control his own administration. Johnson refused to recognize the constitutionality of the law and dismissed his secretary of war, Edwin M. Stanton. This action provided the Radicals with the excuse they needed to attempt to remove

Johnson from office through the impeachment process. (See IMPEACHMENT POWER.) In a Senate trial the president escaped removal by a single vote. If the Radicals' effort had succeeded, the presidency would have gone to Senator Wade, since the vice presidency was vacant and, under the law at that time, the Senate president pro tempore—the post held by Wade—was next in the line of succession. (See JOHNSON IMPEACHMENT TRIAL.)

Congressional Republicans remained in control of most of the reconstructed states well into the 1870s. Control was maintained by an alliance of blacks and Radical Republicans. The latter were of two types: "carpetbaggers," northerners who came to the South for political and economic profit; and "scalawags," southern white renegades. This situation led to a dreadful record of misrule, political corruption, human exploitation, and economic dislocation, including staggering budget deficits.

By the early 1870s the Radicals' drastic policies toward the South had lost most of their popular appeal. In 1874 Democrats gained control of the House of Representatives, and the policy of Reconstruction was finally rejected. The last Union troops were withdrawn from South Carolina and Louisiana in 1877 by order of President Rutherford B. Hayes.

*Thomas Brackett Reed, who held office near the turn of the century, was one of the most powerful Speakers in the history of the House of Representatives. Although resented by some for his assumption of power, "Czar" Reed was admired widely for his wit.*
Source: National Portrait Gallery, Smithsonian Institution

## Reed, Thomas Brackett

Thomas Brackett Reed (1839–1902) of Maine, known as "Czar" Reed, was one of the most powerful Speakers in House history. Determined to put an end to the obstructionist tactics of the minority party, Reed made a series of rulings from the chair that allowed the Republican majority to conduct the business of the House without hindrance. His biting wit, determination, and physical presence made Reed impressive and aided him in forming a Republican voting bloc. (See SPEAKER OF THE HOUSE.)

After practicing law in Portland, Maine, and serving in city and state offices (including the state legislature), Reed was elected to the House of Representatives in 1876. In 1882 he was appointed to the Rules Committee, where he acquired power and the respect of fellow members of his party. When Republicans assumed control of the House in 1889, they elected Reed Speaker. He led Republicans when they were out of power from 1891 to 1895 and resumed the job of Speaker from 1895 to 1899.

The House of which Reed took control was plagued by filibusters that slowed the conduct of business. Democratic representatives refused to answer quorum calls (even when they were present on the House floor) and introduced a flurry of delaying motions to harry their opponents and lengthen the passage of legislation. Reed's insistence that all members present—whether answering or not—be counted toward a quorum caused pandemonium on the floor.

Members tried to hide and were prevented from leaving by the sergeant-at-arms, who was ordered to lock the door. Reed ruled further that the chair would not entertain motions whose purpose was to delay business. These and other "Reed Rules" were formally incorporated into the rules of the House in 1890.

The rules revisions and Czar Reed's exercise of power allowed the House to pass an unprecedented number of bills during the so-called "Billion-dollar Congress" of 1889–1891. Although resented for his assumption of power, Reed was admired as a wit. (When a member stated that he would rather be right than be president, Reed replied: "The gentleman need not be disturbed, he never will be either.")

Reed was an unsuccessful candidate for the Republican presidential nomination in 1896. He resigned from Congress in 1899 in protest over U.S. involvement in the Philippines and Hawaii.

## Reform, Congressional

Making Congress work better is a never-ending process that has preoccupied senators and representatives ever since reformers turned the Continental Congress into the House of Representatives and Senate. Once institutional reforms are in place, they may turn out to be ineffective or cause new, unexpected problems—prompting yet another set of institutional reforms.

Reforms are changes that have been made deliberately, but changes in the House and Senate also happen gradually, as the institutions adapt to new circumstances and new members. The story of the evolving Congress encompasses far more than reorganizations and formal revisions of rules. (See HOUSE OF REPRESENTATIVES; SENATE.)

### Changing the Rules

Like many institutions, Congress is biased toward maintaining the status quo. Reform does not come easily, and it frequently threatens the existing power structure. In 1910 the House ended the autocratic rule of Speaker Joseph G. CANNON, a conservative Illinois Republican, but only after a two-year struggle by Democrats and insurgent Republicans. They finally succeeded in stripping the Speaker of his power base on the Rules Committee and removing his authority to appoint House committee members and their chairs. (See COMMITTEE SYSTEM; RULES COMMITTEE, HOUSE.)

The Rules Committee, which controls access to the House floor for major bills, has been the focus of lengthy reform efforts. For many years the committee was dominated by a coalition of conservative Democrats and Republicans who repeatedly blocked or delayed liberal legislation. In 1959 Speaker Sam RAYBURN, a Texas Democrat, headed off a liberal effort to curb the Rules panel by giving his "personal assurance" that civil rights and other social legislation "would not be bottled up in the committee." Rayburn often was unable to deliver on his promise, however, and two years later the House voted to add three additional members to the committee, thus diluting the power of its conservative members. The dramatic 217–212 House vote in January 1961 was an early signal of the wave of reform that came in the next decade.

In the 1970s the party caucuses in each chamber voted institutional reforms that enabled junior members to share power held by their older and more experienced colleagues. Among the changes was a sweeping attack on the SENIORITY SYSTEM, which used length of service to determine committee chairmanships. Democrats and Republicans in both chambers agreed to elect their committee leaders, using secret ballots in most cases. The most vivid evidence of the new system at work came in 1975, when House Democrats deposed three chairs. Seniority nonetheless remained a major factor in choosing leaders. (See CAUCUSES, PARTY.)

The House rejected proposals for wholesale reorganization of its committee structure, but the Senate approved substantial changes in its committee system in 1977. Several of the most important Senate reforms centered on the FILIBUSTER, the use of unlimited debate to block the will of the majority. The reforms aimed to strengthen Senate restrictions on the filibuster, which were first adopted in 1917.

Reformers of the 1970s also sought to increase members' accountability by opening to the public and press the inner workings of Congress. The House began gavel-to-gavel TELEVISION broadcasts of its floor proceedings in 1979; the Senate followed suit in 1986.

## Statutory Changes

Other major reforms have been achieved by statute. The Legislative Reorganization Act of 1946 streamlined the committee structure, reduced and redistributed the workload of Congress, and improved staff assistance. Budget control provisions included in the act soon proved unworkable and were dropped. A section on lobby regulation was too weak to be effective. Although there were fewer committees under the new structure, subcommittees proliferated.

Another legislative reorganization act, this one in 1970, opened Congress to more public scrutiny and curbed the power of committee chairs. Among other things, the law changed House VOTING procedures to allow for recorded votes on amendments offered on the House floor, required public disclosure of all committee roll calls, authorized radio and television broadcasts of committee hearings, made it more difficult for committees to meet in closed sessions, and required committees to have written rules. The 1970 law authorized additional staff, strengthened Congress's research and information sources, and required the administration to provide Congress with more information about the federal budget. The act also included changes in Senate rules that limited the ability of the most senior members to monopolize choice committee assignments.

The Congressional Budget and Impoundment Control Act of 1974 established a process that for the first time forced lawmakers to coordinate their spending and revenue decisions in a single budget package. It also curbed presidential impoundment of funds appropriated by Congress. The 1974 act was less effective than its sponsors had hoped; in 1985 and again in 1990, as budget deficits rose to alarming levels, lawmakers made substantial changes in the BUDGET PROCESS. They also revised laws dealing with CAMPAIGN FINANCING and ETHICS.

Two important twentieth-century reforms were achieved through constitutional amendments. The Seventeenth Amendment, ratified in 1913, provided for DIRECT ELECTION OF SENATORS; previously, senators had been chosen by state legislatures. The Twentieth Amendment, ratified in 1933, advanced to January from March the date for beginning a new Congress. The change ended the regular practice of lame-duck sessions that ran from the December after an election until the new Congress convened the following March.

## Push for Further Reforms

Despite these reforms, legislators in the 1980s became increasingly dissatisfied with the way Congress worked. By the early 1990s Congress appeared ready to tackle reform once again. Congress in 1992 created a Joint Committee on the Organization of Congress to develop a bipartisan plan for improving legislative operations. (See ORGANIZATION OF CONGRESS COMMITTEE, JOINT.)

Although there were partisan differences, many members on both sides shared views about what was wrong with Congress. One of the most common complaints was that the committee system was an unwieldy anachronism. Critics said the system—troubled by turf battles, overlapping jurisdiction, and outdated delineations of issues—was a significant obstacle to prompt consideration of legislation. For example, a clean air bill in 1990 was handled by seven committees in the House, and that chamber sent 140 members to the conference with the Senate. Major contemporary issues, such as health and international economics, were split among several committees in the House and Senate.

Critics also complained that the Democratic and Republican party LEADERSHIP in Congress had trouble offering a cohesive legislative agenda because of its weak hold on rank-and-file party members. In 1990, for example, Republican and Democratic leaders agreed to a budget deal with the White House, but neither party was able to deliver its share of the votes in the House. Majority party leaders faced an additional problem, since many powerful committee chairs did not feel compelled to answer to party leaders. (See PARTIES, POLITICAL.)

Congressional floor debate was also cited as a problem. The House was criticized for being too restrictive

*Frustrations over how Congress works have been expressed both within and outside the walls of Congress. Here, at the 1992 Republican National Convention in Houston, a Republican raises a hand-painted sign calling for congressional reform.*
*Source: R. Michael Jenkins*

in its rules for limiting amendments; the Senate was criticized for not being restrictive enough. Both were faulted for giving too much time to political side-shows. (See LEGISLATIVE PROCESS.)

Others wanted changes in the legislative and budget processes. Most policy questions had to be addressed in three processes: the budget process, which set general spending priorities; AUTHORIZATION BILLS, which set policy; and APPROPRIATIONS BILLS, which provided year-by-year financing for government programs. Critics charged that procedures were complex, redundant, and ill suited to addressing long-term problems, such as the budget deficit, health care, and international competition.

Some saw these problems as arising from the last round of reforms. The drive to break up the power of committee chairs in the 1970s complicated the job of party leaders. Until then, majority party leaders had been able to cut deals with only a handful of power-brokers; after the reforms, they had to build consensus within a much broader constituency. Opening Congress to greater public scrutiny made members more accountable, but it also made debate more partisan, unruly, and beholden to special interests. Efforts

to give Congress a stronger hand in budgeting ended up obscuring responsibility for fiscal decisions.

Reformers faced significant obstacles in their attempts to change the status quo, but many thought the impetus was there. Congress had been battered by ethics scandals, deadlocked over vital legislative issues, abandoned out of frustration by talented colleagues, and subjected to public scorn. The 103rd Congress (1993–1995) had the largest freshman class since 1949. Many of the newcomers were sent to Washington by an electorate weary of business as usual.

### Additional Readings

Davidson, Roger H., and Walter J. Oleszek. *Congress against Itself.* Bloomington: Indiana University Press, 1977.

Dodd, Lawrence C., and Bruce I. Oppenheimer, eds. *Congress Reconsidered.* 4th ed. Washington, D.C.: CQ Press, 1989.

Hinckley, Barbara. *Stability and Change in Congress.* 4th ed. New York: Harper and Row, 1988.

Rieselbach, Leroy N. *Congressional Reform.* Washington, D.C.: CQ Press, 1986.

Sheppard, Burton D. *Rethinking Congressional Reform: The Reform Roots of the Special Interest Congress.* Cambridge, Mass.: Schenkman, 1985.

## Removal Power

The Senate can approve or reject presidential nominations through its APPOINTMENT POWER, but the congressional role in removing individuals from office is limited. The Constitution does not mention removal except for the impeachment provisions of Article II, Section 4. Presidents have resisted numerous efforts by Congress to restrict their ability to dismiss officials.

Early presidents exercised great restraint in their use of the removal power. But in the 1830s Congress resisted President Andrew Jackson's partisan use of the removal power and his insistence on political loyalty as a requirement for government jobs, a practice known as PATRONAGE. The Senate passed a series of resolutions requesting Jackson to inform it of his reasons for removing various officials.

The legislative and executive branches clashed again over removal power during the administration of Andrew Johnson, who sought to control the post–Civil War Reconstruction effort by giving key posts to his followers. The result was the Tenure of Office Act, passed over Johnson's veto in 1867. The act stated that officials appointed by the president and confirmed by the Senate could not be removed without the consent of the Senate. Johnson's defiance of the act led to his impeachment by the House in 1868. (See JOHNSON IMPEACHMENT TRIAL.)

The Tenure of Office Act was weakened in 1869 and repealed in 1887, ending Congress's most aggressive effort to curb the president's removal power. The Senate also has attempted to force removal of officials, but without much success.

The courts have upheld the president's right to remove government officials without the approval of Congress, except in certain cases. After nearly 140 years of controversy over the issue, the Supreme Court in 1926 ruled that the Constitution gives the president unrestricted power of removal. The Court modified this position in a 1935 decision, *Humphrey's Executor v. United States,* which allowed Congress to restrict the president's authority to remove officials from independent agencies or regulatory bodies.

## Report

*See* LEGISLATIVE PROCESS.

## Reprimand

*See* DISCIPLINING MEMBERS.

## Rescission

*See* IMPOUNDMENT OF FUNDS.

## Resident Commissioner

*See* DELEGATES.

## Resolution

*See* LEGISLATION.

## Rider

An amendment that is not germane, or pertinent, to the subject matter of a bill is called a rider. Riders are most frequently used in the Senate, where nongermane amendments are considered fair play. But they also turn up in the House of Representatives, even though House rules prohibit them.

A rider is often a proposal that would be unlikely to become law as a separate bill, either because one chamber would not pass it or because the president would veto it. Riders are more likely to be accepted if they are attached to urgent LEGISLATION, such as bills providing funds to operate the federal government. Emergency funding bills, called continuing resolutions, have become magnets for unrelated amendments because they must be passed quickly to keep government agencies from shutting down. For example, a CONTINUING RESOLUTION approved in 1984 included, almost as a footnote, a sweeping revision of federal criminal law.

Sometimes a rider is used as a "sweetener" to win the president's approval of a measure he opposes. A tax bill that President Ronald Reagan had vowed to veto became law in 1983 after Congress attached to the measure a trade plan favored by the president. Other riders have been used to rescue bills that had become stalled in hostile committees. A notable example occurred in 1960 when Senate majority leader Lyndon B. Johnson made good on a promise to act on civil rights legislation. When the Senate Judiciary Committee failed to produce such legislation, Johnson called up a minor bill that had been passed by the House, and a landmark civil rights measure was added to it on the Senate floor.

Riders may also obstruct the passage of a bill. An urgent debt-ceiling measure had to be pulled from the Senate floor in 1982 after a five-week filibuster over unrelated amendments involving abortion and school busing. Some 1,400 additional amendments had been prepared on these and other issues.

Tax legislation is frequently subject to riders. The Constitution says tax bills must originate in the House, but the Senate Finance Committee has learned how to initiate major tax proposals by attaching them to minor bills passed by the House. That happened with a far-reaching tax increase in 1982.

The Senate also has a fondness for loading tax or trade bills with nongermane amendments that benefit special interests. Such a measure is known as a CHRISTMAS TREE BILL.

Even though House rules prohibit nongermane amendments, members have found ways to get around the restrictions. Antiabortion riders became a regular feature of annual government appropriations bills beginning in the 1970s and continuing into the early 1990s; they met the House germaneness standard because they were worded to restrict the use of federal funds for abortions. The House may also waive—or ignore—its germaneness rule, a practice that sometimes makes for strange legislative bedfellows. A 1980 House bill, for example, simultaneously set new nutritional requirements for infant formulas and increased federal penalties for marijuana trafficking. A House bill enacted into law in 1991 included not only its original provisions on the trading status of Czechoslovakia and Hungary but also provisions expanding unemployment benefits and imposing sanctions to limit the spread of chemical and biological weapons.

## Rule for House Debate

Most major legislation that reaches the House floor is debated and amended under a resolution, known as a rule, that governs floor consideration of the measure. The rule establishes time limits for debate and determines what amendments, if any, may be offered; it may include other provisions as well. A bill goes to the Rules Committee after it has been reported by a legislative committee. The Rules Committee then writes the rule and presents it to the full House. House approval of the rule precedes floor debate and amendments. (See LEGISLATIVE PROCESS; RULES COMMITTEE, HOUSE.)

In devising rules for floor consideration, the Rules Committee works closely with the House leadership. Before the 1975 reforms, the committee frequently was able to frustrate leadership goals.

## Rules, House and Senate

*See* LEGISLATIVE PROCESS.

## Rules and Administration Committee, Senate

The task of overseeing Senate operations is handled by the Senate Rules and Administration Committee. Its focus is usually on the nuts and bolts of running the Senate: committee budgets, assignment of office space, and other housekeeping matters. The panel also has jurisdiction over election law, including restrictions on CAMPAIGN FINANCING, corrupt practices, presidential succession, and contested elections. Although the committee is responsible for Senate rules and organization, most efforts to reform Senate procedures have been handled by special temporary committees. The rules committee, central to the Senate establishment, has had little enthusiasm for change.

The committee has two House counterparts, the HOUSE ADMINISTRATION COMMITTEE and Rules Committee. (See RULES COMMITTEE, HOUSE.) Although rarely in the limelight, the Senate rules committee has had a role in several key decisions. In the 1950s, reacting to Sen. Joseph R. McCarthy's abusive treatment of witnesses before his subcommittee, the rules panel pushed committees to adopt safeguards giving witnesses a chance for rebuttal. A 1960s investigation into misconduct by Bobby Baker, secretary of the Senate from 1955 to 1963, was handled by the rules committee. Republicans on the panel said Democrats limited their probe to protect Lyndon B. Johnson, who had hired Baker while he was the Democratic leader.

Various reforms went through the Rules Committee in the 1970s, though it often did not originate the changes. The panel endorsed opening the Senate chamber to TELEVISION cameras in the early 1980s; the rest of the Senate went along in 1986. (See REFORM, CONGRESSIONAL.) While Republicans controlled the Senate (1981–1987), Charles McC. Mathias, Jr., of Maryland chaired the committee. Wendell H. Ford of Kentucky assumed the post when the Democrats took control of the Senate in 1987.

---

# Rules Committee, House

The House Rules Committee occupies a unique place in the congressional COMMITTEE SYSTEM. Almost all major legislation that is debated on the floor of the HOUSE OF REPRESENTATIVES must first win the committee's blessing. Its opposition can kill a bill that another House committee spent months preparing.

The Rules Committee is frequently described as a traffic cop for the House: it determines which bills get to the floor, which amendments—if any—can be considered, and in what order they will come up. By controlling the amendment procedure, the Rules Committee is able to influence the substance of legislation. In addition, the panel has broad jurisdiction over House rules of procedure and House reorganization issues.

The committee is strictly partisan. It is an agent of the SPEAKER OF THE HOUSE, who is both the presiding officer of the House and the overall leader of the majority party in the chamber. Democrats have held almost unbroken control of the House since 1931. As the majority party, they occupy more seats on the committee than the Republicans do—in fact, a disproportionate ratio. Nine Democrats and only four Republicans served on the panel in 1992. The committee's Democrats are put there by the Speaker, and with rare exceptions they do what the Speaker wants. The outnumbered Republican members have little say in the matter.

## Granting a Rule

All but the most routine legislation passes through the Rules Committee. A bill goes to the panel after it has been considered and approved by a legislative committee that specializes in the subject involved. During a hearing before the Rules Committee the legislative committee's chair, senior minority party member, and others explain the content of the bill and how they want it to be handled on the floor.

After the hearing the Rules Committee generally approves a resolution, known as a rule, that sets time limits for general debate on the entire bill and establishes ground rules for considering amendments to it. Some rules permit any germane, or relevant, amendment to be offered from the floor. These are known as open rules. Others, called closed rules, prohibit all floor amendments. Frequently, bills are given modified rules that allow only specified amendments to be introduced or permit floor amendments only to certain sections of the bill.

In recent years the committee has become increasingly creative in devising rules to meet the leadership's objectives, keep debate under control, and ensure that members are given an opportunity to debate

*Often described as a traffic cop for the House, the Rules Committee determines which bills reach the floor, which amendments can be considered, and in what order they will come up.    Source: R. Michael Jenkins*

the major amendments and alternatives to a particular bill. Republicans complain that there has been an increase in restrictive rules that prohibit them from offering amendments that might win.

The rule must be adopted on the House floor before the bill is debated. Occasionally rules are amended or defeated when they reach the floor, but most receive routine approval. (See LEGISLATIVE PROCESS.)

### Shifting Role

The Rules Committee was established on a temporary basis in 1789, but originally it had jurisdiction only over House rules. Its influence over legislation did not develop until after the Speaker was made a member of the panel in 1858. The panel became a standing committee in 1880 and began issuing rules for floor debate in 1883. Until 1910 the committee worked closely with the House leadership in deciding

what legislation could come to the floor. It was made independent of the leadership in the 1910–1911 Progressive revolt against the arbitrary reign of Speaker Joseph G. CANNON, a Republican from Illinois.

A coalition of conservative Democrats and Republicans took control of the committee in the late 1930s and frustrated the Democratic leadership for decades. Under the twelve-year chairmanship of Virginia Democrat Howard W. SMITH (1955–1967), the panel repeatedly blocked or delayed civil rights measures sought by the Democratic majority. Because the committee had no regular meeting day and could be called together only by the chair, it was frequently unable to clear any bills for floor action during the final days of a session when Smith simply "disappeared" to his Virginia farm.

Several attempts to break the conservative grip on the committee proved unsuccessful. Finally in 1975 the House Democratic Caucus gave the Speaker the power to name all Democratic members of the panel, subject to caucus approval. The Rules Committee thus returned to leadership control. (See CAUCUSES, PARTY.)

A seat on the Rules Committee is still considered an important post. Sometimes it is a springboard to House leadership. Rules Committee member Thomas P. O'NEILL, Jr., earned a place on the leadership ladder for his role in a House reorganization effort advanced by the Rules Committee in 1970. O'Neill, a Massachusetts Democrat, went on to become Speaker in 1977.

Rules Committee members also have an opportunity to leave their imprint on bills that come before them. The committee may require changes in one measure as the price of granting a rule; it may bar a floor amendment that would transform another. Legislative committees sometimes woo votes for their bills in the Rules Committee by appealing to the interests of individual members of the panel—adding a flood control project in one member's district, perhaps, or revising a foreign policy provision opposed by another.

The committee has become even more influential in recent years by mediating legislative disputes between committees. This has occurred because of the House Appropriations Committee's practice of adding legislative provisions to spending bills and because of the referral of bills to more than one committee.

For these reasons, among others, Rules Committee assignments are highly prized. The panel's members do not serve on other major committees. They tend to represent the dominant political currents of the House. They come from politically safe districts; what little turnover occurs on the panel typically results from death or retirement, not election defeat.

Joe Moakley, a Democrat from Massachusetts, became chair in 1989 after the death of Florida Democrat Claude Pepper. Pepper had taken over the committee in 1983 when Richard BOLLING, a Democrat from Missouri, retired. As chair, Bolling had done much to transform the internal operations of the committee as well as its role in the House. During his tenure, two standing subcommittees were created, the committee's staff and budget were increased, and the committee's own legislative initiatives were expanded.

## Russell, Richard B.

Richard B. Russell (1897–1971) was at the heart of the Senate power structure for most of his long career (1933–1971). Even before seniority made him chair of two top committees, Armed Services and then Appropriations, the Georgia Democrat was leader of a tightly knit bloc of southern conservatives who dominated the Senate for years. He also worked closely with Lyndon B. JOHNSON, who had been a freshman senator when Russell backed him for the Democratic leadership in the early 1950s. For his own leadership role, Russell preferred working behind the scenes and on the Democratic policy and steering committees, where he usually held sway.

Patrician in his demeanor and gracious in his dealings with others, Russell built his reputation on what he called "doing homework." His byword was caution. "When I am in doubt about a question, I always vote no," Russell once said. His assessment of leadership was straightforward: "Any man who dares to vote independently is a leader . . . and any man who can persuade three or four men to vote with him is a power."

Russell was an opponent of civil rights legislation, but he avoided racist statements, invoking instead the traditional states' rights arguments against federal interference. His politics, though generally conservative, could not be neatly categorized; for example, Russell opposed U.S. involvement in Vietnam from the beginning.

As chair of the Armed Services Committee (1951–1953, 1955–1969), Russell never took as gospel the military policies proposed by the executive branch; he questioned and criticized without hesitation. Russell also learned how to steer defense contracts toward Georgia, which became a major center of the military industry. Russell chaired the Appropriations Subcommittee on Defense in the 1960s, which gave him a powerful dual role of controlling first the authorization of military programs and then the actual spending.

Born and raised in Winder, Georgia, Russell was the fourth of thirteen children. His father, who had made unsuccessful bids for governor and senator, served as chief justice of the Georgia supreme court. Russell, who practiced law in Winder, was elected in 1921 to the Georgia legislature; in six years he was chosen Speaker. The next step for the young politician was the governor's mansion; he won a two-year term as governor in 1930. When he took office in 1931 at the age of thirty-four, he was the youngest chief executive in the state's history. But his tenure was brief. When a Georgia senator died, Russell was selected to fill the unexpired term, and he joined the Senate in January 1933. Except for a bid for the Democratic presidential nomination in 1952, which he lost on the third ballot, Russell focused his life on the Senate for the next thirty-eight years.

Russell became the most senior senator in 1969, a standing that gave him the title president pro tempore. His health by that time was poor, and he died in 1971. The following year his colleagues marked their affection and respect by naming one of two existing Senate office buildings in his honor.

# S

## Science and Technology Committee, House

Once preoccupied with space exploration, the House Science and Technology Committee in the last decade has focused on a wide array of government research and development programs. Energy, aviation, transportation, and environment are among the research topics within the committee's jurisdiction. It also reviews overall government science policy.

Most legislators consider the science and technology panel their secondary committee. The legislation written by the committee often becomes part of a broader measure that other committees have also helped draft. In floor action on major bills, the science panel often ends up as partner of a more aggressive committee that dominates the debate. For example, nuclear waste disposal is an issue shared with the Natural Resources and Commerce committees, which have usually overshadowed the Science and Technology Committee.

Within its own territory—research and space—the science panel was showing more independence by the late 1980s. The committee was often lobbied by aerospace, energy, and high-technology companies competing for government support. Committee members sought to keep research compatible with overall government science policy. They even began to engage in critical questioning of the National Aeronautics and Space Administration (NASA). Under George E. Brown, Jr., a California Democrat who became chair in 1991, the panel has pressured NASA to shift its emphasis toward unmanned space exploration.

The Science and Technology Committee was established in 1958 as the Select Committee on Astronautics and Space Exploration. In 1959 it became the Science and Astronautics Committee. When reorganization proposals became commonplace as part of reform efforts in the 1970s, the science panel at first seemed vulnerable to efforts to streamline committee jurisdictions. Instead the committee ended up with a broader mandate, a move that gave it higher standing within the House. It was renamed the Science and Technology Committee in 1975.

## Seating Disputes

The Constitution authorized each house of Congress to judge the fairness of the elections of its members. Under that authority the Senate and House of Representatives have settled hundreds of contested elections. Defeated candidates have challenged election results after close tallies or apparent voting irregularities. Although Congress has tried to give a judicial tone to its decisions, the result usually is partisan: the party in power gives the seat to its candidate.

The House is governed by the Federal Contested Election Act of 1969. No comparable law guides the Senate, but it handles far fewer elections and thus fewer disputes. The entire membership of the House, but only a third of the Senate, is elected every two years, so that the House oversees 435 elections every other November, while the Senate oversees only about 33. The Senate has been elected by popular vote since 1913. Previously, senators were chosen by state legislatures. (See DIRECT ELECTION OF SENATORS.)

The closest Senate election since 1913 was a 1974 New Hampshire contest that ultimately was settled by a new election. The initial tally was so close that one count showed only two votes separating the contenders. Senators spent seven months wrangling over the results. After forty-one roll-call votes on the question, John A. Durkin, the Democratic candidate, asked for a new election. The Senate declared the seat vacant and set the second election for September

1975. It was the first time senators had ever declared a vacancy because they could not make up their minds. Durkin handily defeated Republican Louis C. Wyman the second time around.

The closest House contest of the twentieth century was resolved in 1985 by a vote along party lines. The decision, which came after an acrimonious four-month struggle, made Republicans so angry they walked out of the House chamber in protest. For the next several days they used parliamentary tactics to disrupt proceedings on the House floor. The dispute centered on Democratic incumbent Frank McCloskey, who appeared to have narrowly lost his Indiana House seat in November 1984 to Republican Richard D. McIntyre. After a recount of votes McCloskey claimed the seat. The House in early 1985 declared the seat vacant and called for an investigation. A special investigating committee then declared McCloskey the winner by four votes. The House, dominated by Democrats, voted to accept the committee recommendation, triggering the Republican walkout. In a 1986 rematch, McCloskey beat McIntyre by a comfortable margin.

## Secretary of the Senate

The secretary of the Senate is the chief administrative officer of the Senate. The secretary's responsibilities are similar to those of the CLERK OF THE HOUSE: providing equipment and supplies, disbursing payroll, and making periodic reports. Like the House clerk, the secretary of the Senate is elected by the majority party in the chamber and generally continues in the post as long as that party maintains its majority.

## Senate

Although the Constitution says the two chambers of Congress are equal, senators rarely leave the Senate to run for the House of Representatives. Representatives, however, often decide to run for the Senate.

The two chambers share the tasks of legislating, overseeing the federal government, and representing their constituencies. But there are striking differences between the two legislative bodies and how they go about their work. The Senate, once known as the "world's most exclusive club," projects an image of influence and prestige that the House does not match. The Senate has 100 members—two from each state—while the House has 435 members, allocated among the states according to population. Senators are elected for six years, House members for two. Senators have a broad, statewide constituency, while most House members represent districts within states. These differences have shaped the practices and procedures of the two chambers.

Thanks to its small size, the Senate is informal and flexible, in contrast to the highly structured House. It is also more individualistic, with power more evenly distributed among its members. The Senate shares certain executive powers with the president, which contributes to the chamber's prestige. With fewer members to share the limelight, senators enjoy more attention. But, by the same token, there are fewer members to share the workload, which is as heavy in the Senate as in the House. As a result, senators tend to be policy generalists, while representatives develop specialties. The Senate takes longer to consider legislation, in part because it sees its chief role as one of deliberation.

Representatives who move to the Senate feel a sort of political "culture shock" in their new environment. They welcome the Senate's tradition of deference to individual senators. But some look back with nostalgia on the efficient procedures of the House. Many miss the camaraderie of the House, though few wish to return to it. "Rules and tradition make it possible for every member of the Senate to play a significant role in legislating," said Colorado Republican William L. Armstrong, who was elected to the Senate in 1978 after six years in the House. "It's possible even for a brand new member to jump right in."

"A senator has greater access to virtually anyone inside or outside of government," remarked Paul Simon, an Illinois Democrat who moved from the House to the Senate in 1985. "There are very few people who won't return a phone call from a U.S. senator."

## Origins

The differences between the two chambers were not an accident of history but rather the result of a carefully crafted plan of the framers of the Constitution in 1787. The Senate was born of compromise—one so significant it was called the "Great Compromise" of the Constitutional Convention. Without it, the convention would have collapsed. When it was decided that representation in the House would be proportional to a state's population, the small states sounded the alarm. Fearful of domination by the more populous states, they insisted that states have equal representation in the Senate. The large states resisted until agreement was reached that, in return for equality of state representation in the Senate, the House would be given sole power to originate money bills, which the Senate could accept or reject but could not modify. This last provision was changed in the final draft to allow the Senate to alter or amend revenue bills.

The convention also decided that voters would elect House members but that the Senate should be insulated from popular sentiments. To this end, the convention directed that senators be elected by the state legislatures and for six-year terms. James MADISON explained the delegates' thinking: "The use of the Senate is to consist in its proceeding with more coolness, with more system, and with more wisdom, than the popular branch."

State legislatures no longer elect senators, since the Seventeenth Amendment provided for DIRECT ELECTION OF SENATORS. Despite their long terms, senators today devote considerable time and energy to running for reelection, so that they are no longer insulated from public opinion. Some observers would also question whether the Senate has stayed aloof from popular legislative battles.

Nonetheless, the framers' views can still be heard two centuries later. During a 1986 debate over whether to televise Senate proceedings, the discussion was laced with references to the differences between the two chambers, with the Senate depicted as the voice of reason and the House as the more impulsive voice of popular demands. The Senate ultimately voted to allow television cameras into the chamber, as the House had done earlier.

## Powers

Contrasting views of the roles of the Senate and House were apparent in the Constitutional Convention's debates over congressional powers. For the most part, the two chambers were given equal powers, but there were several important exceptions. (See STRUCTURE AND POWERS.)

### Power of the Purse

One of the most significant instances in which one chamber was given precedence over the other was in the exercise of the power of the purse. The Constitution required that the House originate tax legislation. The convention's debate over the question of whether the Senate should be allowed to amend the House tax bills reflected the contrasting views of the Senate as likely to be either the most responsible branch or the most aristocratic one, to be strengthened or checked accordingly. (See PURSE, POWER OF.)

The question eventually was resolved in favor of the Senate's right to amend. This is a right the Senate does not hesitate to use, particularly toward the end of a session. Because the Senate has few procedures or rules to ward off amendments, the Senate often has turned a tax measure into a CHRISTMAS TREE BILL by attaching to it amendments that bestow benefits on various economic interests.

The Senate has even on occasion circumvented the constitutional stricture on originating tax bills. In 1982 it wrote the largest peacetime tax increase in the nation's history by attaching the plan to a minor tax bill passed by the House that went straight to a House-Senate conference committee.

### Power of Confirmation

Counterbalancing the House's precedence in money matters are the Senate's executive powers, which it shares with the president. These are the powers of confirmation of appointments and treaty ratification.

*Matthew Brady's photograph of the sixty-eight members of the Senate in 1859.*

The Constitution requires that the president appoint government officials with the advice and consent of the Senate. The vast majority of nominations receive routine confirmation, but those for top positions in the federal government and judiciary are closely scrutinized by Senate committees and sometimes hotly debated on the Senate floor. For example, there were grueling battles over President Ronald Reagan's Supreme Court nominations in 1987. One nominee was defeated, and a second withdrew under intense Senate scrutiny before a third finally received Senate approval. (See APPOINTMENT POWER.)

### Treaty Power

The Constitution requires that the Senate give its advice and consent to a treaty. A two-thirds vote of the senators present is necessary for treaty ratification. The Senate's voting record on treaties has been overwhelmingly favorable. Outright rejection is rare. In 1920, however, after prolonged debate the Treaty of Versailles was ultimately rejected. The Treaty of Versailles was the World War I treaty of peace with Germany and also covered U.S. membership in the League of Nations.

Congressional involvement in the treaty process reached an unprecedented level in modern times during negotiation in the late 1970s of the SALT II agreement with the Soviet Union and during consideration of the Panama Canal treaties and related legislation. The Panama Canal treaties were eventually approved by the Senate, but the arms agreement was shelved after the Soviet invasion of Afghanistan. (See TREATY-MAKING POWER.)

### Impeachment Power

The Senate and House share the power to impeach high federal officials. The House conducts the investigation, brings charges (called articles of impeachment) against an official, and argues for removal during a trial conducted in the Senate. The final decision is the Senate's. The Constitution requires a two-thirds vote of the senators present to convict on any article of impeachment. Between 1789 and 1992, the Senate sat as a court of impeachment fifteen times. Seven cases ended in conviction and six in acquittal. In two cases the Senate dismissed the charges. (See IMPEACHMENT POWER.)

### Election Power

Both chambers have the responsibility of counting the electoral votes for president and vice president. If no candidate for the presidency has a majority of the electoral votes, the House chooses the president. If no vice-presidential candidate has a majority, the Senate makes the choice. (See ELECTING THE PRESIDENT.)

Only once has the Senate resolved a vice-presidential contest. In 1837, when Martin Van Buren was elected president, his running mate, Richard M. Johnson, was one vote short of a majority because Van Buren electors from Virginia had boycotted Johnson. The Senate elected Johnson vice president.

## Development

The framers of the Constitution assumed that the House would be the preeminent chamber, with the Senate functioning as a revisory body and a restraining influence. Initially the House did overshadow the Senate. In fact, it was reported that in the First Congress (1789–1791), the Senate often adjourned its own tedious sessions so that its twenty-six members could go listen to the livelier floor debates in the House.

The Senate's influence was soon felt. The importance of its treaty and appointment powers, in which the House had no share, was a factor; in addition, membership in the smaller Senate became more desirable than election to the rapidly expanding House. The Senate's longer term and more stable membership also made it more attractive.

The Senate's legislative importance increased gradually. In the early years the House dominated the great debates, such as those surrounding the War of 1812. But the Senate took the lead in the struggle over the Missouri Compromise of 1820 and succeeded in imposing on the House an amendment barring slavery in future northern states. In the years leading up to the Civil War, the Senate became the chief forum for the great antislavery debates. Illustrious figures, such as Daniel WEBSTER of Massachusetts, Henry CLAY of Kentucky, and John C. CAL-

*Forceful senators such as Daniel Webster (center) and Henry Clay (right) challenged the policies and executive prerogatives used by President Andrew Jackson (left).* Source: The New-York Historical Society

HOUN of South Carolina, dominated this "golden age" of the Senate.

Alexis de Tocqueville, French aristocrat, scholar, and astute observer of American life, wrote in 1834 that "the Senate is composed of eloquent advocates, distinguished generals, wise magistrates, and statesmen of note, whose arguments would do honor to the most remarkable parliamentary debates of Europe." He had harsher words for the House of Representatives: "One is struck by the vulgar demeanor of that great assembly. Often there is not a distinguished man in the whole number."

### Legislative Process

Courtesy, dignity, and informality marked the proceedings of the early Senate. Sometimes on a chilly morning members would leave their seats and gather around the fireplace to conduct Senate business.

There was little need for elaborate procedures or for a formal division of labor because there was not much labor to divide. As the duties of Congress grew and as legislation increased in volume and complexity, however, a discernible LEGISLATIVE PROCESS began to evolve. "Rules are never observed in this body; they are only made to be broken. We are a law unto ourselves," claimed Republican senator John J. Ingalls of Kansas in 1876. In the smaller, more individualistic Senate, rules have been far less important than in the larger House.

The Senate today operates largely by UNANIMOUS CONSENT, suspending or adjusting its rules as needed. Because the early Senate saw its primary function as deliberation, no restrictions were placed on debate, and thus was born the Senate's cherished tradition of unlimited debate. There was little obstruction in the early Senate, but the FILIBUSTER—the practice by which a minority employs extended debate and delaying tactics to put off or block action on a bill—became increasingly common in the nineteenth century. There was a virtual epidemic of filibusters in the 1880s and 1890s. A rule to cut off filibusters was finally adopted in 1917 and was first used several years later during the seemingly interminable debates on the Treaty of Versailles. Further reforms to curtail obstructionism in the Senate were adopted over the years. Yet the filibuster—or even the threat of one—remained a potent weapon.

The Senate originally conducted most of its deliberations in its chamber. Senators would consider questions brought before them and indicate the line of action to be followed before appointing a temporary committee to work out the details of proposed legislation. Ad hoc select committees soon grew to an unmanageable number (nearly 100 in the 1815–1816 session), and the Senate established permanent legislative committees.

Committees developed into powerful, autonomous institutions during the nineteenth century. The important practice of having the majority party's most senior member of a committee serve as chair was begun at this time. These committee chairs often served as floor managers of bills until formal floor leaders were established. (See COMMITTEE SYSTEM; SENIORITY SYSTEM.)

The Constitution mentioned only two Senate officers: the VICE PRESIDENT of the United States was to serve as the president of the Senate, and a PRESIDENT PRO TEMPORE was to act in his absence. But neither officer was given any real power, and as a result neither has done much more than preside over the Senate.

Eventually the Senate developed a formal LEADERSHIP hierarchy, but it did not build a tradition of strong leadership like that in the House. As Webster put it in 1830, "This is a Senate, a Senate of equals, of men of individual honor and personal character, and of absolute independence. We know no masters, we acknowledge no dictators."

Leadership was provided by powerful individuals or groups until political parties began to dominate. Modern party discipline made its appearance in the

Senate in the 1890s, and formally designated majority and minority floor leaders followed in the early 1900s. These leaders came to play an important role in organizing the Senate to carry out their parties' programs. Senators reached top leadership positions after years of spending time on the floor, mastering parliamentary rules, and constantly doing favors for other members. (See Appendix.)

No Senate leader in modern times has rivaled the effectiveness of Lyndon B. JOHNSON, a Texas Democrat who served as minority leader in 1953–1954 and as majority leader from 1955 until 1961, when he resigned to become John F. Kennedy's vice president.

Johnson's influence was the accumulation of hundreds of intense one-to-one relationships. He got his way by subjecting senators to his legendary " treatment" —cajoling, accusing, threatening, and promising—until he had won.

Johnson's power was not something that could be passed on to successors, partly because it was uniquely his but also because the climate in the Senate was changing. Organizational and procedural changes in the 1970s enabled less senior members of the Senate to gain power at the expense of older and more experienced legislators. With more staff, more money, and more power, individual senators were able to maintain their independence from party leaders and more easily pursue their own interests and legislative goals. (See REFORM, CONGRESSIONAL.)

## The Modern Senate

By the 1980s members were increasingly frustrated by the legislative system and the Senate's bouts of legislative paralysis. A few highly publicized retirements focused attention on the problems of the modern Senate. "We are legislators. Like baseball players who like to play nine innings, like farmers who like to plant all of their fields, we like to pass laws," said South Dakota Democrat Thomas A. Daschle, who moved to the Senate from the House in 1987. "In an era of fast moving, globalized issues, the possibility that the world could pass the Senate by increases immeasurably."

Complaints about the Senate's cumbersome processes are as old as the institution itself. Because of

# A TYPICAL DAY IN THE SENATE

*A typical day in the Senate might run as follows:*

• The Senate is called to order by the presiding officer. The constitutional presiding officer, the vice president, is seldom in attendance. Usually the president pro tempore presides over the opening minutes of the Senate session. During the course of the day, other members of the majority party take turns presiding for an hour at a time.

• The Senate chaplain delivers the opening prayer.

• The majority leader and the minority leader are recognized for opening remarks. The majority leader usually announces the plan for the day's business, which is developed in consultation with the minority leadership.

• Senators who have requested time in advance are recognized for special orders; they may speak about any topic for five minutes.

• After special orders, the Senate usually conducts morning business. During morning business—which need not take place in the morning, in spite of its name—members conduct routine chores. They introduce bills and receive reports from committees and messages from the president.

• After morning business, the Senate considers legislative or executive matters. If the majority leader wants the Senate to begin work on a piece of legislation, he normally asks for unanimous consent to call up the measure. If any member objects, the leader may make a debatable motion that the Senate take up the bill. The debatable motion gives opponents the opportunity to launch a filibuster, or extended debate, even before the Senate officially begins considering the bill. A few measures, such as budget resolutions and reports from Senate-House conference committees, are privileged, and a motion to consider them is not debatable.

• After the Senate begins work on a bill, floor debate is generally handled by managers, usually the chair and ranking minority member of the committee that has jurisdiction over the measure. Some measures are considered under a time agreement in which the Senate unanimously agrees to limit debate and to divide the time in some prearranged fashion. In the absence of a time agreement, any senator may seek recognition from the chair and, once recognized, may speak for as long as he or she wishes. Unless the Senate has unanimously agreed to limit amendments, senators may offer as many as they wish. Generally, amendments need not be germane, or directly related, to the bill. Most bills are passed by a voice vote with only a handful of senators present.

• Any member can request a roll call, or recorded vote, on an amendment or on final passage of a measure. Senate roll calls are casual affairs. Few members answer the clerk as their names are called. Instead, senators stroll in from the cloakrooms or their offices and congregate in the well (the area in the front of the chamber). When they are ready to vote, senators catch the eye of the clerk and vote, often by indicating thumbs up or thumbs down. Roll-call votes are supposed to last fifteen minutes, but some have dragged on for more than an hour.

• Often, near the end of the day, the majority leader and the minority leader quickly move through a wrap-up period, during which minor bills that have been cleared by all members are passed by unanimous consent.

• Just before the Senate finishes its work for the day, the majority leader seeks unanimous consent for the agenda for the next session: when the Senate will convene, which senators will be given special orders, and sometimes specific time agreements for consideration of legislation.

*The Senate Chamber.*    Source: *U.S. Senate Commission on Art and Antiquities*

its privileges of unlimited debate and virtually unlimited amending powers, the Senate may well spend days considering a measure that the House debated and passed in one afternoon.

To keep business moving, the Senate in the early 1970s began operating on a two-track system, with a certain period of time reserved daily for particularly controversial bills. It was hoped that in this way a much-debated bill would not interfere with other business. Nonetheless, delays and obstructionism continued to increase.

Filibusters, which a generation ago were reserved for civil rights and a handful of other divisive issues,

came to be used on dozens of less important subjects. A few intransigent senators—just one, if he or she was sufficiently determined—could block action on any bill that did not have the sixty votes required to end a filibuster. Probably no one voiced the growing frustration felt by many senators better than Barry Goldwater, who retired in 1987 after thirty years as a Republican senator from Arizona. "If this is the world's greatest deliberative body," he told a colleague one day in 1982, "I'd hate to see the world's worst."

Efforts to streamline procedures were made in the 1980s. Yet, in an institution as traditional as the Senate, those seeking changes in procedures and organi-

*The restored old Senate Chamber.*    Source: *U.S. Senate Commission on Art and Antiquities*

zation inevitably faced a battle. Senior members jealously guarded their power bases. Others resisted change because they thought the Senate's constitutional role and its identity as a "deliberative" body were inextricably linked to its inefficiency. They feared that changes would weaken the power of the minority party—and even individual senators—to affect the outcome of legislation. The burden of proof rested heavily on those seeking procedural revisions.

The leadership in the 100th Congress inaugurated a new system to answer one frustration of senators: the chamber's erratic schedule. The new plan called for the Senate to be in session for three five-day work weeks and then off for a week. Until then, the Senate generally had had floor business four days a week. Members had complained that the unpredictable schedule interfered with family events, meetings with constituents, and campaign fund-raising events. But the Senate quickly returned to four-day weeks and unpredictable schedules. Majority Leader Robert C. BYRD, a West Virginia Democrat, had cautioned against expecting too much. "There is no magic solution that will automatically make the Senate a 9-to-5 job," Byrd said in 1987. "We could make it a 9-to-5 job but it would no longer be the United States Senate."

## Elections

Senators were elected by state legislatures until the early twentieth century. But in the PROGRESSIVE ERA with its movement toward more democratic control of government, public opinion increasingly favored popular election of senators. Eventually the Senate was forced to participate in its own reform. The Seventeenth Amendment, approved by Congress in 1912 and ratified by the states the following year, provided for the direct election of senators.

The six-year terms of senators are staggered so that one-third of the Senate seats are up for election every two years, rather than all the seats being open at one time. In the event of a vacancy, a state governor may make a temporary appointment until the vacancy can be filled by a special election.

The length of a senator's term has always been considered a real advantage, especially by House members who face elections every two years. Historically, senators were able to act as statesmen for the first half of their terms and deal with politics in the last few years. But Senate seats today are not so secure as they once were, and senators are increasingly becoming permanent candidates, like their House colleagues. Senate races are not only more competitive but also more costly, with multimillion-dollar campaigns common. According to former majority leader Byrd, one of his biggest problems as leader was accommodating the senators' need for time away from the floor to raise campaign money. (See CAMPAIGN FINANCING.)

## Qualifications

To serve in the U.S. Senate, the Constitution requires that a person be at least thirty years of age, have been a citizen of the United States for not less than nine years, and live in the state he or she is to represent.

## Characteristics

Few senators in modern times have found the age requirement to be a problem. The average senator in the 103rd Congress was fifty-eight years old. (See MEMBERS OF CONGRESS: CHARACTERISTICS.)

The Senate in 1993 counted six women among its ranks, one African American, and one Native American. These small numbers were hardly surprising, given the fact that only twenty-one women had been elected or appointed to the Senate since its beginning. (Of these, one served just a day and another never was sworn in because Congress was not in session.) Only three African Americans had served in the Senate before Carol Moseley-Braun, the first black woman senator, was elected by Illinois in 1992. (See BLACKS IN CONGRESS; WOMEN IN CONGRESS.)

One telling statistic from the 103rd Congress was the number of former representatives serving in the Senate: thirty-five, more than a third of the Senate's membership. Although representatives tend to bristle when the House is referred to as the "lower chamber," they recognize the incentives to make a run for the Senate: the Senate's greater prestige and publicity; its longer term, larger staff, and more generous perquisites; the opportunity for increased effectiveness; a greater role in foreign affairs; and the challenge of dealing with a statewide constituency.

Only one former senator sat in the House in recent years. This was Florida Democrat Claude Pepper who, after serving as a senator from 1936 through 1951, became a House member in 1963 and served until his death in 1989. Even after Pepper's several decades in the House, people still called him by his more prestigious title, "Senator Pepper."

### Additional Readings

Byrd, Robert C. *The Senate 1789–1989: Addresses on the History of the United States Senate.* Washington, D.C.: Government Printing Office, 1988.

Davidson, Roger H., and Oleszek, Walter J. *Congress and Its Members.* 4th ed. Washington, D.C.: CQ Press, 1993.

Haynes, George H. *The Senate of the United States: Its History and Practice.* 2 vols. Boston: Houghton Mifflin, 1938.

## Senate Manual

The Senate Manual is a handbook of rules and other requirements for Senate operations, comparable to the HOUSE MANUAL in the House of Representatives. In addition to the forty-three standing rules of the Senate, it includes other orders and resolutions dealing with Senate operations, as well as the sections of U.S. laws that apply to Senate business. Among the matters covered are FINANCIAL DISCLOSURE requirements, rules for CAMPAIGN FINANCING, senators' salaries, and rules for impeachment trials. (See IMPEACHMENT POWER.) In the back of the document is an appendix that includes charts of electoral votes and lists of every senator, cabinet secretary, and Supreme Court justice who has ever served.

## Senatorial Courtesy

The Senate has derived from its APPOINTMENT POWER a custom, called senatorial courtesy, that gives senators additional influence over presidential nominations to federal positions within their own states. According to the custom the full Senate usually goes along when a senator from the president's party objects to a nominee in his or her state. The custom primarily affects nominations of judges, U.S. attorneys, federal marshals, and other federal officials based locally.

The custom of senatorial courtesy dates from 1789, when President George Washington replaced his nominee for a post in Georgia with the candidate endorsed by the state's two senators. Among the most aggressive advocates of senatorial courtesy was

Roscoe CONKLING, a New York Republican who served in the Senate from 1867 to 1881. The importance of senatorial courtesy diminished as positions once filled by PATRONAGE were brought into the civil service.

Another aspect of senatorial courtesy is the "hold" a senator can place on a nomination. A hold, considered a temporary delay, is possible even when a job has national significance. Usually the leadership of a senator's party will honor the hold, delaying the vote on the nomination. The senator may be waiting for written answers to questions or other information; when the information is received, the hold is released. Like other aspects of senatorial courtesy, the hold is not always honored by a senator's colleagues.

## Seniority System

For many decades positions of authority in Congress were routinely given to the members who had served in the institution the longest. The practice of reserving power to the most veteran senators and representatives is known as the seniority system.

The seniority system still exists in Congress today. However, seniority is a less important factor now than it was in earlier decades in selecting members for leadership positions.

The seniority system has been a unique aspect of Congress's internal organization. In no other major legislative body in the world has sheer length of service determined which members will have power and influence. Even when it was followed most closely in Congress, the seniority system was not a formal law or rule of the House of Representatives or Senate. Rather, it has always been an informal custom or tradition voluntarily observed by members.

There are two types of seniority. The first is seniority within the House or Senate as a whole. Members are ranked within their parties according to when their current period of continuous service began. This type of seniority has limited significance. Senior members have access to the most desirable office space, and they have a few other privileges. For example, the most senior member of the majority party in the Senate holds the post of PRESIDENT PRO TEMPORE, a virtually powerless position. But the most important positions—Speaker of the House and majority and minority leaders in each chamber—have never been filled on the basis of seniority. (See LEADERSHIP.)

The seniority system has had its greatest effect within committees. Seniority on a committee is determined by when a member joined that committee, not when he or she became a member of Congress. During its heyday the seniority system ensured that the member with the longest service on each committee became the chair. Other veteran committee members automatically became subcommittee chairs. (See COMMITTEE SYSTEM.)

Congress did not always follow the seniority system. The practice of awarding committee chairmanships solely on the basis of length of service evolved slowly in the late nineteenth and early twentieth centuries. It reached its peak in the decades after World War II. From 1949 to 1963 there was only one instance in which a House committee chairmanship was *not* awarded on the basis of seniority.

The revolt against the seniority system began in the early 1970s. Many younger House members, who resented the iron control of a handful of veteran members, pushed through a series of reforms that greatly weakened the importance of seniority. For example, the decision was made to choose committee chairs without regard to seniority; members of the majority party were permitted to choose committee chairs on a secret-ballot vote.

The reforms did not obliterate the seniority system entirely. Today, the most senior member of the majority party on a committee or subcommittee usually will be chosen chair, unless there is strong political or personal opposition to that individual. Seniority still is normally followed in positioning members on committees and in filling vacancies; new members are ranked at the bottom of their committees. If members, even senior members, transfer from one committee to another, they are ranked at the bottom in seniority of their new committees.

Efforts to change the seniority system have provoked heated debate. One argument for the system is simple: experience counts. It often takes many years for members to master the difficult subjects before their committees. The most experienced members often have more of the political skills needed to provide strong leadership for a committee. Moreover, the practice of automatically awarding posts according to seniority prevents periodic internal battles for power.

Critics of seniority view it as a rigid, inefficient system that deprives vigorous younger members of influence while reserving power to a small group of senior members. In some cases the system produced very elderly chairs whose talents and intellect had faded with the years. In others it encouraged chairs to run their committees in an arrogant, autocratic manner, ignoring the wishes of other members.

Several factors led to the development of the seniority system. One was the trend toward longer congressional careers that became evident in the early twentieth century. In earlier times, when most members served for only a few terms, seniority meant little. But the arrival on Capitol Hill of members who viewed Congress as a lifetime job tended to emphasize the importance of seniority.

The seniority system also developed as a result of conflicts between leaders and the congressional rank and file. In the late nineteenth century, all-powerful leaders—the House Speaker and the chair of the majority party caucus in the Senate—controlled committee assignments and chairmanships. The revolt against that system led to the use of seniority to fill key posts. (See CAUCUSES, PARTY; SPEAKER OF THE HOUSE.)

The Legislative Reorganization Act of 1946 solidified the rule of seniority. The act consolidated many committees into a smaller number of panels, thus giving a few seniority-selected chairs wide power over every aspect of congressional activity.

A key consequence of the seniority system was to give members from the South an unusual amount of power. The Democrats, who were the majority party throughout most of this period, had a monopoly on southern House and Senate seats. Individual members from the South tended to win reelection easily

for decades. As a result, the senior members on most committees were southern Democrats who were able to control their committees for many years. They tended to be more conservative than the rest of their party.

The seniority-based power of the southern Democrats became a major point of conflict at the time when national Democratic leaders were seeking to push civil rights and social legislation through Congress. The ability of the committee chairs to block such legislation led to many bitter disputes. James O. Eastland, a Mississippi Democrat who chaired the Senate Judiciary Committee from 1956 to 1979, was notorious for bottling up civil rights bills sought by party leaders.

The rule of the veteran members caused intense frustration on the part of less senior members. By the 1970s most committee chairs were over sixty-five and had decades of service. That left many middle-aged members, who might otherwise have been at the peak of their careers, with little more power than the most junior members.

The revolt against the seniority system was a major element in the reform movement that transformed Congress in the 1970s. The key battleground for this movement was the House Democratic Caucus, which over the course of a few years took a series of actions that greatly reduced the importance of seniority in allocating power. As the minority party, the Republicans had far less power to allocate, but they too took steps to reduce the dominance of seniority. The Senate also acted to reduce the iron-clad rule of seniority at about this time, although the changes there were less marked than in the House. (See REFORM, CONGRESSIONAL.)

The changes approved by the House Democratic Caucus during the 1970s made it possible for party members to reject committee chairs, as well as subcommittee chairs of the Appropriations Committee, by secret ballot. (In the early 1990s subcommittee chairs of the Ways and Means Committee also became subject to a caucus vote.) Another change barred members from chairing more than one subcommittee, thus opening up the posts to more junior members. (See APPROPRIATIONS COMMIT-

TEE, HOUSE; WAYS AND MEANS COMMITTEE, HOUSE.)

As a result of the changes made in the 1970s, senior members are no longer guaranteed chairmanships if they have angered their colleagues for some reason. A key development in this movement came in 1975, when House Democrats defeated three autocratic committee chairs. Ten years later they deposed a fourth, eighty-year-old Melvin Price. Price, who had taken over the Armed Services Committee in the 1975 revolt, was replaced by the committee's seventh-ranking Democrat, Les Aspin of Wisconsin. Members considered that Price, a representative from Illinois since 1945, was too old and infirm to provide adequate leadership.

Two chairs were deposed when House Democrats organized for the 102nd Congress (1991–1993). The Public Works Committee chair, Glenn M. Anderson of California, and the House Administration Committee chair, Frank Annunzio of Illinois, were regarded as weak, ineffective leaders. They were replaced by younger, more aggressive Democrats: Robert A. Roe of New Jersey, the number-two Democrat on the public works panel, and Charlie Rose of North Carolina, the third-ranking Democrat on the House Administration Committee.

During the 102nd Congress the aged and ailing Appropriations Committee chair, Jamie L. Whitten, a Mississippi Democrat, turned over most of the public duties of his chairmanship to the second-ranked committee Democrat, William H. Natcher of Kentucky. In letting go of those duties, Whitten bowed to heavy pressure from friends, committee colleagues, and the House leadership. In the next Congress the change was formalized, when House Democrats ousted Whitten and replaced him with Natcher.

Members organizing for the 103rd Congress (1993–1995) made further inroads on the seniority system. House Democrats voted to allow their Steering and Policy Committee at any time to declare the chairmanship of a committee or a subcommittee vacant, and the matter then would go to the full caucus for a vote. House Republicans prohibited anyone in their caucus from holding any committee's top post for more than six consecutive years, which would mean a complete turnover of every full committee's ranking Republican position in 1999, unless the rule were changed. The Republican party was hoping to pressure Democrats to follow suit, but that seemed unlikely.

## Separation of Powers

The Constitution established a national government comprising three independent branches: legislative, executive, and judicial. Each has distinct functions and powers derived directly from the Constitution. The resulting arrangement is generally referred to as the separation of powers.

Having experienced forms of arbitrary rule under both the British monarchy and various state legislatures under the Articles of Confederation, the framers of the Constitution were preoccupied with ways of avoiding a repetition of either executive or legislative tyranny. They feared despotism by an elected legislature almost as much as by an autocracy. By dividing the powers of government among three separate bodies, the framers believed that no one branch would be able to dominate the government. Such an arrangement has its price, however, since to some extent government efficiency and speed are sacrificed to protect individual liberties.

### Constitutional Structure

Article I of the Constitution outlines in detail the powers and limitations of the legislative branch, which is divided into two chambers, the HOUSE OF REPRESENTATIVES and the SENATE. Of the three branches of government, the framers of the Constitution were most familiar with the legislature, and its importance is reflected in the attention given it. Almost half of the Constitution is devoted to the operation and powers of Congress. The framers viewed Congress as the "first branch" of the government because they believed strongly in the need for a representative body to formulate national policy.

Article II outlines the powers of the executive

branch, headed by the president. The organization and powers of the presidency are not described in nearly as much detail as those of the legislature. The ambiguities have helped give the modern president great latitude in running the executive branch, particularly in foreign affairs.

The authors of the Constitution had serious reservations about establishing a strong executive. At the same time, they realized that it was primarily the lack of a strong national executive under the Articles of Confederation that had doomed the nation's first experiment in representative government. Indeed, under the Confederation there was no independent presidency; the legislature controlled and directed executive functions. At the Constitutional Convention in 1787, the delegates gradually were won over to the necessity of a stronger chief executive, though the extent of the president's powers remained a matter of dispute until the final days of the Convention.

Article III describes the powers and organization of the national judiciary, including the Supreme Court.

The other articles of the Constitution confer additional powers on the legislative and executive branches and spell out various government procedures and guarantees.

### Sharing of Powers

The American system is based on separation of powers, but those powers are not neatly divided. In many instances executive, legislative, and judicial powers overlap. Mixing the various powers of government among the three branches was another way of checking arbitrary rule. Thus the framers saw a network of checks and balances as an essential corollary to the separation of powers.

Separation of powers, if it is to be effective as a governing doctrine, requires officials of all three branches, particularly legislators and the president, to work together in making national policy. From time to time in the nation's history, executive-legislative cooperation has broken down. Particularly divisive eras, such as the periods immediately before and after the Civil War, resulted in the near collapse of this necessary cooperation.

Since no one branch or political party can govern alone under this system, senators and representatives of the two major political parties must work out compromises with each other as well as with the executive branch. The president must become involved in the LEGISLATIVE PROCESS by formulating a legislative agenda and working hard for its enactment. Since the early years of the twentieth century, and particularly since the administration of Franklin D. Roosevelt, the president has in large part set the legislative agenda. Congress generally reacts to presidential initiatives. Still, the president depends on members of Congress to help promote and pass his legislative program.

### Division of Powers

The Constitution grants many powers and responsibilities to one branch exclusively. All appointed and elected officials of the U.S. government are prohibited from serving in more than one branch simultaneously. The VICE PRESIDENT is an exception: as second in command, the vice president is next in line of succession as the nation's chief executive, but the vice president also serves as president of the Senate. (See EXECUTIVE BRANCH AND CONGRESS; PRESIDING OFFICER.)

The Supreme Court periodically is called upon to resolve issues involving the separation of powers. For example, a provision of the 1985 deficit-reduction law known as Gramm-Rudman-Hollings was declared unconstitutional by the Supreme Court in 1986 on grounds that it violated the separation of powers. The Court struck down the law's provision for automatic spending cuts because it assigned certain executive powers and duties to the General Accounting Office, an agency controlled by the legislative branch. The separation of powers figured in a 1983 Supreme Court decision declaring Congress's use of the LEGISLATIVE VETO unconstitutional. In a 1976 decision the Supreme Court declared that congressional appointment of Federal Election Commission officials who exercised executive powers violated the constitutional clauses concerning separation of powers and appointments.

### Checks and Balances

As an additional safeguard against the exercise of arbitrary power, the framers incorporated in the Constitution provisions in which the legislative, executive, and judicial branches were checked by overlapping functions of one or both of the other branches. For example, the president wields two important legislative functions: formulation of a legislative agenda, and thus the ability to set national priorities; and the veto power that allows the president to kill legislation he opposes, subject to the congressional power to override such VETOES. The president also exerts influence on the judicial branch through the power to appoint judges and Supreme Court justices, subject to congressional confirmation.

Many powers granted to Congress infringe upon executive branch functions, including the power to declare war and to organize and maintain the armed forces. (See WAR POWERS.) Congress was given the power to impeach (in the House) and to try impeachments (in the Senate) of executive and judicial branch officials, including the president and federal judges. (See IMPEACHMENT POWER.) Congress exerts influence on the other two branches through its power to confirm appointments. (See APPOINTMENT POWER.) Legislators also are granted, in Article III, the power to establish lower courts—the district and appeals courts—and to reorganize the federal court system. (See COURTS AND CONGRESS.)

The judicial branch has the ultimate check on Congress. Soon after the new republic was established, the Supreme Court declared and exercised the right to decide the constitutionality of laws passed by Congress.

### Problems

Throughout the nation's history, the separation of powers has worked well in protecting the people against arbitrary rule and domination by any branch of government. Whether separation of powers provides effective government in an increasingly complex age is debatable. Many political scientists believe the present system fails to provide enough concentrated authority and harmony to ensure decisive governmental action. They also worry that a system of fragmented powers does not clearly identify responsibility for setting government policies or make officials accountable for their actions. For example, in such a system, how can the nation's voters apportion re-

sponsibility between the executive and legislative branches for the staggering budget deficits of recent years?

The U.S. system of two-year House terms, a four-year presidential term, and six-year Senate terms is another form of checks and balances, one that tends to diffuse power and responsibility.

Divided government also complicates matters. Divided government occurs when one political party controls the White House and the opposing party controls one or both house of Congress, as happened during the Republican administrations of Ronald Reagan and George Bush. For two of the eight years of Reagan's administration, the Democratic party controlled both houses of Congress; the House of Representatives was in Democratic hands for all eight years. Both houses were controlled by the Democrats during Bush's four years in office. Conflict between the executive and legislative branches resulted in deadlocks in policy making and confusion about the role of the two branches in foreign policy.

## Sequestration

*See* BUDGET PROCESS.

## Sergeant-at-Arms

The House and Senate sergeants-at-arms are the police officers of their respective chambers. They attend all sessions and are responsible for enforcing rules and maintaining decorum, ensuring the security of buildings and visitors, and supervising the Capitol police force. Each was paid at an annual rate of $119,000 in early 1993.

The House sergeant-at-arms is in charge of the mace, the symbol of legislative power and authority, and carries it when enforcing order in the House chamber.

Sergeants-at-arms are also responsible for rounding up members for floor votes. This authority, unused since 1942, became an issue during a 1988 filibuster in which Republican senators boycotted votes on campaign finance legislation. Senate majority leader Robert C. Byrd, a West Virginia Democrat, directed the sergeant-at-arms to arrest absent members and bring them to the Senate floor. Carrying out this order, sergeant-at-arms Henry K. Giugni tracked down Bob Packwood, an Oregon Republican, who was arrested and carried feet first into the Senate chamber. Packwood, whose broken finger was reinjured in the escapade, took his arrest in good humor, although other Republicans spoke bitterly of the incident.

## Sessions of Congress

*See* TERMS AND SESSIONS OF CONGRESS.

## Sherman, John

John Sherman (1823–1900) became a fixture of the Republican party in the nineteenth century, serving both in Congress and in the executive branch. As an influential member, and later chair, of the Senate Finance Committee, the Ohio Republican played a major role in formulating national financial policies. Later in his Senate career he sponsored antitrust legislation that carries his name to this day.

Sherman was elected to the House of Representatives in 1854 as part of the wave of antislavery sentiment that had led to the founding of the Republican party that year. In 1859 he was involved in a hotly contested race for House Speaker. Sherman led in the early voting, but he was abhorred by the proslavery camp. The Republicans finally concluded he could not be elected, and he withdrew on the thirty-ninth ballot. Sherman became chair of the House Ways and Means Committee instead.

When he moved to the Senate in 1861, he was assigned to the Senate Finance Committee and became its chair in 1867. From this base, Sherman played an important role in the nation's finances during the Civil War and in the Reconstruction period. He supported wartime legislation authorizing paper money, or "greenbacks," and helped plan a new national banking system. In the postwar period he backed legislation calling for the redemption of paper money in gold.

Sherman's efforts were rewarded when he was named secretary of the Treasury in 1877. He failed to win the Republican presidential nomination in 1880 (and again in 1884 and 1888) and returned to the Senate in 1881. His legislative achievements included the Sherman Antitrust Act of 1890, a basic antitrust statute that is still on the books, and the Sherman Silver Purchase Act of 1890. He was named president pro tempore of the Senate in 1886, the year he also became chair of the Senate Foreign Relations Committee.

Sherman left the Senate to become President William McKinley's secretary of state in 1897. Ineffectual in the role, Sherman resigned the next year in protest against the Spanish-American War. He died two years later.

## Small Business Committees, House and Senate

Popular with legislators, whose districts always include small businesses, the House and Senate Small Business committees have survived several attempts to reorganize them out of existence. Usually bipartisan in their actions, the two committees often serve as advocates, reminding other congressional panels of the special problems of small businesses.

The committees' main focus in the last decade was preserving the Small Business Administration, which the Reagan administration during the 1980s wanted to make part of the Commerce Department. Another concern was to guarantee the participation of small businesses in federal procurement and government contracts.

The Senate committee was set up in 1950 as a select committee. It gained standing committee status in 1980. Alabama Democrat John J. Sparkman was the panel's first chair and had a long tenure in the post (1950–1953, 1955–1967). Connecticut Republican Lowell P. Weicker, Jr., chaired the committee from 1981 to 1987, when Arkansas Democrat Dale Bumpers took over.

The House committee was set up in 1947 as the Select Committee to Conduct a Study and Investigation of the Problems of Small Business. Two representatives served several terms as chair: Texas Democrat Wright Patman (1949–1953, 1955–1963) and Tennessee Democrat Joe L. Evins (1963–1979). The panel became the Small Business Committee in a 1974 reorganization. John J. LaFalce (D-N.Y.) took over as chair in 1987.

## Smith, Howard W.

Howard W. Smith (1883–1976) served as a representative from Virginia from 1931 to 1967. A leader of the conservative southern Democrats, or "Dixiecrats," and chair of the Rules Committee, Smith often was called the second most powerful member of the House of Representatives.

Smith began his career as a lawyer and went on to become a circuit judge and a banker. He became a foe of Franklin D. Roosevelt's New Deal and opposed social welfare programs throughout his career. Smith also spoke out against legislation aiding organized labor and voted against the 1935 National Labor Relations Act. He sponsored a bill in 1939 that called for the imprisonment of resident foreigners who recommended changes in the U.S. system of government. In 1940 he authored the Smith Act, which made it a crime to be a communist. The act was later struck down by the Supreme Court.

Roosevelt called Smith "the greatest obstructionist in Congress," and it was as a dissenter that Smith made his career. From his seat on the Rules Committee, Smith harried opponents from both political parties. By forming an alliance with conservative Democrats and Republicans on the committee, Smith was able to bottle up legislation, which had to move through the rules panel before going to the House

President Franklin D. Roosevelt called him "the greatest obstructionist in Congress," and it was as a dissenter that Howard W. Smith, left, made his career.    Source: House Rules Committee

floor. In 1939 this CONSERVATIVE COALITION began demanding changes in bills before it would approve a rule. Dominated by these conservatives, the committee often flouted the wishes of the Democratic Speaker.

Smith became chair of the Rules Committee in 1955. He once held up consideration of legislation for days by disappearing to Virginia because, he said, his barn had burned down and it had taken a while to repair. The committee could meet only when convened by the chair.

In 1958 liberals sought to restructure the Rules Committee, but the proposal was rejected by Speaker Sam Rayburn, who promised that the committee would not hold up civil rights and welfare legislation. In 1961 Rayburn himself recognized the need to reorganize the committee and supported a successful attempt to increase its membership. The addition of loyal Democrats to the committee diminished Smith's authority. He was defeated for reelection in 1966.

## Smith, Margaret Chase

Margaret Chase Smith (1897– ), a Maine Republican, entered the House of Representatives in 1940 after the death of her husband, Rep. Clyde H. Smith. In 1948 she was elected to the Senate, where she served until 1973. An independent-minded Republican, Smith was the first of her party to denounce Sen. Joseph R. MCCARTHY on the Senate floor for his virulent anticommunist activities.

Before her marriage, Smith worked as a teacher and then as an executive with a newspaper and a woolen mill. After her husband entered Congress, she worked as his assistant in his congressional office. He encouraged her to run for his House seat after he suffered a heart attack in 1940. He died later that year, and she was elected to the seat in a special election.

In the House Smith served on the Naval Affairs Committee, where she was a strong advocate of military preparedness. Her reputation as a "hawk" was borne out by her 1961 speech in the Senate criticizing President John F. Kennedy's seeming reluctance to use nuclear weapons. She charged that this reluctance put the United States at a disadvantage with the Soviet Union. The speech prompted Nikita S. Khrushchev, then Soviet premier, to call her "the devil in the disguise of a woman."

In 1950 Smith presented a "declaration of conscience" on the Senate floor. The declaration, supported by six other Republican senators, criticized McCarthy's anticommunist campaign. She said, "I am not proud of the way we spear outsiders from the floor of the Senate. . . . I do not want to see the party ride to political victory on the Four Horsemen of Calumny—fear, ignorance, bigotry, and smear."

Smith was proud of her congressional attendance

record and late in her career introduced measures to regulate senators' attendance on the floor. From June 1955 to July 1968 she never missed a Senate roll-call vote. Smith was defeated for reelection in 1972.

## Speaker of the House

The Speaker is both the PRESIDING OFFICER of the HOUSE OF REPRESENTATIVES and the overall leader of the majority party in the chamber. The Constitution says that the House shall choose its Speaker, but it does not describe the Speaker's duties. The role has developed over more than two centuries of parliamentary give-and-take.

The formal duties of the Speaker are broad. The Speaker officially has authority to refer bills to committees for preliminary consideration and to schedule LEGISLATION for House floor action. When presiding over the House, the Speaker has the power to recognize members wishing to speak, subject to certain limitations spelled out in the House rules. With the advice of the parliamentarian the Speaker also may decide points of order, objections raised by members who think House rules have been violated. The Speaker chooses members to chair the COMMITTEE OF THE WHOLE, a parliamentary framework the House adopts when it considers bills for amendment. The Speaker appoints members to various special House committees, as well as to conference committees, which work out the differences between bills passed by the House and Senate. (See COMMITTEE SYSTEM.)

These are usually routine tasks, governed by House customs and rules that limit the Speaker's options. Skillful Speakers nonetheless find ways to make the rules work to their advantage.

The Speaker's formal powers are less critical than political mastery in determining the Speaker's influence in the House. A successful Speaker enjoys personal prestige as head of the party LEADERSHIP structure and commands a high degree of party loyalty. Such a Speaker combines a deep understanding of the LEGISLATIVE PROCESS with strong persuasive skills. In the mid-1970s Democrats increased the Speaker's power by allowing the Speaker to appoint Democratic members of the House Rules Committee. The powerful committee works in concert with the majority leadership to control the flow of legislation to the floor and set the terms of floor debate. (See RULES COMMITTEE, HOUSE.)

The Constitution does not specify that a Speaker must be a member of the House, but no nonmember has ever been elected to the post. Speakers are chosen by the caucus of the majority party's members, whose decision is confirmed by the full House at the beginning of each new Congress. (See CAUCUSES, PARTY.) In the twentieth century only senior members have been chosen; since 1925 all Speakers have advanced from the position of either majority or minority leader. All but one Speaker retained the post as long as their party held a majority in the House or until their own retirement. The exception was Jim WRIGHT, who became embroiled in an ethics scandal and in 1989 became the first Speaker to be forced to resign in midterm.

Like any other member, the Speaker may participate in debate and vote. Modern Speakers occasionally speak from the floor; they rarely vote except to break a tie. They do not serve on legislative committees.

Under the Twenty-fifth Amendment to the Constitution, adopted in 1967, the Speaker follows the vice president in the line of presidential succession. (See PRESIDENTIAL DISABILITY AND SUCCESSION.)

### Historical Highlights

In the early years of Congress the Speaker was largely a figurehead. The first Speaker, Frederick A.C. Muhlenberg of Pennsylvania, was necessarily a nonpartisan presiding officer because political parties had not yet been formed when he assumed the post in 1789.

The authority of the office ebbed and flowed during the nineteenth century, but by the 1880s the Speaker had become the dominant leader of the House. The office reached its peak of status in the early 1900s under a series of autocratic Speakers, but their arbitrary use of power led to a 1910 "revolt" that

---

### LONGEST-SERVING HOUSE SPEAKERS

| Name | Years* |
|------|--------|
| Sam Rayburn | 17 |
| Henry Clay | 10 |
| Thomas P. O'Neill, Jr. | 10 |
| John W. McCormack | 9 |
| Joseph G. Cannon | 8 |
| James B. "Champ" Clark | 8 |
| Andrew Stevenson | 7 |
| Carl Albert | 6 |
| James G. Blaine | 6 |
| John G. Carlisle | 6 |
| Schuyler Colfax | 6 |
| Frederick H. Gillett | 6 |
| Nicholas Longworth | 6 |
| Nathaniel Macon | 6 |
| Thomas Brackett Reed | 6 |

*Figures have been rounded to the nearest year.

---

stripped the Speaker of most formal authority. In the 1960s and 1970s party discipline weakened in Congress, and Speakers found that to lead the House they had to rely chiefly on their own persuasive arts. (See Appendix.)

### Clay

The first really influential Speaker of the House was Henry CLAY, a popular Kentuckian who held the post for six terms between 1811 and 1825. The seven Speakers before him had presided over the House only ceremonially; Clay was the first to lead it.

Clay was elected Speaker the day he arrived in the House at age thirty-four. He promptly set out to assert the supremacy of Congress over the other branches of government and of the Speaker over the affairs of the

House. Clay owed his election as Speaker to a faction of young representatives known as the War Hawks, and he used the influence of his office to push the nation into the War of 1812. He stacked key House committees with supporters of his war policy, exploited House rules to reinforce his control of the chamber, and used his great oratorical skills to pressure President James Madison into declaring war against England.

### Reed

The next great expansion of the Speaker's power came under Thomas Brackett REED, who won the nickname "Czar Reed" for his efforts. Reed, a Maine Republican, served as Speaker in 1889–1891 and 1895–1899. When he assumed the post, delaying tactics by the Democratic minority often prevented the majority from working its will. Through a succession of floor rulings, Reed firmly established the right of the majority to control the legislative process.

The minority's chief stalling tactic was the "disappearing quorum." A majority of the chamber's members, known as a quorum, was required to transact business. But when the roll was called to establish the presence of a quorum, minority members who were present in the chamber refused to answer to their names. Thus the vote fell short of the number required. Reed solved the problem of the disappearing quorum by counting all the members who were present, not just those who answered the roll. The Democrats were furious, but the Speaker held firm. Asked to explain the function of the minority, Reed is said to have replied: "The right of the minority is to draw its salary, and its function is to make a quorum."

Reed's rulings later became part of a new set of House rules, which was drafted by the Rules Committee under his chairmanship. Speakers had chaired the Rules Committee since 1858, and much of their power resulted from that arrangement.

### Cannon

The power of the Speaker reached its peak when Illinois Republican Joseph G. CANNON held the post from 1903 to 1911. Although "Uncle Joe" Cannon instituted few parliamentary changes in the House, he used fully those made by his predecessors. His dictatorial rule ended in 1910 when insurgent Republicans joined Democrats in a revolt against him, stripping the Speaker of the authority to chair—or even to serve on—the Rules Committee, to appoint committee members, and to control all floor action.

### Longworth

During his tenure from 1925 to 1931, Nicholas LONGWORTH, an Ohio Republican, tried to restore the centralized authority of the Speaker that had been lost in the revolt against Cannon. Aided by a small group of trusted associates, Longworth personally assumed control of the House. He was able to achieve through persuasion what Cannon had done by arbitrary interpretation of the rules.

### Rayburn

Legend surrounds the tenure of Speaker Sam RAYBURN, who served in the post from 1940 until his death in 1961, except for two short stints as minority leader when the Republicans controlled the House in 1947–1949 and 1953–1955. Rayburn exerted such influence as Speaker that the Texas Democrat was said to run the House out of his hip pocket.

Confronted after World War II with a party badly split over civil rights and other domestic issues, Rayburn found he could minimize disunity by making party decisions himself and bargaining with individuals rather than with the party as a whole. "To get along, you've got to go along," he routinely advised House freshmen, and they generally complied.

Rayburn's leadership style demonstrated the profound changes that had occurred in Congress since Cannon's reign. As party discipline declined, the Speaker found he had to rely on his personal style to achieve his goals. "The old day of pounding on the desk and giving people hell is gone," Rayburn said as early as 1950. "A man's got to lead by persuasion and kindness and the best reason—that's the only way he can lead people."

### O'Neill

A continuing decline in party discipline weakened the leadership of Thomas P. O'NEILL, Jr., a Massachu-

*The decline of party discipline has made the job of Speaker much more difficult than it once was. Speaker Thomas P. O'Neill's attempts at unity were not as successful as those of legendary Speaker Sam Rayburn, pictured in the painting behind O'Neill. Source: AP/Wide World Photos*

setts Democrat who was Speaker from 1977 until his retirement in 1987. O'Neill himself was known for his party loyalty and partisanship. But younger and generally more liberal Democrats criticized him for failing to crack down on conservative members who voted against positions supported by a majority of the party. O'Neill maintained that the party's diversity made it nearly impossible to discipline or even threaten to discipline disloyal members.

On one of the rare occasions when discipline was attempted, it backfired. Texas Democrat Phil Gramm was removed from his seat on the Budget Committee in 1983, in reprisal for his two-year collaboration with the White House on President Ronald Reagan's budget. Gramm promptly resigned his House seat, won

reelection as a Republican, and returned to the Budget Committee. Gramm was elected to the Senate in 1984.

O'Neill did eventually warm to the role thrust upon him in 1981 by Republican control of the White House: that of chief national spokesperson for Democratic positions.

### Wright

Controversy surrounded Jim Wright, the flamboyant Texas Democrat who succeeded O'Neill in 1987. As Speaker, Jim Wright was determined to give House Democrats the policy leadership many of them had found O'Neill to lack. But in pursuing his ambitious agenda for the House, Wright overstepped the limits of the modern Speaker's powers.

Wright was criticized for his aggressive tactics in getting legislation passed; Republicans considered him a match for Cannon in his treatment of the minority. Although Wright's Democratic colleagues took pride in the legislative achievements, many resented Wright's failure to include them in the process of achieving them. Wright, sometimes dubbed the "Lone Ranger," had a record of springing major decisions without consulting key colleagues.

As allegations of financial misconduct developed into a full-blown investigation, Wright found that Democrats who were willing to support him when he—and they—were winning were not as willing to back him on a question of personal ethics. Wright became the first Speaker to be forced from office at midterm, when he resigned the post of Speaker and his House seat in June 1989. The House Democratic leadership was further shaken at this time by the resignation of Democratic whip Tony Coelho of California, who gave up his House seat in the face of allegations of financial irregularities.

### Foley

Democrat Thomas S. FOLEY of Washington was chosen to succeed Wright. Known for his low-key, nonconfrontational style, Foley was a striking contrast to the hard-charging Wright. The new Speaker received a great deal of credit for restoring stability to the House after the resignations of Wright and

Coelho. Even Republicans who had been extremely critical of Wright praised Foley for his civil manner and attempts at bipartisanship.

Foley was a cautious, careful political navigator. He preferred to let the legislative process work, however slowly, than to impose his own views or push specific legislation. He was not one to play hardball with his colleagues or use his influence to reward people who stuck with the leadership and to punish those who did not. But some Democrats occasionally found Foley too accommodating and lacking the aggression they thought was necessary to push their agenda. Such criticism surfaced in 1992 when the House was torn by scandals involving the House bank and post office. (See HOUSE BANK SCANDAL.)

Foley's position, however, was secured when Democratic incumbents did well in the 1992 elections, and his leadership style seemed more appropriate when the initiative shifted to the White House under President Bill Clinton. For the first time since entering the upper reaches of leadership as majority whip in 1981, Foley had the chance to work with a Democratic president. Freed from serving as the party's human symbol and media spokesperson, the Speaker could concentrate on running the House and pressing a program with which he was in sympathy.

Some expected Foley to run the House with a firmer hand. Foley's removal of Dave McCurdy, an Oklahoma Democrat, as head of the Intelligence Committee at the beginning of the 103rd Congress suggested to some observers that a stronger Foley might emerge. Foley himself said that he expected to be "more decisive" if "not necessarily more controlling." The timing would be right, with more and more members weary of turf wars and gridlock and looking for stronger leadership.

### Additional Readings

Hardeman, D. B., and Donald C. Bacon. *Rayburn: A Biography.* Austin: Texas Monthly Press, 1987.

O'Neill, Thomas P., Jr., with William Novak. *Man of the House: The Life and Political Memoirs of Speaker Tip O'Neill.* New York: Random House, 1987.

Peters, Ronald M., Jr. *The American Speakership: The Office in Historical Perspective.* Baltimore: Johns Hopkins University Press, 1990.

Sinclair, Barbara. *Majority Leadership in the U.S. House.* Baltimore: Johns Hopkins University Press, 1983.

## Special Orders

Legislators who want to address the House or Senate on a topic that is not necessarily part of the day's legislative agenda can reserve a block of time in advance. This is called a special order.

In the House members who have requested special orders are allowed to speak for up to sixty minutes at the end of the day's session—before the House adjourns but after legislative business has been completed. TELEVISION cameras record the speeches, which often are made to an almost empty chamber.

Controversy about the routine practice erupted in 1984, after Republicans repeatedly used special orders for speeches attacking the Democratic leadership. Infuriated, Speaker Thomas P. O'NEILL, Jr., ordered the television cameras to pan the House chamber, showing viewers how few members were present to hear the emotional speakers. The practice has been continued; periodically during the period reserved for special orders, the cameras show the House chamber—and its rows of empty seats.

In the Senate members are recognized for special orders at the beginning of a day's session; they may speak for five minutes. Fifteen-minute speeches were permitted until 1986, when Senate sessions began to be televised and requests for special orders increased. Some senators ask for special-order time almost every day.

The term *special order* also refers to the resolution approved by the House Rules Committee setting guidelines for floor consideration of a bill. The resolution is more commonly known as a rule. (See LEGISLATIVE PROCESS; RULE FOR HOUSE DEBATE; RULES COMMITTEE, HOUSE.)

## Speech or Debate Clause

*See* IMMUNITY, CONGRESSIONAL.

*These five sisters worked as secretaries for members of Congress in the 1920s.*    Source: Library of Congress

## Staff

Thousands of people work for Congress, and its elected members depend heavily on these employees. Staff members cannot vote, but their imprint is on every other step in getting a bill passed. They draft legislation, negotiate with lobbyists, and plot strategy for floor action.

The influence of congressional staff is vast. Critics complain that the staff exercises too much power and costs too much money. But others argue that legislators are asked to debate and vote on a wide range of complex issues, and that they need staff to provide the expertise that one person alone simply could not master.

The congressional bureaucracy is well entrenched. There are nearly twenty thousand aides who work directly for Congress and its 540 members. Another ten thousand or so congressional employees are "support staff." These include workers who handle security, maintenance, and other support services, as well as staff at the Congressional Research Service of the LIBRARY OF CONGRESS, the CONGRESSIONAL BUDGET OFFICE, the OFFICE OF TECHNOLOGY ASSESSMENT, and the GENERAL ACCOUNTING OFFICE.

By the early 1990s Congress was spending more than six times as much on its operations as it had in 1970. Legislative branch appropriations, which include some nonlegislative activities, are the best measure of its cost that Congress has provided over the years. That figure rose from more than $361 million in fiscal 1970 to about $2.3 billion in fiscal 1992. More than two-thirds of that money goes to pay salaries.

### Growth in Staff Size

The size of House and Senate staff has grown enormously since World War II. In 1947 there were fewer than 500 aides on House and Senate committees; by 1991 that number had jumped to about 3,800. Similarly, in 1947 there were about 2,000 House and Senate personal aides, and in 1991, about 12,000. Several thousand more worked in administrative and leadership offices.

This enormous growth changed the fabric of life on Capitol Hill. It crowded existing offices, spurred construction of large new office buildings for the House and Senate, and prompted expansion into "annex" buildings formerly used as hotels or apartments. The presence of so many employees made Capitol Hill more and more like a small city, bustling with restaurants, barbershops, stationery stores, gymnasiums, and its own subways linking office buildings to the Capitol.

The congressional staff explosion came about for a variety of reasons. After World War II, and again in the 1960s and 1970s, the federal government expanded rapidly and became more complex. Congress wanted its own sources of information, independent of the executive branch and interest groups, so it added staff. Changes within Congress also spurred the hiring of more people. In the 1970s the erosion of the SENIORITY SYSTEM shifted new authority to junior and minority members; they wanted aides to help with their new responsibilities. Subcommittees were given higher status, and by the late 1970s as many people worked for subcommittees as had worked for full committees in the 1960s.

Congress also became the last resort for those dealing with the federal bureaucracy. Each legislator usually had several employees whose sole job was handling voters' requests and complaints, a task known as casework or constituent services. Casework is usually the primary function of district and state offices. A measure of its importance is that more than a third of members' personal staffs work outside of Washington. (See VOTERS AND CONGRESS.)

The dramatic growth in staff leveled off in the 1980s and early 1990s as Congress, trying to cut overall federal spending, responded to criticism about increases in its own budget. Staffing was one of the issues on the agenda of the Joint Committee on the Organization of Congress, a special committee set up in 1992 to study and recommend reforms in congressional operations. (See ORGANIZATION OF CONGRESS COMMITTEE, JOINT; REFORM, CONGRESSIONAL.)

## Partisanship

Congressional employees are drawn from a mix of backgrounds, but most are young, male, and well educated. Campaign workers may end up on a legislator's payroll, but jobs also go to others who have no ties to the politician or the district. An economist might be hired for a committee post, for example. Many veteran "Hill" employees outlast the legislator who originally hired them; they simply find a job with someone else.

Sometimes staff members become politicians themselves. President Lyndon B. JOHNSON began his career as a congressional aide; later he was elected to Congress and served twenty-four years in the House and Senate, including six years as Senate majority leader.

Traditionally, many nonlegislative posts have been PATRONAGE jobs. The chauffeur, the elevator operator, the parking garage attendant, and even jobs closer to legislative action, such as the doorkeepers, have been controlled by party leaders and their top aides. But the system began to erode in the 1960s, when secretary of the Senate Bobby Baker, a Johnson protégé, was convicted of using his office—and his control of numerous Senate jobs—for personal gain. Since then the number of patronage jobs has been drastically reduced. Further reductions were expected in the wake of scandals involving the House bank and post office. In 1992 the House voted to bring its nonlegislative functions under the control of a professional, nonpartisan HOUSE ADMINISTRATOR and to prohibit patronage for positions controlled by the new official. (See HOUSE BANK SCANDAL.)

Although merit, not friendship with a legislator, is usually the basis for being hired today, the political parties still maintain control over numerous jobs. The top leaders of both parties have their own staff. Party affiliation is usually a factor when legislators hire their personal aides. Committee hiring is also partisan, with the majority usually responsible for about two-thirds of the jobs and the minority for about one-third. In reality, however, other qualifications often take precedence over party allegiance. A few committees, such as the ethics panels and the Joint Committee on Taxa-

*Speaker Tom Foley's staff, pictured here in 1989, includes his wife, seated beside him; under the nepotism rule, she serves without pay as his chief of staff.* Source: R. Michael Jenkins

tion, have removed partisanship from their hiring practices.

Despite partisanship in hiring, a line is drawn between congressional work and campaign work. House rules allow a House employee to work on a campaign if assigned congressional duties are also being fulfilled. The Senate has no formal procedures to govern the practice. Sometimes House and Senate staff members take a leave from their congressional posts to become campaign workers, paid by the campaign. Another practice is to divide duties, with a staff member's congressional pay reduced to reflect time spent on the campaign.

## Personal Staff

Clerks were hired by Congress even in its earliest years, for jobs such as recording floor debate and handling committee paperwork. But authority—and funding—for a member's personal staff was not provided until 1885 in the Senate and 1893 in the House.

By 1919 a ceiling had been placed on the number of personal staff members each legislator could hire. (Committee staffs were handled separately.) In 1946 a House member could hire a maximum of five people, and a senator, six. By the early 1990s a House member could hire a staff of up to twenty-two people; in 1991 each member had a budget of $475,000 to pay them. Senators had no limit on the size of their staff, but most employed thirty to forty people. In 1991 each senator received an allowance of between $814,000 and $1.76 million, depending on state population. Most senators received an additional legislative assistance allowance of $269,000.

Legislators divide their personal staff between their Washington and local offices. Representatives usually have at least one office in their district; senators often have three or more spread across their state.

For their Washington office, most legislators hire an administrative assistant (AA) responsible for overall operations, including casework, and a legislative assistant (LA) who concentrates on committee action, floor votes, and a member's own political agenda. Often a press secretary handles questions from reporters and writes newsletters. Other employees report to these top aides. Hiring policies, job descriptions, pay scales, and vacations differ from office to office.

### Committee Staff

Each committee, like each legislator, sets its own hiring policies. Most have a professional staff and a clerical staff, with staff director, legislative counsel, and chief clerk among the top posts. Reporting to them are legislative aides, researchers, investigators, and secretaries. Although those on a legislator's personal staff must focus on reelection efforts and casework, committee staff members concentrate on legislation and can be very influential. The House since 1946 has restricted committee staff to handling committee business.

Authority for hiring full-time committee staff existed by 1900, but the Legislative Reorganization Act of 1946 provided the funding for each committee to hire a roster of aides. In the 1970s the size of the committee staffs was greatly increased. The House in 1974 tripled the size of each committee's professional staff, from six to eighteen, and doubled the clerical staff, from six to twelve. This brought the total number of permanent staff on most committees to thirty, where it remained as of the early 1990s. No strict limits apply in the Senate, where committees usually employ forty or more people, often with another five or more working for each subcommittee. In 1975 the Senate gave each member authority to hire three legislative aides to help with committee work.

In addition to permanent staff, House and Senate committees also hire investigative aides. These aides are considered to be temporary employees, but they often remain with a committee year after year.

### Employment Practices

For all the power that many Capitol Hill employees possess, they are not covered by most federal labor, safety, and health laws. Members of Congress argue that their employment practices should not be regulated like the private sector's because of the politi-cal nature of Congress; members must be free, they say, to choose employees who will be loyal to them. Many members also insist that the principle of separation of powers would be violated if the executive branch had the power to enforce employment laws in the legislature.

Although members of Congress have followed voluntary rules against discrimination on Capitol Hill, some critics have dubbed it "the last plantation." They complain that women and African Americans are clustered in low-paying jobs and that African Americans are underrepresented on the congressional payroll.

Until recent years, congressional aides have had little recourse if they felt they were being mistreated or discriminated against, underpaid, or dismissed without good cause. Although Congress had procedures for staff to bring complaints against members through the ethics committees, critics argued that these procedures were poorly understood and little used. They said that staff members were more likely to go to the press with their complaints or quit their jobs than to go to the ethics committees. After a rash of media reports alleging mistreatment of staff, the House in 1988 adopted new complaint procedures and set up a separate fair employment office to handle complaints. The Senate followed suit in 1991.

The House in 1989 extended to its employees the rights and protections provided by the Fair Labor Standards Act of 1938, such as minimum wage, overtime compensation, and pay equity measures. Civil rights protections were extended in 1990 to congressional employees with physical disabilities.

Another avenue for settling congressional employee grievances is the court system. The Supreme Court ruled in 1979 that congressional employees have the right to sue for damages if they believe they are victims of job discrimination.

Congress also has specific rules against hiring relatives, a practice known as nepotism. The ban on nepotism was slipped into a House bill in 1967 and, once under consideration, was politically impossible to oppose. A senator or representative can still recommend a relative for employment in another office, and a legislator's relatives can still work in his or her office, but without pay. For example, Heather Foley for years has been a top, unpaid assistant to her husband, Speaker of the House Thomas S. FOLEY.

### Additional Readings

Bisnow, Mark. *In the Shadow of the Dome: Chronicles of a Capitol Hill Aide.* New York: William Morrow, 1990.

Fox, Harrison W., Jr., and Susan Webb Hammond. *Congressional Staffs: The Invisible Force in American Lawmaking.* New York: The Free Press, 1979.

Malbin, Michael J. *Unelected Representatives: Congressional Staff and the Future of Representative Government.* New York: Basic Books, 1980.

# Standards of Official Conduct Committee, House

Commonly known as the House ethics committee, the Committee on Standards of Official Conduct investigates representatives charged with ethical misconduct, such as misuse of campaign funds, failure to disclose personal finances, or improper acceptance of gratuities. The committee then reports to the full House and in some cases recommends punishment, such as reprimand, censure, or, in rare cases, expulsion from the House. The Senate has a Select Ethics Committee that monitors senators' conduct. (See DISCIPLINING MEMBERS; ETHICS; ETHICS COMMITTEE, SENATE SELECT.)

Unlike most House committees, where the majority party dominates, the ethics panel is bipartisan, with seven members from each party. The chair is from the majority party. The committee has its own investigative staff and counsel but has hired outside attorneys. For example, former Watergate special prosecutor Leon Jaworski handled allegations of influence peddling by Korean business executives in the late 1970s.

Committee investigations are usually triggered by complaints from colleagues or from news stories. The committee also gives advice to members who are confused about ethics rules. In 1987 it published an ethics manual for members and staff, including its advisory opinions on some of the most frequently asked questions about gifts, outside income, and allowances.

### Wright Investigation

Few representatives seek a seat on the panel, which has the awkward responsibility of passing judgment on colleagues' behavior. In 1988 the committee assumed the most uncomfortable task it had ever faced: an investigation of charges, brought by Republicans, that the Speaker of the House, Texas Democrat Jim WRIGHT, had abused his office to enrich himself. The committee vote to undertake the investigation was unanimous.

To consider the six major allegations against Wright, the committee instituted a new two-part procedure. First came a "preliminary investigation" to hear witnesses, including Wright; this resembled a grand jury procedure. Next would come a staff report and recommendations, followed by a hearing, resembling a trial, to decide whether to discipline the accused. Chicago lawyer Richard A. Phelan was hired as special counsel to head the investigation.

Ten months later the committee formally charged Wright with the acceptance of improper gifts, use of book royalties to circumvent limits on earned income, and numerous other violations of House rules. But in 1989, before the disciplinary hearing took place, Wright resigned from Congress, making him the first Speaker forced from office at midterm.

### History

The committee was established in 1967 in response to public outrage over a series of congressional scandals. The first chair was Illinois Democrat Melvin Price. The House gave the panel only a limited mission at first: to write a code of conduct. Approved in 1968, the code expanded the committee's responsibility, giving it authority to enforce the new rules.

But the code was couched in general terms, and FINANCIAL DISCLOSURE was confined to sources, not amounts, of income. The House and Senate revised their codes in 1977, and in 1978 Congress applied ethics codes to the entire federal government. In 1989 the ethics law was revised and strengthened, increasing the size of the House committee to fourteen members, from twelve.

Critics complain that the committee is too lenient, reporting violations and then recommending no punishment. But California Democrat Julian C. Dixon, chair from 1985 to 1991, said, "I think the committee does a good job of, one, being nonpartisan and, two, investigating facts, evaluating facts, and taking appropriate action. But is the committee on a constant search for improprieties by members of Congress? The answer is no. I think the members of Congress have a right to feel the committee is not on a witch hunt."

Although the House usually goes along with the recommendations of the ethics committee, it has acted independently. In 1983 the committee recommended that Massachusetts Democrat Gerry E. Studds and Illinois Republican Daniel B. Crane be reprimanded because of improper relationships with teenage pages; the House opted for the stiffer penalty of censure. Seven years later the House went along with the committee in reprimanding Massachusetts Democrat Barney Frank for befriending a male prostitute, despite widespread criticism that the penalty was too lenient.

In the committee's first twenty-five years of existence, about a dozen members received the House's harshest punishments of censure, reprimand, or, in one case, expulsion.

Besides Price and Dixon, the committee had had four other chairs as of mid-1993. Democrat Jim McDermott of Washington took over at the beginning of the 103rd Congress.

## State of the Union

Early each year the president addresses a joint session of Congress, spelling out his legislative program and goals for the year in a State of the Union message. Since early in the twentieth century, the annual address has been the way that presidents comply with a constitutional directive to "from time to time give to the Congress Information of the State of the Union." It has also become a key way in which presidents seek to influence the national agenda.

*President Bill Clinton delivers his first State of the Union address in 1993. Source: R. Michael Jenkins*

The evening session of Congress, usually in late January, brings a rare mood of pageantry to the House chamber, which is seldom so full. Seated in the front rows are the Supreme Court justices and members of the president's cabinet. Nearby are foreign diplomats. Galleries are packed with family members, visitors, and reporters. A special escort committee, dispatched by the Speaker of the House, greets the president and accompanies him down the aisle.

The president's speech is usually interrupted several times with applause. On rare occasions members of an opposing party groan to indicate their disagreement with a statement. More typical is the reaction of the Democratic-controlled Congress to Republican president Ronald Reagan in 1988. Even when he was criticizing Congress for its catchall spending bills, and hefting a forty-three-pound stack of documents in demonstration, the legislators reacted with applause and cheers.

The nation's first two presidents, George Washington and John Adams, delivered their annual messages as speeches to Congress. The third president, Thomas Jefferson, chose in 1801 to avoid what was an elaborate, formal ceremony, complete with a chair called "the president's throne." Instead he had his private secretary carry the message to Capitol Hill.

No president addressed Congress again until 1913, when Woodrow Wilson renewed the custom of delivering the message in person, a decision that was quite controversial. He eventually appeared before Congress twenty-six times, a record that still held in 1993. Since Wilson's time, only President Herbert Hoover has declined to visit Capitol Hill at all.

President Lyndon B. JOHNSON in 1965 shifted the time of the State of the Union address from midday to evening, a move designed to attract the large television audience during prime time. The next year Republicans received a half-hour slot from each network to offer their own assessment of national affairs. By 1976 television time was available to the opposing party immediately following the State of the Union broadcast.

In 1986 the State of the Union address was postponed for the first time. On the morning of President Reagan's scheduled January 28 address to Congress, the space shuttle *Challenger* exploded, killing all seven crew members. Reagan delayed the speech until February 4.

## States and Congress

The states and Congress have never fully agreed on how to share—or divide—responsibility for governing the nation. For two centuries the states have protested acts of Congress that in the states' opinion have undermined their autonomy and independence. That conflict erupted once into civil war and has spawned numerous other political disputes.

Certain areas, such as national defense, clearly lie in the federal domain. But the Constitution left many gray areas in which no clear rules stated what level of government was in charge. Often the Supreme Court has been forced to referee disputes, deciding whether the federal government or the states are ultimately responsible.

The sharing of responsibility for governing is called federalism. In the United States federalism means that a national government, fifty state governments, and thousands of local governments all operate at different levels. By the late twentieth century, the federal government clearly dominated the relationship; several Supreme Court decisions had enhanced federal authority, as had the enormous flow of federal money to state and local governments.

State and local officials found it almost impossible to refuse their share of tax dollars, even when the money came with rules and regulations that encroached on their autonomy. Congress, for its part, became accustomed in the 1960s and 1970s to setting national goals and giving other governments money to use in reaching those goals.

By the early 1990s constraints on the federal budget had made the pattern increasingly difficult to sustain. Sweeping new programs were out of the question, and existing policies were at risk. Congress continued to set national goals but could no longer be counted on to accompany the rules with the "carrot" of federal money for state and local governments to use in carrying out the rules. Governors and mayors, who began LOBBYING Washington heavily in the 1970s and 1980s, called these policies "mandates without money." They were asked to spend their own governments' money to implement federal goals. Even worse, from their point of view, was the use of the federal "stick"—potential loss of federal funds in other areas if they failed to comply with new national policies. Clean air laws, for example, called for cuts in federal highway funds for states that failed to meet national goals.

A once beneficial relationship with the federal government suddenly became less attractive to state and local governments, and they began to resist federal demands. Old arguments about states' rights had a new appeal, two centuries after the Constitution tried to divide local and national responsibilities.

## Constitutional Responsibilities

The Constitution enumerated several powers of Congress, including authority over the federal purse, interstate commerce, taxes and tariffs, and war. But it left untouched a wide area for the states to handle, such as education, property transactions, marriage, inheritance, contracts, and maintenance of domestic order, called the "police power." (See COMMERCE POWER; PURSE, POWER OF; STRUCTURE AND POWERS; WAR POWERS.)

The Tenth Amendment addressed the division of state and federal authority: "The powers not delegated to the United States by the Constitution, nor prohibited by it to the states, are reserved to the states respectively, or to the people."

Federal authority had an early test in Maryland, where opponents of the national bank tried to tax it into ruin. The Supreme Court in an 1819 decision, *McCulloch v. Maryland,* sided with the federal government, saying its law prevailed over any conflicting state laws or constitutions because of the "supremacy clause" of the Constitution.

But numerous Court decisions after that gave the upper hand to the states. Not until 1937, in a landmark case upholding the Social Security system *(Helvering v. Davis),* did the Court elaborate the power of the "general welfare" clause. That was followed by other decisions endorsing a broad application of the interstate commerce clause, opening the door to broad federal regulations. Since then, federal authority has rarely been checked.

In setting up the national government, the Constitution protected state interests in several ways. Each state was to be represented in Congress by two senators and one or more representatives. States were to govern the election of presidents and vice presidents through the electoral college. No changes could be made in the Constitution itself without the approval of three-fourths of the states. (See CONSTITUTIONAL AMENDMENTS; ELECTING THE PRESIDENT.)

The Constitution left voter qualifications up to the states, but it has been amended five times to overrule state restrictions on voting rights. Congress and the Supreme Court have also acted against state attempts to limit voting. Males without property, blacks, women, and young people were among those benefiting from the changes.

Three constitutional amendments ratified after the Civil War were designed to guarantee individual rights, even against action by states. The Thirteenth, Fourteenth, and Fifteenth amendments outlawed slavery; affirmed that voting was a right regardless of race, color, or previous condition of servitude; and promised due process and equal protection to all citizens. Not until the 1960s, however, did Supreme Court decisions and congressional action on civil rights laws put the full authority of the federal government behind the concept of equal rights.

## States' Rights

The philosophical debate over states' rights influenced the drafting of the nation's first documents. Statesmen such as Alexander Hamilton, who favored a strong national government, and Thomas Jefferson, who favored the states, continued the dialogue even after the Constitution appeared to resolve many issues.

### Virginia and Kentucky Resolutions

The discussion was rekindled in 1798, when the Federalist Congress enacted the Alien and Sedition Acts, which were thinly disguised attempts to weaken the Republicans. Under the Sedition Act, the most vigorously enforced of four new laws, twenty-five people, including Republican newspaper editors, were arrested for publishing articles criticizing Federalist policies. Virginia and Kentucky reacted to the restrictive law by writing resolutions asserting the right of states to resist laws they considered unconstitutional. James MADISON drafted the Virginia Resolution, Jefferson the Kentucky Resolution.

Seven northern states protested the resolutions, particularly Kentucky's advocacy of the theory of nullification. Under that theory, a state—as opposed to the Supreme Court—could declare null and void any federal law it found to violate constitutional rights. In 1814 Massachusetts, Connecticut, and Rhode Island borrowed the theory when they met at the Hartford Convention to consider secession as a protest against the War of 1812.

## Nullification

The concept of nullification was revived in the late 1820s and used to support the proslavery argument of the southern states. South Carolinian John C. CAL-HOUN was an eloquent advocate of states' rights. He resigned the vice presidency in 1832 and returned to the Senate to defend the nullification doctrine. South Carolina that year voted to nullify a new federal tariff act and to prohibit its enforcement in the state. Southern opposition to protective tariffs, and to the national bank, was connected to the slavery issue; if the southern states could assert their rights on tariffs, they might also be able to nullify any federal law banning slavery.

President Andrew Jackson responded by denouncing nullification, contending that states had surrendered a part of their sovereignty to the federal government. "Disunion by armed force is treason," Jackson said. A compromise on the tariff averted a direct confrontation, but the debate continued. Georgia in the 1830s tried to nullify a Supreme Court decision favoring the Cherokee Indians in its western territories.

## Civil War

The southern states took their concept of states' rights to its ultimate test in 1860 and 1861 when eleven states voted to secede from the Union. Their action was triggered by the election of President Abraham Lincoln; he opposed slavery and argued that the states, by joining the Union, had given up certain rights.

The victory of the Union in 1865 made the national government supreme and settled the argument about secession. But other aspects of the debate remained in dispute. The concept of states' rights continued to be identified with those reluctant to end racial discrimination.

## Dixiecrats and Desegregation

Champions of states' rights renewed their battle in the late 1940s and 1950s, as federal efforts to end racial discrimination intensified. When the Democratic National Convention in 1948 adopted a procivil rights platform, disgruntled southerners from

thirteen states established a States' Rights, or Dixiecrat, party. They nominated for president Strom Thurmond, a South Carolina governor; Thurmond eventually won in Alabama, Louisiana, Mississippi, and South Carolina. (Thurmond went on to enter the Senate as a Democrat in 1954 and became a Republican in 1964.)

Southern states also rallied around the states' rights cry in 1954, when the Supreme Court outlawed racially segregated public schools. For the next decade, congressional opponents of civil rights laws often made the claim that states had constitutional rights to resist federal policy. A 1956 "manifesto" signed by 101 southern members of Congress declared, "We commend the motives of those states which have declared the intention to resist forced integration by any lawful means." In 1957 President Dwight D. Eisenhower sent federal troops to enforce civil rights in Little Rock, Arkansas, where black students enrolled at the previously all-white Central High School.

## Grants-in-Aid

The debate over states' rights has at times been deeply philosophical, but a more powerful factor in the federal-state relationship has little to do with philosophy. Federal grants-in-aid to state and local governments steadily increased in the twentieth century, particularly in the mid-1960s and after. Such grants escalated from 5 percent of total federal outlays in fiscal 1955 to nearly 12 percent in fiscal 1992. Conditions on use of this money gave the federal government increasing control over local matters.

The patchwork of grant programs developed piecemeal, as Congress responded to various problems. Conditions were devised rather haphazardly and have grown increasingly complex. To be eligible for federal health funds, for example, states must have overall plans for how health care is delivered. Federally insured mortgages are available only to states with flood control programs. Highway grants come with a host of rules about how roads and bridges must be built, and also with links to other federal policies, such as speed limits and the minimum legal age for drinking alcoholic beverages.

Applicable to all grants are several "cross-cutting"

*Highway legislation passed by Congress in 1916 became the model for later federal grant programs. Highway aid still makes up more than 15 percent of total federal transfers to state and local governments.    Source: Jim Wells Photographers*

rules on civil rights, affirmative action, environmental impact, labor, and accessibility for the handicapped.

## Land Grants

The earliest federal grants consisted of land; as western territories were divided, a portion of every parcel, often one-sixteenth of each township, was set aside, with proceeds used to support local education. Application of the same approach to roads and canals met resistance. Several presidents, from Madison to Andrew Jackson, opposed as improper a federal role in "internal improvements," despite the idea's popularity in Congress.

Land grants were sometimes controversial. President Franklin Pierce in 1854 vetoed Congress's plan to provide land to states for facilities aiding the mentally handicapped. In 1859 President James Buchanan vetoed a congressional attempt to fund agricultural colleges. Both presidents argued that such federal funding was unconstitutional. Lincoln supported a stronger federal role and in 1862 signed the Morrill Act, which provided grants of federal land to establish agricultural colleges.

### Highways

A new era began in 1916 with federal highway legislation. Matching grants and formulas for distributing funds were among the procedures devised then, which became standard practice for decades afterward. To qualify for the aid, states were required to establish a highway department; by 1917 every state had managed to do so. (Highway aid still makes up more than 15 percent of total federal transfers to state and local governments.) It was no coincidence that the highway bill was passed just three years after enactment of a federal income tax, which for the first time guaranteed a steady flow of funds into federal coffers.

### The New Deal and the 1950s

Coping with economic upheaval during the Depression of the 1930s, President Franklin D. Roosevelt proposed an array of federal programs, many of which were based on grants to states and also to cities. The most sweeping new law was the Social Security Act, which set up programs to benefit dependent children, the blind, and the elderly; these were administered by the states. Annual federal grants quadrupled between 1932 and 1940. By 1950, $2.3 billion was being spent on grants-in-aid.

Although the NEW DEAL clearly changed the framework of federal-state relations, debate about the proper federal role had not ended. In the 1950s, Congress spent several years arguing about federal aid to elementary and secondary education, which had traditionally been handled by state and local governments. Some critics fought any federal aid, while churches insisted that funds should also be channeled to parochial schools. The deadlock was broken by the Soviet Union's launching of the first artificial satellite in 1957. In an effort to catch up with and surpass Soviet technology, Congress approved the National Defense Education Act the following year.

### The Great Society

Democratic presidents John F. KENNEDY and Lyndon B. JOHNSON led Congress in a sweeping expansion of federal welfare programs that required state and local governments to handle billions of additional federal dollars—according to federal rules. "This administration today here and now declares unconditional war on poverty in America," Johnson proclaimed in 1964. Food stamps, urban housing programs, community development, health care for the poor (Medicaid), health care for the elderly (Medicare), and education programs for disadvantaged children (such as Head Start) were among the bills passed in the 1960s and 1970s. Johnson called his policy "creative federalism." (See GREAT SOCIETY.)

### The New Federalism

President Richard NIXON pushed a "new federalism" that would return responsibility to the state and local levels. He wanted to accompany that with an infusion of federal money, which he called "revenue sharing." Congress in 1972 approved the revenue-sharing program, which provided virtually unrestricted grants to state and local governments. However, it resisted Nixon's efforts to combine most "categorical grant" programs, aimed at specific problems, into "block grants," a move designed to give more flexibility to local administrators.

### The Reagan Revolution

The 1980s brought another attempt at "new federalism," this time by President Ronald Reagan, who argued that "our nation of sovereign states has come dangerously close to becoming one great national government." Reagan saw block grants as the first step in the redirection of money and power to state and local governments. But Congress, anxious to have national policy carried out uniformly in every state and city, resisted major shifts of responsibility back to the local level. As part of his program, Reagan sought sweeping cuts in federal payments to states and cities; Congress cut funding, though not so deeply as Reagan proposed in each annual budget request.

The Reagan years also brought an end to revenue sharing, which between 1973 and 1986 transferred more than $80 billion to state and local governments with few strings attached. More than 39,000 local governments benefited from the program; states did not receive revenue-sharing funds after 1980. Revenue-sharing money was used to pay police and fire personnel, provide health care to residents, buy library books, build and repair highways, support education, and meet dozens of other needs.

In the 1990s continuing federal budget deficits threatened levels of funding for other aid programs to the states.

### Additional Reading

Conlon, Timothy. *New Federalism: Intergovernmental Reform from Nixon to Reagan.* Washington, D.C.: Brookings Institution, 1988.

---

# Steering and Policy Committee

*See* LEADERSHIP.

---

# Stennis, John C.

By the time he announced his retirement in 1988, Mississippi Democrat John C. Stennis (1901– ) had become an anachronistic figure in the Senate, a link to another era. But his physical frailty never diminished the dignity and rectitude that marked more than forty years of Senate service. His colleagues always held him in high esteem, as they demonstrated with the displays of public affection that greeted him when, barely a month after he lost a leg to cancer in late 1984, Stennis returned to the Senate floor in a wheelchair.

Born in 1901 on a Mississippi cotton and cattle farm, Stennis served in the state legislature and as a prosecuting attorney. He then spent ten years on the bench as a circuit judge. Stennis was elected to the Senate in 1947 after the death of Sen. Theodore G. Bilbo, a race-baiting demagogue. Two of the five candidates in the special election copied Bilbo's white supremacist style; Stennis, while ready to preserve "the southern way of life," did not make race the center of his campaign.

Stennis brought a judicial bearing to the Senate. A member of the committee that investigated the conduct of Sen. Joseph R. MCCARTHY in 1954, Stennis was the first Democrat to take the Senate floor to denounce him, charging that McCarthy had poured "slush and slime" on the Senate.

When the Senate Ethics Committee was established in 1965, Stennis was immediately chosen to chair the panel, even though he had not advocated establishing it. He chaired the committee until 1975. In 1973 Stennis suffered critical gunshot wounds during a holdup in front of his Washington, D.C., home. He was absent from the Senate for several months.

Stennis voted as a southern Democrat, advocating fiscal conservatism and opposing civil rights legislation. But he was overshadowed by more aggressive southern senators. Most of Stennis's career was focused on the Armed Services Committee, which he chaired from 1969 to 1981. He was also able to promote defense spending on the Appropriations Committee, where he chaired the Defense Subcommittee.

Stennis usually supported presidents in their military policies, even when his Democratic colleagues did not. But he also defended congressional prerogatives. In 1971 Stennis introduced WAR POWERS legislation to require congressional approval of sustained military action, and he supported the law enacted two years later over President Richard Nixon's veto.

When Democrats regained control of the Senate in 1987, Stennis, as the party's senior senator, became president pro tempore. He also became chair of the Appropriations Committee. "I want to plow a straight furrow," he once said, "right down to the end of my row."

## Stevens, Thaddeus

Thaddeus Stevens (1792–1868) served in the House of Representatives as a Whig (1849–1853) and as a Republican (1859–1868) from Pennsylvania. An accomplished orator, Stevens held several important committee chairmanships, and on occasion his power surpassed that of the Speaker. Above all, Stevens hated slavery, and his career was devoted to its eradication and to the punishment of the rebellious southern states.

Before entering national politics, Stevens practiced law, owned a forge, and served in the Pennsylvania state legislature. Once in Congress he allied himself with the Free Soilers, who opposed the spread of slavery to western states. Stevens spoke and voted against the Compromise of 1850 because it failed to prohibit slavery in the territories of Utah and New Mexico. He also opposed the Fugitive Slave Act, which required the return of fugitive slaves to their owners. An uncompromising man, Stevens left Congress in 1853 to protest what he considered to be his party's indecisive stand on slavery.

Returning to the House in 1859, Stevens served as chair of the Ways and Means Committee from 1861 until he became chair of the new Appropriations Committee in 1865. During the Civil War Stevens controlled the House, unchecked by a weak Republican Speaker.

Stevens often spoke of the South with bitterness and vindictiveness. He objected to President Abraham Lincoln's plans for Reconstruction, declaring that the South had put itself beyond the protection of the Constitution. Stevens hoped to reduce the South to territorial status, thereby preventing an influx of southern representatives who would almost certainly be Democrats. (See RECONSTRUCTION ERA.)

When President Andrew Johnson pursued Lin-

*An accomplished orator of the nineteenth century, Rep. Thaddeus Stevens here closes the House debate on the impeachment of President Andrew Johnson in 1868.     Source: Library of Congress*

coln's plan for Reconstruction, conservative and radical Republicans joined together to impeach him on the grounds that his firing of Secretary of War Edwin M. Stanton violated the Tenure of Office Act. Stevens was a manager of the case against Johnson. Suffering from ill health and disappointed by Johnson's acquittal, Stevens died in 1868. (See JOHNSON IMPEACHMENT TRIAL.)

He was buried in a biracial cemetery; the inscription on his tombstone states that he chose to be buried there "that I might illustrate in my death the principles which I advocated through a long life—Equality of Man before his Creator."

## Structure and Powers

Under the Constitution Congress is charged with carrying out the legislative functions of government. The framers of the Constitution wanted the lawmaking role to be in the hands of a representative body. They considered Congress, the collective name for the SENATE and HOUSE OF REPRESENTATIVES, to be the "first branch" of the U.S. government, the primary maker of national policy. The powers, structure, and procedures of the national legislature are outlined in considerable detail, unlike those of the presidency and the judiciary, the other independent branches in the

American system of SEPARATION OF POWERS. (See Appendix.)

## Checks and Balances

Each branch is structured so that it may restrain the others' excesses, resulting in a form of institutionalized "checks and balances." Within Congress itself the legislative power is checked in many ways. To a degree the House and Senate are competitors, even when both are controlled by the same party. Each seeks to protect its own powers and prerogatives. The Constitution helps to create the competition—that is, the checks—by giving some powers to the Senate alone and others to the House. Powers reserved to the Senate include approval of treaties, confirmation of presidential nominations, and the power to try impeachments. Granted to the House alone is the authority to originate impeachments and all revenue-raising bills.

Although competition and conflict are built into the system, cooperation between House and Senate is essential because legislation must be passed in identical form by both chambers before it can be sent to the president for approval or veto. A form of checks and balances between branches comes into play once Congress has finished acting on a bill. The president may veto any bill that Congress sends him, forcing legislators to consider the chief executive's opinions and priorities. Congress, however, may override the president's action by a two-thirds vote of both chambers. (See VETOES.) The actions of both the legislative and executive branches are at least implicitly checked by the review functions of the national judiciary.

Another form of checks and balances derives from the system of federalism, the countervailing forces of the state and federal governments. Federalism is a factor to be reckoned with in the legislative process. Because members of Congress are elected either from a state or from a congressional district within a state, local and regional interests strongly influence how the laws are drafted. This often creates tensions between the House and Senate and between Congress and the executive branch. (See STATES AND CONGRESS.)

Members in modern Congresses are seldom dependent on their national party apparatus for their election. Senators or representatives who are popular back home usually cannot be forced to heed the wishes of the president or their party's congressional leaders. This independence is a result of many modern developments, including television, direct mail, and campaign-financing trends. It is a significant change from historical patterns, under which political parties and major party leaders were able to control the political conduct and votes of members.

## Congress's Many Roles

Congress by design is untidy, unwieldy, and unrestrained. But an independent, decentralized, and deliberative legislature is exactly what the framers of Article I of the Constitution had in mind.

Members' constituents are not united on most issues most of the time, and a halting, indecisive Congress usually mirrors the public at large. The framers of the Constitution did not look upon efficiency as the primary goal in lawmaking. Sensitive to what they viewed as the denial of basic human rights under British rule, and to other failings of eighteenth-century governments, they were mainly concerned with ensuring individual rights and liberties. Within the federal government they feared the potential excesses or domination of one branch over the others, and in Congress they feared the domination of a majority over the minority.

The Constitution, then, provides the framework of a complicated system of government. Some of the complexities become quickly apparent when tracing the steps involved in the LEGISLATIVE PROCESS. Legislation must follow an intricate course before it can become law. Each step presents potential barriers to passage and gives legislators opportunities to kill or modify bills or provisions they oppose.

Many experts on Congress have observed that the legislative process resembles an obstacle course that favors the opponents of legislation over the proponents. There are many points at which bills can be stymied or delayed and relatively few effective tools for speeding passage through Congress, particularly when members differ strongly over issues. Although opponents have the upper hand in most situations, members also are under pressure to get legislation enacted, especially programs in the domestic field that

*A nineteenth century scene in the Old Senate Chamber.*   Source: Library of Congress

can benefit their districts, states, or regions—a public works project, for example, or a navy ship-building contract. Therefore, bargaining, compromise, and LOGROLLING are necessary to offset the institutional bias against speedy enactment of bills.

### President as Legislative Leader

The modern president plays the principal role in setting the legislative agenda. Congress expects the White House to submit proposals for new laws dealing with the whole spectrum of foreign and domestic policy. When existing programs come up for renewal, Congress generally waits for the executive branch to present its recommendations before setting the legislative wheels in motion. Although the Constitution

implies that the president should play the leading role, this was not the general practice during the nineteenth century.

The president uses a variety of vehicles and forums to present his program to Congress and the nation. Best known is the annual STATE OF THE UNION address, which is a constitutional requirement. Article II, Section 3 of the Constitution directs the president periodically to "give to the Congress Information of the State of the Union, and recommend to their Consideration such Measures as he shall judge necessary and expedient."

Equally important is the president's annual budget message, with its accompanying documents. The budget message contains many of the president's legislative goals for the coming year, as well as requests for money to run the federal government. The agenda also is shaped by periodic messages and statements proposing new measures or changes in pending bills. Even presidential veto messages may contain recommendations for future legislation.

## Structure

The legislative branch is bicameral, meaning that it consists of two houses, or chambers. The terms of service in the House and Senate differ. Representatives are elected for two-year terms, senators for six-year terms. Before adoption of the Seventeenth Amendment to the Constitution in 1913, senators were elected by their state legislatures. (See DIRECT ELECTION OF SENATORS.)

Senators represent entire states, while House members represent population-based districts within the states. States that have very small populations relative to the others qualify for only one representative in the House. For these, the entire state is the congressional district and is referred to as an at-large district. In the 103rd Congress (1993–1995) there were seven at-large districts. Congress has passed a law prohibiting House members from being elected at large in states that have more than one representative.

Traditionally House members were considered to represent the people more closely than senators, because of their short terms and small constituencies. Although facing reelection every two years does tend to force representatives to view their roles somewhat differently than senators do, this distinction is fast disappearing. The major factors are the pervasive influence of television—including gavel-to-gavel coverage of both Senate and House floor debates—and other media coverage, and the ease with which members can return to their states and districts. These factors make senators and representatives equally accessible to the public and aware of the views of the citizens they represent. Earlier, senators were drawn closer to their constituents when they became subject to direct election.

The complexities of the legislative process require Congress to operate through elaborate rules as well as informal practices that have been refined, modified, and changed over the years. Except where the Constitution delineates the powers and parliamentary procedures, each chamber has developed its own set of rules from the body of traditions and precedents that developed during more than 200 years of legislating. Size alone accounts for many of the differences in the organization of the two bodies and in the rules and customs each has adopted. The House requires a more formal structure and detailed rules; the smaller Senate legislates in an informal setting and may not follow its formal rules if it prefers not to.

### Qualifications

The Constitution sets only three qualifications for membership in Congress. They are:

*Age:* A House member must be at least twenty-five years old, a senator at least thirty.

*U.S. citizenship:* A House member must have been a citizen for at least seven years, a senator for at least nine.

*Residency:* A senator or representative must be a resident of the state from which he or she is elected.

Since adoption of the Twentieth Amendment in 1933, members' terms have begun on January 3 of the year following their election. That amendment also made January 3 the beginning of each new two-year term of Congress, and January 20 the date that newly elected presidents take office. The original constitutional language regulating when sessions of Congress began, and the precedents Congress followed in its first 140 years, proved inefficient for timely lawmaking and unrepresentative of the most recent general-election results. Elections are held on the first Tuesday following the first Monday in November in even-numbered years. (See LAME-DUCK AMENDMENT; TERMS AND SESSIONS OF CONGRESS.)

### Size

The Senate, as mandated by the Constitution, consists of two senators from each state. Senators' terms are staggered. Only thirty-three or thirty-four Senate seats—one-third of the membership—are at stake in each biennial general election. For this reason the Senate considers itself a continuing body, and its rules continue in effect from one Congress to the next. The House adopts its rules at the beginning of each Congress.

The size of the House is determined by Congress itself, within certain constitutional prescriptions. Throughout the nineteenth century the membership of the House was increased to reflect the growth of the nation's population and the addition of new states to the Union. In 1910 the size of the House was set at 435 members, where it has remained ever since, except for a brief period (1959–1963) after Alaska and Hawaii were admitted to statehood, when it was increased to 437.

The size of each state's House delegation is determined by the results of the census, which is conducted every ten years. The Constitution specifies that House seats must be reapportioned among the states after every census to reflect population growth and shifts in population from one state to another since the last census. (There was no reapportionment after the 1920 census because Congress could not agree on any plan to reapportion House seats.)

Ever since the House decided to keep its membership at 435, reapportionment has resulted in some states gaining seats at the expense of others. After the reapportionment following the 1990 census, House districts averaged about 572,000 constituents. (See REAPPORTIONMENT AND REDISTRICTING.) In addition to its 435 voting members, the House has five DELEGATES. They represent the District of Columbia, Puerto Rico, the Virgin Islands, Guam, and American Samoa.

## Powers of Congress

The many explicit powers of Congress enumerated in the Constitution reflect in part the framers' experience with the woefully weak Congress under the Articles of Confederation, the nation's original plan of government. Under the Articles Congress was practically powerless to protect the national interest. It could not limit encroachment on the federal government's authority by the thirteen independent states. The Constitution's detailed, precise enumeration of many of Congress's powers, principally in Article I, Section 8, reflects the fears and distrust between the various states and blocs of states at the time the document was drafted. Although these powers are extensive, most of them are shared with the other two branches, particularly the executive. Thus the Constitution really established a system not of separate powers but of separate institutions sharing powers and functions.

The Tenth Amendment specifies that powers not expressly delegated to Congress or the other branches, and not prohibited by the Constitution, are reserved to the states or to the people.

### Domestic Powers

Foremost among Congress's powers is the right "to lay and collect taxes, duties, imposts and excises, to pay the debts [and] . . . to borrow money on the credit of the United States." Article I, Section 9 stipulates that no federal funds can be spent except "in consequence of appropriations made by law." Three key powers are involved here: taxing, borrowing, and spending. They are known collectively as the power of the purse. (See PURSE, POWER OF.)

Most of the time members spend on legislative work is occupied with measures that either directly or indirectly involve these three powers. Although there are certain limitations on how Congress can legislate under these powers, raising and spending money, or committing the federal government to spend money in the future, lie at the heart of congressional decision making. (See BUDGET PROCESS.)

Congress also is charged with providing for the "general welfare." These two words have provided the underpinning for the whole list of public assistance programs enacted by the modern Congress that are taken for granted today: Social Security, agricultural subsidies, workers' unemployment and disability insurance, food stamps, Medicare and Medicaid, and many other programs.

Also very important is Congress's power to regulate foreign and domestic commerce. Since the earliest days of the republic, Congress has vigorously used the power to regulate foreign trade through tariffs, import quotas, and licenses and trade embargoes. Through its power to regulate domestic commerce, Congress has vastly expanded its powers to cope with national problems in areas never imagined by the framers of the Constitution. (See COMMERCE POWER.)

The Constitution simply states that Congress shall have the power to regulate commerce with foreign countries "and among the several states." This general and rather innocuous language gave Congress the latitude it needed, beginning in the 1880s, to expand its power over commerce to meet the needs of an increasingly industrialized and urbanized society linked by rapid transportation and communication. In the early and mid-nineteenth century the Supreme Court accepted congressional regulation of interstate commerce, but viewed this power narrowly. It accepted regulation of common carriers, such as the railroads, but rejected regulation of private property rights, states' rights, and most businesses, as well as legislation concerning social evils, such as child labor.

Only in the late 1930s and 1940s did the Court embrace Congress's broad interpretation of interstate commerce to include business activity even where it had only an indirect effect on interstate commerce. The power was expanded further in the 1960s to deal with racial discrimination and other social problems and in the 1970s to encompass conservation and environmental issues.

Today congressional power in this area is practically limitless. Congress sets the rules conferring citizenship on foreign-born persons, and it regulates the admission into the country and the deportation of aliens. Congressional power extends to bankruptcy, patent and copyright issues, regulation of the U.S. currency, the right to set standard weights and measures, and authority to establish a national postal system.

### Foreign Policy Powers

It is in foreign affairs that Congress most clearly shares its powers with the executive branch. The Constitution presupposes that the two branches will maintain a delicate balance in exercising their foreign policy prerogatives. Nonetheless, both branches still debate vigorously the scope of and limits on Congress's power in the formulation of U.S. foreign and defense policies. The extent of Congress's involve-

*Congress shares its powers with the executive branch in the field of foreign affairs. Here Russian President Boris Yeltsin addresses a joint meeting of Congress.* Source: R. Michael Jenkins

ment in and influence over foreign policy has varied throughout American history. Since the early years of the Vietnam War in the 1960s, Congress and the White House have actively competed with each other for control of foreign policy.

Certain specific foreign policy powers granted to Congress are not disputed. These include the power to raise, support, and regulate the armed forces; the power to declare war and, through its power of the purse, to finance or withhold financing for U.S. participation in foreign wars; and the requirement that the Senate give its consent to all treaties and executive branch nominations of diplomatic officials. Although these powers have been important in ensuring that the legislative branch remains an independent force in U.S. foreign affairs, its role in some cases has been altered or diminished by international developments since World War I.

Probably the most important change is the erosion of the power of Congress to declare war. In the nuclear age, when decisions about war must be made in minutes, rather than in days or weeks, the power of the national legislature to declare war seems impractical. Presidents since World War II have committed U.S. armed forces without first asking Congress's consent. World War II was the last in which Congress exercised its power to declare war. Since then U.S. military forces have engaged in several major armed conflicts, including those in Korea and Vietnam.

In early 1991, however, Congress—at the request of President George Bush—debated heatedly before approving a resolution authorizing the president to send U.S. troops to the Persian Gulf to force Iraqi troops to leave Kuwait. In August 1990 Iraq had sent its armies to occupy Kuwait, claiming that that country was by right a province of Iraq.

Reacting to its inability to curtail or, ultimately, end U.S. involvement in the Vietnam War in the 1960s and early 1970s, Congress in 1973 enacted the War Powers Resolution over President Richard Nixon's veto. This measure was an effort by Congress to reinvigorate its war-making—or war-curtailing—power. But later presidents avoided its use, maintaining that it was an unconstitutional infringement on their powers.

Similarly, congressional control of the purse strings has not been very effective in preventing U.S. armed intervention abroad. Once presidential decisions have been made to deploy U.S. military personnel overseas in hostile situations, it is difficult for Congress to force a halt to such operations, especially since doing so might jeopardize the lives of Americans stationed in those areas. Congress did, however, use the power of the purse to wind down the Vietnam War. (See WAR POWERS.)

Another change in Congress's foreign policy powers has been the increasing reliance on executive agreements, which are compacts with other nations informally drawn up and agreed to by the executive branch alone, without any requirement for Senate consent. In certain areas of U.S. foreign policy, executive agreements have largely replaced treaties. (See TREATY-MAKING POWER.)

Although some of Congress's formal constitutional powers in foreign affairs have decreased in importance, lawmakers' influence in this field has greatly expanded in other ways. Congressional backing is indispensable to the array of programs for foreign economic and military aid and international lending that the United States launched after World War II. These programs have expanded greatly since then, which gives Congress significant leverage over presidential policies. For example, when Congress approves such aid programs, it often writes laws giving itself a voice on how they are funded and administered, and mandating what actions the White House can and cannot take.

### Institutional Powers

Congress employs a wealth of institutional powers to buttress its position as an equal branch of government.

In the procedure for amending the Constitution, Congress and the states act alone; the president may propose constitutional amendments but has no formal role in their ratification. Article V provides that Congress, "whenever two-thirds of both Houses shall deem it necessary, shall propose" amendments to the Constitution, which take effect when ratified by three-fourths of the states. Alternatively, the states themselves, if two-thirds agree, can call a constitutional convention to propose amendments. The latter route, however, has never been used successfully. (See CONSTITUTIONAL AMENDMENTS.)

The Senate alone possesses the key power to confirm or reject presidential appointments to many government positions. Most are confirmed routinely, but the few hundred top-level appointments requiring confirmation give the Senate a potent policy voice. Besides appointments at and beneath the cabinet level, the Senate's advice and consent power covers nominees for the Supreme Court and lower courts; for top-level diplomatic and military posts; and for federal regulatory agencies and boards. (See AP-POINTMENT POWER.)

The power to conduct INVESTIGATIONS is not mentioned in the Constitution. It is an implied power, derived from the introductory clause in Article I declaring that "all legislative Powers herein granted shall be vested" in Congress. Investigations can cover the entire range of congressional activity. They are used to review the effectiveness of existing laws, to assess the need for new ones, and to probe into government waste, inefficiency, and corruption.

Congress is also charged with making the "Rules for the Government." It can add or abolish federal agencies and departments and can even alter the size of the Supreme Court. Indeed, the entire federal court structure was established by Congress. The power to admit new states into the Union also is conferred on Congress.

Several congressional powers directly affect the presidency. Congress is given the duty, now largely ceremonial, of counting the electoral votes for president and vice president after every election and formally announcing the winners. More important is the House's power to choose the president, and the Senate's power to choose the vice president, in the event that no candidate receives a clear majority of the vote. (See ELECTING THE PRESIDENT.)

The Twentieth and Twenty-fifth amendments also give Congress powers dealing with PRESIDENTIAL DISABILITY AND SUCCESSION, including the power to confirm presidential choices to fill vacancies in the vice presidency. The House and Senate share the power to impeach the president and other officials and remove them from office for treason, bribery, or other "high crimes and misdemeanors." Although rarely used, the IMPEACHMENT POWER is perhaps Congress's most formidable weapon against the executive branch. The House draws up impeachment charges; the Senate acts as judge and jury.

Finally, the Constitution declares that Congress may "make all laws which shall be necessary and proper for carrying into Execution the foregoing Powers." This catchall provision was originally intended to help Congress exercise the powers specifically enu-

merated in the Constitution. It was broadly defined by the Supreme Court in 1819 in the case of *McCulloch v. Maryland.* In practice, the provision has allowed Congress to extend its role and has led to far-reaching debates over the scope of congressional powers.

### Additional Readings

Congressional Quarterly. *Guide to Congress.* 4th ed. Washington, D.C.: Congressional Quarterly, Inc., 1991.

Davidson, Roger H., and Walter J. Oleszek. *Congress and Its Members.* 4th ed. Washington, D.C.: CQ Press, 1993.

Josephy, Alvin M., Jr. *On the Hill: A History of the American Congress.* New York: Simon and Schuster, 1980.

Wilson, Woodrow. *Congressional Government: A Study in American Politics.* Boston: Houghton Mifflin, 1885. Rpt., Cleveland: Meridian Books, 1956.

## Subpoena Power

The power to issue subpoenas enables congressional committees to compel the cooperation of reluctant witnesses. A subpoena is a legal order that requires a witness to testify or to produce documents upon demand of a committee. A witness who refuses may be cited for CONTEMPT OF CONGRESS and prosecuted in the courts. Committees of both the Senate and the House of Representatives routinely issue subpoenas as part of their INVESTIGATIONS.

The Supreme Court has upheld Congress's subpoena power. "Issuance of subpoenas . . . has long been held to be a legitimate use by Congress of its power to investigate," the Court wrote in 1927. "Experience has taught that mere requests for . . . information often are unavailing."

## Substitute

When a motion or amendment is pending in the House or Senate, legislators can offer a substitute proposal dealing with the same subject. Under parliamentary rules, if a substitute is accepted, it supplants the original amendment, thus killing it. Also possible is an "amendment in the nature of a substitute," which usually replaces the entire text of a bill with a new version.

Substitute bills are used less often in the Senate than in the House, where major legislation is often handled by more than one committee. The separate House committees work out their differences and draft a compromise bill, which is offered on the floor as a substitute. (See LEGISLATIVE PROCESS.)

## Sumner, Charles

Charles Sumner (1811–1874) served as a senator from Massachusetts at the time of the Civil War. His energies were directed toward the outlawing of slavery and later the radical Reconstruction of the South. Like his Radical Republican colleagues, Sumner supported the impeachment of President Andrew Johnson. (See RECONSTRUCTION ERA.)

Sumner was a practicing lawyer when Massachusetts Democrats and Free Soilers proposed him as a candidate for the Senate. He entered the Senate in 1851. Sumner remained a Democrat until 1857, when he became a Republican. As a new senator, Sumner began speaking out against slavery. His assertion that he would not comply with the Fugitive Slave Act, which required the return of escaped slaves to their owners, provoked an unsuccessful Senate petition to expel him.

Debates in the Senate on matters pertaining to slavery were fiery and personal. In 1856, while addressing the status of Kansas, Sumner vilified many individuals, including Illinois senator Stephen A. DOUGLAS, a Popular Sovereignty Democrat, whom he called a "noisome, squat and nameless animal." Two days after the speech, while Sumner was sitting at his desk on the Senate floor, he was bludgeoned by Rep. Preston S. Brooks, a States Rights Democrat from South Carolina, whose uncle Sumner had criticized. It took Sumner three years to recover from the injuries Brooks inflicted using a walking stick.

Sumner's hatred of slavery also led him into vindictiveness against the South. He believed that the Confederates had relinquished their right to constitutional protections. Disliking the more moderate Reconstruction program of Abraham Lincoln and Andrew Johnson, Sumner advocated complete congressional control over the process. He played a major role in the impeachment of Johnson, saying that if he could, he would vote on the charges, "Guilty of all and infinitely more." (See JOHNSON IMPEACHMENT TRIAL.)

In 1861 Sumner was made chair of the Foreign Relations Committee. As such, he was involved in the *Trent* affair, in which Confederate agents were seized from a British ship. Later Sumner was so upset by President Ulysses S. Grant's plan to annex Santo Domingo that he was removed as chair of the committee. Republicans felt they needed a chair who was at least speaking to the president and the secretary of state.

Sumner died in 1874 while still a member of the Senate.

## Supreme Court

The Supreme Court is the most powerful court the world has ever known. It can override the will of the majority by declaring acts of Congress unconstitutional. It can remind presidents that in the United States all persons are subject to the rule of law. It can require the states to redistribute political power. And it can persuade the nation's citizens that society must move in new directions.

The Supreme Court can do all this because it functions as both the nation's highest court of appeals and the ultimate interpreter of the Constitution. Many key parts of the Constitution are vague or ambiguous, leaving room for the Court to set limits on the proper exercise of power by Congress, the president, and the states. As a result, the Court has often surpassed the executive and legislative branches in shaping the course of American politics. Two landmark rulings among many are *Brown v. Board of Education of Topeka* (1954), which outlawed racial segregation in public schools, and *Roe v. Wade* (1973), which legalized abortion in most instances.

Supreme Court justices are appointed by the presi-

*Above the main entrance to the Supreme Court Building are the words "Equal Justice Under Law."*    *Source: R. Michael Jenkins*

dent and confirmed by the Senate. Justices are appointed for life, and for most members that has been literally true. The majority of justices either have died while still on the bench or have retired shortly before their deaths. Prior judicial service is not required, although most nominees in recent decades have had such experience. Indeed, some of the most highly regarded justices had never before sat on a court. The list includes five chief justices of the United States— John Marshall, Roger Brooke Taney, Charles Evans Hughes, Harlan Fiske Stone, and Earl Warren.

### The Court at Work

Cases come before the Supreme Court in three ways. First, the Constitution designates two classes of cases as being in the Court's "original" jurisdiction—

that is, eligible for hearing without prior review by a lower court. Such cases, which account for only a small portion of the total number on the Supreme Court docket, are those in which a state is a party and those involving senior foreign diplomats.

Second, the Supreme Court has authority to hear appeals from the lower federal courts. Although the Supreme Court is required by law to hear certain types of appeals, most cases come before it through a writ of certiorari. In seeking such a writ, a litigant who has lost a case in a lower court petitions the Supreme Court to review the case, setting forth the reasons why review should be granted. The Supreme Court, under its rules, may grant a writ of certiorari by a vote of at least four justices—an exception to the rule that all business be controlled by majority decision. In general, the Court grants certiorari only if the case touches on a question of fundamental public importance. About 90 percent of petitions for certiorari fail to win approval.

Third, the Supreme Court reviews appeals from state supreme courts that present a "substantial federal question." Such questions usually arise when a U.S. constitutional right has been denied in the state courts.

The number of justices on the Supreme Court is fixed by Congress, not the Constitution. Under the Judiciary Act of 1789, Congress created a six-member Court. Congress later changed the Court's size from time to time, but since 1869 the Court has consisted of a chief justice and eight associate justices. In early 1937 President Franklin D. Roosevelt proposed that Congress add as many as six justices to the Court, in an effort to obtain more favorable rulings on the constitutionality of New Deal legislation, but his attempt to "pack" the Court failed. (See COURTS AND CONGRESS.)

The Supreme Court convenes on the first Monday in October of each year. It usually hears oral arguments for two weeks at a time, at two-week intervals, but the schedule may vary. It usually recesses in late June until the following autumn. On Friday of a week of argument (and Saturday, if need be), the nine justices meet in closed session. At the Friday conference the cases ready for decision are discussed and voted upon. If the chief justice votes with the majority, the chief justice assigns the writing of the majority opinion. If the chief justice is in the minority, the senior associate justice voting with the majority makes the assignment. Decisions usually are announced to the public on Mondays, but in recent years the press of business has meant that some important rulings have been announced on Tuesdays.

In arriving at decisions, the Court largely relies on precedent. Except in rare cases where there is no judicial opinion to be cited, decisions are based primarily on earlier relevant opinions of the Court or of lower courts as interpreted in light of the case under consideration.

The most dramatic and far-reaching of the Court's decisions have been instances where it has arrived at

## VISITING THE SUPREME COURT

The Supreme Court building comprises six levels, only two of which are open to the public. The basement contains a parking garage, a printing press, and offices for security guards and maintenance personnel. A public information office is on the ground floor, and the courtroom itself is on the main floor. The second floor contains the justices' dining rooms and library, as well as various offices; the third floor, the Court library; and the fourth floor, the gym, and storage areas.

From October to the end of April, the Court hears oral arguments from Monday to Wednesday for about two weeks a month. These sessions begin at 10 a.m. and continue until 3 p.m., with a one-hour recess beginning at noon. They are open to the public on a first-come, first-served basis.

Visitors may inspect the Supreme Court chamber at any time the Court is not in session. Historical exhibits and a film on how the Court works also are presented throughout the year. The Supreme Court building is open from 9 a.m. to 4:30 p.m. Monday through Friday, except for legal holidays. When the Court is not in session, lectures are given in the courtroom every hour on the half hour between 9:30 a.m. and 3:30 p.m.

a clear-cut reversal of one of its earlier landmark opinions, especially one where basic constitutional questions are involved. The 1954 decision in *Brown v. Board of Education* reversed more than a century of earlier Court decisions in civil rights cases—decisions that the Court, in effect, now declared to have been unconstitutional.

Among the Court's most important traditions is secrecy, which applies to formal deliberations and also to disclosure of personal disagreements and animosities among the justices. The unwritten code of secrecy has made the Court the most leakproof of Washington institutions. Still, there have been, and no doubt will continue to be, occasional glimpses into the Court's inner workings and conflicts.

Justices have good reason to maintain the veil of secrecy that surrounds their conference deliberations and their personal relations with other justices. Widespread disclosure of what goes on in conference might reduce public esteem for the Court and its rulings.

### The Court's Quarters

Of the federal government's three branches, the Supreme Court has the newest home. Its building in the classical Greek style at One First Street, N.E. faces the Capitol to the west and the Library of Congress's main Jefferson Building to the south. The building was opened in 1935.

Before 1935 the Court held its sessions in about a dozen different places. Some of its early courtrooms were shared with other tribunals. After the federal government moved to Washington in 1801, the Court sat in various rooms of the Capitol—and, some sources say, in two local taverns as well.

Because the wing of the Capitol where the Court was initially housed needed renovation, the Court in 1808 moved into a library formerly occupied by the House of Representatives. According to Capitol architect Benjamin H. Latrobe, the Court's 1809 sessions took place at Long's Tavern, where the main building of the Library of Congress now stands. The following year, the Court returned to the Capitol and met in a room designed for it, beneath the Senate chamber.

There the Court remained until the Capitol was burned by the British on August 24, 1814, during the War of 1812. The justices then moved to the temporary "Brick Capitol" at the site of the present Supreme Court building and then—during the two years when the Capitol was being restored—to a rented house that later became Bell Tavern. The Court returned to the Capitol for its February 1817 term and occupied an undamaged section in the north wing until 1819, when its regular quarters beneath the Senate were ready to be occupied again.

In 1860, with the Civil War imminent, the Court moved from the basement to the old Senate chamber on the first floor of the Capitol. The new courtroom was situated on the east side of the main corridor between the Rotunda and the current Senate chamber. The large room, with a dozen anterooms for office space and storage, was by far the roomiest and most pleasing space the Court had occupied. Still, none of the justices had individual office space in the Capitol.

President William Howard Taft began promoting the idea of a separate building for the Supreme Court about 1912. Taft continued his campaign when he became chief justice of the United States in 1921. At his urging, Congress finally agreed in 1929 and authorized funds for the construction of a permanent home for the Court.

---

# Suspension of the Rules

The suspension of the rules is a convenient shortcut procedure that the House uses for floor action on noncontroversial legislation. By avoiding the regular, time-consuming parliamentary procedures, bills—even major ones—facing little or no opposition can be approved quickly.

Debate on legislation considered under suspension of the rules is limited to forty minutes. Floor amendments are prohibited—another reason why this shortcut is so effective. Only one vote to pass the bill is in order; a two-thirds majority of members voting is required for passage.

Suspension of the rules is in order on Mondays and Tuesdays of every week and during the last six days of the session, when there is usually a great backlog of legislation awaiting action. The SPEAKER OF THE HOUSE has control over the procedure because of the authority to recognize members. Members make arrangements in advance to receive recognition to offer a suspension motion.

The Speaker has the authority to postpone recorded votes until all the bills have been debated, and then to vote on them at one time, cutting voting time on each bill to as little as five minutes. A bill that fails to pass under suspension of the rules may be considered later under the regular parliamentary rules used in the House. (See LEGISLATIVE PROCESS.)

In the late 1970s, after Republicans accused the Democrats of using the procedure for complex and controversial legislation, the House Democratic Caucus set guidelines for its use. Major legislation, however, is still passed under suspension, either because there is substantial bipartisan support for it or because an emergency situation warrants suspension.

In the Senate, motions to suspend the rules are rare because they are debatable and thus open to filibusters and other delaying tactics. The shortcut procedure also is considered an affront to the committee system. As in the House, a two-thirds vote is needed in the Senate to pass measures by this method.

# T

## Table, Motion to

Motions to table, or to "lay on the table," are used to block or kill amendments or other parliamentary questions. When approved, a tabling motion is considered the final disposition of that issue. One of the most widely used parliamentary procedures, the motion to table is not debatable, and adoption requires a simple majority vote.

Motions to table are used regularly with motions to reconsider. (See RECONSIDER, MOTION TO.) The tabling of a motion to reconsider makes final a previous legislative action, whether approval or rejection of a bill, amendment, or other parliamentary question. (See LEGISLATIVE PROCESS.)

Members of Congress often prefer procedural votes, particularly the motion to table, over direct votes for or against a substantive proposal. By voting to table, they can avoid being recorded directly on a controversial bill or politically sensitive issue. The motion to table often will win more support than a vote to defeat the issue.

Motions to table are not used when the House of Representatives considers bills in the COMMITTEE OF THE WHOLE; they are used only after the Committee of the Whole has been dissolved and the legislation returned to the full House.

In the Senate, tabling motions on amendments are effective devices to end debate.

## Taft, Robert A.

Robert A. Taft (1889–1953), an Ohio Republican, entered the Senate in 1939. A leader of the conservative wing of the Republican party, Taft generally opposed President Franklin D. Roosevelt's NEW DEAL programs. Before the Japanese attack on Pearl Harbor in 1941, he advocated "America first" isolationism.

Taft was extremely intelligent and hardworking, although he lacked charisma. In power and authority he was the leading Republican in the Senate from the 1940s to his death. Not until 1953, the year he died, however, did Taft officially lead his Senate colleagues as majority leader.

As the son of President William Howard Taft, Robert Taft was no stranger to politics. He practiced law in Cincinnati and in 1919 went to Paris to help Herbert Hoover (then head of the Food Administration) oversee the distribution of postwar aid to Europe. Shortly after his return, he entered the state legislature, where he stayed until he was elected to the U.S. Senate.

As a senator, Taft approved of only some elements of the New Deal, such as Social Security and public housing. He opposed generous farm subsidies and, until he reversed positions in 1946, federal involvement in education. Taft thought the power of organized labor had become excessive; in 1947 he cosponsored the Taft-Hartley Act, which restricted the right of unions to strike.

Taft felt that Europe's problems were its own and spoke out against the lend-lease program, through which the United States helped supply the Allies during World War II. He believed that the only organization capable of promoting world peace would be an international court buttressed by a body of strong international laws. He put little faith in the United Nations and objected to the North Atlantic Treaty Organization (NATO). He thought NATO would only antagonize the Soviet Union, which, he believed, had no interest in hegemony over western Europe.

Earnest and well-briefed, Taft earned the respect of his colleagues. His power was centered in the Senate Policy Committee, which he headed from its establishment in 1947. He was a candidate for the Republican presidential nomination in 1940, 1948, and 1952. In 1952 he lost to Dwight D. Eisenhower, to whom he gave his support (after Eisenhower agreed to some general conservative conditions) and his unconditional friendship.

## Tax and Tariff Powers

*See* PURSE, POWER OF.

## Taxation Committee, Joint

The principal function of the Joint Taxation Committee is to provide a neutral home for the nonpartisan tax experts who advise both the House Ways and Means and Senate Finance committees. The staff comprises more than sixty lawyers, economists, accountants, and other tax specialists. The joint committee of five senators and five representatives is headed by the chairs of the two tax panels, who rotate as chair and vice chair. (See FINANCE COMMITTEE, SENATE; WAYS AND MEANS COMMITTEE, HOUSE.)

Established in 1926, today the Joint Taxation Committee rarely meets. It has no legislative authority, but it does from time to time conduct investigations. One of the most notable was a probe of President Richard Nixon's taxes, undertaken at his request. The committee is also responsible for approving any tax refunds of more than $200,000, a task that involves committee staff reviewing decisions made by the Internal Revenue Service.

## Teapot Dome

Teapot Dome is the enduring legacy of Warren G. Harding's presidency, a code name for scandal in government. After the disclosures of a long congressional investigation, one member of the president's cabinet, Interior Secretary Albert B. Fall, went to prison for accepting bribes to lease government-owned oil land to favored persons. Teapot Dome was the most prominent of several shady activities that left a taint of corruption on the Harding administration.

The name Teapot Dome comes from a sandstone formation, faintly resembling a teapot, that rises above the plains of north-central Wyoming. Deep below the rock outcropping is a reservoir of oil in the shape of a dome. This underground oil and the land above it make up a tiny portion of the vast federal holdings in the West.

In 1915 President Woodrow Wilson assigned control of Teapot Dome to the Navy Department as a reserve source of fuel for U.S. warships. It was designated Reserve No. 3; two other oil sites, Elk Hills and Buena Vista in California, already had been selected as numbers 1 and 2. The U.S. Navy, spurred by the outbreak of World War I in Europe, was converting its fleet from the use of coal to oil. The nation's petroleum supply turned out to be far bigger than geologists had envisioned at the war's onset, and Teapot Dome did not have to be tapped.

Teapot Dome was coveted by America's fast-growing oil industry. The industry had strong support from western lawmakers who clung to the frontier belief in exploitation of natural resources. Fall, a rancher and lawyer who had represented New Mexico in the Senate, was outspoken in that view. As head of the Interior Department under Harding, Fall quickly won agreement to bring the naval reserve oil lands under the Interior Department's control. In 1922 the department leased the Elk Hills reserve to Edward L. Doheny of the Pan-American Petroleum and Transport Co., and the Teapot Dome reserve to Harry F. Sinclair's Mammoth Oil Co.

Pressure soon grew for a congressional investigation of the transactions. Tight Republican control blocked action in the House. But Senate Democrats and insurgent Republicans managed to push through a resolution that authorized the Senate Committee on Public Lands and Surveys (renamed Interior and Insular Affairs in 1948) to investigate the leases. The committee was headed by a series of Republican chairs, but a Democrat on the panel, Thomas J. Walsh of Montana, took charge of the inquiry.

When the hearings opened in October 1923, they concentrated at first on the legality of the two leases. Then Walsh learned that Fall had accepted bribes from Doheny and Sinclair. The committee's evidence revealed that Doheny had given Fall at least $100,000 and Sinclair had given the interior secretary at least $300,000. Fall, who had meanwhile resigned his cabinet post, protested that he had received only "gifts and loans."

Fall eventually was convicted of having accepted a bribe from Doheny in connection with the Elk Hills lease. However, in a separate trial Doheny was acquitted on charges of having made the bribe. Fall entered prison in June 1931 and served eleven months. Sinclair went to jail twice: first for three months for contempt of Congress over his refusal to answer questions, and then for six months for contempt of court for attempting to bribe a juror at his bribery trial. He ultimately was acquitted of those charges.

The memory of Teapot Dome lived on, a reminder of the potential for corruption in high places. "It is the dome we live under here at the Interior Department," Interior Secretary Stewart Udall told a congressional committee in 1967, assuring the panel that department officials recalled the lessons of the past.

---

# Television

Once Congress worried that live televised coverage of its daily proceedings would prompt grandstanding or erode the dignity of its operations. Now that televised floor coverage is commonplace, those fears have virtually disappeared. The gavel-to-gavel broadcasts of floor action have not caused significant changes in the way Congress works. For many members, television coverage has proven politically expedient, allowing them to gain public exposure when national and local news programs air excerpts from floor debates. The broadcasts are also convenient, allowing members to follow floor action from their offices or review a debate they missed.

The House was first to open its chamber to television, in 1979. The Senate held out against the television era until 1986. Even senators who once opposed television applauded the results a year later. "It seems to be an unalloyed success at this point. . . . Our fears were unfounded," said Sen. J. Bennett Johnston, a Louisiana Democrat who had been a vocal opponent. The Senate painted the walls of its chamber a new color after Kansas Republican Robert Dole complained that the old backdrop made senators on television "look like they're standing in split-pea soup."

Long before broadcasts of floor debate, television had captured dramatic events on Capitol Hill. Presidential STATE OF THE UNION messages were televised from the packed House chamber. Senate committee hearings were opened to cameras several times, enabling viewers to watch the KEFAUVER probe of organized crime and the Army-MCCARTHY investigation in the 1950s, testimony on the Vietnam War in the 1960s, and the hearings in the WATERGATE SCANDAL in 1973. The House banned cameras from committee sessions until 1970; in 1974 it won a large national audience for committee sessions on impeachment of President Richard Nixon. (See NIXON IMPEACHMENT EFFORT.)

Representatives and senators have learned to exploit television by consenting to interviews, appearing on news programs, and crafting "photo opportunities" with constituents. Legislators have used the press to lobby internally. "If you want to reach your colleagues, sometimes the best way is to let them see you on TV or read your name in the paper," said Thomas J. Downey, a Democratic representative from New York. Some legislators have even devised a video version of the press release, a prepackaged statement that can be shipped, or beamed via satellite, back to local stations.

Both the House and Senate have special studios, equipped with technicians and cameras, that legislators can use for interviews or statements. The studios cannot be used for political advertisements. The Democratic and Republican parties also operate separate Capitol Hill studios that legislators can use without restrictions; political campaign spots are often made there.

## Floor Proceedings

Recordings of House and Senate floor action are not edited. Each chamber does, however, keep close control over its broadcasts, using cameras owned by Congress and operated by congressional staff. The coverage provides only a limited view of floor action, usually focusing on the rostrum or on the member who is speaking. The cameras are operated by remote

*House proceedings have been televised since 1979, but the Senate did not allow television coverage until 1986 (pictured here).    Source: C-SPAN/ Nan M. Gibson*

control from basement studios beneath each chamber. Senators speak from their desks; representatives go to one of two lecterns in the House well or use the tables on each side of the central aisle. When votes are in progress, the cameras show the full chamber, with information about the vote superimposed on the screen. Recordings of House and Senate floor action cannot be used for political or commercial purposes.

Although networks and local television stations use excerpts from the recordings, the only gavel-to-gavel coverage is on a cable network, Cable Satellite Public Affairs Network (C-SPAN). In addition to its floor coverage, C-SPAN selectively broadcasts other major congressional events, such as committee hearings, press conferences, and the like.

### Entering the TV Era

The House first allowed cameras in its chamber in 1947 to record its opening session. For the next three decades television coverage was permitted only for special joint sessions. A key opponent of broadcasts was Speaker Sam RAYBURN, who in 1952 banned cameras even from House committee sessions, a dictum that later Speakers left in place.

Reforms of overall legislative procedure in 1970 included a new ruling that let each committee decide whether to televise its sessions. By the time Thomas P. O'NEILL, Jr., became Speaker in 1977, the House included a new generation of members who were comfortable with television and eager for coverage of floor debate. Members quickly agreed to a test of a closed-circuit system.

The 1977 test, which lasted seven months, was considered successful, and by a lopsided vote later that year the House endorsed gavel-to-gavel coverage. In 1978 the House agreed to let broadcasters tap into its audio system. By early 1979 the House had invested $1.2 million in modern cameras, microphones, and lighting. Efforts by the networks to win access to the chamber for their own cameras failed. The first live

House coverage occurred briefly on March 19, 1979. C-SPAN coverage began on April 3.

Controversy about the broadcasts has been rare. In 1984, however, O'Neill angered a group of militant House Republicans when he ordered cameras to pan the chamber, revealing to the television audience that the fiery Republican speakers were addressing an empty House. O'Neill could do this because House rules give the Speaker control of the broadcast system. Now cameras routinely show the House chamber during speeches made under SPECIAL ORDERS, a period at the end of each day's session when legislators may address the often-deserted chamber.

Television cameras were first allowed in the Senate chamber in December 1974, when Nelson A. Rockefeller was sworn in as vice president. In 1978 the Senate permitted radio broadcasts of its debate on the Panama Canal treaty.

Despite support from top Democratic and Republican leaders, the Senate spent several more years arguing about broadcasts. Opponents, who threatened to filibuster, argued that television would erode the Senate's historic role as the slower, more deliberative body. But proponents of television prevailed, and a two-month experiment began June 2, 1986. At the end of July, the Senate voted by a four-to-one margin to keep the television cameras rolling permanently.

---

## Terms and Sessions of Congress

The meetings of Congress are divided into two-year cycles embracing the two-year period for which representatives are elected. The system is based on constitutional requirements that members of the HOUSE OF REPRESENTATIVES must be elected "every second year" and that Congress must meet at least once each year.

A new term of Congress begins at noon on January 3 in odd-numbered years, following the election of representatives the previous November. The term expires, and the next term begins, on January 3 two years later. Each two-year term is known as a "Congress." The Congress that convened in January 1991 was the 102nd Congress because it was the 102nd to convene since the ratification of the Constitution. It lasted until January 3, 1993, when the 103rd Congress began.

Each Congress has two regular sessions. The first begins in January of the odd-numbered year, and members elected the previous November are sworn in at that time. Because they are elected for two-year terms, all representatives must be sworn in at the beginning of each new Congress. Senators are elected for staggered six-year terms, and only about a third of the SENATE is sworn in every two years. The second regular session of a Congress begins in January of the even-numbered year and may run until a new Congress takes office the following year. (See ADJOURNMENT.)

Bills introduced in the first year of a Congress remain alive until that Congress ends; legislative action carries over from session to session. Unfinished measures die at the end of a Congress and may be begun again in the next. (See LEGISLATIVE PROCESS.)

The modern schedule of terms and sessions was established in 1933 by the Twentieth Amendment to the Constitution. Until then members of Congress took office on March 4, and Congress met annually in December. When it met in December of an even-numbered year, following the election of its successor, it could remain in session until March 4 of the next year, when the term of the new Congress began. Members who had been defeated for reelection could vote in this short LAME-DUCK SESSION, which was characterized by filibusters and other efforts to stall legislative action.

The Twentieth Amendment, known as the LAME-DUCK AMENDMENT, established January 3 as the day on which the term of members of Congress would begin. It also provided that Congress should meet annually on January 3 "unless they shall by law appoint a different day." Congress frequently takes advantage of that option and convenes later in the month. The Twentieth Amendment failed to eliminate postelection sessions. Seven were held between 1948 and 1992. They were called either by Congress itself or by the president, who has authority under the Constitution to convene special sessions of Congress.

## Tie Votes

*See* VOTING IN CONGRESS.

## Treaty-Making Power

Under the Constitution, the president and the Senate share the power to make treaties with other countries. Although the precise division of labor is ambiguous, the treaty clause has been interpreted to give the president the sole authority to conduct negotiations with foreign governments on treaties and other international agreements. The Senate has the power to approve, amend, or reject treaties once they have been formally submitted to it by the president. The House of Representatives has no authority over treaties, although efforts are sometimes made there to block or change a treaty by withholding the funds needed to fulfill its terms.

The Senate's treaty powers have been a major source of congressional influence over foreign affairs. Beginning with the first treaty it approved—the Jay Treaty with Great Britain in 1795—the Senate has used its approval power to force changes in international agreements. On a few occasions the Senate has rejected major treaties. The most notable example was the 1919 Treaty of Versailles, which formally concluded World War I and established the League of Nations.

There has been ample evidence in recent decades that the Senate's treaty power continues to be a potent tool for affecting foreign policy. Members of the Senate participated directly in negotiations with Panama over conditions attached to the Panama Canal treaties in 1978. In 1988 the Senate held up approval of an arms control treaty until negotiators had clarified several issues. And in the late 1980s the House joined with the Senate in forcing continued U.S. compliance with two earlier arms agreements with the Soviet Union, even though one of them was not ratified.

### Ratification Process

Senate consideration of a treaty is open to presidential discretion at several points. The president may refuse to submit a treaty, may withdraw it after it has been submitted, or may refuse to ratify it even after the Senate has given its consent.

Once the president has submitted a treaty to the Senate, it remains before the Senate until it is approved or rejected or until the president requests its return and the Senate agrees to withdraw it. The Senate also may take the initiative to return a treaty to the president.

The Foreign Relations Committee has jurisdiction over all treaties, even if an agreement covers a subject that is not under the committee's usual jurisdiction. After treaties have been reported by the committee, they are considered by the full Senate.

Contrary to a widespread misconception, the Senate does not have the power under the Constitution to ratify treaties. Ratification means the formal acceptance of a treaty by the government and is a power of the president. But the Constitution provides that the president can take that step only with the approval of two-thirds of the senators present and voting. Technically speaking, what the Senate actually votes on is not the text of a treaty but rather a resolution approving ratification by the president.

Once approved by the Senate and ratified by the president, the terms of a treaty become the law of the land, as legally valid as any legislation.

Between the founding of the republic and mid-1992, the full Senate rejected outright only twenty treaties. The most recent was an agreement on international air traffic, which failed to win a two-thirds majority in 1983. The Senate also uses other means than rejection to thwart treaties. (See Appendix.)

Although there are no provisions in the Constitution pertaining to treaty amendments, the Senate has claimed the authority since 1795, when it consented to ratification of the Jay Treaty only on condition that an additional article be negotiated. Since then many treaties have been subjected to amendments, reservations, conditions, and qualifications, some of which have been added at the request of the president.

A Senate amendment to a treaty, if it is accepted by

the president and the other parties to the treaty, changes it for all parties. Instead of amending a treaty, the Senate may add a reservation, which limits only the treaty obligation of the United States. A reservation, however, may be so significant that the other parties to the treaty may file similar reservations or refuse to ratify the treaty.

In many cases the Senate adds relatively minor understandings, or subtle interpretations of treaty language, which usually do not significantly affect the substance of the treaty and do not require any additional negotiations with the other parties to the treaty. Sometimes declarations are attached; these are statements of intent or policy that are not directly related to provisions of the treaty itself.

Reservations, understandings, and declarations are used more frequently than amendments. But the differences among these various conditions have become blurred over the years. Amendments to a treaty automatically require the concurrence of the other parties to the accord if it is to take effect. But the substance of reservations and understandings dictates whether the conditions must be formally communicated to the other parties and whether they must be agreed to before the treaty can take effect.

The Senate's assertion of its treaty authority sometimes is criticized by those who see it as representing excessive interference in the president's foreign policy powers. Efforts have been made over the years to amend the Constitution to reduce the two-thirds vote required for ratification to a simple majority or to include the House in the ratification process. None of these attempts has succeeded.

In the 1950s Sen. John W. Bricker, an Ohio Republican, led an effort with the opposite aim: to curb the president's powers to make treaties and other international agreements. Bricker's proposed constitutional amendment would have provided that the provisions of a treaty or other international agreement take effect only when implemented through separate legislation passed by Congress. The amendment provoked heated debate during President Dwight D. Eisenhower's first term. A revised version, requiring congressional action on agreements other than treaties, was rejected by the Senate by a one-vote margin in 1954.

## History

The division of authority over treaties was a subject of considerable debate during the Constitutional Convention, but the delegates finally reached agreement. Spelling out presidential authority, Article II, Section 2, Clause 2 declares that the president "shall have Power, by and with the Advice and Consent of the Senate, to make Treaties, provided two-thirds of the Senators present concur."

The ambiguity of the compromise language set the stage for several disputes over the treaty-making authority. The Senate established almost immediately its authority to amend treaties. But was it entitled to offer the president advice during the course of treaty negotiations? Could the Senate initiate treaty talks? Did it have the right to confirm, and thus to some extent control, negotiators appointed by the president?

In general, these and similar issues have been resolved in favor of the president. The Senate's role is basically limited to considering treaties submitted by the president. However, twentieth-century presidents have often found it politically advisable to consult with key senators during the course of treaty negotiations to try to ensure that the prospective agreement has broad support in the Senate.

Disputes between the president and Congress over foreign policy issues are often played out during debates on treaties. Perhaps the most dramatic example was the Senate's rejection of the Treaty of Versailles, ending World War I. The treaty, worked out by President Woodrow Wilson and the leaders of the other nations that had defeated Germany, included provisions establishing a League of Nations for the resolution of international disputes. A faction of the Senate, led by Foreign Relations Committee chair Henry Cabot LODGE, a Massachusetts Republican, strongly opposed the part of the treaty providing for U.S. membership in the league. Lodge proposed "reservations" making clear that membership in the league would not lead to encroachment on the sovereignty of the United States or the powers of Congress. Wilson was adamantly opposed to any changes, however, and the failure of his administration to reach a compromise with key groups of senators led to the final defeat of the treaty.

# TREATIES KILLED BY THE SENATE

## (As of December 1992)

| Date of Vote | Country | Vote Yea-Nay | Subject |
|---|---|---|---|
| March 9, 1825 | Colombia | 0–40 | Suppression of African Slave Trade |
| June 11, 1836 | Switzerland | 14–23 | Personal and Property Rights |
| June 8, 1844 | Texas | 16–35 | Annexation |
| June 15, 1844 | German Zollverein | 26–18 | Reciprocity |
| May 31, 1860 | Mexico | 18–27 | Transit and Commercial Rights |
| June 27, 1860 | Spain | 26–17 | Cuban Claims Commission |
| April 13, 1869 | Great Britain | 1–54 | Arbitration of Claims |
| June 1, 1870 | Hawaii | 20–19 | Reciprocity |
| June 30, 1870 | Dominican Republic | 28–28 | Annexation |
| Jan. 29, 1885 | Nicaragua | 32–23 | Interoceanic Canal |
| April 20, 1886 | Mexico | 32–26 | Mining Claims |
| Aug. 21, 1888 | Great Britain | 27–30 | Fishing Rights |
| Feb. 1, 1889 | Great Britain | 15–38 | Extradition |
| May 5, 1897 | Great Britain | 43–26 | Arbitration |
| March 19, 1920 | Multilateral | 49–35 | Treaty of Versailles |
| Jan. 18, 1927 | Turkey | 50–34 | Commercial Rights |
| March 14, 1934 | Canada | 46–42 | St. Lawrence Seaway |
| Jan. 29, 1935 | Multilateral | 52–36 | World Court |
| May 26, 1960 | Multilateral | 49–30 | Law of the Sea Convention |
| March 8, 1983 | Multilateral | 50–42 | Montreal Aviation Protocol |

SOURCE: Compiled by Senate Historical Office from W. Stull Holt, *Treaties Defeated by the Senate* (Baltimore: Johns Hopkins University Press, 1933) and from *Senate Executive Journal.*

NOTE: A two-thirds majority vote is required for Senate consent to the ratification of treaties. In many cases, treaties were blocked in committee or withdrawn before ever coming to a vote in the Senate.

Partly as a result of the rejection of the Treaty of Versailles and partly because foreign affairs were becoming more complicated, presidents began to rely on the executive agreement to conduct business with other countries. Executive agreements are understandings with other countries that are not subject to Senate approval. Although most executive agreements cover routine matters, such as regulation of fishing rights, some have had an important impact on U.S. foreign policy. An example is the World War II summit agreements reached by Allied leaders at Cairo, Tehran, Yalta, and Potsdam.

Some lawmakers have been alarmed at the use of executive agreements, seeing them as presidential usurpation of the Senate's treaty power. However, the treaty power continues to play a significant role in major foreign policy issues, particularly in shaping the debate on arms control agreements.

### Additional Readings

Crabb, Cecil V., Jr., and Pat M. Holt. *Invitation to Struggle: Congress, the President, and Foreign Policy.* 4th ed. Washington, D.C.: CQ Press, 1991.

Fisher, Louis. *Constitutional Conflicts between Congress and the President.* Princeton, N.J.: Princeton University Press, 1985.

Johnson, Loch K. *The Making of International Agreements: Congress Confronts the Executive.* New York: New York University Press, 1984.

Margolis, Lawrence. *Executive Agreements and Presidential Power in Foreign Policy.* Westport, Conn.: Greenwood Press, 1986.

## Truman, Harry S.

Unpretentious and unassuming, Harry S. Truman (1884–1972) represented Missouri in the Senate from 1935 to 1945. Truman's diligence and honesty as the head of a Senate investigation of defense programs drew national attention and led to his selection as President Franklin D. Roosevelt's running mate in 1944. Truman had served as vice president for less than four months when Roosevelt died and Truman assumed the presidency.

Truman's career began in Missouri's local Democratic politics. After working for years as a farmer and serving in the military in World War I, Truman was elected to a county court judgeship. The job was nonjudicial; he was responsible for the maintenance of county roads and buildings. Truman owed his election in part to Kansas City's corrupt political machine, which was run by Thomas Pendergast. It was Pendergast who in 1934 persuaded Truman not to run for the House of Representatives but to try instead for a Senate seat. Pendergast's support was a mixed blessing. While it made Truman's political career possible, it also alienated many supporters.

After joining the Senate in 1935, Truman served on the Appropriations and Interstate Commerce committees and compiled a voting record supporting the NEW DEAL. In 1941 he traveled around the country to visit defense companies and concluded that there were abuses in defense contracting and in the location of defense plants. He succeeded in setting up the Senate Special Committee to Investigate the National Defense Program with himself as chair. Known as the Truman Committee, the panel set about uncovering and correcting waste and abuse in defense preparations for World War II. Truman's role on the commit-

*Sen. Harry S. Truman, center, meets with some of his colleagues in the early 1940s, just a few years before becoming president.*
Source: Library of Congress

tee earned him national prominence and the gratitude of Roosevelt. In later years Truman said he was genuinely surprised to be selected as Roosevelt's running mate in 1944.

Truman's experience as a senator and his native good sense and diligence helped ease his transition to the presidency when Roosevelt died in 1945. After finishing Roosevelt's term, Truman was elected to the presidency in his own right in 1948. As president he oversaw the use of the atomic bomb against the Japanese, the end of World War II, the Marshall Plan for postwar European recovery, and the establishment of the North Atlantic Treaty Organization. His domestic program followed the lines of the New Deal and was named the Fair Deal. Truman retired from public life in 1953 at the end of his first full term as president.

## Un-American Activities Committee

*See* INVESTIGATIONS.

## Unanimous Consent

Proceedings of the House and Senate and action on legislation often take place upon the unanimous consent of the chamber. A unanimous consent request, as its name implies, can be blocked by a single objection.

Unanimous consent is used in both chambers to expedite floor action. In the House, for example, noncontroversial bills on the CONSENT CALENDAR are considered and passed by unanimous consent. In the Senate almost anything can be done by unanimous consent. Besides considering noncontroversial matters by unanimous consent, the Senate also uses a complex device called a UNANIMOUS CONSENT AGREEMENT to govern the consideration of most major legislation.

Minor matters in both chambers are frequently handled by unanimous consent. A senator or representative will say, "I ask unanimous consent that . . ." and make a request. A legislator might ask to add additional material to the *Congressional Record,* or seek permission to have a staff aide on the floor during debate. Such requests are handled routinely, and objections are extremely rare.

## Unanimous Consent Agreement

The Senate has no procedure equivalent to the formal House rule that governs floor consideration of legislation, but senators often agree to restrict amendments, limit the time allowed for debate, and schedule votes for specific times. The device they use to expedite business is called a unanimous consent agreement. Senate leaders from both parties work out such agreements, which are then formally proposed on the Senate floor. Because a single objection from a senator can prevent unanimous consent, the leaders are careful to accommodate even minor objections. Once reached, an agreement is binding on senators unless it is changed by unanimous consent. For major legislation the details of a proposed agreement, which can be quite specific, are written and circulated to members in advance. (See LEADERSHIP; LEGISLATIVE PROCESS; RULE FOR HOUSE DEBATE.)

## Underwood, Oscar W.

Oscar W. Underwood (1862–1929), an Alabama Democrat, served in the House of Representatives from 1895 to 1915, except for one brief interlude in 1896–1897. In 1915 he moved to the Senate, where he served until 1927. Underwood benefited from a House revolt in 1910 against the autocratic rule of Speaker Joseph G. CANNON, an Illinois Republican. When rules changes weakened the Speaker's authority, Underwood became the de facto ruler of the House.

Underwood was practicing law in Birmingham, Alabama, when he first ran for the House in 1894. He won but served only until June 1896, when he was replaced by his opponent. Undaunted, he ran again that year and won.

Underwood's particular legislative interest was tariffs. The Underwood Tariff Act of 1913 reduced protective tariffs on most imported goods; it also established the modern income tax system.

In 1910, after years of suffering under Speaker

Cannon's despotic rule, a coalition of Democrats and Republicans changed House rules to strip the Speaker of much of his power. The elections of that year gave the Democrats a majority in the House. Anxious to organize into a voting bloc but unwilling to risk giving power to their own Speaker, the Democrats vested new authority in the chair of the Ways and Means Committee and in the majority leader. At the same time, they elected Underwood to both positions. (See WAYS AND MEANS COMMITTEE, HOUSE.)

As chair of Ways and Means, Underwood had the power to make committee assignments. He also con- trolled the Democratic caucus, which at that time had the power to tell members how to vote on the floor and in committee. The House Speaker, Missouri Dem- ocrat James B. "Champ" CLARK, was only a figure- head.

In the Senate, Underwood served as Democratic floor leader from 1921 to 1923. He resigned from the Senate after two terms. Twice, in 1912 and in 1924, Underwood was considered a candidate for the presi- dency. In 1924 he took a courageous stand against the popular Ku Klux Klan, a move that killed any presi- dential hopes he may have harbored.

# V

## Vandenberg, Arthur H.

Arthur H. Vandenberg (1884–1951) was a Republican senator from Michigan from 1928 until his death. Vandenberg was an isolationist turned internationalist, and his influential position in the Senate allowed him to play a critical role in the conduct of international relations in the years following World War II.

After a long career as editor of the Grand Rapids *Herald,* Vandenberg entered the Senate in 1928 to finish an unexpired term. He also was elected to a full term in the elections of the same year. In 1929, at the beginning of his first full term, Vandenberg joined the Senate Foreign Relations Committee. Vandenberg made his mark in the Senate as a member and later as chair of this committee.

Vandenberg supported ratification of the Treaty of Versailles and League of Nations covenant following World War I. Later he became an outspoken isolationist. During the 1930s he supported legislation that would keep the United States free of foreign entanglements. During World War II, however, Vandenberg underwent a dramatic change of heart, in part because of his distrust of the Soviet Union.

Vandenberg took part in the planning of the United Nations and was one of eight U.S. representatives at the San Francisco Conference that drafted the United Nations Charter. Later he played a critical role in planning and implementing the Marshall Plan (economic aid to war-torn European countries) and Truman Doctrine (aid to Turkey and Greece). He sponsored the Vandenberg Resolution of 1948, which formed the basis of U.S. participation in the North Atlantic Treaty Organization. A bipartisan spirit characterized all his efforts in the field of foreign affairs.

Vandenberg was a colorful and emotional speaker. He enjoyed the national attention paid to him in 1947–1949, when Republicans controlled the Senate

Sen. Arthur Vandenberg, right, in an informal moment, pauses with his friend Jim Preston.    Source: Library of Congress

and he became chair of the Foreign Relations Committee, as well as president pro tempore of the Senate. Vandenberg wielded an unusual amount of power in the largely ceremonial post of president pro tempore; he participated in planning the legislative program and involved himself in debate while he was presiding over the chamber.

## Veterans' Affairs Committees, House and Senate

Federal programs for veterans, ranging from health care to job counseling, are the responsibility of the House and Senate Veterans' Affairs committees. Both committees act within Congress as advocates of improved veterans' benefits.

The House committee, set up in 1946, has been dominated by conservative southerners, who have had close ties to traditional veterans' lobbying groups, such as the American Legion and Veterans of Foreign Wars. The Senate created its committee in 1971, bucking a movement to eliminate committees with narrow jurisdictions. Its leaders have been considered more sympathetic than their House counterparts toward Vietnam-era veterans. Despite budget constraints in the late 1980s, they were successful in passing several measures, including a new version of the education benefits under the GI Bill of Rights, first provided after World War II.

Texas Democrat Olin E. Teague, a decorated World War II veteran, spent almost two decades as chair of the House committee (1955–1973). His strong support of the military was typical of committee members. That approach continued under Mississippi Democrat G. V. "Sonny" Montgomery, who became chair in 1981. By the late 1980s, however, the committee had begun to shift its outlook, as younger members began questioning the panel's traditional orientation. At the same time the conflict between old-line veterans' lobbying groups and those representing Vietnam veterans had eased.

California Democrat Alan Cranston chaired the Senate committee from 1977 to 1981 and took over again from 1987 to 1993 when Democrats regained control of the Senate. More skeptical about expanding veterans' benefits was Wyoming Republican Alan Simpson, who led the committee until 1985, when he became the second-ranking Republican leader and, under his party's rules, had to give up the chairmanship. Democrat John D. Rockefeller IV, of West Virginia, became chair of the Senate panel in 1993.

## Vetoes

Perhaps the president's most potent power in dealing with Congress is the ability to veto legislation. A chief executive may use the veto as a negative weapon for blocking legislation he opposes, or he may use the threat of a veto to persuade Congress to approve the administration's legislative program or at least to compromise on key issues.

Article I, Section 7 of the Constitution requires the president to approve or disapprove all legislation passed by Congress. If the president opposes a bill, he vetoes it and returns the legislation to Congress, together with a message giving his reasons for disapproving it.

The president's veto power is not absolute. Article I, Section 7 gives Congress an opportunity to enact vetoed bills into law by repassing them by a two-thirds majority vote in each house. Congress, however, sustains far more vetoes than it overrides.

### Veto Procedure

After both houses of Congress have passed a bill in identical form, the measure is sent to the White House. The president has ten days, excluding Sundays, in which to sign or veto it; the ten-day period begins at midnight on the day the bill is received. If the president takes no action on the measure within ten days, and Congress is in session, the bill automatically becomes law without the president's signature. However, if Congress has already adjourned and the president does not sign it within the ten-day period, the measure is killed, or "pocket-vetoed."

The Constitution specifies that the president shall return a rejected bill along with his objections to the house that originated the legislation. There is no deadline by which Congress must try to override the veto. It may act at any time during the Congress in which the bill is vetoed. Override attempts usually are made within weeks or even days of the veto. If the LEADERSHIP decides Congress is unlikely to override the veto, it may decide not to schedule a vote. Or it may return the vetoed bill to the committee that had considered it. Occasionally, when the political climate is favorable, the committee will quickly draft a new version of the vetoed bill that satisfies the president's objections.

To override a veto, a quorum must be present, and the bill must be supported by two-thirds of the members voting in each chamber. If the first chamber to vote does not muster a two-thirds majority, the bill is dead and no further action is taken. If there is a two-thirds majority, the bill goes to the other chamber; a two-thirds vote there enacts the measure into law. (All LEGISLATION not enacted into law dies at the end of the Congress in which it was introduced.)

In the Senate, the question whether to override a presidential veto is debatable (and it may be filibustered, although this is rarely tried). A vetoed bill may not be amended. Only one vote to override is permitted. The Constitution requires recorded votes in each house on override attempts. (See VOTING IN CONGRESS.)

## Historical Use

In the early years of the nation, the veto was seldom used. Until the administration of Andrew Jackson, presidents usually vetoed bills only if they believed the legislation was unconstitutional or defective in some manner. Three of the first six presidents did not veto a single bill. That pattern changed under Jackson, who vetoed twelve bills, more than the combined total of all his predecessors. More important, Jackson was the first chief executive to use the veto as a political weapon to further his own legislative agenda and to kill bills he personally opposed.

After Jackson's administration, members of Congress saw the veto as a powerful weapon in the president's hands. The first attempt to impeach a president, John Tyler, resulted from his veto of a tariff bill. Proposals were introduced at the time to allow Congress to override vetoes by a simple majority rather than by a two-thirds vote. Nothing came of those attempts. President Andrew Johnson's post–Civil War struggle with the Radical Republicans in Congress led him to veto twenty-nine bills, a record up to that time. Congress responded with the first successful effort to override a veto on a major legislative issue.

President Grover Cleveland used the veto 584 times, a record that stood until the administration of Franklin D. Roosevelt. Many of Cleveland's vetoes were directed at preventing corruption that had mounted through the abuse of private pension bills.

Roosevelt vetoed 635 bills during his twelve years in office. All types of bills were targeted, including, for the first time, a revenue bill. Until that time it had been assumed that by precedent tax bills were immune from the presidential veto. Roosevelt dramatized his disapproval of one bill by personally delivering his veto message to a joint session of Congress.

## Recent Use

Every president since World War II has made extensive use of the veto power. President Harry S. TRUMAN used it effectively to protect organized labor until the Republicans took control of Congress in the late 1940s, making it likely that his vetoes would be overridden. Republican president Dwight D. Eisenhower used the veto to block or limit new social welfare programs promoted by the Democrats when they controlled Congress during his final six years in office. Eisenhower's threat to use the veto power was just as important as the veto itself in stopping legislation he opposed.

Presidents John F. KENNEDY and Lyndon B. JOHNSON vetoed few bills; Johnson in particular had a large Democratic majority in Congress that favored his activist legislative agenda. Republican presidents Richard NIXON and Gerald R. FORD, however, followed Eisenhower's example in frequently vetoing social programs passed by Democratic-controlled Congresses. One of Nixon's most controversial vetoes was the 1973 War Powers Resolution, which Congress passed near the end of the Vietnam War in an effort to limit the president's flexibility to commit U.S. forces in battle zones overseas without congressional approval. Nixon argued that the bill was unconstitutional, claiming it infringed upon the president's powers as commander in chief. But with Nixon weakened politically by an unpopular war and the Watergate scandal, the House and Senate were able to override his veto. (See WAR POWERS; WATERGATE SCANDAL.)

Ford's use of the veto demonstrated its effective-

# VETOES AND VETOES OVERRIDDEN, 1789–1992

| President | All bills vetoed | Regular vetoes | Pocket vetoes | Vetoes overridden |
|---|---|---|---|---|
| Washington | 2 | 2 | 0 | 0 |
| J. Adams | 0 | 0 | 0 | 0 |
| Jefferson | 0 | 0 | 0 | 0 |
| Madison | 7 | 5 | 2 | 0 |
| Monroe | 1 | 1 | 0 | 0 |
| J. Q. Adams | 0 | 0 | 0 | 0 |
| Jackson | 12 | 5 | 7 | 0 |
| Van Buren | 1 | 0 | 1 | 0 |
| W. H. Harrison | 0 | 0 | 0 | 0 |
| Tyler | 10 | 6 | 4 | 1 |
| Polk | 3 | 2 | 1 | 0 |
| Taylor | 0 | 0 | 0 | 0 |
| Fillmore | 0 | 0 | 0 | 0 |
| Pierce | 9 | 9 | 0 | 5 |
| Buchanan | 7 | 4 | 3 | 0 |
| Lincoln | 7 | 2 | 5 | 0 |
| A. Johnson | 29 | 21 | 8 | 15 |
| Grant | 93[1] | 45 | 48[1] | 4 |
| Hayes | 13 | 12 | 1 | 1 |
| Garfield | 0 | 0 | 0 | 0 |
| Arthur | 12 | 4 | 8 | 1 |
| Cleveland (first term) | 414 | 304 | 110 | 2 |
| B. Harrison | 44 | 19 | 25 | 1 |
| Cleveland (second term) | 170 | 42 | 128 | 5 |
| McKinley | 42 | 6 | 36 | 0 |
| T. Roosevelt | 82 | 42 | 40 | 1 |
| Taft | 39 | 30 | 9 | 1 |
| Wilson | 44 | 33 | 11 | 6 |
| Harding | 6 | 5 | 1 | 0 |
| Coolidge | 50 | 20 | 30 | 4 |
| Hoover | 37 | 21 | 16 | 3 |
| F. D. Roosevelt | 635 | 372 | 263 | 9 |
| Truman | 250 | 180 | 70 | 12 |
| Eisenhower | 181 | 73 | 108 | 2 |
| Kennedy | 21 | 12 | 9 | 0 |
| Johnson | 30 | 16 | 14 | 0 |
| Nixon | 43[2] | 26 | 17[2] | 7 |
| Ford | 66 | 48 | 18 | 12 |
| Carter | 31 | 13 | 18 | 2 |
| Reagan | 78 | 39 | 39 | 9 |
| Bush | 44[3] | 29 | 15 | 1 |

[1]Veto total listed for Grant does not include a pocket veto of a bill that apparently never was placed before him for his signature.

[2]Includes Nixon pocket veto of a bill during the 1970 congressional Christmas recess which was later ruled invalid by the District Court for the District of Columbia and the U.S. Court of Appeals for the District of Columbia.

[3]Bush's total number of vetoes, listed here as 44, is controversial. Two additional actions by Bush, involving the pocket-veto procedure, have been described as vetoes. Bush asserted that he had issued pocket vetoes of HJ Res 390, involving thrift bailout rules, on Aug. 16, 1989, and S 1176, involving a foundation named for former Rep. Morris K. Udall, on Dec. 20, 1991. The first came during a congressional recess and the second following adjournment of the first session of the 102nd Congress. Senate experts say Bush's claim that these measures were pocket vetoed would not stand constitutional scrutiny.

The Constitution's veto provisions and Supreme Court cases on the power have established for many constitutional scholars that a true pocket veto can occur only after final adjournment of a Congress and not during recesses or between first and second sessions if Congress has taken certain steps allowing it to receive any veto message the president might send. This view is widely held in Congress but has been challenged by a number of presidents, including Bush. On the two Bush actions in question, HJ Res 390 and S 1176, congressional leaders believe that the measures became law without the president's signature, as occurs under the Constitution if a president takes no action on legislation sent to him before Congress' final adjournment. The issue is further muddied in the case of S 1176 because Congress later repealed it with a new bill, S 2184, which Bush signed while at the same time asserting that although he agreed with the measure he did not accept the congressional disclaimer that S 2184 repealed S 1176.

*At a 1991 press conference House Democrats hold the veto pen—which they referred to as "President George Bush's domestic agenda."*   Source: R. Michael Jenkins

ness. Despite large Democratic gains in Congress in 1974 after Nixon's resignation, Ford was sustained on thirteen of the seventeen bills he vetoed in 1975. Another major bill was never sent to him because he had threatened to veto it.

Jimmy Carter was the first president since Truman to have a veto overridden by a Congress controlled by the president's own party. He suffered two such ignominious defeats in 1980.

Republican presidents Ronald Reagan and George Bush both used the veto and veto threat to great advantage. Faced with sizable Democratic majorities in both chambers, Bush made the veto and the veto threat the cornerstone of his legislative strategy. Bush was overridden only once, just before the end of the 1992 session, on a bill regulating cable television that was popular among consumers and both parties. Before that he had prevailed on thirty-five vetoes, often by shifting his position enough to win the support he needed. In 1991, for example, when recession deepened enough to make a second veto of extended unemployment benefits politically unwise, he negotiated a compromise.

## Importance of Veto Power

The veto is a powerful tool because most presidents most of the time can muster the necessary support to defeat override attempts in Congress. A president needs the support of only one-third plus one member in either house to sustain a veto. Those odds give the chief executive a great advantage. Even when Congress is controlled by the opposition political party, a president who mobilizes all the LOBBYING and public relations resources at his disposal usually can find the needed votes. President Woodrow Wilson once said the veto power made the president "a third branch of the legislature."

At each stage of the legislative process, senators and representatives, their staffs, and lobbyists for special interests must weigh the risk of a presidential veto if provisions opposed by the president are retained in legislation pending before Congress. Normally, most members of Congress would rather compromise with the president to gain his support than have a bill vetoed and face the task of trying to rally a two-thirds majority in each house to override the veto.

Decisions to veto legislation are scarcely made in a

vacuum. Presidents receive advice from all sides of the issue. In the end, a president's veto decision is a collective one involving the White House staff, the heads of interested federal departments, the director of the Office of Management and Budget, key legislators of the president's party in Congress—and, when their interests are seriously affected, state and local officials, special interest groups, and influential private citizens. Some presidential vetoes are cast on principle, because the legislation is diametrically opposed to the president's policies or political philosophy. Many others are close calls, in which the president and his advisers must balance the provisions of the bill they support against those they oppose.

## Congressional Leverage

The power to override is not the only leverage Congress can exert over presidential vetoes. Lawmakers have devised several ways to frustrate attempts by presidents to veto bills. The Senate often attaches riders to legislation regarded as essential or highly desirable by the White House, forcing the president to approve provisions he strongly opposes because they are part of bills he "must" sign. Essential legislation includes APPROPRIATIONS BILLS to maintain and run the federal departments, measures to raise the national DEBT LIMIT, AUTHORIZATION BILLS for programs or activities actively promoted by the president, and various emergency measures.

In the 1980s Congress relied heavily on the CONTINUING RESOLUTION. This is legislation incorporating many or all of the thirteen annual appropriations bills needed to run the federal government into one giant money bill, passed near the end of a session of Congress. The president must either sign the bill or, if he vetoes it, watch the U. S. government run out of money and be forced to shut down temporarily. In such situations Congress often can disregard many of the president's recommendations and enact much of its own spending agenda. In 1988 President Reagan used his State of the Union address to denounce such practices.

Congress occasionally uses the presidential veto as a foil for its own legislative goals. Particularly when the legislature is controlled by one party and the executive by the other, lawmakers who oppose the president may pass legislation with the expectation that it will be vetoed, or they may add amendments that they know will force the president to veto a particular bill. If it is an election year, they can then go home to their constituents and portray the president as heartless, indifferent, or out of touch with the public interest.

Presidents, of course, can do the same thing, by denouncing lawmakers or members of the opposition party as big spenders or the ones wanting to raise voters' taxes.

## Pocket Veto Dispute

If the president does not act on a bill within the ten-day period specified in the Constitution, and Congress has adjourned, the bill is pocket-vetoed. The measure dies because the president is prevented from returning the legislation to Congress so that lawmakers can consider the vetoed bill. James MADISON was the first president to pocket-veto a bill, in 1812.

The pocket-veto provision continues to raise controversy. Nowhere in the veto provision is the meaning of adjournment spelled out. Presidents have interpreted it loosely, as covering short recesses and interim adjournments within a session. Congress has applied a very narrow definition, so that the word means only the final adjournment of a two-year Congress.

In the twentieth century presidents routinely pocket-vetoed bills during congressional recesses and adjournments of varying lengths. The practice unleashed a major controversy in the late 1920s when President Calvin Coolidge's pocket veto of a bill during a four-month recess was challenged. The case went all the way to the Supreme Court, which decided in favor of the president. The Court at that time broadly interpreted the president's power, holding that the president could pocket-veto bills any time a congressional recess or adjournment prevented the return of a vetoed bill to Congress within the ten-day period specified in the Constitution. Another Supreme Court decision nine years later limited this interpretation somewhat, but the issue remained murky.

In the early 1970s the question came up again. A pocket-veto controversy between Nixon and the Congress in 1973 was decided by a U.S. court of appeals in favor of the lawmakers' position. The court ruled that Nixon had acted improperly in pocket-vetoing a bill during a six-day congressional recess. A second case decided by the same court in 1976 broadened the ruling to prohibit the president from pocket-vetoing a bill during adjournments between sessions of the same Congress.

Despite these rulings, the pocket veto remains a contentious issue between the executive and legislative branches. In 1981 and 1983 Reagan pocket-vetoed bills between the first and second sessions of the 97th and 98th congresses. In August 1985 a U.S. appeals court ruled that the president's veto between sessions of Congress was unconstitutional. Reagan was not prevented from returning the bill to Congress, the court ruled, because the House and Senate had appointed agents to receive the president's veto messages in the interim.

Bush challenged these rulings by pocket-vetoing measures while Congress was in recess. Congress has sometimes responded by passing compromise versions of the measures that include a repeal of the original legislation. Bush also claimed to have pocket-vetoed measures that he returned to Congress with a message explaining his objections. In those cases, Congress has responded as if the rejection were a direct veto. Congress still insists that a pocket veto is valid only when a Congress has adjourned *sine die*. It seems likely that a definitive ruling on the issue will have to await action by the Supreme Court.

### Line-Item Veto

Like many presidents before him, Bush asked that presidents be given a line-item veto over appropriations bills. A line-item veto would empower chief executives to reject the funding level approved by Congress for specific programs in an appropriations bill without being forced to veto the entire legislation. As in a regular veto, Congress could override the president's line-item veto by a two-thirds majority vote in each house.

Republicans, and some Democrats, contended that the president should be given the line-item veto as a tool to control the federal budget. They maintained that it would give presidents an effective way to eliminate wasteful pork-barrel spending projects that members slip into the yearly appropriations bills.

Opponents argued that the veto might usurp the powers of Congress and give presidents a club to use on members to pressure them to vote his way on legislation. They claimed it would also achieve limited fiscal results since some of the biggest federal spending would be beyond its reach, including programs for which spending was required by law. (See BUDGET PROCESS.)

In February 1992 the Senate rejected a Republican-sponsored amendment that would have given the president a line-item veto. A milder compromise was adopted by the House in October 1992, but it died when Congress adjourned.

In May 1993 the House passed a bill requiring (for a two-year test period) Congress to vote on proposals the president makes to rescind, or cancel, specific spending items in appropriations bills after he has signed the measures. Substitutes could be offered, but only if the president's proposal fails. The House bill then went to the Senate for consideration.

## Vice President

In addition to the role of presidential understudy, the vice president of the United States also serves as the president of the Senate. Because the framers of the Constitution gave the position no real authority and the Senate has been disinclined to delegate power to an outsider, it is for the most part a ceremonial position.

The vice president does not participate in debates, unless permitted by a majority of the Senate, and votes only to break a tie. It is rare to see a vice president presiding over the chamber; the job usually falls to the PRESIDENT PRO TEMPORE.

When the vice president presides, it is often by design. If close votes on administration bills are expected, the vice president is on hand to break the tie in favor of the president's position. The vice president occasionally uses the role of president of the Senate to issue parliamentary rulings that advance party floor strategy and to assist in the administration's legislative liaison efforts.

## Origins and Development

The framers of the Constitution decided to give the vice president the Senate position to provide a job for the runner-up in the electoral vote and to give the Senate an impartial presiding officer without depriving any state of one of its two votes. Some objections to this arrangement were raised when the proposal was debated at the Constitutional Convention. George Mason complained that "it mixed too much the Legislative and the Executive." Elbridge Gerry thought it tantamount to putting the president himself at the head of the Senate because of "the close intimacy that must subsist between the president and the vice president." But Roger Sherman pointed out that "if the Vice President were not to be President of the Senate, he would be without employment."

Although the framers solved the problem of a job for the runner-up, the vice president was powerless to supply effective legislative leadership. Precedent was set by the first vice president, John Adams. Although he was clearly in general agreement with the majority of the Senate during his term as vice president, Adams perceived his role as simply that of presiding officer and made little effort to guide Senate action.

His successor, Democratic-Republican Thomas Jefferson, could not have steered the Federalist-controlled Senate if he had wanted to, but he did make an important contribution by compiling a manual of parliamentary procedure. (See *JEFFERSON'S MANUAL*.)

The next vice president, Aaron Burr, was so impartial that he even cost the Jefferson administration a victory or two in the Senate.

There have been other vice presidents who were not content to sit on the sidelines. John C. CALHOUN, for example, was a commanding figure as vice president, and his influence was felt in the Senate before he resigned in 1832 to become a senator himself.

Examples in the twentieth century include Charles Dawes, Calvin Coolidge's vice president, who campaigned actively though unsuccessfully against Senate rules allowing the FILIBUSTER and often openly supported legislation opposed by Coolidge. John Nance Garner, a former Speaker of the House, helped win congressional votes for New Deal legislation in Franklin D. Roosevelt's first term, although the two became estranged when Garner opposed the pace and scope of later proposals.

The most blatant power play in recent times occurred when Lyndon B. JOHNSON, a legendary Senate majority leader, sought to preside over Senate Democratic caucus meetings even after he became John F. Kennedy's vice president. The proposal was rejected.

## Presiding Officers

Vice presidents have been given certain powers as presiding officers. For the most part, these powers can be overridden by the chamber. The duties include recognizing members seeking the floor; deciding points of order, subject to appeal to the full Senate; appointing senators to House-Senate conference committees (though the presiding officer usually appoints senators recommended by the floor manager of the bill); enforcing decorum; administering oaths; and appointing members to special committees.

Vice presidents occasionally become involved in parliamentary struggles while presiding over the Senate. In 1987, for example, Vice President George Bush became embroiled in a confrontation over an energy standards bill and some fairly obscure points of order under Senate rules. When the Democratic leadership began to take up the bill, which the Republicans hoped to delay, Bush rushed over from the White House to assist the Republican minority. After the Republicans had succeeded in their tactics to block immediate action, Bush was chastised by Senate majority leader Robert C. BYRD of West Virginia for a ruling that facilitated the delay. Bush insisted that he had done nothing wrong.

Ten years earlier, Byrd had delivered a similar rebuke to a vice president from his own party, Walter F. Mondale, who presided over the Senate in 1977 during a prolonged battle over natural gas legislation. In a stinging, lengthy public lecture to Mondale, Byrd upbraided the vice president for trying to recognize Carter administration allies ahead of Minority Leader Howard H. Baker, Jr., a Tennessee Republican. Byrd

*Although the vice president serves as president of the Senate, the position is largely ceremonial, especially during such major events as the State of the Union address, when the vice president sits next to the House Speaker and directly behind the president. Here President George Bush greets Speaker Tom Foley while Vice President Dan Quayle looks on.*
*Source: R. Michael Jenkins*

reminded the vice president in cold, clear terms that Senate custom dictated that party leaders always be recognized when they sought the floor. Less than two weeks later Mondale demonstrated how useful a vice president can be, when he and Byrd teamed up to bring to a halt a filibuster-by-amendment on that same gas bill. Mondale, reading from a typed script given him by Byrd, ruled a series of amendments out of order, while ignoring senators seeking to exercise their right to appeal his rulings.

### Tie Votes

The vice president's constitutional authority to vote in the Senate in the event of a tie is a rarely used power, but a vital one when administration proposals are at stake. (See Appendix.)

By the end of 1992, vice presidents had cast 223 votes in the Senate. Some of these votes were recorded against questions that would have failed even if the vice president had not voted, because a question on which the Senate is evenly divided auto-

matically dies. In such cases the vice president's negative vote is superfluous. Its only purpose is to make known the vice president's opposition to the proposal. There are no records available showing how many of the tie-breaking votes cast by vice presidents were in the affirmative and thus decisive.

One crucial vote by a vice president was cast in 1846 when George M. Dallas broke a tie in favor of a Polk administration bill for tariff reform. Among other important vice-presidential votes were two cast by Woodrow Wilson's vice president, Thomas R. Marshall, on foreign policy issues. In 1916 his vote carried an amendment on a bill pledging full independence to the Philippines by March 4, 1921. (The amendment later was modified in conference.) In 1919 Marshall cast the deciding vote to table a resolution calling for withdrawal of U.S. troops from Russia.

In the 1980s Bush used his vote to stave off attacks on Reagan administration defense programs, including chemical weapons, the MX missile, and the Strategic Defense Initiative. Altogether Bush was called upon seven times to break tie votes. Bush's vice president, Dan Quayle, never had to cast a tie-breaking vote.

### Legislative Liaison

Many vice presidents have been well suited to the job of lobbying on behalf of their administration's policies—and of carrying back to the president advice and information from members of Congress. As of 1993, thirty-two of forty-five vice presidents previously had served in either the House or Senate, or both.

Yet only in recent decades have vice presidents been formally assigned liaison duties. Earlier vice presidents were considered to be legislative officers who could not be assigned executive duties without violating the SEPARATION OF POWERS doctrine. This view was held as recently as the 1940s and 1950s, although vice presidents were used in behind-the-scenes lobbying efforts.

Mondale, operating out of offices in the Capitol and a Senate office building, proved to be an effective spokesperson for the Carter White House on numerous occasions, as did George Bush later for the Reagan administration. Both men served presidents who lacked legislative experience themselves.

### *Additional Readings*

Light, Paul C. *Vice-Presidential Power: Advice and Influence in the White House.* Baltimore: Johns Hopkins University Press, 1984.

Nelson, Michael. *A Heartbeat Away.* New York: Unwin Hyman, 1988.

---

## Voters and Congress

Members of Congress play a dual role. As legislators, they pass laws and oversee the federal government's implementation of laws. As representatives, they listen to the views of voters back home and give voice to those views in Washington.

Members have attempted to balance the needs of the country as a whole against local concerns since the First Congress in 1789. The job has become even more challenging as the country and its national government have grown. Serving in Congress has become a full-time, year-round job. Constituencies have grown in size, diversity, and sophistication.

The president, congressional leaders, and national lobbyists all compete to win the support of legislators. But the home constituents hold the ultimate power. By definition, senators and representatives are successful politicians whose skills brought them to Congress in the first place. Not surprisingly, most are adept at courting public favor in their home states and districts.

Legislators keep themselves before the voters' eyes by making frequent trips back home, helping constituents with particular problems, sending out newsletters, and keeping a high profile in the local news. Paying attention to the voters back home has become even more important as the grass-roots influence of the political parties has waned in the decades since World War II.

Members also defend their electoral bases by playing the time-honored game of PORK-BARREL POLITICS, the effort to obtain federal projects and grants to benefit the home state or district. In addition to doling out the public works projects and other benefits traditionally known as pork, Congress makes countless decisions that can help or hurt a member's constituents—from the closing of a military base to the inclusion of a particular provision in the tax code. Legislators often attempt to influence decisions in their constituents' favor, especially if the constituents are individuals, corporations, or institutions powerful enough to influence the outcome of an election.

It is difficult to tell where constituent service ends and campaigning begins. This is especially true for House members, whose two-year terms keep them on a perpetual quest for reelection. In spite of the heavy advantage that incumbents enjoyed during the 1980s, many House members felt anything but secure and campaigned continuously to keep their seats. This insecurity intensified in the early 1990s as a wave of anti-incumbent sentiment swept the nation. Only fifteen House members lost their seats in 1990, but many others saw their margins of victory shrink. In

1992 anti-incumbent sentiment was even stronger, and redistricting was also a factor. In that year a record number of House members retired rather than face election challenges. Only twenty-four House incumbents were defeated in 1992, but once again others won by smaller margins. (See REAPPORTIONMENT AND REDISTRICTING.)

At one time the six-year Senate term provided at least a modest shelter from outside pressures, allowing a senator to concentrate on national issues, free from political distractions, during the first part of his or her term. Although senators have had to wage longer, more grueling campaigns in recent years, most incumbents who ran for reelection in 1992 retained their seats despite public dissatisfaction with Congress.

Senate and House races have become intensely competitive and often enormously expensive. The struggle to raise funds continues throughout the tenure of many members, as they seek to pay off campaign debts or to amass a war chest for the next campaign.(See CAMPAIGN FINANCING.)

## Constituent Casework

Members court constituents by helping them deal with the federal government, an activity known as casework. Congressional caseworkers help constituents obtain Social Security and veterans' benefits, apply for passports and patents, interpret immigration laws, make unemployment claims, and resolve disputes with the Internal Revenue Service.

The number of services performed for constituents has skyrocketed as the federal government has expanded into many areas directly affecting the private lives of individuals. Most casework is handled by the lawmaker's STAFF; more and more of it is being done in district and state offices. Because of the volume of constituent problems, federal agencies and the military services have special liaison offices to assist members. The Veterans Administration, military services, and Office of Personnel Management maintain offices on Capitol Hill.

Many "cases" are simply requests for information about legislation, government programs and regulations, or tourist information about Washington, D.C. Schools and other organizations often ask for an American flag that has flown over the CAPITOL BUILDING. Many members willingly supply such flags, which are hoisted over the Capitol on a flagpole put up especially for this constituent service.

## Constituent Communications

Successful members of Congress communicate frequently and effectively with their constituents. They rely on constituent mail, surveys, polls, district office reports, and trips home to monitor voters' sentiments. They keep constituents informed about their activities through mass mailings, radio and television appearances, and meetings. These contacts are financed at least in part by special allowances to incumbent members of Congress. (See PAY AND PERQUISITES.)

At one time a single clerk could handle a member's mail, but mail now consumes a large share of congressional staff time. Despite the volume of mail, letters are an imprecise measure of voter sentiment, since few Americans ever write to their representatives and senators. Much legislative mail—along with telegrams and telephone calls—is inspired by pressure groups through well-organized grass-roots LOBBYING campaigns. (See Appendix.)

Outgoing mail also has mushroomed in recent years. One of members' most valuable perquisites is the FRANKING PRIVILEGE, which allows them to mail letters and packages under their signatures without being charged for postage. Members use the franking privilege to mail public documents, such as bill texts and committee reports, as well as copies of speeches and articles reprinted in the *Congressional Record.* Legislators also use the frank to send out newsletters, express concern about state and district problems, and ask for constituents' views on particular issues.

Controversy surrounding the frank led Congress to restrict the kinds of mail that can be sent out free and to prohibit mass mailings sixty days before elections. Despite these restrictions, there are more mailings in election years.

Effective members make good use of the news media to communicate with their constituents. The party organizations in the House and Senate operate radio and television facilities that members use to prepare programs for broadcast back home at a fraction of the cost of private taping facilities. Some members tape

*Walter Faulkner, candidate for election to the U.S. Congress, speaks to a farmer in Tennessee in 1938.*   Source: Library of Congress

periodic reports to constituents that are broadcast courtesy of local radio and television stations. Members often respond to breaking news by taping a short commentary that can be incorporated into local newscasts.

Most members and their staffs also go out of their way to accommodate the newspapers back home. Members cultivate good relations with Washington-based reporters for local papers, make themselves available for interviews, and offer reporters a steady stream of press releases touting their accomplishments in Congress.

Benefiting from the revolution in communications technology, senators and representatives use the computer, the fax machine, and sophisticated telephone services to stay in touch with constituents. Members use computers to print and address their mail and to target mailings to constituents who have indicated an interest in a particular issue. Members use fax ma-

chines and telephones to disseminate press releases and other materials.

High-tech communications aside, members know the importance of meeting with their constituents in person, both in Washington and back home. Most constituents who visit Capitol Hill are tourists hoping to pose for a photograph with their representative, shake hands, or perhaps receive passes to the House or Senate visitors' gallery. Members and their staffs usually are eager to welcome these visitors, aware that good impressions are remembered at election time.

But the number of constituents who visit Washington is limited, and a member of Congress must return home frequently to stay in touch. Only a few decades ago, most members remained in Washington for the duration of the legislative session. Jets now make it possible to go home every week, even when home is as far away as Hawaii. Most junior House members can be seen in their districts at least two weekends a month. Senators and representatives are permitted to take an unlimited number of trips home and to spend as much as they wish within their official expense accounts.

Legislative business is scheduled to accommodate members' travel. The House operates on a Tuesday-through-Thursday working week, allowing members to spend four-day "weekends" in their home districts. Frequent "district work periods" permit longer stays. The Senate, which previously had a four-day working week, established a new schedule in 1988 that generally called for three full five-day workweeks followed by one week off. The new schedule was designed to allow senators to plan for their visits home and to stay longer once they got there.

On trips home, members sandwich in speeches, civic meetings, ribbon cuttings, fund-raising events, district office hours, political consultations, coffee hours, breakfasts, luncheons, dinners, and picnics. While making the rounds, members are presenting what has been called their "home styles" to convince voters to trust them.

A classic example of "home style" is provided by former House Speaker Sam RAYBURN. A powerful Democrat who served as speaker during the 1940s and 1950s, Rayburn became a plain dirt farmer when he returned home to his east Texas district. His drawl thickened, his attire changed from a business suit to khakis and a slouch hat, and he traveled in an old pickup truck rather than a limousine.

Members maintain offices in their home districts or states and sometimes even have mobile offices to make themselves more accessible to voters. The offices are funded by members' allowances. With the aid of computers, legislators have been shifting some constituent services—such as answering letters and casework—away from Washington and back to their local offices.

### Additional Readings

Davidson, Roger H., and Walter J. Oleszek. *Congress and Its Members.* 4th ed. Washington, D.C.: CQ Press, 1993.

Dodd, Lawrence C., and Bruce I. Oppenheimer, eds. *Congress Reconsidered.* 5th ed. Washington, D.C.: CQ Press, 1993.

Fenno, Richard F., Jr. *Home Style: House Members in Their Districts.* Boston: Little, Brown, 1978.

Johannes, John R. *To Serve the People: Congress and Constituency Service.* Lincoln: University of Nebraska Press, 1984.

Miller, James A. *Running in Place: Inside the Senate.* New York: Simon and Schuster, 1986.

## Voting in Congress

Every law must be voted on by the House and Senate. Although many votes are taken informally, with verbal yeas and nays and no record of individual positions, senators and representatives cast formal floor votes at least several hundred times a year. On those votes, each individual position is recorded in the *CONGRESSIONAL RECORD.* Months and sometimes years of work in committees come to fruition, or fail, as the House and Senate vote.

The House and Senate have each developed their own procedures for voting. Guiding them in many cases are voting rules spelled out in the Constitution. Most specific are requirements for roll-call votes, or what the Constitution calls the "yeas and nays." One

rule is aimed at preventing secret ballots: "The yeas and nays of the members of either house on any question shall, at the desire of one fifth of those present, be entered on the Journal." For votes to override presidential vetoes, the Constitution is even more specific: "In all such cases the votes of both houses shall be determined by yeas and nays, and the names of persons voting for and against the bill shall be entered on the Journal."

The ritual of voting is interesting to watch even when the question is minor, and votes on major issues can be quite dramatic. When a vote is pending, buzzers are used to summon senators and representatives from their offices to the Capitol. (See LEGISLATIVE PROCESS.)

House members stream into their chamber through several different entrances. They pull from their pockets white plastic cards, which they insert into one of more than forty voting boxes mounted on the backs of chairs along the aisles. Each member punches a button to indicate his or her position, and a giant electronic board behind the Speaker's desk immediately flashes green for yes and red for no next to the member's name. For those who are more cautious, yellow signals a vote of present, usually changed later to reflect support or opposition. On close votes, tension builds as the fifteen minutes allowed for the vote run out. Boisterous members sometimes shout when the tally for their side hits the number needed for victory.

The House seems a bastion of high technology when compared with the Senate, where there is no electronic voting. When the Senate takes a roll-call vote, a clerk goes through the alphabet, reading each name aloud and pausing for an answer. Most senators miss the name call; when they enter the chamber, the clerk calls their name again, and they vote. On major questions the chamber fills with senators staying to hear the final result. Although party leaders keep a tally, the official vote is not announced until voting has been completed. In contrast to the rowdier House, the noise level is kept low by the gavel of the presiding officer, who must be able to hear the clerk and the senators' replies.

Voting has been a frequent target of reformers on

*Since 1973 the House has used an electronic voting system for recorded votes. Members insert plastic cards in voting boxes like the one shown. Their votes are displayed on a lighted board behind the Speaker's rostrum. Source: Warren K. Leffler, U.S. News & World Report*

Capitol Hill. In response to House members' complaints that all too often they must interrupt other business to come to the floor for votes, party leaders have tried to schedule several votes together and discourage members from seeking votes on unimportant questions, or those on which they have little chance of victory. Senators have had similar complaints about time-consuming votes, which often have taken more than the fifteen minutes set aside, because party leaders waited for late arrivals. In recent years the Senate leadership has tried to be stricter about keeping votes within the time limit.

Voting records are not a perfect measure of a member's politics. Controversial questions are often resolved without a clear vote. The language of AMEND- MENTS is often complicated, leaving members confused about what position to take. Local considerations can prompt a member to reject a bill that he or she supports philosophically. Party leaders sometimes intentionally avoid a vote to protect members from having to take an unpopular stand. As a result of these shortcomings, voting records are inevitably incomplete, but they are still the best available yardstick of members' views. The records also provide a way to measure how far Congress supports the president and whether parties or regions are voting together. (See CONSERVATIVE COALITION; EXECUTIVE BRANCH AND CONGRESS.)

### House Voting

Four types of votes are used regularly in the House. The vast majority of House votes are cast when the House sits as the COMMITTEE OF THE WHOLE, a type of session used often for amending legislation because rules governing it are less restrictive than those that apply to the full House.

#### Voice Vote

The quickest method of voting is by voice vote. Even on controversial questions, voice votes may be held first, followed by more elaborate voting methods. The presiding officer calls first for the ayes and then for the noes. A chorus of members shouts in response to each question. The chair determines the results. If the chair is in doubt, or if a single member requests a further test, a standing vote is in order.

#### Standing Vote

In a standing, or division, vote those in favor and then those opposed to the question stand while a head count is taken by the chair. Only the total vote on each side is recorded; no determination is made of how individual members voted. Few issues are resolved at this stage. If the issue was important enough for members to seek a standing vote, then the losing side, hoping to reverse the outcome, usually will ask for a recorded vote. The recorded vote draws many more members to the chamber.

### Recorded Vote

Recorded votes, which use the electronic voting system, make up the largest part of members' voting records. Members' votes are recorded individually as they insert their voting cards in the voting boxes in the chamber. A recorded vote may be ordered upon demand of one-fourth of a quorum (twenty-five) when the House is meeting as the Committee of the Whole. One-fifth of a quorum (forty-four) is required when the House is meeting in regular session.

Until 1971 votes in the Committee of the Whole were taken by methods that did not reveal the stands of individual members. Many questions were decided by teller votes; the chair appointed tellers representing opposite sides on a vote and directed members to pass between them up the center aisle to be counted—first the ayes, then the noes.

Only vote totals were announced on traditional teller votes, but the Legislative Reorganization Act of 1970 opened the way for "tellers with clerks," or recorded teller votes. This procedure, for the first time in the Committee of the Whole, made it possible to record the votes of individual members. After the electronic voting system was installed in 1973, the recorded teller vote became known simply as a recorded vote.

Old-style teller votes in which members walked by stations where the number for and against a question were counted were abolished in 1993 on the grounds that they wasted time.

### Yeas and Nays

Until the teller vote changes of the 1970s, yeas and nays were the only votes on which House members were individually recorded. Yeas and nays are ordered upon demand of one-fifth of those present, and they are not taken in the Committee of the Whole. The Constitution requires yea-and-nay votes on the question of overriding a veto.

Use of the electronic system has blurred the distinction between yeas and nays and other recorded votes. Before the electronic voting system was installed, yeas and nays were taken by calling the roll, a time-consuming process in the 435-member House; each roll call took about half an hour. The Speaker still retains the right to call the roll rather than use the electronic system. Also, the old-fashioned method is used when the electronic system breaks down, as it does from time to time.

During roll calls, members are required to vote yea or nay. Members who do not wish to vote may answer present. The Speaker's name is called only at the Speaker's request. The Speaker is required to vote only if that vote would be deciding.

### Senate Voting

Only two types of votes are in everyday use in the Senate: voice votes and roll-call votes. Standing, or division, votes are seldom employed. The Senate does not use the teller vote and has no electronic voting system.

As in the House, the most common method of deciding issues is by voice vote. The presiding officer determines the outcome.

To obtain a roll-call vote, the backing of one-fifth of the senators present on the floor is needed. Roll calls are required by the Constitution on attempts to override presidential vetoes; by tradition the Senate always uses roll calls when voting on treaties.

The Senate usually allows fifteen minutes for a roll-call vote, although UNANIMOUS CONSENT requests may shorten the voting time in specific situations.

### Pairs, House and Senate

Both the House and Senate permit their members to "pair" on recorded votes as a way of canceling out the effect of absences. A member who expects to be absent for a vote pairs off with another member, usually someone on the opposite side of the issue in question, and both agree not to vote. Pairs are voluntary, informal arrangements. They are not counted in tabulating the final results and have no official standing.

However, members pairing are identified in the *Congressional Record,* along with their positions on such votes, if known.

There are three types of pairs:

A *live pair* involves a member who is present for a vote and another who is absent. The member in attendance votes and then withdraws the vote, announcing that he or she has a live pair with a certain colleague and stating how the two members would have voted, one in favor, the other opposed. A live pair may affect the outcome of a closely contested vote, since it subtracts one yea or one nay vote from the final tally. A live pair may cover one or several specific issues.

A *general pair,* widely used in the House, does not entail any arrangement between two members and does not affect the vote. Members who expect to be absent notify the clerk that they wish to make a general pair. Each member then is paired with another desiring a pair, and their names are listed in the *Congressional Record.* The stands of members pairing are not identified.

A *specific pair* is similar to a general pair, except that the opposing stands of the two members are identified and printed in the *Record.*

### Informal Votes

Not all legislative or parliamentary questions are decided by formal votes. Uncontested bills, amendments, and motions, such as quorum calls, may be disposed of quickly if no one voices an objection. The terms used on the floor are "without objection" and "unanimous consent."

## War Powers

Article I, Section 8 of the Constitution assigns several different powers to Congress. Among these are the so-called war powers, which include the authority to declare war, raise and support an army, provide and maintain a navy, and make rules regulating the armed forces. At the same time, the Constitution in Article II, Section 2 designates the president to be the commander in chief of the military. How these powers of the legislative and executive branches mesh—or conflict—is the subject of a debate that dates back to the Constitutional Convention.

### Constitutional Background

During the drafting of the Constitution in Philadelphia in the summer of 1787, the framers debated whether to give the war-making power to Congress or the executive branch. Notes of the convention reflect how the framers struggled with the issue. At that time the war-making power in all other countries was vested in the executive. But the excesses of the British monarchy were still fresh in the delegates' minds, so they decided to split the responsibility. Congress was given the power to "declare" war, while the president was assigned the responsibility for conducting wars. James MADISON expressed the majority view at the Constitutional Convention when he said that government officials who wage wars are not the best judges of "whether a war ought to be commenced." The Convention delegates recognized, however, that if Congress declared war, the president as commander in chief should conduct it. The delegates agreed that the president should have the flexibility to repel an armed attack or a sudden invasion without first seeking a declaration of war from Congress.

### Congress's War Powers

Despite this explicit division of the powers to declare and conduct war, the roles of the legislative and executive branches have not evolved as the framers of the Constitution envisioned. Throughout history the chief executive has been the dominant force in decisions of war and peace, while Congress has played a secondary role.

Since the nation's founding, American armed forces have engaged in numerous major and minor conflicts overseas. Estimates of the number of times military forces have been used abroad vary, ranging from more than a hundred to several hundred. But Congress has formally declared war on only five occasions, and only once, in the War of 1812, did Congress debate the merits of committing the nation to war.

In the 1846 war with Mexico, and in the first and second world wars, the president committed the nation to war, and Congress merely ratified his decision. In the Spanish-American War in 1898, a strongly expansionist Congress forced a declaration of war on President William McKinley. Only with America's entry into World War II, in response to Japan's bombing of Pearl Harbor, could it be said that the president took military action in the face of a sudden armed attack on the United States.

In the Civil War, the Union insisted that it was putting down a rebellion in the southern states and, technically, not waging a war with the Confederacy. By that reasoning, a declaration of war could not be considered. No declaration was made or requested in the Naval War with France (1798–1800), the First Barbary War (1801–1805), the Second Barbary War (1815), or the various Mexican-American clashes of 1914–1917.

Similarly, in modern times there was no formal declaration of war in the full-scale wars in Korea in the 1950s and in Vietnam in the 1960s and 1970s. In a few instances, however, Congress passed a policy resolution supporting a presidential decision to use force. The Persian Gulf resolution of 1991, in which Congress supported the use of force if needed to oust Iraqi invading forces from Kuwait, was regarded by many as the functional equivalent of a declaration of war. There was no such consensus on claims by Lyndon Johnson's administration that a 1964 resolution, known as the Tonkin Gulf resolution, authorized the executive to wage war in Vietnam.

## Funding Powers

Besides its constitutional power to declare war, Congress also has the power to raise and support the armed forces of the United States. Through the use of its power of the purse, Congress provides appropriations to fund the military establishment. (See APPROPRIATIONS BILLS; PURSE, POWER OF.)

The funding power can be a potent weapon. Congress has used it to influence foreign policies dealing with, among other things, economic and military aid and arms control. For example, in the 1980s, over President Ronald Reagan's objections, Congress refused to continue funding the efforts by Nicaraguan rebels (known as "contras") to overthrow Nicaragua's leftist Sandinista government.

Congress has rarely used this power to shut off funds for ongoing military operations abroad. Despite congressional complaints in recent years that the president had committed U.S. forces to trouble spots overseas without consulting Congress, lawmakers repeatedly have refused to use their power over appropriations as a way of forcing the chief executive to reverse policy. Once U.S. forces are engaged in hostilities, the last thing members of Congress want to do is to expose themselves to accusations that they are jeopardizing national security or the lives of Americans. Even during the unpopular war in Vietnam, Congress repeatedly voted funds to carry on the fighting. Only after the United States had pulled out of Vietnam but was continuing to bomb Cambodia and Laos did Congress vote to bar funds for further combat activity in Indochina.

## Other Powers

Congress also retains authority to regulate the size and makeup of the armed forces. Through legislation it limits the number of personnel in the various military services.

The Constitution places an important qualification on the legislature's power to raise and support the armed forces. Congress is prohibited from appropriating such funds for more than two years, ensuring that its decisions will be debated and reviewed periodically. In actual practice, Congress today appropriates annually the money to maintain the armed forces.

## Presidential War Powers

Presidential assertion of the war power has drastically eroded Congress's prerogatives. Presidents have not hesitated to use their power as commander in chief to the fullest. Since the early days of the nation, presidents have sent armed forces into battle without first consulting Congress, much less asking for a declaration of war. Since World War II, presidential exercise of war powers has increased. In addition to the wars in Korea, Vietnam, and the Persian Gulf, the United States has been involved in lesser fights on land, sea, and in the air—none under a declaration of war. The list includes two Marine landings in Lebanon, air strikes against Libya, the taking of the island of Grenada, and the overthrow of the Manuel Noriega government in Panama. There have been harbor minings, Persian Gulf patrols, a blockade of Cuba, interdictions of shipping, seizures at sea, and combat in the sky. Beyond that were various surrogate wars fought with U.S. encouragement and equipment on three continents.

## Justifications for Actions

Presidents have justified their use of the armed forces abroad on a variety of grounds, including their position as commander in chief; their sworn duty to preserve, protect, and defend the Constitution; their responsibility to protect the United States against invasion or surprise attack and to protect American citizens and interests; and their claims to inherent and exclusive powers as the nation's chief executive.

The president's responsibility to defend the country and protect American citizens has been invoked to explain U.S. participation in wars and limited armed actions in which the United States was not threatened by imminent invasion or attack. The word *security* has acquired a much broader meaning than was understood by the framers of the Constitution. Modern

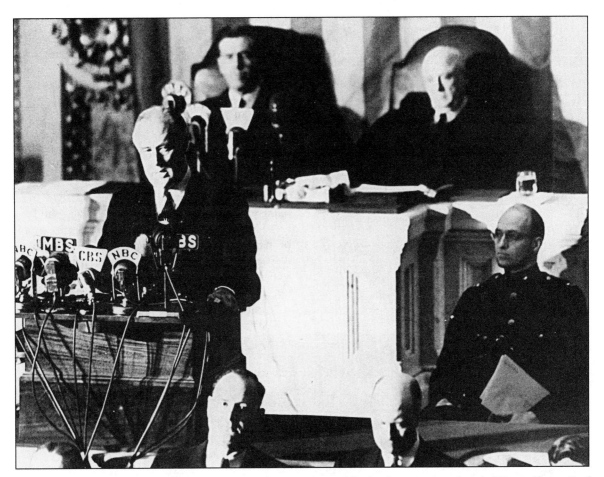

*President Franklin D. Roosevelt in 1941 asks Congress to declare war on Japan following the Japanese attack on the U.S. naval base at Pearl Harbor, Hawaii.* Source: Franklin D. Roosevelt Library

presidents have come to view major economic dislocations and international terrorism as posing as much of a threat to U.S. security as military attacks.

With a large standing military force, and an annual defense budget in the hundreds of billions of dollars, the president has been able to make military commitments without first requesting additional funds from Congress.

### Congressional Role

Congress itself has been a party to this expansion of the president's war powers. When U.S. troops entered combat in Korea and in Vietnam, Congress did not make a serious effort to debate the merits of declaring war or to encourage the president to seek its approval. In neither war did the chief executive acknowledge that a declaration of war was warranted or required by the Constitution. In Korea, U.S. troops were sent to battle under the auspices of the United Nations; in Vietnam, Congress approved the controversial Gulf of Tonkin Resolution, which President Lyndon B. JOHNSON later insisted was equivalent to a declaration of war. Congress repealed the resolution in 1970.

In addition to the Tonkin Resolution, Congress passed other joint resolutions authorizing or approv-

*One of the most controversial actions ever taken by Congress was its approval in August 1964 of the Gulf of Tonkin Resolution, which sanctioned President Lyndon Johnson's prior use of U.S. naval forces against North Vietnam. Here Johnson, right, talks with Senate leaders Mike Mansfield and Everett McKinley Dirksen.*

ing the president's determination to used armed forces as he deemed necessary to repel armed attacks or threats against certain nations or geographical areas, including Taiwan (Formosa), the Middle East, Cuba, and Berlin.

Congress also enacted numerous open-ended authorizations, as well as laws conferring emergency powers on the president.

## Changing World

Presidential war powers have also been enhanced by a rapidly changing world. The framers wrote the Constitution with a much different world in mind. In the eighteenth century, battles usually came only after formal declarations of war. For the most part, professional armies were affected, not the general population. War was clearly defined and separate from other forms of international relations. After 1945 the United States emerged as a superpower, with major and minor interests and commitments in every part of the world. In the prewar period, diplomacy and defense had been distinct and separate entities. In the postwar world, the military establishment began to play an integral, and at some levels even a dominant, role in the foreign policy process. The Cold War between Western and Soviet-bloc nations, involving a state of tension just short of armed conflict, helped to merge traditional foreign policy concerns and defense issues.

The decades following World War II brought a massive arms race, United Nations "police actions" and peacekeeping forces, worldwide terrorism, round-the-clock surveillance against Soviet nuclear attack, and sophisticated intelligence gathering. Such a state of defense preparedness blurred the distinction between war and peace and between foreign policy and domestic policy. Unlike the prewar period, the United States now had a large armed force, global treaty obligations, and numerous foreign assistance programs. One example of how these developments contributed to the erosion of Congress's war power is the network of military alliances that grew up to contain the Soviet Union. A provision of the treaty establishing the North Atlantic Treaty Organization stated that an attack on any member nation was considered an attack on all the members, committing the United States to war in the defense of all other member states.

In the nuclear age, the traditional view embodied in the Constitution—that Congress is in the best position to make decisions about war and peace—no longer seemed valid. As the framers of the Constitution saw it, the process of deciding whether to go to war would be carefully weighed and debated by Congress over days or perhaps even weeks. Such a procedure became obsolete. Through modern means of communications and transportation, and especially through military technology and the nature of modern warfare, the world became much smaller. Geographic remoteness no longer ensured security. If war became imminent, the decision of whether to counterattack with nuclear missiles might have to be made in a matter of minutes, possibly even seconds. There would be no time to consult Congress, and few members of Congress would insist on consultation in such a situation.

## 1973 War Powers Act

Efforts to redress the imbalance in war powers between the two branches began in the late 1960s as the Vietnam War was expanded despite repeated promises by both the Johnson and Nixon administrations to bring the conflict quickly to an end. At the height of U.S. involvement in the late 1960s, more than 500,000 U.S. troops were in Southeast Asia. As the fighting dragged on, the death tallies rose, and the antiwar movement gained momentum, members of Congress increasingly challenged the executive branch's prosecution of the war.

Frustrated by its ineffective role in the Indochina war, Congress in 1973 passed the War Powers Resolution over the veto of President Richard NIXON. Through this law, Congress sought to check the president's war-making powers. It required the president "in every possible instance" to consult Congress before committing U.S. forces to ongoing or imminent hostilities. If the president undertakes to commit military personnel to a combat situation, he must report to Congress on the action within forty-eight hours. U.S. forces must be withdrawn from such operations within sixty (sometimes ninety) days unless Congress declares war or otherwise authorizes the operation to continue, extends the withdrawal deadline, or is unable to act because of an armed attack on the United States.

Under the original law Congress could pass a concurrent resolution at any time directing the president to withdraw U.S. forces from a foreign mission. However, this use of a concurrent resolution, which does not require the signature of the president, became constitutionally suspect in 1983 when the Supreme Court declared the so-called LEGISLATIVE VETO unconstitutional.

## Presidential Opposition

As of mid-1993, every president has refused to acknowledge the constitutionality of the War Powers Resolution. Presidents have contended that no act of Congress can curtail or modify their constitutional powers as commander in chief to take such actions as they alone think necessary to protect national security or the lives of Americans.

Further—with one exception—each chief executive has been careful to avoid taking any action that implied Congress had the authority, under the act, to control or delay any military or quasi-military action taken by the president. The exception was in 1983, when Reagan reluctantly agreed to a compromise with Congress and signed into law a time limit for the deployment of U.S. marines in Lebanon. However, he insisted that the war powers act was not valid.

From the White House point of view, Congress has only one legitimate means of controlling the deployment of military forces overseas: by refusing to appropriate funds to support a foreign military operation.

## Congressional Disagreement

Congress itself is divided on the desirability and the constitutionality of the war powers act. There is disagreement about how much power and flexibility the president should have to run the military and defend the country.

Some members think the act has served as a restraint on the executive branch. Others say it is inadequate; they have proposed amendments to strengthen the congressional role in decisions to use force. Still others agree with many executive branch officials that the law is an unconstitutional and impractical restraint on the president.

The diverse views were apparent in the debate over Reagan's 1987 decision to provide U.S. Navy escorts for Kuwaiti-owned oil tankers in the Persian Gulf. Reagan had refused to invoke the war powers law when he adopted the policy, despite a series of armed confrontations with Iran. Attempts in the Senate to initiate war powers procedures failed in 1987 and 1988. A lawsuit to force the president to initiate the procedures, brought by 111 House members, was dismissed by the federal courts. Reagan thus was essentially free to commit the navy to the operation.

## Persian Gulf War

The lessons of Vietnam and the track record of the War Powers Resolution provided the backdrop for the 1990–1991 debate over the U.S. decision to go to war to end Iraq's occupation of Kuwait.

After several months of voicing concerns over congressional prerogatives but doing little about it, a divided Congress passed a joint resolution backing a presidential decision to go to war if necessary to oust the Iraqi army from Kuwait. Although this was not a formal declaration of war, it was the closest Congress had come to that step since World War II. Most legal experts agreed that the vote by Congress authorizing President George Bush to use force qualified as an exercise of its constitutional authority to "declare war."

But underlying much of the somber and historic debate was a sense that the legislative branch had acted too late to have any real choice except to back Bush in his showdown with Iraq. By the time Congress finally debated the authorization for war, months of feuding with the White House over the constitutional role of the two branches seemed beside the point.

Nonetheless, the broader dispute over constitutional powers lingered in a reference to the war powers act incorporated in the Persian Gulf resolution and in the president's signing statement. The legislation stated that the 1973 law granted Congress specific statutory authority for using force. Bush insisted that his request for congressional action and his signing of the Persian Gulf resolution did not constitute any change in the long-standing executive position on the president's constitutional authority to use U.S. forces to defend vital U.S. interests or the constitutionality of the war powers act.

## Politics of War Powers

The exercise of the war powers by the executive and legislative branches is governed by many factors besides the formal constitutional provisions. In the end, the effectiveness of Congress in exercising its powers, whether they are derived from the Constitution or from legislation, such as the war powers act and other laws, depends on political factors. When Congress favors presidential policies involving the deployment of forces abroad, there is little concern about constitutional or legal niceties. If there is substantial opposition by lawmakers, demands are quickly raised about the need to assert Congress's prerogatives.

Many factors may influence how and when the war power is used: the party composition of Congress; the influence, prestige, and popularity of the president; foreign policy successes and failures; the nature and length of a military operation; the views of U.S. allies; and international developments, among others.

## Alternatives to War Powers

In the absence of effective war powers, Congress has turned to various legislative actions as a way to participate in presidential decisions committing armed forces to combat. In very few instances has Congress actually tried to restrain or block such presidential decisions.

As one substitute for formal declarations of war, Congress has used policy resolutions to show its support for executive decisions either to send armed forces to foreign trouble spots or to commit forces to hostilities if U.S. allies or interests were attacked.

Presidents since World War II have often pointed to legislative actions by Congress as substitutes for declarations of war when it suited their purposes. Other congressional acts used by the Johnson and Nixon administrations to justify waging war in Southeast Asia included extension of the military draft and military appropriations bills during the war years.

Where there is strong disagreement with the president, Congress tends to adopt amendments limiting presidential actions, as it did in the 1980s when it barred U.S. aid to the Nicaraguan Contras. In the late 1960s, hearings on the Vietnam conflict conducted by the Senate Foreign Relations Committee helped galvanize opposition to the war. The Senate adopted a succession of antiwar amendments, but most were weakened by the House.

Through concurrent resolutions, Congress may express its sentiment on major foreign policy and defense issues. In 1969 the Senate adopted a resolution expressing the sense of the Senate that national commitments involving armed forces result only from actions taken by both the legislative and executive branches—through joint resolutions, for example. However, the House did not consider the measure, and it was not binding on the president. Nixon, in fact, ignored the resolution less than a year later when he ordered U.S. troops into Cambodia.

After the Vietnam War, Congress terminated several grants of emergency powers to the president that had been approved during the Depression, the Korean War, and other national crises.

Although the war power has lost much of its importance for Congress, this does not mean that the legislative branch has little or no voice in foreign policy. In many ways, Congress's influence has grown immensely since World War II. More than ever before in the nation's history, the making of foreign policy is shared by both branches. (See STRUCTURE AND POWERS; TREATY-MAKING POWER.)

### Additional Readings

Crabb, Cecil V., Jr., and Pat M. Holt. *Invitation to Struggle: Congress, the President, and Foreign Policy.* 4th ed. Washington, D.C.: CQ Press, 1991.

Reveley, W. Taylor III. *War Powers of the President and Congress: Who Holds the Arrows and Olive Branch?* Charlottesville: University Press of Virginia, 1981.

Smyrl, Marc E. *Conflict or Codetermination? Congress, the President, and the Power to Make War.* Cambridge, Mass.: Ballinger, 1988.

Wormuth, Francis D., and Edwin B. Firmage. *To Chain the Dog of War: The War Power of Congress in History and Law.* 2nd ed. Urbana: University of Illinois Press, 1989.

# Watergate Scandal

The word *Watergate* has a permanent place in the American political lexicon as the name of a tangle of scandals that destroyed the presidency of Richard NIXON and dwarfed all other scandals in U.S. political history.

The Watergate is a posh apartment-office complex in Washington, D.C., where the Democratic National Committee had its headquarters in the spring of 1972, as the presidential election of that year got under way. On June 17 there was a break-in at the Democrats' office, committed by five men connected to the Republican campaign committee. The break-in touched off the revelations of wrongdoing that toppled the Nixon administration and profoundly shook public confidence in government.

The break-in appeared insignificant at first. But the evidence of lawbreaking that emerged in the following months led directly to the White House, implicating the president himself. Facing impeachment charges in Congress, Nixon became the first president ever to resign from office. His departure from the White House on August 9, 1974, ended a constitutional crisis brought on by the president's defiance of Congress and the courts. (See IMPEACHMENT POWER.)

Nixon was spared the possibility of criminal prosecution when he received a pardon from his successor, Gerald R. FORD. But nearly a score of others in the government and in Nixon's 1972 reelection campaign, including several of his close associates, drew prison sentences. Still others paid fines or went to prison for Watergate-related activities, such as making illegal campaign contributions and attempting to sabotage Nixon's political "enemies."

### The Break-In

The break-in that set the scandal in motion took place at the Democrats' headquarters on the sixth floor of the Watergate building, not far from the White House. In the early morning hours of June 17, 1972, District of Columbia police caught and arrested five men who had forced their way into the office. The intruders wore surgical gloves and carried walkie-talkies and photographic and electronic eavesdropping equipment. It was later disclosed that, among other things, they intended to replace a faulty tap on the telephone of the Democratic party's national chair, Lawrence F. O'Brien. Later some insiders said they believed that the burglars were looking for information they suspected the Democrats might have gathered to embarrass Nixon during the campaign.

Four of the five burglars became known as "the

Cubans." They were Bernard L. Barker, Virgilio R. Gonzalez, Eugenio R. Martinez, and Frank Sturgis—all from Miami and identified with Cuban groups bitterly opposed to Fidel Castro. They had ties to the Central Intelligence Agency (CIA), as did the fifth man, James W. McCord, Jr. He had been a former agent of the CIA and the Federal Bureau of Investigation (FBI) before becoming director of security for the Committee for the Re-Election of the President, an organization sometimes known by the initials CRP or CREEP.

O'Brien called the break-in "an incredible act of political espionage" and on June 20 filed a $1 million civil lawsuit against the Nixon reelection committee. The suit eventually was settled out of court, but O'Brien did not accept the word of spokespersons for Nixon who insisted that the Republicans had had nothing to do with in the break-in. The day after the break-in, John N. Mitchell, a former attorney general in the Nixon administration who was now running the president's reelection campaign, stated flatly that "McCord and the other four men arrested in Democratic headquarters Saturday were not operating on our behalf or with our consent in the alleged bugging." Ronald L. Ziegler, the White House press secretary, characterized the break-in as a "third-rate burglary" and nothing more. Nixon reinforced that view at a news conference on June 22, saying: "This kind of activity . . . has no place in the electoral process. And, as Mr. Ziegler has stated, the White House has no involvement whatever in this particular incident."

Despite these denials, the top echelon at the White House was busy devising a cover-up strategy. White House aides pressured the CIA to ask the FBI to call off its investigation of the case by falsely warning that intelligence operations in Mexico would be jeopardized. The Watergate schemers feared, among other things, that money "laundered" through a Mexican bank to pay the burglars would be traced to its source, the Nixon campaign headquarters. All of this and much more came to light over the next two years.

Nixon's direct participation in the cover-up was not known with certainty until his final days in office. Once his denials had been refuted, his presidency was doomed. Until then, the Watergate drama was played

out in the courts, in congressional committees, in the headlines, and before the television cameras.

Without the aggressive reporting of several newspapers and magazines, the full story might never have come out. The *Washington Post* took the lead in breaching the administration's "stonewalling," as the Watergate principals called their concealment effort. The paper's reporting team of Carl Bernstein and Bob Woodward was especially adept at obtaining Watergate information from anonymous sources, including a celebrated executive branch official identified only as "Deep Throat." For its Watergate coverage, the *Post* endured the administration's wrath and won the Pulitzer Prize for "meritorious service."

During the summer of 1972, Rep. Wright Patman, a Texas Democrat who chaired the House Banking and Currency Committee, began inquiring into news reports of money laundering by the Nixon campaign. But the White House convinced friendly members of Patman's committee to abort his investigation. The public showed little interest in the allegations of scandal: Americans went to the polls on November 7 and reelected Nixon in a landslide.

### The Hearings and the Trial

But Watergate would not go away. At the beginning of the new 93rd Congress in January 1973, the Senate unanimously approved a resolution by Majority Leader Mike MANSFIELD, a Montana Democrat, to create a seven-member, bipartisan investigating committee. Called the Select Committee on Presidential Campaign Activities, it was generally known as the Watergate Committee. Its chair was Sam J. ERVIN, Jr., an elderly North Carolina Democrat serving out his last Senate term. Ervin, a former judge and a trial lawyer, became a folk hero when the committee's televised hearings displayed his courtly manners, wry humor, and penchant for quoting the Bible.

Also in January 1973, in a federal courtroom near the Capitol, the five break-in defendants and two others went on trial. The two added defendants were E. Howard Hunt and G. Gordon Liddy. Hunt was an ex-CIA agent and writer of spy novels who was then serving as a consultant to White House aide Charles W. Colson. Liddy was a former FBI agent who had subsequently worked for John D. Ehrlichman,

Nixon's chief domestic adviser, and then moved on to Nixon's reelection campaign—first under Mitchell and then under Maurice H. Stans, the former secretary of commerce, who was directing fund raising.

Liddy, Hunt, and McCord belonged to a secret White House group set up to take on administration projects that might require unorthodox tactics. They called themselves "the plumbers" because their original purpose had been to stop news leaks. Headed by White House aide Egil Krogh, Jr., the plumbers carried out numerous acts of political sabotage, including the Watergate break-in and another break-in the previous year at the office of a psychiatrist who had treated a man Nixon considered an enemy, Daniel Ellsberg. The plumbers were seeking derogatory information about Ellsberg, who had given the press the so-called Pentagon Papers, an official but hitherto secret study of U.S. involvement in the Vietnam War.

In federal court before Judge John J. Sirica, the Cubans and Hunt pleaded guilty. McCord and Liddy underwent a jury trial and were convicted January 30, 1973, on charges stemming from the break-in. Judge Sirica delayed sentencing until March 23, when he stunned the court by reading a letter from McCord saying that others had been involved in the break-in but that the defendants had been under political pressure to remain silent. Moreover, McCord wrote, perjury had been committed during the trial. McCord was intensely loyal to his former employer, the CIA, and expressed fear that the White House might try to portray the Watergate break-in as the agency's work.

During the trial Judge Sirica had often complained that he was not getting the full story about the case. Hoping to convince the defendants to tell more of what they knew to a sitting federal grand jury or to the Senate Watergate Committee, he provisionally handed out maximum terms of up to forty years. "Should you decide to speak freely," he said, "I would have to weigh that factor in appraising what sentence will be finally imposed."

McCord, whose sentencing was delayed indefinitely, told the Senate committee that Mitchell, Colson, John W. Dean III, and Jeb Stuart Magruder had known in advance about the break-in. Magruder was deputy director of the reelection committee; Dean was the White House counsel. Fearful of what lay

ahead, Dean and Magruder agreed to tell the committee what they knew in return for partial immunity ("use" immunity) from prosecution. Several other Watergate figures followed suit. Judge Sirica's pivotal role in unraveling the Watergate cover-up brought him prominence after an undistinguished earlier career. *Time* magazine selected him as its "man of the year" in 1973.

Nixon's problems continued to grow. At the Senate Judiciary Committee's confirmation hearings on the nomination of L. Patrick Gray as FBI director, Gray implicated several administration officials in the effort to thwart the FBI's investigation of Watergate. Gray's testimony doomed his nomination and prompted Ehrlichman to tell Dean, "Well, I think we ought to let him hang there. Let him twist slowly, slowly in the wind." Gray, abandoned by the White House, withdrew his nomination and resigned as acting FBI director in early April.

At a brief news conference on April 17, Nixon said he had begun "intensive new inquiries" into the Watergate affair "as a result of serious charges which came to my attention." On April 30, 1973, the president announced Dean's firing and the resignations of White House chief of staff H. R. Haldeman, chief domestic affairs adviser Ehrlichman, and Attorney General Richard G. Kleindienst. The last three, all implicated in the Watergate scandal through news leaks, said they could no longer carry out their duties amid the Watergate controversies. In a television address that night, Nixon took full responsibility for any improper activities in his 1972 presidential campaign. He pledged that justice would be pursued "fairly, fully, and impartially, no matter who is involved." The president named Elliot L. Richardson as the new attorney general, placing him in charge of the administration's own investigation and giving him authority to appoint a special prosecutor in the case. Richardson chose Archibald Cox, a Harvard law professor who had served as solicitor general under presidents John F. Kennedy and Lyndon B. Johnson.

The nationally televised Senate Watergate hearings opened on May 17, 1973, in the ornate Caucus Room of the Old Senate Office Building. The room had been the site of earlier famous hearings, including Sen. Joseph R. McCarthy's inquiries into alleged communist subversion in the early 1950s and the investigation of the Teapot Dome oil-leasing scandal of the Harding administration. McCord, the first witness, took the stand on May 18 and told of White House pressure on him to remain silent and plead guilty to break-in charges in return for a promise of executive clemency.

As the hearings continued throughout the summer and into the fall, the committee's ranking Republican, Sen. Howard H. BAKER, Jr., of Tennessee, asked repeatedly: "How much did the president know, and when did he know it?" Dean, who took the witness stand for five days beginning on June 25, became the first witness publicly to accuse the president of direct involvement in the cover-up. But it was Dean's word against the president's until tapes of some of the disputed conversations became available. In mid-July, the committee was startled to learn—almost by accident—that the president had secretly recorded many of the relevant Oval Office conversations.

### The Tapes

From that time on, the Watergate struggle focused on the investigators' attempts to gain control of the tapes and Nixon's claim that the doctrine of EXECUTIVE PRIVILEGE allowed him to withhold them. After Nixon had refused to obey subpoenas from Cox and the Watergate Committee to produce more of the tapes, Judge Sirica ruled on August 29, 1973, that the president should let him review them privately to decide whether the claim of executive privilege was justified. Nixon appealed, and while the case was on the way to the Supreme Court for a historic constitutional test, he offered to prepare summaries of nine tapes Cox sought and to let John C. STENNIS, a Mississippi Democrat and Senate elder known for his integrity, check their accuracy against the tapes themselves. Cox, in turn, would have to agree to request no more tapes.

When Cox rejected the deal, Nixon ordered Richardson to fire him. Richardson refused and resigned, as did deputy attorney general William D. Ruckelshaus. Robert H. Bork, elevated to the post of acting attorney general, complied with the order to fire Cox. This dramatic chain of events, announced on Saturday evening, October 20, 1973, quickly became known as "the Saturday night massacre." It provoked, in the words of the new White House chief of staff, Gen. Alexander M. Haig, Jr., "a firestorm" of public outrage. According to a Gallup poll, Nixon's popularity among the American people dropped to a low of 27 percent, a plunge of forty points during the year.

The nation's confidence in its president had also been damaged by the forced resignation of Vice President Spiro T. Agnew and by reports that Nixon had paid only nominal federal income taxes during most of his first term. He later settled the tax matter by paying $476,561 in back taxes and interest. Agnew resigned on October 10, 1973, and on the same day pleaded no contest to a charge of tax evasion. He was sentenced to three years of unsupervised probation and fined $10,000. The charge, which was the result of an investigation into Agnew's political activities as Baltimore County executive and Maryland governor, was not directly related to Watergate. But Agnew's downfall reflected on the president's judgment of people and the moral climate of the Nixon administration. Nixon named Ford, the House minority leader, as the new vice president. Ford was confirmed by the House and Senate without difficulty and sworn into office December 6, 1973.

### Impeachment Drive

Shaken by the erosion of his public support, Nixon on October 23, 1973, agreed to surrender the tapes to Judge Sirica for review. His reversal came too late; the NIXON IMPEACHMENT EFFORT had begun. That day forty-four Watergate bills were introduced in Congress, many of them calling for impeachment. Rep. Peter W. Rodino, Jr., a New Jersey Democrat who chaired the Judiciary Committee, said on October 24 that he would proceed "full steam ahead" with an impeachment investigation. With only four dissenting votes, the House on February 6, 1974, formally authorized the committee to investigate whether Nixon should be impeached.

In the meantime, Nixon's lawyers had told Judge Sirica that two long-sought tapes did not exist and that an eighteen-minute segment of conversation had been erased from another tape—eliminating evidence that was thought to be damning to Nixon. Leon Ja-

*The Senate Watergate Committee's televised hearings exposed a web of political scandals in the Nixon administration. The committee's chair was Sam J. Ervin, Jr., center. Left is Sen. Howard Baker, ranking Republican on the committee.* Source: Senate Historical Office

worski, a former president of the American Bar Association who had been named the new special prosecutor, demanded more tapes. Nixon refused to release them, and as Jaworski awaited a Supreme Court ruling on the tapes, his staff prepared evidence for the Watergate grand jury.

On March 1, 1974, the grand jury indicted Mitchell, Haldeman, Ehrlichman, and Colson for their roles in covering up the truth about the break-in. They were later convicted in federal district court and, after a long appeals process, went to prison. (At the time of the indictments, Mitchell and Stans were being tried in federal court in New York on charges of interfering with a government investigation of Robert L. Vesco, an international financier, in return for a

$200,000 contribution to the Nixon campaign. Mitchell and Stans were acquitted; Vesco fled the country and never was tried.) The same grand jury that indicted Mitchell, Haldeman, and Ehrlichman named Nixon a coconspirator but at Jaworski's request did not indict him. The prosecutor explained later that an indictment would have resulted in a trial interfering with and probably delaying the impeachment proceedings.

On April 30, 1974, hoping to end the dispute over the tapes, Nixon released heavily edited transcripts of forty-six tapes of Watergate discussions between himself and his advisers. The transcripts failed to satisfy the demands of Watergate investigators, but the unflattering details they revealed—Nixon's frequent use of obscenity, his suspicion of outsiders, his political cynicism—did him further damage.

Hours before the House Judiciary Committee began its public debate on impeachment, on July 24, 1974, the Supreme Court ruled unanimously against the president's refusal to submit sixty-four tapes to Judge Sirica. Three in particular contained incriminating material, but the White House did not release them until August 5—after the committee had voted on impeachment. The contents of the three tapes ended any remaining hopes Nixon and his few congressional supporters harbored of turning back the impeachment effort. Recorded on June 23, 1972, six days after the Watergate break-in, the tapes clearly contradicted the president's earlier claims that he was not involved in the cover-up.

On July 27, 29, and 30, the House Judiciary Committee approved three of five proposed articles of impeachment: for obstruction of justice, abuse of presidential power, and contempt of Congress. Ten of the seventeen Republicans on the thirty-eight-member committee voted against all five articles. But the release of the tapes on August 5 ended all doubt about Nixon's involvement, and each of the ten called for his resignation or impeachment.

The president chose resignation, which came on August 9 in a tearful, televised farewell at the White House. Nixon acknowledged no wrongdoing but attributed his departure to loss of political support in Congress. Ford immediately was sworn in as the nation's thirty-eighth president. In his brief inaugural address, Ford said: "My fellow Americans, our long national nightmare is over. Our Constitution works. Our great republic is a government of laws and not of men. Here, the people rule."

Most Americans shared Ford's sense of relief. But speculation and debate continued over whether Nixon would or should be indicted for his role in the Watergate cover-up. Ford put an end to that a month after the resignation, on September 8, when he granted Nixon a "full, free and absolute" pardon for federal offenses he may have committed during his presidency. Ford argued that Nixon had suffered enough, and that the pardon would spare the nation the painful spectacle of a former president brought to trial. The pardon set off a storm of controversy. Some critics charged that Ford had agreed to pardon Nixon in exchange for his resignation, an accusation that was never substantiated. Ford denied the accusation in an unprecedented appearance before the House Judiciary Committee.

Judge Sirica later lamented that while Nixon's associates went to prison, the former president "received a large government pension and retired to his lovely home in San Clemente [California]." The judge said he believed Nixon should have faced a criminal trial after his resignation and, if convicted by a jury, should have gone to prison.

Many of Nixon's Watergate associates did go to prison, but they spent relatively little time behind bars. Liddy served the longest term, fifty-two months. Several, including Liddy, were greeted on their release by lucrative contracts and a ready audience for their books and lectures. Others found new career opportunities in business and, in the case of Colson and Magruder, the ministry.

In retirement, Nixon wrote extensively about his years in office and about world affairs. But he never admitted that he had broken the law as president. In May 1977, in a television interview with David Frost, Nixon said: "I have let the American people down. And I have to carry that burden with me the rest of my life." Twenty years after the break-in, Sen. William S. Cohen of Maine, one of the Republicans on the House Judiciary Committee who had voted for impeachment, asked a question that continued to haunt many Americans: "Why didn't Nixon ever come before the American people, condemn the break-in, explain his involvement and ask to be forgiven?" Cohen said he believed that Nixon might well have saved his presidency with such a statement, even as late as the spring of 1974.

### Additional Readings

Kutler, Stanley. *The Wars of Watergate: The Last Crisis of Richard Nixon.* New York: Knopf, 1990.

Lukas, J. Anthony. *Nightmare: The Underside of the Nixon Years.* New York: Viking, 1976.

Schudson, Michael. *Watergate in American Memory.* New York: Basic Books, 1992.

White, Theodore. *Breach of Faith: The Fall of Richard Nixon.* New York: Atheneum, 1975.

Woodward, Bob, and Carl Bernstein. *All the President's Men.* New York: Simon and Schuster, 1974.

Woodward, Bob, and Carl Bernstein. *The Final Days.* New York: Simon and Schuster, 1976.

# Ways and Means Committee, House

The House Ways and Means Committee has a pivotal role in Congress. Charged with raising revenues to run the government, the committee is also responsible for disbursing more than 45 percent of the federal budget. The panel approves taxes and tariffs, and it also makes rules about public assistance, Social Security, health insurance, and unemployment compensation.

The importance of the Ways and Means Committee was somewhat reduced in the reforms of the 1970s, but it is still one of the most powerful committees in the House. (See REFORM, CONGRESSIONAL.) Because the House originates most tax legislation, the Ways and Means Committee usually sets the agenda; the Senate Finance Committee then reacts to House proposals. But sometimes a Senate plan prevails, as in 1990 when a "soak the rich" plan of the Ways and Means Committee that was vehemently opposed by President George Bush was superseded by the Senate's bill.

Made a permanent committee in 1802, the Ways and Means Committee handled all aspects of federal finances until the mid-1860s, when the Appropriations Committee was set up to oversee spending. At that time the Senate also split an appropriations panel away from the Finance Committee. After Social Security was set up in the 1930s, both taxing panels saw their plates fill with spending questions as Congress created welfare, health, and retirement programs financed by special federal levies. Funding of these programs has been kept separate from the regular appropriations process. (See APPROPRIATIONS COMMITTEE, HOUSE; APPROPRIATIONS COMMITTEE, SENATE; FINANCE COMMITTEE, SENATE.)

In the nineteenth century the Ways and Means Committee focused on tariffs. Its source of revenues in the twentieth century, however, has been taxes.

Congress has spent decades manipulating tax laws, with breaks and loopholes for an endless list of causes that range from oil production to home ownership. The tax code affects every business and individual; no lobbyist can afford not to know what the Ways and Means Committee is doing.

Dan Rostenkowski, a Chicago Democrat who entered the House in 1959, became chair of the Ways and Means Committee in 1981. His background as a skillful insider in House politics was expected to help bring the chaotic committee into line. His predecessor, Oregon Democrat Al Ullman (1914–1986), served as chair from 1974 to 1981. Ullman was more timid politically, and competing factions on the panel rarely worked in harmony during his chairmanship. But Rostenkowski's first major tax bill was rejected by the House, which instead took a substitute measure backed by President Ronald Reagan and House Republicans. That loss was eventually overshadowed by the 1986 tax reform bill, which Rostenkowski helped engineer. The measure eliminated many special tax breaks and lowered tax rates.

In the 103rd Congress (1993–1995) the Ways and Means Committee had thirty-eight members, only fourteen of them Republicans. That favorable ratio was a legacy of a Democratic caucus vote in 1974 to expand the committee, which previously had only twenty-five members split almost evenly between Democrats and Republicans. The smaller group had been cohesive, at least publicly, and had promoted its tax work as being too complex for outsiders to understand. Arkansas Democrat Wilbur D. MILLS, the committee's chair from 1957 to 1974, put a premium on consensus, keeping the members in closed meetings until they hashed out a bipartisan approach. An expert on the tax code, Mills was legendary for his successes on the House floor, where the united committee could resist major amendments to its tax bills. Rostenkowski resurrected the closed meetings in the mid-1980s, claiming that members worked better without public scrutiny.

Between 1910 and 1974 Democrats on the Ways and Means Committee had a special role in the party leadership. They were given responsibility for making Democratic committee assignments after a 1910 revolt by House members stripped that authority from the autocratic Speaker, Joseph G. CANNON. At the time, Majority Leader Oscar W. UNDERWOOD of Alabama was also chair of the tax-writing panel. Controlling committee assignments gave Democratic members of the Ways and Means Committee extra clout to win votes for tax bills and made them key players in House politics.

Later critics saw the House as a closed system, dominated by older, senior members. They wanted those making committee assignments to be more accountable to the party. In 1974 these reformers convinced Democrats to shift the task to the Democratic Steering and Policy Committee, a group of about thirty members, including top party leaders and a dozen members elected by region. (See LEADERSHIP.)

## Webster, Daniel

Daniel Webster (1782–1852) was a lawyer, a member of the House of Representatives and Senate, and twice secretary of state. Above all, however, he was an orator in an era of American politics when oratory was a high art. Webster used his skill as a debater to protect the commercial interests of his constituency, to benefit his legal clients, and to sway the emotions of crowds. He is best remembered for his eloquence when, putting aside special interests, he analyzed the nature of the Union and pleaded for its preservation in the years leading up to the Civil War.

Before entering the House of Representatives from his native state of New Hampshire in 1813, Webster practiced law, pamphleteering, and occasional oratory. Once in Congress, he spoke out against the War of 1812 and protective tariffs. He continued to practice law and was retained to plead before the Supreme Court in several well-known cases. He left the House in 1817 and moved to Boston to pursue his lucrative legal career. In 1823 he again entered the House as a Federalist, although this time as a representative from Boston. He remained a member of the Federalist party until 1845, when he became a Whig. In the House Webster continued his legal career and was made chair of the Judiciary Committee. Reflecting the com-

*Sen. Daniel Webster was a skilled orator in an era when oratory was a high art. The best known of his speeches was his 1830 reply to Sen. Robert Y. Hayne of South Carolina on the subject of nullification.*    Source: Library of Congress

mercial interests of his constituents, he supported protective tariffs and continued to do so throughout the remainder of his career.

In 1827 he entered the Senate, where he stayed until 1850, leaving to serve as secretary of state in 1841–1843 and again in 1850–1852. The best known of his speeches and an example of Webster at his finest was his 1830 reply to South Carolina senator Robert Y. HAYNE on the subject of nullification, or the right of a state to nullify an act of the federal government. Above all, Webster believed in the sanctity of the Union; he ended his oration with the words, "Liberty *and* Union, now and forever, one and inseparable!"

It was his belief in the importance of maintaining the union of states that led Webster to criticize both the South and the North on the issue of slavery. He angered both sides by urging compromise on the western expansion of slavery.

An extravagant man, Webster was often in financial difficulties despite his large legal fees. The Bank of the United States paid him a retainer while he was a senator, and eastern business interests supplemented his congressional salary to keep him in Washington. These financial arrangements did not enhance his reputation, but his devotion to the union of states and his extraordinary eloquence made him one of the most notable members in a Senate that also included Henry CLAY, John C. CALHOUN, and Thomas Hart BENTON.

---

## Wesberry v. Sanders

*See* REAPPORTIONMENT AND REDISTRICTING.

---

## Whips

*See* LEADERSHIP.

---

## White House

The White House, which rivals the U.S. Capitol for the distinction of being Washington's most revered building, serves three main functions. It is the president's home, the president's office, and one of the city's leading tourist attractions. About 1.5 million unofficial visitors a year tour the White House. Official guests at dinners and receptions swell the annual total of visitors by about 50,000.

The White House is the oldest public structure in the nation's capital; its cornerstone was laid in 1792. Called "the Palace" in the original plans, the building was designed by architect James Hoban and occupies a site chosen by George Washington.

Many persons viewing the White House for the first time express surprise at its relatively modest size. The main building, which is four stories high, is about 170 feet long and 85 feet wide. New space has been added over the years, including east and west terraces, the president's Oval Office (originally built in 1909 and moved to a different part of the West Wing twenty-five years later), the East Wing (1942), and a penthouse and a bomb shelter (1952). The colonnade at the east end of the White House is the public entrance for the daily tours of the public rooms on the main floor.

The public rooms shown to tour groups are all on the main floor. Each of the rooms is heavily used. Large receptions (and, during recent administrations, presidential news conferences as well) usually are held in the East Room. Dinners for visiting dignitaries are held in the State Dining Room at the opposite end of the building. Three smaller rooms lie between these two large chambers. The Blue Room is the scene of many diplomatic and social receptions, while the Red Room and the Green Room are used for private and semiofficial gatherings.

### Early Years

In November 1800, only four months before his single term in office ended, John Adams became the first president to live in the White House. His wife Abigail was not impressed by their new home. The place was "habitable," she wrote to her daughter in Massachusetts, but bells for summoning servants were "wholly wanting to assist us in this great castle." She also complained about the lack of warmth, noting that "wood is not to be had, because people cannot be found to cut and cart it!"

Fourteen years later, during the War of 1812, British troops set fire to the White House as well as to the Capitol. Only a torrential rainstorm saved both buildings from total ruin.

Among the items salvaged from the Executive Mansion by Dolley Madison, the wife of President James Madison, was the famed full-length portrait of George Washington by Gilbert Stuart. It is the only object known to have remained in the White House since the Adamses first occupied it.

Restoration of the White House, supervised by Hoban, took three years. To hide unsightly smoke stains, the exterior walls of gray stone were painted white. Even before then, however, the building had

*Called "the Palace" in the original plans, the White House was designed by architect James Hoban and occupies a site chosen by George Washington.    Source: Folio Inc.*

been known as the White House. Many years later, when President Theodore Roosevelt had it engraved upon his stationery, the name became official.

From the outside the main portion of the White House looks much the same today as it did when its first residents moved in. But the interior has undergone many changes. In 1817, for example, Hoban added twelve new fireplaces. Heating the high-ceilinged public rooms remained a problem even after the addition of a central heating system in 1853.

Plumbing was also a worry. It was not until 1833, during President Andrew Jackson's second term, that the White House was provided with running water. A zinc-lined bathtub was installed around 1855, but the White House still had only one full bathroom when President Benjamin Harrison was inaugurated in

1889. During his administration, the White House was first wired for electric lighting. This change, plus others in later years, meant that floors and walls were continually being pierced to accommodate new flues, pipes, and wires. All these "improvements" eventually took their toll on the structural stability of the aging building.

## Truman Restoration

Signs of serious trouble became impossible to ignore shortly after World War II. In late 1947 President Harry S. Truman became increasingly disturbed about vibrations in the floor of certain rooms of the White House family quarters. As a result, he ordered an engineering survey, whose findings led to follow-up studies of the condition of the entire building. The

White House was found to be in such precarious condition that it needed immediate and drastic renovation.

A complete restoration of the White House followed, lasting from late 1949 to early 1952. During that time, the Trumans lived at Blair House, just across Pennsylvania Avenue from the White House. In their absence the Executive Mansion's original exterior walls were given a new underpinning of concrete, and the interior was provided with new foundations, a two-story basement, and a steel frame.

President Truman visited the reconstructed White House on March 27, 1952, two days before announcing that he would not seek reelection. The building now had fifty-four rooms instead of the previous forty-eight. On arrival, the president was given a gold key, which he held aloft for reporters and onlookers to see before he turned to enter the house.

The furnishings of the White House have varied greatly over the years, reflecting shifting tastes in society at large. Even today, each presidential family may decorate the second- and third-floor private quarters as they wish.

Four rooms of the second-floor family quarters are worth special mention. The Yellow Oval Room, a formal drawing room with eighteenth-century French furniture, opens onto the Truman balcony (added in 1948). The view from there of the Washington Monument and the Jefferson Memorial is regarded as one of the city's finest prospects. Next to the Yellow Oval Room on the east is the Treaty Room, which was used for cabinet meetings until the Theodore Roosevelt administration. Farther to the east lie the Queen's Bedroom and the Lincoln Bedroom.

Other parts of the family quarters on the second and third floors of the White House were redecorated by President Ronald Reagan and his wife Nancy in 1981–1982. They raised nearly $1 million from friends and supporters to have the work done. The redecoration gave a lighter, more contemporary atmosphere to living spaces that some presidential families had found confining.

It is difficult nowadays to change the appearance of the public rooms on the main floor of the White House. These rooms have come to be regarded as al-

## VISITING THE WHITE HOUSE

The White House ranks high on the sightseeing lists of most visitors to Washington, D.C. A free, self-guided tour takes them through the public rooms on the main floor. Visitors are welcome Tuesday through Saturday, from 10 a.m. to noon.

The White House is also open for such tours on certain major public holidays, including Memorial Day and Labor Day. A special weekend garden tour is scheduled each fall and spring; dates vary.

The White House Visitor's Office uses a ticket system to minimize long lines and help visitors schedule their day's activities. On tour days, tickets for that day become available at 8 a.m. from a special kiosk on the Ellipse, the grassy area just south of the White House. Each person planning to join the tour must be present in order to receive a free entrance ticket. Each ticket is valid for a particular time that same morning; visitors need not show up at the White House until the time their visit is scheduled. The supply of tickets is limited, but for most of the year the 7,000 usually available each day are enough to accommodate visitors. However, during the crush of the summer tourist season, some ticket-seekers are turned away from the kiosk.

Another route to the White House requires advance planning. Most senators and representatives will arrange for their constituents to take part in special guided White House tours conducted before 10 a.m. Write your own senator or representative and request the tour on a specific date.

most a museum, especially since Jacqueline Kennedy, the wife of President John F. Kennedy, launched a campaign in the early 1960s to furnish them with authentic items from the late eighteenth and early nineteenth centuries. Any major alterations to the public rooms must now be approved by the Committee for the Preservation of the White House, established by executive order in 1964.

### White House Grounds

Presidents and their families have left their imprint on the White House grounds as well as on the building itself. It has long been customary, for example, for each president to plant at least one tree on the grounds. In the 1820s President John Quincy Adams hoped to make the grounds a living museum of native American plants, particularly trees.

One of the best-known landscaping features of the White House is the Rose Garden, which lies just beyond the French doors of the Oval Office. Roses were first planted there in 1913 by Ellen Wilson, President Woodrow Wilson's first wife. But the garden as it appears today dates from 1962 when, at the request of President Kennedy, the Rose Garden was redesigned by Rachel Lambert Mellon. The Rose Garden has been the setting for many official functions.

---

# Women in Congress

Women always have been underrepresented in Congress. Still, their numbers in the male-dominated Senate and House have grown slowly ever since Jeannette Rankin was elected in 1916 as a Republican representative from Montana. Her state gave women the vote before the Nineteenth Amendment to the Constitution was ratified in 1920, extending the franchise to all female citizens of the United States. (See WOMEN'S SUFFRAGE.)

Rebecca L. Felton, the first woman to serve in the Senate, did so for only one day. The Georgia Democrat, appointed in 1922 to fill a vacancy, stepped aside one day after she was sworn in to make way for a man who had been elected to fill the vacancy.

More than seventy-five years after Rankin took

her seat in the House, the 102nd Congress (1991–1993) included only twenty-eight female representatives and two senators.

Although women remained underrepresented, 1992 was a banner year in which record numbers of women ran for and were elected to Congress. The 103rd Congress, which opened in 1993, included forty-seven women in the House, an increase of nineteen, and six in the Senate, an increase of four. In addition, Democrat Eleanor Holmes Norton was elected to a second term as delegate from the District of Columbia. (See DELEGATES.)

Several factors contributed to the success of women candidates in 1992. Many capitalized on an unusually large number of retirements to run in open seats. They also benefited from reapportionment, which created dozens of opportunities for newcomers in the South and West. Another factor was public dissatisfaction with Congress, which allowed women to portray themselves positively as outsiders. The 1991 confirmation hearings of Supreme Court nominee Clarence Thomas also had an impact. The televised image of an all-male Senate Judiciary panel sharply questioning a woman, law professor Anita F. Hill, about sexual harassment charges she had made against Thomas brought home dramatically to many women their lack of representation in Congress. (See APPOINTMENT POWER.)

Despite their record gains in 1992, women still made up only about 10 percent of the Congress, even though they accounted for more than half of the U.S. population. (See Appendix.)

Many women got their start in Congress by way of the "widow's mandate." According to this custom, widows were appointed to replace their husbands who had died in office. This practice allowed state leaders extra time to choose a successor or hold a special election. Sometimes a widow was chosen by her late husband's party to run for his seat on the theory that a strong sympathy vote would sweep her into office.

Whatever the motive, the widow's mandate marked the beginning of long careers in Congress for several women. Margaret Chase SMITH, a Maine Republican, filled her late husband's House seat after his death in 1940 and then went on to serve four terms

*These seven women were members of the 71st Congress (1929–1931).*
*Source: Library of Congress*

*One month after their 1992 victory, these Democratic House members conferred before a press conference. From left, Pat Danner, Elizabeth Furse, Karen Shepherd, Lynn Schenk, and Marjorie Margolies-Mezvinsky.*
*Source: R. Michael Jenkins*

## NUMBER OF WOMEN MEMBERS IN CONGRESS

Listed here in reverse chronological order by Congress is the number of women members of the Senate and House of Representatives in each Congress from the 103rd back to the 80th. The figures include women appointed to office as well as those chosen by voters in general elections and special elections. (See Appendix.)

| Congress | Senate | House |
|---|---|---|
| 103rd (1993*–) | 7 | 47 |
| 102nd (1991–1993) | 2 | 28 |
| 101st (1989–1991) | 2 | 28 |
| 100th (1987–1989) | 2 | 23 |
| 99th (1985–1987) | 2 | 23 |
| 98th (1983–1985) | 2 | 22 |
| 97th (1981–1983) | 2 | 21 |
| 96th (1979–1981) | 1 | 16 |
| 95th (1977–1979) | 1 | 8 |
| 94th (1975–1977) | 0 | 19 |
| 93rd (1973–1975) | 0 | 16 |
| 92nd (1971–1973) | 2 | 13 |
| 91st (1969–1971) | 1 | 10 |
| 90th (1967–1969) | 1 | 11 |
| 89th (1965–1967) | 2 | 10 |
| 88th (1963–1965) | 2 | 11 |
| 87th (1961–1963) | 2 | 17 |
| 86th (1959–1961) | 1 | 16 |
| 85th (1957–1959) | 1 | 15 |
| 84th (1955–1957) | 1 | 16 |
| 83rd (1953–1955) | 3 | 12 |
| 82nd (1951–1953) | 1 | 10 |
| 81st (1949–1951) | 1 | 9 |
| 80th (1947–1949) | 1 | 7 |

* as of June 1993

in the Senate. Edith Nourse Rogers, a Massachusetts Republican, entered the House after her husband's death in 1925 and remained there for thirty-five years, until her own death in 1960. Hattie W. Caraway, an Arkansas Democrat, took her late husband's Senate seat after his death in 1931 and continued to serve until 1945. Democrat Corinne "Lindy" Boggs of Louisiana, widow of House Democratic leader Thomas Hale Boggs, took over her late husband's seat in 1973 and held it until she retired in 1991.

The tradition of the widow's mandate faded as women became more active in politics. Of the fifty-three women elected in 1992, only one, Democrat Cardiss Collins of Illinois, had entered Congress to replace a husband. Collins took over the House seat of her late husband, George Washington Collins, in 1973.

In 1978 Republican Nancy Landon Kassebaum of Kansas became the first woman ever elected to the Senate without being preceded by her husband. She and Democrat Barbara Mikulski of Maryland, elected to the Senate in 1987, were joined in 1993 by four new women for a record total of six women senators. Two, Barbara Boxer and Dianne Feinstein, were from California, making their state the first to send two women to the Senate at one time. Another, Democrat Carol Moseley-Braun of Illinois, was the first African American woman elected to the Senate.

The backgrounds of the women elected to Congress in 1992 reflected several decades of advances for women in politics and government. Democrat Patty Murray of Washington, the fourth of the new female senators, called herself "a mom in tennis shoes," but she had served for four years on a school board and for four years in her state's senate. Democrat Corrine Brown of Florida, one of nine African American women elected to Congress in 1992, had been a member of the Florida legislature for almost a decade.

Most of the other women elected in 1992 had similar experience in state legislatures, city councils, and other local government positions. One who did not was Democrat Blanche Lambert of Arkansas, who had worked as a receptionist for Rep. Bill Alexander and defeated her twelve-term former boss in the Democratic primary.

As of 1992 no woman had chaired a standing committee in either chamber since Rep. Leonor K. Sullivan, a Missouri Democrat, headed the Merchant Marine and Fisheries Committee from 1973 to 1977. Mae Ella Nolan, a California Republican who served from 1923 to 1925, was the first woman to chair a congressional committee; she headed the House Committee on Expenditures in the Post Office Department.

Congress has been an important starting point for women seeking national office. Shirley Chisholm, a Democratic representative from New York, ran for president in 1972, and Geraldine Ferraro, another New York Democrat who served in the House, was her party's vice-presidential nominee in 1984.

## Women's Suffrage

Although several states gave women the right to vote in the nineteenth century, full voting rights were not extended to all American women until 1920, when the Nineteenth Amendment to the Constitution was ratified. That year, for the first time, women in every state had the right to participate in the November election.

The amendment states: "The right of citizens of the United States to vote shall not be denied or abridged by the United States or by any State on account of sex."

The decades-long effort for women's suffrage was under way as early as the 1830s. Women working to abolish slavery were struck by the similarity of their lot, under law, to that of slaves. A key event was the 1848 Women's Rights Convention at Seneca Falls, New York, where women passed a Declaration of Principles, a broad manifesto that included a call for the vote.

After the Civil War, some women contended they were granted equal rights, including voting privileges, by the Fourteenth Amendment, which freed slaves. Susan B. Anthony urged women to claim their right to vote at the polls; she did so in Rochester, New York, in 1872. Anthony was arrested and later convicted of

*For decades before passage of the Nineteenth Amendment in 1920, suffragettes battled to win the right to vote, even when it meant picketing the White House in the cold.    Source: Library of Congress*

"voting without having a lawful right to vote." Anthony and her followers pressed Congress for a constitutional amendment granting the franchise to women, but in 1887 the Senate rejected the proposal, 16–34.

The suffragists then turned to the states, where they were more successful. By the turn of the century, four western states had extended the franchise to women: Wyoming, Colorado, Utah, and Idaho. Then, as the Progressive movement gained influence, additional states gave women the vote: Washington in 1910; California in 1911; Arizona, Kansas, and Oregon in 1912; Montana and Nevada in 1914; New York in 1917; and Michigan, South Dakota, and Oklahoma in 1918. (See PROGRESSIVE ERA.)

Arguments for and against the vote included extravagant claims; some said women's enfranchisement would end corruption in American politics, while others cautioned that it would lead to free love. By 1914 some advocates of women's suffrage, led by Alice Paul, were using more militant tactics. They opposed every Democratic candidate in the eleven states where women could vote, regardless of the candidate's position on women's suffrage. They reasoned that the majority party should be held responsible for the failure of Congress to endorse a constitutional amendment. More than half of the forty-three Democrats running in those states were defeated.

Many suffragists saw President Woodrow Wilson as a major obstacle to their movement. Wilson, who endorsed women's suffrage, preferred to let the states handle voting qualifications and opposed a constitutional amendment. Women responded by demonstrating in Washington, and thousands were arrested and jailed.

In January 1918 Wilson finally announced his support for the proposed amendment. The House agreed the next day. Only after a new Congress met in 1919, however, did the Senate join the House in mustering the two-thirds majority required to send the amendment to the states for ratification. The amendment took effect in August 1920, when three-fourths of the states consented to ratification.

By the early 1990s well over a hundred women had served as senators and representatives. The first woman in Congress was Jeannette RANKIN, a Montana Republican (1917–1919, 1941–1943). When Rankin first ran for the House of Representatives in 1916, only a handful of states permitted women to vote. (See WOMEN IN CONGRESS.)

### Additional Readings

Commission on the Bicentenary of the U.S. House of Representatives. *Women in Congress, 1917–1990.* Washington, D.C.: Government Printing Office, 1991.

Flexner, Eleanor. *Century of Struggle: The Women's Rights Movement in the United States.* Rev. ed. Cambridge, Mass.: Belknap Press, 1975.

Kraditor, Aileen S. *The Ideas of the Woman Suffrage Movement: 1880–1920.* New York: W. W. Norton, 1981.

## Wright, Jim

Jim Wright (1922–   ) became in 1989 the first House Speaker in history to be forced by scandal to leave the office in the middle of a term. Only two years before, barely into his first term leading the House, the Texas Democrat had been hailed as one of the strongest leaders of the postwar Congress. (See SPEAKER OF THE HOUSE.)

"Let me give you back this job you gave me as a propitiation for all of this season of bad will that has grown up among us," Wright said in a dramatic hour-long speech on the House floor in May 1989 announcing his impending resignation. He portrayed himself as a victim of "mindless cannibalism" on the part of Republicans and an overzealous official investigator.

Wright's problem was his personal finances. After months of newspaper stories about them, the House ethics committee in 1988 opened an investigation headed by an outside attorney to look into suggestions that Wright had used a book contract to circumvent House rules limiting outside income and had received improper favors from a Texas developer. (See STANDARDS OF OFFICIAL CONDUCT COMMITTEE, HOUSE.)

In April 1989 the panel dropped a bombshell, announcing on the basis of the investigator's report that it would look into sixty-nine instances in which

*Just as the Washington community accords automatic status to out-of-towners who take high offices, so it revokes that status when they leave office. Former Speaker of the House Jim Wright, D-Texas, once one of the most powerful people in Washington, "vanished to Texas" when he resigned his speakership in June 1989. Accompanied by his wife, Betty, he returned to Washington for the first time in July 1990 for the unveiling of his official portrait at the Capitol.*
Source: The Washington Post

Wright might have violated House rules. The prospect of open hearings was not appealing to Democrats, particularly since their third-ranking House leader, whip Tony Coelho, had resigned in May rather than face an ethics investigation of his financial affairs.

Wright's hard-charging style was that of a political loner who governed more by fear than by respect. It left him with few friends, and he quit rather than drag out a demise that appeared inevitable.

Wright's one full Congress as Speaker, the 100th, was one of the most legislatively productive terms in a generation. Wright himself was at the center of it all. He began by calling for higher taxes to cut the deficit; by the end of the year President Ronald Reagan had dropped his opposition and signed a modest tax increase into law. Wright's lone-wolf drive for conciliation in Nicaragua, many Democrats believed, contributed as much to the eventual downfall of an anti-American leftist regime as did the Reagan administration's support of armed rebellion.

The 100th Congress enacted landmark welfare, health, and trade laws. It also featured an unusual vote that sealed Republican enmity to Wright. The Speaker kept a close vote on a cherished budget bill open ten minutes longer than usual, announced it closed, and then let a Texas colleague—brought to the floor by one of Wright's assistants—change his vote for a 206–205 victory.

Wright, who entered the House in 1955, built his power base on the Public Works Committee. He gave attention to his colleagues' needs, making sure there was a dam here or a highway there, a courtesy that paid off later when he began his climb up the ladder of the Democratic LEADERSHIP.

When Wright ran for majority leader in 1976, he offered himself as an alternative to the bitterly antagonistic front-runners, Richard Bolling of Missouri and Phillip Burton of California. He eliminated Bolling by three votes on the second ballot and Burton by one vote on the third. In 1985, no sooner had Speaker Thomas P. O'Neill, Jr., announced he would retire at the end of the term than Wright declared, two years before the vote, that he had the support to win the post. The preemptive strike was effective; Wright had no challengers.

# Y

## Yeas and Nays

*See* VOTING IN CONGRESS.

## Yield

When a member of Congress has been recognized to speak, no other member may speak unless he or she obtains permission from the person recognized. Permission usually is requested in this form: "Will the gentleman [or gentlewoman] yield?" A legislator who has the floor, perhaps for a specified period of time to make the case for a bill or amendment, may yield some of that time to supporters who also want to speak: "I yield two minutes to the gentlewoman [from Arizona, Illinois, etc.]." The rules, which are enforced by the presiding officer, protect the legislator who has the floor.

## Youth Franchise

The Twenty-sixth Amendment to the Constitution, ratified in 1971, extended voting rights to citizens eighteen years of age or older. Until then, most states had required voters to be at least twenty-one years old.

The key argument for the amendment linked voting rights to the military draft, which was then in effect for males aged eighteen to twenty-six, many of whom were sent to Vietnam. The same rationale had prompted Georgia in 1943 to lower its voting age to eighteen. The war-inspired slogan was: "Old enough to fight, old enough to vote." But few other states extended the franchise. Kentucky lowered its voting age to eighteen in 1955; Alaska and Hawaii, which be-

came states in 1959, adopted minimum voting ages of nineteen and twenty, respectively.

In 1954 President Dwight D. Eisenhower proposed a constitutional amendment lowering the voting age to eighteen, but it was rejected by the Senate.

In passing the Voting Rights Act of 1970, Congress agreed to lower the voting age to eighteen years. The Supreme Court, in a quick test of the provision's constitutionality, ruled late that year that Congress could set qualifications by law only for federal elections; a constitutional amendment was needed to regulate voting in state and local elections.

By March 1971 Congress had sent the Twenty-sixth Amendment to the states for ratification. Moving more quickly than ever before on a proposed amendment, the states endorsed the change; the required three-fourths (thirty-eight) of the states ratified the amendment by the end of June.

The youth franchise amendment was the fourth constitutional amendment to enlarge the electorate since the Constitution was adopted in 1789:

•The Fifteenth Amendment gave the vote to blacks, although additional civil rights laws were necessary to guarantee against discrimination.

•The Nineteenth Amendment provided for WOMEN'S SUFFRAGE.

•The Twenty-third Amendment gave citizens in the District of Columbia the right to vote for president.

More than 11 million people were given the franchise by the Twenty-sixth Amendment, but the eighteen- to twenty-year-old age group has had the poorest record of voting participation of any age group. U.S. census surveys in the 1970s and 1980s found that less than 40 percent of that age group said they voted in presidential elections, compared with a national average of about 60 percent. In congressional election years, reported turnout among the age group fell to 20 percent.

Despite their poor participation rates, young voters—more broadly defined as those under thirty—have become a significant voting bloc, especially in presidential races. Republican presidents Ronald Reagan and George Bush lured a majority of these voters away from their traditional loyalty to the Democrats in 1984 and 1988, but Bill Clinton, the Democrat who was elected president in 1992, brought them back. Clinton, who wooed young voters with appearances on college campuses and late-night television, achieved a ten-point advantage over Bush with voters under thirty.

# Z

## Zone Whips

Party leaders in the 435-member House of Representatives need layers of assistant leaders to help them ride herd on their members. Zone whips, the lowest level of the Democratic LEADERSHIP structure, keep in touch with party members from a particular area of the country and try to make sure they turn up for important votes. House Republicans have a similar, though less extensive, regional whip structure to perform this function. Senate Democrats also organize their deputy whips by region.

# Reference Material

# Appendixes

# *Appendixes*

## Speakers of the House of Representatives, 1789–1993

| Congress | | Speaker | Congress | | Speaker |
|---|---|---|---|---|---|
| 1st | (1789–91) | Frederick A. C. Muhlenberg, Pa. | 38th | (1863–65) | Schuyler Colfax, R–Ind. |
| 2nd | (1791–93) | Jonathan Trumbull, F–Conn. | 39th | (1865–67) | Colfax |
| 3rd | (1793–95) | Muhlenberg | 40th | (1867–68) | Colfax |
| 4th | (1795–97) | Jonathan Dayton, F–N.J. | | (1868–69) | Theodore M. Pomeroy, R–N.Y. |
| 5th | (1797–99) | Dayton | 41st | (1869–71) | James G. Blaine, R–Maine |
| 6th | (1799–1801) | Theodore Sedgwick, F–Mass. | 42nd | (1871–73) | Blaine |
| 7th | (1801–03) | Nathaniel Macon, D–N.C. | 43rd | (1873–75) | Blaine |
| 8th | (1803–05) | Macon | 44th | (1875–76) | Michael C. Kerr, D–Ind. |
| 9th | (1805–07) | Macon | | (1876–77) | Samuel J. Randall, D–Pa. |
| 10th | (1807–09) | Joseph B. Varnum, Mass. | 45th | (1877–79) | Randall |
| 11th | (1809–11) | Varnum | 46th | (1879–81) | Randall |
| 12th | (1811–13) | Henry Clay, R–Ky. | 47th | (1881–83) | Joseph Warren Keifer, R–Ohio |
| 13th | (1813–14) | Clay | 48th | (1883–85) | John G. Carlisle, D–Ky. |
| | (1814–15) | Langdon Cheves, D–S.C. | 49th | (1885–87) | Carlisle |
| 14th | (1815–17) | Clay | 50th | (1887–89) | Carlisle |
| 15th | (1817–19) | Clay | 51st | (1889–91) | Thomas Brackett Reed, R–Maine |
| 16th | (1819–20) | Clay | 52nd | (1891–93) | Charles F. Crisp, D–Ga. |
| | (1820–21) | John W. Taylor, D–N.Y. | 53rd | (1893–95) | Crisp |
| 17th | (1821–23) | Philip P. Barbour, D–Va. | 54th | (1895–97) | Reed |
| 18th | (1823–25) | Clay | 55th | (1897–99) | Reed |
| 19th | (1825–27) | Taylor | 56th | (1899–1901) | David B. Henderson, R–Iowa |
| 20th | (1827–29) | Andrew Stevenson, D–Va. | 57th | (1901–03) | Henderson |
| 21st | (1829–31) | Stevenson | 58th | (1903–05) | Joseph G. Cannon, R–Ill. |
| 22nd | (1831–33) | Stevenson | 59th | (1905–07) | Cannon |
| 23rd | (1833–34) | Stevenson | 60th | (1907–09) | Cannon |
| | (1834–35) | John Bell, W–Tenn. | 61st | (1909–11) | Cannon |
| 24th | (1835–37) | James K. Polk, D–Tenn. | 62nd | (1911–13) | James B. "Champ" Clark, D–Mo. |
| 25th | (1837–39) | Polk | 63rd | (1913–15) | Clark |
| 26th | (1839–41) | Robert M. T. Hunter, D–Va. | 64th | (1915–17) | Clark |
| 27th | (1841–43) | John White, W–Ky. | 65th | (1917–19) | Clark |
| 28th | (1843–45) | John W. Jones, D–Va. | 66th | (1919–21) | Frederick H. Gillett, R–Mass. |
| 29th | (1845–47) | John W. Davis, D–Ind. | 67th | (1921–23) | Gillett |
| 30th | (1847–49) | Robert C. Winthrop, W–Mass. | 68th | (1923–25) | Gillett |
| 31st | (1849–51) | Howell Cobb, D–Ga. | 69th | (1925–27) | Nicholas Longworth, R–Ohio |
| 32nd | (1851–53) | Linn Boyd, D–Ky. | 70th | (1927–29) | Longworth |
| 33rd | (1853–55) | Boyd | 71st | (1929–31) | Longworth |
| 34th | (1855–57) | Nathaniel P. Banks, R–Mass. | 72nd | (1931–33) | John Nance Garner, D–Texas |
| 35th | (1857–59) | James L. Orr, D–S.C. | 73rd | (1933–34) | Henry T. Rainey, D–Ill. [1] |
| 36th | (1859–61) | William Pennington, R–N.J. | 74th | (1935–36) | Joseph W. Byrns, D–Tenn. |
| 37th | (1861–63) | Galusha A. Grow, R–Pa. | | (1936–37) | William B. Bankhead, D–Ala. |

| Congress | | Speaker | Congress | | Speaker |
|---|---|---|---|---|---|
| 75th | (1937–39) | Bankhead | 89th | (1965–67) | McCormack |
| 76th | (1939–40) | Bankhead | 90th | (1967–69) | McCormack |
| | (1940–41) | Sam Rayburn, D–Texas | 91st | (1969–71) | McCormack |
| 77th | (1941–43) | Rayburn | 92nd | (1971–73) | Carl Albert, D–Okla. |
| 78th | (1943–45) | Rayburn | 93rd | (1973–75) | Albert |
| 79th | (1945–47) | Rayburn | 94th | (1975–77) | Albert |
| 80th | (1947–49) | Joseph W. Martin, Jr., R–Mass. | 95th | (1977–79) | Thomas P. O'Neill, Jr., D–Mass. |
| 81st | (1949–51) | Rayburn | 96th | (1979–81) | O'Neill |
| 82nd | (1951–53) | Rayburn | 97th | (1981–83) | O'Neill |
| 83rd | (1953–55) | Martin | 98th | (1983–85) | O'Neill |
| 84th | (1955–57) | Rayburn | 99th | (1985–87) | O'Neill |
| 85th | (1957–59) | Rayburn | 100th | (1987–89) | Jim Wright, D–Texas |
| 86th | (1959–61) | Rayburn | 101st | (1989) | Wright [2] |
| 87th | (1961) | Rayburn | | (1989–91) | Thomas S. Foley, D–Wash. |
| | (1962–63) | John W. McCormack, D–Mass. | 102nd | (1991–93) | Foley |
| 88th | (1963–65) | McCormack | 103rd | (1993–95) | Foley |

SOURCES: *1991–1992 Congressional Directory, 102nd Congress* (Washington, D.C.: Government Printing Office, 1991); *Congressional Quarterly Weekly Report*, selected issues.

NOTE: Party abbreviations: (D) Democrat, (F) Federalist, (R) Republican, (W) Whig.

[1] Rainey died in 1934, but was not replaced until the next Congress.

[2] Wright resigned and was succeeded by Foley on June 6, 1989.

# Party Leadership in Congress, 1977–1993

## 95TH CONGRESS (1977–79)

### Senate
President Pro Tempore—James O. Eastland, D–Miss.
Deputy President Pro Tempore—Hubert H. Humphrey, D–Minn.
Majority Leader—Robert C. Byrd, D–W.Va.
Majority Whip—Alan Cranston, D–Calif.

Minority Leader—Howard H. Baker, Jr., R–Tenn.
Minority Whip—Ted Stevens, R–Alaska

### House
Speaker—Thomas P. O'Neill, Jr., D–Mass.
Majority Leader—Jim Wright, D–Texas
Majority Whip—John Brademas, D–Ind.

Minority Leader—John J. Rhodes, R–Ariz.
Minority Whip—Robert H. Michel, R–Ill.

## 96TH CONGRESS (1979–81)

### Senate
President Pro Tempore—Warren G. Magnuson, D–Wash.
Majority Leader—Robert C. Byrd, D–W.Va.
Majority Whip—Alan Cranston, D–Calif.

Minority Leader—Howard H. Baker, Jr., R–Tenn.
Minority Whip—Ted Stevens, R–Alaska

### House
Speaker—Thomas P. O'Neill, Jr., D–Mass.
Majority Leader—Jim Wright, D–Texas
Majority Whip—John Brademas, D–Ind.

Minority Leader—John J. Rhodes, R–Ariz.
Minority Whip—Robert H. Michel, R–Ill.

## 97TH CONGRESS (1981–83)

### Senate
President Pro Tempore—Strom Thurmond, R–S.C.
Majority Leader—Howard H. Baker, Jr., R–Tenn.
Majority Whip—Ted Stevens, R–Alaska

Minority Leader—Robert C. Byrd, D–W.Va.
Minority Whip—Alan Cranston, D–Calif.

### House
Speaker—Thomas P. O'Neill, Jr., D–Mass.
Majority Leader—Jim Wright, D–Texas
Majority Whip—Thomas S. Foley, D–Wash.

Minority Leader—Robert H. Michel, R–Ill.
Minority Whip—Trent Lott, R–Miss.

## 98TH CONGRESS (1983–85)

### Senate
President Pro Tempore—Strom Thurmond, R–S.C
Majority Leader—Howard H. Baker, Jr., R–Tenn.
Majority Whip—Ted Stevens, R–Alaska

Minority Leader—Robert C. Byrd, D–W.Va.
Minority Whip—Alan Cranston, D–Calif.

### House
Speaker—Thomas P. O'Neill, Jr., D–Mass.
Majority Leader—Jim Wright, D–Texas
Majority Whip—Thomas S. Foley, D–Wash.

Minority Leader—Robert H. Michel, R–Ill.
Minority Whip—Trent Lott, R–Miss.

## 99TH CONGRESS (1985–87)

### Senate
President Pro Tempore—Strom Thurmond, R–S.C.
Majority Leader—Robert Dole, R–Kan.
Assistant Majority Leader—Alan K. Simpson, R–Wyo.

Minority Leader—Robert C. Byrd, D–W.Va.
Minority Whip—Alan Cranston, D–Calif.

### House
Speaker—Thomas P. O'Neill, Jr., D–Mass.
Majority Leader—Jim Wright, D–Texas
Majority Whip—Thomas S. Foley, D–Wash.

Minority Leader—Robert H. Michel, R–Ill.
Minority Whip—Trent Lott, R–Miss.

## 100TH CONGRESS (1987–89)

### Senate
President Pro Tempore—John C. Stennis, D–Miss.
Majority Leader—Robert C. Byrd, D–W.Va.
Majority Whip—Alan Cranston, D–Calif.

Minority Leader—Robert Dole, R–Kan.
Assistant Minority Leader—Alan K. Simpson, R–Wyo.

### House
Speaker—Jim Wright, D–Texas
Majority Leader—Thomas S. Foley, D–Wash.

Majority Whip—Tony Coelho, D–Calif.

Minority Leader—Robert H. Michel, R–Ill.
Minority Whip—Trent Lott, R–Miss.

### 101ST CONGRESS (1989–91)

**Senate**
President Pro Tempore—Robert C. Byrd, D–W.Va.
Majority Leader—George J. Mitchell, D–Maine
Majority Whip—Alan Cranston, D–Calif.

Minority Leader—Robert Dole, R–Kan.
Assistant Minority Leader—Alan K. Simpson, R–Wyo.

**House**
Speaker—Jim Wright, D–Texas/Thomas S. Foley, D–Wash. [1]
Majority Leader—Foley/Richard A. Gephardt, D–Mo. [2]
Majority Whip—Tony Coelho, D–Calif./
    William H. Gray III, D–Pa. [3]

Minority Leader—Robert H. Michel, R–Ill.
Minority Whip—Dick Cheney, R–Wyo./Newt Gingrich, R–Ga. [4]

### 102ND CONGRESS (1991–93)

**Senate**
President Pro Tempore—Robert C. Byrd, D–W.Va.
Majority Leader—George J. Mitchell, D–Maine
Majority Whip—Wendell H. Ford, D–Ky.

Minority Leader—Robert Dole, R–Kan.
Assistant Minority Leader—Alan K. Simpson, R–Wyo.

**House**
Speaker—Thomas S. Foley, D–Wash.
Majority Leader—Richard A. Gephardt, D–Mo.
Majority Whip—William H. Gray III, D–Pa./
    David E. Bonior, D–Mich. [5]

Minority Leader—Robert H. Michel, R–Ill.
Minority Whip—Newt Gingrich, R–Ga.

### 103RD CONGRESS (1993–95)

**Senate**
President Pro Tempore—Robert C. Byrd, D–W.Va.
Majority Leader—George J. Mitchell, D–Maine
Majority Whip—Wendell H. Ford, D–Ky.

Minority Leader—Robert Dole, R–Kan.
Assistant Minority Leader—Alan K. Simpson, R–Wyo.

**House**
Speaker—Thomas S. Foley, D–Wash.
Majority Leader—Richard A. Gephardt, D–Mo.
Majority Whip—David E. Bonior, D–Mich.

Minority Leader—Robert H. Michel, R–Ill.
Minority Whip—Newt Gingrich, R–Ga.

SOURCE: *Congressional Quarterly Almanac*, selected years.
    [1] Wright resigned as Speaker and was succeeded by Foley on June 6, 1989.
    [2] Gephardt became majority leader on June 14, 1989, filling the vacancy created when Foley succeeded Wright as Speaker of the House on June 6, 1989.
    [3] Gray became majority whip on June 14, 1989, filling the vacancy caused by Coelho's resignation.
    [4] Gingrich became minority whip on March 23, 1989, filling the vacancy caused by the resignation of Cheney on March 17, 1989, to become secretary of defense.
    [5] Bonior became majority whip on Sept. 11, 1991, filling the vacancy caused by Gray's resignation from Congress on the same day.

# House Floor Leaders, 1899–1993

| Congress | | Majority | Minority |
|---|---|---|---|
| 56th | (1899–1901) | Sereno E. Payne, R–N.Y. | James D. Richardson, D–Tenn |
| 57th | (1901–03) | Payne | Richardson |
| 58th | (1903–05) | Payne | John Sharp Williams, D–Miss. |
| 59th | (1905–07) | Payne | Williams |
| 60th | (1907–09) | Payne | Williams/Champ Clark, D–Mo. [1] |
| 61st | (1909–11) | Payne | Clark |
| 62nd | (1911–13) | Oscar W. Underwood, D–Ala. | James R. Mann, R–Ill. |
| 63rd | (1913–15) | Underwood | Mann |
| 64th | (1915–17) | Claude Kitchin, D–N.C. | Mann |
| 65th | (1917–19) | Kitchin | Mann |
| 66th | (1919–21) | Franklin W. Mondell, R–Wyo. | Clark |
| 67th | (1921–23) | Mondell | Claude Kitchin, D–N.C. |
| 68th | (1923–25) | Nicholas Longworth, R–Ohio | Finis J. Garrett, D–Tenn. |
| 69th | (1925–27) | John Q. Tilson, R–Conn. | Garrett |
| 70th | (1927–29) | Tilson | Garrett |
| 71st | (1929–31) | Tilson | John N. Garner, D–Texas |
| 72nd | (1931–33) | Henry T. Rainey, D–Ill. | Bertrand H. Snell, R–N.Y. |
| 73rd | (1933–35) | Joseph W. Byrns, D–Tenn. | Snell |
| 74th | (1935–37) | William B. Bankhead, D–Ala.[2] | Snell |
| 75th | (1937–39) | Sam Rayburn, D–Texas | Snell |
| 76th | (1939–41) | Rayburn/John W. McCormack, D–Mass.[3] | Joseph W. Martin, Jr., R–Mass. |
| 77th | (1941–43) | McCormack | Martin |
| 78th | (1943–45) | McCormack | Martin |
| 79th | (1945–47) | McCormack | Martin |
| 80th | (1947–49) | Charles A. Halleck, R–Ind. | Sam Rayburn, D–Texas |
| 81st | (1949–51) | McCormack | Martin |
| 82nd | (1951–53) | McCormack | Martin |
| 83rd | (1953–55) | Halleck | Rayburn |
| 84th | (1955–57) | McCormack | Martin |
| 85th | (1957–59) | McCormack | Martin |
| 86th | (1959–61) | McCormack | Charles A. Halleck, R–Ind. |
| 87th | (1961–63) | McCormack/Carl Albert, D–Okla.[4] | Halleck |
| 88th | (1963–65) | Albert | Halleck |
| 89th | (1965–67) | Albert | Gerald R. Ford, R–Mich. |
| 90th | (1967–69) | Albert | Ford |

| | Congress | Majority | Minority |
|---|---|---|---|
| 91st | (1969–71) | Albert | Ford |
| 92nd | (1971–73) | Hale Boggs, D–La. | Ford |
| 93rd | (1973–75) | Thomas P. O'Neill, Jr., D–Mass. | Ford/John J. Rhodes, R–Ariz. [5] |
| 94th | (1975–77) | O'Neill | Rhodes |
| 95th | (1977–79) | Jim Wright, D–Texas | Rhodes |
| 96th | (1979–81) | Wright | Rhodes |
| 97th | (1981–83) | Wright | Robert H. Michel, R–Ill. |
| 98th | (1983–85) | Wright | Michel |
| 99th | (1985–87) | Wright | Michel |
| 100th | (1987–89) | Thomas S. Foley, D–Wash. | Michel |
| 101st | (1989–91) | Foley/Richard A. Gephardt, D–Mo. [6] | Michel |
| 102nd | (1991–93) | Gephardt | Michel |
| 103rd | (1993–95) | Gephardt | Michel |

SOURCES: Randall B. Ripley, *Party Leaders in the House of Representatives* (Washington, D.C.: Brookings Institution, 1967); *Congressional Directory* (Washington, D.C.: Government Printing Office), selected years; *Biographical Directory of the American Congress, 1774–1971*, comp. Lawrence F. Kennedy, 92nd Cong., 1st sess., 1971 S Doc 8; *Congressional Quarterly Weekly Report*, selected issues.

[1] Clark became minority leader in 1908.

[2] Bankhead became Speaker of the House on June 4, 1936, after Speaker Joseph W. Byrns's death. The post of majority leader remained vacant until the next Congress.

[3] McCormack became majority leader on Sept. 26, 1940, filling the vacancy caused by the elevation of Rayburn to the post of Speaker of the House on Sept. 16, 1940, after Bankhead's death.

[4] Albert became majority leader on Jan. 10, 1962, filling the vacancy caused by the elevation of McCormack to the post of Speaker of the House on Jan. 10, 1962, after Rayburn's death.

[5] Rhodes became minority leader on Dec. 7, 1973, filling the vacancy caused by the resignation of Ford on Dec. 6, 1973, to become vice president.

[6] Gephardt became majority leader on June 14, 1989, filling the vacancy caused by the elevation of Foley to the post of Speaker of the House on June 6, 1989, after Wright's resignation.

## Senate Floor Leaders, 1911–1993

| Congress | | Majority | Minority |
|---|---|---|---|
| 62nd | (1911–13) | Shelby M. Cullom, R–Ill. | Thomas S. Martin, D–Va. |
| 63rd | (1913–15) | John W. Kern, D–Ind. | Jacob H. Gallinger, R–N.H. |
| 64th | (1915–17) | Kern | Gallinger |
| 65th | (1917–19) | Thomas S. Martin, D–Va. | Gallinger/Henry Cabot Lodge, R–Mass. [1] |
| 66th | (1919–21) | Henry Cabot Lodge, R–Mass. | Martin/Oscar W. Underwood, D–Ala. [2] |
| 67th | (1921–23) | Lodge | Underwood |
| 68th | (1923–25) | Lodge/Charles Curtis, R–Kan. [3] | Joseph T. Robinson, D–Ark. |
| 69th | (1925–27) | Curtis | Robinson |
| 70th | (1927–29) | Curtis | Robinson |
| 71st | (1929–31) | James E. Watson, R–Ind. | Robinson |
| 72nd | (1931–33) | Watson | Robinson |
| 73rd | (1933–35) | Joseph T. Robinson, D–Ark. | Charles L. McNary, R–Ore. |
| 74th | (1935–37) | Robinson | McNary |
| 75th | (1937–39) | Robinson/Alben W. Barkley, D–Ky. [4] | McNary |
| 76th | (1939–41) | Barkley | McNary |
| 77th | (1941–43) | Barkley | McNary |
| 78th | (1943–45) | Barkley | McNary |
| 79th | (1945–47) | Barkley | Wallace H. White, Jr., R–Maine |
| 80th | (1947–49) | Wallace H. White, Jr., R–Maine | Alben W. Barkley, D–Ky. |
| 81st | (1949–51) | Scott W. Lucas, D–Ill. | Kenneth S. Wherry, R–Neb. |
| 82nd | (1951–53) | Ernest W. McFarland, D–Ariz. | Wherry/Styles Bridges, R–N.H. [5] |
| 83rd | (1953–55) | Robert A. Taft, R–Ohio/ William F. Knowland, R–Calif. [6] | Lyndon B. Johnson, D–Texas Johnson |
| 84th | (1955–57) | Lyndon B. Johnson, D–Texas | William F. Knowland, R–Calif. |
| 85th | (1957–59) | Johnson | Knowland |
| 86th | (1959–61) | Johnson | Everett McKinley Dirksen, R–Ill. |
| 87th | (1961–63) | Mike Mansfield, D–Mont. | Dirksen |
| 88th | (1963–65) | Mansfield | Dirksen |
| 89th | (1965–67) | Mansfield | Dirksen |
| 90th | (1967–69) | Mansfield | Dirksen |
| 91st | (1969–71) | Mansfield | Dirksen/Hugh Scott, R–Pa. [7] |
| 92nd | (1971–73) | Mansfield | Scott |
| 93rd | (1973–75) | Mansfield | Scott |
| 94th | (1975–77) | Mansfield | Scott |
| 95th | (1977–79) | Robert C. Byrd, D–W.Va. | Howard H. Baker, Jr., R–Tenn. |

| Congress | | Majority | Minority |
|---|---|---|---|
| 96th | (1979–81) | Byrd | Baker |
| 97th | (1981–83) | Howard H. Baker, Jr., R–Tenn. | Robert C. Byrd. D–W.Va. |
| 98th | (1983–85) | Baker | Byrd |
| 99th | (1985–87) | Robert Dole, R–Kan. | Byrd |
| 100th | (1987–89) | Byrd | Robert Dole, R–Kan. |
| 101st | (1989–91) | George J. Mitchell, D–Maine | Dole |
| 102nd | (1991–93) | Mitchell | Dole |
| 103rd | (1993–95) | Mitchell | Dole |

SOURCES: *Congressional Directory* (Washington, D.C.: Government Printing Office), selected years; *Biographical Directory of the American Congress, 1774–1971,* comp. Lawrence F. Kennedy, 92nd Cong., 1st sess., 1971, S Doc 8; *Majority and Minority Leaders of the Senate,* comp. Floyd M. Riddick, 94th Cong., 1st sess., 1975, S Doc 66; *Congressional Quarterly Weekly Report,* selected issues.

[1] Lodge became minority leader on Aug. 24, 1918, filling the vacancy caused by the death of Gallinger on Aug. 17, 1918.

[2] Underwood became minority leader on April 27, 1920, filling the vacancy caused by the death of Martin on Nov. 12, 1919. Gilbert M. Hitchcock, D–Neb., served as acting minority leader in the interim.

[3] Curtis became majority leader on Nov. 28, 1924, filling the vacancy caused by the death of Lodge on Nov. 9, 1924.

[4] Barkley became majority leader on July 22, 1937, filling the vacancy caused by the death of Robinson on July 14, 1937.

[5] Bridges became minority leader on Jan. 8, 1952, filling the vacancy caused by the death of Wherry on Nov. 29, 1951.

[6] Knowland became majority leader on Aug. 4, 1953, filling the vacancy caused by the death of Taft on July 31, 1953. Taft's vacant seat was filled by a Democrat, Thomas Burke, on Nov. 10, 1953. The division of the Senate changed to 48 Democrats, 47 Republicans, and 1 Independent, thus giving the Democrats a numerical majority. However, Knowland remained as majority leader until the end of the 83rd Congress.

[7] Scott became minority leader on Sept. 24, 1969, filling the vacancy caused by the death of Dirksen on Sept. 7, 1969.

# Congressional Committee Chairs since 1947

Following is a list of House and Senate standing committee chairs from 1947 through January 1993. Years reflect tenure as committee chair.

## HOUSE

### Agriculture

Clifford R. Hope  (R–Kan. 1947–49)
Harold D. Cooley (D–N.C. 1949–53)
Clifford R. Hope (R–Kan. 1953–55)
Harold D. Cooley (D–N.C. 1955–67)
W. R. Poage (D–Texas 1967–75)
Thomas S. Foley (D–Wash. 1975–81)
E. "Kika" de la Garza (D–Texas 1981–    )

### Appropriations

John Taber (R–N.Y. 1947–49)
Clarence Cannon (D–Mo. 1949–53)
John Taber (R–N.Y. 1953–55)
Clarence Cannon (D–Mo. 1955–64)
George H. Mahon (D–Texas 1964–79)
Jamie L. Whitten (D–Miss. 1979–93)
William H. Natcher (D–Ky. 1993–    )

### Armed Services

Walter G. Andrews (R–N.Y. 1947–49)
Carl Vinson (D–Ga. 1949–53)
Dewey Short (R–Mo. 1953–55)
Carl Vinson (D–Ga. 1955–65)
L. Mendel Rivers (D–S.C. 1965–71)
F. Edward Hébert (D–La. 1971–75)
Melvin Price (D–Ill. 1975–85)
Les Aspin (D–Wis. 1985–93)
Ronald V. Dellums (D–Calif. 1993–    )

### Banking and Currency

Jesse P. Wolcott (R–Mich. 1947–49)
Brent Spence (D–Ky. 1949–53)
Jesse P. Wolcott (R–Mich. 1953–55)
Brent Spence (D–Ky. 1955–63)
Wright Patman (D–Texas 1963–75)

### Banking, Currency, and Housing
*(renamed in 1975)*

Henry S. Reuss (D–Wis. 1975–77)

### Banking, Finance, and Urban Affairs
*(renamed in 1977)*

Henry S. Reuss (D–Wis. 1977–81)
Fernand J. St Germain (D–R.I. 1981–89)
Henry B. Gonzalez (D–Texas 1989–    )

### Budget

Brock Adams (D–Wash. 1975–77)
Robert N. Giaimo (D–Conn. 1977–81)
James R. Jones (D–Okla. 1981–85)
William H. Gray III (D–Pa. 1985–89)
Leon E. Panetta (D–Calif. 1989–93)
Martin Olav Sabo (D–Minn. 1993–    )

### District of Columbia

Everett McKinley Dirksen
    (R–Ill. 1947–49)
John L. McMillan (D–S.C. 1949–53)
Sidney Elmer Simpson (R–Ill. 1953–55)
John L. McMillan (D–S.C. 1955–73)
Charles C. Diggs, Jr. (D–Mich. 1973–79)
Ronald V. Dellums (D–Calif. 1979–93)
Pete Stark (D–Calif. 1993–    )

### Education and Labor

Fred A. Hartley, Jr. (R–N.J. 1947–49)
John Lesinski (D–Mich. 1949–50)
Graham A. Barden (D–N.C. 1950–53)
Samuel K. McConnell, Jr.
    (R–Pa. 1953–55)
Graham A. Barden (D–N.C. 1955–61)
Adam Clayton Powell, Jr.
    (D–N.Y. 1961–67)
Carl D. Perkins (D–Ky. 1967–84)
Augustus F. Hawkins
    (D–Calif. 1984–91)
William D. Ford (D–Mich. 1991–  )

### Foreign Affairs

Charles A. Eaton (R–N.J. 1947–49)
John Kee (D–W.Va. 1949–51)
James P. Richards (D–S.C. 1951–53)
Robert B. Chiperfield (R–Ill. 1953–55)
James P. Richards (D–S.C. 1955–57)
Thomas S. Gordon (D–Ill. 1957–59)
Thomas E. Morgan (D–Pa. 1959–75)

### International Relations
*(renamed in 1975)*

Thomas E. Morgan (D–Pa. 1975–77)
Clement J. Zablocki (D–Wis. 1977–79)

### Foreign Affairs
*(renamed in 1979)*

Clement J. Zablocki (D–Wis. 1979–83)
Dante B. Fascell (D–Fla. 1984–93)
Lee H. Hamilton (D–Ind. 1993–    )

### Expenditures in the Executive Departments

Clare E. Hoffman (R–Mich. 1947–49)
William L. Dawson (D–Ill. 1949–52)

### Government Operations
*(renamed in 1952)*

William L. Dawson (D–Ill. 1952–53)
Clare E. Hoffman (R–Mich. 1953–55)
William L. Dawson (D–Ill. 1955–71)
Chet Holifield (D–Calif. 1971–75)
Jack Brooks (D–Texas 1975–89)
John Conyers, Jr. (D–Mich. 1989–    )

### House Administration

Karl M. LeCompte (R–Iowa 1947–49)
Mary T. Norton (D–N.J. 1949–51)
Thomas B. Stanley (D–Va. 1951–53)
Karl M. LeCompte (R–Iowa 1953–55)
Omar Burleson (D–Texas 1955–68)
Samuel N. Friedel (D–Md. 1968–71)
Wayne L. Hays (D–Ohio 1971–76)
Frank Thompson, Jr. (D–N.J. 1976–80)
Augustus F. Hawkins
    (D–Calif. 1981–84)
Frank Annunzio (D–Ill. 1985–91)
Charlie Rose (D–N.C. 1991–  )

### Intelligence, Select Committee on

Lucien N. Nedzi (D–Mich. 1975)
Otis G. Pike (D–N.Y. 1975–76)

### Intelligence, Permanent Select Committee on

Edward P. Boland (D–Mass. 1977–85)
Lee H. Hamilton (D–Ind. 1985–87)
Louis Stokes (D–Ohio 1987–89)
Anthony C. Beilenson
    (D–Calif. 1989–91)
Dave McCurdy (D–Okla. 1991–93)
Dan Glickman (D–Kan. 1993–    )

### Interstate and Foreign Commerce

Charles A. Wolverton (R–N.J. 1947–49)
Robert Crosser (D–Ohio 1949–53)
Charles A. Wolverton (R–N.J. 1953–55)
J. Percy Priest (D–Tenn. 1955–57)
Oren Harris (D–Ark. 1957–66)
Harley O. Staggers (D–W.Va. 1966–81)

## Energy and Commerce
*(renamed in 1981)*

John D. Dingell (D–Mich. 1981–   )

## Judiciary

Earl C. Michener (R–Mich. 1947–49)
Emanuel Celler (D–N.Y. 1949–53)
Chauncey W. Reed (R–Ill. 1953–55)
Emanuel Celler (D–N.Y. 1955–73)
Peter W. Rodino, Jr. (D–N.J. 1973–89)
Jack Brooks (D–Texas 1989–   )

## Merchant Marine and Fisheries

Fred Bradley (R–Mich. 1947)
Alvin F. Weichel (R–Ohio 1947–49)
Schuyler Otis Bland (D–Va. 1949–50)
Edward J. Hart (D–N.J. 1950–53)
Alvin F. Weichel (R–Ohio 1953–55)
Herbert C. Bonner (D–N.C. 1955–65)
Edward A. Garmatz (D–Md. 1966–73)
Leonor K. Sullivan (D–Mo. 1973–77)
John M. Murphy (D–N.Y. 1977–81)
Walter B. Jones (D–N.C. 1981–92)
Gerry E. Studds (D–Mass. 1992–   )

## Post Office and Civil Service

Edward H. Rees (R–Kan. 1947–49)
Tom Murray (D–Tenn. 1949–53)
Edward H. Rees (R–Kan. 1953–55)
Tom Murray (D–Tenn. 1955–67)
Thaddeus J. Dulski (D–N.Y. 1967–75)
David N. Henderson (D–N.C. 1975–77)
Robert N. C. Nix, Sr. (D–Pa. 1977–79)
James M. Hanley (D–N.Y. 1979–81)
William D. Ford (D–Mich. 1981–91)
William L. Clay (D–Mo. 1991–   )

## Public Lands

Richard J. Welch (R–Calif. 1947–49)
Andrew L. Somers (D–N.Y. 1949)
J. Hardin Peterson (D–Fla. 1949–51)

## Interior and Insular Affairs
*(renamed in 1951)*

John R. Murdock (D–Ariz. 1951–53)
A. L. Miller (R–Neb. 1953–55)
Clair Engle (D–Calif. 1955–59)
Wayne N. Aspinall (D–Colo. 1959–73)
James A. Haley (D–Fla. 1973–77)
Morris K. Udall (D–Ariz. 1977–91)
George Miller (D–Calif. 1991–92)

## Natural Resources
*(renamed in 1993)*

George Miller (D–Calif. 1993–   )

## Public Works

George A. Dondero (R–Mich. 1947–49)
William M. Whittington
    (D–Miss. 1949–51)
Charles A. Buckley (D–N.Y. 1951–53)
George A. Dondero (R–Mich. 1953–55)
Charles A. Buckley (D–N.Y. 1955–65)
George H. Fallon (D–Md. 1965–71)
John A. Blatnik (D–Minn. 1971–75)

## Public Works and Transportation
*(renamed in 1975)*

Robert E. Jones, Jr. (D–Ala. 1975–77)
Harold T. Johnson (D–Calif. 1977–81)
James J. Howard (D–N.J. 1981–88)
Glenn M. Anderson (D–Calif. 1988–91)
Robert A. Roe (D–N.J. 1991–93)
Norman Y. Mineta (D–Calif. 1993–   )

## Rules

Leo E. Allen (R–Ill. 1947–49)
Adolph J. Sabath (D–Ill. 1949–53)
Leo E. Allen (R–Ill. 1953–55)
Howard W. Smith (D–Va. 1955–67)
William M. Colmer (D–Miss. 1967–73)
Ray J. Madden (D–Ind. 1973–77)
James J. Delaney (D–N.Y. 1977–78)
Richard Bolling (D–Mo. 1979–83)
Claude Pepper (D–Fla. 1983–89)
Joe Moakley (D–Mass. 1989–   )

## Science and Astronautics

Overton Brooks (D–La. 1959–61)
George P. Miller (D–Calif. 1961–73)
Olin E. Teague (D–Texas 1973–75)

## Science and Technology
*(renamed in 1975)*

Olin E. Teague (D–Texas 1975–79)
Don Fuqua (D–Fla. 1979–87)

## Science, Space, and Technology
*(renamed in 1987)*

Robert A. Roe (D–N.J. 1987–91)
George E. Brown, Jr. (D–Calif. 1991–   )

## Small Business, Select Committee on

Walter C. Ploeser (R–Mo. 1947–49)
Wright Patman (D–Texas 1949–53)
William S. Hill (R–Colo. 1953–55)
Wright Patman (D–Texas 1955–63)
Joe L. Evins (D–Tenn. 1963–75)

### Small Business

Joe L. Evins (D–Tenn. 1975–77)
Neal Smith (D–Iowa 1977–81)
Parren J. Mitchell (D–Md. 1981–87)
John J. LaFalce (D–N.Y. 1987–   )

## Standards of Official Conduct

Melvin Price (D–Ill. 1969–75)
John J. Flynt, Jr. (D–Ga. 1975–77)
Charles E. Bennett (D–Fla. 1977–81)
Louis Stokes (D–Ohio 1981–85)
Julian C. Dixon (D–Calif. 1985–91)
Louis Stokes (D–Ohio 1991–93)
Jim McDermott (D–Wash. 1993–   )

## Un-American Activities

J. Parnell Thomas (R–N.J. 1947–49)
John S. Wood (D–Ga. 1949–53)
Harold H. Velde (R–Ill. 1953–55)
Francis E. Walter (D–Pa. 1955–63)
Edwin E. Willis (D–La. 1963–69)

## Internal Security
*(renamed in 1969)*

Richard H. Ichord (D–Mo. 1969–75)
*(The panel was abolished in 1975.)*

## Veterans' Affairs

Edith Nourse Rogers (R–Mass. 1947–49)
John E. Rankin (D–Miss. 1949–53)
Edith Nourse Rogers (R–Mass. 1953–55)
Olin E. Teague (D–Texas 1955–73)
William Jennings Bryan Dorn
    (D–S.C. 1973–75)
Ray Roberts (D–Texas 1975–81)
G. V. "Sonny" Montgomery
    (D–Miss. 1981–   )

## Ways and Means

Harold Knutson (R–Minn. 1947–49)
Robert L. Doughton (D–N.C. 1949–53)
Daniel A. Reed (R–N.Y. 1953–55)
Jere Cooper (D–Tenn. 1955–57)
Wilbur D. Mills (D–Ark. 1958–75)
Al Ullman (D–Ore. 1975–81)
Dan Rostenkowski (D–Ill. 1981–   )

# SENATE

## Aeronautical and Space Sciences

Lyndon B. Johnson (D–Texas 1958–61)
Robert S. Kerr (D–Okla. 1961–63)
Clinton P. Anderson (D–N.M. 1963–73)
Frank E. Moss (D–Utah 1973–77)

*(Abolished in 1977, when its jurisdiction was consolidated under Commerce.)*

## Agriculture and Forestry

Arthur Capper (R–Kan. 1947–49)
Elmer Thomas (D–Okla. 1949–51)
Allen J. Ellender (D–La. 1951–53)
George D. Aiken (R–Vt. 1953–55)
Allen J. Ellender (D–La. 1955–71)
Herman E. Talmadge (D–Ga. 1971–77)

## Agriculture, Nutrition, and Forestry

*(renamed in 1977)*

Herman E. Talmadge (D–Ga. 1977–81)
Jesse Helms (R–N.C. 1981–87)
Patrick J. Leahy (D–Vt. 1987–   )

## Appropriations

Styles Bridges (R–N.H. 1947–49)
Kenneth McKellar (D–Tenn. 1949–53)
Styles Bridges (R–N.H. 1953–55)
Carl Hayden (D–Ariz. 1955–69)
Richard B. Russell (D–Ga. 1969–71)
Allen J. Ellender (D–La. 1971–72)
John L. McClellan (D–Ark. 1972–77)
Warren G. Magnuson
   (D–Wash. 1978–81)
Mark O. Hatfield (R–Ore. 1981–87)
John C. Stennis (D–Miss. 1987–89)
Robert C. Byrd (D–W.Va. 1989–   )

## Armed Services

Chan Gurney (R–S.D. 1947–49)
Millard E. Tydings (D–Md. 1949–51)
Richard B. Russell (D–Ga. 1951–53)
Leverett Saltonstall (R–Mass. 1953–55)
Richard B. Russell (D–Ga. 1955–69)
John C. Stennis (D–Miss. 1969–81)
John Tower (R–Texas 1981–85)
Barry Goldwater (R–Ariz. 1985–87)
Sam Nunn (D–Ga. 1987–   )

## Banking and Currency

Charles W. Tobey (R–N.H. 1947–49)
Burnet R. Maybank (D–S.C. 1949–53)
Homer E. Capehart (R–Ind. 1953–55)

J. W. Fulbright (D–Ark. 1955–59)
A. Willis Robertson (D–Va. 1959–67)
John J. Sparkman (D–Ala. 1967–71)

## Banking, Housing, and Urban Affairs

*(renamed in 1971)*

John J. Sparkman (D–Ala. 1971–75)
William Proxmire (D–Wis. 1975–81)
Jake Garn (R–Utah 1981–87)
William Proxmire (D–Wis. 1987–89)
Donald W. Riegle, Jr. (D–Mich. 1989–   )

## Budget

Edmund S. Muskie (D–Maine 1975–79)
Ernest F. Hollings (D–S.C. 1979–81)
Pete V. Domenici (R–N.M. 1981–87)
Lawton Chiles, Jr. (D–Fla. 1987–89)
Jim Sasser (D–Tenn. 1989–   )

## Interstate and Foreign Commerce

Wallace H. White (R–Maine 1947–49)
Edwin C. Johnson (D–Colo. 1949–53)
Charles W. Tobey (R–N.H. 1953)
John W. Bricker (R–Ohio 1953–55)
Warren G. Magnuson
   (D–Wash. 1955–61)

## Commerce

*(renamed in 1961)*

Warren G. Magnuson
   (D–Wash 1961–77)

## Commerce, Science, and Transportation

*(renamed in 1977)*

Warren G. Magnuson
   (D–Wash. 1977–78)
Howard W. Cannon (D–Nev. 1978–81)
Bob Packwood (R–Ore. 1981–85)
John C. Danforth (R–Mo. 1985–87)
Ernest F. Hollings (D–S.C. 1987–   )

## District of Columbia

C. Douglass Buck (R–Del. 1947–49)
J. Howard McGrath (D–R.I. 1949–51)
Matthew M. Neely (D–W.Va. 1951–53)
Francis Case (R–S.D. 1953–55)
Matthew M. Neely (D–W.Va. 1955–59)
Alan Bible (D–Nev. 1959–69)
Joseph D. Tydings (D–Md. 1969–71)
Thomas Eagleton (D–Mo. 1971–77)

*(Abolished in 1977 and its responsibilities transferred to Governmental Affairs.)*

## Energy and Natural Resources

Henry M. Jackson (D–Wash. 1977–81)
James A. McClure (R–Idaho 1981–87)
J. Bennett Johnston (D–La. 1987–   )

## Expenditures in the Executive Departments

George D. Aiken (R–Vt. 1947–49)
John L. McClellan (D–Ark. 1949–52)

## Government Operations

*(renamed in 1952)*

John L. McClellan (D–Ark. 1952–53)
Joseph R. McCarthy (R–Wis. 1953–55)
John L. McClellan (D–Ark. 1955–72)
Sam J. Ervin, Jr. (D–N.C. 1972–74)
Abraham A. Ribicoff (D–Conn. 1975–77)

## Governmental Affairs

*(renamed in 1977)*

Abraham A. Ribicoff (D–Conn. 1977–81)
William V. Roth, Jr. (R–Del. 1981–87)
John Glenn (D–Ohio 1987–   )

## Finance

Eugene D. Millikin (R–Colo. 1947–49)
Walter F. George (D–Ga. 1949–53)
Eugene D. Millikin (R–Colo. 1953–55)
Harry Flood Byrd (D–Va. 1955–65)
Russell B. Long (D–La. 1965–81)
Robert Dole (R–Kan. 1981–85)
Bob Packwood (R–Ore. 1985–87)
Lloyd Bentsen (D–Texas 1987–93)
Daniel Patrick Moynihan
   (D–N.Y. 1993–   )

## Foreign Relations

Arthur H. Vandenberg
   (R–Mich. 1947–49)
Tom Connally (D–Texas 1949–53)
Alexander Wiley (R–Wis. 1953–55)
Walter F. George (D–Ga. 1955–57)
Theodore Francis Green (D–R.I. 1957–59)
J. W. Fulbright (D–Ark. 1959–75)
John J. Sparkman (D–Ala. 1975–79)
Frank Church (D–Idaho 1979–81)
Charles Percy (R–Ill. 1981–85)
Richard G. Lugar (R–Ind. 1985–87)
Claiborne Pell (D–R.I. 1987–   )

## Intelligence Activities, Select Committee on

Daniel K. Inouye (D–Hawaii 1976–78)
Birch Bayh (D–Ind. 1978–81)

Barry Goldwater (R–Ariz. 1981–85)
Dave Durenberger (R–Minn. 1985–87)
David L. Boren (D–Okla. 1987–93)
Dennis DeConcini (D–Ariz. 1993–    )

## Judiciary

Alexander Wiley (R–Wis. 1947–49)
Pat McCarran (D–Nev. 1949–53)
William Langer (R–N.D. 1953–55)
Harley M. Kilgore (D–W.Va. 1955–56)
James O. Eastland (D–Miss. 1956–78)
Edward M. Kennedy (D–Mass. 1979–81)
Strom Thurmond (R–S.C. 1981–87)
Joseph R. Biden, Jr. (D–Del. 1987–    )

## Labor and Public Welfare

Robert A. Taft (R–Ohio 1947–49)
Elbert D. Thomas (D–Utah 1949–51)
James E. Murray (D–Mont. 1951–53)
H. Alexander Smith (R–N.J. 1953–55)
Lister Hill (D–Ala. 1955–69)
Ralph W. Yarborough (D–Texas 1969–71)
Harrison A. Williams, Jr.(D–N.J. 1971–77)

### Human Resources
*(renamed in 1977)*

Harrison A. Williams, Jr.(D–N.J. 1977–79)

### Labor and Human Resources
*(renamed in 1979)*

Harrison A. Williams, Jr. (D–N.J. 1979–81)
Orrin G. Hatch (R–Utah 1981–87)
Edward M. Kennedy (D–Mass. 1987–    )

## Post Office and Civil Service

William Langer (R–N.D. 1947–49)
Olin D. Johnston (D–S.C. 1949–53)
Frank Carlson (R–Kan. 1953–55)
Olin D. Johnston (D–S.C. 1955–65)
A. S. Mike Monroney
     (D–Okla. 1965–69)
Gale W. McGee (D–Wyo. 1969–77)

*(Abolished in 1977 and its responsibilities transferred to Governmental Affairs.)*

## Public Lands

Hugh Butler (R–Neb. 1947–48)

### Interior and Insular Affairs
*(renamed in 1948)*

Hugh Butler (R–Neb. 1948–49)
Joseph C. O'Mahoney (D–Wyo. 1949–53)
Hugh Butler (R–Neb. 1953–54)
Guy Cordon (R–Ore. 1954–55)
James E. Murray (D–Mont. 1955–61)
Clinton P. Anderson (D–N.M. 1961–63)
Henry M. Jackson (D–Wash. 1963–77)

*(Most of its jurisdiction transferred to Energy and Natural Resources in 1977.)*

## Public Works

Chapman Revercomb
     (R–W.Va. 1947–49)
Dennis Chavez (D–N.M. 1949–53)
Edward Martin (R–Pa. 1953–55)
Dennis Chavez (D–N.M. 1955–62)
Pat McNamara (D–Mich. 1963–66)
Jennings Randolph (D–W.Va. 1966–77)

### Environment and Public Works
*(renamed in 1977)*

Jennings Randolph (D–W.Va. 1977–81)
Robert T. Stafford (R–Vt. 1981–87)
Quentin N. Burdick (D–N.D. 1987–92)
Daniel Patrick Moynihan (D–N.Y. 1992)
Max Baucus (D–Mont. 1993–    )

## Rules and Administration

C. Wayland Brooks (R–Ill. 1947–49)
Carl Hayden (D–Ariz. 1949–53)
William E. Jenner (R–Ind. 1953–55)
Theodore Francis Green
     (D–R.I. 1955–57)
Thomas C. Hennings, Jr. (D–Mo. 1957–60)
Mike Mansfield (D–Mont. 1961–63)
B. Everett Jordan (D–N.C. 1963–72)
Howard W. Cannon (D–Nev. 1973–77)
Claiborne Pell (D–R.I. 1978–81)
Charles McC. Mathias, Jr.
     (R–Md. 1981–87)
Wendell H. Ford (D–Ky. 1987–    )

## Small Business, Select Committee on

John J. Sparkman (D–Ala. 1950–53)
Edward J. Thye (R–Minn. 1953–55)
John J. Sparkman (D–Ala. 1955–67)
George A. Smathers (D–Fla. 1967–69)
Alan Bible (D–Nev. 1969–75)
Gaylord Nelson (D–Wis. 1975–81)

### Small Business

Lowell P. Weicker, Jr.
     (R–Conn. 1981–87)
Dale Bumpers (D–Ark. 1987–    )

## Standards and Conduct, Select Committee on

John C. Stennis (D–Miss. 1966–75)
Howard W. Cannon (D–Nev. 1975–77)

### Ethics, Select Committee on
*(renamed in 1977)*

Adlai Ewing Stevenson III
     (D–Ill. 1977–81)
Malcolm Wallop (R–Wyo. 1981–83)
Ted Stevens (R–Alaska 1983–85)
Warren B. Rudman (R–N.H. 1985–87)
Howell Heflin (D–Ala. 1987–1991)
Terry Sanford (D–N.C. 1991–93)
Richard H. Bryan (D–Nev. 1993–    )

## Veterans' Affairs

Vance Hartke (D–Ind. 1971–77)
Alan Cranston (D–Calif. 1977–81)
Alan K. Simpson (R–Wyo. 1981–85)
Frank H. Murkowski (R–Alaska 1985–87)
Alan Cranston (D–Calif. 1987–93)
John D. Rockefeller IV
     (D– W.Va. 1993–    )

# Women Members of Congress, 1917–1993

As of January 1993, a total of 160 women had been elected or appointed to Congress.* Of the 157 women who actually served in Congress (two others were never sworn in and another resigned her seat the day after she was sworn in), 138 served in the House only, sixteen in the Senate, and three—Maine Republican Margaret Chase Smith, Maryland Democrat Barbara Mikulski, and California Democrat Barbara Boxer—in both chambers. Following is a list of the women members, their parties and states, and the years in which they served. In addition, Mary E. Farrington, R–Hawaii (1954–57), and Eleanor Holmes Norton, D–D.C. (1991–   ), served as delegates.

## Senate

| | |
|---|---|
| Rebecca L. Felton, Ind. D–Ga. [1] | 1922 |
| Hattie W. Caraway, D–Ark. | 1931–45 |
| Rose McConnell Long, D–La. | 1936–37 |
| Dixie Bibb Graves, D–Ala. | 1937–38 |
| Gladys Pyle, R–S.D. [2] | 1938–39 |
| Vera C. Bushfield, R–S.D. | 1948 |
| Margaret Chase Smith, R–Maine | 1949–73 |
| Hazel H. Abel, R–Neb. | 1954 |
| Eva K. Bowring, R–Neb. | 1954 |
| Maurine B. Neuberger, D–Ore. | 1960–67 |
| Elaine S. Edwards, D–La. | 1972 |
| Maryon Pittman Allen, D–Ala. | 1978 |
| Muriel Buck Humphrey, D–Minn. | 1978 |
| Nancy Landon Kassebaum, R–Kan. | 1978– |
| Paula Hawkins, R–Fla. | 1981–87 |
| Barbara Mikulski, D–Md. | 1987– |
| Jocelyn B. Burdick, D–N.D. | 1992–93 |
| Dianne Feinstein, D–Calif. | 1992– |
| Barbara Boxer, D–Calif. | 1993– |
| Carol Moseley-Braun, D–Ill. | 1993– |
| Patty Murray, D–Wash. | 1993– |

## House

| | |
|---|---|
| Jeannette Rankin, R–Mont. | 1917–19; 1941–43 |
| Alice M. Robertson, R–Okla. | 1921–23 |
| Winnifred S. M. Huck, R–Ill. | 1922–23 |
| Mae E. Nolan, R–Calif. | 1923–25 |
| Florence P. Kahn, R–Calif. | 1925–37 |
| Mary T. Norton, D–N.J. | 1925–51 |
| Edith N. Rogers, R–Mass. | 1925–60 |
| Katherine G. Langley, R–Ky. | 1927–31 |
| Ruth H. McCormick, R–Ill. | 1929–31 |
| Pearl P. Oldfield, D–Ark. | 1929–31 |
| Ruth B. Owen, D–Fla. | 1929–33 |
| Ruth S. B. Pratt, R–N.Y. | 1929–33 |
| Effiegene Wingo, D–Ark. | 1930–33 |
| Willa M. B. Eslick, D–Tenn. | 1932–33 |
| Marian W. Clarke, R–N.Y. | 1933–35 |
| Virginia E. Jenckes, D–Ind. | 1933–39 |

| | |
|---|---|
| Kathryn O'Loughlin McCarthy, D–Kan. | 1933–35 |
| Isabella S. Greenway, D–Ariz. | 1933–37 |
| Caroline L. G. O'Day, D–N.Y. | 1935–43 |
| Nan W. Honeyman, D–Ore. | 1937–39 |
| Elizabeth H. Gasque, D–S.C. [2] | 1938–39 |
| Clara G. McMillan, D–S.C. | 1939–41 |
| Jessie Sumner, R–Ill. | 1939–47 |
| Frances P. Bolton, R–Ohio | 1940–69 |
| Florence R. Gibbs, D–Ga. | 1940–41 |
| Margaret Chase Smith, R–Maine | 1940–49 |
| Katherine E. Byron, D–Md. | 1941–43 |
| Veronica G. Boland, D–Pa. | 1942–43 |
| Clare Boothe Luce , R–Conn. | 1943–47 |
| Winifred C. Stanley, R–N.Y. | 1943–45 |
| Willa L. Fulmer, D–S.C. | 1944–45 |
| Emily T. Douglas, D–Ill. | 1945–47 |
| Helen G. Douglas, D–Calif. | 1945–51 |
| Chase G. Woodhouse, D–Conn. | 1945–47; 1949–51 |
| Helen D. Mankin, D–Ga. | 1946–47 |
| Eliza J. Pratt, D–N.C. | 1946–47 |
| Georgia L. Lusk, D–N.M. | 1947–49 |
| Katherine P. C. St. George, R–N.Y. | 1947–65 |
| Reva Z. B. Bosone, D–Utah | 1949–53 |
| Cecil M. Harden, R–Ind. | 1949–59 |
| Edna F. Kelly, D–N.Y. | 1949–69 |
| Vera D. Buchanan, D–Pa. | 1951–55 |
| Marguerite S. Church, R–Ill. | 1951–63 |
| Maude E. Kee, D–W.Va. | 1951–65 |
| Ruth Thompson , R–Mich. | 1951–57 |
| Gracie B. Pfost, D–Idaho | 1953–63 |
| Leonor K. Sullivan, D–Mo. | 1953–77 |
| Iris F. Blitch, D–Ga. | 1955–63 |
| Edith Green, D–Ore. | 1955–75 |
| Martha W. Griffiths, D–Mich. | 1955–74 |
| Coya G. Knutson, DFL–Minn. | 1955–59 |
| Kathryn E. Granahan, D–Pa. | 1956–63 |
| Florence P. Dwyer, R–N.J. | 1957–73 |
| Catherine D. May, R–Wash. | 1959–71 |
| Edna O. Simpson, R–Ill. | 1959–61 |
| Jessica McC. Weis, R–N.Y. | 1959–63 |

| | | | |
|---|---|---|---|
| Julia B. Hansen, D–Wash. | 1960–74 | Marcy Kaptur, D–Ohio | 1983– |
| Catherine D. Norrell, D–Ark. | 1961–63 | Barbara Vucanovich, R–Nev. | 1983– |
| Louise G. Reece, R–Tenn. | 1961–63 | Helen Delich Bentley, R–Md. | 1985– |
| Corinne B. Riley, D–S.C. | 1962–63 | Jan Meyers, R–Kan. | 1985– |
| Charlotte T. Reid, R–Ill. | 1963–71 | Cathy Long, D–La. | 1985–87 |
| Irene B. Baker, R–Tenn. | 1964–65 | Constance A. Morella, R–Md. | 1987– |
| Patsy T. Mink, D–Hawaii | 1965–77; 1990– | Elizabeth J. Patterson, D–S.C. | 1987–93 |
| Lera M. Thomas, D–Texas | 1966–67 | Patricia Saiki, R–Hawaii | 1987–91 |
| Margaret M. Heckler, R–Mass. | 1967–83 | Louise M. Slaughter, D–N.Y. | 1987– |
| Shirley Chisholm, D–N.Y. | 1969–83 | Nancy Pelosi, D–Calif. | 1987– |
| Bella S. Abzug, D–N.Y. | 1971–77 | Nita M. Lowey, D–N.Y. | 1989– |
| Ella T. Grasso, D–Conn. | 1971–75 | Jolene Unsoeld, D–Wash. | 1989– |
| Louise Day Hicks, D–Mass. | 1971–73 | Jill Long, D–Ind. | 1989– |
| Elizabeth B. Andrews, D–Ala. | 1972–73 | Ileana Ros-Lehtinen, R–Fla. | 1989– |
| Yvonne B. Burke, D–Calif. | 1973–79 | Susan Molinari, R–N.Y. | 1990– |
| Marjorie S. Holt, R–Md. | 1973–87 | Barbara-Rose Collins, D–Mich. | 1991– |
| Elizabeth Holtzman, D–N.Y. | 1973–81 | Rosa DeLauro, D–Conn. | 1991– |
| Barbara C. Jordan, D–Texas | 1973–79 | Joan Kelly Horn, D–Mo. | 1991–93 |
| Patricia Schroeder, D–Colo. | 1973– | Maxine Waters, D–Calif. | 1991– |
| Corinne C. Boggs, D–La. | 1973–91 | Corrine Brown, D–Fla. | 1993– |
| Cardiss R. Collins, D–Ill. | 1973– | Leslie L. Byrne, D–Va. | 1993– |
| Marilyn Lloyd, D–Tenn. | 1975– | Maria Cantwell, D–Wash. | 1993– |
| Millicent Fenwick, R–N.J. | 1975–83 | Eva Clayton, D–N.C. | 1993– |
| Martha E. Keys, D–Kan. | 1975–79 | Pat Danner, D–Mo. | 1993– |
| Helen S. Meyner, D–N.J. | 1975–79 | Jennifer Dunn, R–Wash. | 1993– |
| Virginia Smith, R–Neb. | 1975–91 | Karan English, D–Ariz. | 1993– |
| Gladys Noon Spellman, D–Md. | 1975–81 | Anna G. Eshoo, D–Calif. | 1993– |
| Shirley N. Pettis, R–Calif. | 1975–79 | Tillie Fowler, R–Fla. | 1993– |
| Barbara A. Mikulski, D–Md. | 1977–87 | Elizabeth Furse, D–Ore. | 1993– |
| Mary Rose Oakar, D–Ohio | 1977–93 | Jane Harman, D–Calif. | 1993– |
| Beverly Byron, D–Md. | 1979–93 | Eddie Bernice Johnson, D–Texas | 1993– |
| Geraldine Ferraro, D–N.Y. | 1979–85 | Blanche Lambert, D–Ark. | 1993– |
| Olympia J. Snowe, R–Maine | 1979– | Carolyn B. Maloney, D–N.Y. | 1993– |
| Bobbi Fiedler, R–Calif. | 1981–87 | Cynthia McKinney, D–Ga. | 1993– |
| Lynn M. Martin, R–Ill. | 1981–91 | Carrie Meek, D–Fla. | 1993– |
| Marge Roukema, R–N.J. | 1981– | Marjorie Margolies-Mezvinsky, D–Pa. | 1993– |
| Claudine Schneider, R–R.I. | 1981–91 | Deborah Pryce, R–Ohio | 1993– |
| Jean Ashbrook, R–Ohio | 1982–83 | Lucille Roybal-Allard, D–Calif. | 1993– |
| Barbara B. Kennelly, D–Conn. | 1982– | Lynn Schenk, D–Calif. | 1993– |
| Katie Hall, D–Ind. | 1982–85 | Karen Shepherd, D–Utah | 1993– |
| Sala Burton, D–Calif. | 1983–87 | Karen L. Thurman, D–Fla. | 1993– |
| Barbara Boxer, D–Calif. | 1983–93 | Nydia M. Velazquez, D–N.Y. | 1993– |
| Nancy L. Johnson, R–Conn. | 1983– | Lynn Woolsey, D–Calif. | 1993– |

SOURCES: *Women in Congress, 1917–1990,* Commission on the Bicentenary of the U.S. House of Representatives (Washington, D.C.: Government Printing Office, 1991); *Congressional Quarterly Weekly Report,* selected issues.

[1] Felton was sworn in Nov. 21, 1922, to fill the vacancy created by the death of Thomas E. Watson, D. The next day she gave up her seat to Walter F. George, D, the elected candidate for the vacancy.

[2] Never sworn in because Congress was not in session between election and expiration of term.

NOTE* Another woman was elected to the Senate in a June 1993 special election: Kay Bailey Hutchison, R–Texas.

## Black Members of Congress, 1870–1993

As of January 1993, eighty–six black Americans had served in Congress; four in the Senate and eighty–two in the House.* Following is a list of the black members, their parties and states, and the years in which they served. In addition, John W. Menard, R–La., won a disputed election in 1868 but was not permitted to take his seat in Congress. In addition to the blacks listed below, Walter E. Fauntroy, D (1971–91) and Eleanor Holmes Norton, D (1991–   ) served as delegates from the District of Columbia.

### Senate

| | |
|---|---|
| Hiram R. Revels, R–Miss. | 1870–71 |
| Blanche K. Bruce, R–Miss. | 1875–81 |
| Edward W. Brooke, R–Mass. | 1967–79 |
| Carol Moseley-Braun, D–Ill. | 1993– |

### House

| | |
|---|---|
| Joseph H. Rainey, R–S.C. | 1870–79 |
| Jefferson F. Long, R–Ga. | 1870–71 |
| Robert C. De Large, R–S.C. | 1871–73 |
| Robert B. Elliott, R–S.C. | 1871–74 |
| Benjamin S. Turner, R–Ala. | 1871–73 |
| Josiah T. Walls, R–Fla. | 1871–76 |
| Richard H. Cain, R–S.C. | 1873–75; 1877–79 |
| John R. Lynch, R–Miss. | 1873–77; 1882–83 |
| Alonzo J. Ransier, R–S.C. | 1873–75 |
| James T. Rapier, R–Ala. | 1873–75 |
| Jeremiah Haralson, R–Ala. | 1875–77 |
| John A. Hyman, R–N.C. | 1875–77 |
| Charles E. Nash, R–La. | 1875–77 |
| Robert Smalls, R–S.C. | 1875–79; 1882–83; 1884–87 |
| James E. O'Hara, R–N.C. | 1883–87 |
| Henry P. Cheatham, R–N.C. | 1889–93 |
| John M. Langston, R–Va. | 1890–91 |
| Thomas E. Miller, R–S.C. | 1890–91 |
| George W. Murray, R–S.C. | 1893–95; 1896–97 |
| George H. White, R–N.C. | 1897–1901 |
| Oscar De Priest, R–Ill. | 1929–35 |
| Arthur W. Mitchell, D–Ill. | 1935–43 |
| William L. Dawson, D–Ill. | 1943–70 |
| Adam Clayton Powell, Jr., D–N.Y. | 1945–67; 1969–71 |
| Charles C. Diggs, Jr., D–Mich. | 1955–80 |
| Robert N. C. Nix, D–Pa. | 1958–79 |
| Augustus F. Hawkins, D–Calif. | 1963–91 |
| John Conyers, Jr., D–Mich. | 1965– |
| Shirley Chisholm, D–N.Y. | 1969–83 |
| William L. Clay, D–Mo. | 1969– |
| Louis Stokes, D–Ohio | 1969– |
| George W. Collins, D–Ill. | 1970–72 |
| Ronald V. Dellums, D–Calif. | 1971– |
| Ralph H. Metcalfe, D–Ill. | 1971–78 |
| Parren J. Mitchell, D–Md. | 1971–87 |
| Charles B. Rangel, D–N.Y. | 1971– |
| Yvonne B. Burke, D–Calif. | 1973–79 |
| Cardiss Collins, D–Ill. | 1973– |
| Barbara C. Jordan, D–Texas | 1973–79 |
| Andrew Young, D–Ga. | 1973–77 |
| Harold E. Ford, D–Tenn. | 1975– |
| Julian C. Dixon, D–Calif. | 1979– |
| William H. Gray III, D–Pa. | 1979–91 |
| George T. Leland, D–Texas | 1979–89 |
| Bennett McVey Stewart, D–Ill. | 1979–81 |
| George W. Crockett, Jr., D–Mich. | 1981–91 |
| Mervin M. Dymally, D–Calif. | 1981–93 |
| Gus Savage, D–Ill. | 1981–93 |
| Harold Washington, D–Ill. | 1981–83 |
| Katie Hall, D–Ind. | 1983–85 |
| Charles A. Hayes, D–Ill. | 1983–93 |
| Major R. Owens, D–N.Y. | 1983– |
| Edolphus Towns, D–N.Y. | 1983– |
| Alan Wheat, D–Mo. | 1983– |
| Alton R. Waldon, Jr., D–N.Y. | 1986–87 |
| Mike Espy, D–Miss. | 1987–93 |
| Floyd H. Flake, D–N.Y. | 1987– |
| John Lewis, D–Ga. | 1987– |
| Kweisi Mfume, D–Md. | 1987– |
| Donald M. Payne, D–N.J. | 1989– |
| Craig Washington, D–Texas | 1990– |
| Barbara-Rose Collins, D–Mich. | 1991– |
| Gary Franks, R–Conn. | 1991– |
| William J. Jefferson, D–La. | 1991– |
| Maxine Waters, D–Calif. | 1991– |
| Lucien E. Blackwell, D–Pa. | 1991– |
| Eva Clayton, D–N.C. | 1992– |
| Sanford Bishop, D–Ga. | 1993– |
| Corrine Brown, D–Fla. | 1993– |

| | | | | |
|---|---|---|---|---|
| James E. Clyburn, D–S.C. | 1993– | | Mel Reynolds, D–Ill. | 1993– |
| Cleo Fields, D–La. | 1993– | | Bobby L. Rush, D–Ill. | 1993– |
| Alcee L. Hastings, D–Fla. | 1993– | | Robert C. Scott, D–Va. | 1993– |
| Earl F. Hilliard, D–Ala. | 1993– | | Walter R. Tucker, D–Calif. | 1993– |
| Eddie Bernice Johnson, D–Texas | 1993– | | Melvin Watt, D–N.C. | 1993– |
| Cynthia McKinney, D–Ga. | 1993– | | Albert R. Wynn, D–Md. | 1993– |
| Carrie Meek, D–Fla. | 1993– | | | |

SOURCES: Maurine Christopher, *America's Black Congressmen* (Thomas Y. Crowell, 1971); U.S. Congress, Joint Committee on Printing, *Biographical Directory of the American Congress, 1774–1989* (Washington, D.C.: Government Printing Office, 1989); *Congressional Quarterly Weekly Report,* selected issues.

* Another African-American was elected to the House in an April 1993 special election: Bennie Thompson, D–Miss.

# Hispanic Members of Congress, 1877–1993

As of January 1993, thirty-one Hispanics had served in Congress; one in both the Senate and the House, one in the Senate only, and twenty-nine in the House only. Following is a list of the Hispanic members, their parties and states, and the years in which they served. Not included are Hispanics who served as territorial delegates (ten), resident commissioners of Puerto Rico (fourteeen), or delegates of Guam (one) or the Virgin Islands (one).

**Senate**

| | |
|---|---|
| Dennis Chavez, D–N.M. | 1935–62 |
| Joseph Montoya, D–N.M. | 1964–77 |

**House**

| | |
|---|---|
| Romualdo Pacheco, R–Calif. | 1877–78; 1879–83 |
| Ladislas Lazaro, D–La. | 1913–27 |
| Benigno Cardenas Hernandez, R–N.M. | 1915–17; 1919–21 |
| Nestor Montoya, R–N.M. | 1921–23 |
| Dennis Chavez, D–N.M. | 1931–35 |
| Joachim Octave Fernandez, D–La. | 1931–41 |
| Antonia Manuel Fernandez, D–N.M. | 1943–56 |
| Henry B. Gonzalez, D–Texas | 1961– |
| Edward R. Roybal, D–Calif. | 1963–93 |
| E. "Kika" de la Garza, D–Texas | 1965– |
| Manuel Lujan, Jr., R–N.M. | 1969–89 |
| Herman Badillo, D–N.Y. | 1971–77 |
| Robert Garcia, D–N.Y. | 1978–90 |
| Tony Coelho, D–Calif. | 1979–89 |
| Matthew G. Martinez, D–Calif. | 1982– |
| Solomon P. Ortiz, D–Texas | 1983– |
| William B. Richardson, D–N.M. | 1983– |
| Esteban E. Torres, D–Calif. | 1983– |
| Albert G. Bustamante, D–Texas | 1985–93 |
| Ileana Ros-Lehtinen, R–Fla. | 1989– |
| José E. Serrano, D–N.Y. | 1990– |
| Ed Pastor, D–Ariz. | 1991– |
| Xavier Becerra, D–Calif. | 1993– |
| Henry Bonilla, R–Texas | 1993– |
| Lincoln Diaz-Balart, R–Fla. | 1993– |
| Luis V. Gutierrez, D–Ill. | 1993– |
| Robert Menendez, D–N.J. | 1993– |
| Lucille Roybal-Allard, D–Calif. | 1993– |
| Frank Tejeda, D–Texas | 1993– |
| Nydia M. Velázquez, D–N.Y. | 1993– |

SOURCES: *Congressional Quarterly Weekly Report,* selected issues; Congressional Hispanic Caucus.

## Cases of Expulsion in the House

| Year | Member | Grounds | Disposition |
|------|--------|---------|-------------|
| 1798 | Matthew Lyon, Anti–Fed–Vt. | Assault on representative | Not expelled |
| 1798 | Roger Griswold, Fed–Conn. | Assault on representative | Not expelled |
| 1799 | Matthew Lyon, Anti–Fed–Vt. | Sedition | Not expelled |
| 1838 | William J. Graves, Whig–Ky. | Killing of representative in duel | Not expelled |
| 1839 | Alexander Duncan, Whig–Ohio | Offensive publication | Not expelled |
| 1856 | Preston S. Brooks, State Rights Dem.–S.C. | Assault on senator | Not expelled |
| 1857 | Orsamus B. Matteson, Whig–N.Y. | Corruption | Not expelled |
| 1857 | William A. Gilbert, Whig–N.Y. | Corruption | Not expelled |
| 1857 | William W. Welch, American–Conn. | Corruption | Not expelled |
| 1857 | Francis S. Edwards, American–N.Y. | Corruption | Not expelled |
| 1858 | Orsamus B. Matteson, Whig–N.Y. | Corruption | Not expelled |
| 1861 | John B. Clark, D–Mo. | Support of rebellion | Expelled |
| 1861 | Henry C. Burnett, D–Ky. | Support of rebellion | Expelled |
| 1861 | John W. Reid, D–Mo. | Support of rebellion | Expelled |
| 1864 | Alexander Long, D–Ohio | Treasonable utterance | Not expelled [1] |
| 1864 | Benjamin G. Harris, D–Md. | Treasonable utterance | Not expelled [1] |
| 1866 | Lovell H. Rousseau, R–Ky. | Assault on representative | Not expelled [1] |
| 1870 | Benjamin F. Whittemore, R–S.C. | Corruption | Not expelled [1] |
| 1870 | Roderick R. Butler, R–Tenn. | Corruption | Not expelled [1] |
| 1873 | Oakes Ames, R–Mass. | Corruption | Not expelled [1] |
| 1873 | James Brooks, D–N.Y. | Corruption | Not expelled [1] |
| 1875 | John Y. Brown, D–Ky. | Insult to representative | Not expelled [1] |
| 1875 | William S. King, R–Minn. | Corruption | Not expelled |
| 1875 | John G. Schumaker, D–N.Y. | Corruption | Not expelled |
| 1884 | William P. Kellogg, R–La. | Corruption | Not expelled |
| 1921 | Thomas L. Blanton, D–Texas | Abuse of leave to print | Not expelled [1] |
| 1979 | Charles C. Diggs, Jr., D–Mich. | Misuse of clerk–hire funds | Not expelled [1] |
| 1980 | Michael J. "Ozzie" Myers, D–Pa. | Corruption | Expelled |
| 1988 | Mario Biaggi, D–N.Y | Corruption | Not expelled [2] |
| 1990 | Barney Frank, D–Mass. | Discrediting House | Not expelled [3] |

SOURCES: Hinds and Cannon, *Precedents of the House of Representatives of the United States,* 11 vols. (1935–41); Joint Committee on Congressional Operations, *House of Representatives Exclusion, Censure, and Expulsion Cases from 1789 to 1973,* 93rd Cong., 1st sess., 1973, committee print; *Congressional Quarterly Almanac 1980; Congressional Quarterly Weekly Report,* selected issues.

[1] Censured after expulsion move failed or was withdrawn.
[2] Facing probable expulsion, Biaggi resigned from Congress on August 8, 1988.
[3] Reprimanded after expulsion and censure moves failed.

# Cases of Expulsion in the Senate

| Year | Member | Grounds | Disposition |
|------|--------|---------|-------------|
| 1797 | William Blount, Ind–Tenn. | Anti–Spanish conspiracy | Expelled |
| 1808 | John Smith, D–Ohio | Disloyalty | Not expelled |
| 1858 | Henry M. Rice, D–Minn. | Corruption | Not expelled |
| 1861 | James M. Mason, D–Va. | Support of rebellion | Expelled |
| 1861 | Robert M. T. Hunter, D–Va. | Support of rebellion | Expelled |
| 1861 | Thomas L. Clingman, D–N.C. | Support of rebellion | Expelled |
| 1861 | Thomas Bragg, D–N.C. | Support of rebellion | Expelled |
| 1861 | James Chestnut, Jr., States Rights–S.C. | Support of rebellion | Expelled |
| 1861 | Alfred O. P. Nicholson, D–Tenn. | Support of rebellion | Expelled |
| 1861 | William K. Sebastian, D–Ark. | Support of rebellion | Expelled [1] |
| 1861 | Charles B. Mitchel, D–Ark. | Support of rebellion | Expelled |
| 1861 | John Hemphill, State Rights D–Texas | Support of rebellion | Expelled |
| 1861 | Louis T. Wigfall, D–Texas [2] | Support of rebellion | Not expelled |
| 1861 | Louis T. Wigfall, D–Texas | Support of rebellion | Expelled |
| 1861 | John C. Breckinridge, D–Ky. | Support of rebellion | Expelled |
| 1861 | Lazarus W. Powell, D–Ky. | Support of rebellion | Not expelled |
| 1862 | Trusten Polk, D–Mo. | Support of rebellion | Expelled |
| 1862 | Jesse D. Bright, D–Ind. | Support of rebellion | Expelled |
| 1862 | Waldo P. Johnson, D–Mo. | Support of rebellion | Expelled |
| 1862 | James F. Simmons, Whig–R.I. | Corruption | Not expelled |
| 1873 | James W. Patterson, R–N.H. | Corruption | Not expelled |
| 1893 | William N. Roach, D–N.D. | Embezzlement | Not expelled |
| 1905 | John H. Mitchell, R–Ore. | Corruption | Not expelled |
| 1907 | Reed Smoot, R–Utah | Mormonism | Not expelled |
| 1919 | Robert M. La Follette, R–Wis. | Disloyalty | Not expelled |
| 1934 | John H. Overton, D–La. | Corruption | Not expelled |
| 1934 | Huey P. Long, D–La. | Corruption | Not expelled |
| 1942 | William Langer, R–N.D. | Corruption | Not expelled |
| 1982 | Harrison A. Williams, Jr., D–N.J. | Corruption | Not expelled [3] |

SOURCES: Senate Committee on Rules and Administration, Subcommittee on Privileges and Elections, *Senate Election, Expulsion, and Censure Cases from 1793 to 1972,* comp. Richard D. Hupman, 92nd Cong., 1st sess., 1972, S Doc 92–7; *Congress and the Nation 1981–84,* vol. 6. (Washington, D.C.: Congressional Quarterly Inc.)

[1] The Senate reversed its decision on Sebastian's expulsion March 3, 1877. Sebastian had died in 1865, but his children were paid an amount equal to his Senate salary between the time of his expulsion and the date of his death.

[2] The Senate took no action on an initial resolution expelling Wigfall because he represented a state that had seceded from the Union; three months later he was expelled for supporting the Confederacy.

[3] Facing probable expulsion, Williams resigned March 11, 1982.

# Censure Proceedings in the House

| Year | Member | Grounds | Disposition |
|---|---|---|---|
| 1798 | Matthew Lyon, Anti–Fed–Vt. | Assault on representative | Not censured |
| 1798 | Roger Griswold, Fed–Conn. | Assault on representative | Not censured |
| 1832 | William Stanbery, JD–Ohio | Insult to Speaker | Censured |
| 1836 | Sherrod Williams, Whig–Ky. | Insult to Speaker | Not censured |
| 1838 | Henry A. Wise, Tyler Dem.–Va. | Service as second in duel | Not censured |
| 1839 | Alexander Duncan, Whig–Ohio | Offensive publication | Not censured |
| 1842 | John Q. Adams, Whig–Mass. | Treasonable petition | Not censured |
| 1842 | Joshua R. Giddings, Whig–Ohio | Offensive paper | Censured |
| 1856 | Henry A. Edmundson, D–Va. | Complicity in assault on senator | Not censured |
| 1856 | Laurence M. Keitt, D–S.C. | Complicity in assault on senator | Censured |
| 1860 | George S. Houston, D–Ala. | Insult to representative | Not censured |
| 1864 | Alexander Long, D–Ohio | Treasonable utterance | Censured |
| 1864 | Benjamin G. Harris, D–Md. | Treasonable utterance | Censured |
| 1866 | John W. Chanler, D–N.Y. | Insult to House | Censured |
| 1866 | Lovell H. Rousseau, R–Ky. | Assault on representative | Censured |
| 1867 | John W. Hunter, Ind–N.Y. | Insult to representative | Censured |
| 1868 | Fernando Wood, D–N.Y. | Offensive utterance | Censured |
| 1868 | E. D. Holbrook, D–Idaho[1] | Offensive utterance | Censured |
| 1870 | Benjamin F. Whittemore, R–S.C. | Corruption | Censured |
| 1870 | Roderick R. Butler, R–Tenn. | Corruption | Censured |
| 1870 | John T. Deweese, D–N.C. | Corruption | Censured |
| 1873 | Oakes Ames, R–Mass. | Corruption | Censured |
| 1873 | James Brooks, D–N.Y. | Corruption | Censured |
| 1875 | John Y. Brown, D–Ky. | Insult to representative | Censured[2] |
| 1876 | James G. Blaine, R–Maine | Corruption | Not censured |
| 1882 | William D. Kelley, R–Pa. | Offensive utterance | Not censured |
| 1882 | John D. White, R–Ky. | Offensive utterance | Not censured |
| 1883 | John Van Voorhis, R–N.Y. | Offensive utterance | Not censured |
| 1890 | William D. Bynum, D–Ind. | Offensive utterance | Censured |
| 1921 | Thomas L. Blanton, D–Texas | Abuse of leave to print | Censured |
| 1978 | Edward R. Roybal, D–Calif. | Lying to House committee | Not censured[3] |
| 1979 | Charles C. Diggs, Jr., D–Mich. | Misuse of clerk–hire funds | Censured |
| 1980 | Charles H. Wilson, D–Calif. | Financial misconduct | Censured |
| 1983 | Gerry E. Studds, D–Mass. | Sexual misconduct | Censured |
| 1983 | Daniel B. Crane, R–Ill. | Sexual misconduct | Censured |
| 1990 | Barney Frank, D–Mass. | Discrediting House | Not censured[3] |

SOURCES: Hinds and Cannon, *Precedents of the House of Representatives of the United States,* 11 vols. (1935–41); Joint Committee on Congressional Operations, *House of Representatives Exclusion, Censure, and Expulsion Cases from 1789 to 1973,* 93rd Cong., 1st sess., 1973, committee print; *Congress and the Nation 1977–80, 1981–84, 1985–88,* vols. 5–7 (Washington, D.C.: Congressional Quarterly Inc.); *Congressional Quarterly Almanac 1990.*

[1] Holbrook was a territorial delegate, not a representative.

[2] The House later rescinded part of the censure resolution against Brown.

[3] Reprimanded after censure resolution failed or was withdrawn.

## Censure Proceedings in the Senate

| Year | Member | Grounds | Disposition |
|------|--------|---------|-------------|
| 1811 | Timothy Pickering, Fed–Mass. | Breach of confidence | Censured |
| 1844 | Benjamin Tappan, D–Ohio | Breach of confidence | Censured |
| 1850 | Thomas H. Benton, D–Mo. | Disorderly conduct | Not censured |
| 1850 | Henry S. Foote, Unionist–Miss. | Disorderly conduct | Not censured |
| 1902 | John L. McLaurin, D–S.C. | Assault | Censured |
| 1902 | Benjamin R. Tillman, D–S.C. | Assault | Censured |
| 1929 | Hiram Bingham, R–Conn. | Bringing Senate into disrepute | Condemned [1] |
| 1954 | Joseph R. McCarthy, R–Wis. | Obstruction of legislative process, insult to senators, etc. | Condemned [1] |
| 1967 | Thomas J. Dodd, D–Conn. | Financial misconduct | Censured |
| 1979 | Herman E. Talmadge, D–Ga. | Financial misconduct | Denounced [2] |
| 1990 | Dave Durenberger, R–Minn. | Financial misconduct | Denounced [2] |
| 1991 | Alan Cranston, D–Calif. | Improper conduct | Reprimanded [3] |

SOURCES: Senate Committee on Rules and Administration, Subcommittee on Privileges and Elections, *Senate Election, Expulsion, and Censure Cases from 1793 to 1972,* comp. Richard D. Hupman, 92nd Cong., 1st sess., 1972, S Doc 92–7; *Congress and the Nation 1977–80,* vol. 5 (Washington, D.C.: Congressional Quarterly Inc.); *Congressional Quarterly Almanac 1990.*

[1]The word *condemned* as used in the Bingham and McCarthy cases is regarded as the same as *censured.*

[2]As in the Bingham and McCarthy cases, the word *denounced* as applied to Talmadge and Durenberger is considered virtually synonymous with *censured.*

[3]The Ethics Committee reprimanded Cranston on behalf of the full Senate, after determining that it lacked the authority to issue a censure in the same manner. The reprimand was delivered on the Senate floor by committee leaders, but there was no vote or formal action by the full Senate. It was the first use of *reprimand* in the Senate.

## Incumbents Reelected, Defeated, or Retired, 1946–1992

| Year | Retired[1] | Total seeking reelection | Defeated in primaries | Defeated in general election | Total reelected | Percentage of those seeking reelection |
|------|-----------|-------------------------|----------------------|------------------------------|-----------------|----------------------------------------|
| HOUSE | | | | | | |
| 1946 | 32 | 398 | 18 | 52 | 328 | 82.4 |
| 1948 | 29 | 400 | 15 | 68 | 317 | 79.3 |
| 1950 | 29 | 400 | 6 | 32 | 362 | 90.5 |
| 1952 | 42 | 389 | 9 | 26 | 354 | 91.0 |
| 1954 | 24 | 407 | 6 | 22 | 379 | 93.1 |
| 1956 | 21 | 411 | 6 | 16 | 389 | 94.6 |
| 1958 | 33 | 396 | 3 | 37 | 356 | 89.9 |
| 1960 | 26 | 405 | 5 | 25 | 375 | 92.6 |
| 1962 | 24 | 402 | 12 | 22 | 368 | 91.5 |
| 1964 | 33 | 397 | 8 | 45 | 344 | 86.6 |
| 1966 | 22 | 411 | 8 | 41 | 362 | 88.1 |
| 1968 | 23 | 409 | 4 | 9 | 396 | 96.8 |
| 1970 | 29 | 401 | 10 | 12 | 379 | 94.5 |
| 1972 | 40 | 390 | 12 | 13 | 365 | 93.6 |
| 1974 | 43 | 391 | 8 | 40 | 343 | 87.7 |
| 1976 | 47 | 384 | 3 | 13 | 368 | 95.8 |
| 1978 | 49 | 382 | 5 | 19 | 358 | 93.7 |
| 1980 | 34 | 398 | 6 | 31 | 361 | 90.7 |
| 1982 | 40 | 393 | 10 | 29 | 354 | 90.1 |
| 1984 | 22 | 409 | 3 | 16 | 390 | 95.4 |
| 1986 | 38 | 393 | 2 | 6 | 385 | 98.0 |
| 1988 | 23 | 408 | 1 | 6 | 401 | 98.3 |
| 1990 | 27 | 406 | 1 | 15 | 390 | 96.0 |
| 1992 | 65 | 368 | 19 | 24 | 325 | 88.3 |
| SENATE | | | | | | |
| 1946 | 9 | 30 | 6 | 7 | 17 | 56.7 |
| 1948 | 8 | 25 | 2 | 8 | 15 | 60.0 |
| 1950 | 4 | 32 | 5 | 5 | 22 | 68.8 |
| 1952 | 4 | 31 | 2 | 9 | 20 | 64.5 |
| 1954 | 6 | 32 | 2 | 6 | 24 | 75.0 |
| 1956 | 6 | 29 | 0 | 4 | 25 | 86.2 |
| 1958 | 6 | 28 | 0 | 10 | 18 | 64.3 |
| 1960 | 5 | 29 | 0 | 1 | 28 | 96.6 |
| 1962 | 4 | 35 | 1 | 5 | 29 | 82.9 |
| 1964 | 2 | 33 | 1 | 4 | 28 | 84.8 |
| 1966 | 3 | 32 | 3 | 1 | 28 | 87.5 |
| 1968 | 6 | 28 | 4 | 4 | 20 | 71.4 |
| 1970 | 4 | 31 | 1 | 6 | 24 | 77.4 |
| 1972 | 6 | 27 | 2 | 5 | 20 | 74.1 |

| ·Year | Retired[1] | Total seeking reelection | Defeated in primaries | Defeated in general election | Total reelected | Percentage of those seeking reelection |
|-------|---------|--------------------------|----------------------|------------------------------|-----------------|-----------------------------------------|
| 1974 | 7 | 27 | 2 | 2 | 23 | 85.2 |
| 1976 | 8 | 25 | 0 | 9 | 16 | 64.0 |
| 1978 | 10 | 25 | 3 | 7 | 15 | 60.0 |
| 1980 | 5 | 29 | 4 | 9 | 16 | 55.2 |
| 1982 | 3 | 30 | 0 | 2 | 28 | 93.3 |
| 1984 | 4 | 29 | 0 | 3 | 26 | 89.6 |
| 1986 | 6 | 28 | 0 | 7 | 21 | 75.0 |
| 1988 | 6 | 27 | 0 | 4 | 23 | 85.2 |
| 1990 | 3 | 32 | 0 | 1 | 31 | 96.9 |
| 1992 | 7 | 28 | 1 | 4 | 23 | 82.1 |

SOURCE: Norman J. Ornstein, Thomas E. Mann, and Michael J. Malbin, *Vital Statistics on Congress, 1993–1994* (Washington, D.C.: Congressional Quarterly, 1993).
[1] Does not include persons who died or resigned before the election.

## Party Affiliations in Congress and the Presidency, 1789-1993

| Year | Congress | HOUSE Majority party | HOUSE Principal minority party | SENATE Majority party | SENATE Principal minority party | President |
|------|----------|---------------|------------------|---------------|------------------|-----------|
| 1993–1995 | 103rd | D–258 | R–176 | D–57 | R–43 | D (Clinton) |
| 1991–1993 | 102nd | D–267 | R–167 | D–56 | R–44 | R (Bush) |
| 1989–1991 | 101st | D–259 | R–174 | D–55 | R–45 | R (Bush) |
| 1987–1989 | 100th | D–258 | R–177 | D–55 | R–45 | R (Reagan) |
| 1985–1987 | 99th | D–252 | R–182 | R–53 | D–47 | R (Reagan) |
| 1983–1985 | 98th | D–269 | R–165 | R–54 | D–46 | R (Reagan) |
| 1981–1983 | 97th | D–243 | R–192 | R–53 | D–46 | R (Reagan) |
| 1979–1981 | 96th | D–276 | R–157 | D–58 | R–41 | D (Carter) |
| 1977–1979 | 95th | D–292 | R–143 | D–61 | R–38 | D (Carter) |
| 1975–1977 | 94th | D–291 | R–144 | D–60 | R–37 | R (Ford) |
| 1973–1975 | 93rd | D–239 | R–192 | D–56 | R–42 | R (Ford) |
| | | | | | | R (Nixon) |
| 1971–1973 | 92nd | D–254 | R–180 | D–54 | R–44 | R (Nixon) |
| 1969–1971 | 91st | D–243 | R–192 | D–57 | R–43 | R (Nixon) |
| 1967–1969 | 90th | D–247 | R–187 | D–64 | R–36 | D (L. Johnson) |
| 1965–1967 | 89th | D–295 | R–140 | D–68 | R–32 | D (L. Johnson) |
| 1963–1965 | 88th | D–258 | R–177 | D–67 | R–33 | D (L. Johnson) |
| | | | | | | D (Kennedy) |
| 1961–1963 | 87th | D–263 | R–174 | D–65 | R–35 | D (Kennedy) |
| 1959–1961 | 86th | D–283 | R–153 | D–64 | R–34 | R (Eisenhower) |
| 1957–1959 | 85th | D–233 | R–200 | D–49 | R–47 | R (Eisenhower) |
| 1955–1957 | 84th | D–232 | R–203 | D–48 | R–47 | R (Eisenhower) |
| 1953–1955 | 83rd | R–221 | D–211 | R–48 | D–47 | R (Eisenhower) |
| 1951–1953 | 82nd | D–234 | R–199 | D–49 | R–47 | D (Truman) |
| 1949–1951 | 81st | D–263 | R–171 | D–54 | R–42 | D (Truman) |
| 1947–1949 | 80th | R–245 | D–188 | R–51 | D–45 | D (Truman) |
| 1945–1947 | 79th | D–242 | R–190 | D–56 | R–38 | D (Truman) |
| 1943–1945 | 78th | D–218 | R–208 | D–58 | R–37 | D (F. Roosevelt) |
| 1941–1943 | 77th | D–268 | R–162 | D–66 | R–28 | D (F. Roosevelt) |
| 1939–1941 | 76th | D–261 | R–164 | D–69 | R–23 | D (F. Roosevelt) |
| 1937–1939 | 75th | D–331 | R–89 | D–76 | R–16 | D (F. Roosevelt) |
| 1935–1937 | 74th | D–319 | R–103 | D–69 | R–25 | D (F. Roosevelt) |
| 1933–1935 | 73rd | D–310 | R–117 | D–60 | R–35 | D (F. Roosevelt) |
| 1931–1933 | 72nd | D–220 | R–214 | R–48 | D–47 | R (Hoover) |
| 1929–1931 | 71st | R–267 | D–167 | R–56 | D–39 | R (Hoover) |
| 1927–1929 | 70th | R–237 | D–195 | R–49 | D–46 | R (Coolidge) |
| 1925–1927 | 69th | R–247 | D–183 | R–56 | D–39 | R (Coolidge) |

N O T E :  (Key to abbreviations: AD—Administration; AM—Anti–Masonic; D—Democratic; DR—Democratic-Republican; F—Federalist; J—Jacksonian; NR—National Republican; Op—Opposition; R—Republican; U—Unionist; W—Whig. Figures are for the beginning of the first session of each Congress.

| Year | Congress | HOUSE | | SENATE | | President |
| | | Majority party | Principal minority party | Majority party | Principal minority party | |
|------|----------|------|------|------|------|------|
| 1923–1925 | 68th | R–225 | D–205 | R–51 | D–43 | R (Coolidge) |
| 1921–1923 | 67th | R–301 | D–131 | R–59 | D–37 | R (Harding) |
| 1919–1921 | 66th | R–240 | D–190 | R–49 | D–47 | D (Wilson) |
| 1917–1919 | 65th | D–216 | R–210 | D–53 | R–42 | D (Wilson) |
| 1915–1917 | 64th | D–230 | R–196 | D–56 | R–40 | D (Wilson) |
| 1913–1915 | 63rd | D–291 | R–127 | D–51 | R–44 | D (Wilson) |
| 1911–1913 | 62nd | D–228 | R–161 | R–51 | D–41 | R (Taft) |
| 1909–1911 | 61st | R–219 | D–172 | R–61 | D–32 | R (Taft) |
| 1907–1909 | 60th | R–222 | D–164 | R–61 | D–31 | R (T. Roosevelt) |
| 1905–1907 | 59th | R–250 | D–136 | R–57 | D–33 | R (T. Roosevelt) |
| 1903–1905 | 58th | R–208 | D–178 | R–57 | D–33 | R (T. Roosevelt) |
| 1901–1903 | 57th | R–197 | D–151 | R–55 | D–31 | R (T. Roosevelt) |
| | | | | | | R (McKinley) |
| 1899–1901 | 56th | R–185 | D–163 | R–53 | D–26 | R (McKinley) |
| 1897–1899 | 55th | R–204 | D–113 | R–47 | D–34 | R (McKinley) |
| 1895–1897 | 54th | R–244 | D–105 | R–43 | D–39 | D (Cleveland) |
| 1893–1895 | 53rd | D–218 | R–127 | D–44 | R–38 | D (Cleveland) |
| 1891–1893 | 52nd | D–235 | R–88 | R–47 | D–39 | R (B. Harrison) |
| 1889–1891 | 51st | R–166 | D–159 | R–39 | D–37 | R (B. Harrison) |
| 1887–1889 | 50th | D–169 | R–152 | R–39 | D–37 | D (Cleveland) |
| 1885–1887 | 49th | D–183 | R–140 | R–43 | D–34 | D (Cleveland) |
| 1883–1885 | 48th | D–197 | R–118 | R–38 | D–36 | R (Arthur) |
| 1881–1883 | 47th | R–147 | D–135 | R–37 | D–37 | R (Arthur) |
| | | | | | | R (Garfield) |
| 1879–1881 | 46th | D–149 | R–130 | D–42 | R–33 | R (Hayes) |
| 1877–1879 | 45th | D–153 | R–140 | R–39 | D–36 | R (Hayes) |
| 1875–1877 | 44th | D–169 | R–109 | R–45 | D–29 | R (Grant) |
| 1873–1875 | 43rd | R–194 | D–92 | R–49 | D–19 | R (Grant) |
| 1871–1873 | 42nd | R–134 | D–104 | R–52 | D–17 | R (Grant) |
| 1869–1871 | 41st | R–149 | D–63 | R–56 | D–11 | R (Grant) |
| 1867–1869 | 40th | R–143 | D–49 | R–42 | D–11 | R (A. Johnson) |
| 1865–1867 | 39th | U–149 | D–42 | U–42 | D–10 | R (A. Johnson) |
| | | | | | | R (Lincoln) |
| 1863–1865 | 38th | R–102 | D–75 | R–36 | D–9 | R (Lincoln) |
| 1861–1863 | 37th | R–105 | D–43 | R–31 | D–10 | R (Lincoln) |
| 1859–1861 | 36th | R–114 | D–92 | D–36 | R–26 | D (Buchanan) |
| 1857–1859 | 35th | D–118 | R–92 | D–36 | R–20 | D (Buchanan) |
| 1855–1857 | 34th | R–108 | D–83 | D–40 | R–15 | D (Pierce) |

N O T E : (Key to abbreviations: AD—Administration; AM—Anti–Masonic; D—Democratic; DR—Democratic-Republican; F—Federalist; J—Jacksonian; NR—National Republican; Op—Opposition; R—Republican; U—Unionist; W—Whig. Figures are for the beginning of the first session of each Congress.

| Year | Congress | HOUSE | | SENATE | | President |
|------|----------|-------|--|--------|--|-----------|
| | | Majority party | Principal minority party | Majority party | Principal minority party | |
| 1853–1855 | 33rd | D–159 | W–71 | D–38 | W–22 | D (Pierce) |
| 1851–1853 | 32nd | D–140 | W–88 | D–35 | W–24 | W (Fillmore) |
| 1849–1851 | 31st | D–112 | W–109 | D–35 | W–25 | W (Fillmore) |
| | | | | | | W (Taylor) |
| 1847–1849 | 30th | W–115 | D–108 | D–36 | W–21 | D (Polk) |
| 1845–1847 | 29th | D–143 | W–77 | D–31 | W–25 | D (Polk) |
| 1843–1845 | 28th | D–142 | W–79 | W–28 | D–25 | W (Tyler) |
| 1841–1843 | 27th | W–133 | D–102 | W–28 | D–22 | W (Tyler) |
| | | | | | | W (W. Harrison) |
| 1839–1841 | 26th | D–124 | W–118 | D–28 | W–22 | D (Van Buren) |
| 1837–1839 | 25th | D–108 | W–107 | D–30 | W–18 | D (Van Buren) |
| 1835–1837 | 24th | D–145 | W–98 | D–27 | W–25 | D (Jackson) |
| 1833–1835 | 23rd | D–147 | AM–53 | D–20 | NR–20 | D (Jackson) |
| 1831–1833 | 22nd | D–141 | NR–58 | D–25 | NR–21 | D (Jackson) |
| 1829–1831 | 21st | D–139 | NR–74 | D–26 | NR–22 | DR (Jackson) |
| 1827–1829 | 20th | J–119 | AD–94 | J–28 | AD–20 | DR (John Q. Adams) |
| 1825–1827 | 19th | AD–105 | J–97 | AD–26 | J–20 | DR (John Q. Adams) |
| 1823–1825 | 18th | DR–187 | F–26 | DR–44 | F–4 | DR (Monroe) |
| 1821–1823 | 17th | DR–158 | F–25 | DR–44 | F–4 | DR (Monroe) |
| 1819–1821 | 16th | DR–156 | F–27 | DR–35 | F–7 | DR (Monroe) |
| 1817–1819 | 15th | DR–141 | F–42 | DR–34 | F–10 | DR (Monroe) |
| 1815–1817 | 14th | DR–117 | F–65 | DR–25 | F–11 | DR (Madison) |
| 1813–1815 | 13th | DR–112 | F–68 | DR–27 | F–9 | DR (Madison) |
| 1811–1813 | 12th | DR–108 | F–36 | DR–30 | F–6 | DR (Madison) |
| 1809–1811 | 11th | DR–94 | F–48 | DR–28 | F–6 | DR (Madison) |
| 1807–1809 | 10th | DR–118 | F–24 | DR–28 | F–6 | DR (Jefferson) |
| 1805–1807 | 9th | DR–116 | F–25 | DR–27 | F–7 | DR (Jefferson) |
| 1803–1805 | 8th | DR–102 | F–39 | DR–25 | F–9 | DR (Jefferson) |
| 1801–1803 | 7th | DR–69 | F–36 | DR–18 | F–13 | DR (Jefferson) |
| 1799–1801 | 6th | F–64 | DR–42 | F–19 | DR–13 | F (John Adams) |
| 1797–1799 | 5th | F–58 | DR–48 | F–20 | DR–12 | F (John Adams) |
| 1795–1797 | 4th | F–54 | DR–52 | F–19 | DR–13 | F (Washington) |
| 1793–1795 | 3rd | DR–57 | F–48 | F–17 | DR–13 | F (Washington) |
| 1791–1793 | 2nd | F–37 | DR–33 | F–16 | DR–13 | F (Washington) |
| 1789–1791 | 1st | AD–38 | Op–26 | AD–17 | Op–9 | F (Washington) |

SOURCES: *Congressional Quarterly Weekly Report*, selected issues; U.S. Bureau of the Census, *Historical Statistics of the United States, Colonial Times to 1970* (Washington, D.C.: Government Printing Office, 1975); and *Congressional Directory*, selected years.

NOTE: (Key to abbreviations: AD—Administration; AM—Anti-Masonic; D—Democratic; DR—Democratic-Republican; F—Federalist; J—Jacksonian; NR—National Republican; Op—Opposition; R—Republican; U—Unionist; W—Whig. Figures are for the beginning of the first session of each Congress.

# Presidents and Vice Presidents of the United States

| President | Term of service | Vice president |
|---|---|---|
| George Washington, F (1732–1799) | April 30, 1789–March 4, 1793 | John Adams |
| Washington | March 4, 1793–March 4, 1797 | Adams |
| John Adams, F (1735–1826) | March 4, 1797–March 4, 1801 | Thomas Jefferson |
| Thomas Jefferson, DR (1743–1826) | March 4, 1801–March 4, 1805 | Aaron Burr |
| Jefferson | March 4, 1805–March 4, 1809 | George Clinton |
| James Madison, DR (1751–1836) | March 4, 1809–March 4, 1813 | Clinton |
| Madison | March 4, 1813–March 4, 1817 | Elbridge Gerry |
| James Monroe, DR (1758–1831) | March 4, 1817–March 4, 1821 | Daniel D. Tompkins |
| Monroe | March 4, 1821–March 4, 1825 | Tompkins |
| John Q. Adams, DR (1767–1848) | March 4, 1825–March 4, 1829 | John C. Calhoun |
| Andrew Jackson, DR (1767–1845) | March 4, 1829–March 4, 1833 | Calhoun |
| Jackson, D | March 4, 1833–March 4, 1837 | Martin Van Buren |
| Martin Van Buren, D (1782–1862) | March 4, 1837–March 4, 1841 | Richard M. Johnson |
| W. H. Harrison, W (1773–1841) | March 4, 1841–April 4, 1841 | John Tyler |
| John Tyler, W (1790–1862) | April 6, 1841–March 4, 1845 | |
| James K. Polk, D (1795–1849) | March 4, 1845–March 4, 1849 | George M. Dallas |
| Zachary Taylor, W (1784–1850) | March 4, 1849–July 9, 1850 | Millard Fillmore |
| Millard Fillmore, W (1800–1874) | July 10, 1850–March 4, 1853 | |
| Franklin Pierce, D (1804–1869) | March 4, 1853–March 4, 1857 | William R. King |
| James Buchanan, D (1791–1868) | March 4, 1857–March 4, 1861 | John C. Breckinridge |
| Abraham Lincoln, R (1809–1865) | March 4, 1861–March 4, 1865 | Hannibal Hamlin |
| Lincoln | March 4, 1865–April 15, 1865 | Andrew Johnson |
| Andrew Johnson, R (1808–1875) | April 15, 1865–March 4, 1869 | |
| Ulysses S. Grant, R (1822–1885) | March 4, 1869–March 4, 1873 | Schuyler Colfax |
| Grant | March 4, 1873–March 4, 1877 | Henry Wilson |
| Rutherford B. Hayes, R (1822–1893) | March 4, 1877–March 4, 1881 | William A. Wheeler |
| James A. Garfield, R (1831–1881) | March 4, 1881–Sept. 19, 1881 | Chester A. Arthur |
| Chester A. Arthur, R (1830–1886) | Sept. 20, 1881–March 4, 1885 | |
| Grover Cleveland, D (1837–1908) | March 4, 1885–March 4, 1889 | Thomas A. Hendricks |
| Benjamin Harrison, R (1833–1901) | March 4, 1889–March 4, 1893 | Levi P. Morton |
| Grover Cleveland, D (1837–1908) | March 4, 1893–March 4, 1897 | Adlai E. Stevenson |
| William McKinley, R (1843–1901) | March 4, 1897–March 4, 1901 | Garret A. Hobart |
| McKinley | March 4, 1901–Sept. 14, 1901 | Theodore Roosevelt |
| Theodore Roosevelt, R (1858–1919) | Sept. 14, 1901–March 4, 1905 | |
| Roosevelt | March 4, 1905–March 4, 1909 | Charles W. Fairbanks |
| William H. Taft, R (1857–1930) | March 4, 1909–March 4, 1913 | James S. Sherman |
| Woodrow Wilson, D (1856–1924) | March 4, 1913–March 4, 1917 | Thomas R. Marshall |
| Wilson | March 4, 1917–March 4, 1921 | Marshall |
| Warren G. Harding, R (1865–1923) | March 4, 1921–Aug. 2, 1923 | Calvin Coolidge |
| Calvin Coolidge, R (1872–1933) | Aug. 3, 1923–March 4, 1925 | |
| Coolidge | March 4, 1925–March 4, 1929 | Charles G. Dawes |

| President | Term of service | Vice president |
|---|---|---|
| Herbert Hoover, R (1874–1964) | March 4, 1929–March 4, 1933 | Charles Curtis |
| Franklin D. Roosevelt, D (1882–1945) | March 4, 1933–Jan. 20, 1937 | John N. Garner |
| Roosevelt | Jan. 20, 1937–Jan. 20, 1941 | Garner |
| Roosevelt | Jan. 20, 1941–Jan. 20, 1945 | Henry A. Wallace |
| Roosevelt | Jan. 20, 1945–April 12, 1945 | Harry S. Truman |
| Harry S. Truman, D (1884–1972) | April 12, 1945–Jan. 20, 1949 | |
| Truman | Jan. 20, 1949–Jan. 20, 1953 | Alben W. Barkley |
| Dwight D. Eisenhower, R (1890–1969) | Jan. 20, 1953–Jan. 20, 1957 | Richard Nixon |
| Eisenhower | Jan. 20, 1957–Jan. 20, 1961 | Nixon |
| John F. Kennedy, D (1917–1963) | Jan. 20, 1961–Nov. 22, 1963 | Lyndon B. Johnson |
| Lyndon B. Johnson, D (1908–1973) | Nov. 22, 1963–Jan. 20, 1965 | |
| Johnson | Jan. 20, 1965–Jan. 20, 1969 | Hubert H. Humphrey |
| Richard Nixon, R (1913– ) | Jan. 20, 1969–Jan. 20, 1973 | Spiro T. Agnew |
| Nixon | Jan. 20, 1973–Aug. 9, 1974 | Agnew |
| | | Gerald R. Ford |
| Gerald R. Ford, R (1913– ) | Aug. 9, 1974–Jan. 20, 1977 | Nelson A. Rockefeller |
| Jimmy Carter, D (1924– ) | Jan. 20, 1977–Jan. 20, 1981 | Walter F. Mondale |
| Ronald Reagan, R (1911– ) | Jan. 20, 1981–Jan. 20, 1985 | George Bush |
| Reagan | Jan. 20, 1985–Jan. 20, 1989 | Bush |
| George Bush, R (1924– ) | Jan. 20, 1989–Jan. 20, 1993 | Dan Quayle |
| Bill Clinton, D (1946– ) | Jan. 20, 1993– | Al Gore |

Abbreviations: D—Democrat, DR—Democratic-Republican, F—Federalist, R—Republican, W—Whig

## Senate Votes Cast by Vice Presidents

Following is a list of the number of votes cast by each vice president through January 20, 1993:

| Period | Vice President | Votes Cast | Period | Vice President | Votes Cast |
| --- | --- | --- | --- | --- | --- |
| 1789–1797 | John Adams | 29 | 1893–1897 | Adlai E. Stevenson | 2 |
| 1797–1801 | Thomas Jefferson | 3 | 1897–1899 | Garret A. Hobart | 1 |
| 1801–1805 | Aaron Burr | 3 | 1901 | Theodore Roosevelt | 0 |
| 1805–1812 | George Clinton | 11 | 1905–1909 | Charles W. Fairbanks | 0 |
| 1813–1814 | Elbridge Gerry | 8 | 1909–1912 | James S. Sherman | 4 |
| 1817–1825 | Daniel D. Tompkins | 5 | 1913–1921 | Thomas R. Marshall | 4 |
| 1825–1832 | John C. Calhoun | 28 | 1921–1923 | Calvin Coolidge | 0 |
| 1833–1837 | Martin Van Buren | 4 | 1925–1929 | Charles G. Dawes | 2 |
| 1837–1841 | Richard M. Johnson | 14 | 1929–1933 | Charles Curtis | 3 |
| 1841 | John Tyler | 0 | 1933–1941 | John N. Garner | 3 |
| 1845–1849 | George M. Dallas | 19 | 1941–1945 | Henry A. Wallace | 4 |
| 1849–1850 | Millard Fillmore | 3 | 1945 | Harry S. Truman | 1 |
| 1853 | William R. King | 0 | 1949–1953 | Alben W. Barkley | 7 |
| 1857–1861 | John C. Breckinridge | 10 | 1953–1961 | Richard M. Nixon | 8 |
| 1861–1865 | Hannibal Hamlin | 7 | 1961–1963 | Lyndon B. Johnson | 0 |
| 1865 | Andrew Johnson | 0 | 1965–1969 | Hubert H. Humphrey | 4 |
| 1869–1873 | Schuyler Colfax | 13 | 1969–1973 | Spiro T. Agnew | 2 |
| 1873–1875 | Henry Wilson | 1 | 1973–1974 | Gerald R. Ford | 0 |
| 1877–1881 | William A. Wheeler | 5 | 1974–1977 | Nelson A. Rockefeller | 0 |
| 1881 | Chester A. Arthur | 3 | 1977–1981 | Walter F. Mondale | 1 |
| 1885 | Thomas A. Hendricks | 0 | 1981–1989 | George Bush | 7 |
| 1889–1893 | Levi P. Morton | 4 | 1989–1993 | Dan Quayle | 0 |
| | | | | Total | 223 |

SOURCE: Library of Congress, Congressional Research Service.

# Salaries, 1993

| Position | 1993 pay level |
|---|---|
| **EXECUTIVE BRANCH** | |
| President | $200,000 |
| Vice president | $171,500 |
| Level I includes cabinet officers | 148,400 |
| Level II includes deputy secretaries of cabinet departments, and heads of offices and agencies such as the CIA, FBI, EPA, NASA, and OMB | 133,600 |
| Level III includes under secretaries of cabinet departments and chairs of regulatory commissions such as the FTC, FDIC, and the NLRB | 123,100 |
| Level IV includes assistant secretaries of cabinet departments, members of regulatory commissions, and cabinet department general counsels | 115,700 |
| Level V includes directors of major bureaus of cabinet departments | 108,200 |
| **LEGISLATIVE BRANCH** | |
| Speaker of the House | 171,500 |
| President pro tempore, majority and minority leaders | 148,400 |
| Senators, representatives, four delegates to Congress, resident commissioner of Puerto Rico, comptroller general | 133,600 |
| Director of CBO, deputy comptroller general, librarian of Congress, and the architect of the Capitol | 123,000 |
| Deputy director of CBO, general counsel of GAO, deputy librarian of Congress, and the assistant architect of the Capitol | 115,700 |
| **JUDICIAL BRANCH** | |
| Chief justice | 171,500 |
| Retired chief justice | 171,500 |
| Associate justices | 164,100 |
| Judges, circuit courts of appeal and court of military appeals | 141,700 |
| Judges, district courts; court of international trade; tax court; assistant to the chief justice; director, Administrative Office—U.S. Courts; director, Federal Judicial Center | 133,600 |
| Judges, U.S. Claims Court | 133,600 |
| Deputy director, Administrative Office—U.S. Courts; circuit executives | 133,600 |
| Bankruptcy judges, U.S. magistrates | 122,912 |

SOURCES: U.S. Office of Personnel Management; Administrative Office of the U.S. Courts; Congressional Budget Office.

## Legislative Branch Appropriations, 1946–1993

| Fiscal Year | Appropriation | Fiscal Year | Appropriation | Fiscal Year | Appropriation |
|---|---|---|---|---|---|
| 1946 | $ 54,065,614 | 1962 | $ 136,686,715 | 1978 | $ 1,009,225,350 |
| 1947 | 61,825,020 | 1963 | 150,426,185 | 1979 | 1,124,766,400 |
| 1948 | 62,119,714 | 1964 | 168,467,869 | 1980 | 1,199,061,463 |
| 1949 | 62,057,678 | 1965 | 221,904,318 | 1981 | 1,285,943,826 |
| 1950 | 64,313,460 | 1966 | 197,965,307 | 1982 | 1,365,272,433 |
| 1951 | 71,888,244 | 1967 | 221,715,643 | 1983 | 1,467,318,263 |
| 1952 | 75,673,896 | 1968 | 282,003,322 | 1984 | 1,644,160,600 |
| 1953 | 77,670,076 | 1969 | 311,542,399 | 1985 | 1,599,977,138 |
| 1954 | 70,925,361 | 1970 | 361,024,327 | 1986 | 1,783,255,000 |
| 1955 | 86,304,923 | 1971 | 443,104,319 | 1987 | 1,635,190,214 |
| 1956 | 94,827,986 | 1972 | 564,107,992 | 1988 | 1,745,201,500 |
| 1957 | 120,775,798 | 1973 | 645,127,365 | 1989 | 1,804,624,000 |
| 1958 | 107,785,560 | 1974 | 662,180,668 | 1990 | 1,968,441,000 |
| 1959 | 136,153,580 | 1975 | 785,618,833 | 1991 | 2,161,367,000 |
| 1960 | 131,055,385 | 1976 | 947,185,778 | 1992 | 2,306,231,000 |
| 1961 | 140,930,781 | 1977 | 963,921,185 | 1993 | 2,275,148,000 |

SOURCE: Norman J. Ornstein, Thomas E. Mann, and Michael J. Malbin, *Vital Statistics on Congress, 1991–1992* (Washington, D.C.: Congressional Quarterly, 1992); *Congressional Quarterly Weekly Report,* selected issues.

NOTE: A portion of the appropriation to the legislative branch is not spent directly on congressional operations. See detailed breakdown of fiscal 1993 appropriations, below.

## Fiscal 1993 Legislative Appropriations

| CONGRESSIONAL OPERATIONS | | RELATED AGENCIES | |
|---|---|---|---|
| Senate | $451,451,000 | Botanic Garden | $ 4,906,000 |
| House of Representatives | 671,333,000 | Library of Congress | 252,808,000 |
| Joint Items | 80,476,000 | Architect of the Capitol | |
| Office of Technology Assessment | 21,025,000 | (library buildings) | 9,733,000 |
| Congressional Budget Office | 22,542,000 | Copyright Royalty Tribunal | 130,000 |
| Architect of the Capitol | 149,613,000 | Government Printing Office | |
| Congressional Research Service | 57,291,000 | (noncongressional) | 29,082,000 |
| Government Printing Office | | General Accounting Office | 435,167,000 |
| (congressional printing) | 89,591,000 | | |
| | | Subtotal | 731,826,000 |
| Subtotal | $1,543,322,000 | | |
| TOTAL LEGISLATIVE APPROPRIATIONS | | | $2,275,148,000 |

SOURCE: House Appropriations Committee.

## U.S. House of Representatives

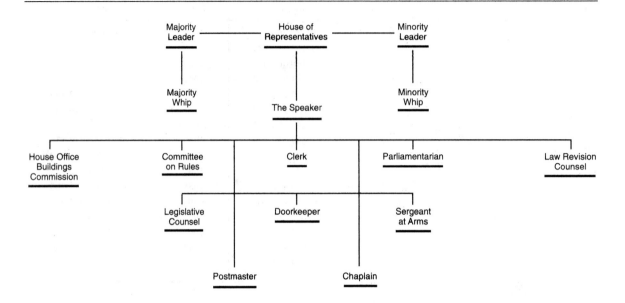

S O U R C E : *United States Government Manual*, 1990-91 (Washington, D.C.: Government Printing Office, 1990), 27.

# U.S. Senate

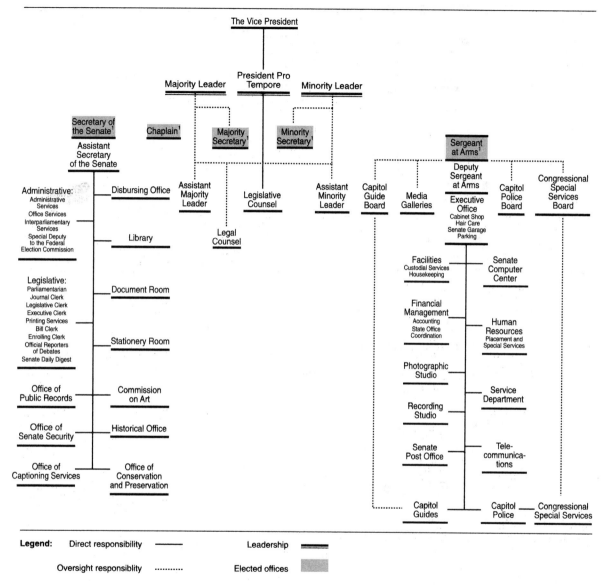

The Vice President

President Pro Tempore

Majority Leader

Minority Leader

Secretary of the Senate[1]

Assistant Secretary of the Senate

Chaplain[1]

Majority Secretary[1]

Minority Secretary[1]

Sergeant at Arms[1]

Deputy Sergeant at Arms

**Administrative:**
Administrative Services
Office Services
Interparliamentary Services
Special Deputy to the Federal Election Commission

Disbursing Office

Assistant Majority Leader

Legislative Counsel

Assistant Minority Leader

Capitol Guide Board

Media Galleries

Executive Office
Cabinet Shop
Hair Care
Senate Garage
Parking

Capitol Police Board

Congressional Special Services Board

**Legislative:**
Parliamentarian
Journal Clerk
Legislative Clerk
Executive Clerk
Printing Services
Bill Clerk
Enrolling Clerk
Official Reporters of Debates
Senate Daily Digest

Library

Legal Counsel

Facilities
Custodial Services
Housekeeping

Senate Computer Center

Document Room

Financial Management
Accounting
State Office Coordination

Human Resources
Placement and Special Services

Stationery Room

Office of Public Records

Commission on Art

Photographic Studio

Service Department

Office of Senate Security

Historical Office

Recording Studio

Office of Captioning Services

Office of Conservation and Preservation

Senate Post Office

Tele-communications

Capitol Guides

Capitol Police

Congressional Special Services

**Legend:**   Direct responsibility ———   Leadership ▀▀▀

Oversight responsiblity ·········   Elected offices ▓

[1] Elected officers of the Senate.

477

## Sessions of the U.S. Congress, 1789–1992

| Congress | Session | Date of beginning [1] | Date of adjournment [2] | Length in days | President pro tempore of the Senate [3] | Speaker of the House of Representatives |
|----------|---------|-----------------------|-------------------------|----------------|------------------------------------------|-----------------------------------------|
| **1st**  | 1 | Mar. 4, 1789 | Sept. 29, 1789 | 210 | John Langdon of New Hampshire [4] | Frederick A. C. Muhlenberg of Pennsylvania |
|          | 2 | Jan. 4, 1790 | Aug. 12, 1790 | 221 | | |
|          | 3 | Dec. 6, 1790 | Mar. 3, 1791 | 88 | | |
| **2nd**  | 1 | Oct. 24, 1791 | May 8, 1792 | 197 | Richard Henry Lee of Virginia | Jonathan Trumbull of Connecticut |
|          | 2 | Nov. 5, 1792 | Mar. 2, 1793 | 119 | John Langdon of New Hampshire | |
| **3rd**  | 1 | Dec. 2, 1793 | June 9, 1794 | 190 | Langdon / Ralph Izard of South Carolina | Frederick A. C. Muhlenberg of Pennsylvania |
|          | 2 | Nov. 3, 1794 | Mar. 3, 1795 | 121 | Henry Tazewell of Virginia | |
| **4th**  | 1 | Dec. 7, 1795 | June 1, 1796 | 177 | Tazewell / Samuel Livermore of New Hampshire | Jonathan Dayton of New Jersey |
|          | 2 | Dec. 5, 1796 | Mar. 3, 1797 | 89 | William Bingham of Pennsylvania | |
| **5th**  | 1 | May 15, 1797 | July 10, 1797 | 57 | William Bradford of Rhode Island | Dayton |
|          | 2 | Nov. 13, 1797 | July 16, 1798 | 246 | Jacob Read of South Carolina / Theodore Sedgwick of Massachusetts | George Dent of Maryland [5] |
|          | 3 | Dec. 3, 1798 | Mar. 3, 1799 | 91 | John Laurence of New York / James Ross of Pennsylvania | |
| **6th**  | 1 | Dec. 2, 1799 | May 14, 1800 | 164 | Samuel Livermore of New Hampshire / Uriah Tracy of Connecticut | Theodore Sedgwick of Massachusetts |
|          | 2 | Nov. 17, 1800 | Mar. 3, 1801 | 107 | John E. Howard of Maryland / James Hillhouse of Connecticut | |
| **7th**  | 1 | Dec. 7, 1801 | May 3, 1802 | 148 | Abraham Baldwin of Georgia | Nathaniel Macon of North Carolina |
|          | 2 | Dec. 6, 1802 | Mar. 3, 1803 | 88 | Stephen R. Bradley of Vermont | |
| **8th**  | 1 | Oct. 17, 1803 | Mar. 27, 1804 | 163 | John Brown of Kentucky / Jesse Franklin of North Carolina | Macon |

478

| Congress | Session | Date of beginning[1] | Date of adjournment[2] | Length in days | President pro tempore of the Senate[3] | Speaker of the House of Representatives |
|---|---|---|---|---|---|---|
|  | 2 | Nov. 5, 1804 | Mar. 3, 1805 | 119 | Joseph Anderson of Tennessee |  |
| 9th | 1 | Dec. 2, 1805 | Apr. 21, 1806 | 141 | Samuel Smith of Maryland | Macon |
|  | 2 | Dec. 1, 1806 | Mar. 3, 1807 | 93 | Smith |  |
| 10th | 1 | Oct. 26, 1807 | Apr. 25, 1808 | 182 | Smith | Joseph B. Varnum of Massachusetts |
|  | 2 | Nov. 7, 1808 | Mar. 3, 1809 | 117 | Stephen R. Bradley of Vermont John Milledge of Georgia |  |
| 11th | 1 | May 22, 1809 | June 28, 1809 | 38 | Andrew Gregg of Pennsylvania | Varnum |
|  | 2 | Nov. 27, 1809 | May 1, 1810 | 156 | John Gaillard of South Carolina |  |
|  | 3 | Dec. 3, 1810 | Mar. 3, 1811 | 91 | John Pope of Kentucky |  |
| 12th | 1 | Nov 4, 1811 | July 6, 1812 | 245 | William H. Crawford of Georgia | Henry Clay of Kentucky |
|  | 2 | Nov. 2, 1812 | Mar. 3, 1813 | 122 | Crawford |  |
| 13th | 1 | May 24, 1813 | Aug. 2, 1813 | 71 | Crawford | Clay |
|  | 2 | Dec. 6, 1813 | Apr. 18, 1814 | 134 | Joseph B. Varnum of Massachusetts |  |
|  | 3 | Sept. 19, 1814 | Mar. 3, 1815 | 166 | John Gaillard of South Carolina | Langdon Cheves of South Carolina[6] |
| 14th | 1 | Dec. 4, 1815 | Apr. 30, 1816 | 148 | Gaillard | Henry Clay of Kentucky |
|  | 2 | Dec. 2, 1816 | Mar. 3, 1817 | 92 | Gaillard |  |
| 15th | 1 | Dec. 1, 1817 | Apr. 20, 1818 | 141 | Gaillard | Clay |
|  | 2 | Nov. 16, 1818 | Mar. 3, 1819 | 108 | James Barbour of Virginia |  |
| 16th | 1 | Dec. 6, 1819 | May 15, 1820 | 162 | John Gaillard of South Carolina | Clay |
|  | 2 | Nov. 13, 1820 | Mar. 3, 1821 | 111 | Gaillard | John W. Taylor of New York[7] |
| 17th | 1 | Dec. 3, 1821 | May 8, 1822 | 157 | Gaillard | Philip P. Barbour of Virginia |
|  | 2 | Dec. 2, 1822 | Mar. 3, 1823 | 92 | Gaillard |  |
| 18th | 1 | Dec. 1, 1823 | May 27, 1824 | 178 | Gaillard | Henry Clay of Kentucky |
|  | 2 | Dec. 6, 1824 | Mar. 3, 1825 | 88 | Gaillard |  |
| 19th | 1 | Dec. 5, 1825 | May 22, 1826 | 169 | Nathaniel Macon of North Carolina | John W. Taylor of New York |
|  | 2 | Dec. 4, 1826 | Mar. 3, 1827 | 90 | Macon |  |
| 20th | 1 | Dec. 3, 1827 | May 26, 1828 | 175 | Samuel Smith of Maryland | Andrew Stevenson of Virginia |
|  | 2 | Dec. 1, 1828 | Mar. 3, 1829 | 93 | Smith |  |

| Congress | Session | Date of beginning[1] | Date of adjournment[2] | Length in days | President pro tempore of the Senate[3] | Speaker of the House of Representatives |
|---|---|---|---|---|---|---|
| **21st** | 1 | Dec. 7, 1829 | May 31, 1830 | 176 | Smith | Stevenson |
| | 2 | Dec. 6, 1830 | Mar. 3, 1831 | 88 | Littleton Waller Tazewell of Virginia | |
| **22nd** | 1 | Dec. 5, 1831 | July 16, 1832 | 225 | Tazewell | Stevenson |
| | 2 | Dec. 3, 1832 | Mar. 2, 1833 | 91 | Hugh Lawson White of Tennessee | |
| **23rd** | 1 | Dec. 2, 1833 | June 30, 1834 | 211 | George Poindexter of Mississippi | Stevenson |
| | 2 | Dec. 1, 1834 | Mar. 3, 1835 | 93 | John Tyler of Virginia | John Bell of Tennessee [8] |
| **24th** | 1 | Dec. 7, 1835 | July 4, 1836 | 211 | William R. King of Alabama | James K. Polk of Tennessee |
| | 2 | Dec. 5, 1836 | Mar. 3, 1837 | 89 | King | |
| **25th** | 1 | Sept. 4, 1837 | Oct. 16, 1837 | 43 | King | Polk |
| | 2 | Dec. 4, 1837 | July 9, 1838 | 218 | King | |
| | 3 | Dec. 3, 1838 | Mar. 3, 1839 | 91 | King | |
| **26th** | 1 | Dec. 2, 1839 | July 21, 1840 | 233 | King | Robert M. T. Hunter of Virginia |
| | 2 | Dec. 7, 1840 | Mar. 3, 1841 | 87 | King | |
| **27th** | 1 | May 31, 1841 | Sept. 13, 1841 | 106 | Samuel L. Southard of New Jersey | John White of Kentucky |
| | 2 | Dec. 6, 1841 | Aug. 31, 1842 | 269 | Willie P. Mangum of North Carolina | |
| | 3 | Dec. 5, 1842 | Mar. 3, 1843 | 89 | Mangum | |
| **28th** | 1 | Dec. 4, 1843 | June 17, 1844 | 196 | Mangum | John W. Jones of Virginia |
| | 2 | Dec. 2, 1844 | Mar. 3, 1845 | 92 | Mangum | |
| **29th** | 1 | Dec. 1, 1845 | Aug. 10, 1846 | 253 | David R. Atchison of Missouri | John W. Davis of Indiana |
| | 2 | Dec. 7, 1846 | Mar. 3, 1847 | 87 | Atchison | |
| **30th** | 1 | Dec. 6, 1847 | Aug. 14, 1848 | 254 | Atchison | Robert C. Winthrop of Massachusetts |
| | 2 | Dec. 4, 1848 | Mar. 3, 1849 | 90 | Atchison | |
| **31st** | 1 | Dec. 3, 1849 | Sept. 30, 1850 | 302 | William R. King of Alabama | Howell Cobb of Georgia |
| | 2 | Dec. 2, 1850 | Mar. 3, 1851 | 92 | King | |
| **32nd** | 1 | Dec. 1, 1851 | Aug. 31, 1852 | 275 | King | Linn Boyd of Kentucky |
| | 2 | Dec. 6, 1852 | Mar. 3, 1853 | 88 | David R. Atchison of Missouri | |
| **33rd** | 1 | Dec. 5, 1853 | Aug. 7, 1854 | 246 | Atchison | Boyd |
| | 2 | Dec. 4, 1854 | Mar. 3, 1855 | 90 | Jesse D. Bright of Indiana Lewis Cass of Michigan | |
| **34th** | 1 | Dec. 3, 1855 | Aug. 18, 1856 | 260 | Jesse D. Bright of Indiana | Nathaniel P. Banks of Massachusetts |

| Congress | Session | Date of beginning[1] | Date of adjournment[2] | Length in days | President pro tempore of the Senate[3] | Speaker of the House of Representatives |
|---|---|---|---|---|---|---|
| | 2 | Aug. 21, 1856 | Aug. 30, 1856 | 10 | Bright | |
| | 3 | Dec. 1, 1856 | Mar. 3, 1857 | 93 | James M. Mason of Virginia | |
| | | | | | Thomas J. Rusk of Texas | |
| **35th** | 1 | Dec. 7, 1857 | June 14, 1858 | 189 | Benjamin Fitzpatrick of Alabama | James L. Orr of South Carolina |
| | 2 | Dec. 6, 1858 | Mar. 3, 1859 | 88 | Fitzpatrick | |
| **36th** | 1 | Dec. 5, 1859 | June 25, 1860 | 202 | Fitzpatrick | William Pennington of New Jersey |
| | | | | | Jesse D. Bright of Indiana | |
| | 2 | Dec. 3, 1860 | Mar. 3, 1861 | 93 | Solomon Foot of Vermont | |
| **37th** | 1 | July 4, 1861 | Aug. 6, 1861 | 34 | Foot | Galusha A. Grow of Pennsylvania |
| | 2 | Dec. 2, 1861 | July 17, 1862 | 228 | Foot | |
| | 3 | Dec. 1, 1862 | Mar. 3, 1863 | 93 | Foot | |
| **38th** | 1 | Dec. 7, 1863 | July 4, 1864 | 209 | Foot | Schuyler Colfax of Indiana |
| | | | | | Daniel Clark of New Hampshire | |
| | 2 | Dec. 5, 1864 | Mar. 3, 1865 | 89 | Clark | |
| **39th** | 1 | Dec. 4, 1865 | July 28, 1866 | 237 | Lafayette S. Foster of Connecticut | Colfax |
| | 2 | Dec. 3, 1866 | Mar. 3, 1867 | 91 | Benjamin F. Wade of Ohio | |
| **40th** | 1 | Mar. 4, 1867[9] | Dec. 2, 1867 | 274 | Wade | Colfax |
| | 2 | Dec. 2, 1867[10] | Nov. 10, 1868 | 345 | Wade | |
| | 3 | Dec. 7, 1868 | Mar. 3, 1869 | 87 | Wade | Theodore M. Pomeroy of New York[11] |
| **41st** | 1 | Mar. 4, 1869 | Apr. 10, 1869 | 38 | Henry B. Anthony of Rhode Island | James G. Blaine of Maine |
| | 2 | Dec. 6, 1869 | July 15, 1870 | 222 | Anthony | |
| | 3 | Dec. 5, 1870 | Mar. 3, 1871 | 89 | Anthony | |
| **42nd** | 1 | Mar. 4, 1871 | Apr. 20, 1871 | 48 | Anthony | Blaine |
| | 2 | Dec. 4, 1871 | June 10, 1872 | 190 | Anthony | |
| | 3 | Dec. 2, 1872 | Mar. 3, 1873 | 92 | Anthony | |
| **43rd** | 1 | Dec. 1, 1873 | June 23, 1874 | 204 | Matthew H. Carpenter of Wisconsin | Blaine |
| | 2 | Dec. 7, 1874 | Mar. 3, 1875 | 87 | Carpenter | |
| | | | | | Henry B. Anthony of Rhode Island | |
| **44th** | 1 | Dec. 6, 1875 | Aug. 15, 1876 | 254 | Thomas W. Ferry of Michigan | Michael C. Kerr of Indiana[12] |
| | | | | | | Samuel S. Cox of New York, pro tempore[13] |
| | | | | | | Milton Sayler of Ohio, pro tempore[14] |

| Congress | Session | Date of beginning[1] | Date of adjournment[2] | Length in days | President pro tempore of the Senate[3] | Speaker of the House of Representatives |
|---|---|---|---|---|---|---|
| | 2 | Dec. 4, 1876 | Mar. 3, 1877 | 90 | Ferry | Samuel J. Randall of Pennsylvania |
| **45th** | 1 | Oct. 15, 1877 | Dec. 3, 1877 | 50 | Ferry | Randall |
| | 2 | Dec. 3, 1877 | June 20, 1878 | 200 | Ferry | |
| | 3 | Dec. 2, 1878 | Mar. 3, 1879 | 92 | Ferry | |
| **46th** | 1 | Mar. 18, 1879 | July 1, 1879 | 106 | Allen G. Thurman of Ohio | Randall |
| | 2 | Dec. 1, 1879 | June 16, 1880 | 199 | Thurman | |
| | 3 | Dec. 6, 1880 | Mar. 3, 1881 | 88 | Thurman | |
| **47th** | 1 | Dec. 5, 1881 | Aug. 8, 1882 | 247 | Thomas F. Bayard of Delaware | J. Warren Keifer of Ohio |
| | 2 | Dec. 4, 1882 | Mar. 3, 1883 | 90 | David Davis of Illinois<br>George F. Edmunds of Vermont | |
| **48th** | 1 | Dec. 3, 1883 | July 7, 1884 | 218 | Edmunds | John G. Carlisle of Kentucky |
| | 2 | Dec. 1, 1884 | Mar. 3, 1885 | 93 | Edmunds | |
| **49th** | 1 | Dec. 7, 1885 | Aug. 5, 1886 | 242 | John Sherman of Ohio | Carlisle |
| | 2 | Dec. 6, 1886 | Mar. 3, 1887 | 88 | John J. Ingalls of Kansas | |
| **50th** | 1 | Dec. 5, 1887 | Oct. 20, 1888 | 321 | Ingalls | Carlisle |
| | 2 | Dec. 3, 1888 | Mar. 3, 1889 | 91 | Ingalls | |
| **51st** | 1 | Dec. 2, 1889 | Oct. 1, 1890 | 304 | Ingalls | Thomas B. Reed of Maine |
| | 2 | Dec. 1, 1890 | Mar. 3, 1891 | 93 | Charles F. Manderson of Nebraska | |
| **52nd** | 1 | Dec. 7, 1891 | Aug. 5, 1892 | 251 | Manderson | Charles F. Crisp of Georgia |
| | 2 | Dec. 5, 1892 | Mar. 3, 1893 | 89 | Isham G. Harris of Tennessee | |
| **53rd** | 1 | Aug. 7, 1893 | Nov. 3, 1893 | 89 | Harris | Crisp |
| | 2 | Dec. 4, 1893 | Aug. 28, 1894 | 268 | Harris | |
| | 3 | Dec. 3, 1894 | Mar. 3, 1895 | 97 | Matt W. Ransom of North Carolina<br>Isham G. Harris of Tennessee | |
| **54th** | 1 | Dec. 2, 1895 | June 11, 1896 | 193 | William P. Frye of Maine | Thomas B. Reed of Maine |
| | 2 | Dec. 7, 1896 | Mar. 3, 1897 | 87 | Frye | |
| **55th** | 1 | Mar. 15, 1897 | July 24, 1897 | 131 | Frye | Reed |
| | 2 | Dec. 6, 1897 | July 8, 1898 | 215 | Frye | |
| | 3 | Dec. 5, 1898 | Mar. 3, 1899 | 89 | Frye | |
| **56th** | 1 | Dec. 4, 1899 | June 7, 1900 | 186 | Frye | David B. Henderson of Iowa |
| | 2 | Dec. 3, 1900 | Mar. 3, 1901 | 91 | Frye | |
| **57th** | 1 | Dec. 2, 1901 | July 1, 1902 | 212 | Frye | Henderson |
| | 2 | Dec. 1, 1902 | Mar. 3, 1903 | 93 | Frye | |

| Congress | Session | Date of beginning[1] | Date of adjournment[2] | Length in days | President pro tempore of the Senate[3] | Speaker of the House of Representatives |
|---|---|---|---|---|---|---|
| **58th** | 1 | Nov. 9, 1903 | Dec. 7, 1903 | 29 | Frye | Joseph G. Cannon of Illinois |
| | 2 | Dec. 7, 1903 | Apr. 28, 1904 | 144 | Frye | |
| | 3 | Dec. 5, 1904 | Mar. 3, 1905 | 89 | Frye | |
| **59th** | 1 | Dec. 4, 1905 | June 30, 1906 | 209 | Frye | Cannon |
| | 2 | Dec. 3, 1906 | Mar. 3, 1907 | 91 | Frye | |
| **60th** | 1 | Dec. 2, 1907 | May 30, 1908 | 181 | Frye | Cannon |
| | 2 | Dec. 7, 1908 | Mar. 3, 1909 | 87 | Frye | |
| **61st** | 1 | Mar. 15, 1909 | Aug. 5, 1909 | 144 | Frye | Cannon |
| | 2 | Dec. 6, 1909 | June 25, 1910 | 202 | Frye | |
| | 3 | Dec. 5, 1910 | Mar. 3, 1911 | 89 | Frye | |
| **62nd** | 1 | Apr. 4, 1911 | Aug. 22, 1911 | 141 | Frye[15] | Champ Clark of Missouri |
| | 2 | Dec. 4, 1911 | Aug. 26, 1912 | 267 | Augustus O. Bacon of Georgia;[16] Frank B. Brandegee of Connecticut;[17] Charles Curtis of Kansas;[18] Jacob H Gallinger of New Hampshire;[19] Henry Cabot Lodge of Massachusetts[20] | |
| | 3 | Dec. 2, 1912 | Mar. 3, 1913 | 92 | Bacon;[21] Gallinger[22] | |
| **63rd** | 1 | Apr. 7, 1913 | Dec. 1, 1913 | 239 | James P. Clarke of Arkansas | Clark |
| | 2 | Dec. 1, 1913 | Oct. 24, 1914 | 328 | Clarke | |
| | 3 | Dec. 7, 1914 | Mar. 3, 1915 | 87 | Clarke | |
| **64th** | 1 | Dec. 6, 1915 | Sept. 8, 1916 | 278 | Clarke[23] | Clark |
| | 2 | Dec. 4, 1916 | Mar. 3, 1917 | 90 | Willard Saulsbury of Delaware | |
| **65th** | 1 | Apr. 2, 1917 | Oct. 6, 1917 | 188 | Saulsbury | Clark |
| | 2 | Dec. 3, 1917 | Nov. 21, 1918 | 354 | Saulsbury | |
| | 3 | Dec. 2, 1918 | Mar. 3, 1919 | 92 | Saulsbury | |
| **66th** | 1 | May 19, 1919 | Nov. 19, 1919 | 185 | Albert B. Cummins of Iowa | Frederick H. Gillett of Massachusetts |
| | 2 | Dec. 1, 1919 | June 5, 1920 | 188 | Cummins | |
| | 3 | Dec. 6, 1920 | Mar. 3, 1921 | 88 | Cummins | |
| **67th** | 1 | Apr. 11, 1921 | Nov. 23, 1921 | 227 | Cummins | Gillett |
| | 2 | Dec. 5, 1921 | Sept. 22, 1922 | 292 | Cummins | |
| | 3 | Nov. 20, 1922 | Dec. 4, 1922 | 15 | Cummins | |
| | 4 | Dec. 4, 1922 | Mar. 3, 1923 | 90 | Cummins | |
| **68th** | 1 | Dec. 3, 1923 | June 7, 1924 | 188 | Cummins | Gillett |
| | 2 | Dec. 1, 1924 | Mar. 3, 1925 | 93 | Cummins | |

| Congress | Session | Date of beginning[1] | Date of adjournment[2] | Length in days | President pro tempore of the Senate[3] | Speaker of the House of Representatives |
|---|---|---|---|---|---|---|
| **69th** | 1 | Dec. 7, 1925 | July 3, 1926 | 209 | George H. Moses of New Hampshire | Nicholas Longworth of Ohio |
| | 2 | Dec. 6, 1926 | Mar. 3, 1927 | 88 | Moses | |
| **70th** | 1 | Dec. 5, 1927 | May 29, 1928 | 177 | Moses | Longworth |
| | 2 | Dec. 3, 1928 | Mar. 3, 1929 | 91 | Moses | |
| **71st** | 1 | Apr. 15, 1929 | Nov. 22, 1929 | 222 | Moses | Longworth |
| | 2 | Dec. 2, 1929 | July 3, 1930 | 214 | Moses | |
| | 3 | Dec. 1, 1930 | Mar. 3, 1931 | 93 | Moses | |
| **72nd** | 1 | Dec. 7, 1931 | July 16, 1932 | 223 | Moses | John N. Garner of Texas |
| | 2 | Dec. 5, 1932 | Mar. 3, 1933 | 89 | Moses | |
| **73rd** | 1 | Mar. 9, 1933 | June 15, 1933 | 99 | Key Pittman of Nevada | Henry T. Rainey of Illinois [24] |
| | 2 | Jan. 3, 1934 | June 18, 1934 | 167 | Pittman | |
| **74th** | 1 | Jan. 3, 1935 | Aug. 26, 1935 | 236 | Pittman | Joseph W. Byrns of Tennessee [25] |
| | 2 | Jan. 3, 1936 | June 20, 1936 | 170 | Pittman | William B. Bankhead of Alabama [26] |
| **75th** | 1 | Jan. 5, 1937 | Aug. 21, 1937 | 229 | Pittman | Bankhead |
| | 2 | Nov. 15, 1937 | Dec. 21, 1937 | 37 | Pittman | |
| | 3 | Jan. 3, 1938 | June 16, 1938 | 165 | Pittman | |
| **76th** | 1 | Jan. 3, 1939 | Aug. 5, 1939 | 215 | Pittman | Bankhead [27] |
| | 2 | Sept. 21, 1939 | Nov. 3, 1939 | 44 | Pittman | |
| | 3 | Jan. 3, 1940 | Jan. 3, 1941 | 366 | Pittman [28] William H. King of Utah [30] | Sam Rayburn of Texas [29] |
| **77th** | 1 | Jan. 3, 1941 | Jan. 2, 1942 | 365 | Pat Harrison of Mississippi;[31] Carter Glass of Virginia [32] | Rayburn |
| | 2 | Jan. 5, 1942 | Dec. 16, 1942 | 346 | | |
| **78th** | 1 | Jan. 6, 1943 [33] | Dec. 21, 1943 | 350 | Glass | Rayburn |
| | 2 | Jan. 10, 1944 [34] | Dec. 19, 1944 | 345 | Glass | |
| **79th** | 1 | Jan. 3, 1945 [35] | Dec. 21, 1945 | 353 | Kenneth McKellar of Tennessee | Rayburn |
| | 2 | Jan. 14, 1946 [36] | Aug. 2, 1946 | 201 | McKellar | |
| **80th** | 1 | Jan. 3, 1947 [37] | Dec. 19, 1947 | 351 | Arthur H. Vandenberg of Michigan | Joseph W. Martin, Jr. of Massachusetts |
| | 2 | Jan. 6, 1948 [38] | Dec. 31, 1948 | 361 | Vandenberg | |
| **81st** | 1 | Jan. 3, 1949 | Oct. 19, 1949 | 290 | Kenneth McKellar of Tennessee | Sam Rayburn of Texas |
| | 2 | Jan. 3, 1950 [39] | Jan. 2, 1951 | 365 | McKellar | |
| **82nd** | 1 | Jan. 3, 1951 [40] | Oct. 20, 1951 | 291 | McKellar | Rayburn |
| | 2 | Jan. 8, 1952 [41] | July 7, 1952 | 182 | McKellar | |
| **83rd** | 1 | Jan. 3, 1953 [42] | Aug. 3, 1953 | 213 | Styles Bridges of New Hampshire | Joseph W. Martin, Jr. of Massachusetts |
| | 2 | Jan. 6, 1954 [43] | Dec. 2, 1954 | 331 | Bridges | |

| Congress | Session | Date of beginning[1] | Date of adjournment[2] | Length in days | President pro tempore of the Senate[3] | Speaker of the House of Representatives |
|---|---|---|---|---|---|---|
| **84th** | 1 | Jan. 5, 1955[44] | Aug. 2, 1955 | 210 | Walter F. George of Georgia | Sam Rayburn of Texas |
|  | 2 | Jan. 3, 1956[45] | July 27, 1956 | 207 | George | |
| **85th** | 1 | Jan. 3, 1957[46] | Aug. 30, 1957 | 239 | Carl Hayden of Arizona | Rayburn |
|  | 2 | Jan. 7, 1958[47] | Aug. 24, 1958 | 230 | Hayden | |
| **86th** | 1 | Jan. 7, 1959[48] | Sept. 15, 1959 | 252 | Hayden | Rayburn |
|  | 2 | Jan. 6, 1960[49] | Sept. 1, 1960 | 240 | Hayden | |
| **87th** | 1 | Jan. 3, 1961[50] | Sept. 27, 1961 | 268 | Hayden | Rayburn[51] |
|  | 2 | Jan. 10, 1962[52] | Oct. 13, 1962 | 277 | Hayden | John W. McCormack of Massachusetts[53] |
| **88th** | 1 | Jan. 9, 1963[54] | Dec. 30, 1963 | 356 | Hayden | McCormack |
|  | 2 | Jan. 7, 1964[55] | Oct. 3, 1964 | 270 | Hayden | |
| **89th** | 1 | Jan. 4, 1965 | Oct. 23, 1965 | 293 | Hayden | McCormack |
|  | 2 | Jan. 10, 1966[56] | Oct. 22, 1966 | 286 | Hayden | |
| **90th** | 1 | Jan. 10, 1967[57] | Dec. 15, 1967 | 340 | Hayden | McCormack |
|  | 2 | Jan. 15, 1968[58] | Oct. 14, 1968 | 274 | Hayden | |
| **91st** | 1 | Jan. 3, 1969[59] | Dec. 23, 1969 | 355 | Richard B. Russell of Georgia | McCormack |
|  | 2 | Jan. 19, 1970[60] | Jan. 2, 1971 | 349 | Russell | |
| **92nd** | 1 | Jan. 21, 1971[61] | Dec. 17, 1971 | 331 | Russell;[62] Allen J. Ellender of Louisiana[63] | Carl Albert of Oklahoma |
|  | 2 | Jan. 18, 1972[64] | Oct. 18, 1972 | 275 | Ellender;[65] James O. Eastland of Mississippi[66] | |
| **93rd** | 1 | Jan. 3, 1973[67] | Dec. 22, 1973 | 354 | Eastland | Albert |
|  | 2 | Jan. 21, 1974[68] | Dec. 20, 1974 | 334 | Eastland | |
| **94th** | 1 | Jan. 14, 1975[69] | Dec. 19, 1975 | 340 | Eastland | Albert |
|  | 2 | Jan. 19, 1976[70] | Oct. 2, 1976 | 258 | Eastland | |
| **95th** | 1 | Jan. 4, 1977[71] | Dec. 15, 1977 | 346 | Eastland | Thomas P. O'Neill, Jr. of Massachusetts |
|  | 2 | Jan. 19, 1978[72] | Oct. 15, 1978 | 270 | Eastland | |
| **96th** | 1 | Jan. 15, 1979[73] | Jan. 3, 1980 | 354 | Warren G. Magnuson of Washington | O'Neill |
|  | 2 | Jan. 3, 1980[74] | Dec. 16, 1980 | 349 | Magnuson | |
| **97th** | 1 | Jan. 5, 1981[75] | Dec. 16, 1981 | 347 | Strom Thurmond of South Carolina | O'Neill |
|  | 2 | Jan. 25, 1982[76] | Dec. 23, 1982 | 333 | Thurmond | |
| **98th** | 1 | Jan. 3, 1983[77] | Nov. 18, 1983 | 320 | Thurmond | O'Neill |
|  | 2 | Jan. 23, 1984[78] | Oct. 12, 1984 | 264 | Thurmond | |

| Congress | Session | Date of beginning[1] | Date of adjournment[2] | Length in days | President pro tempore of the Senate[3] | Speaker of the House of Representatives |
|---|---|---|---|---|---|---|
| **99th** | 1 | Jan. 3, 1985[79] | Dec. 20, 1985 | 352 | Thurmond | O'Neill |
| | 2 | Jan. 21, 1986[80] | Oct. 18, 1986 | 271 | Thurmond | |
| **100th** | 1 | Jan. 6, 1987[81] | Dec. 22, 1987 | 351 | John C. Stennis of Mississippi | Jim Wright of Texas |
| | 2 | Jan. 25, 1988[82] | Oct. 22, 1988 | 272 | Stennis | |
| **101st** | 1 | Jan. 3, 1989[83] | Nov. 22, 1989 | 324 | Robert C. Byrd of West Virginia | Wright; Thomas S. Foley of Washington[84] |
| | 2 | Jan. 23, 1990[85] | Oct. 28, 1990 | 279 | Byrd | Foley |
| **102nd** | 1 | Jan. 3, 1991[86] | Nov. 27, 1991 | 329 | Byrd | Foley |
| | 2 | Jan. 3, 1992[87] | Oct. 9, 1992 | 281 | Byrd | Foley |

SOURCE: For 1789–1990: *Official Congressional Directory*. For 1991–1992: Calendars of the United States House of Representatives and History of Legislation and the U.S. Senate Library.

1. The Constitution (art. I, sec. 4) provided that "The Congress shall assemble at least once in every year . . . on the first Monday in December, unless they shall by law appoint a different day." Pursuant to a resolution of the Continental Congress, the first session of the First Congress convened March 4, 1789. Up to and including May 20, 1820, 18 acts were passed providing for the meeting of Congress on other days in the year. After 1820 Congress met regularly on the first Monday in December until 1934, when the Twentieth Amendment to the Constitution became effective changing the meeting date to Jan. 3. (Until then, brief special sessions of the Senate only were held at the beginning of each presidential term to confirm Cabinet and other nominations—and occasionally at other times for other purposes. The Senate last met in special session from March 4 to March 6, 1933.) The first and second sessions of the First Congress were held in New York City. Subsequently, including the first session of the Sixth Congress, Philadelphia was the meeting place; since then, Congress has convened in Washington.

2. Until adoption of the Twentieth Amendment, the deadline for adjournment of Congress in odd-numbered years was March 3. However, the expiring Congress often extended the "legislative day" of March 3 up to noon of March 4, when the new Congress came officially into being. After ratification of the Twentieth Amendment, the deadline for adjournment of Congress in odd-numbered years was noon on Jan. 3.

3. At one time, the appointment or election of a president pro tempore was considered by the Senate to be for the occasion only, so that more than one appear in several sessions, and in others none was chosen. Since March 12, 1890, they have served until "the Senate otherwise ordered."

4. Elected to count the vote for president and vice president, which was done April 6, 1789, because there was a quorum of the Senate for the first time. John Adams, vice president, appeared April 21, 1789, and took his seat as president of the Senate.

5. Elected Speaker pro tempore for April 20, 1798, and again for May 28, 1798.

6. Elected Speaker Jan. 19, 1814, to succeed Henry Clay, who resigned Jan. 19, 1814.

7. Elected Speaker Nov. 15, 1820, to succeed Henry Clay, who resigned Oct. 28, 1820.

8. Elected Speaker June 2, 1834, to succeed Andrew Stevenson of Virginia, who resigned.

9. There were recesses in this session from Saturday, Mar. 30, to Wednesday, July 1, and from Saturday, July 20, to Thursday, Nov. 21.

10. There were recesses in this session from Monday, July 27, to Monday, Sept. 21, to Friday, Oct. 16, and to Tuesday, Nov. 10. No business was transacted subsequent to July 27.

11. Elected Speaker Mar. 3, 1869, and served one day.

12. Died Aug. 19, 1876.

13. Appointed Speaker pro tempore Feb. 17, May 12, June 19.

14. Appointed Speaker pro tempore June 4.

15. Resigned as president pro tempore Apr. 27, 1911.

16. Elected to serve Jan. 11–17, Mar. 11–12, Apr. 8, May 10, May 30 to June 1 and 3, June 13 to July 5, Aug. 1–10, and Aug. 27 to Dec. 15, 1912.

17. Elected to serve May 25, 1912.

18. Elected to serve Dec. 4–12, 1911.

19. Elected to serve Feb. 12–14, Apr. 26–27, May 7, July 6–31, Aug. 12–26, 1912.

20. Elected to serve Mar. 25–26, 1912.

21. Elected to serve Aug. 27 to Dec. 15, 1912, Jan. 5–18, and Feb. 2–15, 1913.

22. Elected to serve Dec. 16, 1912, to Jan. 4, 1913, Jan. 19 to Feb. 1, and Feb. 16 to Mar. 3, 1913.

23. Died Oct. 1, 1916.

24. Died Aug. 19, 1934.

25. Died June 4, 1936.

26. Elected June 4, 1936.

27. Died Sept. 15, 1940.

28. Died Nov. 10, 1940.

29. Elected Sept. 16, 1940.

30. Elected Nov. 19, 1940.

31. Elected Jan. 6, 1941; died June 22, 1941.

32. Elected July 10, 1941.

33. There was a recess in this session from Thursday, July 8, to Tuesday, Sept. 14.

34. There were recesses in this session from Saturday, Apr. 1, to Wednesday, Apr. 12; from Friday, June 23, to Tuesday, Aug. 1; and from Thursday, Sept. 21, to Tuesday, Nov. 14.

35. The House was in recess in this session from Saturday, July 21, 1945, to Wednesday, Sept. 5, 1945, and the Senate from Wednesday, Aug. 1, 1945, to Wednesday, Sept. 5, 1945.

36. The House was in recess in this session from Thursday, Apr. 18, 1946, to Tuesday, Apr. 30, 1946.

37. There was a recess in this session from Sunday, July 27, 1947, to Monday, Nov. 17, 1947.

38. There were recesses in this session from Sunday, June 20, 1948, to Monday, July 26, 1948, and from Saturday, Aug. 7, 1948, to Friday, Dec. 31, 1948.

39. The House was in recess in this session from Thursday, Apr. 6, 1950, to Tuesday, Apr. 18, 1950, and both the Senate and the House were in recess from Saturday, Sept. 23, 1950, to Monday, Nov. 27, 1950.

40. The House was in recess in this session from Thursday, Mar. 22, 1951, to Monday, Apr. 2, 1951, and from Thursday, Aug. 23, 1951, to Wednesday, Sept. 12, 1951.

41. The House was in recess in this session from Thursday, Apr. 10, 1952, to Tuesday, Apr. 22, 1952.

42. The House was in recess in this session from Thursday, Apr. 2, 1953, to Monday, Apr. 13, 1953.

43. The House was in recess in this session from Thursday, Apr. 15, 1954, to Monday, Apr. 26, 1954, and adjourned sine die Aug. 20, 1954. The Senate was in recess in this session from Friday, Aug. 20, 1954, to Monday, Nov. 8, 1954; from Thursday, Nov. 18, 1954, to Monday, Nov. 29, 1954, and adjourned sine die Dec. 2, 1954.

44. There was a recess in this session from Monday, Apr. 4, 1955, to Wednesday, Apr. 13, 1955.

45. There was a recess in this session from Thursday, Mar. 29, 1956, to Monday, Apr. 9, 1956.

46. There was a recess in this session from Thursday, Apr. 18, 1957, to Monday, Apr. 29, 1957.

47. There was a recess in this session from Thursday, Apr. 3, 1958, to Monday, Apr. 14, 1958.

48. There was a recess in this session from Thursday, Mar. 26, 1959, to Tuesday, Apr. 7, 1959.

49. The Senate was in recess in this session from Thursday, Apr. 14, 1960, to Monday, Apr. 18, 1960; from Friday, May 27, 1960, to Tuesday, May 31, 1960, and from Sunday, July 3, 1960, to Monday, Aug. 8, 1960. The House was in recess in this session from Thursday, Apr. 14, 1960, to Monday, Apr. 18, 1960; from Friday, May 27, 1960, to Tuesday, May 31, 1960, and from Sunday, July 3, 1960, to Monday, Aug. 15, 1960.

50. The House was in recess in this session from Thursday, Mar. 30, 1961, to Monday, Apr. 10, 1961.

51. Died Nov. 16, 1961.

52. The House was in recess in this session from Thursday, Apr. 19, 1962, to Monday, Apr. 30, 1962.

53. Elected Jan. 10, 1962.

54. The House was in recess in this session from Thursday, Apr. 11, 1963, to Monday, Apr. 22, 1963.

55. The House was in recess in this session from Thursday, Mar. 26, 1964, to Monday, Apr. 6, 1964; from Thursday, July 2, 1964, to Monday, July 20, 1964; from Friday, Aug. 21, 1964, to Monday, Aug. 31, 1964. The Senate was in recess in this session from Friday, July 10, 1964, to Monday, July 20, 1964; from Friday, Aug. 21, 1964, to Monday, Aug. 31, 1964.

56. The House was in recess in this session from Thursday, Apr. 7, 1966, to Monday, Apr. 18, 1966; from Thursday, June 30, 1966, to Monday, July 11, 1966. The Senate was in recess in this session from Thursday, Apr. 7, 1966, to Wednesday, Apr. 13, 1966; from Thursday, June 30, 1966, to Monday, July 11, 1966.

57. There was a recess in this session from Thursday, Mar. 23, 1967, to Monday, Apr. 3, 1967; from Thursday, June 29, 1967, to Monday, July 10, 1967; from Thursday, Aug. 31, 1967, to Monday, Sept. 11, 1967; and from Wednesday, Nov. 22, 1967, to Monday, Nov. 27, 1967.

58. The House was in recess this session from Thursday, Apr. 11, 1968, to Monday, Apr. 22, 1968; from Wednesday, May 29, 1968, to Monday, June 3, 1968; from Wednesday, July 3, 1968, to Monday, July 8, 1968; from Friday, Aug. 2, 1968, to Wednesday, Sept. 4, 1968. The Senate was in recess this session from Thursday, Apr. 11, 1968, to Wednesday, Apr. 17, 1968; from Wednesday, May 29, 1968, to Monday, June 3, 1968; from Wednesday, July 3, 1968, to Monday, July 8, 1968; from Friday, Aug. 2, 1968, to Wednesday, Sept. 4, 1968.

59. The House was in recess this session from Friday, Feb. 7, 1969, to Monday, Feb. 17, 1969; from Thursday, Apr. 3, 1969, to Monday, Apr. 14, 1969; from Wednesday, May 28, 1969, to Monday, June 2, 1969; from Wednesday, July 2, 1969, to Monday, July 7, 1969; from Wednesday, Aug. 13, 1969, to Wednesday, Sept. 3, 1969; from Thursday, Nov. 6, 1969, to Wednesday, Nov. 12, 1969; from Wednesday, Nov. 26, 1969, to Monday, Dec. 1, 1969. The Senate was in recess this session from Friday, Feb. 7, 1969, to Monday, Feb. 17, 1969; from Thursday, Apr. 3, 1969, to Monday, Apr. 14, 1969; from Wednesday, July 2, 1969, to Monday, July 7, 1969; from Wednesday, Aug. 13, 1969, to Wednesday, Sept. 3, 1969; from Wednesday, Nov. 26, 1969, to Monday, Dec. 1, 1969.

60. The House was in recess this session from Tuesday, Feb. 10, 1970, to Monday, Feb. 16, 1970; from Thursday, Mar. 26, 1970, to Tuesday, Mar. 31, 1970; from Wednesday, May 27, 1970, to Monday, June 1, 1970; from Wednesday, July 1, 1970, to Monday, July 6, 1970; from Friday, Aug. 14, 1970, to Wednesday, Sept. 9, 1970; from Wednesday, Oct. 14, 1970, to Monday, Nov. 16, 1970; from Wednesday, Nov. 25, 1970, to Monday, Nov. 30, 1970; from Tuesday, Dec. 22, 1970, to Tuesday, Dec. 29, 1970. The Senate was in recess this session from Tuesday, Feb. 10, 1970, to Monday, Feb. 16, 1970; from Thursday, Mar. 26, 1970, to Tuesday, Mar. 31, 1970; from Wednesday, Sept. 2, 1970, to Tuesday, Sept. 8, 1970; from Wednesday, Oct. 14, 1970, to Monday, Nov. 16, 1970; from Wednesday, Nov. 25, 1970, to Monday, Nov. 30, 1970; from Tuesday, Dec. 22, 1970, to Monday, Dec. 28, 1970.

61. The House was in recess this session from Wednesday, Feb. 10, 1971, to Wednesday, Feb. 17, 1971; from Wednesday, Apr. 7, 1971, to Monday, Apr. 19, 1971; from Thursday, May 27, 1971, to Tuesday, June 1, 1971; from Thursday, July 1, 1971, to Tuesday, July 6, 1971; from Friday, Aug. 6, 1971, to Wednesday, Sept. 8, 1971; from Thursday, Oct. 7, 1971, to Tuesday, Oct. 12, 1971; from Thursday, Oct. 21, 1971, to Tuesday, Oct. 26, 1971; from Friday, Nov. 19, 1971, to Monday, Nov. 29, 1971. The Senate was in recess this session from Thursday, Feb. 11, 1971, to Wednesday, Feb. 17, 1971; from Wednesday, Apr. 7, 1971, to Wednesday, Apr. 14, 1971; from Wednesday, May 26, 1971, to Tuesday, June 1, 1971; from Wednesday, June 30, 1971, to Tuesday, July 6, 1971; from Friday, Aug. 6, 1971, to Wednesday, Sept. 8, 1971; from Thursday, Oct. 21, 1971, to Tuesday, Oct. 26, 1971; from Wednesday, Nov. 24, 1971, to Monday, Nov. 29, 1971.

62. Died Jan. 21, 1971.

63. Elected Jan. 22, 1971.

64. The House was in recess this session from Wednesday, Feb. 9, 1972, to Wednesday, Feb. 16, 1972; from Wednesday, Mar. 29, 1972, to Monday, Apr. 10, 1972; from Wednesday, May 24, 1972, to Tuesday, May 30, 1972; from Friday, June 30, 1972, to Monday, July 17, 1972; from Friday, Aug. 18, 1972, to Tuesday, Sept. 5, 1972. The Senate was in recess this session from Wednesday, Feb. 9, 1972, to Monday, Feb. 14, 1972; from Thursday, Mar. 30, 1972, to Tuesday, Apr. 4, 1972; from Thursday, May 25, 1972, to Tuesday, May 30, 1972; from Friday, June 30, 1972, to Monday, July 17, 1972; from Friday, Aug. 18, 1972, to Tuesday, Sept. 5, 1972.

65. Died July 27, 1972.

66. Elected July 28, 1972.

67. The House was in recess this session from Thursday, Feb. 8, 1973, to Monday, Feb. 19, 1973; from Thursday, Apr. 19, 1973, to Monday, Apr. 30, 1973; from Thursday, May 24, 1973, to Tuesday, May 29, 1973; from Saturday, June 30, 1973, to Tuesday, July 10, 1973; from Friday, Aug. 3, 1973, to Wednesday, Sept. 5, 1973; from Thursday, Oct. 4, 1973, to Tuesday, Oct. 9, 1973; from Thursday, Oct. 18, 1973, to Tuesday, Oct. 23, 1973; from Thursday, Nov. 15, 1973 to Monday, Nov. 26, 1973. The Senate was in recess this session from Thursday, Feb. 8, 1973, to Thursday, Feb. 15, 1973; from Wednesday, Apr. 18, 1973, to Monday, Apr. 30, 1973; from Wednesday, May 23, 1973, to Tuesday, May 29, 1973; from Saturday, June 30, 1973, to Monday, July 9, 1973; from Friday, Aug. 3, 1973, to Wednesday, Sept. 5, 1973; from Thursday, Oct. 18, 1973, to Tuesday, Oct. 23, 1973; from Wednesday, Nov. 21, 1973, to Monday, Nov. 26, 1973.

68. The House was in recess this session from Thursday, Feb. 7, 1974, to Wednesday, Feb. 13, 1974; from Thursday, Apr. 11, 1974, to Monday, Apr. 22, 1974; from Thursday, May 23, 1974, to Tuesday, May 28, 1974; from Thursday, Aug. 22, 1974, to Wednesday, Sept. 11, 1974; from Thursday, Oct. 17, 1974, to Monday, Nov. 18, 1974; from Tuesday, Nov. 26, 1974, to Tuesday, Dec. 3, 1974. The Senate was in recess this session from Friday, Feb. 8, 1974, to Monday, Feb. 18, 1974; from Wednesday, Mar. 13, 1974, to Tuesday, Mar. 19, 1974; from Thursday, Apr. 11, 1974, to Monday, Apr. 22, 1974; from Wednesday, May 23, 1974, to Tuesday, May 28, 1974; from Thursday, Aug. 22, 1974, to Wednesday, Sept. 4, 1974; from Thursday, Oct. 17, 1974, to Monday, Nov. 18, 1974; from Tuesday, Nov. 26, 1974, to Monday, Dec. 2, 1974.

69. The House was in recess this session from Wednesday, Mar. 26, 1975, to Monday, Apr. 7, 1975; from Thursday, May 22, 1975, to Monday, June 2, 1975; from Thursday, June 26, 1975, to Tuesday, July 8, 1975; from Friday, Aug. 1, 1975, to Wednesday, Sept. 3, 1975; from Thursday, Oct. 9, 1975, to Monday, Oct. 20, 1975; from Thursday, Oct. 23, 1975, to Tuesday, Oct. 28, 1975; from Thursday, Nov. 20, 1975, to Monday, Dec. 1, 1975. The Senate was in recess this session from Wednesday, Mar. 26, 1975, to Monday, Apr. 7, 1975; from Thursday, May 22, 1975, to Monday, June 2, 1975; from Friday, June 27, 1975, to Monday, July 7, 1975; from Friday, Aug. 1, 1975, to Wednesday, Sept. 3, 1975; from Thursday, Oct. 9, 1975, to Monday, Oct. 20, 1975; from Thursday, Oct. 23, 1975, to Tuesday, Oct. 28, 1975; from Thursday, Nov. 20, 1975, to Monday, Dec. 1, 1975.

70. The House was in recess this session from Wednesday, Feb. 11, 1976, to Monday, Feb. 16, 1976; from Wednesday, Apr. 14, 1976, to Monday, Apr. 26, 1976; from Thursday, May 27, 1976, to Tuesday, June 1, 1976; from Friday, July 2, 1976, to Monday, July 19, 1976; from Tuesday, Aug. 10, 1976, to Monday, Aug. 23, 1976; from Thursday, Sept. 2, 1976, to Wednesday, Sept. 8, 1976. The Senate was in recess this session from Friday, Feb. 6, 1976, to Monday, Feb. 16, 1976; from Wednesday, Apr. 14, 1976, to Monday, Apr. 26, 1976; from Friday, May 28, 1976, to Wednesday, June 2, 1976; from Friday, July 2, 1976, to Monday, July 19, 1976; from Tuesday, Aug. 10, 1976, to Monday, Aug. 23, 1976; from Wednesday, Sept. 1, 1976, to Tuesday, Sept. 7, 1976.

71. The House was in recess this session from Wednesday, Feb. 9, 1977, to Wednesday, Feb. 16, 1977; from Wednesday, Apr. 6, 1977, to Monday, Apr. 18, 1977; from Thursday, May 26, 1977, to Wednesday, June 1, 1977; from Thursday, June 30, 1977, to Monday, July 11, 1977; from Friday, Aug. 5, 1977, to Wednesday, Sept. 7, 1977; from Thursday, Oct. 6, 1977, to Tuesday, Oct. 11, 1977. The Senate was in recess this session from Friday, Feb. 11, 1977, to Monday, Feb. 21, 1977; from Thursday, Apr. 7, 1977, to Monday, Apr. 18, 1977; from Friday, May 27, 1977, to Monday, June 6, 1977; from Friday, July 1, 1977, to Monday, July 11, 1977; from Saturday, Aug. 6, 1977, to Wednesday, Sept. 7, 1977.

72. The House was in recess this session from Thursday, Feb. 9, 1978, to Tuesday, Feb. 14, 1978; from Wednesday, Mar. 22, 1978, to Monday, Apr. 3, 1978; from Thursday, May 25, 1978, to Wednesday, May 31, 1978; from Thursday, June 29, 1978, to Monday, July 10, 1978; from Thursday, Aug. 17, 1978, to Wednesday, Sept. 6, 1978. The Senate was in recess this session from Friday, Feb. 10, 1978, to Monday, Feb. 20, 1978; from Thursday, Mar. 23, 1978, to Monday, Apr. 3, 1978; from Friday, May 26, 1978, to Monday, June 5, 1978; from Thursday, June 29, 1978, to Monday, July 10, 1978; from Friday, Aug. 25, 1978, to Wednesday, Sept. 6, 1978.

73. The House was in recess this session from Thursday, Feb. 8, 1979, to Tuesday, Feb. 13, 1979; from Tuesday, Apr. 10, 1979, to Monday, Apr. 23, 1979; from Thursday, May 24, 1979, to Wednesday, May 30, 1979; from Friday, June 29, 1979, to Monday, July 9, 1979; from Thursday, Aug. 2, 1979, to Wednesday, Sept. 5, 1979; from Tuesday, Nov. 20, 1979, to Monday, Nov. 26, 1979. The Senate was in recess this session from Friday, Feb. 9, 1979, to Monday, Feb. 19, 1979; from Tuesday, Apr. 10, 1979, to Monday, Apr. 23, 1979; from Friday, May 25, 1979, to Monday, June 4, 1979; from Friday, Aug. 3, 1979, to Wednesday, Sept. 5, 1979; from Tuesday, Nov. 20, 1979, to Monday, Nov. 26, 1979.

74. The House was in recess this session from Wednesday, Feb. 13, 1980, to Tuesday, Feb. 19, 1980; from Wednesday, Apr. 2, 1980, to Tuesday, Apr. 15, 1980; from Thursday, May 22, 1980, to Wednesday, May 28, 1980; from Wednesday, July 2, 1980, to Monday, July 21, 1980; from Friday, Aug. 1, 1980, to Monday, Aug. 18, 1980; from Thursday, Aug. 28, 1980, to Wednesday, Sept. 13, 1980. The Senate was in

recess this session from Monday, Feb. 11, 1980, to Thursday, Feb. 14, 1980; from Thursday, Apr. 3, 1980, to Tuesday, Apr. 15, 1980; from Thursday, May 22, 1980, to Wednesday, May 28, 1980; from Wednesday, July 2, 1980, to Monday, July 21, 1980; from Wednesday, Aug. 6, 1980, to Monday, Aug. 18, 1980; from Wednesday, Aug. 27, 1980, to Wednesday, Sept. 3, 1980; from Wednesday, Oct. 1, 1980, to Wednesday, Nov. 12, 1980; from Monday, Nov. 24, 1980, to Monday, Dec. 1, 1980.

75. The House was in recess this session from Friday, Feb. 6, 1981, to Tuesday, Feb. 17, 1981; from Friday, Apr. 10, 1981, to Monday, Apr. 27, 1981; from Friday, June 26, 1981, to Wednesday, July 8, 1981; from Tuesday, Aug. 4, 1981, to Wednesday, Sept. 9, 1981; from Wednesday, Oct. 7, 1981, to Tuesday, Oct. 13, 1981; from Monday, Nov. 23, 1981, to Monday, Nov. 30, 1981. The Senate was in recess this session from Friday, Feb. 6, 1981, to Monday, Feb. 16, 1981; from Friday, Apr. 10, 1981, to Monday, Apr. 27, 1981; from Thursday, June 25, 1981, to Wednesday, July 8, 1981; from Monday, Aug. 3, 1981, to Wednesday, Sept. 9, 1981; from Wednesday, Oct. 7, 1981, to Wednesday, Oct. 14, 1981; from Tuesday, Nov. 24, 1981, to Monday, Nov. 30, 1981.

76. The House was in recess this session from Wednesday, Feb. 10, 1982, to Monday, Feb. 22, 1982; from Tuesday, Apr. 6, 1982, to Tuesday, Apr. 20, 1982; from Thursday, May 27, 1982, to Wednesday, June 2, 1982; from Thursday, July 1, 1982, to Monday, July 12, 1982; from Friday, Aug. 20, 1982, to Wednesday, Sept. 8, 1982; from Friday, Oct. 1, 1982, to Monday, Nov. 29, 1982. The Senate was in recess this session from Thursday, Feb. 11, 1982, to Monday, Feb. 22, 1982; from Thursday, Apr. 1, 1982, to Tuesday, Apr. 13, 1982; from Thursday, May 27, 1982, to Tuesday, June 8, 1982; from Thursday, July 1, 1982, to Monday, July 12, 1982; from Friday, Aug. 20, 1982, to Wednesday, Sept. 8, 1982; from Friday, Oct. 1, 1982, to Monday, Nov. 29, 1982.

77. The House adjourned for recess this session Friday, Jan. 7, 1983, to Tuesday, Jan. 25, 1983; Thursday, Feb. 17, 1983, to Tuesday, Feb. 22, 1983; Thursday, March 24, 1983, to Tuesday, Apr. 5, 1983; Thursday, May 26, 1983, to Wednesday, June 1, 1983; Thursday, June 30, 1983, to Monday, July 11, 1983; Friday, Aug. 5, 1983, to Monday, Sept. 12, 1983; Friday, Oct. 7, 1983, to Monday, Oct. 17, 1983. The Senate adjourned for recess this session Monday, Jan. 3, 1983, to Tuesday, Jan. 25, 1983; Friday, Feb. 4, 1983, to Monday, Feb. 14, 1983; Friday, March 25, 1983, to Tuesday, Apr. 5, 1983; Friday, May 27, 1983, to Monday, June 6, 1983; Friday, July 1, 1983, to Monday, July 11, 1983; Friday, Aug. 5, 1983, to Monday, Sept. 12, 1983; Monday Oct. 10, 1983, to Monday, Oct. 17, 1983.

78. The House adjourned for recess this session Thursday, Feb. 9, 1984, to Tuesday, Feb. 21, 1984; Friday, Apr. 13, 1984, to Tuesday, Apr. 24, 1984; Friday, May 25, 1984, to Wednesday, May 30, 1984; Friday, June 29, 1984, to Monday, July 23, 1984; Friday, Aug. 10, 1984, to Wednesday, Sept. 5, 1984. The Senate adjourned for recess this session Friday, Feb. 10, 1984, to Monday, Feb. 20, 1984; Friday, Apr. 13, 1984, to Tuesday, Apr. 24, 1984; from Friday, May 25, 1984, to Thursday, May 31, 1984; from Friday, June 29, 1984, to Monday, July 23, 1984; Friday, Aug. 10, 1984, to Wednesday, Sept. 5, 1984.

79. The House adjourned for recess this session Monday, Jan. 7, 1985, to Monday, Jan. 21, 1985; Thursday, Feb. 7, 1985, to Tuesday, Feb. 19, 1985; Thursday, March 7, 1985, to Tuesday, March 19, 1985; Thursday, Apr. 4, 1985, to Monday, Apr. 15, 1985; Thursday, May 23, 1985, to Monday, June 3, 1985; Thursday, June 27, 1985, to Monday, July 8, 1985; Thursday, Aug. 1, 1985, to Wednesday, Sept. 4, 1985; Thursday, Nov. 21, 1985, to Monday, Dec. 2, 1985. The Senate adjourned for recess this session Monday, Jan. 7, 1985, to Monday, Jan. 21, 1985; Thursday, Feb. 7, 1985, to Monday, Feb. 18, 1985; Tuesday, March 12, 1985, to Thursday, March 14, 1985; Thursday, Apr. 4, 1985, to Monday, Apr. 15, 1985; Friday, May 24, 1985, to Monday, June 3, 1985; Thursday, June 27, 1985, to Monday, July 8, 1985; Thursday, Aug. 1, 1985, to Monday, Sept. 9, 1985; Saturday, Nov. 23, 1985, to Monday, Dec. 2, 1985.

80. The House adjourned for recess this session Tuesday, Jan. 7, 1986, to Tuesday, Jan. 21, 1986; Friday, Feb. 7, 1986, to Tuesday, Feb. 18, 1986; Tuesday, March 25, 1986, to Tuesday, Apr. 8, 1986; Thursday, May 22, 1986, to Tuesday, June 3, 1986; Thursday, June 26, 1986, to Monday, July 14, 1986; Friday, Aug. 15, 1986, to Monday, Sept. 8, 1986. The Senate adjourned for recess this session Tuesday, Jan. 7, 1986, to Tuesday, Jan. 21, 1986; Friday, Feb. 7, 1986, to Monday, Feb. 17, 1986; Thursday, March 27, 1986, to Tuesday, Apr. 8, 1986; Wednesday, May 21, 1986, to Monday, June 2, 1986; Thursday, June 26, 1986, to Monday, July 14, 1986; Friday, Aug. 15, 1986, to Monday, Sept. 8, 1986.

81. The House adjourned for recess this session Thursday, Jan. 8, 1987, to Tuesday, Jan. 20, 1987; Wednesday, Feb. 11, 1987, to Wednesday, Feb. 18, 1987; Thursday, Apr. 9, 1987, to Tuesday, Apr. 21, 1987; Thursday, May 21, 1987, to Wednesday, May 27, 1987; Wednesday, July 1, 1987, to Tuesday, July 7, 1987; Wednesday, July 15, 1987, to Monday, July 20, 1987; Friday, Aug. 7, 1987, to Wednesday, Sept. 9, 1987; Tuesday, Nov. 10, 1987, to Monday, Nov. 16, 1987; Friday, Nov. 20, 1987, to Monday, Nov. 30, 1987. The Senate adjourned for recess this session Tuesday, Jan. 6, 1987, to Monday, Jan. 12, 1987; Thursday, Feb. 5, 1987, to Monday, Feb. 16, 1987; Friday, Apr. 10, 1987, to Tuesday, Apr. 21, 1987; Thursday, May 21, 1987, to Wednesday, May 27, 1987; Wednesday, July 1, 1987, to Tuesday, July 7, 1987; Friday, Aug. 7, 1987, to Wednesday, Sept. 9, 1987; Friday, Nov. 20, 1987, to Monday, Nov. 30, 1987.

82. The House adjourned for recess this session Tuesday, Feb. 9, 1988, to Tuesday, Feb. 16, 1988; Thursday, March 31, 1988, to Monday, Apr. 11, 1988; Thursday, May 26, 1988, to Wednesday, June 1, 1988; Thursday, June 30, 1988, to Thursday, July 7, 1988; Thursday, July 14, 1988, to Tuesday, July 26, 1988; Thursday, Aug. 11, 1988, to Wednesday, Sept. 7, 1988. The Senate adjourned for recess this session Thursday, Feb. 4, 1988, to Monday, Feb. 15, 1988; Friday, March 4, 1988, to Monday, March 14, 1988; Thursday, March 31, 1988, to Monday, Apr. 11, 1988; Friday, Apr. 29, 1988, to Monday, May 9, 1988; Friday, May 27, 1988, to Monday, June 6, 1988; Wednesday, June 29, 1988, to Wednesday, July 6, 1988; Thursday, July 14, 1988, to Monday, July 25, 1988, Thursday, Aug. 11, 1988, to Wednesday, Sept. 7, 1988.

83. The House adjourned for recess this session Wednesday, Jan. 4, 1989, to Thursday, Jan. 19, 1989; Thursday, Feb. 9, 1989, to Tuesday, Feb. 21, 1989; Thursday, March 23, 1989, to Monday, Apr. 3, 1989; Tuesday, Apr. 18, 1989, to Tuesday, Apr. 25, 1989; Thursday, May 25, 1989, to Wednesday, May 31, 1989; Thursday, June 29, 1989, to Monday, July 10, 1989; Saturday, Aug. 5, 1989, to Wednesday, Sept. 6, 1989. The Senate adjourned for recess this session Wednesday, Jan. 4, 1989, to Friday, Jan. 20, 1989; Friday, Jan. 20, 1989, to Wednesday, Jan. 25, 1989; Thursday, Feb. 9, 1989, to Tuesday, Feb. 21, 1989; Friday, March 17, 1989, to Tuesday, Apr. 4, 1989; Wednesday, Apr. 19, 1989, to Monday, May 1, 1989; Thursday, May 18, 1989, to Wednesday, May 31, 1989; Friday, June 23, 1989, to Tuesday, July 11, 1989; Friday, Aug. 4, 1989, to Wednesday, Sept. 6, 1989.

84. Elected Speaker June 6, 1989, to succeed Jim Wright, who resigned the Speakership that day.

85. The House adjourned for recess this session Wednesday, Feb. 7, 1990, to Tuesday, Feb. 20, 1990; Wednesday, Apr. 4, 1990, to

Wednesday, Apr. 18, 1990; Friday, May 25, 1990, to Tuesday, June 5, 1990; Thursday, June 28, 1990, to Tuesday, July 10, 1990; Saturday, Aug. 4, 1990, to Wednesday, Sept. 5, 1990. The Senate adjourned for recess this session Thursday, Feb. 8, 1990, to Tuesday, Feb. 20, 1990; Friday, March 9, 1990, to Tuesday, March 20, 1990; Thursday, Apr. 5, 1990, to Wednesday, Apr. 18, 1990; Thursday, May 24, 1990, to Tuesday, June 5, 1990; Thursday, June 28, 1990, to Tuesday, July 10, 1990; Saturday, Aug. 4, 1990, to Monday, Sept. 10, 1990.

86. The House adjourned for recess this session Wednesday, Feb. 6, 1991, to Tuesday, Feb. 19, 1991; Friday, March 22, 1991, to Tuesday, Apr. 9, 1991; Thursday, June 27, 1991, to Tuesday, July 9, 1991; Friday, Aug. 2, 1991, to Wednesday, Sept. 11, 1991. The Senate adjourned for recess this session Wednesday, Feb. 6, 1991, to Tuesday, Feb. 19, 1991; Friday, March 22, 1991, to Tuesday, Apr. 9, 1991; Thursday, Apr. 25, 1991, to Monday, May 6, 1991; Friday, May 24, 1991, to Monday, June 3, 1991; Friday, June 28, 1991, to Monday, July 8, 1991; Friday, Aug. 2, 1991, to Tuesday, Sept. 10, 1991.

87. The House adjourned for recess this session Friday, Jan. 3, 1992, to Wednesday, Jan. 22, 1992; Friday, Apr. 10, 1992, to Tuesday, April 28, 1992; Thursday, July 2, 1992, to Tuesday, July 7, 1992; Friday, July 9, 1992, to Tuesday, July 21, 1992; Wednesday, Aug. 12, 1992, to Wednesday, Sept. 9, 1992. The Senate adjourned for recess this session Monday, Jan. 6, 1992, to Monday, Jan. 20, 1992; Monday, Feb. 10, 1992, to Monday, Feb. 17, 1992; Monday, Apr. 13, 1992, to Friday, Apr. 24, 1992; Monday, May 25, 1992, to Friday, May 29, 1992; Monday, July 6, 1992, to Friday, July 17, 1992; Thursday, Aug. 13, 1992, to Monday, Sept. 7, 1992.

### 1. Executive Proposals

*In 1983 Congress enacted legislation designed to save the Social Security system from threatened insolvency. The measure was based on recommendations of the National Commission on Social Security Reform, which issued its report early that year. The commission had been established by President Ronald Reagan in 1981.*

REPORT OF THE

## NATIONAL COMMISSION

ON

## SOCIAL SECURITY

## REFORM

JANUARY 1983

H.R. 1900

98TH CONGRESS
1ST SESSION

To assure the solvency of the Social Security Trust Fund, to extend the Federal reimbursement of hospitals, and for other purposes.

IN THE HOUSE OF REP...

MARCH 3,...

Mr. ROSTENKOWSKI (for himself, Mr. PICK...
following bill, which was referred to...

A

To assure the solvency of...
reform the medicare...
the Federal supple...
other purposes.

1    Be it enact...
2    tives of the Uni...

98TH CONGRESS
1ST SESSION

# S. 1

To implement the consensus recommendations of the National Commission on Social Security Reform.

### IN THE SENATE OF THE UNITED STATES

JANUARY 26 (legislative day, JANUARY 25), 1983

Mr. DOLE (for himself, Mr. MOYNIHAN, Mr. HEINZ, Mr. BAKER, Mr. STEVENS, Mr. LAXALT, Mr. DANFORTH, Mr. KENNEDY, Mr. BENTSEN, and Mr. MUR-KOWSKI) introduced the following bill, which was read twice and referred to the Committee on Finance.

# A BILL

To implement the consensus recommendations of the National Commission on Social Security Reform.

1    *Be it enacted by the Senate and House of Representa-*
2    *tives of the United States of America in Congress assembled,*
3    SHORT TITLE
4    SECTION 1. This Act, with the following table of con-
5    tents, may be cited as the "Social Security Amendments of
6    1983".

TABLE OF CONTENTS

Sec. 1. Short title.

TITLE I—CHANGES IN COVERAGE

Sec. 101. Coverage of newly hired Federal employees.
Sec. 102. Coverage of employees of nonprofit organizations.
Sec. 103. Duration of agreement for coverage of State and local employees.

### 2. Introduction of Bills

*In the Senate, Finance Committee chair Robert Dole introduced S 1, to carry out the commission's recommendations, on January 26. In the House, Ways and Means Committee chair Dan Rostenkowski introduced HR 1900, a companion bill, on March 3, 1983.*

**98TH CONGRESS** 1st Session — HOUSE OF REPRESENTATIVES

SOCIAL SECURITY ACT AMENDMENTS OF 1983

REPORT
OF THE
COMMITTEE ON WAYS AND MEANS
U.S. HOUSE OF REPRESENTATIVES
ON
H.R. 1900
together
ADDITIONAL AND

MARCH 4, 1983 —Committee
State of

Calendar No. 41

| 98TH CONGRESS 1st Session | SENATE | REPORT No. 98-23 |

SOCIAL SECURITY ACT AMENDMENTS OF 1983

MARCH 11 (legislative day, MARCH 7), 1983.—Ordered to be printed

Mr. DOLE, from the Committee on Finance, submitted the following

REPORT

[To accompany S. 1]

The Committee on Finance to which was referred the bill (S. 1) to implement the consensus recommendations of the National Commission on Social Security Reform, having considered the same, reports favorably thereon with an amendment and recommend that the bill do pass.

SOCIAL SECURITY (OASDI) PROVISIONS

ACTUARIAL ANALYSIS

The OASDI estimates in the following sectional descriptions were prepared by the office of the Actuary, SSA and are based on 1983 Trustees II-B assumptions. Under those assumptions, the Committee amendments described below would permit the timely payment of social security cash benefits through the short-range (1983-89). In the long-range, the Committee amendments are projected to meet or slightly exceed the long-deficit identified by the National Commission on Social Security Reform of 1.80 percent of taxable payroll (revised under 1983 Trustees II-B assumptions to 2.09 percent of taxable payroll).

These amendments are also projected to have a significant impact on the Hospital Insurance (HI) trust fund. CBO estimates project an increase in the HI trust fund of $14.6 billion over the period fiscal years 1983-88.

The amendments also impact on other Federal programs. To the extent the cost/savings are reflected in the following descriptions, they have been provided by CBO and are based on CBO's February 1983 assumptions. A table showing the impact of these amend-

17-743 O

### 3. Committee Reports

*The Ways and Means Committee reported HR 1900 to the full House on March 4. The report included an explanation of the purpose and scope of the bill, a summary of principal provisions, cost estimates, committee votes, and additional and dissenting views by committee members. The Finance Committee reported S 1 to the Senate on March 11.*

98TH CONGRESS 1ST SESSION **H. R. 1900**

### AN ACT

To assure the solvency of the Social Security Trust Funds, to reform the medicare reimbursement of hospitals, to extend the Federal supplemental compensation program, and for other purposes.

1     *Be it enacted by the Senate and House of Representa-*
2 *tives of the United States of America in Congress assembled,*
3              SHORT TITLE
4     SECTION 1. This Act, with the following table of con-
5 tents, may be cited as the "Social Security Act Amendments
6 of 1983".

TABLE OF CONTENTS

Sec. 1. Short title.

MARCH 9, 1983
Considered, amended and passed

### 4. Passage of Bills

*The House passed HR 1900 on March 9. The Senate never passed S 1. Instead, on March 23 it passed HR 1900, after substituting the text of S 1 for the text of the House-passed bill.*

## 5. Conference Report

*A joint Senate-House conference committee worked out a compromise version of the bill, which required approval by each chamber. Conferees filed their report on March 24. The House and Senate quickly approved the report, and HR 1900 was sent to the White House for the president's signature.*

---

98TH CONGRESS | HOUSE OF REPRESENTATIVES | REPORT
1st Session | | No. 98-47

SOCIAL SECURITY AMENDMENTS OF 1983

MARCH 24, 1983.—Ordered to be printed

Mr. ROSTENKOWSKI, from the committee of conference,
submitted the following

CONFERENCE REPORT

[To accompany H.R. 1900]

The committee of conference on the disagreeing votes of the two Houses on the amendment of the Senate to the bill (H.R. 1900) to assure the solvency of the Social Security Trust Funds, to reform the medicare reimbursement of hospitals, to extend the Federal supplemental compensation program, and for other purposes, having met, after full and free conference, have agreed to recommend and do recommend to their respective Houses as follows:

That the House recede from its disagreement to the amendment of the Senate and agree to the same with an amendment as follows:

In lieu of the matter proposed to be inserted by the Senate amendment insert the following:

SHORT TITLE

SECTION 1. This Act, with the following table of contents, may be cited as the "Social Security Amendments of 1983".

TABLE OF CONTENTS

Sec. 1. Short title.

TITLE I—PROVISIONS AFFECTING THE FINANCING OF THE SOCIAL
SECURITY SYSTEM

PART A—COVERAGE

Sec. 101. Coverage of newly hired Federal employees.
Sec. 102. Coverage of employees of nonprofit organizations.
Sec. 103. Duration of agreements for coverage of State and local employees.

PART B—COMPUTATION OF BENEFIT AMOUNTS

Sec. 111. Shift of cost-of-living adjustments to calendar year basis.
Sec. 112. Cost-of-living increases to be based on either wages or prices (whichever is lower) when balance in OASDI trust funds falls below specified level.

19-370 O

---

## 6. Public Law

*The president signed the bill into law on April 20, 1983, and it became PL 98-21. Public laws are first presented in a pamphlet called a "slip law."*

---

PUBLIC LAW 98-21—APR. 20, 1983 97 STAT. 65

Public Law 98-21
98th Congress

An Act

To assure the solvency of the Social Security Trust Funds, to reform the medicare reimbursement of hospitals, to extend the Federal supplemental compensation program, and for other purposes.

Apr. 20, 1983
[H.R. 1900]

*Be it enacted by the Senate and House of Representatives of the United States of America in Congress assembled,*

Social Security
Amendments of
1983.

SHORT TITLE

SECTION 1. This Act, with the following table of contents, may be cited as the "Social Security Amendments of 1983".

42 USC 1305
note.

TABLE OF CONTENTS

Sec. 1. Short title.

TITLE I—PROVISIONS AFFECTING THE FINANCING OF THE SOCIAL
SECURITY SYSTEM

PART A—COVERAGE

Sec. 101. Coverage of newly hired Federal employees.
Sec. 102. Coverage of employees of nonprofit organizations.
Sec. 103. Duration of agreements for coverage of State and local employees.

PART B—COMPUTATION OF BENEFIT AMOUNTS

Sec. 111. Shift of cost-of-living adjustments to calendar year basis.
Sec. 112. Cost-of-living increases to be based on either wages or prices (whichever is lower) when balance in OASDI trust funds falls below specified level.
Sec. 113. Elimination of windfall benefits for individuals receiving pensions from noncovered employment.
Sec. 114. Increase in old-age insurance benefit amounts on account of delayed retirement.

PART C—REVENUE PROVISIONS

Sec. 121. Taxation of social security and tier 1 railroad retirement benefits.
Sec. 122. Credit for the elderly and the permanently and totally disabled.
Sec. 123. Acceleration of increases in FICA taxes; 1984 employee tax credit.
Sec. 124. Taxes on self-employment income; credit against such taxes for years before 1990; deduction of such taxes for years after 1989.
Sec. 125. Treatment of certain faculty practice plans.
Sec. 126. Allocations to disability insurance trust fund.

PART D—BENEFITS FOR CERTAIN SURVIVING, DIVORCED, AND DISABLED SPOUSES

Sec. 131. Benefits for surviving divorced spouses and disabled widows and widowers who remarry.
Sec. 132. Entitlement to divorced spouse's benefits without regard to entitlement of insured individual to benefits; exemption of divorced spouse's benefits from deduction on account of work.
Sec. 133. Indexing of deferred surviving spouse's benefits to recent wage levels.
Sec. 134. Limitation on benefit reduction for early retirement in case of disabled widows and widowers.

PART E—MECHANISMS TO ASSURE CONTINUED BENEFIT PAYMENTS IN UNEXPECTEDLY
ADVERSE CONDITIONS

Sec. 141. Normalized crediting of social security taxes to trust funds.
Sec. 142. Interfund borrowing extension.

## How to Write a Member of Congress

Citizens with complaints, suggestions, and comments on how the government is being run can voice their views directly to Congress.

### Writing Tips

The following hints on how to write a member of Congress were suggested by congressional sources and the League of Women Voters.

•Write to your own senators or representative. Letters sent to other members will end up on the desk of members from your state.

•Write at the proper time, when a bill is being discussed in committee or on the floor.

•Use your own words and your own stationery. Avoid signing and sending a form or mimeographed letter.

•Don't be a pen pal. Don't try to instruct the representative or senator on every issue that comes up.

•Don't demand a commitment before all the facts are in. Bills rarely become law in the same form as introduced.

•Whenever possible, identify all bills by their number.

•If possible, include pertinent editorials from local papers.

•Be constructive. If a bill deals with a problem you admit exists but you believe the bill is the wrong approach, tell what you think the right approach is.

•If you have expert knowledge or wide experience in particular areas, share it with the member. But don't pretend to wield vast political influence.

•Write to members when they do something you approve of. A note of appreciation will make them remember you more favorably the next time.

•Feel free to write when you have a question or problem dealing with procedures of government departments.

•Be brief, write legibly, and be sure to use the proper form of address.

### Suggested Form for Letters

#### Senator

Honorable —————— ———————
United States Senate
Washington, DC 20510
Dear Senator——————————:
Sincerely yours,

#### Representative

Honorable —————— ——————
House of Representatives
Washington, DC 20515
Dear Representative ——————:
Sincerely yours,

# Capital Attractions

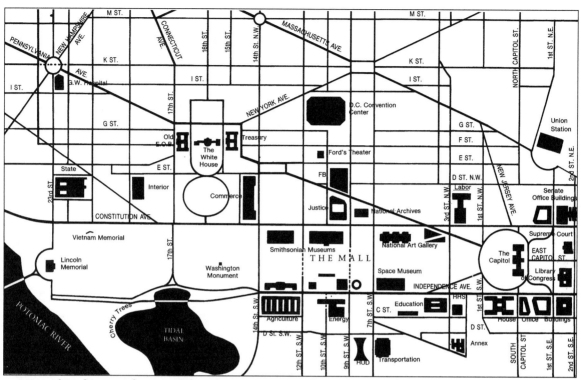

Many of Washington's foremost sightseeing attractions are clustered around the Mall, the grassy strip that stretches from the Capitol west to the Lincoln Memorial.

TOURMOBILE shuttle buses provide narrated sightseeing service to eighteen sites in the Mall area and to nearby Arlington National Cemetery. Passengers pay a single daily fee; they may board and reboard the buses as often as they like. For information, call 554-7950. For information on METRO bus and subway service in the Washington area, call 637-7000. The Washington, D.C., area code is 202.

The sites listed below are open daily unless otherwise noted.

**CAPITOL**
224-3121, 225-6827 (tours)

*North side of the Mall:*

**National Gallery of Art**
Constitution Avenue at Sixth Street, NW
737-4215

**National Archives**
Constitution Avenue at Eighth Street, NW
523-3220

**Washington Monument**
Constitution Avenue at Fifteenth Street, NW
426-6839

**Vietnam Veterans Memorial**
Constitution Avenue at Twenty-first Street, NW

**Lincoln Memorial**
Constitution Avenue at Twenty-third Street, NW
426-6895

*Smithsonian Institution*

Smithsonian museums line both sides of the Mall between Seventh and Fourteenth Streets. General information: 357-2700.

National Museum of Natural History
Constitution Avenue at Tenth Street, NW

National Museum of American History
Constitution Avenue at Fourteenth Street, NW

*South side of the Mall:*

National Air and Space Museum
Independence Avenue at Seventh Street, SW

Hirshhorn Museum and Sculpture Garden
Independence Avenue at Seventh Street, SW

Arts and Industries Building
900 Jefferson Drive, SW

Smithsonian Castle
1000 Jefferson Drive, SW

National Museum of African Art
950 Independence Ave, SW

Arthur M. Sackler Gallery
1050 Independence Avenue, SW

Freer Gallery of Art
Jefferson Drive at Twelfth Street, SW

*Beyond the Mall:*

White House
1600 Pennsylvania Avenue
Open Tuesday-Saturday
456-7041

Jefferson Memorial
Tidal Basin, SW
426-6821

Library of Congress
10 First Street, SE
287-5108

Ford's Theatre
511 Tenth Street, NW
Museum/tours: 426-6924

Arlington National Cemetery
Arlington, Virginia
703-695-3175

National Zoological Park (Smithsonian)
3000 Connecticut Avenue, NW
673-4800

# Government of the United States

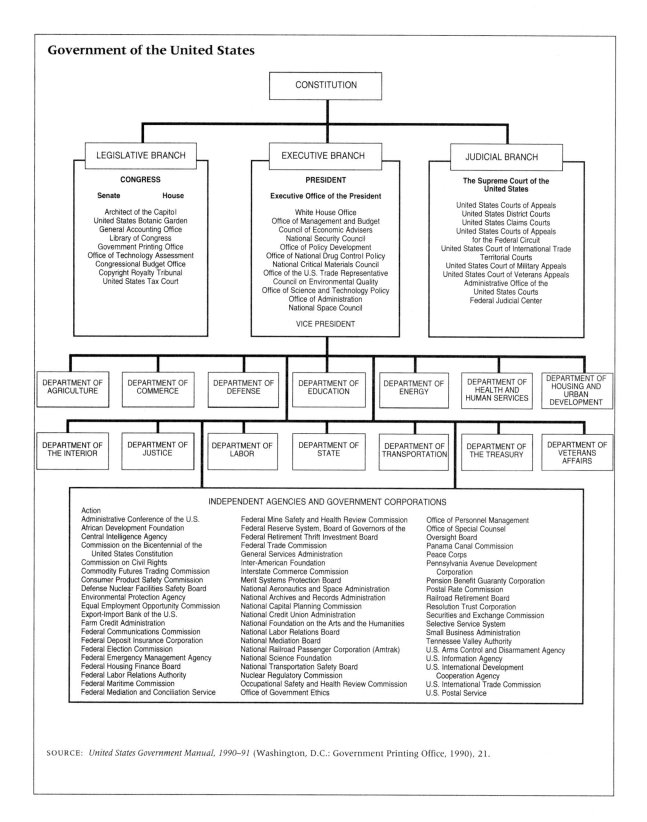

CONSTITUTION

## LEGISLATIVE BRANCH

### CONGRESS

**Senate**      **House**

Architect of the Capitol
United States Botanic Garden
General Accounting Office
Library of Congress
Government Printing Office
Office of Technology Assessment
Congressional Budget Office
Copyright Royalty Tribunal
United States Tax Court

## EXECUTIVE BRANCH

### PRESIDENT

**Executive Office of the President**

White House Office
Office of Management and Budget
Council of Economic Advisers
National Security Council
Office of Policy Development
Office of National Drug Control Policy
National Critical Materials Council
Office of the U.S. Trade Representative
Council on Environmental Quality
Office of Science and Technology Policy
Office of Administration
National Space Council

VICE PRESIDENT

## JUDICIAL BRANCH

### The Supreme Court of the United States

United States Courts of Appeals
United States District Courts
United States Claims Courts
United States Courts of Appeals
for the Federal Circuit
United States Court of International Trade
Territorial Courts
United States Court of Military Appeals
United States Court of Veterans Appeals
Administrative Office of the
United States Courts
Federal Judicial Center

---

DEPARTMENT OF AGRICULTURE
DEPARTMENT OF COMMERCE
DEPARTMENT OF DEFENSE
DEPARTMENT OF EDUCATION
DEPARTMENT OF ENERGY
DEPARTMENT OF HEALTH AND HUMAN SERVICES
DEPARTMENT OF HOUSING AND URBAN DEVELOPMENT

DEPARTMENT OF THE INTERIOR
DEPARTMENT OF JUSTICE
DEPARTMENT OF LABOR
DEPARTMENT OF STATE
DEPARTMENT OF TRANSPORTATION
DEPARTMENT OF THE TREASURY
DEPARTMENT OF VETERANS AFFAIRS

## INDEPENDENT AGENCIES AND GOVERNMENT CORPORATIONS

Action
Administrative Conference of the U.S.
African Development Foundation
Central Intelligence Agency
Commission on the Bicentennial of the
   United States Constitution
Commission on Civil Rights
Commodity Futures Trading Commission
Consumer Product Safety Commission
Defense Nuclear Facilities Safety Board
Environmental Protection Agency
Equal Employment Opportunity Commission
Export-Import Bank of the U.S.
Farm Credit Administration
Federal Communications Commission
Federal Deposit Insurance Corporation
Federal Election Commission
Federal Emergency Management Agency
Federal Housing Finance Board
Federal Labor Relations Authority
Federal Maritime Commission
Federal Mediation and Conciliation Service

Federal Mine Safety and Health Review Commission
Federal Reserve System, Board of Governors of the
Federal Retirement Thrift Investment Board
Federal Trade Commission
General Services Administration
Inter-American Foundation
Interstate Commerce Commission
Merit Systems Protection Board
National Aeronautics and Space Administration
National Archives and Records Administration
National Capital Planning Commission
National Credit Union Administration
National Foundation on the Arts and the Humanities
National Labor Relations Board
National Mediation Board
National Railroad Passenger Corporation (Amtrak)
National Science Foundation
National Transportation Safety Board
Nuclear Regulatory Commission
Occupational Safety and Health Review Commission
Office of Government Ethics

Office of Personnel Management
Office of Special Counsel
Oversight Board
Panama Canal Commission
Peace Corps
Pennsylvania Avenue Development
   Corporation
Pension Benefit Guaranty Corporation
Postal Rate Commission
Railroad Retirement Board
Resolution Trust Corporation
Securities and Exchange Commission
Selective Service System
Small Business Administration
Tennessee Valley Authority
U.S. Arms Control and Disarmament Agency
U.S. Information Agency
U.S. International Development
   Cooperation Agency
U.S. International Trade Commission
U.S. Postal Service

SOURCE: *United States Government Manual, 1990–91* (Washington, D.C.: Government Printing Office, 1990), 21.

# Constitution of the United States

*We the People of the United States, in Order to form a more perfect Union, establish Justice, insure domestic Tranquility, provide for the common defence, promote the general Welfare, and secure the Blessings of Liberty to ourselves and our Posterity, do ordain and establish this Constitution for the United States of America.*

ARTICLE I

**Section 1.** All legislative Powers herein granted shall be vested in a Congress of the United States, which shall consist of a Senate and House of Representatives.

**Section 2.** The House of Representatives shall be composed of Members chosen every second Year by the People of the several States, and the Electors in each State shall have the Qualifications requisite for Electors of the most numerous Branch of the State Legislature.

No Person shall be a Representative who shall not have attained to the age of twenty five Years, and been seven Years a Citizen of the United States, and who shall not, when elected, be an Inhabitant of that State in which he shall be chosen.

[Representatives and direct Taxes shall be apportioned among the several States which may be included within this Union, according to their respective Numbers, which shall be determined by adding to the whole Number of free Persons, including those bound to Service for a Term of Years, and excluding Indians not taxed, three fifths of all other Persons.][1] The actual Enumeration shall be made within three Years after the first Meeting of the Congress of the United States, and within every subsequent Term of ten Years, in such Manner as they shall by Law direct. The Number of Representatives shall not exceed one for every thirty Thousand, but each State shall have at Least one Representative; and until such enumeration shall be made, the State of New Hampshire shall be entitled to chuse three, Massachusetts eight, Rhode-Island and Providence Plantations one, Connecticut five, New-York six, New Jersey four, Pennsylvania eight, Delaware one, Maryland six, Virginia ten, North Carolina five, South Carolina five, and Georgia three.

When vacancies happen in the Representation from any State, the Executive Authority thereof shall issue Writs of Election to fill such Vacancies.

The House of Representatives shall chuse their Speaker and other Officers; and shall have the sole Power of Impeachment.

**Section 3.** The Senate of the United States shall be composed of two Senators from each State, [chosen by the Legislature thereof,][2] for six Years; and each Senator shall have one Vote.

Immediately after they shall be assembled in Consequence of the first Election, they shall be divided as equally as may be into three Classes. The Seats of the Senators of the first Class shall be vacated at the Expiration of the second Year, of the second Class at the Expiration of the fourth Year, and of the third Class at the Expiration of the sixth Year, so that one third may be chosen every second Year; [and if Vacancies happen by Resignation, or otherwise, during the Recess of the Legislature of any State, the Executive thereof may make temporary Appointments until the next Meeting of the Legislature, which shall then fill such Vacancies.][3]

No Person shall be a Senator who shall not have attained to the Age of thirty Years, and been nine Years a Citizen of the United States, and who shall not, when elected, be an Inhabitant of that State for which he shall be chosen.

The Vice President of the United States shall be President of the Senate, but shall have no Vote, unless they be equally divided.

The Senate shall chuse their other Officers, and also a President pro tempore, in the Absence of the Vice President, or when he shall exercise the Office of President of the United States.

The Senate shall have the sole Power to try all Impeachments. When sitting for that Purpose, they shall be on Oath or Affirmation. When the President of the United States is tried, the Chief Justice shall preside: And no Person shall be convicted without the Concurrence of two thirds of the Members present.

Judgment in Cases of Impeachment shall not extend further than to removal from Office, and disqualification to hold and enjoy any Office of honor, Trust or Profit under the United States: but the Party convicted shall nevertheless be liable and subject to Indictment, Trial, Judgment and Punishment, according to Law.

***Section 4.*** The Times, Places and Manner of holding Elections for Senators and Representatives, shall be prescribed in each State by the Legislature thereof; but the Congress may at any time by Law make or alter such Regulations, except as to the Places of chusing Senators.

The Congress shall assemble at least once in every Year, and such Meeting shall [be on the first Monday in December],[4] unless they shall by Law appoint a different Day.

***Section 5.*** Each House shall be the Judge of the Elections, Returns and Qualifications of its own Members, and a Majority of each shall constitute a Quorum to do Business; but a smaller Number may adjourn from day to day, and may be authorized to compel the Attendance of absent Members, in such Manner, and under such Penalties as each House may provide.

Each House may determine the Rules of its Proceedings, punish its Members for disorderly Behaviour, and, with the Concurrence of two thirds, expel a Member.

Each House shall keep a Journal of its Proceedings, and from time to time publish the same, excepting such Parts as may in their Judgment require Secrecy; and the Yeas and Nays of the Members of either House on any question shall, at the Desire of one fifth of those Present, be entered on the Journal.

Neither House, during the Session of Congress, shall, without the Consent of the other, adjourn for more than three days, nor to any other Place than that in which the two Houses shall be sitting.

***Section 6.*** The Senators and Representatives shall receive a Compensation for their Services, to be ascertained by Law, and paid out of the Treasury of the United States. They shall in all Cases, except Treason, Felony and Breach of the Peace, be privileged from Arrest during their Attendance at the Session of their respective Houses, and in going to and returning from the same; and for any Speech or Debate in either House, they shall not be questioned in any other Place.

No Senator or Representative shall, during the Time for which he was elected, be appointed to any civil Office under the Authority of the United States, which shall have been created, or the Emoluments whereof shall have been encreased during such time; and no Person holding any Office under the United States, shall be a Member of either House during his Continuance in Office.

***Section 7.*** All Bills for raising Revenue shall originate in the House of Representatives; but the Senate may propose or concur with Amendments as on other Bills.

Every Bill which shall have passed the House of Representatives and the Senate, shall, before it become a Law, be presented to the President of the United States; If he approve he shall sign it, but if not he shall return it, with his Objections to that House in which it shall have originated, who shall enter the Objections at large on their Journal, and proceed to reconsider it. If after such Reconsideration two thirds of that House shall agree to pass the Bill, it shall be sent, together with the Objections, to the other House, by which it shall likewise be reconsidered, and if approved by two thirds of that House, it shall become a Law. But in all such Cases the Votes of both Houses shall be determined by yeas and Nays, and the Names of the Persons voting for and against the Bill shall be entered on the Journal of each House respectively. If any Bill shall not be returned by the President within ten Days (Sundays excepted) after it shall have been presented to him, the Same shall be a Law, in like Manner as if he had signed it, unless the Congress by their Adjournment prevent its Return, in which Case it shall not be a Law.

Every Order, Resolution, or Vote to which the Concurrence of the Senate and House of Representatives may be necessary (except on a question of Adjournment) shall be presented to the President of the United States; and before the Same shall take Effect, shall be approved by him, or being disapproved by him, shall be repassed by two thirds of the Senate and House of Representatives, according to the Rules and Limitations prescribed in the Case of a Bill.

***Section 8.*** The Congress shall have Power To lay and collect Taxes, Duties, Imposts and Excises, to pay the Debts and provide for the common Defence and general Welfare of the United States; but all Duties, Imposts and Excises shall be uniform throughout the United States;

To borrow Money on the credit of the United States;

To regulate Commerce with foreign Nations, and among the several States, and with the Indian Tribes;

To establish an uniform Rule of Naturalization, and uniform Laws on the subject of Bankruptcies throughout the United States;

To coin Money, regulate the Value thereof, and of foreign Coin, and fix the Standard of Weights and Measures;

To provide for the Punishment of counterfeiting the Securities and current Coin of the United States;

To establish Post Offices and post Roads;

To promote the Progress of Science and useful Arts, by securing for limited Times to Authors and Inventors the exclusive Right to their respective Writings and Discoveries;

To constitute Tribunals inferior to the supreme Court;

To define and punish Piracies and Felonies committed on the high Seas, and Offences against the Law of Nations;

To declare War, grant Letters of Marque and Reprisal, and make Rules concerning Captures on Land and Water;

To raise and support Armies, but no Appropriation of Money to that Use shall be for a longer Term than two Years;

To provide and maintain a Navy;

To make Rules for the Government and Regulation of the land and naval Forces;

To provide for calling forth the Militia to execute the Laws of the Union, suppress Insurrections and repel Invasions;

To provide for organizing, arming, and disciplining, the Militia, and for governing such Part of them as may be employed in the Service of the United States, reserving to the States respectively, the Appointment of the Officers, and the Authority of training the Militia according to the discipline prescribed by Congress;

To exercise exclusive Legislation in all Cases whatsoever, over such District (not exceeding ten Miles square) as may, by Cession of particular States, and the Acceptance of Congress, become the Seat of the Government of the United States, and to exercise like Authority over all Places purchased by the Consent of the Legislature of the State in which the Same shall be, for the Erection of Forts, Magazines, Arsenals, dock-Yards, and other needful Buildings; —And

To make all Laws which shall be necessary and proper for carrying into Execution the foregoing Powers, and all other Powers vested by this Constitution in the Government of the United States, or in any Department or Officer thereof.

*Section 9.* The Migration or Importation of such Persons as any of the States now existing shall think proper to admit, shall not be prohibited by the Congress prior to the Year one thousand eight hundred and eight, but a Tax or duty may be imposed on such Importation, not exceeding ten dollars for each Person.

The Privilege of the Writ of Habeas Corpus shall not be suspended, unless when in Cases of Rebellion or Invasion the public Safety may require it.

No Bill of Attainder or ex post facto Law shall be passed.

No Capitation, or other direct, Tax shall be laid, unless in Proportion to the Census or Enumeration herein before directed to be taken.[5]

No Tax or Duty shall be laid on Articles exported from any State.

No Preference shall be given by any Regulation of Commerce or Revenue to the Ports of one State over those of another; nor shall Vessels bound to, or from, one State, be obliged to enter, clear, or pay Duties in another.

No Money shall be drawn from the Treasury, but in Consequence of Appropriations made by Law; and a regular Statement and Account of the Receipts and Expenditures of all public Money shall be published from time to time.

No Title of Nobility shall be granted by the United States: And no Person holding any Office of Profit or Trust under them, shall, without the Consent of the Congress, accept of any present, Emolument, Office, or Title, of any kind whatever, from any King, Prince, or foreign State.

*Section 10.* No State shall enter into any Treaty, Alliance, or Confederation; grant Letters of Marque and Reprisal; coin Money; emit Bills of Credit; make any Thing but gold and silver Coin a Tender in Payment of Debts; pass any Bill of Attainder, ex post facto Law, or Law impairing the Obligation of Contracts, or grant any Title of Nobility.

No State shall, without the Consent of the Congress, lay any Imposts or Duties on Imports or Exports, except what may be absolutely necessary for executing it's inspection Laws: and the net Produce of all Duties and Imposts, laid by any State on Imports or Exports, shall be for the Use of the Treasury of the United States; and all such Laws shall be subject to the Revision and Controul of the Congress.

No State shall, without the Consent of Congress, lay any Duty of Tonnage, keep Troops, or Ships of War in time of Peace, enter into any Agreement or Compact with another State, or with a foreign Power, or engage in War, unless actually invaded, or in such imminent Danger as will not admit of delay.

ARTICLE II

*Section 1.* The executive Power shall be vested in a President of the United States of America. He shall hold his Office during the Term of four Years, and, together with the Vice President, chosen for the same Term, be elected, as follows

Each State shall appoint, in such Manner as the Legislature thereof may direct, a Number of Electors, equal to the whole Number of Senators and Representatives to which the State may be entitled in the Congress: but no Senator or Representative, or Person holding an Office of Trust or Profit under the United States, shall be appointed an Elector.

[The Electors shall meet in their respective States, and vote by Ballot for two Persons, of whom one at least shall not be an Inhabitant of the same State with themselves. And they shall make a List of all the Persons voted for, and of the Number of Votes for each; which List they shall sign and certify, and transmit sealed to the Seat of the Government of the United States, directed to the President of the Senate. The President of the Senate shall, in the Presence of the Senate and House of Representatives, open all the Certificates, and the Votes shall then be counted. The Person having the greatest Number of Votes shall be the President, if such Number be a Majority of the whole Number of Electors appointed; and if there be more than one who have such Majority, and have an equal Number of Votes, then the House of Representatives shall immediately chuse by Ballot one of them for President; and if no Person have a Majority, then from the five highest on the list the said House shall in like Manner chuse the President. But in chusing the President, the Votes shall be taken by States, the Representation from each State having one Vote; A quorum for this Purpose shall consist of a Member or Members from two thirds of the States, and a Majority of all the States shall be necessary to a Choice. In every Case, after the Choice of the President, the Person having the greatest Number of Votes of the Electors shall be the Vice President. But if there should remain two or more who have equal Votes, the Senate shall chuse from them by Ballot the Vice President.][6]

The Congress may determine the Time of chusing the Electors, and the Day on which they shall give their Votes; which Day shall be the same throughout the United States.

No Person except a natural born Citizen, or a Citizen of the United States, at the time of the Adoption of this Constitution, shall be eligible to the Office of President; neither shall any Person be eligible to that Office who shall not have attained to the Age of thirty five Years, and been fourteen Years a Resident within the United States.

In Case of the Removal of the President from Office, or of his Death, Resignation, or Inability to discharge the Powers and Duties of the said Office,[7] the Same shall devolve on the Vice President, and the Congress may by Law provide for the Case of Removal, Death, Resignation or Inability, both of the President and Vice President, declaring what Officer shall then act as President, and such Officer shall act accordingly, until the Disability be removed, or a President shall be elected.

The President shall, at stated Times, receive for his Services, a Compensation, which shall neither be encreased nor diminished during the Period for which he shall have been elected, and he shall not receive within that Period any other Emolument from the United States, or any of them.

Before he enter on the Execution of his Office, he shall take the following Oath or Affirmation:—"I do solemnly swear (or affirm) that I will faithfully execute the Office of President of the United States, and will to the best of my Ability, preserve, protect and defend the Constitution of the United States."

**Section 2.** The President shall be Commander in Chief of the Army and Navy of the United States, and of the Militia of the several States, when called into the actual Service of the United States; he may require the Opinion, in writing, of the principal Officer in each of the executive Departments, upon any Subject relating to the Duties of their respective Offices, and he shall have Power to grant Reprieves and Pardons for Offences against the United States, except in Cases of Impeachment.

He shall have Power, by and with the Advice and Consent of the Senate, to make Treaties, provided two thirds of the Senators present concur; and he shall nominate, and by and with the Advice and Consent of the Senate, shall appoint Ambassadors, other public Ministers and Consuls, Judges of the supreme Court, and all other Officers of the United States, whose Appointments are not herein otherwise provided for, and which shall be established by Law: but the Congress may by Law vest the Appointment of such inferior Officers, as they think proper, in the President alone, in the Courts of Law, or in the Heads of Departments.

The President shall have Power to fill up all Vacancies that may happen during the Recess of the Senate, by granting Commissions which shall expire at the End of their next Session.

**Section 3.** He shall from time to time give to the Congress Information of the State of the Union, and recommend to their Consideration such Measures as he shall judge necessary and expedient; he may, on extraordinary Occasions, convene both Houses, or either of them, and in Case of Disagreement between them, with Respect to the Time of Adjournment, he may adjourn them to such Time as he shall think proper; he shall receive Ambassadors and other public Ministers; he shall take Care that the Laws be faithfully executed, and shall Commission all the Officers of the United States.

***Section 4.*** The President, Vice President and all civil Officers of the United States, shall be removed from Office on Impeachment for, and Conviction of, Treason, Bribery, or other high Crimes and Misdemeanors.

ARTICLE III

***Section 1.*** The judicial Power of the United States, shall be vested in one supreme Court, and in such inferior Courts as the Congress may from time to time ordain and establish. The Judges, both of the supreme and inferior Courts, shall hold their Offices during good Behaviour, and shall, at stated Times, receive for their Services, a Compensation, which shall not be diminished during their Continuance in Office.

***Section 2.*** The judicial Power shall extend to all Cases, in Law and Equity, arising under this Constitution, the Laws of the United States, and Treaties made, or which shall be made, under their Authority; — to all Cases affecting Ambassadors, other public Ministers and Consuls; — to all Cases of admiralty and maritime Jurisdiction; — to Controversies to which the United States shall be a Party; — to Controversies between two or more States; — between a State and Citizens of another State;[8] — between Citizens of different States; — between Citizens of the same State claiming Lands under Grants of different States, and between a State, or the Citizens thereof, and foreign States, Citizens or Subjects.[8]

In all Cases affecting Ambassadors, other public Ministers and Consuls, and those in which a State shall be Party, the supreme Court shall have original Jurisdiction. In all the other Cases before mentioned, the supreme Court shall have appellate Jurisdiction, both as to Law and Fact, with such Exceptions, and under such Regulations as the Congress shall make.

The Trial of all Crimes, except in Cases of Impeachment, shall be by Jury; and such Trial shall be held in the State where the said Crimes shall have been committed; but when not committed within any State, the Trial shall be at such Place or Places as the Congress may by Law have directed.

***Section 3.*** Treason against the United States, shall consist only in levying War against them, or in adhering to their Enemies, giving them Aid and Comfort. No Person shall be convicted of Treason unless on the Testimony of two Witnesses to the same overt Act, or on Confession in open Court.

The Congress shall have Power to declare the Punishment of Treason, but no Attainder of Treason shall work Corruption of Blood, or Forfeiture except during the Life of the Person attainted.

ARTICLE IV

***Section 1.*** Full Faith and Credit shall be given in each State to the public Acts, Records, and judicial Proceedings of every other State. And the Congress may by general Laws prescribe the Manner in which such Acts, Records and Proceedings shall be proved, and the Effect thereof.

***Section 2.*** The Citizens of each State shall be entitled to all Privileges and Immunities of Citizens in the several States.

A Person charged in any State with Treason, Felony, or other Crime, who shall flee from Justice, and be found in another State, shall on Demand of the executive Authority of the State from which he fled, be delivered up, to be removed to the State having Jurisdiction of the Crime.

[No Person held to Service or Labour in one State, under the Laws thereof, escaping into another, shall, in Consequence of any Law or Regulation therein, be discharged from such Service or Labour, but shall be delivered up on Claim of the Party to whom such Service or Labour may be due.][9]

***Section 3.*** New States may be admitted by the Congress into this Union; but no new State shall be formed or erected within the Jurisdiction of any other State; nor any State be formed by the Junction of two or more States, or Parts of States, without the Consent of the Legislatures of the States concerned as well as of the Congress.

The Congress shall have Power to dispose of and make all needful Rules and Regulations respecting the Territory or other Property belonging to the United States; and nothing in this Constitution shall be so construed as to Prejudice any Claims of the United States, or of any particular State.

***Section 4.*** The United States shall guarantee to every State in this Union a Republican Form of Government, and shall protect each of them against Invasion; and on Application of the Legislature, or of the Executive (when the Legislature cannot be convened) against domestic Violence.

ARTICLE V

The Congress, whenever two thirds of both Houses shall deem it necessary, shall propose Amendments to this Constitution, or, on the Application of the Legislatures of two thirds of the several States, shall call a Convention for proposing Amendments, which, in either Case, shall be valid to all Intents and Purposes, as Part of this Constitution, when ratified by the Legislatures of three fourths of the several States, or by Conventions in three fourths thereof, as the one or the other Mode of Ratification may be proposed by the Congress; Provided [that no Amendment which may be made prior to the Year One thousand eight hundred and eight shall in any Manner affect the first and fourth Clauses in the Ninth Section of the first Article; and][10] that no State, without its Consent, shall be deprived of its equal Suffrage in the Senate.

ARTICLE VI

All Debts contracted and Engagements entered into, before the Adoption of this Constitution, shall be as valid against the United States under this Constitution, as under the Confederation.

This Constitution, and the Laws of the United States which shall be made in Pursuance thereof; and all Treaties made, or which shall be made, under the Authority of the United States, shall be the supreme Law of the Land; and the Judges in every State shall be bound thereby, any Thing in the Constitution or Laws of any State to the Contrary notwithstanding.

The Senators and Representatives before mentioned, and the Members of the several State Legislatures, and all executive and judicial Officers, both of the United States and of the several States, shall be bound by Oath or Affirmation, to support this Constitution; but no religious Test shall ever be required as a Qualification to any Office or public Trust under the United States.

ARTICLE VII

The Ratification of the Conventions of nine States, shall be sufficient for the Establishment of this Constitution between the States so ratifying the Same.

Done in Convention by the Unanimous Consent of the States present the Seventeenth Day of September in the Year of our Lord one thousand seven hundred and Eighty seven and of the Independence of the United States of America the Twelfth. IN WITNESS whereof We have hereunto subscribed our Names,

George Washington,
*President and deputy from Virginia.*

*New Hampshire:* John Langdon, Nicholas Gilman.
*Massachusetts:* Nathaniel Gorham, Rufus King.
*Connecticut:* William Samuel Johnson, Roger Sherman.
*New York:* Alexander Hamilton.
*New Jersey:* William Livingston, David Brearley, William Paterson, Jonathan Dayton.
*Pennsylvania:* Benjamin Franklin, Thomas Mifflin, Robert Morris, George Clymer, Thomas FitzSimons, Jared Ingersoll, James Wilson, Gouverneur Morris.
*Delaware:* George Read, Gunning Bedford Jr., John Dickinson, Richard Bassett, Jacob Broom.
*Maryland:* James McHenry, Daniel of St. Thomas Jenifer, Daniel Carroll.
*Virginia:* John Blair, James Madison Jr.
*North Carolina:.* William Blount, Richard Dobbs Spaight, Hugh Williamson.
*South Carolina:* John Rutledge, Charles Cotesworth Pinckney, Charles Pinckney, Pierce Butler.
*Georgia:* William Few, Abraham Baldwin.

[The language of the original Constitution, not including the Amendments, was adopted by a convention of the states on September 17, 1787, and was subsequently ratified by the states on the following dates: Delaware, December 7, 1787; Pennsylvania, December 12, 1787; New Jersey, December 18, 1787; Georgia, January 2, 1788; Connecticut, January 9, 1788; Massachusetts, February 6, 1788; Maryland, April 28, 1788; South Carolina, May 23, 1788; New Hampshire, June 21, 1788.

Ratification was completed on June 21, 1788.

The Constitution subsequently was ratified by Virginia, June 25, 1788; New York, July 26, 1788; North Carolina, November 21, 1789; Rhode Island, May 29, 1790; and Vermont, January 10, 1791.]

AMENDMENTS

*AMENDMENT I*
*(First ten amendments ratified December 15, 1791.)*
Congress shall make no law respecting an establishment

of religion, or prohibiting the free exercise thereof; or abridging the freedom of speech, or of the press; or the right of the people peaceably to assemble, and to petition the Government for a redress of grievances.

*AMENDMENT II*

A well regulated Militia, being necessary to the security of a free State, the right of the people to keep and bear Arms, shall not be infringed.

*AMENDMENT III*

No Soldier shall, in time of peace be quartered in any house, without the consent of the Owner, nor in time of war, but in a manner to be prescribed by law.

*AMENDMENT IV*

The right of the people to be secure in their persons, houses, papers, and effects, against unreasonable searches and seizures, shall not be violated, and no Warrants shall issue, but upon probable cause, supported by Oath or affirmation, and particularly describing the place to be searched, and the persons or things to be seized.

*AMENDMENT V*

No person shall be held to answer for a capital, or otherwise infamous crime, unless on a presentment or indictment of a Grand Jury, except in cases arising in the land or naval forces, or in the Militia, when in actual service in time of War or public danger; nor shall any person be subject for the same offence to be twice put in jeopardy of life or limb; nor shall be compelled in any criminal case to be a witness against himself, nor be deprived of life, liberty, or property, without due process of law; nor shall private property be taken for public use, without just compensation.

*AMENDMENT VI*

In all criminal prosecutions, the accused shall enjoy the right to a speedy and public trial, by an impartial jury of the State and district wherein the crime shall have been committed, which district shall have been previously ascertained by law, and to be informed of the nature and cause of the accusation; to be confronted with the witnesses against him; to have compulsory process for obtaining witnesses in his favor, and to have the Assistance of Counsel for his defence.

*AMENDMENT VII*

In Suits at common law, where the value in controversy shall exceed twenty dollars, the right of trial by jury shall be preserved, and no fact tried by a jury, shall be otherwise re-examined in any Court of the United States, than according to the rules of the common law.

*AMENDMENT VIII*

Excessive bail shall not be required, nor excessive fines imposed, nor cruel and unusual punishments inflicted.

*AMENDMENT IX*

The enumeration in the Constitution, of certain rights, shall not be construed to deny or disparage others retained by the people.

*AMENDMENT X*

The powers not delegated to the United States by the Constitution, nor prohibited by it to the States, are reserved to the States respectively, or to the people.

*AMENDMENT XI* *(Ratified February 7, 1795)*

The Judicial power of the United States shall not be construed to extend to any suit in law or equity, commenced or prosecuted against one of the United States by Citizens of another State, or by Citizens or Subjects of any Foreign State.

*AMENDMENT XII* *(Ratified June 15, 1804)*

The Electors shall meet in their respective states and vote by ballot for President and Vice-President, one of whom, at least, shall not be an inhabitant of the same state with themselves; they shall name in their ballots the person voted for as President, and in distinct ballots the person voted for as Vice-President, and they shall make distinct lists of all persons voted for as President, and of all persons voted for as Vice-President, and of the number of votes for each, which lists they shall sign and certify, and transmit sealed to the seat of the government of the United States, directed to the President of the Senate; — The President of the Senate shall, in the presence of the Senate and House of Representatives, open all the certificates and the votes shall then be counted; — The person having the greatest number of votes for President, shall be the President, if such number be a majority of the whole number of Electors appointed; and if no person have such majority, then from the persons having the highest numbers not exceeding three on the list of those voted for as President, the House of Representatives shall choose immediately, by ballot, the President. But in choosing the President, the votes shall be taken by states, the representation from each state having one vote; a quorum for this purpose shall consist of a member or members from two-thirds of the states, and a majority of all the states shall be necessary to a choice. [And if the House of Representatives shall not choose a President whenever the right of choice shall devolve upon them, before the fourth day of March next following, then the Vice-President shall act as President, as in the case of the death or other constitutional disability of the President. —][11] The person having the greatest number of votes as Vice-President, shall be the Vice-President, if such number be a majority of the whole number of Electors appointed, and if no person have a majority, then from the two highest numbers on the list, the Senate shall choose the Vice-President; a quorum for the purpose shall consist of two-thirds of the whole number of Senators, and a majority of the whole number shall be necessary to a choice. But no person constitutionally ineligible to the office of President shall be eligible to that of Vice-President of the United States.

*AMENDMENT XIII (Ratified December 6, 1865)*

**Section 1.** Neither slavery nor involuntary servitude, except as a punishment for crime whereof the party shall have been duly convicted, shall exist within the United States, or any place subject to their jurisdiction.

**Section 2.** Congress shall have power to enforce this article by appropriate legislation.

*AMENDMENT XIV (Ratified July 9, 1868)*

**Section 1.** All persons born or naturalized in the United States, and subject to the jurisdiction thereof, are citizens of the United States and of the State wherein they reside. No State shall make or enforce any law which shall abridge the privileges or immunities of citizens of the United States; nor shall any State deprive any person of life, liberty, or property, without due process of law; nor deny to any person within its jurisdiction the equal protection of the laws.

**Section 2.** Representatives shall be apportioned among the several States according to their respective numbers, counting the whole number of persons in each State, excluding Indians not taxed. But when the right to vote at any election for the choice of electors for President and Vice

President of the United States, Representatives in Congress, the Executive and Judicial officers of a State, or the members of the Legislature thereof, is denied to any of the male inhabitants of such State, being twenty-one years of age,[12] and citizens of the United States, or in any way abridged, except for participation in rebellion, or other crime, the basis of representation therein shall be reduced in the proportion which the number of such male citizens shall bear to the whole number of male citizens twenty-one years of age in such State.

**Section 3.** No person shall be a Senator or Representative in Congress, or elector of President and Vice President, or hold any office, civil or military, under the United States, or under any State, who, having previously taken an oath, as a member of Congress, or as an officer of the United States, or as a member of any State legislature, or as an executive or judicial officer of any State, to support the Constitution of the United States, shall have engaged in insurrection or rebellion against the same, or given aid or comfort to the enemies thereof. But Congress may by a vote of two-thirds of each House, remove such disability.

**Section 4.** The validity of the public debt of the United States, authorized by law, including debts incurred for payment of pensions and bounties for services in suppressing insurrection or rebellion, shall not be questioned. But neither the United States nor any State shall assume or pay any debt or obligation incurred in aid of insurrection or rebellion against the United States, or any claim for the loss or emancipation of any slave; but all such debts, obligations and claims shall be held illegal and void.

**Section 5.** The Congress shall have power to enforce, by appropriate legislation, the provisions of this article.

*AMENDMENT XV (Ratified February 3, 1870)*

**Section 1.** The right of citizens of the United States to vote shall not be denied or abridged by the United States or by any State on account of race, color, or previous condition of servitude.

**Section 2.** The Congress shall have power to enforce this article by appropriate legislation.

*AMENDMENT XVI (Ratified February 3, 1913)*

The Congress shall have power to lay and collect taxes on incomes, from whatever source derived, without apportionment among the several States, and without regard to any census or enumeration.

*AMENDMENT XVII (Ratified April 8, 1913)*

The Senate of the United States shall be composed of two Senators from each State, elected by the people thereof, for six years; and each Senator shall have one vote. The electors in each State shall have the qualifications requisite for electors of the most numerous branch of the State legislatures.

When vacancies happen in the representation of any State in the Senate, the executive authority of such State shall issue writs of election to fill such vacancies: *Provided,* That the legislature of any State may empower the executive thereof to make temporary appointments until the people fill the vacancies by election as the legislature may direct.

This amendment shall not be so construed as to affect the election or term of any Senator chosen before it becomes valid as part of the Constitution.

[*AMENDMENT XVIII (Ratified January 16, 1919)*

**Section 1.** After one year from the ratification of this article the manufacture, sale, or transportation of intoxicating liquors within, the importation thereof into, or the exportation thereof from the United States and all territory subject to the jurisdiction thereof for beverage purposes is hereby prohibited.

**Section 2.** The Congress and the several States shall have concurrent power to enforce this article by appropriate legislation.

**Section 3.** This article shall be inoperative unless it shall have been ratified as an amendment to the Constitution by the legislatures of the several States, as provided in the Constitution, within seven years from the date of the submission hereof to the States by the Congress.][13]

*AMENDMENT XIX (Ratified August 18, 1920)*

The right of citizens of the United States to vote shall not be denied or abridged by the United States or by any State on account of sex.

Congress shall have power to enforce this article by appropriate legislation.

*AMENDMENT XX (Ratified January 23, 1933)*

**Section 1.** The terms of the President and Vice President shall end at noon on the 20th day of January, and the terms of Senators and Representatives at noon on the 3d day of January, of the years in which such terms would have ended if this article had not been ratified; and the terms of their successors shall then begin.

**Section 2.** The Congress shall assemble at least once in every year, and such meeting shall begin at noon on the 3d day of January, unless they shall by law appoint a different day.

**Section 3.**[14] If, at the time fixed for the beginning of the term of the President, the President elect shall have died, the Vice President elect shall become President. If a President shall not have been chosen before the time fixed for the beginning of his term, or if the President elect shall have failed to qualify, then the Vice President elect shall act as President until a President shall have qualified; and the Congress may by law provide for the case wherein neither a President elect nor a Vice President elect shall have qualified, declaring who shall then act as President, or the manner in which one who is to act shall be selected, and such person shall act accordingly until a President or Vice President shall have qualified.

**Section 4.** The Congress may by law provide for the case of the death of any of the persons from whom the House of Representatives may choose a President whenever the right of choice shall have devolved upon them, and for the case of the death of any of the persons from whom the Senate may choose a Vice President whenever the right of choice shall have devolved upon them.

**Section 5.** Sections 1 and 2 shall take effect on the 15th day of October following the ratification of this article.

**Section 6.** This article shall be inoperative unless it shall have been ratified as an amendment to the Constitution by the legislatures of three-fourths of the several States within seven years from the date of its submission.

*AMENDMENT XXI (Ratified December 5, 1933)*

**Section 1.** The eighteenth article of amendment to the Constitution of the United States is hereby repealed.

**Section 2.** The transportation or importation into any State, Territory, or possession of the United States for delivery or use therein of intoxicating liquors, in violation of the laws thereof, is hereby prohibited.

**Section 3.** This article shall be inoperative unless it shall have been ratified as an amendment to the Constitution by conventions in the several States, as provided in the Constitution, within seven years from the date of the submission hereof to the States by the Congress.

*AMENDMENT XXII (Ratified February 27, 1951)*

**Section 1.** No person shall be elected to the office of the President more than twice, and no person who has held the office of President, or acted as President, for more than two years of a term to which some other person was elected President shall be elected to the office of the President more than once. But this Article shall not apply to any person holding the office of President when this Article was proposed by the Congress, and shall not prevent any person who may be holding the office of President, or acting as President, during the term within which this Article becomes operative from holding the office of President or acting as President during the remainder of such term.

**Section 2.** This article shall be inoperative unless it shall have been ratified as an amendment to the Constitution by the legislatures of three-fourths of the several States within seven years from the date of its submission to the States by the Congress.

*AMENDMENT XXIII (Ratified March 29, 1961)*

**Section 1.** The District constituting the seat of Government of the United States shall appoint in such manner as the Congress may direct:

A number of electors of President and Vice President equal to the whole number of Senators and Representatives in Congress to which the District would be entitled if it were a State, but in no event more than the least populous State; they shall be in addition to those appointed by the States, but they shall be considered, for the purposes of the election of President and Vice President, to be electors appointed by a State; and they shall meet in the District and perform such duties as provided by the twelfth article of amendment.

**Section 2.** The Congress shall have power to enforce this article by appropriate legislation.

*AMENDMENT XXIV (Ratified January 23, 1964)*

**Section 1.** The right of citizens of the United States to vote in any primary or other election for President or Vice President, for electors for President or Vice President, or for Senator or Representative in Congress, shall not be denied or abridged by the United States or any State by reason of failure to pay any poll tax or other tax.

**Section 2.** The Congress shall have power to enforce this article by appropriate legislation.

*AMENDMENT XXV (Ratified February 10, 1967)*

**Section 1.** In case of the removal of the President from office or of his death or resignation, the Vice President shall become President.

**Section 2.** Whenever there is a vacancy in the office of the Vice President, the President shall nominate a Vice President who shall take office upon confirmation by a majority vote of both Houses of Congress.

**Section 3.** Whenever the President transmits to the President pro tempore of the Senate and the Speaker of the House of Representatives his written declaration that he is unable to discharge the powers and duties of his office, and until he transmits to them a written declaration to the contrary, such powers and duties shall be discharged by the Vice President as Acting President.

**Section 4.** Whenever the Vice President and a majority of either the principal officers of the executive departments or of such other body as Congress may by law provide, transmit to the President pro tempore of the Senate and the Speaker of the House of Representatives their written declaration that the President is unable to discharge the powers and duties of his office, the Vice President shall immediately assume the powers and duties of the office as Acting President.

Thereafter, when the President transmits to the President pro tempore of the Senate and the Speaker of the House of Representatives his written declaration that no inability exists, he shall resume the powers and duties of his office unless the Vice President and a majority of either the principal officers of the executive departments or of such other body as Congress may by law provide, transmit within four days to the President pro tempore of the Senate and the Speaker of the House of Representatives their written declaration that the President is unable to discharge the powers and duties of his office. Thereupon Congress shall decide the issue, assembling within forty-eight hours for that purpose if not in session. If the Congress, within twenty-one days after receipt of the latter written declaration, or, if Congress is not in session, within twenty-one days after Congress is required to assemble, determines by two-thirds vote of both Houses that the President is unable to discharge the powers and duties of his office, the Vice President shall continue to discharge the same as Acting President; otherwise, the President shall resume the powers and duties of his office.

*A M E N D M E N T   X X V I  (Ratified July 1, 1971)*

**Section 1.** The right of citizens of the United States, who are eighteen years of age or older, to vote shall not be denied or abridged by the United States or by any State on account of age.

**Section 2.** The Congress shall have power to enforce this article by appropriate legislation.

*A M E N D M E N T   X X V I I  (Ratified May 7, 1992)*

No law varying the compensation for the services of the Senators and Representatives shall take effect, until an election of Representatives shall have intervened.

SOURCE: U.S. Congress, House, Committee on the Judiciary, *The Constitution of the United States of America, as Amended,* 100th Cong., 1st sess., 1987, H Doc 100–94.

NOTES
1. The part in brackets was changed by section 2 of the Fourteenth Amendment.

2. The part in brackets was changed by the first paragraph of the Seventeenth Amendment.

3. The part in brackets was changed by the second paragraph of the Seventeenth Amendment.

4. The part in brackets was changed by section 2 of the Twentieth Amendment.

5. The Sixteenth Amendment gave Congress the power to tax incomes.

6. The material in brackets was superseded by the Twelfth Amendment.

7. This provision was affected by the Twenty-fifth Amendment.

8. These clauses were affected by the Eleventh Amendment.

9. This paragraph was superseded by the Thirteenth Amendment.

10. Obsolete.

11. The part in brackets was superseded by section 3 of the Twentieth Amendment.

12. See the Nineteenth and Twenty-sixth amendments.

13. This amendment was repealed by section 1 of the Twenty-first Amendment.

14. See the Twenty-fifth Amendment.

# Selected Bibliography

*(The following general bibliography supplements the "Additional Readings" found at the end of many of the longer individual entries in* Congress A to Z.*)*

Aberbach, Joel D. *Keeping a Watchful Eye: The Politics of Congressional Oversight.* Washington, D.C.: Brookings Institution, 1990.

Abraham, Henry Julian. *Justices and Presidents: A Political History of Appointments to the Supreme Court.* 2nd ed. New York: Oxford University Press, 1985.

Aikman, Lonnelle. *We, the People: The Story of the United States Capitol.* 14th ed. Washington, D.C.: United States Capitol Historical Society, 1991.

Alexander, De Alva Stanwood. *History and Procedure of the House of Representatives.* Boston: Houghton Mifflin, 1916.

Alexander, Herbert E. *Financing Politics: Money, Elections, and Political Reform.* 4th ed. Washington, D.C.: CQ Press, 1992.

American Political Science Association and American Historical Association. *This Constitution: From Ratification to the Bill of Rights.* Washington, D.C.: CQ Press, 1988.

American Political Science Association and American Historical Association. *This Constitution: Our Enduring Legacy.* Washington, D.C.: CQ Press, 1986.

Arnold, R. Douglas. *Congress and the Bureaucracy: A Theory of Influence.* New Haven, Conn.: Yale University Press, 1979.

Bacchus, William I. *Inside the Legislative Process.* Boulder, Colo.: Westview Press, 1983.

Bach, Stanley, and Steven S. Smith. *Managing Uncertainty in the House of Representatives: Adaptation and Innovation of Special Rules.* Washington, D.C.: Brookings Institution, 1988.

Bailey, Stephen K. *Congress Makes a Law.* New York: Columbia University Press, 1950.

Baker, Richard A. *The Senate of the United States: A Bicentennial History.* Malabar, Fla.: Robert E. Krieger, 1988.

Baker, Richard A., and Roger H. Davidson, eds. *First Among Equals: Senate Leaders of the 20th Century.* Washington, D.C.: Congressional Quarterly, 1991.

Baker, Ross K. *House and Senate.* New York: W. W. Norton, 1989.

Barbash, Fred. *The Founding: A Dramatic Account of the Writing of the Constitution.* New York: Linden Press/Simon and Schuster, 1987.

Barone, Michael, and Grant Ujifusa. *The Almanac of American Politics 1992.* Washington, D.C.: National Journal, 1992.

Baum, Lawrence. *The Supreme Court.* 4th ed. Washington, D.C.: CQ Press, 1991.

Benjamin, Gerald, and Michael J. Malbin, eds. *Limiting Legislative Terms.* Washington, D.C.: CQ Press, 1992.

Benson, Paul R. *Supreme Court and the Commerce Clause, 1937–1970.* Port Washington, N.Y.: Dunellen Publishing, 1971.

Berger, Raoul. *Congress v. The Supreme Court.* Cambridge, Mass.: Harvard University Press, 1969.

———. *Executive Privilege.* Cambridge, Mass.: Harvard University Press, 1974.

———. *Impeachment: The Constitutional Problems.* Cambridge, Mass.: Harvard University Press, 1973.

Berman, Daniel M. *How a Bill Becomes a Law: Congress Enacts Civil Rights Legislation.* New York: Macmillan, 1966.

———. *In Congress Assembled: The Legislative Process in the National Government.* New York: Macmillan, 1964.

Bibby, John F. *Congress off the Record: The Candid Analysis of Seven Members.* Washington, D.C.: American Enterprise Institute, 1983.

———. *Government by Consent: An Introduction to American Politics.* Washington, D.C.: CQ Press, 1992.

Binkley, Wilfred E., and Malcolm C. Moos. *A Grammar of American Politics: The National Government*. New York: Alfred A. Knopf, 1958.

Birnbaum, Jeffrey H., and Alan S. Murray. *Showdown at Gucci Gulch: Lawmakers, Lobbyists, and the Unlikely Triumph of Tax Reform*. New York: Random House, 1987.

Bisnow, Mark. *In the Shadow of the Dome: Chronicles of a Capitol Hill Aide*. New York: William Morrow, 1990.

Bolling, Richard W. *House Out of Order*. New York: E. P. Dutton, 1965.

———. *Power in the House: A History of the Leadership of the House of Representatives*. New York: Capricorn Books, 1974.

Bowles, Nigel. *The White House and Capitol Hill: The Politics of Presidential Persuasion*. New York: Oxford University Press, 1987.

Brady, David W. *Critical Elections and Congressional Policy Making*. Stanford, Calif.: Stanford University Press, 1988.

Brenner, Phillip. *The Limits and Possibilities of Congress*. New York: St. Martin's Press, 1983.

Bronner, Ethan. *Battle for Justice: How the Bork Nomination Shook America*. New York: W. W. Norton, 1989.

Brown, Glenn. *History of the United States Capitol*. 2 vols. Washington, D.C.: Government Printing Office, 1903. Rpt., New York: Da Capo Press, 1970.

Burdette, Franklin L. *Filibustering in the Senate*. Princeton, N.J.: Princeton University Press, 1940.

Byrd, Robert C. *The Senate 1789–1989: Addresses on the History of the United States Senate*. Washington, D.C.: Government Printing Office, 1988.

Cain, Bruce, John Ferejohn, and Morris Fiorina. *The Personal Vote: Constituency Service and Electoral Independence*. Cambridge, Mass.: Harvard University Press, 1987.

Chamberlin, Hope. *A Minority of Members: Women in the U.S. Congress*. New York: Praeger, 1973.

Cigler, Allan J., and Burdett A. Loomis. *Interest Group Politics*. 3rd ed. Washington, D.C.: CQ Press, 1991.

Clark, Peter, and Susan H. Evans. *Covering Campaigns: Journalism in Congressional Elections*. Stanford, Calif.: Stanford University Press, 1983.

Clausen, Aage R. *How Congressmen Decide: A Policy Focus*. New York: St. Martin's Press, 1973.

Congressional Quarterly. *Guide to Congress*. 4th ed. Washington, D.C.: Congressional Quarterly, 1991.

———. *Guide to U.S. Elections*. 2nd ed. Washington, D.C.: Congressional Quarterly, 1985.

———. *The Iran-Contra Puzzle*. Washington, D.C.: Congressional Quarterly, 1987.

———. *The Washington Lobby*. 5th ed. Washington, D.C.: Congressional Quarterly, 1987.

———. *Watergate: Chronology of a Crisis*. Washington, D.C.: Congressional Quarterly, 1975.

Cook, Timothy E. *Making Laws and Making News: Media Strategies in the U.S. House of Representatives*. Washington, D.C.: Brookings Institution, 1989.

Cooper, Joseph, and G. Calvin Mackenzie. *The House at Work*. Austin: University of Texas Press, 1981.

Corwin, Edward S. *The Commerce Power vs. States Rights*. Princeton, N.J.: Princeton University Press, 1936.

———. *The Doctrine of Judicial Review: Its Legal and Historical Basis and Other Essays*. Princeton, N.J.: Princeton University Press, 1914. Rpt., Gloucester, Mass.: Peter Smith, 1963.

Crabb, Cecil V., Jr., and Pat M. Holt. *Invitation to Struggle: Congress, the President, and Foreign Policy*. 4th ed. Washington, D.C.: CQ Press, 1991.

Craig, Barbara H. *Chadha*. New York: Oxford University Press, 1988.

———. *The Legislative Veto: Congressional Control of Regulation*. Boulder, Colo.: Westview Press, 1983.

Crawford, Kenneth G. *The Pressure Boys: The Inside Story of Lobbying in America*. New York: Arno Press, 1974.

Davidson, Roger H., and Walter J. Oleszek. *Congress Against Itself*. Bloomington: Indiana University Press, 1979.

———. *Congress and Its Members*. 4th ed. Washington, D.C.: CQ Press, 1993.

———. *Governing: Readings and Cases in American Politics*. 2d ed. Washington, D.C.: CQ Press, 1991.

Deakin, James. *Lobbyists*. Washington, D.C.: Public Affairs Press, 1966.

Deering, Christopher J. *Congressional Politics*. Chicago: Dorsey, 1989.

deKieffer, Donald. *How to Lobby Congress: A Guide for the Citizen Lobbyist*. New York: Dodd, Mead, 1981.

Dodd, Lawrence C., and Bruce I. Oppenheimer, eds. *Congress Reconsidered*. 5th ed. Washington, D.C.: CQ Press, 1993.

Dodd, Lawrence C., and Richard L. Schott. *Congress and the Administrative State.* New York: Wiley, 1979.

Dole, Bob. *Historical Almanac of the United States Senate.* Washington, D.C.: Government Printing Office, 1989.

Drew, Elizabeth. *Politics and Money: The New Road to Corruption.* New York: Macmillan, 1983.

Duncan, Phil, ed. *Politics in America 1994: The 103rd Congress.* Washington, D.C.: Congressional Quarterly, 1993.

Edwards, George C. III. *At the Margins: Presidential Leadership of Congress.* New Haven, Conn.: Yale University Press, 1989.

Ehrenhalt, Alan. *The United States of Ambition: Politicians, Power, and the Pursuit of Office.* New York: Times Books, 1991.

Fenno, Richard F., Jr. *Congressmen in Committees.* Boston: Little, Brown, 1973.

———. *Home Style: House Members in Their Districts.* Boston: Little, Brown, 1978.

———. *The Power of the Purse: Appropriation Politics in Congress.* Boston: Little, Brown, 1973.

Fiorina, Morris P. *Congress: Keystone of the Washington Establishment.* New Haven, Conn.: Yale University Press, 1977.

Fiorina, Morris P., and David W. Rohde, eds. *Home Style and Washington Work: Studies of Congressional Politics.* Ann Arbor: University of Michigan Press, 1989.

Fisher, Louis. *Constitutional Conflicts between Congress and the President.* Princeton, N.J.: Princeton University Press, 1985.

———. *The Politics of Shared Power: Congress and the Executive.* 3rd ed. Washington, D.C.: CQ Press, 1992.

Follett, Mary P. *The Speaker of the House of Representatives.* New York: Longmans, Green, 1896. Rpt., New York: Burt Franklin Reprints, 1974.

Fowler, Linda, and Robert D. McClure. *Political Ambition: Who Decides to Run for Congress.* New Haven, Conn.: Yale University Press, 1989.

Fox, Harrison W., Jr., and Susan Webb Hammond. *Congressional Staffs: The Invisible Force in American Lawmaking.* New York: Free Press, 1979.

Franck, Thomas M., ed. *The Tethered Presidency: Congressional Restraints on Executive Power.* New York: New York University Press, 1981.

Franck, Thomas M., and Edward Weisband. *Foreign Policy by Congress.* New York: Oxford University Press, 1979.

Franklin, Daniel P. *Making Ends Meet: Congressional Budgeting in the Age of Deficits.* Washington, D.C.: CQ Press, 1992.

Frantzich, Stephen E. *Write Your Congressman: Constituent Communications and Representation.* New York: Praeger, 1986.

Fritz, Sara, and Dwight Morris. *Gold-Plated Politics: Running for Congress in the 1990s.* Washington, D.C.: CQ Press, 1992.

Froman, Lewis A., Jr. *The Congressional Process: Strategies, Rules, and Procedures.* Boston: Little, Brown, 1967.

Galloway, George B. *History of the House of Representatives.* Rev. ed. New York: Thomas Y. Crowell, 1976.

———. *The Legislative Process in Congress.* New York: Thomas Y. Crowell, 1953.

Gavit, Bernard C. *Commerce Clause of the United States Constitution.* New York: AMS Press, 1970.

Gertzog, Irwin N. *Congressional Women: Their Recruitment, Treatment, and Behavior.* New York: Praeger, 1984.

Goldenberg, Edie N., and Michael W. Traugott. *Campaigning for Congress.* Washington, D.C.: CQ Press, 1984.

Goldwin, Robert A., and Art Kaufman, eds. *Separation of Powers: Does It Still Work?* Washington, D.C.: American Enterprise Institute, 1986.

Goldwin, Robert A., and Robert A. Licht, eds. *Foreign Policy and the Constitution.* Washington, D.C.: AEI Press, 1990.

Goodwin, George, Jr. *The Little Legislatures: Committees of Congress.* Amherst: University of Massachusetts Press, 1970.

Graber, Doris A. *Mass Media and American Politics.* 4th ed. Washington, D.C.: CQ Press, 1992.

———. *Media Power in Politics.* 3rd ed. Washington, D.C.: CQ Press, 1993.

Gross, Bertram M. *The Legislative Struggle: A Study in Social Combat.* New York: McGraw-Hill, 1953.

Hamilton, Alexander, John Jay, and James Madison. *The Federalist.* Introduction by Edward Gaylord Bourne. New York: Tudor, 1937.

Hamilton, James. *The Power to Probe: A Study of Congressional Investigations.* New York: Random House, 1976.

Hansen, Orval, and Ellen Miller. *Congressional Operations: The Role of Mail in Decisionmaking in Congress.* Washington, D.C.: Center for Responsive Politics, 1987.

Harris, Joseph P. *The Advice and Consent of the Senate: A Study of the Confirmation of Appointments by the United States Senate.* 1953. Rpt. Westport, Conn.: Greenwood, 1968.

Haynes, George H. *The Senate of the United States: Its History and Practice.* 2 vols. Boston: Houghton Mifflin, 1938.

Hess, Stephen. *Live from Capitol Hill! Studies of Congress and the Media.* Washington, D.C.: Brookings Institution, 1991.

Hinckley, Barbara. *Stability and Change in Congress.* 4th ed. New York: Harper and Row, 1988.

Hunter, Robert E., Wayne L. Berman, and John F. Kennedy, eds. *Making Government Work: From White House to Congress.* Boulder, Colo.: Westview Press, 1986.

Jacobson, Gary C. *Money in Congressional Elections.* New Haven, Conn.: Yale University Press, 1980.

———. *The Politics of Congressional Elections.* 2nd ed. Boston: Little, Brown, 1987.

Jewell, Malcolm E., and Samuel C. Patterson. *The Legislative Process in the United States.* 4th ed. New York: McGraw-Hill, 1985.

Johannes, John R. *To Serve the People: Congress and Constituency Service.* Lincoln: University of Nebraska Press, 1984.

Jones, Charles O. *The Minority Party in Congress.* Boston: Little, Brown, 1970.

———. *The United States Congress: People, Place, and Policy.* Homewood, Ill.: Dorsey, 1982.

Jones, Rochelle, and Peter Woll. *The Private World of Congress.* New York: Free Press, 1979.

Josephy, Alvin M., Jr. *On the Hill: A History of the American Congress.* New York: Simon and Schuster, 1980. (Published in 1975 under the title *The American Heritage History of the Congress of the United States.*)

Keefe, William J. *Congress and the American People.* 3rd ed. Englewood Cliffs, N.J.: Prentice-Hall, 1988.

———. *Parties, Politics, and Public Policy in America.* 6th ed. Washington, D.C.: CQ Press, 1991.

Keefe, William J., and Morris S. Ogul. *The American Legislative Process: Congress and the States.* 7th ed. Englewood Cliffs, N.J.: Prentice-Hall, 1989.

Keefe, William J., and Samuel Kernell. *Strategy and Choice in Congressional Elections.* New Haven: Yale University Press, 1981.

Kennon, Donald R., ed. *The Speakers of the U.S. House of Representatives.* Baltimore: The Johns Hopkins University Press, 1986.

Kernell, Samuel. *Going Public: New Strategies of Presidential Leadership.* 2nd ed. Washington, D.C.: CQ Press, 1992.

Key, V.O. *The Responsible Electorate.* New York: Vintage Books, 1966.

King, Anthony, ed. *Both Ends of the Avenue: The Presidency, the Executive Branch, and Congress in the 1980s.* Washington, D.C.: American Enterprise Institute, 1983.

Kingdon, John W. *Congressmen's Voting Decisions.* 3rd ed. New York: Harper and Row, 1989.

Kornacki, John J., ed. *Leading Congress: New Styles, New Strategies.* Washington, D.C.: CQ Press, 1990.

Kozak, David C. *Contexts of Congressional Decision Behavior.* Lanham, Md.: University Press of America, 1984.

Kozak, David C., and John D. Macartney, eds. *Congress and Public Policy.* 2nd ed. Chicago: Dorsey, 1987.

Kravitz, Walter. *Congressional Quarterly's American Congressional Dictionary.* Washington, D.C.: Congressional Quarterly, 1993.

Longley, Lawrence D., and Walter J. Oleszek. *Bicameral Politics: Conference Committees in Congress.* New Haven, Conn.: Yale University Press, 1989.

Loomis, Burdett A. *The New American Politician.* New York: Basic Books, 1988.

Maass, Arthur. *Congress and the Common Good.* New York: Basic Books, 1983.

McGeary, M. Nelson. *The Development of Congressional Investigative Power.* New York: Octagon Books, 1966.

Mackaman, Frank H., ed. *Understanding Congressional Leadership.* Washington, D.C.: CQ Press, 1981.

Mackenzie, G. Calvin. *The Politics of Presidential Appointments.* New York: Free Press, 1981.

MacNeil, Neil. *Forge of Democracy: The House of Representatives.* New York: David McKay, 1963.

Magleby, David B., and Candice J. Nelson. *The Money Chase: Congressional Campaign Finance Reform.* Washington, D.C.: Brookings Institution, 1990.

Maisel, Louis Sandy. *From Obscurity to Oblivion: Running in the Congressional Primary.* Knoxville: University of Tennessee Press, 1982.

Maisel, Louis Sandy, and Joseph Cooper, eds. *Congressional Elections.* Beverly Hills, Calif.: Sage, 1981.

Makinson, Larry. *The Cash Constituents of Congress.* Washington, D.C.: Congressional Quarterly, 1992.

Malbin, Michael J. *Unelected Representatives: Congressional Staff and the Future of Representative Government.* New York: Basic Books, 1980.

———, ed. *Money and Politics in the United States: Financing Elections in the 1980s.* Chatham, N.J.: Chatham House/American Enterprise Institute, 1984.

———, ed. *Parties, Interest Groups, and Campaign Finance Laws.* Washington, D.C.: American Enterprise Institute, 1980.

Marcuss, Stanley J. *Effective Washington Representation.* New York: Harcourt Brace Jovanovich, 1983.

Matsunaga, Spark M., and Ping Chen. *Rulemakers of the House.* Urbana: University of Illinois Press, 1976.

Matthews, Donald R. *U.S. Senators and Their World.* 1960. Rpt. Westport, Conn.: Greenwood Press, 1980.

Mayhew, David R. *Congress: The Electoral Connection.* New Haven, Conn.: Yale University Press, 1974.

———. *Divided We Govern: Party Control, Lawmaking and Investigations, 1946-1990.* New Haven, Conn.: Yale University Press, 1991.

Miller, Clem. *Member of the House: Letters of a Congressman.* New York: Charles Scribner's Sons, 1962.

Miller, James A. *Running in Place: Inside the Senate.* New York: Simon and Schuster, 1986.

Muskie, Edmund S., Kenneth Rush, and Kenneth W. Thompson, eds. *The President, the Congress and Foreign Policy.* Lanham, Md.: University Press of America, 1986.

Mutch, Robert E. *Campaigns, Congress, and the Courts: The Making of Federal Campaign Finance Law.* New York: Praeger, 1988.

Nelson, Garrison. *Committees in the U.S. Congress, 1947-1992.* 2 vols. Washington, D.C.: Congressional Quarterly, 1993.

Nelson, Michael, ed. *Congressional Quarterly's Guide to the Presidency.* Washington, D.C.: Congressional Quarterly, 1989.

Neustadt, Richard E. *Presidential Power and the Modern Presidents: The Politics of Leadership from Roosevelt to Reagan.* New York: Free Press, 1990.

Nugent, Margaret Latus, and John R. Johannes. *Money, Elections, and Democracy: Reforming Congressional Campaign Finance.* Boulder, Colo.: Westview Press, 1990.

Oleszek, Walter J. *Congressional Procedures and the Policy Process.* 3rd ed. Washington, D.C.: CQ Press, 1989.

Ornstein, Norman J., Thomas E. Mann, and Michael J. Malbin. *Vital Statistics on Congress, 1993–1994.* Washington, D.C.: Congressional Quarterly, 1993.

Parker, Glenn R. *Characteristics of Congress: Politics and Congressional Behavior.* Englewood Cliffs, N.J.: Prentice Hall, 1989.

———. *Homeward Bound: Exploring Changes in Congressional Behavior.* Pittsburgh: University of Pittsburgh Press, 1986.

———, ed. *Studies of Congress.* Washington, D.C.: CQ Press, 1985.

Parker, Glenn R., and Suzanne L. Parker. *Factions in House Committees.* Knoxville: University of Tennessee Press, 1985.

Peabody, Robert L. *Leadership in Congress: Stability, Succession and Change.* Boston: Little, Brown, 1976.

Peirce, Neal R., and Lawrence D. Longley. *The People's President: The Electoral College in American History and the Direct Vote Alternative.* Rev. ed. New Haven, Conn.: Yale University Press, 1981.

Peterson, Mark A. *Legislating Together: The White House and Capitol Hill from Eisenhower to Reagan.* Cambridge, Mass.: Harvard University Press, 1990.

Plano, Jack C., and Milton Greenberg. *The American Political Dictionary.* 9th ed. New York: Holt, Rinehart and Winston, 1992.

Polsby, Nelson. *Congress and the Presidency.* 4th ed. Englewood Cliffs, N.J.: Prentice Hall, 1986.

Pritchett, C. Herman. *The American Constitution.* 3rd ed. New York: McGraw-Hill, 1977.

Ragsdale, Bruce A., and Joel D. Treese. *Black Americans in Congress, 1870–1989.* Office of the Historian, U.S. House of Representatives. Washington, D.C.: Government Printing Office, 1990.

Redman, Eric. *The Dance of Legislation.* New York: Simon and Schuster, 1973.

Reedy, George E. *The U.S. Senate.* New York: Crown, 1986.

Reid, T. R. *Congressional Odyssey: The Saga of a Senate Bill.* San Francisco: W. H. Freeman, 1980.

Rieselbach, Leroy N. *Congressional Reform.* Washington, D.C.: CQ Press, 1986.

Ripley, Randall B. *Congress: Process and Policy.* 4th ed. New York: W. W. Norton, 1988.

———. *Majority Party Leadership in Congress.* Boston: Little, Brown, 1969.

———. *Power in the Senate.* New York: St. Martin's Press, 1969.

Ripley, Randall B., and Grace A. Franklin. *Congress, the Bureaucracy, and Public Policy.* 4th ed. Homewood, Ill.: Dorsey, 1987.

Rothman, David J. *Politics and Power: The United States Senate, 1869–1901.* New York: Atheneum, 1969.

Rourke, John. *Congress and the Presidency in U.S. Foreign Policymaking: A Study of Interaction and Influence, 1945–1982.* Boulder, Colo.: Westview Press, 1983.

Sabato, Larry J. *PAC Power: Inside the World of Political Action Committees.* New York: W. W. Norton, 1984.

Salmore, Stephen A., and Barbara G. Salmore. *Candidates, Parties, and Campaigns: Electoral Politics in America.* 2nd ed. Washington, D.C.: CQ Press, 1989.

Schick, Allen. *Congress and Money: Budgeting, Spending, and Taxing.* Washington, D.C.: Urban Institute, 1980.

———. *Crisis in the Budget Process: Exercising Political Choice.* Washington, D.C.: American Enterprise Institute, 1986.

———, ed. *Making Economic Policy in Congress.* Washington, D.C.: American Enterprise Institute, 1984.

Schlesinger, Arthur M., Jr., ed. *History of U.S. Political Parties.* 4 vols. New York: Chelsea House, 1981.

Schlesinger, Arthur M., Jr., and Roger Burns, eds. *Congress Investigates: A Documentary History, 1792–1974.* 5 vols. New York: R. R. Bowker, 1975.

Schneider, Jerrold E. *Ideological Coalitions in Congress.* Westport, Conn.: Greenwood, 1979.

Shafritz, Jay M. *The HarperCollins Dictionary of American Government and Politics.* New York: HarperCollins, 1992.

Shelley, Mack C. *The Permanent Majority: The Conservative Coalition in the United States Congress.* University: University of Alabama Press, 1983.

Sheppard, Burton D. *Rethinking Congressional Reform: The Reform Roots of the Special Interest Congress.* Cambridge, Mass.: Schenkman, 1985.

Shuman, Howard E. *Politics and the Budget.* Englewood Cliffs, N.J.: Prentice-Hall, 1984.

Siff, Ted, and Alan Weil. *Ruling Congress: How House and Senate Rules Govern the Legislative Process.* New York: Grossman, 1975.

Simon, Paul. *The Glass House.* New York: Continuum Publishing, 1984.

Sinclair, Barbara. *Majority Leadership in the U.S. House.* Baltimore: Johns Hopkins University Press, 1983.

———. *The Transformation of the U.S. Senate.* Baltimore: Johns Hopkins University Press, 1989.

Smith, Gene. *High Crimes and Misdemeanors: The Impeachment and Trial of Andrew Johnson.* New York: McGraw-Hill, 1985.

Smith, Hedrick. *The Power Game: How Washington Works.* New York: Random House, 1988.

Smith, Steven S. *Call to Order: Floor Politics in the House and Senate.* Washington, D.C.: Brookings Institution, 1989.

Smith, Steven S., and Christopher J. Deering. *Committees in Congress.* 2nd ed. Washington, D.C.: CQ Press, 1990.

Sorauf, Frank J. *Money in American Elections.* Glenview, Ill.: Scott, Foresman/Little, Brown, 1988.

Sullivan, Terry. *Procedural Structure: Success and Influence in Congress.* New York: Praeger, 1984.

Sundquist, James L. *Constitutional Reform and Effective Government.* Rev. ed. Washington, D.C.: Brookings Institution, 1992.

———. *The Decline and Resurgence of Congress.* Washington, D.C.: Brookings Institution, 1981.

Swisher, Carl Brent. *American Constitutional Development.* 1954. Rpt. Westport, Conn.: Greenwood, 1978.

Tacheron, Donald G., and Morris K. Udall. *The Job of the Congressman: An Introduction to Service in the U.S. House of Representatives.* 2nd ed. New York: Macmillan, 1970.

Taylor, Telford. *Grand Inquest.* New York: Simon and Schuster, 1955.

Thurber, James A. *Divided Democracy: Cooperation and Conflict between the President and Congress.* Washington, D.C.: CQ Press, 1991.

Tocqueville, Alexis de. *Democracy in America.* 2 vols. New York: Schocken, 1967.

Truman, David B. *The Governmental Process: Political Interests and Public Opinion.* New York: Alfred A. Knopf, 1981.

Vogler, David J. *The Third House: Conference Committees in the United States Congress.* Evanston, Ill.: Northwestern University Press, 1971.

Vogler, David J., and Sidney R. Waldman. *Congress and Democracy.* Washington, D.C.: CQ Press, 1985.

Wander, Thomas W., Ted F. Hebert, and Gary W. Copeland, eds. *Congressional Budgeting.* Baltimore: The Johns Hopkins University Press, 1984.

Warren, Charles. *Congress as Santa Claus.* 1932. Rpt. New York: Arno, 1978.

———. *Congress, the Constitution, and the Supreme Court.* Boston: Little, Brown, 1925.

———. *The Supreme Court in United States History.* 2 vols. 1922, 1926. Rpt. Littleton, Colo.: Rothman, 1987.

Wattenberg, Martin P. *The Decline of American Political Parties, 1952 to 1980.* Cambridge, Mass.: Harvard University Press, 1984.

Wayne, Stephen J. *The Legislative Presidency.* New York: Harper and Row, 1978.

Weatherford, J. McIver. *Tribes on the Hill: The U.S. Congress—Rituals and Realities.* South Hadley, Mass.: Bergin and Garvey, 1985.

Whalen, Charles. *The House and Foreign Policy: The Irony of Congressional Reform.* Chapel Hill: University of North Carolina Press, 1985.

Whalen, Charles, and Barbara Whalen. *The Longest Debate: A Legislative History of the 1964 Civil Rights Act.* Washington, D.C.: Seven Locks Press, 1985.

Wildavsky, Aaron. *The New Politics of the Budgetary Process.* Glenview, Ill.: Scott, Foresman/Little, Brown, 1988.

Wilson, Woodrow. *Congressional Government: A Study in American Politics.* 1885. Rpt. Baltimore: The Johns Hopkins University Press, 1981.

Witt, Elder. *Congressional Quarterly's Guide to the Supreme Court.* 2nd ed. Washington, D.C.: Congressional Quarterly, 1990.

Wolpe, Bruce C. *Lobbying Congress: How the System Works.* Washington, D.C.: Congressional Quarterly, 1990.

*Women in Congress, 1917-1990.* Commission on the Bicentenary of the U.S. House of Representatives. Washington, D.C.: Government Printing Office, 1991.

Woodward, Bob. *The Final Days.* New York: Touchstone, 1989.

Woodward, Bob, and Carl Bernstein. *All the President's Men.* New York: Touchstone, 1987.

# Index

PRODUCTION NOTES

*Congress A to Z*

was designed, composed, and paged by Kachergis Book Design,
Pittsboro, North Carolina. The text type is 9.5/12 Meridien,
with Centaur display type. Using word-processing files supplied
by CQ Books and illustrations scanned by R. R. Donnelley, page
layouts were prepared in QuarkXPress 3.1 on a Macintosh IIFX,
and files were output to imposed negatives by R. R. Donnelley.
The book was printed on #50 Finch Opaque paper and bound
in Kivar 6 by R. R. Donnelley, Harrisonburg, Virginia.